DATE DUE

OC 06 '10			

Computing the Mind

The only book explaining how the mind works that also contains a usable map of the London Tube (see p. 274). You'll need a magnifying glass, though.

Computing the Mind

How the Mind Really Works

Shimon Edelman

OXFORD
UNIVERSITY PRESS

OXFORD

UNIVERSITY PRESS

Oxford University Press, Inc., publishes works that further
Oxford University's objective of excellence
in research, scholarship, and education.

Oxford New York
Auckland Cape Town Dar es Salaam Hong Kong Karachi
Kuala Lumpur Madrid Melbourne Mexico City Nairobi
New Delhi Shanghai Taipei Toronto

With offices in
Argentina Austria Brazil Chile Czech Republic France Greece
Guatemala Hungary Italy Japan Poland Portugal Singapore
South Korea Switzerland Thailand Turkey Ukraine Vietnam

Published by Oxford University Press, Inc.
198 Madison Avenue, New York, New York 10016
www.oup.com

Oxford is a registered trademark of Oxford University Press

Library of Congress Cataloging-in-Publication Data
Edelman, Shimon.
Computing the mind : how the mind really works / Shimon Edelman.
p.   cm.
Includes bibliographical references and index.
ISBN 978–0–19–532067–1
1. Cognition.   2. Computational neuroscience.   3. Thought and
thinking–Mathematical models.   I. Title.
[DNLM: 1. Mental Processes–physiology.   2. Brain–physiology. BF 441 E21c 2008]
BF311.E328   2008
153–dc22   2008011578

3 5 7 9 8 6 4

Printed in the United States of America
on acid-free paper

To Esti —

אֵשֶׁת־חַיִל, מִי יִמְצָא;   וְרָחֹק מִפְּנִינִים מִכְרָהּ.
רַבּוֹת בָּנוֹת, עָשׂוּ חָיִל;   וְאַתְּ, עָלִית עַל־כֻּלָּנָה.

Contents

Preface

When you set out on your journey to Ithaka,
wish that the road be long,
full of adventures, full of discoveries.

Ithaka
CONSTANTINE PETER CAVAFY

T O A TRAVELER setting out on a quest to understand how the mind works, the conceptual terrain of cognitive psychology appears in a typical textbook bird's eye view as mountain ranges rising from thick fog: here is Perception Plateau, over there Memory Massif, Thinking Peak, and Language Ridge, with the Consciousness Cordillera circling the horizon. On a closer examination, the mountains resolve into multiple summits of theories, each surrounded by a scree of data and often guarded by its own scholarly *genius loci*. Each peak seems to stand alone: whether the fog conceals an impassable chasm or a strait of an inland sea, one cannot tell.

This book is different. Rather than airlifting the reader from peak to peak, it aims to dispel the fog and show that the Mountains of the Mind all rise from the same plain; indeed, that they are within hiking distance from each other. The common foundation of cognition that will emerge from the fog as we journey together is *computation* — a key concept that is yet to be universally recognized in psychology, neuroscience, and the philosophy of mind as the unifying explanatory principle behind all these disciplines.

In composing this conceptual atlas of cognition, I sifted through many trail reports, stitched together numerous existing maps, and threw in a few of my own making. Like any book that has around 800 items in its bibliography section, this one is in a sense a collective effort. I am happy to acknowledge the hundreds of people from whose published work and insights I have benefited while writing it.

During the last eight years, I also had the privilege of learning from a unique scholarly community: the students and faculty of Cornell University in Ithaca, New York. I thank the Cornell students, to whom I regularly tried to communicate the ideas presented here, for the many shared thrilling moments and for their patience with me. To my colleagues in the Department of

Psychology I owe a debt of gratitude, for accepting me — an outsider, with a professed interest but little knowledge in their discipline — into their midst, and then proceeding to train me, gently, one mailroom chat, party conversation, and seminar discussion at a time, to think like a psychologist. If the Cornell experience has not been entirely successful in educating me, it is no doubt because this old dog could only be taught so many new tricks.

A part of this book was written during a sabbatical leave, most of which I spent away from Ithaca, at Tel Aviv University. I thank the School of Computer Science there for hosting me, Eytan Ruppin and David Horn for arranging for support, and Zach Solan for company and conversations while hiking in the Negev and in the Judean Desert.

Over the years, I have discussed various aspects of this project with many people, among them Morten Christiansen, Rick Dale, Dave Dunning, Nathan Intrator, Wendy Jones, Viorica Marian, Dennis Regan, Eytan Ruppin, Ben-Ami Scharfstein, Tadashi Sugihara, Heidi Waterfall, and Yanek Yontef. Their advice is greatly appreciated.

Mor Amitai, Jonathan Berant, Peter Brodsky, Andrew Carr, Jackie Cerretani, Eric Dietrich, Barb Finlay, Tom Gilovich, Claudia Hunter Gilson, Catalina Iricinschi, Wendy Jones, Barbara Lust, Dick Neisser, Dennis Regan, Eytan Ruppin, Michael Spivey, Anne Warlaumont, and Heidi Waterfall were kind enough to have read portions of the manuscript and to offer comments and suggestions. Many, but likely not nearly enough, of these I had the good sense to act upon.

I thank my editor Catharine Carlin and the Oxford University Press team for support and encouragement, and Aaron Sloman and three anonymous reviewers for constructive reading of the book proposal. John Cleese, who was an A. D. White Professor-at-Large and is now a Provost's Visiting Professor at Cornell, kindly interceded to help secure permissions for the use of excerpts from Monty Python skits.

Quasi-periodic gatherings of the local argument clinic whose founding members are Tim DeVoogd, Dave Dunning, David Field, Barb Finlay, Mike Goldstein, Jen Schwade, Harry Segal, and Michael Spivey helped me maintain just the right degree of sanity needed to keep working on this book, and to stop doing so when it seemed to be complete. I am particularly grateful to Barb the bright-eyed (γλαυκῶπις), without whose help I would have probably never set out to seek my Ithaca, and whose knowledge, wit, and wisdom more than once kept me from getting lost along the way.

Last, I thank Esti, my Penelope, for everything.

A woman of valor who can find? For her price is far above rubies. Many women have done valiantly, but you surpass them all.

Shimon Edelman
Ithaca, New York
August 2007

Part I

Foundations

1

Brains, Minds, and Numbers

Know thyself.

An inscription above the entrance to the Delphic Oracle

You drive a car, not knowing how its engine works. You ride as passenger in someone else's car, not knowing how that driver works. And strangest of all, you sometimes drive yourself to work, not knowing how you work, yourself.

From the afterword to Vernor Vinge's *True Names*
MARVIN MINSKY

IF YOU ARE READING THIS in the first couple of decades of the third millennium of the common era, chances are that (1) the human brain is the most complex toy you'll ever come near, let alone get to play with, and (2) you're trapped inside one for the foreseeable future. Wouldn't it be fun to get to know how it works? Even if you are not by inclination a tinkerer, eager to find out how everything works, you may resent being confined in this manner. Indeed, you may wish to evaluate the prospects of upgrading the game console to a better model, or at least to learn how to make the most of the current one. For that, it is necessary to understand the relationship between minds (which is *what* we are) and brains (which is *where* we are).

The process whereby alert brains generate minds used to be utterly mysterious, but is now better and better understood by the scientists who study cognition. The tools of their trade are similar to those found in any other science: a cycle of theoretical analysis and theory-motivated experimentation, often accompanied by computer simulations. The use of these tools in cognition can be illustrated on easily graspable yet profound problems in perception, memory, language, thought, action, and consciousness, leading to real, non-metaphorical understanding of how the mind/brain works. This is what this book is about.

Self-knowledge seen as the basis for all knowledge: the inscription above the entrance to the temple of Apollo at Delphi in ancient Greece read "KNOW THYSELF," ΓΝΩΘΙ ΣΕΑΥΤΟΝ. The Delphic Oracle is shown here in Michelangelo's painting in the Cappella Sistina in the Vatican.

3

1.1   Minds as organizational entities

To investigate the relationship between minds and brains, we may reason from the rather uncontroversial double premise that I just stated in passing, namely, that we *are* minds, and that we inhabit brains. To begin, consider the riddle illustrated in Figure 1.1: what is common to the minds of all sentient creatures that look at the same scene? Note that the mind states need not be perceptual for the riddle to retain its poignancy. For example, they may relate to some abstract mathematical truth such as $3 \times 3 = 9$, in which case cats, but presumably not intelligent robots, would be excluded (just for the record, there is a sense in which cats are great natural mathematicians; by the time this story gets to Figure 9.15 on page 428, you'll know exactly what I mean).

You and I. When you and I are regarding a scene, our perceptions of it are in many important respects identical: awake, sober observers rarely argue about the shared visual world, and so we probably agree that the group of shiny shapes in Figure 1.1 contains three objects. Such an agreement (in this case, about visual perception) implies something common to our mind states, because these minds is what we *are*. What is this commonality, and how is it related to what is common to our brain states (something must be, insofar as brains harbor minds)?

WHY THE MIND IS IN THE HEAD is the title of a remarkable paper by Warren McCulloch (1951), who set out to "bridge the traditional gulf between mind and body and the technical gap between things begotten and things made." Pointing out that the BRAIN is an information processing device, McCulloch notes: "To understand its proper function, we need to know what it computes." Analyzing cognition at this level is an integral part of cognitive science.

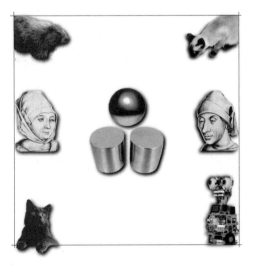

Figure 1.1 — The BRAIN/MIND RIDDLE. What is common to the minds of various sentient creatures that look at the scene in the center of this picture and see three objects? This question can be elaborated (by asking it about two cylinders and a sphere rather than "three objects"), or extended to other cognitive processes such as thought or discourse that need not involve vision or any other particular perceptual modality.

1.2 Minds as computational entities

A fancy way of expressing the insight we just gained is to say that minds are ORGANIZATIONAL INVARIANTS: two minds implemented in different substrates will be identical (invariant) as long as they are organized in the same way. Is there any convenient way of describing collections of objects so that their organizational properties are easy to grasp and to relate to? Indeed there is, and it is provided by a conceptual framework that has been familiar to each of us since elementary school. This framework is called computation.

The fundamental fact about computation — that computational concepts relate to the *organization of systems of objects*, rather than to the nature of the objects that comprise those systems — is easy to visualize with the help of a simple example. Imagine returning from the grocery store where you bought some apples and some oranges. You count the apples and find out that there are nine of them. You divide the apples into three groups of three and set them aside. Next, you discover that of the oranges there are also nine. These too you divide into three equal groups. Thanks to your computational prowess, the two kinds of fruit are now identically organized. Now, there is a clear parallel between the apple-orange correspondence in this example and the correspondence among mind states in various creatures discussed earlier. In each case, what matters and what is identical across systems — two piles of different fruit, or two differently embodied minds — is the *organization* of their constituent items.

We can now begin putting the vast resources of the theory of computation, which is a general framework for dealing with organizational phenomena, to work in understanding cognition. For that, we first need to convince ourselves that computational operations such as multiplying three by three to obtain nine are actually relevant to cognition.

To see that number manipulation is at the core of cognition, consider the example of an everyday perceptual phenomenon, LIGHTNESS CONSTANCY, which relates to the unchanging perception of the reflectance — the shade of gray or the color — of a surface, in the face of a possible drastic variability in the illumination and other viewing conditions. The human visual system is very good at solving this problem. For an immediate demonstration, switch off your reading light or otherwise darken the room; the page in front of you will still appear white, even though less light may now be reflected by the blank areas of the paper than by those covered with print when the page is seen under the full illumination.

The essence of THE NUMBER 9 is expressed in this ad for Florida fruit in three different ways, using apples, oranges and pears. Nineness is thus an ORGANIZATIONAL INVARIANT, independent of the objects that may be used to embody it.

The expression "organizational invariant" is due to Chalmers (1994).

The amount of light falling on the various surfaces in this early setup for studying LIGHTNESS CONSTANCY can be manipulated independently; the subjects have to report the lightness (perceived shade of gray) of each central square.

Because of the unavoidable confounding between surface reflectance and illumination, the problem of lightness recovery is beset with AMBIGUITY — and so are many other problems, all across cognition. In language, for example, ambiguity commonly arises in the interpretation of phrases that lack context, such as headlines ("China Cabinet Orders a Drive Against Inflation"), or church signs ("Hurting people loved here").[2] The standard computational approach taken by the brain in all these cases is statistical: infer, from experience, any regularities that hold for the domain at hand, and turn these into extra prior ASSUMPTIONS that can help disambiguate the situation. We shall see numerous examples of this approach in later chapters.

Let us see how the problem of attaining lightness constancy can be reduced to arithmetics. The signal that any visual system (human, feline, alien, or robotic) must use to find out the reflectance of a viewed surface is the amount of light that arrives from it at the measurement device, whether an eye or a camera (Figure 1.3). That amount can be represented by a number, say, the number of photons reflected by the surface in question that strike the detector each second. Note, however, that the measured number of photons is AMBIGUOUS, because it contains information both about the light source (the number of photons emitted per second) and the surface (the ratio of the incident number of photons to the number of those reflected by the surface). Specifically, these two pieces of information are *confounded* multiplicatively: a visual system can measure their product (the amount of light that arrives at the detector), but it has no direct access to the individual numbers.

The product of the two numbers that the visual system is after can be factored in an infinity of different ways: for example, if the detector measures 30 photons per second, the possibilities are that the surface is 50% reflective and the source emits 60 photons per second, or that the surface is 20% reflective and the source emits 150 photons per second, and so on. It is absolutely

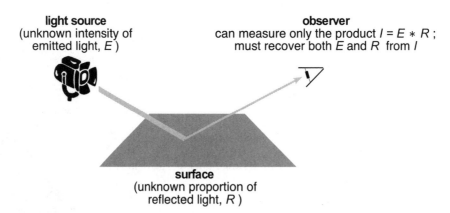

light source
(unknown intensity of
emitted light, E)

observer
can measure only the product $I = E * R$;
must recover both E and R from I

surface
(unknown proportion of
reflected light, R)

Figure 1.3 — The PROBLEM OF LIGHTNESS (computing the value of the surface reflectance R) is precisely equivalent to the problem of prying apart two numbers (R and E) that are only available to a visual system in the form of their product. I shall describe the possible solutions to this problem in a later chapter; for now, the conclusion is that at least some aspects of cognition are inherently computational.

crucial to note that the confounding of information about surface reflectance and source intensity stems from the physics of the imaging process and is inherent to the PROBLEM of lightness, not to any particular solution. As such, it constitutes a challenge to *any* visual system, natural or artificial, terrestrial or Martian. Furthermore, because the problem of lightness is most naturally, concisely, and completely described by a multiplicative relationship between two quantities of interest, it is the concept of computation that provides just the right tools to think about the *cognitive process* of lightness perception.

I shall describe the computational principle that allows the recovery both of surface reflectance and of light source intensity in Chapter 5. Meanwhile, let us review the lessons that we have learned so far:

- Reasoning from the riddle illustrated in Figure 1.1, we realized that minds must be organizational entities: a mind emerges from the relationships among elements of the substrate that implements it.

- The example of lightness indicates that at least some of those aspects of the world with which minds are concerned are best described computationally.

Computation is therefore doubly indispensable for understanding the mind. First, it provides a uniquely powerful framework within which organizational entities such as minds can be described. Second, minds are essentially computational because the challenges they must necessarily deal with are inherently computational.

1.3 About this book

1.3.1 On what this book is intended to be

> *Giving your son a skill is better than giving him one thousand pieces of gold.*
>
> — a Chinese proverb

I would like to help you to understand your own mind, and how it is related to your brain. The standard way of going about this, in an educational setting, is to write a textbook, or an encyclopedia. All the psychology textbooks I know, and many of the popular books that purport to tell everything

賜子千金, 不如賜子一技
This Chinese proverb[3] seems related to the following better-known one: "Give a man a fish and you feed him for a day; teach a man to fish and you feed him for a lifetime." I sincerely hope that the Hanzi text, which I cannot read, is authentic; an automatic translation that came from the same Web portal as the original did is only mildly encouraging in that respect: "Lu son wife, son and a better technology grant."

about how the mind works, do the equivalent of giving you a thousand pieces of gold (and with some you have to settle for just a couple of hundred). Instead of writing yet another compendium of facts about the mind (however skillfully dressed), I choose to communicate a set of skills, throwing in just enough examples to illustrate how these can be used.

To that end, I set out to write a book that would describe the *principles of operation of the human mind, considered as an information-processing, or computational, system.* Understanding the basic principles and mastering their application to a wide variety of problems in cognition will, I believe, instill in you the skills needed for informed thinking about all the faculties of the mind and the phenomena they give rise to, and for delving further into the relevant literature.

1.3.2   On how to use this book

It is difficult to do justice to the manifold and complex theme of brain/mind within the confines of a linear narrative imposed by the printed book form. I aim to circumvent this difficulty by several means. First, the main text is accompanied by side notes, which offer additional references, on-the-spot remarks, and some illustrations. In particular, concepts highlighted in the main text by SMALL CAPITALS usually have an explanatory margin note. Second, each chapter is followed by end notes, containing longer comments, explanations of the more complex issues,[4] and pointers into technical literature. Third, the book includes a complete bibliography. Although it is certainly possible to enjoy this book by reading the main text only, making use of all the extra materials is highly recommended.

The remainder of the book describes the application of the insights afforded by the computational approach to a broad range of issues in cognition. In pursuit of understanding, we shall venture across the traditional borders of cognitive psychology and into neighboring areas — neurobiology, ethology, linguistics — only to find that we never really left home, and that computation reigns there too. At times, the chase will lead us into conceptual minefields such as aesthetics or ethics; even there we shall be quite safe, most of the mines having been set off by my predecessors. A rough map of the ground I shall cover follows on the next page.

❦   ❦   ❦

Notes

[1]MARGIN NOTES, as well as END NOTES such as this one, may be skipped if you prefer to read the book as an uninterrupted narrative.

[2]Both these AMBIGUITY examples are from the Language Log blog. For the ambiguous headline, see http://itre.cis.upenn.edu/~myl/languagelog/archives/003912.html. For the ambiguous church sign, see http://itre.cis.upenn.edu/~myl/languagelog/archives/004438.html.

[3]I found this Chinese PROVERB at http://www.openface.ca/~dstephen/chprov.htm.

[4]The easily introduced idea that MINDS ARE ORGANIZATIONAL INVARIANTS is in fact one of the more complex issues presented in this book. Organizational identity as defined by Chalmers (1994) calls for a strict correspondence both between the states of the two minds

and between their respective state transitions. This means that to embody a copy of your mind it is not enough for a system to be capable of separately mirroring the various individual states of your brain. It must also mirror the orderly progression from state to state over time, while obeying any causal relationships that hold among the brain states, as well as between the brain and the state of affairs "out there" in the world. You'll find more about this in the next chapter, where the idea of computation is introduced properly, using state transitions as the main conceptual tool.

2

Computing Minds

Consider the nature of signs the mind makes use of for the
understanding of things, or conveying its knowledge to others.
For, since the things the mind contemplates are none of them,
besides itself, present to the understanding, it is necessary that
something else, as a sign or representation of the thing it
considers, should be present to it.

JOHN LOCKE (1690)

No cognition without representation!

A rallying cry of the cognitive revolution (*ca.* 1960)

2.1   Representations, and what they are good for

THE ARGUMENTS I outlined in the preceding chapter suggest that minds
are best explained in computational terms. To persuade you that the
quest for such an explanation is worth our while, I must now show that the
chain of explanatory reasoning connecting the proposed theory of the mind
to computation is sound, and that the concept of computation itself is solid
and intuitive enough to anchor that reasoning in the bedrock of empirical
knowledge and, indeed, common sense.

The three successive links in the chain of explanation that I am setting
out to forge can be conveniently cast in the form of three tightly interwoven
observations, as illustrated in Figure 2.1 on the next page. I propose to explain
the nature of minds in terms of the function of brains, brain function in terms
of computation, and computation itself in terms of principled manipulation of
representations. The opening observation — "minds are what brains do" (a
quip by Marvin Minsky, a co-founder of the MIT Artificial Intelligence Laboratory) — leads naturally to the next question: "what *is* it that brains do?"

Representations are good for planning ahead, and planning is a
hallmark of cognitive sophistication. Very appropriately, the name
of humanity's mythical educator
and the bringer of the gift of
fire, Prometheus, means FORE-
THOUGHT.

13

minds are what   ↗   **brains** embody varieties   ↗   **computation** is formally constrained
brains do   of **computation**   manipulation of **representations**

Figure 2.1 — The chain of explanation that grounds the understanding of minds in the understanding of computation.

The answer that this book offers — "brains compute" — is informative, plausible, and, as we shall see soon, fully consistent with the available knowledge in the neurosciences.

It is not surprising that computation can serve as a firm foundation for the emerging explanatory framework: we already learned that the problems that brains must contend with are inherently computational. In particular, the lightness example (illustrated in Figure 1.3 on page 8) made it clear that any visual system that aims to recover illumination and surface reflectance in a scene must be capable of arithmetical operations such as division, because the two quantities of interest are inexorably confounded by the viewing process, and are only available — to *any* observer — in the form of a product. This is where the notion of REPRESENTATION comes in: if the arithmetics the brain engages in (for example, while attempting to determine the illumination and the reflectance from their product, as measured by the eye) is to be of any use, the numbers being processed must represent — stand for — the actual entities "out there" in the world (illumination, reflectance, and so on, depending on

Figure 2.2 — Unlike in this New Yorker cartoon that makes gentle fun of the idea that ballet can serve as a reliable medium of communication, the relationship between mental REPRE-SENTATIONS and the REALITY they stand for is solid enough to support the weight of our cognitive worlds. The question of how this could possibly be — how a "mental" entity can refer to something "out there" in the world — has been keeping many philosophers busy ever since Brentano (1874). The good news is that this question *can* be put to rest, but doing so requires an appropriate conceptual armamentarium, so it will have to wait until section 5.5.

the problem at hand). My goal in this chapter is to survey the various ways in which the world can be represented, and in which its representations can support computation that is the essence of cognition.

2.1.1 The building blocks of representations: physical symbols

Let me define computation most simply as manipulation of numbers according to the rules of arithmetic (this is a provisional definition; in section 2.3 we shall see how it can and should be extended). Now, consider a system whose function is to manipulate numbers: a calculating device. Such a device needs a physical means for embodying the numbers, so that the subsystems that are charged with actually carrying out the arithmetical operations can do so. Recall what happens when you use a calculator to add two numbers. You type in the first number, then press the "+" key to choose the desired operation. Although that makes the first number disappear from the display, it certainly does not vanish without a trace: somewhere in the calculator's innards the number is still *represented* — embodied in the state of some electrical circuit — and is waiting to be called up the moment the second number is entered. Such embodiments of representations are called PHYSICAL SYMBOLS.

The entire raison d'être of symbols is to allow the representational system to deal by proxy with all manner of objects that the symbols signify. To the system that harbors them, the symbols themselves are therefore nothing more than vehicles for meaning, mediating between objects or events[1] that you cannot plausibly fit inside your head (such as an elephant, or the Battle of Lexington and Concord on April 19, 1775) and your various cognitive faculties. In philosophy, where the idea of symbols as mediators between the external world and the mind has originated, a symbol is defined as a SIGN that represents some entity for the benefit of some user. For millennia, it has been assumed that only rational, language-using entities — humans, for example — can imbue symbols with meaning. Indeed, it would seem that a heap of nine apples can mean "nine" only to a counting human, or something that can pass for one, such as Count von Count, the likable vampire muppet from Sesame Street.

Compelling as they are, the intuitions behind this assumption are wrong. First, it turns out that you don't have to be a rational, linguistically capable human to harbor meaningful symbolic representations. In particular, human adults whose language does not have words for numbers or for counting, preverbal human infants, and non-human animals, from rats to insects, have

PHYSICAL SYMBOLS. "The hypothesis [is] that intelligence is the work of symbol systems. Stated a little more formally, the hypothesis is that a physical symbol system ... has the necessary and sufficient means for general intelligent action." (Simon, 1996).

According to Charles Sanders Peirce, one of the fathers of semiotics (the philosophy of signs), "A SIGN, or representamen, is something which stands *to somebody* for something in some respect or capacity. It addresses *somebody*, that is, creates in the mind of that *person* an equivalent sign, or perhaps a more developed sign" (see Peirce 1960, 2.228; italics mine).

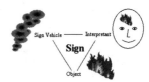

all been shown capable of representing numerosity (Gelman and Gallistel, 2004). Second, and more important, the capacity for symbolic representation is found not only at the level of "complete" cognitive systems (an entire rat; a whole preschooler), but also down at the level of their components — single neurons. Indeed, if you could wire a neuron so that its state covaries reliably with some quality or quantity that is external to it, the neuron would thereby become capable of representing it symbolically, for the potential benefit of the rest of the brain[2] (if you find this difficult to believe, take a peek at section 3.3 on page 50, whose title is *Neural Computation*).

The realization that it is not necessary to invite the Count to be present at every counting event has all but knocked the wind out of the traditional, anthropic view of symbols and meaning. Nevertheless, in the dark corners of certain philosophy departments, the Count Theory of Representation survives to the present day, having mutated into the claim that even the most complex instance of symbol manipulation by neural tissue or machine don't mean a thing if it ain't got a human consumer for the symbols it produces. The equivalent of a bunch of garlic for shooing away this Theory, which remains undead even as progress in the cognitive sciences drives it deeper and deeper into the shadows, is the realization that a physical symbol that is a part of a representational system can stand for something *for the benefit of the rest of the system*. By virtue of that, a symbol can exert causal influence on the other symbolic structures in the system, or even on the rest of the world "out there." What more can one ask of a mere representation?

Although symbols cannot be anything but physical,[3] precisely what they are made of is entirely unimportant insofar as using them for computing is concerned. This is because computation has to do with a certain level of *organization* of the entities on which it operates (as we already saw in Figure 1.1 on page 4). So, representations can have the same meaning, yet take on diverse physical forms, just as the number nine can be represented by nine apples or nine oranges. If the computing device consists of the arithmomanic Count sequestered with some fruit in the kitchen, apple "stuff" and orange "stuff" will prove to serve equally well in forming symbols for the number nine (say), provided that two conditions are met. First, representational *consistency* must be observed: there must be indeed nine of each fruit when the computation calls for the presence of the number nine. Second, the relevant subsystems must have *access* to the representations: the Count, who in this example outsources part of his brain's representational needs to the fruit, must have the opportunity to observe each pile of fruit as needed.

ARITHMOMANIA [Greek *arithmos* number + *mania*]: compulsive counting, as paces when walking, steps in a staircase, etc.; a common symptom in obsessive-compulsive disorder (Dorlands Medical Dictionary).

Crucially, symbols can be made completely abstract, if we give up the quite unnecessary requirement of *resemblance* between the symbol and the number it stands for. A pile of nine apples does resemble a pile of nine oranges in its numerosity. In contrast, the Roman symbol for "nine" bears resemblance neither to the Chinese symbol for "nine" nor to nine apples, however arranged. Indeed, of the various symbols for "nine" shown in the margins here, only one (the ancient cuneiform) may rely on resemblance by numerosity for generating its meaning.

Likewise, even the simplest mechanical computation aid, the abacus, does not use nine beads to represent the number nine; in fact, such representation by numerosity would render the abacus much less useful. Instead, the abacus uses *positional* coding: by convention, the positions of the beads on each wire, and the relative locations of the wires, code for numbers. And when the little human computers watching Sesame Street graduate to counting larger numbers, they quickly learn that the symbol "9" in "91" stands for quite a different number than in "19."

It is difficult to overstate the importance of such abstract modes of representation or symbolizing. Abstract symbols being made to refer consistently to diverse entities without having to resemble them is what enables systems that seemingly have nothing to do with numbers — such as neuronal networks in a brain, or transistor circuits in a computer — to represent and manipulate quantities, such as the lightness of a visible surface. As we shall see in detail in Chapter 4, the activity of a neuron may represent a certain number to the rest of the brain, as long as the conditions of consistency and accessibility are met. It is amusing to think that, way before a child masters single-digit numbers (let alone positional notation) in arithmetic, his or her brain will have already developed into an accomplished symbol-processing device. Brains juggle symbols (and, in particular, crunch numbers) for a living; without the representations they maintain and use, there would be no cognition.

2.1.2 Basic representations: mind states mirroring world states

Representational capacity is necessary for cognition (remember, "no cognition without representation") because the mind must relate to the world, and the world does not fit inside a brain — except vicariously, through the representations that the brain maintains. The examples of representations we looked at so far focused on quantities, or numbers. In a trivial sense, one *must* look at numbers when the task consists of dealing with numbers in the

These symbols, taken from some of the writing systems invented on this planet, share the same meaning. They are brought to you courtesy of the number nine.

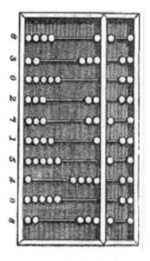

ABSTRACT SYMBOLS. On an abacus, quantities are represented not merely by the numbers of displaced beads on each wire, but also by the relative *positions* of the wires.

first place (as in counting). Less trivially, numbers that capture various aspects of the world need to be represented in perception (as when the sense of vision is used to gauge the lightness of surfaces). Yet the truly profound import of the idea of representation in cognition emerges only when we extend the domain of application of symbolic representation from quantitative to any and all aspects of the world, effectively trying to fit the entire world inside the representational system.

Although some cognitive systems got quite good at doing just that (and even at writing about the experience), most are much less ambitious. Consider the bay scallop, a bivalve mollusk that is equipped with fifty or so beautiful blue eyes, complete with reflective mirror optics (Llinás, 2001, p.104). Rapid changes in the ambient illumination cause the scallop's shell to snap closed, propelling it away from presumed danger (perhaps a cuttlefish passing overhead). This kind of information processing clearly does not amount to representing everything that could be represented about the scallop's habitat (the marine littoral teeming with colorful flora and fauna, the shape of the cuttlefish, and so on). Still, the scallops' capacity for processing visual information, limited as it may be, is manifestly sufficient for them to avoid being eaten, on the average, often enough to propagate their genes to the next generation: witness the longevity of bivalves, which first emerged in the Ordovician Period, more than 450 million years ago.

There is a continuity between the simple representations and straightforward algorithms that are behind the scallop's escape mechanism (many functional equivalents of which can be found in humans in the form of RE-FLEXES) and the sophistication of, say, Emily Dickinson's thinking about how her brain encompasses the sky. This continuity is satisfying, because it suggests that the powers of human mind, which appear (even to a scientifically literate non-specialist) to be nothing short of miraculous, are amenable to a standard evolutionary explanation. This explanation is greatly helped by findings of "missing links" between organisms that exhibit extreme characteristics on some performance scale. In the case of the capacity for representing the world, a useful example of a middle position between what scallops can represent and what humans can is found in pinyon jays.

This species of jays (which are relatives of crows) is highly social, with a strict pecking order in each flock. As you would expect, this means that each member of a flock knows which other birds are stronger than itself, and which are weaker. A recent study (Paz-y-Miño, Bond, Kamil, and Balda, 2004) demonstrated that jays are capable of putting this knowledge to pro-

The Brain – is wider than the Sky –
For – put them side by side –
The one the other will contain
With ease – and You – beside –

Emily Dickinson

THE REFLEX ARC — a simple, hard-wired prediction mechanism. The reflex arc that controls withdrawal prompted by contact with fire or some other noxious stimulus, illustrated in this engraving from a 1637 book by Descartes, requires very little in the manner of internal representation.

ductive use: the degree of submissiveness in their behavior toward a member of another flock (in a showdown over a shelled peanut) depends on the outcome of a previously observed match between the stranger and a familiar bird. If the competition is staged between two birds that are unfamiliar to the observer, its outcome has no effect on its behavior toward the stranger.

Of course, jays also represent many other characteristics of their environment. For example, sensitivity to social relations among conspecifics would be unthinkable without the ability to recognize individuals.[4] The beauty of the results just described is in that they demonstrate the capacity of jays for representing *abstract* information such as the dominance relations in a social ordering (see Figure 2.3). Even more important is the dynamical nature of this information: for jays to modify their behavior in response to an observed encounter, the representations they maintain must involve reflection of sorts, rather than merely a reflex.

2.1.3   Advanced representations: mind processes modeling world processes

An old Russian joke defines a member of the intelligentsia as someone who does not have enough muscle to put a hooligan in his place, but has enough brains not to get into a brawl with one. In some sense, this is the essence of forethought — a quality with which humankind has been endowed, according to the Greek mythology, by Prometheus. Ovid (in *Metamorphoses* 1.85)

REPRESENTING SOCIAL ORDER. Pinyon jays such as this one represent the dominance relations ("pecking order") among the members of their flock.

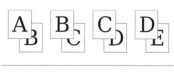

1. A ←→ E   ?

2. B ←→ D   ?

Figure 2.3 — A TRANSITIVE INFERENCE task. In this abstract example, five objects — A, B, C, D, E — are assumed to satisfy a set of dominance relations: A beats B, which in turn beats C, etc. (*top*). This data set implies additional relations, for which no direct observational evidence is available. Because A always wins in the observed cases, inferring that it would beat E (*bottom*, novel case 1) is trivial; not so in the other case, involving B and D, each of which wins and loses in half of the observed encounters (*bottom*, novel case 2). Humans, as well as certain species of birds (Paz-y-Miño et al., 2004) and fish (Grosenick et al., 2007), are capable of inferring that B would beat D in this example, showing that they maintain abstract, LATTICE-like relational representations, which must be *computed* from data (such as observed fights) by transitive inference.

describes how this Titan, whose name *means* "forethought," shaped the first human out of clay, and

> "...bade him to stand erect and turn his eyes to heaven."

The ability of certain species of birds to figure out, effectively, who would beat whom in an encounter with a rival, without running the risk of an actual confrontation, suggests that they were paying close attention when Prometheus decided to fight the monopolistic practices of the gods, and started releasing proprietary Olympian technology such as the use of fire into the public domain. The gift of forethought is a hallmark of advanced cognition — more so than the Promethean fire (without which primates such as us would survive just fine, even if this would mean a return to fighting hyenas over wildebeest bones).

Kenneth J. W. Craik, who pondered deeply the role of predictive capacity in cognition, suggested in his book, *The nature of explanation* (originally published in 1943) that a sophisticated cognitive system would do best by maintaining an **internal model** of the world — a representation whose form mirrors the apparent *causal structure* of the external events and processes relevant to the system's behavioral needs (Craik, 1952). Within this framework, the system's internal states (the embodiments of the symbols that comprise its representations) are linked causally to one another in such a manner that a transition between two states occurs just in case the external event giving rise to the one follows the event corresponding to the other.[5] The idea, thus, is to model the dynamics of the world, so as to be able to dodge (or catch) it better, which is what foresight is about. Indeed, a creature that can **predict** what would happen if it touches fire can avoid it after the first time, and does not need to rely on the action of a reflex arc.

2.2   Varieties of representations

The fundamental characteristic common to all representational systems — from the simplest bundles of reflexes that serve as the minds of scallops to the most sophisticated webs of concepts woven by human brains — is the reliance on mind states that reflect world states. The two basic questions that arise from this defining characteristic are:

- *What to represent?* What constitutes "the world" that needs to be rep-

REPRESENTING PROCESSES. *Armillaries* such as this one are models of the celestial sphere, invented by Eratosthenes in 255 BC. An armillary has a skeleton made of graduated metal circles linking the poles and representing the equator, the ecliptic, meridians and parallels; a ball representing the Earth is at the center. Setting the circles to a position corresponding to a given date allowed the astronomers to calculate the coordinates of the celestial bodies on that date. Note that the orderly procession of celestial bodies across the sky is reflected in the causal structure of the armillary's mechanism. As a consequence, setting it to any target date — past, present or future — can serve as a substitute for (a representation of) time travel to that date (solely for the purposes of observing the sky, that is; there is no way of getting rich from the stock market with this particular time machine).

resented, and what kinds of information about it should be included at a given level of representational detail?

- *How to represent?* What general principles can be used to establish a reliable correspondence between the representation and its object?

Let us examine these questions briefly, in turn.[6]

2.2.1 What to represent?

The answer to this question depends on the needs of the system and on the amount of information processing it can afford — had it but world enough, and time, everything and everywhen would be fair game for representation.

World. THE INANIMATE NATURE. The first order of business of any cognitive agent is to represent (at least some of) its surroundings. THE OTH- ERS. To escape from predators, identify potential mates, and perhaps engage in social interactions with conspecifics, agents include these "others" among the entities to be represented. On a more abstract level, and more in line with Craik's idea of the value of predictive coding, I observe how important it is for me now to represent adequately *you*, the reader, so as to make my writing effective. THE SELF. If what the agent is trying to predict includes the out- comes of its own actions, it may end up — if its organizational complexity affords it — with a sense of self; as Llinás (2001, p.23) puts it, "What is the repository of predictive function? I believe the answer lies in what we call the self: self is the centralization of prediction." The implications of such a development are exciting, because self-awareness is one of the telltale signs of higher-order consciousness.

Time. THE PRESENT. For bundle-of-reflexes creatures that live perpet- ually on the cusp of time that separates the past from the future, only present objects and current events are included. Existence in the present is the in- escapable doom of the scallop, or a robotic vacuum cleaner that scurries un- der your furniture hunting dust bunnies; it is the conscious choice of anyone who heeds the advice of Omar Khayyam not to fret over "unborn tomorrow and dead yesterday." THE PAST. More sophisticated systems include the past in what they represent. There is clearly a range of possibilities here. On the one hand, a reflex whose strength depends on its recent history of activa- tion is a kind of memory (for elucidating the neural basis of such elementary memory abilities in the mollusk *Aplysia*, Eric Kandel was awarded the Nobel Prize in physiology or medicine for the year 2000; see Kandel, 2003). On

WORLD ENOUGH, AND TIME. As contem- porary physics tells us, and as Salvador Dalí seems to have intuited, space and time are inextricably interwoven. In representing the universe, cognitive systems must heed both; some of them got to be very, very good at it.

Ah, fill the Cup: what boots it to repeat
How Time is slipping underneath our Feet:
Unborn TOMORROW, and dead YESTERDAY,
Why fret about them if TODAY be sweet!
Rubaiyat of Omar Khayyam
tr. Edward Fitzgerald
(1983, rubai 37)

the other hand, it's a long way from pliable reflexes to the kind of minutiae-filled remembrance of things past that can precipitate a Proustian outpouring of page-length paragraphs. THE FUTURE. The continuity of the world over time guarantees that a system whose representations extend into the past is automatically well-positioned to predict the future (in fact, one may argue that spending resources on remembering the past makes sense only if it can be used to predict the future).[7]

In the context of representing the future, it is important to realize that forming predictions does not mean simply that the system expects the persistence of recent or current state of affairs (as represented by a set of chosen variables that it monitors). Even the *trends* defined over the measured variables may not suffice, if the phenomenon in question possesses a complex internal causal structure that does not translate well into mere trends (linear, quadratic, or higher-order[8]) over the measured quantities. As usual, it is instructive to consider both simpler and more complex examples of such a situation.

Some, but not much, REMEM-BRANCE OF THINGS PAST: the sea hare, *Aplysia californica*.

For the former, recall the pinyon jay internalizing the relative strengths of the members of its flock: the relevant information here is best described by mathematical structures known as lattices (see Figure 2.3 on page 19),[9] whose inference from sampled relations must be done in adherence to strict rules of logic. At the top end of the sophistication scale, we find the ability of humans to predict where a sentence is going (often down to the very word that is expected to come next). In a later chapter, you'll hear more about the representations that underlie such abilities, and the possible ways of learning these from samples of natural language (which is what human babies excel at).

Detailed and voluminous REMEM-BRANCE OF THINGS PAST: the last page of the manuscript of *À la recherche du temps perdu* by Marcel Proust.

2.2.2 How to represent?

The mechanisms that connect objects and events in the outside world to the symbols that represent them must, first and foremost, be causal. In other words, the activation of a symbol must be a reliable indicator of the presence of the object or event that it came to signify. Beyond that, many possibilities exist; several of them are surveyed below in the form of dichotomies along the most importance dimensions (which also admit intermediate settings).

Analog, digital

The first dimension has to do with the degree of arbitrariness in the relationship between the representation and the thing represented. One extreme possibility — ANALOG representation — describes a situation that contains a causal relationship with no room for any arbitrariness. A good example here is the relationship between an object and its optically formed image — or even its painting. Thus, although René Magritte gave the painting reproduced in Figure 2.4 on the following page, left, the title *The Treachery of Images* (because it is a *picture* of a pipe, not a real pipe), the presence of a picture of a pipe on your retina is normally a good sign that a real, solid pipe is out there. At least, this was the case before Magritte's Cro-Magnon predecessors threw the metaphorical wrench into the cogwheels of representation by making aurochs come to life at Lascaux, in defiance of time (the magnificent aurochs are, sadly, extinct, along with much of the other fauna of paleolithic Europe) and space (there were never real aurochs *in* those caves).

The analog mode of signification is called nomothetic (from the Greek *nomos*, law), because physical laws are at work at the bottom of every instance of analog representation (in the relationship between an object and its image, these are the laws of optics). In contrast, the relationship between the symbol and the thing it stands for may be arbitrary (for example, a matter of contingent association, or even convention). Encoding such relationships by discrete, numerical symbols results in representations that are referred to as DIGITAL. The ultimate maximally abstract, digital representation is a numerical symbol that stands for something not inherently numerical — such as how the number of lanterns in the belfry of the North Church signified, in a purely arbitrary fashion that had been agreed upon between Paul Revere and Robert Newman, the sexton, the mode of advancement of the British troops on Boston on April 18, 1775.[10]

Explicit, implicit

If a symbol represents an object by virtue of encapsulating the relevant information, or pointing toward information that is immediately available elsewhere (as is the case, respectively, with analog and digital representations just discussed), it can be thought of as an EXPLICIT representation. Alternatively, a symbol can represent something by virtue of containing a *blueprint* for it, just as the egg in Magritte's *Clairvoyance* (Figure 2.4 on the next page, right)

ANALOG REPRESENTATION.
Paleolithic drawings of animals from the caves of Lascaux, France.

DIGITAL REPRESENTATION.
Listen my children and you shall hear
Of the midnight ride of Paul Revere,
On the eighteenth of April, in Seventy-five;
Hardly a man is now alive
Who remembers that famous day and year.

He said to his friend, "If the British march
By land or sea from the town to-night,
Hang a lantern aloft in the belfry arch
Of the North Church tower as a signal light,–
ONE IF BY LAND, AND TWO IF BY SEA;
And I on the opposite shore will be,
Ready to ride and spread the alarm
Through every Middlesex village and farm,
For the country folk to be up and to arm."

Paul Revere's Ride
Henry Wadsworth Longfellow

is a blueprint for the bird that is being painted. The best examples of this intriguing possibility — that of an IMPLICIT representation — are found in systems responsible for controlling biological motion. Prior to its execution, the representation of a complex multi-jointed arm movement — its MOTOR PROGRAM — is implicit, because the sequence of commands that is about to be sent to the muscles is meaningful only insofar as one can assume an interaction of the musculature with the skeletal structures (and often with the external world).

To be useful, an implicit symbol needs a more sophisticated interpretation mechanism than an explicit representation does (note that in *Clairvoyance*, the egg is "interpreted" by the painter). Without the proper embodiment, a motor program is worthless: even if you could download into the nervous system of an octopus a motor program that a horse's brain uses to coordinate trotting, the result of pushing the "run" button could only be a total system crash.

As to the role of external props in executing a motor program, I am reminded of my parents' Siamese cat, who, when she was young, used to like turning corners really fast. In many places around the house, the cat did consistently pull off breathtakingly fast turns by bouncing in mid-turn against a conveniently situated wall, which thus served as an integral part of her motor program for corner turning. Where such props were unavailable, the cat's weakness for speed, in combination with low-friction ceramic tile floors, made for some spectacular acrobatics: the cat would skid around the corner,

Figure 2.4 — *Left:* both ANALOG and DIGITAL representations are exemplified by this painting, titled *The Treachery of Images*, by René Magritte. *Right:* Magritte's *Clairvoyance* serves to illustrate the distinction between EXPLICIT and IMPLICIT representations. To represent the world, the brain does not have to replicate it, just as visual art is the most expressive when it transcends photography: as Paul Klee remarked, "art does not reproduce the visible; rather, it makes visible."

the hind paws braking frantically to prevent a roll-over, with the front paws already accelerating in the new direction.

Passive, active

The physical embodiment in the cat's brain of the intention to get up and turn a corner must be ACTIVE enough to cause the rest of the brain to wake up from its all-too-habitual slumber and start executing the appropriate motor program. More generally, a cognitive system cannot make do exclusively with PASSIVE representations that merely make information available, without actively causing things to happen. The active, causal aspects of representations may be highly circumscribed, but they cannot be completely absent from a system that aspires to be autonomous, rather than yoked to some independent control agency, such as the infamous HOMUNCULUS (Noelle, 2001; see Figure 2.5).

Because passing the buck of causality to a homunculus is a sure recipe for an explanatory disaster, a comprehensive theory of the mind has no choice but to posit the existence of active representations. As we shall see in the next section, the computational framework offers a way to banish the homunculus, by allowing representations to manipulate themselves according to a program that specifies their causal interactions and that can in turn be modified by them as needed.

Embodied MOTOR PROGRAM: a photographic proof that some cats indeed practice wall-assisted locomotion, thereby demonstrating the embodied nature of motor control.

Figure 2.5 — The HOMUNCULUS (from Latin, *little man*) is the ultimate consumer and manipulator of representations in those careless theories of the mind that neglect to specify a mechanism whereby symbols can manipulate themselves (Hofstadter, 1985b). If not exorcised (Noelle, 2001) from a theory, a homunculus promptly undermines it by leading to an infinite regress, because its own capacity for manipulating representations needs to be accounted for. This figure illustrates a self-undermining homunculus-based "theory" of vision.

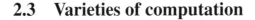

2.3   Varieties of computation

These days, an average person's exposure to the theory and practice of computation typically consists of coaxing an ungainly beige box into doing his or her bidding (Mac users, whose machines are both pleasing to the eye and uncommonly obedient, are exempt from this generalization).[11] Because of that, most of us naturally grow suspicious when offered computation as an explanatory concept: if mind processes are computational, and if computation means what we think it does, who is in charge of the programming and the execution?

A TYPICAL PERSONAL COM-
PUTER system, *ca.* 2004. In a piece of characteristically unforgettable advice, Douglas Adams, the author of *The Hitchhiker's Guide to the Galaxy*, suggested that the best way to annoy the hell out of a cheeky computer is to count quietly within its earshot ("one, two, three..."), the idea being that this is like whispering "blood, blood, ..." into a person's ear.

The evolution of the meaning of the word COMPUTER between the industrial and the information revolutions:

Webster Dictionary, 1828:
COMPUTER, n.   One who computes; a reckoner; a calculator.

Webster Dictionary, 1913:
COMPUTER, n.   One who computes. [– a machine which computes –]

Merriam-Webster Dictionary, 1997:
COMPUTER, n.   One that computes; specifically: a programmable electronic device that can store, retrieve, and process data.

If the word "data" is construed to mean "any symbol" (as it means in computer science), we converge with the definition of computation offered in Figure 2.1 on page 14.

2.3.1   The evolution of the idea of computation: from a person counting to symbols manipulating themselves

These suspicions are excusable, seeing that for most of our species' history, the word COMPUTER used to refer to a person who computes, and computation to mere counting (that is, a manipulation of numbers according to the rules of arithmetic). To understand how computation can explain minds, both these associations need to be relaxed. With the introduction of calculating machines about a century ago, the meaning of "computer" indeed got extended to a machine that calculates, eventually replacing the original sense. Surprisingly, however, that was not the most important development in the history of the concept of computation: the really fundamental change came with Kurt Gödel's use of numbers to represent arbitrary symbolic expressions. This was followed shortly by the emergence, from the work of Alonzo Church, Emil Post, and Alan Turing, of a unified concept of computation as rule-bound manipulation of symbols.

Strangely enough, the ascendancy of general symbol manipulation went unnoticed outside mathematical logic and computer science, even though most people today use computers for anything but number crunching for its own sake. Indeed, when you insert a picture into the middle of a text file using a typical word-processing application such as the OpenOffice[12] Writer, the software must recompute the document's representation, an operation that includes moving around some symbols (words and images). These are represented in your computer's memory by arrays of numbers. However, that numbers are at the basis of our computers' representation is completely immaterial as to the nature of the information processing the computers engage in. The same document would be represented differently if you were to use pencil and paper (and scissors and tape) to carry out the editing task (just remember, or ask your elders, what "cut and paste" used to mean when the Beatles were still playing together).

2.3.2   The Turing Machine

The concern about a possible need for a homunculus — a ghost in the machine of the mind — underscores the critical importance of showing that the computational processes that comprise a mind do not themselves need mindful agents to set them up and carry them out. If this were impossible, the explanation of minds in terms of computation would be hopelessly circular. The now-classical way of avoiding such circularity is to construe computation as dogged adherence to a sequence of instructions each of which is explicit, simple, and unequivocal.

This is precisely what the best-known abstract model of computation — the TURING MACHINE, illustrated in Figure 2.6 — is all about.[13] The basic idea is to reduce complex procedures to sequences of elementary steps whose execution can be mechanized. Suppose you instruct your computer to carry out a computation for you — say, find out what $3 + 2$ is. To comply, it would have to do something like the following: write 3 into a register in its memory, write 2 into another register, then repeatedly increment the content of the first register by 1 while decrementing the content of the second register also by 1, until the latter contains a 0. Note that addition of two numbers has been

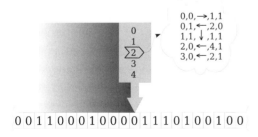

0011000010000111101010100100

Figure 2.6 — A TURING MACHINE is a formalism invented by Alan Turing that allows the specification of an EFFECTIVE mapping between input and output symbolic expressions. In this illustration, the next to last line in the machine's *program* — the table inside the balloon — specifies that **if** the internal *state* is 2 and the *input* (read off the *memory tape*) is '0' (as happens to be the case), **then** the read/write head should *move* to the left, the new state should be 4, and the *output* symbol to be written to the tape should be '1.' That such a machine can compute anything that the largest supercomputer in the world can is a sign, not of a weakness of the latter, but of the remarkable power and generality of the former.

reduced here to the elementary operations of incrementing and decrementing a register by 1 (if you doubt that these operations are indeed simpler than regular arithmetic, consider the addition of 2092423555 and 56097444, which is reducible to the same elementary operations in precisely the same manner).

A critical — and fully intended — byproduct of reducing addition to simpler elementary operations is that it becomes completely mechanical. Using the terminology of computer science, addition is thus shown to be amenable to an EFFECTIVE implementation. Here is how it goes: a procedure for achieving some desired result is called effective if

1. it is specified by a finite number of exact instructions, each expressed in terms of a finite number of symbols;

2. these instructions can, in principle, be carried out by a human being unaided by any machinery save paper and pencil; they require no insight or ingenuity on the part of the human being carrying them out.

In a procedure that is effective in the sense just defined, there is no "devil in the details" and no implicit need for a homunculus, or a divine intervention, on which the ultimate responsibility for making things work would have to be pinned.[14] The requirement of effectiveness is thus an obligatory component of any computation-based strategy for explaining cognition.[15]

2.3.3 Dynamical systems

Alan Turing's idealization of the familiar process of pencil-and-paper computation proved to be an incredibly fruitful idea. In the domain of theoretical computer science, it led to deep insights into the far-reaching capabilities and the fundamental limitations of systems that manipulate symbols. Advances in algorithmics, in turn, translate into the practical breakthroughs that sustain the current information revolution. However, the very idealization that made all this possible is also making Turing-style computation very difficult to apply in theoretical neuroscience. Seeing the brain as hardware for running the mind's software is a fad that should have gone away with the journalistic custom of calling computers "brains." Still, as our reasoning from first principles showed, brains clearly must engage in some kind of computation, so the real challenge is to find a framework for thinking about computation that is relatable to the deep principles behind Turing's formalism, but not necessarily to its surface details.

An EFFECTIVE procedure needs neither a prime mover that sets its metaphorical cogs in motion, nor a supervisor that continually oversees its execution. We need to make sure that computational processes invoked to explain the mind are effective in this sense. The painting (*Prime Mover* by Raphael, Stanza della Segnatura, Palazzi Pontifici, Vatican) shows Urania, the Muse of Astronomy, setting in motion the celestial orb (it does *not* depict a boot about to kick a soccer ball, nor the outline of Italy alongside a strangely circular Sicily — these are artifacts of reducing the ceiling-wide fresco to the size of a postal stamp).

What, then, are the deep principles behind Turing computation? The core notions are (1) distinct *states*, each of which is a complete snapshot of the Turing Machine's registers and any other memory, and (2) *transitions* between states, which are determined by the TM's program on the basis of its current state and the input, if any. In a very deep sense any implementation of a TM is, therefore, merely a special kind of physical system, whose components have been crafted and arranged to obey, in addition to the usual laws of physics, certain constraints that make it useful as an information processor — just as the obstacles and traps in a pinball machine serve to define a mapping between the player's actions and the succession of the machine's internal states, while complying, as they must, with the laws of dynamics that bear the name of Isaac Newton.

The label DYNAMICAL SYSTEM applies to all kinds of physical objects, from personal computers and pinball machines to goats and galaxies. Although only some of these can support Turing-style symbol processing, a larger class of dynamical systems can be set up to perform computation construed in a broad sense as a principled manipulation of representations.[17] A dynamical system is characterized by the number of variables ("degrees of freedom") that are needed to describe it completely. A collection of states of such a system can therefore be naturally described by a A STATE SPACE diagram: a plot in as many dimensions as there are degrees of freedom, in which each point corresponds to a particular state. Points corresponding to successive snapshots of the system's state are usually connected in the plot

A DYNAMICAL SYSTEM "is a mathematical object that unambiguously describes how the state of some system evolves over time" (Beer, 2000).[16] As Beer notes, systems of differential equations and Turing machines are both examples of dynamical systems.

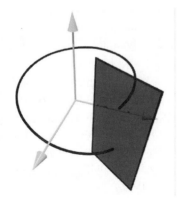

Figure 2.7 — A portion of a STATE SPACE trajectory of a dynamical system with three degrees of freedom. Dynamical systems can be set up to perform computations in a variety of ways. For example, if the system's state is read out periodically when the trajectory reaches the region indicated by the shaded plane, computation could consist of the mapping between the values of the input variables and the coordinates of intersections between the trajectory and this "readout" plane. Note that if the latter is divided into discrete regions, and if these are assigned meanings, this analog mode of representation becomes essentially digital. Indeed, a Turing Machine is nothing but an idealized limiting case of a continuous dynamical system (with some embellishments, such as the infinite input/output tape).

To understand a dragonfly, one must reduce it to simpler subsystems: flight control, digestion, etc. Complex systems such as dragonflies are typically amenable to a hierarchical analysis, as suggested by the diagram below (cf. Rudrauf, Lutz, Cosmelli, Lachaux, and le van Quyen, 2003, fig.3). Yet, it would be futile to seek a complete explanation of a complex system (say, a dragonfly) directly in terms of low-level components such as molecules. Cognitive science (and other sciences of complex systems) must therefore resort to HIERARCHICAL ABSTRACTION, which capitalizes on the separation of levels that characterizes complex systems. It is a fundamental organizational principle of such systems that without hierarchical structuring there would be no complexity (see the quote from Simon (1973) on 2.4 on the facing page).

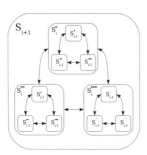

to form a state-space trajectory, which shows how the system's state evolves over time (Figure 2.7 on the previous page illustrates the trajectory of a three-dimensional system).

Whereas in a Turing Machine the entities over which a computation is defined are represented internally by static states or snapshots of the machine's memory, in a dynamical system a representation may be defined, for example, by the region of the state space to which a state-space trajectory is confined during the relevant time interval, or by the shape of the corresponding portion of the trajectory. Tweaking the system's parameters (think of the pinball machine knobs) or providing it with an external input (tilt!) affects its dynamics, changing the progression of states and with it the computation carried out by the system.

2.4   The heart of the mind: hierarchical abstraction

It is difficult to imagine how computation that is constrained to be effective can amount to anything interesting. How can a sequence of operations that are simple enough to be carried out by Turing Machines (Figure 2.6 on page 27) ever be powerful enough to explain cognition? To understand that, we must realize that the requirement that any effective procedure consist of a series of simple and exact steps does not imply that effective computation is good only for doing arithmetic, or only for supporting the kind of behavior that we have developed a bad habit of calling "robotic": inflexible and uninventive (it is a bad habit because conscious robots, who are due to appear on the scene before this century is out, will not appreciate it). Although each step on its own must be simple (to allow execution by mindless entities, such as neurons, or electronic circuits controlling state transitions, memory access, and input/output functions of a computer), representational systems have at their disposal an excellent method for generating complexity: HIERARCHICAL ABSTRACTION.

Let me show what hierarchical abstraction is by pointing out what it is not. First, **hierarchical abstraction is not a luxury.** Invoking it to explain the stunning complexity of so much of cognition is really not a far-reaching leap of the imagination, but rather a dictate of the reality. Simplicity is what complexity must be made of, because there isn't anything else to make it out of,[18] and hierarchical abstraction is the only way in which sufficiently interesting complex stuff can be built out of simple building blocks.

On a related note, **hierarchical abstraction is not a miracle**, but rather a natural by-product of the idea of using symbols as vehicles of representation. The basic requirement of representations is that they *make explicit* certain properties of the world. This insight, which elaborates on John Locke's (1690) observation of the indispensability of representations to minds (as stated in the epigraph to the present chapter), has been formulated by David Marr. In an example that appears in his book *Vision*, Marr (1982) compares the suitability of the Roman numerical notation and the modern one for judging the parity of a number. In the Roman notation, it is impossible simply to read parity off the symbolic representation of the number. In the decimal positional notation, it is easier: you have to look just at the rightmost digit, and remember that 0, 2, 4, 6 and 8 are even. The ultimate representation for telling parity at a glance is binary: the number is even if the rightmost digit is 0, and that's it; the binary notation makes parity explicit. We can imagine a notation that would include an extra bit indicating whether the number represented is prime;[19] although primality can be computed when needed (using one of the many existing precise or approximate algorithms), such a representation would save this work on future occasions by carrying it out once and making the result explicit.

Finally, **hierarchical abstraction is not merely a tool** that the cognitive scientists use to study the mind, but rather, first and foremost, the mind's tool for the study of the world. True, a complex phenomenon such as a mind is seen as fundamentally simpler precisely when it is represented in terms of hierarchically structured components (rather than, say, in terms of a long list of uniformly simple elementary components). Indeed, it is only when each successive layer of representation allows computations to be carried out by simpler means that an infinite explanatory regress and the need for a homunculus are forestalled. Let us, however, look at the situation from the point of view of the mind itself: without appropriately structured mediating states (representations), a cognitive system would be incapable of dealing with the complex real world. Thus, in a very real sense, there would be no cognitive (or any other) scientists on this (or any other) planet, were it not for the mind's capacity for hierarchical abstraction.

More precisely, hierarchical representations are indispensable for cognitive systems that aspire to *scale up* their understanding of the world. The mind of an *Aplysia californica* may do without hierarchical abstraction; the mind of Marcel Proust — definitely not.[20]

Scientific knowledge is organized in levels, not because reduction in principle is impossible, but because nature is organized in levels, and the pattern at each level is most clearly discerned by abstracting from the detail of the levels far below. [...] And nature is organized in levels because hierarchic structures – systems of Chinese boxes – provide the most viable form for any system of even moderate complexity.

— Herbert A. Simon (1973)

THE SKY IS NOT THE LIMIT. The Earth-made probes that are traveling among the outer planets of the solar system even as you are reading these lines ride on the human brain's capacity for acquiring and processing hierarchically structured representations of the complex universe we live in.

As the legend of the Fall illustrates, gods have a habit of taking a personal affront at anyone aiding mortals in their yearning for KNOWLEDGE. Zeus too punished Prometheus, by chaining him to a rock in the Caucasus mountains and sending his eagle to gnaw on the liver of humanity's mythical educator.

2.5 Computation *ad astra*

The power of hierarchical abstraction opens up endless possibilities for the evolution of brains that can acquire, maintain, and improve sophisticated systems of representations, and thus serve as hosts to advanced minds. For such entities, even the sky is not a limit. When scientists control an interplanetary probe on a flyby of Saturn, they can afford to think about the task in terms of the specific impulse and the vectoring provided by the rocket engine, abstracting away the details of its function. The probe's engine, in turn, was built by engineers who could abstract away the chemical composition of nitrogen tetroxide (N_2O_4) and monomethylhydrazine ($N_2H_3CH_3$) and focus on channeling the energy made available by their reaction. All this rocket science is made possible by one and the same overarching principle: the capacity for dealing with any information-processing task on a number of levels of abstraction. Consider this example: in each engineer's brain, there must exist some level of representation capable of treating other members of the team as persons, rather than focusing mindlessly on, say, what they look like (which is the only thing any person's visual cortex really cares about), or what precise words they use to express a given thought (say, "hydrazine running low," or "fuel almost exhausted").

Many of us humans, and certainly most of the human-invented deities, see such unfettered capacity for acquiring and using representations — that is, KNOWLEDGE — of the world as a grave menace. The mythical torments to which Zeus condemned Prometheus and the curse with which Jehovah cursed the biblical Serpent both express the fears that people's predilection for occasionally using their brains to the full extent evokes among the faint of heart.[21]

A contrasting view, found in the Mishna (Avot 2, 13), sees a good mind, along with a good heart, as something to be cherished:

> Rabban Jochanan ben Zakkai said to them: Go and see which is the good a man shall cherish most. Rabbi Eliezer said, a good eye. Rabbi Joshua said, a good companion. Rabbi Yosi said, a good neighbor. Rabbi Shimon said, foresight.[22] Rabbi Elazar said, a good heart. He said to them: I prefer the words of Elazar ben Arach to your words, for in his words yours are included.

To better appreciate this passage, it helps to know that at the time of its writing the Hebrew word for "heart" (*lēb*) stood also for "mind" in all its manifestations: cognitive, affective, and conative (according to Gier (2007), "none of the ancients that we know attributed thinking to the brain, so *lēb* expresses all the functions that we would now ascribe to the brain; Wolff (1974, p.51) lists them as 'the power of perception, reason, understanding, insight, consciousness, memory, knowledge, reflection, judgment, sense of direction, discernment'"). Thus, the conclusion offered by Rabban ("Great Rabbi") ben Zakkai — that a "good heart" is to be cherished above other desiderata because it contains them — resonates surprisingly well with the cognitively informed humanistic ethics that I shall describe in Chapter 10.[23]

Meanwhile, observe that to have a truly good heart, you must know good from evil. How can you do that? Use your brain, of course. The next chapter explains what that means, computationally.

❦ ❦ ❦

Notes

[1] Because NOTHING IS PERMANENT, objects are merely slow events (Hurford, 2003).

[2] BARE-MINIMUM REPRESENTATIONS. Single neurons are not the simplest entities imaginable that are capable of representing things: even a lowly thermostat can represent (the temperature of the room, for the benefit of the furnace). The simplest thermostat consists of a bimetallic strip, which bends this way or that, depending on the ambient temperature, because the two metals have different thermal expansion properties:

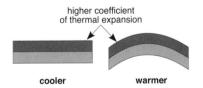

In doing so, the strip closes or opens the circuit that fires the furnace.

[3] PHYSICAL SYMBOLS. Consider for a moment a representational system that harbors symbols that are not physical. Such a system would be totally ineffectual, because anything non-physical is incapable, as a matter of principle, from interacting in any way with the physical world (if it does interact, it becomes by definition physical). This argument has been very effective in keeping cognitive scientists from succumbing to Cartesian dualism.

[4] BIRD COGNITION. A 1989 book on the evolution of language (*The Motor Theory of Language Origin*, R. Allott, pp. 13-30, Lewes: Book Guild) observes:

> If one approaches the question [of language evolution] from the standpoint of more traditional theory, a number of features should be considered together: bipedalism, manipulative skill, good sound discrimination, ability to imitate and respond to differing sound patterns, ability to form concepts, ability to generalise and solve practical problems, better than usual vertebrate sight, bodily agility, close group bonding, [...] Put these elements together and what do you get? A bird!

[5]INTERNAL STATES MIRRORING THE WORLD. The relationship we're after is nomothetic (that is, one that adheres to a law of nature), even if it is only probabilistic. Note that if an internal model succeeds to explain a set of the system's behaviors, such an explanation would necessarily be both *systematic* (because the same model would underlie all aspects of the explanation) and *causal* (because of the inherent causality of any process model). Thus, the two basic requirements concerning the nature of explanation in cognitive psychology as a science would be fulfilled.

[6]PRINCIPLES OF PSYCHOLOGY. A fascinating introduction to these issues can be found in the writings of William James (1890); these are now out of copyright, and most are available online. Not only do James's books offer profound insights into human nature, which are still valid a century later, but his prose is also much better than that of his brother Henry.

[7]PREDICTING THE FUTURE. Philosophically minded readers who think there may be a contradiction between my claims of the importance of prediction in cognition and the unsoundness of induction as a mode of reasoning (Hume's Problem) are advised to read Fogelin (2003, ch. 5). I shall return to discuss induction, causality, and prospective functions of memory in later chapters.

[8]STATISTICAL TRENDS. A data set is said to possess a linear trend if it can be approximated well by an equation in which no independent variable is raised to a power of two or more. In two dimensions, such an equation describes a straight line (hence the word "linear"), as in $y = ax + b$; in three dimensions, it may be a plane, and so on. Likewise, a quadratic trend corresponds to an equation in which variables may be at most squared.

[9]LATTICES are sets in which the elements are ordered according to some relation, yet the order is partial: pairs of elements may exist within which neither element dominates the other.

[10]ANALOG VS. DIGITAL. Two other contrasts found in the literature that parallel the analog-digital distinction are continuous-discrete and iconic-symbolic. The ultimate validity of the former contrast is in doubt because of modern physics, which sees everything as quantized, yet deals with continuous probabilities over such discrete entities. The other contrast is, likewise, questionable. Indeed, symbols are abstract and images iconic by definition, but it seems to me that iconic and symbolic representations actually have a lot in common. Iconicity (the resemblance between a picture and its object) is in the eye of the beholder, and the signification afforded by a symbol needs an interpreting agency to be of any use. Moreover, the degree to which the representation by an icon is free of convention and the degree to which that of an abstract symbol is bound by it both vary: a stylized painting may represent largely due to convention, and a mnemonically convenient symbol may do so by dint of its physical make-up.

[11] THE FUNDAMENTALITY OF COMPUTATION. There is more to the science of computation than constant skirmishes with your PC. Some scientific disciplines posit information processing or computation as the most basic phenomenon, in terms of which everything else has to be explained. In their wide-ranging review of developmental and evolutionary biology,

Szathmáry and Smith (1995, p.231) single out information as "[a] central idea in contemporary biology." This idea reveals the deep connections between biology and memetics: the science of self-replicating information patterns acted upon by natural selection (Dawkins, 1976; cf. section 6.10.2). Then there is information physics — an ontological stance concerning the fabric of reality whose flavor is perfectly captured by the expression "it from bit" coined by John Archibald Wheeler.

[12]OPENOFFICE is a full, open-source office software suite, available free from http://www.openoffice.org.

[13]Formally, a (one-tape) TURING MACHINE is a 7-tuple $M = (Q, \Gamma, \Sigma, s, b, F, \delta)$, where

- Q is a finite set of states;

- Γ is a finite set of the tape alphabet;

- Σ is a finite set of the input alphabet ($\Sigma \subseteq \Gamma$);

- $s \in Q$ is the initial state;

- b is the blank symbol ($b \in \Gamma - \Sigma$);

- $F \subseteq Q$ is the set of final or accepting states;

- $\delta : Q \times \Gamma \rightarrow Q \times \Gamma \times \{L, R\}$ is a partial *transition function*, where L and R denote, respectively, left and right shift of the read/write head.

Given the current state and input symbol, the transition function (or action table) decides whether or not to overwrite the current tape cell (and if yes, with which symbol), and whether to move the read-write head left, right, or to leave it in the same place. Some of the more fascinating basic theorems of computer science state that various enhancements of this basic formalism, such as adding another infinite tape, or more read/write heads, or extra internal registers, do not in fact change its power: the beefed-up machine computes the same set of functions as the original version (Hopcroft and Ullman, 1979). Turing Machines can also *simulate* one another (cf. note 30 on page 232) — an ability that makes Turing computation a particularly useful conceptual tool for thinking about certain key cognitive tasks, as we shall see in later chapters.

[14]The full definition of an EFFECTIVE PROCEDURE includes another clause: if carried out without error, the procedure will always produce the desired result in a finite number of steps. This clause is less relevant to the modeling of cognition, if only because cognition is an open-ended process.

[15]EFFECTIVE REDUCTION. Although an effective computation may be carried out by a human being, note that the contribution of the human is purely mechanical, and is therefore reducible to simple, mindless operations. As such, any successful explanation of a complex information-processing phenomenon in terms of effective computation is truly reductive (cf. note 3 on page 507) and hence non-circular. This is as it should be: after all, a true explanation of the mind may only be coached in terms of entities and processes that are themselves mindless.

[16]Formally, the description of a DYNAMICAL SYSTEM must be a *function* that maps the present value of each of the system's state variables into a corresponding future value. A function is a mapping between two sets such that to every element of the first set corresponds one and only one element of the second set.

[17]ON THE MEANINGFULNESS OF COMPUTATION. If *every* sufficiently complex physical system (such as the collection of molecules that makes up my coffee mug) instantiated *any*

given Turing computation, the explanatory value of the computational theory of the mind would be zilch. It is very important, therefore, to realize that the concept of computation is not vacuously general; the straightforward, if somewhat technical, argument to that effect is given by Chalmers (1994). Note that this does not contradict the "it from bit" view in physics (see note 11 on page 34): on that view, everything is computation, but not *any given* computation.

[18] SIMPLICITY IS WHAT COMPLEXITY MUST BE MADE OF. You may recognize this as a paraphrase of the passage in Robert Penn Warren's novel *All the King's Men* that deals with the relationship between good and evil: "Goodness, yeah, just plain simple goodness. Well, you can't inherit it from anybody. You got to make it, Doc. If you want it. And you got to make it out of badness. And you know why Doc? ... Because there isn't anything else to make it out of."

[19] A natural number is PRIME if it is wholly divisible only by 1 and by itself. Exact and approximate criteria for primality have applications in public-key cryptography. These are based on the following idea: a prime number serving as the key to a message can be multiplied by another prime number to obtain a product that can be safely shared, because the two original factors are very difficult to recover from it.

[20] HIERARCHICAL ABSTRACTION. The realization that complex cognitive systems cannot be understood without resorting to a hierarchical abstraction of details has been articulated by Marr, Poggio and their collaborators in the mid-1970s (Marr and Poggio, 1977). While the three distinct levels of understanding posited by Marr — computational, algorithmic, and implementational — need not (and probably cannot) be as independent as he envisaged (Edelman, 1999), the framework remains valid because of the central role it assigns to representations, which span the levels of understanding and afford hierarchical abstraction. More on this in Chapter 4.

[21] WHO IS AFRAID OF EDUCATION? Those who would rule others by spreading ignorance and fear. Consider the following statement by Karl Rove, a chief political adviser to President George W. Bush (quoted from an interview with *The New Yorker*, February 16, 2001):

> As people do better, they start voting like Republicans — unless they have too much education and vote Democratic, which proves there can be too much of a good thing.

[22] WISDOM AS FORESIGHT. The tradition has it that Rabbi Shimon said: "Whosoever is wise? *He who sees that which is born*" [*ha-roeh et ha-nolad,* הרואה את הנולד] — a curiously Promethean view.

[23] Ben Zakkai's choice ("a good heart") is mirrored across centuries and continents in this Japanese story:

> The layman Sasaki Doppo studied Zen with Ganseki. He later recounted how he had asked his teacher, "What is Buddha?" Ganseki replied, "The good heart is Buddha."

> The layman added, "What is most basic in the human world is a good heart. Therefore the normal mind is called the Way."

> From *Zen Antics: 100 Stories of Enlightenment*,
> translated and edited by Thomas Cleary (1994).

If you can see how Sasaki's conclusion concerning the Way follows from his realization of the value of compassion, you are walking in the footsteps of the patriarchs.

3

Computing Brains

What peculiar privilege has this little agitation of the brain
which we call thought, that we take it to be the model of the
whole universe?

Dialogues Concerning Natural Religion
DAVID HUME (published posthumously in 1779)

H OW CAN BRAINS support computation — not just overt calculations that
minds schooled in arithmetics carry out when balancing a checkbook,
but the pervasive processing of representations that all minds are made of?

As it became clear by the end of Chapter 2, a given computation can be
realized in many different ways, depending on the means available for embodying the representations in question and for manipulating them to achieve
the desired result. You also saw that banishing the homunculus from our
theory of the mind requires that the representations that inhabit the brain be
capable of actively manipulating themselves. On the conceptual level, you
are thus ready to see the brain metaphorically as an arena in which many active representations interact with each other, with the rest of the body, and
with the external world.

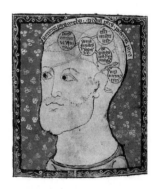

This identification of some of the
faculties of the mind with brain
structures was proposed by the
great Muslim physician and poly-
math IBN SINA (known in the West
by his Latin name Avicenna).

But such preparation appears to be of little help to anyone who is willing
to brave an actual, not metaphorical, look at the brain. Apart from the major
nerve tracts and nuclei, just about the only brain structure that is apparent to
an unaided eye is the system of ventricles that channel the cerebrospinal fluid.
For centuries, the ventricles played a central role in theories of brain function;
the illustration in the margin, taken from a thousand-year-old work of Ibn
Sina, is typical of medieval thinking in that it identifies a specific mental
function or faculty (memory, vision, etc.) with each ventricle.

Although the notion that the brain operates on hydraulic principles became untenable long ago, the real nature of brain function (electrochemical activity) and of the structures that support it (networks of distinct brain

cells, or neurons) was discovered only relatively recently. The minute voltage differentials maintained by the membranes of neurons could not be detected without electronic amplifiers, which were first developed in the 1920s.[1] Moreover, only with the advent of advanced microscopy and tissue-staining techniques a couple of decades prior to that had the neurons themselves come to be seen correctly as discrete cells rather than a continuous tangle of fused filaments.[2]

Neurobiologists now realize that the brain, as any other complex system, must be studied at several different levels of organization (and using a variety of techniques, listed parenthetically):

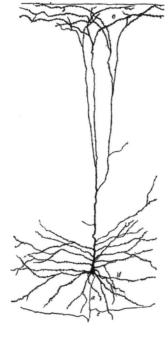

A pyramidal NEURON, so called because of the shape of its body, or soma (the dark blob in the middle of the tangle of fibers in this drawing by Cajal). Many dendrites (including the long, branching apical dendrite) converge on the soma from above, providing the input to the neuron. The output signal is carried by the axon (emerging from the base of the pyramid) and its many collaterals.

- lobes, nuclei, and nerve tracts (which can be seen with a naked eye);

- cytoarchitectonic areas (defined by the spatial distribution of cell shapes and sizes) and their interconnections (traced by anatomical markers);

- NEURONS (seen in specially stained preparations under high magnification, and also recorded from electronically);

- subcellular structures, such as SYNAPSES (seen in electron micrographs);

- molecular structures (tagged by special markers), such as channels, or tube-like protein molecules that straddle the cellular membrane and can close or open to admit ions into the cell, or pump them out.

Finding out what is going on all these levels may help us understand how the brain gives rise to the mind, but two of them are especially relevant for thinking about this process in computational terms: neurons, and synapses.

3.1   The building blocks: neurons and synapses

Every cell in the human body is a complex arrangement of structural elements and organelles, kept alive by the interplay of a staggering variety of complex molecules and by interactions with the rest of the body. The study of the central nervous system cells, or neurons, is a challenging subject: entire scientific careers can be (and are) spent on elucidating the details of neural structures and their function, generating volumes of data that fill thick textbooks on neuroanatomy and neurophysiology.

Mercifully, because we are interested only in the computational function of ensembles of neurons, we can afford to set aside a multitude of technical issues, such as the molecular basis for neural metabolism, that are secondary to neural computation (in the same sense that semiconductor physics is secondary to electronic computer engineering). So what follows is a distillation of the key properties of neurons and synapses, considered as discrete computational elements.

3.1.1 Neurons

The license to seek explanations of brain function at the level of neurons has been articulated by a pioneer in the field of neural computation, Horace B. Barlow, in a programmatic paper titled *Single units and sensation: a neuron doctrine for perceptual psychology* (1972). More than thirty years after the publication of that paper, the balance of the experimental findings and theoretical developments indicates that Barlow's hypothesis — that the functioning of the brain is best understood at the level of neurons — is essentially correct.

THE NEURON IS THE BASIC REPRESENTATIONAL UNIT IN THE BRAIN, because on the next smaller scale — that of ion channels and membrane patches — events are fundamentally local: a change in the electric potential across a patch of neural membrane can affect the rest of the brain only if it contributes to modulating the activity of the neuron of which it is part (for example, by making the firing of the neuron over some period of time more, or less, likely). On the next larger scale, the activity of a nucleus or an area is determined by the activities of its neurons. Thus, the physical nexus where causal chains of local elementary electrochemical brain events must come together before they can influence the rest of the brain is the activity of the neuron.[3]

NEURONS ARE WIRED TOGETHER IN AN ORDERLY MANNER, the pattern of connections being determined both by genetic and by experiential factors.[4] An example of a neural circuit, in Figure 3.1 on the next page, shows the basic wiring of the vertebrate retina. The photoreceptors at the top of the drawing (originally made by Santiago Ramón y Cajal) are wired to the outer plexiform layer, where the so-called horizontal cells connect some of them locally. Bipolar cells link these to the inner plexiform layer, where another dose of lateral interaction is provided by the amacrine cells. Finally, the ganglion cells gather the resulting signals and send them to the rest of the brain (the axons of these cells form the optic nerve).[5]

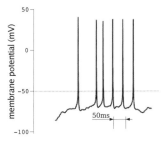

The electrical recording of a burst of action potentials (SPIKES) emitted by a neuron. The combined intensity of the many bursts that typically converge on a destination neuron and the relative timing of their spikes together determine how that neuron responds, and how it may learn from the present signal (by having its synapses modified). Thus, neurons talk to each other in numbers, which is precisely what you would expect from the components of any computation device.

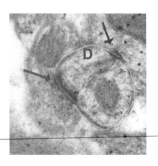

A NEURON SENDS SIGNALS TO OTHER NEURONS BY EMITTING ALL-OR-NONE IMPULSES – ACTION POTENTIALS, OR "SPIKES" – WHOSE TIMING AND FREQUENCY, BOTH GRADED, REFLECT VARIOUS QUALITIES OF ITS COMBINED INPUTS. In a ready, "hyperpolarized" state, the inside of a neuron has a potential of about -70 millivolts with respect to the outside. Signals that arrive from other neurons (or, in the case of sensory receptors, mechanical or optical signals from the outside world) may toggle the membrane potential, depolarizing the neuron and causing it to emit a voltage spike (reaching about $+40$ mV at its peak) that proceeds to travel down its axon. The depolarization and the subsequent repolarization of the neuron (which makes it ready to fire again) together take about two milliseconds. The axon that carries the action potentials may traverse a long distance before splitting (arborizing) to connect to a potentially very large number of other neurons, at junctions called SYNAPSES.

An electron micrograph of two SYNAPSES (arrows) making contact on a dendrite, whose cross-section is marked by D. The round vesicles on the presynaptic side (barely distinguishable in this image) contain small amounts of neurotransmitter. An arriving spike causes some of them to fuse with the membrane, releasing the neurotransmitter molecules into the synaptic cleft. These diffuse across the gap and bind to receptors embedded in the postsynaptic membrane, contributing to its depolarization.

3.1.2 Synapses

THE SYNAPSE IS THE NARROW GAP WHERE A CONNECTION IS MADE between the axon of a presynaptic neuron and some part of the cellular membrane of the postsynaptic neuron (see the illustration in the margin). Most synapses in the brain are electrochemical: the arrival of a spike causes some neurotransmitter molecules to be released into the synaptic gap and to start diffusing across it. Molecules that cross the gap bind to ion channels and

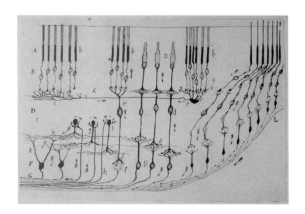

Figure 3.1 — AN EXQUISITE NEURAL NETWORK: a drawing of a frog's retina, made by Cajal in 1901. The precisely wired network of retinal neurons carries out extensive visual signal processing (note that this dispels the common misconception of the eye as a mere camera). The photoreceptors (rods and cones, layers A and B) are connected via the bipolar cells (layer D) to the ganglion cells (layer F), whose axons constitute the optic nerve (G). Lateral interactions among the feedforward signals are supported by the horizontal and amacrine cells, in the outer and inner plexiform layers (C and E).

other proteins embedded in the postsynaptic membrane, precipitating a chain of events that contributes to a possible depolarization of the postsynaptic neuron. With very few exceptions, the EFFICACY of synapses is low, and the coordinated, near-simultaneous action of many presynaptic neurons is required to cause the postsynaptic neuron to fire.

A SYNAPSE MODIFIES THE SIGNAL IT TRANSMITS. The easiest way to conceptualize synaptic efficacy is in terms of a *weight* — a number that multiplies the incoming signal strength to yield the magnitude of the effect that the signal has on the postsynaptic cell. This reveals the fundamental nature of the elementary computation carried out by a neuron: its output is a (nonlinear) function of a weighted sum of its inputs, with each weight controlling the relative contribution of the input in question. The output nonlinearity is a "squashing" function, which prevents the output activity (firing rate) from exceeding a certain fixed, asymptotic value as the inputs become more and more intense.[6]

SYNAPSES LEARN. Clearly, the computation performed by a neuron — the manner in which it maps inputs to outputs — can be controlled by changing the efficacies of its input synapses, as well as by modifying the squashing function. The precise molecular mechanisms behind such changes are of little importance to us; the central issue is how they are brought about, and how they affect the computation that the neuron implements. It turns out that synaptic learning is a common by-product of the routine functioning of the nervous system: the efficacy of a synapse can be significantly affected by the mere activities of the neurons it connects. For example, if the presynaptic and the postsynaptic neurons consistently fire together, the synapse may be strengthened, while another synapse (in the same neuron) for which no such correlation exists is weakened. This synaptic learning rule, under which the rich get richer and the poor poorer, was first proposed by Donald Hebb in 1949.[7]

It's good to be a MAMMAL! The hyrax (*Procavia capensis*) shown here in its native habitat is described in Proverbs 30:24 (along with ants and locusts) as being "the smallest of the earth" yet "exceedingly wise." Mammals such as the hyrax — whose Hebrew name is "rock rabbit" — have relatively large brains for their size (in a sense, so do the ants and the locusts: consider HOW MANY NEURONS there are in an anthill or in a swarm). It *is* brain, not brawn, that made rabbits an evolutionary success story; the film scene in Monty Python's *Holy Grail* that shows the Killer Rabbit of Caerbannog next to the skull of one of its victims has probably been doctored (cf. Figure 9.21 on page 450).

3.2 Functional architecture of the brain

HOW MANY NEURONS does it take to make good in life? "A lot" seems to be a safe answer — that is, if the objective is to be the king of the hill, top of the heap (not merely a tenant in some ecological niche). Indeed, it takes hundreds of millions of neurons to achieve the cognitive sophistication of an average MAMMAL. This suggests both that individual neurons cannot be all that smart, and that how the neurons are connected is likely to be very important.

The mammalian brain is, emphatically, not an undifferentiated clump of randomly interconnected neurons. The orderly nature of its wiring manifests itself in many kinds of regularities, on several levels of organization. Merely tracing and cataloging the anatomical connections in the brain is not enough to understand it: the anatomy can only be properly interpreted in the light of its *functional* significance, because it is the brain's function (to generate the mind) that needs to be elucidated. That is, to understand brain structures and their interconnections, we need to know not only what they are, which is the province of neuroanatomy, but also what they are doing, which is the subject matter of neurophysiology.

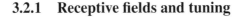

Neuroanatomical and neurophysiological findings all point to the ubiquity in the brain of two main functional features: RECEPTIVE FIELDS and MAPS, which I shall describe shortly. But because the mind is an essentially computational entity, any ultimate answers as to *why* the brain is structured just so and does what it does can only emerge at the level of information processing, which deals with representations and their interactions. Therefore a computational interpretation of receptive fields and maps is of crucial importance to our agenda, to be taken up in section 3.3 on page 50.

3.2.1 Receptive fields and tuning

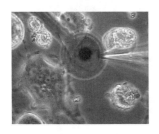

A microphotograph of neuronal precursor cells in vitro, illustrating a parallel intracellular and extracellular recording technique. A cell is seen held by a patch clamp MICRO-ELECTRODE; another electrode approaches it from the right. Similar microelectrodes are used in vivo to record neural activity, or to stimulate neurons, in precisely known locations.

The concept of receptive field was originally defined for neurons that reside in one of the neural pathways leading from the sensory organs (eyes, ears, skin) through the primary sensory cortex[8] areas to the rest of the brain. The receptive field of a sensory neuron is the combination of features that a stimulus has to possess to evoke a response; the choice of features depends on the sensory modality within which the neuron in question operates (sight, hearing, touch). The receptive field of a neuron is mapped by recording its response through a MICROELECTRODE, while stimulating the sensory system in a controlled fashion.

Striking functional parallels exist between the sensory systems. For a visual or a somatosensory neuron, the receptive field is literally a window on the world: to be effective, a stimulus has to appear within a certain region of the visual field, or a certain patch of the skin. However, location is only one of the several feature dimensions to which such neurons may be tuned. Although neurons at the lower levels of the processing hierarchy do respond to very

simple features — dots of light in vision, or pinpricks in touch — the higher
level neurons are much more selective, requiring a particular combination of
features, beyond location, to respond. For example, a neuron situated in the
primary visual cortex may respond optimally to a line segment of a particular
orientation appearing in a particular region of the visual field (Figure 3.2,
left); likewise, a neuron in the primary somatosensory cortex may be tuned to
a straight edge of a particular orientation touching a particular region of the
skin (Figure 3.2, middle).

Only a few synapses upstream in the visual processing pathway from the
level where neurons are tuned to mere line segments, one finds selectivity to
faces (Figure 3.2, right). A face is more than just another kind of effective
stimulus here: these neurons will not respond to anything that does not look
at least a bit like a face. Other neurons in the same area (the inferotemporal cortex, or IT) are found to be tuned to similarly complex objects, such

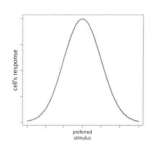

A typical TUNING CURVE of a sensory neuron is smooth, graded, and
compact, reflecting moderate selectivity in the space of possible
stimuli. One of the many computational benefits of this property of
neuronal response tuning is hyperacuity, discussed in section 5.1.

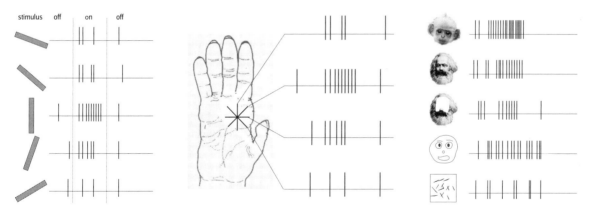

Figure 3.2 — RECEPTIVE FIELDS of sensory neurons. *Left:* a typical tuning profile of a neuron in the primary visual
cortex of a cat, which responds selectively to a line segment of a particular orientation, appearing at a particular
location in the visual field. The neuron's responses are shown alongside the stimuli that evoked them. *Middle:*
the receptive field of a monkey's somatosensory neuron, plotted on the skin of the hand; also shown are the spike
trains evoked by straight-edge stimuli of different orientations. *Right:* the responses of a face-tuned neuron in the
inferotemporal cortex of a monkey to various stimuli (many such neurons were described by Perrett, Mistlin, and
Chitty, 1987).

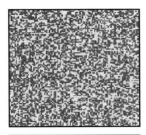

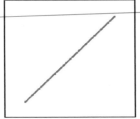

What visual stimuli are SIMPLE
and what are COMPLEX? Of the
two images shown here, the top one
(random dots) is complex, because
its description is long (the shade
of each pixel needs to be specified separately). In comparison,
the bottom image (oriented line)
is relatively simple, because it can
be described by a handful of numbers (essentially, by the coordinates of the segment's endpoints).
There are deep connections here
to the Kolmogorov-Chaitin theory
of algorithmic complexity (Chater
and Vitányi, 2003; Gell-Mann and
Lloyd, 1996; Solomonoff, 1964).

as Mickey Mouse dolls, padlocks, and fire extinguishers (Tsunoda, Yamane, Nishizaki, and Tanifuji, 2001).

Does the discovery of object-tuned neurons mean that the problem of understanding vision, at least, is solved? After all, the brain basis for such high-level functions as face and object recognition seems to have been iden- tified. The answer is "not yet — but we are getting there." On the one hand, in the light of the fundamental premise that minds are what brains do, we should fully expect to find a brain basis for *every* aspect of the mind. More- over, we still need to determine how and why the responses of those neurons are formed, and how the pattern of their activities gives rise to phenomenal visual experience. On the other hand, the importance of the discovery of face and object neurons in the visual pathway is bolstered by the ubiquity of tuned response profiles elsewhere in the cortex; understanding how and why that is so could bring us closer to understanding how the brain does what it does.

To see just how pervasive response tuning is, we should seek, in addition to the examples from the sensory domain, evidence of response selectivity with respect to action rather than perception. One does not have to look far: relevant findings of just the right kind abound in the literature. For instance, in the monkey premotor cortex (a part of the brain involved in the planning and execution of movements), neurons have been found that fire selectively when the animal rehearses a particular action before it is prompted to execute it (Cisek and Kalaska, 2004).

Thus, it seems to be safe to say that **every cortical neuron is tuned** to a certain relatively SIMPLE combination of feature values in its input do- main, be it sensory (visual, auditory, etc.), motor (as in patterns of muscle activations), or entirely abstract (such as subjective utility; cf. section 8.4.2). To realize fully the significance of this general conclusion, observe that it is possible to conceive of a totally different situation: in principle, each neu- ron could have been tuned to a random set of disjoint stimuli (for example, a visual neuron could be tuned to a few very tightly defined orientations, ran- domly scattered over the 180° range of possibilities). Instead, a typical TUN- ING CURVE is smooth, graded and compact, a mere bump over the usually vast space of possible inputs.

One expects such a prominent trait of the functional architecture of the brain to have computational significance, and indeed graded, compact tuning profiles enable neurons to compute what sharp, random tuning could never achieve (including, paradoxically, high-acuity perception and high-precision action; I shall explain how that happens in Chapter 5).

3.2.2 Cortical maps

If the patterns of neural tuning were not so easily interpretable in terms of observable features and events, certain procedures for studying brain function would not be available to us. Here's a captivating description of one such procedure, taken from a book by Greg Egan:

> [The experiment] involved a student volunteer reading poetry in silence, while the scanner subtitled the image of her brain with each line as it was read. There were three independently computed subtitles, based on primary visual data, recognized word-shapes, and the brain's final semantic representations ... the last sometimes only briefly matching the others, before the words' precise meanings diffused out into a cloud of associations.
>
> — Egan (1998, p.72)

An MRI SCANNER. Reading minds by watching brains will not remain science fiction for much longer. For example, Suppes, Han, and Lu (1998) describe how a computer can be trained to recognize, by processing the subject's electrical and magnetic brain waves (EEG and MEG), which of several preset words or sentences he or she is hearing.

Although Egan's book is nominally science fiction (the events it describes are set in the year 2055), the possibility of pinning down words from the patterns of activation they produce in a brain scan is quite close to being a science fact (Edelman, Grill-Spector, Kushnir, and Malach, 1998; Posner and Pavese, 1998). Such feats of brain reading are of interest to us here because the very possibility of detecting a consistent response to a stimulus using the currently available low-resolution non-invasive scanning methods relies on neurons that are tuned to the stimulus (1) being situated in close proximity to each other, and (2) spanning an area that is large enough to appear on a scan. In particular, the scanning technique used in the studies just referred to — functional magnetic resonance imaging (fMRI) — is limited in that, among other things, any activation pattern that is too diffuse, or concentrated in too small an area of the brain, will not register.

The CORTICAL MAPS — which is what the neuroscientists call the orderly arrangements in the cortex of like-minded neurons (those with similar tuning properties) — are patterned on several organizational levels. LO-CALLY, neurons are arranged in a manner that preserves the dimensions and the layout of the relevant aspects of the world. In the visual cortex, for example, neighboring neurons respond to stimuli that are projected onto neighboring locations on the retina, and are selective to similar stimulus properties such as orientation.[9] In the auditory cortex, neighboring neurons may respond to similar sound frequencies. GLOBALLY, the cortical maps preserve the *topology* of the represented feature spaces: their geometry may be distorted, but spatial and feature-based neighborhoods are preserved. Such maps are called *retinotopic* or *tonotopic*, depending on the sensory modality (see Figure 3.3). An example of a retinotopic map appears in Figure 3.3, left, which shows how a bull's-eye pattern seen by a monkey is projected onto the surface of its primary visual cortex.

It is tempting to try to explain such exquisite patterning in functional terms. We can try to reverse-engineer nature by thinking of what these properties of cortical maps could be good for. Here's one suggestion for explaining the functional value of retinotopy: because neighboring points in the primary visual cortex correspond to neighboring locations in the visual field, neurons higher up in the processing stream can be wired to use *local connections* (easier to establish than far-ranging ones) to look for rapid *local changes*, such

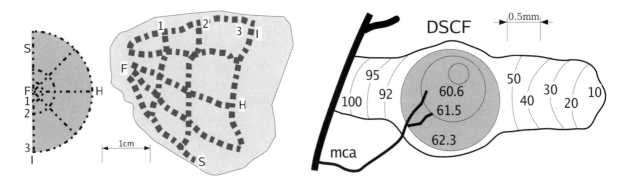

Figure 3.3 — *Left and center:* a RETINOTOPIC MAP, showing how one half of a bull's-eye pattern projects on the surface of the primary visual cortex (brain area V1) of a monkey (Tootell et al., 1988). Points that are neighbors on the retina (and that therefore correspond to nearby visual directions) are mapped to neighboring neurons in V1. Intuitively, this is why neighboring neurons are likely to have similar receptive fields — in the retinal space, and along whatever additional visual dimensions (such as orientation or color-related features) to which they are tuned. Some exceptions to this nice local order are illustrated in Figure 3.4. *Right:* a TONOTOPIC MAP found in the primary auditory cortex of the bat brain (Xiao and Suga, 2002; mca denotes middle cerebral artery). The numbers indicate frequency tuning for each area; the lines mark iso-best frequency contours. Note that sound frequencies between 60.6 and 62.3 kHz are over-represented in the Doppler-shifted constant frequency (DSCF) area (gray).

as those brought about by thin lines or by transitions between light and dark. Such visual features are very important: consider how effective line drawings are, where the shape of an object or an entire scene is conveyed by just a few strokes.

On a yet larger scale, the mapping of the world onto the cortex is discontinuous. The prime example of this discontinuity is the "tear" in the cortical representation of the visual world stemming from the partial crossing-over or DECUSSATION of the optic nerves at the chiasm — a sub-cortical structure so called because it resembles the Greek letter χ (note that Avicenna's diagram reproduced in the beginning of this chapter includes this major anatomical feature of the brain). In mammalian vision, about half of the optic nerve fibers cross over, and half do not, as shown in Figure 3.4, left.

Decussation is a very common neuroanatomical trait found in different sensory modalities in many species. Why does it happen? A bold idea, only partly tongue-in-cheek, has been proposed by the author of the best brief introduction to neuroanatomy, *On the texture of brains* (Braitenberg, 1977): decussation is an evolutionary remnant of hard-wired reflexes corresponding to two most basic emotions, love and hate. The idea, as it is explained by Braitenberg (1984), is illustrated in Figure 3.4, right. Briefly, a crossed connection from the sensors to the actuators in a prototypical mobile sentient

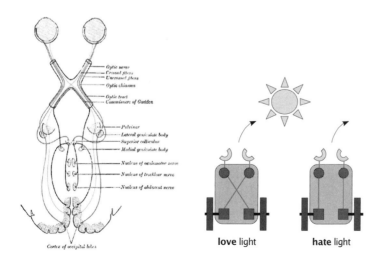

love light   **hate** light

Figure 3.4 — BETWEEN STRUCTURE AND FUNCTION. *Left:* the mapping is disconnected on the global scale, because of the partial crossover of the optic nerves, called DECUSSATION. *Right:* the partly crossed-over connections between sensors and effectors may be thought of as a remnant of hard-wired "love" and "hate" reflexes (Braitenberg, 1984). The sensors in this example are assumed to fire in proportion to their proximity to a light source; the effectors are motors that cause their wheels to turn faster when the received signal is stronger.

agent (a "vehicle") would cause it to turn toward the sensed stimulus (thus embodying, if not "love," a tropism for light), while an uncrossed connection would cause it to flee from the stimulus (implementing "hate").

3.2.3   Cortical resource allocation

The brain is the most expensive organ to maintain, accounting for 20% of the oxygen consumption of the resting body. The sustained expense of keeping the neurons alive and their membranes hyperpolarized results in a persistent evolutionary drive to economize and conserve resources such as the real-time metabolic cost of operating the brain, and the proportion of cortex devoted to various tasks. A typical outcome of the brain conservation effort is the VARIABLE-RESOLUTION representations found in the sensory cortex areas (Figure 3.5; cf. Figure 3.3, right). In vision, for example, the spatial resolution (hence the effective acuity) is highest at the center of gaze, and is drastically reduced in the periphery. (If you find this difficult to believe, hold your gaze steady on the period at the end of this sentence while casting about your attention: you'll see that everything except the immediate vicinity of

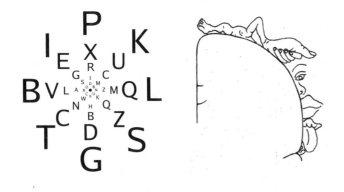

Figure 3.5 — VARIABLE-RESOLUTION REP-RESENTATION. *Left:* our visual acuity is highest at the center of gaze, which is projected to the FOVEA (the highest-resolution spot on the retina); the acuity decreases markedly towards the periphery. Fixating the central dot in this display renders the letters approximately equally discriminable: the fall-off of the effective peripheral resolution is compensated by the increased letter size. *Right:* the effective resolution is variable in the somatosensory (touch) modality, too. In this schematic depiction of the mapping between the skin surface and the somatosensory cortex in the human, the size of each body part symbolically represents the spatial resolution afforded by the corresponding skin area.

the fixation point appears blurry.) This is an entirely reasonable step: why maintain a large, expensive sensor with a uniformly high resolution, when a small steerable one would do just as well?

Stubbornly economizing on resources by keeping a low-resolution representation of a sensory area where information is plentiful would be just as unreasonable as maintaining a high-resolution representation of an informational wasteland. After all, the brain is there to make sense of the world, and if the world *insists* on throwing at it information that is focused in some manner, no matter how peculiar, the brain had better heed it. Indeed, the sensory maps found in mammalian brains are amenable to change following experience — they exhibit considerable PLASTICITY — more so during development, but also in adulthood. For instance, a patch of skin on a monkey's palm that is repeatedly stimulated (by simple touch) eventually becomes over-represented relative to its neighbors in the somatosensory cortex (Figure 3.6).

My use of the word "insists" just now to describe how the stimuli may beat down a path to a particular patch of the cortex hides behind it a computational concept that is absolutely crucial for understanding cognition. That concept is **statistics**: a stimulus is "insistent" enough — and should thus be allowed to leave a special mark on the representation — if and only if it differs significantly from baseline. **The waking brain is constantly engaged in collecting and maintaining a variety of statistical measurements of the world, including traces of past stimulation and of its own past states;**

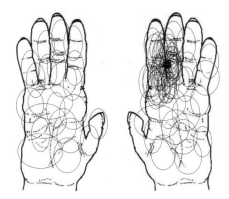

Figure 3.6 — CORTICAL PLASTICITY. The density of receptive fields of somatosensory cortical neurons, mapped onto the monkey palm surface, after prolonged exposure to local stimulation (*right*; the arrow indicates the stimulated spot). The map for the unstimulated hand is shown as a control (*left*). Merely touching the skin repeatedly at the designated location for the period of several days caused that location to become over-represented in the brain.

even during sleep it keeps churning through the accrued data, seeking and consolidating patterns.

I shall address the fundamentally statistical nature of neural computation in the next section, and shall revisit the idea of statistics as the core of cognition throughout the remaining chapters of this book.

3.3   Neural computation

It is time you got some returns on the intellectual investment you've made so far in this book. In Chapter 2, I surveyed the key conceptual tools needed for analyzing minds: representations, computation, and hierarchical abstraction. In the present chapter, I have so far focused on the key facts about brain structure (neurons and synapses), and on the key characteristics of brain function (receptive fields, maps, and experience-driven learning). These key pieces of the puzzle that is the mind/brain are now ready to be brought together. Indeed, the outline of the big picture is already there: the toy example of Braitenberg's "vehicles," which exhibit a tropism because of how their "eyes" are wired to their motors, offers us a glimpse of how a feature of the neural architecture can be interpreted — and hence properly understood — in terms of the computation it supports.

Intuitively, it *may* seem plausible to you that extrapolating this understanding to complex minds and real brains is a straightforward matter, that can be safely left to psycholinguists and neuroscientists — or then again, it may not. We *can* do much better than to rely on overextended intuition: we are now in a position to spell out the real meaning of neural computation, and to support the emerging conceptual structure by examples from real biological information processing systems. So my plan is to prop against that structure a conceptual equivalent of Jacob's ladder: a set of MATHEMATICAL TOOLS for thinking about neural computation.

3.3.1   Multidimensional spaces

The main formal concept that will help the most underlies much of the classical mathematics, yet is exceptionally easy to grasp. It arises in every field, abstract or applied, whose objects of interest must be represented by numbers, yet cannot be reduced to *single* numbers. This is exactly the case with brains: according to the neuron doctrine outlined in section 3.1 on page 38, what matters about the brain is the collective state of its neurons — no more

WHY MATHEMATICS? — Because plain English is just not good enough for what we are going to need; as Led Zeppelin put it in STAIRWAY TO HEAVEN, "you know sometimes words have two meanings." Don't let the anticipation of a bit of mathematics spoil the fun for you: there will be nothing you have not learned about in high school — at least in the beginning ("a ladder set on the earth..."). As to where we end up ("...with its top reaching to heaven") — we shall see.

The UR-LADDER. The Hebrew word *sullam* (ladder) in the description of Jacob's dream in Genesis 28:12 may have originally referred to a structure such as this STAIRWAY TO HEAVEN, situated at the center of the partly restored great ziggurat of Ur in Mesopotamia.

(we don't have to consider parts of neurons), and no less (generally, we cannot lump neurons together). This implies that an *ordered list of numbers*, one per neuron, is required to fully capture a brain state (the list must be consistently ordered to prevent confusion as to which number stands for the activity of which neuron). And this, in turn, means that a brain state can be seen as a point in a MULTIDIMENSIONAL SPACE, whose coordinate axes correspond to the activities of the neurons that comprise the brain.[11]

As Figure 3.7 illustrates, any objects that can be represented by lists of numbers may also be mapped into points in a multidimensional space, by taking each number to signify position along some dimension. We need not worry about the dimensionality getting out of hand: any issues arising in the visualization of high-dimensional spaces are a reasonable price to pay for such a versatile mind tool. Here is one immediate bonus from that deal:

Contrary to what its inclusion in innumerable "science fiction" stories suggests, there is nothing mysterious about the concept of a MULTIDIMENSIONAL SPACE.[10] In fact, your brain state at *this* moment is described completely by a point in a space whose dimensionality is equal to the number of its neurons. And... *now* it's another point... and another one. The moving finger writes; and, having writ, moves on — and the trajectory that emerges is you.

We can conceptualize the kind of computation that neural networks naturally support as mapping the activities of one set of neurons (one multidimensional space) into the activities of another, output set (another multidimensional space).

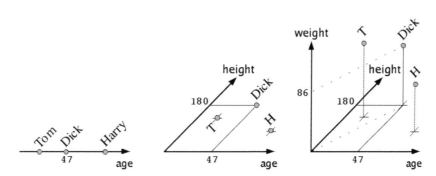

Figure 3.7 — Representing objects in a MULTIDIMENSIONAL SPACE. To illustrate the versatility of the feature space representation, this imaginary example from personal morphometrics plots the data of three people, in one, two, and three dimensions. In the latter case, Dick, for instance, is represented by the list of three numbers [47, 180, 86], which are his age, height in centimeters, and weight in kilograms. If fourteen more features were used, the space would become 17-dimensional — a bit difficult to visualize without proper mathematical tools, but not in any matter of principle different from the familiar cases depicted here.

The possibility of computing merely by establishing connections between
two representation spaces is particularly exciting for two reasons. First, this
idea makes concrete the hitherto abstract definition of computation as *manipulation* of representations, which I offered earlier in the book: "manipulation"
can now be taken to mean simply mapping, or establishing correspondence,
between input and output representations. Second, the very same idea also
serves to tie the abstract computational strand of explanation to actual brain
stuff: the desired mapping can be specified simply by adjusting the strengths
of the synaptic connections between the neurons of the two sets. Let us now
look at some examples of computing with connections.

3.3.2   Computing with connections

Our first example illustrates how wiring together the outputs of some neurons, which respond to spots of light of a particular visual field location and
size, can serve to obtain a more complex receptive field (RF) profile — one
that would be selective to oriented line segments (as in Figure 3.2 on page 43,
left). Functionally, the oriented receptive field is synthesized by assigning a
weight to each portion of the input space, and then computing the response of
the neuron as a weighted sum of the inputs. Anatomically, this computation
can be implemented by the many synapses strewn along the dendrites (the input part) of a typical pyramidal neuron in the cortex, as shown schematically
in Figure 3.8.

In simple creatures, mapping between representation spaces can directly
support the computation of entire chunks of behavior. In the toy example
of an artificial crab equipped with two eyes and an arm, illustrated in Fig-

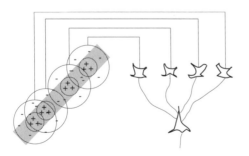

Figure 3.8 — To tailor a visual receptive field (RF) to respond
to a bar of a particular orientation (tilted just so) that appears at a
particular location, it suffices, to a first approximation, to connect
together the outputs of units with simpler response properties (an
excitatory center, marked by +, and an inhibitory surround, marked
by −), situated at strategic positions with respect to the target RF
(after Hubel and Wiesel, 1959).

ure 3.9, the two-dimensional visual input space can be mapped onto the two-dimensional motor control space, resulting in rudimentary visual-motor coordination. This crab's "eyes" can only fixate an object (not produce its image on a retina), thus providing two numbers for each fixation. So, the crab's perceptual space is two-dimensional, the dimensions corresponding to the heading angles from the two eyes to the target object. The crab's arm has two degrees of freedom, corresponding to the two joint angles, which makes its motor space two-dimensional as well. Consequently, to link its perception to action (e.g., to be able to grasp an object that it fixates visually), the crab needs to map the 2D visual space onto the 2D motor space.

As P. M. Churchland (1989) points out, such a mapping can be achieved by choosing a proper setting for the switches (synapses) in a CROSSBAR-like arrangement of input-output lines (Figure 3.10 on the next page, left). The device that communications engineers call a crossbar switch — a matrix of weighted connections (synapses!) between input and output lines — can implement the most general linear mapping[12] between two spaces. Interestingly enough, both this abstract computational device and the crab example that led us to consider it are directly relevant to the understanding of actual biological systems. Anatomical structures that bear an uncanny resemblance to a crossbar switch exist in the cerebellum (a brain structure implicated in the

The male FIDDLER CRAB (*Uca longisignalis*), recognizable by its one hypertrophied claw, is very good at triangulating the location of a rival relative to its own burrow (Hemmi and Zeil, 2003). This shows that you don't have to have a high-school diploma to be capable of doing trigonometry.

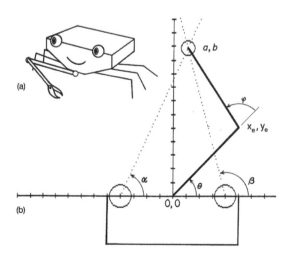

Figure 3.9 — Visual-motor control as a mapping between two REPRESENTATION SPACES in an artificial crab-like creature. The coordinates of the 2D visual space are the angles α, β; the 2D motor space is encoded by θ, ϕ. This example, due to Paul M. Churchland (1986, fig.2), is discussed at length in Chapter 10 of Patricia S. Churchland's excellent book *Neurophilosophy* (Churchland, 1987).

learning of fine-tuned motor programs; see Figure 3.10, right), and in the hippocampus. An even more striking example of convergence between anatomical structure and computational function is found in the superior colliculus (which is a part of the midbrain). There, multimodal maps — some sensory, other motor — are laid out in register with each other. This anatomical arrangement facilitates mapping among multiple sensory and motor spaces by allowing for local connections between the relevant neurons, which are situated in adjacent layers.

3.3.3   What single neurons do: compute statistics of their inputs

The examples of computing with connections that I have just discussed — oriented visual receptive fields and visual-motor coordination — do not in themselves tell us why or how the required intricate patterns of synaptic weights come into being. The answer to both of these questions, which emerges from the groundbreaking ideas of Hebb (1949) and Barlow (1959), is a central pil-

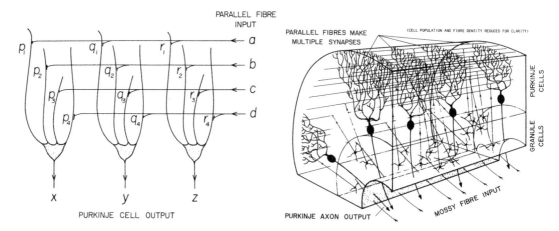

Figure 3.10 — *Left:* this 4×3 neural CROSSBAR switch can implement a general linear mapping from a 4-dimensional input space into a 3-dimensional output space by judiciously setting the synaptic connections of the three output neurons (Churchland, 1986, fig.9). *Right:* an anatomical wiring arrangement that has precisely this structure exists in the cerebellum — a part of the mammalian brain responsible for, among other functions, fine-tuned motor control (Churchland, 1986, fig.10).

lar of contemporary computational cognitive neuroscience: the distribution of weights of the incoming connections of a neuron is determined by the **statistics** of its stimulation.

Neurons can learn to respond to certain statistical properties of their input signal ensemble by letting their synapses be modified by the incoming signals, as mentioned in section 3.1 on page 38.[13] In what follows, I shall focus on a particularly simple rule referred to in that section: Hebbian synaptic learning, which has the advantage of being local (that is, using only the information that is available locally at the synapse in question rather than elsewhere in the brain), hence biologically straightforward to implement. I'll use the conceptual tool introduced earlier — a MULTIDIMENSIONAL DATA SPACE — to explain the key statistical ideas in geometrical terms.

To facilitate visualization, let's work for now in two dimensions: then everything can be plotted in the plane. Accordingly, let's imagine a neuron with two input lines (that is, two incoming connections from other neurons). If each of the two inputs can take on any value between 0 and 1, the entire input space — every possible input — fits inside the unit square in the coordinate system depicted in Figure 3.11. A given input then corresponds to some point in that space or, equivalently, to a *vector* — something we can visualize as a *directed line* connecting the origin to the point in question.

A collection of inputs thus becomes a "cloud" of points, and this is where the conceptual link to statistics becomes obvious: the shape of that cloud captures the statistical relationships among the data points. For example, if the input dimensions are *correlated*, then the cloud of points

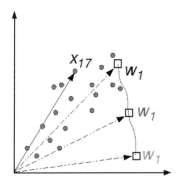

Figure 3.11 — HEBBIAN LEARNING on a cloud of input points, or vectors (only one of which, x_{17}, is labeled), in a two-dimensional space (cf. Figure 3.12 on the following page). The meaning of the dimensions is unimportant in this illustrative example; they could correspond to any two features that are fed to the neuron in question. The positions of the synaptic weight vector **w** at three successive stages of the learning process are marked by open square symbols. See text for the explanation.

is elongated, as in Figures 3.11 and 3.12, so that the value of one of the two coordinates of each point can be predicted with some degree of success from the knowledge of the value of the other coordinate. (In this example, the correlation is positive: if one coordinate is high or low, then the other is, respectively, high or low too.)

The simple two-input neuron in our example has two synapses (one per input dimension), which means that its synaptic weight vector can be plotted in the same space we just used to plot a bunch of possible input vectors. In Figure 3.11, the positions of the weight vector at three successive stages of the Hebbian learning process are marked by open square symbols; the label **w** is a shorthand for an ordered list of the two components, w_1 and w_2. Given an input vector **x**, which likewise consists of two components, x_1 and x_2, the neuron multiplies it component-wise by the synaptic weights and adds the products. When the value of the sum $s = w_1 x_1 + w_2 x_2$ is high, the neuron is more likely to fire, and if it does, the Hebbian rule kicks in, increasing the values of those components of **w** whose corresponding components of **x** are also high.

The value of s is high (and the synaptic enhancement is more likely to happen) when the weights are highly similar, component-wise, to the neuron's inputs. Equivalently, s is high when the weight vector points in the

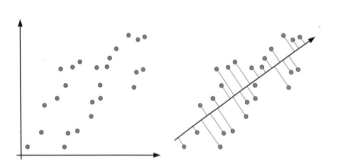

Figure 3.12 — Reducing the dimensionality. *Left:* a cloud of points corresponding to a data set in two dimensions. *Right:* these data can be simplified by projecting them onto the single principal dimension (the direction along which there is the most variability). This kind of dimensionality reduction is known as Principal Component Analysis (Oja, 1989; for one of the many applications of this method in visual information processing, see Jungman, Levi, Aperman, and Edelman, 1994). The reduction to one dimension can also be *nonlinear*, for instance by making the "backbone" for the projection curved rather than straight (Hastie, 1984).

same direction as the input (you might need some back-of-the-envelope calculations to convince yourself that this is indeed so — or you can just trust me). Thus, in each iteration, the Hebbian rule ("the rich get richer") moves the synaptic weight vector closer to the current input. Turning again to Figure 3.11, we can therefore visualize the learning process as follows: over successive iterations, the direction of the weight vector converges to coincide with the direction of the main elongation of the cloud of inputs.

To complete the mental picture of how a single neuron can compute statistics, all that you need to do now is to realize that a data cloud's most important statistical characteristics are its mean (which corresponds to the location of its center) and its direction of elongation. In exploratory multivariate statistics, this direction is computed by a procedure called Principal Component Analysis, illustrated in Figure 3.12 on the facing page. The principal components of a data set can be used for a variety of purposes, including one that is clearly relevant to cognition: *representing* the potentially very high-dimensional data approximately, in a reduced-dimensionality space, with as little information loss as possible. This is done by *rotating* the coordinates into alignment with the data cloud, and *projecting* the points onto a few leading principal components, the most important one being the main direction of elongation.[14]

What, then, can a single neuron compute? As you have just discovered, the answer to this question is this: low-dimensional statistics of its input distribution (Agüera y Arcas, Fairhall, and Bialek, 2001). That the representations maintained and manipulated by neurons relate to the statistics of the world is the central insight into the nature of neural computation that emerges from decades of work in theoretical neuroscience pioneered by Warren McCulloch (1965), Donald Hebb (1949), Horace Barlow (1959; 1990; 1994), David Marr (1970), David Mumford (1994), and others. Statistical computation is a thread that runs through all of cognition; you will be able to discern its manifestations in each and every example of cognitive processing in this book.

Vision: HOW MANY DIMENSIONS? A textbook from which I used to teach cognition (now in its fourth printing) asks: "How do you manage to perceive 3-D space when the proximal stimuli on your retinas comprise only a 2-D projection of what you see?" (Sternberg, 2003, p.118). To be sure, depth perception is a real issue, but the true challenge that is inherent in it (and in other perceptual tasks) arises from something that is never mentioned in that text: the tremendously high dimensionality of the visual signal. If people had compound eyes, this misconception might have been less common.

3.3.4 What multiple neurons do together: compute a multidimensional representation space

Although the individual neurons in a given cortical area may be doing their best to keep a lid on the dimensionality of the data they process, any *ensemble* of neurons necessarily requires a multidimensional space to describe the representations it embodies. Seeing that you are by now fully equipped conceptually for dealing with high-dimensional spaces, let us exercise this ability by considering three edifying examples of multidimensional brain phenomena. These examples share a common distinction: in each case, we can be reasonably sure what the relevant dimensionality is.

The total brain state. Invoking an estimate of the total number of neurons in the human brain, we can claim that about 10 billion dimensions are needed to represent a brain state — as a list of 10^{10} numbers, or, equivalently, a point in a 10^{10}-dimensional space. A sequence of brain states — a thought — is then simply a trajectory in that space. In defense of my use of the word "simply" here, I note that compared to the total mystery that has shrouded brain function since the dawn of humankind, the concreteness of the mental picture offered here — even if it involves a *very* high-dimensional space — is a significant improvement in understanding.

Vision. In psychology textbooks and popular science articles, it is customary to describe vision as a process of recovering the structure of the three-dimensional world that surrounds us from the two-dimensional images projected onto the retina of each eye. As I pointed out elsewhere (Edelman, 1999), this description is deeply misleading: it commits the homunculus fallacy by assuming that the rest of the brain has some kind of a bird's eye's view of the 2D retinal image, and that's what it has to deal with. The truth is quite different: the only vehicle for passing on the information contained in the retinal representation is the pattern of activities of the entire ensemble of retinal neurons that project their axons to the brain (these are the ganglion cells, whose axons form the optic nerve; recall Figure 3.1 on page 40). Thus, vision is really the process of making sense of the million or so simultaneous measurements carried by each optic nerve, whose number determines the dimensionality of the raw visual representation space.

Motor control. The potential for a similar confusion exists in the context of movement generation. Although the problem of controlling the muscles to make your arm reach out and touch something is *defined* in the 3D world space (it takes three numbers to specify the coordinates of the target point), it must be *solved* in the space of muscle activations, which has as many dimensions as there are relevant muscles (assuming for simplicity that the state of each muscle can be captured by a single number).

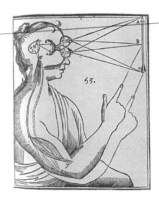

This widely reproduced diagram (from Descartes' *Principles of Philosophy*, published in 1644), gets the DIMENSIONALITY OF VISUAL-MOTOR COORDINATION wrong conceptually, not just anatomically. Still, we should be thankful to Descartes for inventing analytical (algebraic) geometry, thus laying the foundations of the modern treatment of multidimensional spaces.

3.3.5   Dimensionality reduction and hierarchical abstraction

The problem of visual-motor coordination in the toy crab of Figure 3.9 on page 53 was mapping one 2D space into another. For the human brain, the problem in principle is the same, yet its scale is considerably larger, as you just saw. Indeed, were the brain to approach this problem in its raw form — by seeking to map the visual space that has a couple of million dimensions directly into the motor space whose dimensionality runs in the dozens — its fate would have been much sadder than that of the proverbial centipede that becomes paralyzed with confusion when asked how it coordinates the movement of its legs. To computer scientists and engineers, this predicament, which arises from the intractability of various computational problems such as learning and control in high-dimensional spaces, is known as the CURSE OF DIMENSIONALITY (Bellman, 1961).

In the light of the difficulties inherent in any direct onslaught on raw high-dimensional representation spaces, it is easy to see why individual neurons would focus on low-dimensional — hence tractable — aspects of the signal they get from their predecessors in the brain's processing pathways. Each neuron is an information refinery, from which the newly distilled bits go forth to affect the rest of the brain (for example, by acting on other neurons, which may number in the tens of thousands, or by being allowed to tweak a synaptic weight).

By funneling multidimensional data through a narrow-capacity channel, each neuron performs crucial DIMENSIONALITY REDUCTION that mitigates the curse of dimensionality. As a result, even though the *nominal* dimensionality of the data represented by the activities of a bunch of neurons is necessarily equal to their number, the *actual* dimensionality of these representations (how many independent quantities they involve) is usually quite low.

A mnemonic motto for DIMENSIONALITY REDUCTION: out of many, few.

A by-product of this phenomenon is that the brain is considerably less difficult to understand than you might expect from the number of neurons it contains (no cognitive scientist can credibly claim to be capable of reasoning even in as few as a thousand dimensions). Indeed, the traits of the functional architecture of brains discussed earlier, such as tuned receptive fields, are manifestations of precisely this phenomenon. As I noted on p. 44, neurons tend to be tuned to simple combinations of features; a receptive field defined over a 1000-dimensional input space would be virtually impossible to identify, and incomprehensible once identified, if its support (points corresponding to the effective stimuli) were spread evenly throughout that space, rather than being low-dimensional. (An oriented line segment, one might add, is a low-dimensional feature in the space of all possible images.)[15]

However, just as with hierarchical abstraction (discussed in section 2.4 on page 30), the real importance of dimensionality reduction is not in making the life of a cognitive scientist simpler, but in making the functioning of the brain possible. The facility of neurons in implementing dimensionality reduction is what lets the brain curb the astronomical potential complexity stemming from its nominal dimensionality, while it remains capable of dealing with the complex, multi-faceted world. Neural computation thus boils down to mapping rich representation spaces with connections while keeping dimensionality in check. This balancing act, which is repeated at many levels of representation (hierarchical abstraction again!), explains how the managed complexity of cognition can emerge from collective action of relatively simple elements, each focusing on a tractable chunk of the big picture.

Notes

[1]THE BEGINNINGS OF ELECTROPHYSIOLOGY. As soon as electronic devices for amplifying weak signals became available, they were put to use in the study of the electrical activity of neurons by Charles Sherrington, Edgar Adrian, Kenneth Cole, Alan Hogkin, and Andrew Huxley.

[2]DISTINCT CELLS OR A CONTINUOUS SYNCYTIUM? The two pioneers of neuroanatomy, Camillo Golgi and Santiago Ramón y Cajal, who shared the Nobel Prize for 1906, bitterly disagreed as to the basic make-up of the brain. In his acceptance lecture in Stockholm, Golgi, a brilliant scientist and the inventor of a neuron-staining technique that is still in use today, expounded his "reticular" theory, according to which the brain was a diffuse syncytium of cytoplasmically continuous elements. Cajal, who spoke immediately after Golgi, contradicted him and propounded his "neuronal" theory — essentially, the modern view of the brain consisting of metabolically and functionally discrete cells, the neurons. Both these great men, and the productive debate that they sustained over the years, made crucial conceptual and empirical contributions to neuroscience.

[3]ANALOG COMPUTATION IN THE BRAIN. To a certain extent, information processing in the brain is also mediated by "analog," graded membrane potentials within neurons, in addition to the "digital," all-or-none action potentials between neurons.

[4]GENES AND BEHAVIOR. An accessible and insightful summary of the evidence in sup-

port of the contribution of genes to behavior — hence in support of their relevance to the wiring of the brain —- can be found in Steven Pinker's book *The Blank Slate* (2002).

[5]POOR ENGINEERING. Intricate as it is, the retina is not a paragon of engineering design: light has to pass through all those neurons (as well as though the blood vessels that feed them) to reach the photosensitive parts of the receptors in layer A. At the *fovea* (which is Latin for *pit*), where acuity is the highest, the neurons are merely pushed aside, as illustrated in Cajal's drawing (Figure 3.1 on page 40) under (L).

[6]UNIVERSAL COMPUTATION IN THE BRAIN. The simple computations carried out by individual neurons are powerful and versatile when considered as building blocks for complex information processing; in particular, networks of formal neurons can support *logical inference* (McCulloch and Pitts, 1943) and *universal function approximation* (Hartman, Keeler, and Kowalski, 1990).

[7]HEBBIAN RULE of synaptic modification: neurons that fire together, wire together. Hebb (1949) wrote:

> Let us assume that the persistence or repetition of a reverberatory activity (or "trace") tends to induce lasting cellular changes that add to its stability... When an axon of cell A is near enough to excite a cell B and repeatedly or persistently takes part in firing it, some growth process or metabolic change takes place in one or both cells such that A's efficiency, as one of the cells firing B, is increased.

The simplest mathematical expression of this idea makes the rate of change of the strength w of a synapse between neurons i and j proportional to the product of their firing rates:

$$\Delta w_{ij} = \eta x_i x_j$$

where η is the learning rate. Numerous variations on this idea have been developed (Gerstner and Kistler, 2002). Hebb's ideas have been recently validated on cellular, molecular (synaptic), and genetic (neurotransmitter) levels (Lin, Osan, and Tsien, 2006).

[8]The CORTEX is a thin (4-6 mm in humans) sheet of neural tissue that constitutes the evolutionarily new part of the mammalian brain. The anatomy of the cortex is surprisingly uniform: untrained observers find it difficult to distinguish, say, the auditory cortex of a mouse from the somatosensory cortex of the elephant.

[9]FUNCTIONAL ARCHITECTURE OF THE CORTEX. The cortical columns, mentioned on p. 66, are a prominent example of local similarity structure of map-like representations in the brain.

[10]A MULTIDIMENSIONAL SPACE is particularly easy to implement in a network form, simply by wiring up nodes (such as neurons) so that each one has the appropriate number of neighbors (Braitenberg, 1977). Generally, in an *n*-dimensional wireframe cube *n* wires meet at every vertex. The illustration below shows projections of 2-, 3-, 4-, and 5-dimensional cubes (clockwise from top left) into 2D.

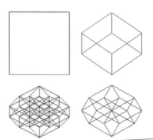

[11]THE BRAIN AS A DYNAMICAL SYSTEM. Seeing each neuron's activity as a dimension of a space in which the total brain state ascribes some complex, yet deterministic, trajectory is equivalent to viewing a brain as a dynamical system, as defined in Chapter 2.

[12]LINEAR MAPPINGS. A function $f(\cdot)$ is called linear if $f(a\mathbf{x}_1 + b\mathbf{x}_2) = af(\mathbf{x}_1) + bf(\mathbf{x}_2)$ for any two numbers a, b and argument values $\mathbf{x}_1, \mathbf{x}_2$.

[13]STATISTICAL COMPUTATIONAL NEUROSCIENCE. For a review of the key early work on the statistical theory of neural computation, see (Barlow, 1990) and (Linsker, 1990). A modern computational statistical theory of synaptic plasticity is presented by Cooper, Intrator, Blais, and Shouval (2004).

[14]DIMENSIONALITY REDUCTION. In Principal Component Analysis, the data are projected onto the directions of the highest variance. In other words, after the coordinates are rotated, one retains in the list of numbers describing each data point only those few that correspond to the dimensions along which the deviation from the mean value — that is, the spread of the data cloud — is the highest.

[15]NOMINAL DIMENSIONALITY OF IMAGES. The nominal dimensionality of a 100×100 (say) image of a solid object is equal to $10,000$. Now, let that object rotate around a fixed axis in front of the camera; its attitude is then completely described by a *single number*: the current angle with respect to some arbitrary fixed reference orientation. Because of that, the collection of snapshots of such a rotating object forms a *manifold* in the $10,000$-dimensional space of all images of all possible objects, and the actual dimensionality of this collection is equal to 1 (see, for example, Edelman, 1999, pp.69ff).

4

The Astonishing Hypothesis

"But does not the way to it lie through the very den of the metaphysician, strewn with the bones of former explorers and abhorred by every man of science?" Let us peacefully answer the first half of his question "Yes," the second half "No," and then proceed serenely.

Through the Den of the Metaphysician,
reprinted in *The Embodiments of Mind* (1965, p.143)
WARREN S. MCCULLOCH

A MIND is a terrible thing to explain. Francis Crick wrote in 1994 that the hypothesis that the mind can be understood in terms of the brain — the central idea in McCulloch's EXPERIMENTAL EPISTEMOLOGY project — was still "so alien to the ideas of most people today that it can truly be called astonishing":

> The Astonishing Hypothesis is that "You," your joys and your sorrows, your memories and your ambitions, your sense of personal identity and free will, are in fact no more than the behavior of a vast assembly of nerve cells and their associated molecules.

— Francis Crick
The Astonishing Hypothesis (1994)

EPISTEMOLOGY: "just say know." Epistemology is the branch of philosophy dealing with the nature and sources of knowledge. Warren McCulloch, who did much to help turn it into a science, called his project "experimental epistemology." The picture shows jnana-mudra — the traditional Indian hand gesture (mudra) that symbolizes teaching. The Sanskrit word *jnana* is cognate with the Russian знание (znanie), Greek γνῶσις (gnosis), and English *knowledge*.

Why is it that an educated person today may still find the idea that he or she is "nothing but a pack of neurons" (to use Crick's expression) so much more repugnant than the idea that those neurons, along with everything else on this planet, are nothing but a pack of atoms swirling in a void? At work here are two factors, which are really two sides of the same coin. The first one is the human visceral predisposition to intuitive animism: as Paul Bloom (2004) argues in his book *Descartes' Baby*, people are "natural-born dualists." The second factor is the human intellectual predisposition to philosophical dualism: although commonly considered to be Descartes's baby, the dualist stance is actually the fallout of millennia of learned discourse, in which some of the smartest people in each generation engaged in protracted and intricate arguments about life, universe, and everything without the slightest shred of what in our age of science would pass as evidence.

The material and the mental in the news: although the headline of a recent article on the study of schizophrenia (Jenette Restivo reporting for the ABC News Online, September 24, 2001) was the factually noncommittal, philosophically orthodox Cartesian *Mystery of the Mind*, its text opened with a truly ASTONISHING HYPOTHESIS: "Destruction of 'gray matter' in the brain may lead to debilitating mental illness."

4.1 Experimental neuroepistemology

Historically, philosophy played an important constructive role in the development of the Western scientific thought. In particular, empirically minded philosophers (think Locke and Hume, not Rousseau; Goethe and Humboldt, not Hegel;[1] Quine and Dennett, not Heidegger) have been instrumental in setting the agenda for the emerging sciences of the mind, and in holding at bay the monotheistic orthodoxy.[2] This came at a price: an inflated role for philosophy in influencing the course of science and in assessing its progress. Even in the pragmatic 20th century, calls for putting science first — including those by philosophers such as Karl Popper (1992) and Willard Van Orman Quine (1960) — fell on many a deaf ear.

Given the special status of the mind as an object of scientific inquiry, the public's perception of the cognitive sciences is particularly vulnerable to undue influence from well-entrenched philosophical doctrines that are clinging to their traditionally privileged place above science. Although this malaise is not widespread among psychologists or neuroscientists, the researchers' freedom from prejudice in those disciplines is often accompanied by an alienation from wider-scope theoretical considerations, which are liable to be misperceived as philosophical diktats.

On placing philosophy above science:

Requiescat
Jade bowl
Of the greatest antiquity
'Bout time it got broke.

Warren S. McCulloch
Embodiments of Mind
MIT Press, 1965

4.1.1 Nullius in verba

Francis Bacon's book *Novum Organum* (1620) — a document that amounted to a declaration of independence of science from stifling scholasticism — states that the aim of science is "...to overcome, not an adversary in argument, but nature in action." This Promethean quest held great appeal for Christopher Wren, Robert Boyle, John Wilkins, Robert Moray, and Robert Hooke, all members of an "invisible college" of *natural philosophers* that had been meeting since the 1640s to discuss Bacon's ideas. In 1660, this group founded the first academy of sciences in the world, the Royal Society of London. The Society chose its motto to be *nullius in verba*, a phrase taken from Horace's *Epistles*:

> *Nullius addictus iurare in verba magistri,*
> *quo me cumque rapit tempestas, deferor hospes.*

> (My words are not owned by any master,
> where the winds [of reason] lead me, there I find home.)

Bacon's *Novum Organum* closes with the observation that "considering the mind in its connexion with things, and not merely relatively to its own powers, we ought to be persuaded that the art of invention can be made to grow with the inventions themselves."[3] Three hundred years after the convening of the Invisible College, the province of the new-fangled natural philosophy — what could and should be studied until understood — came to encompass the world and its fullness. By the 1920s, only one domain was still jealously, and successfully, guarded by *verba magistri* against attempts at empirical understanding: that of the "mental." Embarrassingly, this included the nature of understanding itself.

That too changed when the human mind, within which the scientific method originated on this planet, dared to apply that method to itself. In a lecture titled *Through the Den of the Metaphysician*, delivered to the Philosophical Club of the University of Virginia in 1948, Warren McCulloch noted, "For the first time in the history of science we know how we know and hence are able to state it clearly." Today, we can do more than that: we can put our statement to an empirical test.

The frontispiece of Francis Bacon's NOVUM ORGANUM shows a symbol of pushing against the boundaries of the unknown — a ship venturing beyond the Pillars of Hercules, the Greek name for the Rock of Gibraltar, which guards the passage from the Mediterranean out into the open ocean.

4.1.2 Testing the astonishing hypothesis

The identification of the mind with the activity of the brain, which in 1948 was, and for many in the early 21st century still is, an astonishing hypothesis, can now be studied by standard electrophysiological methods. Electrophysiology, a technique that I described in the previous chapter, involves recording and analyzing the electrical activity of neurons while the organism is engaged in some task of interest. To grasp the full import of the study I am about to recount, let us consider the following corollary of the astonishing hypothesis, as applied to visual perception:

Corollary to the Astonishing Hypothesis: The perception of a given quality or aspect of the visual stimulus **consists** of the activity of identifiable neurons in the cerebral cortex.

This claim is not trivial.[4] It goes beyond assuming that the particular neural activity simply *co-occurs* with the percept in that it posits a *causal* relationship between the former and the latter. In that, it transcends the Cartesian view, often termed "interactionist," according to which the brain is merely a conduit that connects the world to an immaterial soul, the latter being the seat of perception, action, and everything in between.

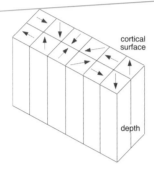

The functional architecture of the medial temporal (MT) cortex exhibits a COLUMNAR structure: neurons with similar tuning properties (here, the selectivity to the direction of visual motion) are clustered in columns, each a couple of hundred micrometers square, that run perpendicular to the cortical surface.

The news from the front lines of neuroscience, where the astonishing hypothesis is being evaluated empirically, do not bode well for Descartes' view. It looks overwhelmingly likely that we don't need anything beyond the activity of the brain itself to account for perception, action, and everything. That this is true for *action* has been accepted knowledge for quite some time: ever since 1791, when Luigi Galvani made a dead frog's leg twitch by touching the exposed sciatic nerve with an electrically charged scalpel, we have known that a muscle can be activated by a weak electrical current. So we don't need to postulate magical and mysterious animal spirits, or interaction with another plane of existence where immaterial souls dwell.[5] That this is also true for *perception* is a more recent discovery, made by the team of William T. Newsome, who showed that a visual percept can be induced through artificial electrical stimulation of the appropriate area of the brain (Salzman, Britten, and Newsome, 1990).[6]

Newsome's experiment relied on earlier work in his laboratory, which had examined the functional architecture of the middle temporal (MT) area in the monkey visual cortex. Neurons in MT had been known to respond selectively to the direction of motion in the visual field (see Figure 4.1, bottom). Newsome and his colleagues discovered that area MT possesses a COLUMNAR layout: neurons situated in neighboring slabs of the cortex have similar directional selectivities. The researchers then established that single neurons in area MT have similar response properties (sensitivity and selectivity) to those of the monkey's entire perceptual system, as assessed behaviorally. That showed that the activity of single neurons *could* in principle account for the animal's perception, but not yet that such activity had a causal role in bringing the perception about, thus stopping one step short of proving the Corollary.

Closing the remaining gap involved an ingenious experimental setup that used controlled motion stimuli: kinetic dot patterns, in which a majority of dots moved randomly, and a small proportion moved coherently (see Figure 4.1, top). The monkey's behavioral task was to detect the direction of coherent motion and report it to the experimenter by moving its eyes to one of several predetermined locations (training monkeys to carry out such a task takes several weeks of reinforcement).

What would a monkey see in such a display when all the dots move about randomly (that is, when the stimulus is 0% coherent)? The same thing you would see: no perception of direction at all, which is just fine, because the visual stimulus in this case contains no directional information. But suppose that the experimenters, having inserted an electrode into area MT and identified there a neuron with a certain directional selectivity, activate that neuron artificially. This can be done by injecting a very weak current into the vicinity of the neuron (a few millionths of an ampere suffice; in comparison, a vacuum cleaner takes about 10 or 20 amperes). Because of the columnar structure of

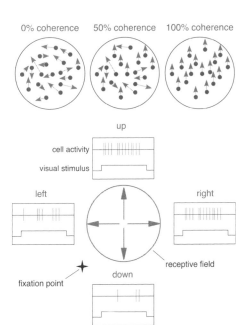

Figure 4.1 — *Top:* visual stimuli consisting of moving dots with controlled COHERENCE (proportion of dots that move in a same fixed direction, rather than randomly) can be used to set up motion perception tasks with varying degrees of difficulty. *Bottom:* a typical receptive field of an MT NEURON. This particular unit responds selectively to upward motion. The hypothesis tested by Newsome and his associates (see text) states that making such a neuron fire even in the absence of coherent motion would cause the subject (a monkey) to perceive movement in the direction corresponding to the neuron's preference.

the MT cortex, this current will kick into action a clump of neurons all of which have approximately the same directional selectivity. As a result, one may expect that the monkey will *see* directional motion, even where there is, in fact, none.

This is precisely what the researchers found: injecting current around neurons known to respond to, say, motion leftwards and upwards, *causes* the monkey to perceive (and to signal) motion leftwards and upwards in a stimulus that is objectively random (see Figure 4.2).[7] It is interesting to note that the possibility of affecting perception by intervening with just a few neurons corroborates Barlow's conjecture concerning the role of individual neurons in shaping cognition (see p. 39).

This experiment (and many more conducted since then) shows that the *causal nexus* in the process of establishing and using internal representations of the world exists at the level of small groups of cortical neurons: the ac-

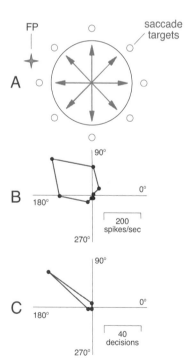

Figure 4.2 — Demonstrating CAUSAL IDENTITY BETWEEN NEURAL ACTIVITY AND PERCEPTION. A, the monkeys in Newsome's studies were trained to signal their perception of directional visual motion by moving their eyes to one of eight target locations (the saccades, or eye movements, were monitored by the computer that controlled the experiment). B, the responses of a chosen neuron to perfectly (100%) coherent motion in each of the eight test directions. The response strength for each direction (in spikes per second) is indicated by the radial distance of the corresponding point from the diagram center. The preferred direction is leftwards and upwards (135°). C, the overt, behavioral responses made by the monkey when current was injected into the vicinity of the neuron whose tuning curve is plotted above, **for 0%-coherence stimuli**. Clearly, the monkey was seeing motion leftwards and upwards, even though the dots in none of the trials plotted here moved in any coherent manner. The results illustrated in (B) and (C) together show that the activity of this neuron and its neighbors is both necessary and sufficient for this monkey to perceive motion in that particular direction. In other monkeys (or, for that matter, in humans, whose visual system is organized similarly), neurons that fulfill an *analogous function* can be found: perception is an organizational – functional – invariant (as we discovered way back on p. 7).

tivation of such a group is both necessary and sufficient for a percept to be registered, or for an action to be initiated. By establishing mappings between perceptual and motor representations, as required by the task at hand and according to the general principles stated in Chapter 3 (p. 53), the brain can bypass the need for a homunculus and close the causal loop — or rather, the multiple, hierarchical, intertwined loops — which is what cognition **consists** of. These findings vindicate McCulloch's insights and Crick's Astonishing Hypothesis, and provide a decisive experimental handle on the mind-body problem, which has been around for millennia, and of which so many bright minds made such an exasperating philosophical mess.

4.2 The Marr-Poggio program

Experiments such as the one I just described are crucial for initiating and sustaining progress in science. But how are we to choose which experiments to undertake? In one of his books, Karl Popper described how he used to start his course on the philosophy of science by telling the students "Observe!" After some milling around, the students would start asking, "What are we supposed to observe?" At that point, Popper would say, "Aha! You must have a THEORY to guide your observations and experimentation."

Indeed, life is too short to waste it on experimentally testing the effects of the prevalence of hay fever in Iowa on the onset of superconductivity in indium-copper alloys. To analyze the available observations, and to come up with a reasonable course of action for further inquiry, we need to act within a theoretical framework that is both explanatory (perhaps in a tentative way), and plausible, at least initially.[8]

4.2.1 Why did the chicken cross the road?

Let's look at what constitutes an adequate explanation with the help of a classical existential puzzle: **why did the chicken cross the road?** Several conjectures, attributed apocryphally to various professional and lay practitioners of the cognitive sciences, are listed in Table 4.1 on the following page.[9]

The disparate nature of the explanations offered suggests that they all should be treated with caution (cf. *Those who cluck do not know; those who know do not cluck*, attributed to Lao Tzu). That very feature of the problem we are facing can, however, be turned into an important lesson: because a

#	explanation	attribution
1	It had a cunning plan.	S. O. Baldrick
2	'Cause it [censored] wanted to. That's the [censored] reason.	Jack Nicholson
3	It was a historical inevitability.	Karl Marx
4	It seemed like the logical thing to do at the time.	Mr. Spock
5	An die andere Seite zu kommen.	Sigmund Freud
6	Because of the catalytical activation of cytosolic creatine kinase isoenzymes during the development of its brain.	anon.
7	Because its nucleus angularis (NA) received ipsilateral excitatory glutaminergic input from the auditory portion of the 8th nerve.	anon.
8	Because of the N-methyl-D-aspartate receptor-mediated modulation of monoaminergic metabolites and amino acids in its forebrain.	anon.

Table 4.1 — Why did the chicken cross the road? The answers offered here represent the following methodological approaches: intuition (1); cognitive psychology (2); social pseudoscience (3); Artificial Intelligence (4); intuition (5); neuroembryology (6); neurophysiology (7); molecular neurobiology (8). The phrases in rows 6–8 were taken from bona fide neuroscience publications (which did not, I must admit, purport to explain chicken road-crossing as such).

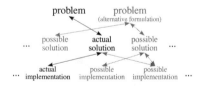

Computational systems such as the mind/brain must be studied at MULTIPLE LEVELS of abstraction: from problems, through representations and algorithms that solve the problems, down to mechanisms that implement the solutions (Marr and Poggio, 1977).

cognitive act can always be explained at several levels, the only *complete* kind of explanation is one that spans them all.

4.2.2 Levels of analysis

In the study of the mind, we do have an overarching explanatory hypothesis: the identification of cognition with computation. Abstract as it is, this idea (along with the lesson just stated) suggests A CONCRETE, MULTIPLE-LEVEL MASTER PLAN, which is applicable to the study of any computational system, including the brain. For an example of this plan in action, let's return to surface lightness constancy — the perceptual phenomenon whose analysis in Chapter 1 (p. 7) convinced us that cognition is computation.

The observation that clinched this conclusion had to do not with the nature of any *solution* to the problem of lightness perception, but rather with the nature of the *problem* itself (which, we realized, consists of having to factor a product of two numbers, corresponding to the quantity of light falling onto the surface in question and the proportion of light reflected from it). The PROB-

LEM LEVEL is the most proper place to start thinking about any instance of computation: if we don't understand why the computation happens and what its inputs and outputs are, even a good understanding of the mechanisms involved (assuming it can be achieved without any idea of the "big picture") would still leave the entire process shrouded in mystery.

For lightness, we do have a problem-level understanding: it's about factoring a product of two unknown numbers. What next? We may be able to understand lightness perception also at the MECHANISM LEVEL — how it is instantiated in the brain — by identifying neurons whose activity is necessary and sufficient for lightness constancy to happen (which is precisely the role that the MT neurons we learned about just now play in motion perception). That, however, would still leave many questions unanswered, such as how, exactly, the recovered lightness is represented in the activities of those neurons, and how, exactly, their input (starting with the retinal signal) gets transformed into the desired output.

Such questions belong at the LEVEL OF REPRESENTATION AND ALGORITHM, whose logical place in the master plan is below that of the problem, and above that of the mechanism. A given computational problem can always be represented in more than one way, and the mapping between the input and output representations called for by the problem can always be attained by more than one algorithm (computational procedure). This multiplicity of possible implementations is mirrored on the next lower level, where a given set of representations and a given procedure that manipulates them can be embodied in various physical substrates — my neurons, your neurons, monkey neurons, my robot's transistors, etc.

4.2.3   Levels of analysis: understanding sound localization in owls

There exist cognitive systems for which our understanding is nearly complete, spanning all the levels just mentioned: problem, representation and algorithm, and neural mechanisms. One of these is the system that supports sound localization in the BARN OWL.

Barn owls hunt mice at night, and are able to locate and catch their prey in total darkness, using for guidance the sounds made by the mice themselves. Let us start with the problem level. The information the owl (or any other airborne hunter) needs to guide its flight consists of the AZIMUTH (heading) and the ELEVATION of the target; the former is needed to steer in the left-right

A BARN OWL (*Tyto alba*). Owls can hunt in complete darkness, homing in on the sound of the mouse scurrying along the ground.

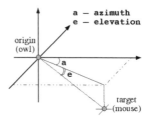

The direction from the hunter to the prey can be conveniently and completely described by two angles: AZIMUTH and ELEVATION.

direction, and the latter – in the up-down direction. What kind of information about these quantities is available in the sounds made by the mouse? That depends on the number and the spatial arrangement of the measurement devices used by the hunter's auditory system.

The only sound measurement devices at the owl's disposal are its ears, of which it has two, just as we do (you cannot see them because they are hidden behind the feathers of the owl's facial ruff). When a mouse situated, say, ahead and to the right of a perched owl rustles on the ground, there is a *delay* in the sound's arrival at the owl's left ear relative to its arrival at the right ear, which in this example happens to be slightly but significantly closer to the source. For the same reason, the *intensity* of the sound at the right ear is somewhat stronger. Both these differences contain information about the azimuth of the mouse relative to the owl (see Figure 4.3).

We may therefore conclude that the owl in principle has access to two kinds of cues that it can use to compute the heading to the mouse:

1. the *intensity difference* between the two ears;

2. the *timing difference* between the two ears.

It is worth noting that any animal or robot equipped with binaural hearing would have access to this information. In identifying its nature, we have analyzed the phenomenon at hand (the owl's prowess in localizing the sound of

Figure 4.3 — OWL HEARING. Just like you, the barn owl has two ears. These are situated in dish-like depressions on the sides of its head, facing forward; the shape of the owl's face and the fine feathers covering it both help focus the sound. The horizontal displacement of the ears relative to each other introduces temporal disparity — a delay in the arrival of sounds to the two ears. The delay varies with the azimuth between head and sound-source directions, vanishing for stimuli located precisely ahead or behind the bird. Because the owl's ears (probably unlike yours) are also displaced vertically — one is a bit higher on the face than the other — the sound differences also carry information about the elevation of the sound source.

the mouse) only at the problem level; nothing at all has yet been said about the representations involved, the algorithms used, or the neural circuits that implement it. In fact, I haven't yet mentioned any evidence suggesting that owls do in fact use binaural hearing... maybe they use telepathy, or divination.

That the owl uses binaural cues can be established simply by measuring its aiming performance in a controlled experiment, with one or the other ear plugged. Such experiments show that the heading errors are very high (20-40 degrees) when only one ear can be used. Moreover, the errors are larger when the earplugs are made of a solid material with better sound insulation properties. We may, therefore, turn to the next levels, and ask how binaural timing information[10] can be used computationally to estimate the direction of the sound source, and what kind of neuronal circuit does in fact implement the necessary computation in the owl brain.

As usual in an information-processing setting, we must consider multiple possibilities when descending from one level of explanation to the next lower one. Indeed, the same computational *problem* (using binaural time differences) can be solved by at least two distinct *procedures* (algorithms). The first possibility is to use some functional equivalent of a stopwatch: a countdown clock, which would start ticking when the first signal arrives, and stop when the second, later signal arrives. The time difference, measured rather directly in this manner, could then be translated into the desired azimuth difference, given the knowledge of the inter-aural distance and the speed of sound.

The second possible way of capitalizing on the binaural time difference is to compensate for the delay in one of the two input streams, then detect

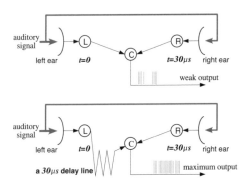

Figure 4.4 — Using COINCIDENCE DETECTION to extract information that comes in the form of a timing difference between two copies of the same signal. Neurons are good coincidence detectors; wiring up a neuron to accept one of the two signals via a *delay line* (which can be implemented simply as an extra length of axon) yields a circuit that capitalizes on this feature.

the simultaneous arrival of the resulting signals at a bank of special COIN-CIDENCE DETECTORS. This alternative has the advantage of being better suited for actual implementation in a neural circuit: neurons are no good at counting, but are very good at responding to synchronous, or near-coincident, inputs. To function as a coincidence detector, a neuron needs to have its firing threshold set to a value just above what a single input can achieve; two simultaneous inputs arriving at the soma would then effectively combine forces to push the neuron over the threshold and make it emit a spike.

The hypothesis that the owl brain uses coincidence detection to process the timing difference information was put forward by Lloyd Jeffress in 1948 (see Figure 4.4 on the previous page). Jeffress realized that the precondition for the use of coincidence detection for this purpose — compensating for the delay in the arrival of one of the two signals, so that they become in fact coincident — can be easily fulfilled with the available neural "hardware." The propagation of the electrochemical signal down axons is slow enough to make it possible for a length of an axon to serve as a *delay line*. If the earlier signal is piped through a somewhat longer axon than the later one, they can be made to arrive at the coincidence detector simultaneously. A system relying on this idea would have to be equipped with a variety of delay lines, tuned to various possible binaural disparities; the actual disparity would be indicated by the identity of the one circuit actually triggered by the incoming signal.

This model was elaborated upon by Masakazu Konishi, who proposed

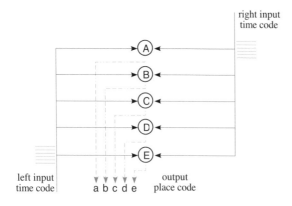

Figure 4.5 — MAPPING TIME INTO LOCATION DIFFER-ENCES. To deal with a range of time differences, the circuit relying on the principle of coincidence detection must incorporate a battery of delay lines of various lengths. Of the five "neurons" shown in this schematic illustration, the topmost one (A) would respond to a signal that arrives at the left input before the right one; the bottommost "neuron" (E) is tuned to the opposite sign of time difference. By means of this hard-wired circuit, the subtle timing differences between the left- and right-ear signals are converted into a robust "place code" in which the location of the neuron determines its functional significance.

an arrangement of axons bearing signals from the two ears and running parallel to each other in opposite directions (Figure 4.5 on the facing page). Coincidence-detecting neurons placed at successive locations within this system of axons would, by virtue of their placement, become tuned to various binaural timing differences. Importantly, this arrangement translates timing information into a spatial representation — a format that requires less precision in the firing properties of the various neurons, and is compatible with some very general principles of information processing in the brain, such as spatially organized maps (of which the tonotopic maps mentioned on p. 46 are an example).

In a stunning confirmation of the theoretical insights of Jeffress and Konishi, anatomical and physiological studies show that the owl's brain uses precisely this approach to the processing of binaural information (Figure 4.6; see Carew (2001, ch.3) for a review). Axons carrying information from the two ears enter the nucleus laminaris from opposite sides, and run parallel to each other, precisely as intuited by the Jeffress-Konishi model (this is an *anatomical* finding, having to do with the "wiring diagram" of the brain; such data are obtained by tracing axons of neurons under a microscope after staining them with a special substance, and noting their course through the tissue).

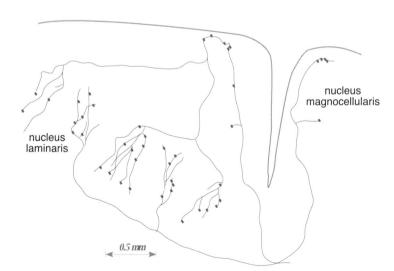

nucleus
magnocellularis

nucleus
laminaris

0.5 mm

Figure 4.6 — ANATOMICAL SUPPORT for the Jeffress-Konishi model: a tracing of the actual neural connections in the part of the owl's brain known as nucleus laminaris reveals a system of axons that bears a striking resemblance to the schematic blueprint shown in Figure 4.5 (Joris et al., 1998).

Moreover, neurons at the top of nucleus laminaris show response time *lead* to the ipsilateral (same-side) ear, changing to *lag* as the recording electrode descends into the nucleus laminaris (this is a *physiological* finding, having to do with the activity of live neurons, which is recorded and visualized as a plot of action potentials unfolding in time).

4.2.4   Levels of analysis: a general method

The kind of comprehensive understanding achieved in the study of sound localization by barn owls would be impossible if the problem were not approached on multiple levels, with computational considerations leading the way, engineering insight sustaining the momentum, and neurobiological findings clinching the case. In the cognitive sciences, a general methodological framework for the study of information-processing systems that incorporates this insight is usually associated with the name of David Marr, who in 1977, in collaboration with Tomaso Poggio, published an influential paper titled ***From understanding computation to understanding neural circuitry***.

The levels of analysis identified by Marr and the manner in which the understanding of sound localization in the barn owl fits into Marr's meta-theoretical, methodological framework are described in Table 4.2. In some disciplines, similar ideas had long been taken for granted; for instance, the

level	*issues*	*the barn owl example*
computational theory	What is the goal of the computation, why is it appropriate, and what is the logic of the strategy by which it can be carried out?	Use timing [and intensity] differences measured at two locations to pinpoint the source.
representation and algorithm	How can this computational theory be implemented? In particular, what is the representation for the input and output, and what is the algorithm for the transformation?	Use coincidence detection and delay lines to transform time difference into a place code in the brain.
hardware implementation	How can the representation and algorithm be realized physically?	Arrange the neurons spatially and wire them up to reflect the algorithmic solution.

Table 4.2 — Marr's levels of understanding, exemplified on sound localization in the barn owl.

distinction between goals, representations, and algorithms in writing computer code may strike an experienced programmer merely as sound software engineering. Marr's ideas did, however, bring about a major paradigm shift in psychology and in the neurosciences, which had lacked a unified, principled approach. In 1957, William Estes, an eminent mathematical psychologist, wrote about his field: "Look at our present theories [...] or at the probabilistic models that are multiplying like overexcited paramecia. Although already too complicated for the average psychologist to handle, these theories are not yet adequate to account for the behavior of a rodent on a runway." The new brand of computational cognitive science brought about a decisive improvement.

4.3 What kind of computer the brain is

The view that an analysis of a cognitive system cannot be considered complete without achieving an understanding on *all* the applicable levels is now a common starting point for most of the research in psychology and in the neurosciences, and the word "computation" itself is common enough in that literature. The transformation of cognitive science will, however, remain incomplete until the fundamental conceptual developments described in this book percolate into the undergraduate texts.

The process has been traditionally hindered by several pervasive misunderstandings of the nature of computation as applied to explaining the mind. The first kind of misunderstanding sees computation at best as a mere embellishment for some independently posited "theory" (itself stated verbally, often using metaphorical language that would make Freud proud). Returning, for the sake of convenience, to Sternberg's *Cognitive Psychology*, we find a typical example of this attitude in a section titled "Add a Dash of Technology":

> Technological developments in telecommunications, in human-factors engineering, and in digital computers led to analogous developments in psychological theory, particularly in regard to the processing of information.

> — Sternberg (2003, p.12)

The truth of the matter is that, in the Bloody Mary of mind theory, computation is neither the dash of Worcestershire nor the three drops of Tabasco:

A neuron grown artificially on a "chip" — a silicon substrate into which a digital integrated circuit had been etched. Neurons resemble programmable digital computers neither in their appearance nor in their details of their operation. Thus, the sense in which brains are like computers needs to be examined carefully, using the concepts and the methodology we have developed so far, to prevent an all too easy misunderstanding.

computation is the vodka that gives the kick and the tomato juice that gives the body.

The second widespread misunderstanding stems from a fixation on *digital* computation at the expense of neglecting all the other ways of computing (note how prominent the word "digital" is in the preceding quote). Let's use what you have learned so far about brains and computation to determine the proper sense in which the brain can be seen as a computer and the mind as a computation.

Claim: the brain is a programmable digital computer

If this were true, the brain would be like hardware to the mind's software. This claim does not stand up to scrutiny, mainly because in the brain it is not possible to separate the "program" from the architecture that executes it. For instance, you cannot upgrade the owl's sound localization routine by downloading new coincidence detection software into its nucleus laminaris. It is very important to remember, however, that a digital computer can simulate the operation of a brain (because a digital computer can simulate any physical system down to an arbitrary precision), and hence the mind. The ramifications of the realization that the mind is what the brain does are far-reaching and profound; I shall describe and discuss them in later chapters.[11]

Claim: the brain is a dynamical system

Insofar as the brain at the levels that matter (from the biochemical innards of neurons and upwards) is a deterministic physical system, this claim is trivially true; as such, it is also remarkably devoid of explanatory value. As you saw just now, we cannot afford to let *all* our explanations take the form "the billiard ball moved because another ball pushed it," or "the chicken crossed the road because its neuron designated as N17.9.821 fired": some of them must involve goals, others — representations, and procedures aimed at achieving those goals. These, in turn, bring into the picture *computation*, construed as principled manipulation of representations — a definition introduced in Figure 2.1 on page 14 to explain the relationship between minds and brains, and substantiated since then by a variety of means, on levels ranging from conceptual-theoretical to concrete-neurobiological.

And the winner is. . .

In the light of these considerations, we may conclude that **the brain is a dynamical system that generates the mind by implementing all manner of computations.** The next part of the book surveys the main categories of activities that human minds engage in: perception, memory, thinking, language, society and culture. For each of these, I examine some of the tasks at hand, the representations involved, the computations that are thought to manipulate them, and, in a few cases, the brain mechanisms at work.

🐛 🐛 🐛

Notes

[1]ON HEGEL. To find out why "few philosophers have had a more baleful influence on modern philosophy and politics than Georg Wilhelm Friedrich Hegel," see http://www.friesian.com/hegel.htm. Here's a hint:

> Frau Edouard Devrient: "Do tell me, who is the stupid fellow sitting next to me?"
> Felix Mendelssohn (behind his napkin): "The stupid fellow next to you is the philosopher Hegel."
>
> from *The Birth of the Modern*
> Paul Johnson, HarperCollins (1991, pp. 817-818).

[2]ORTHODOXY. The word *orthodoxy* is derived from the Greek *doxa*, which means dogma, opinion, or received knowledge. In contrast, the Greek *episteme* (the root of *epistemology*) means universal knowledge based on reason. The adherents of any dogma are the natural opponents of reason. For example, as Miguel de Unamuno (1972, p.79) notes, the Catholic Church considers free thinking ("opposing the known truth") to be a sin against the Holy Ghost, for which there is no remission; in the catechism of St. Pius X, this is sin #3. For an evolutionary computational explanation of fideistic religions viewed as informational replicants, or mind viruses, see (Dawkins, 1976, 2006; Dennett, 2006).

[3]MIND TOOLS. The importance of augmenting the powers of the mind with the right conceptual tools is well illustrated by this passage from the preface to *Novum Organum* (Bacon, 1620):

> Certainly if in things mechanical men had set to work with their naked hands, without help or force of instruments, just as in things intellectual they have set to work with little else than the naked forces of the understanding, very small would the matters have been which, even with their best efforts applied in conjunction, they could have attempted or accomplished. Now (to pause

awhile upon this example and look in it as in a glass) let us suppose that some vast obelisk were (for the decoration of a triumph or some such magnificence) to be removed from its place, and that men should set to work upon it with their naked hands; would not any sober spectator think them mad? And if they should then send for more people, thinking that in that way they might manage it, would he not think them all the madder? And if they then proceeded to make a selection, putting away the weaker hands, and using only the strong and vigorous, would he not think them madder than ever? And if lastly, not content with this, they resolved to call in aid the art of athletics, and required all their men to come with hands, arms, and sinews well anointed and medicated according to the rules of art, would he not cry out that they were only taking pains to show a kind of method and discretion in their madness? Yet just so it is that men proceed in matters intellectual, with just the same kind of mad effort and useless combination of forces, – when they hope great things either from the number and co-operation or from the excellency and acuteness of individual wits; yea, and when they endeavour by Logic (which may be considered as a kind of athletic art) to strengthen the sinews of the understanding; and yet with all this study and endeavour it is apparent to any true judgement that they are but applying the naked intellect all the time; whereas in every great work to be done by the hand of man it is manifestly impossible, without instruments and machinery, either for the strength of each to be exerted or the strength of all to be united.

[4] FUNCTIONALISM AND IDENTITY THEORY OF MIND. Particular care must be taken to understand the relationship between the so-called identity theory of the mind (Smart, 2004), according to which brain activity *is* mind, and the view of mind as an organizational invariant, which I offered in Chapter 1. The statement I just made — that perception *consists* of the activity of some neurons — falls squarely within Smart's (2004) identity theory. At the same time, it is fully compatible with the organizational (functionalist, computational) view, which is solely capable of providing an explanation as to how the same perception can occur in different brains. To remind you, the explanation is this: the neurons in my brain and those in yours whose respective activities give rise to our related perceptions of the same object are singled out by similar response patterns across stimuli, and by similar functional relations to the activities of other neurons.

[5] IMMATERIAL SOULS. You may complicate your ontology all you wish by postulating non-physical modes of existence, but it will not save your worldview from the sanity checks of reason and of the scientific method. By definition, a non-physical ("mental") entity cannot interact causally with any material object. This would make the soul, at best, an impotent observer of the workings of a brain: along for the ride but barred from the steering wheel.

[6] That electrical stimulation of the exposed human brain surface can cause spurious perception has been known since Wilder Penfield's studies in the 1950s. Newsome's experiments stand out in that they addressed the issue in a controlled fashion, on the level of single neurons.

[7] EXPERIMENTAL NEUROEPISTEMOLOGY. The neurophysiologists in Newsome's study essentially played Descartes' "evil spirit" to the monkey's mind:

> I will therefore suppose that, not a true God, who is very good and who is the supreme source of truth, but a certain evil spirit, not less clever and deceitful than powerful, has bent all his efforts to deceiving me. I will suppose that the

sky, the air, the earth, colors, shapes, sounds, and all other objective things that we see are nothing but illusions and dreams that he has used to trick my credulity.

from Descartes (1641)
First Meditation.

[8]THE WORTH OF A THEORY. Theories that do not contribute useful explanations are simply not worth arguing about. An example would be attempting to explain behavior in terms of metaphorical or merely fuzzy concepts such as will to power, or libido; these attempts lead nowhere, because they do not offer a non-circular account of the supposedly explanatory notions they invoke. Here's what Warren McCulloch writes on Freudian psychology:

Dependence of the data on the theory separates psychoanalysis from all true sciences. What Freud thought free associations are not free. The nondirective torture of Catholic inquisitors extracted *mea culpa*'s of previsioned heresies: the communists secure confessions of expected deviations and disloyalties. Interpretations of chaotic dreams are still controlled by theory, and that theory was in the head of Freud. Change this, and you have changed the method and the data.

from *The Past of a Delusion*
reprinted in *Embodiments of Mind*, p.282ff.

[9]CHICKEN CROSSING. A couple of notes to the entries of Table 4.1 on page 70: (1) Baldrick is the manservant of Edmund Blackadder in the eponymous BBC sitcom produced in the 1980s; (2) the uncensored version of Jack Nicholson's entry is available from the author upon request.

[10]TIMING AND INTENSITY. The barn owl uses both timing and intensity cues (Carew, 2001), but only the processing of the timing information is discussed here.

[11]ON SIMULATING THE BRAIN. Why is the possibility of simulating the brain important? Observe that a simulation of a computation and the computation itself are equivalent: try to simulate the addition of 2 and 3, and the result will be just as good as if you "actually" carried out the addition — that is the fundamental nature of numbers (recall the story of the Count in Chapter 2). Therefore, if the mind is a computational entity, a simulation of the relevant computations would constitute its fully functional replica. Note how this realization revives the old Gnostic worries about world-making by a demiurge, which are discernible nowadays in the cyberpunkish notion of the world as computer simulation. More about this later.

Part II

Faculties

5

Perception

Seeing is forgetting the name of the thing one sees.

PAUL VALÉRY

A sage who sees is unaware of the experience of sense objects about which others are aware.

Bhagavad-Gita, 2.69

T HE WAY of the senses is like the way of war: it is easy to see where and how perception starts, but not where and how it ends. When I look at, say, a cat, a causal chain of events is set in motion by photons entering my eyes. Where does it lead? If I actually see the cat while looking at it,[1] one outcome of the perceptual act is usually the activation of a *concept* — a bundle of information containing various generalizations about the category to which the observed object is most readily attributed. The better-entrenched categories have names, which may be concrete ("cat") or abstract ("danger"); these names, of course, are language-dependent. Because the conceptual system is the core of the human mind (Murphy, 2002), the nature of concepts, and their involvement in perception, memory, thinking, and language, must be explained in computational terms, and the next several chapters all focus on doing so.

Conceptualizing a cat cannot, however, be the main — let alone the only — outcome of an act of seeing it, for several reasons. First, I can conceptualize a cat without seeing one (that's what I did when writing this passage, and reading it caused you to do the same).

Second, of all the sentient beings on this planet, only humans seem to be capable of conceptual thinking (that is, deliberately manipulating concepts; cf. Dennett, 1993). Thus, a question that is more pertinent to the nature of perception as such is not what happens in my concept-soaked brain when I see a cat, but rather what happens in the cat's brain when it looks back.

THE CAT LOOKS BACK. What does its seeing you consist of?

85

WORDS AND IMAGES: a composition patterned after a fragment from Magritte's *Les mots et les images*. In the original piece, published in *La Révolution surréaliste*, no. 12, 15 December 1929, this fragment is accompanied by an inscription: "Undefined figures possess as necessary and as perfect a meaning as precise ones." The INEFFABILITY principle suggests that this meaning, albeit precise, is not expressible conceptually, let alone lexically.

The third reason for relegating concepts to the background of a discussion of perception is that many (I would say most, but there is no simple way of quantifying this) of the aspects of the perceived world — those that constitute the *phenomenal* contents of perception — defy conceptualization. This elusive core of perception is my central concern in this chapter alongside the more conventional issues, which have to do with concepts.

Can anything at all intuitive be said about this core of perception, before we plunge into a computational inquiry? By defying conceptualization, the phenomenal content of experience makes its verbal expression very difficult. It seems that there are only two options at my disposal here. For one thing, I can suggest that you exercise your own perceptual powers to literally see what I mean. Thus: when you look at the world, try to *see* without thinking; to *feel* through your eyes, as it were.

Alternatively, I can appeal to your memory, in the hope that it contains a trace of an experience that would allow me to make my point. Here is an attempt: Jackson Pollock's painting *Ocean greyness*[2] is not particularly grey, nor does it look much like any ocean I ever saw. The title of the painting can therefore be safely set aside, letting the viewer focus on the raw phenomenal feel of . . . something quite inexpressible. To know what I mean, you have to have seen the painting.

Somewhat paradoxically, there is a connection between phenomenal cognition, epitomizing that which is difficult to put into words, and the most language-oriented of all human endeavors, literature. Fiction writing as we know it would not exist were it not for writers' implicit appeal to readers' prior perceptual experience. The striking effectiveness of this tool in the hands of master wordsmiths attests to the central role in human cognition of phenomenal experience, and of the memories it leaves behind. Consider this passage:

Just as reading is "externally guided thinking" (Neisser, 1967, p.136), so perception may be a form of controlled hallucination.

— Anne Treisman (1986)

> First (after a long drought) a remote cloud, as light as a bird, appeared on a hill; then, toward the South, the sky took on the rose color of leopard's gums; then came clouds of smoke which rusted the metal of the nights; afterwards came the panic-stricken flight of wild animals.

> — Jorge Luis Borges
> *The Circular Ruins* (1941)[3]

Borges, ever a wizard with words, chooses not so much to *describe* the sky tinted by a forest fire as to *evoke* its image in the reader's brain. There is a price to pay: for readers who never saw a leopard's snarl, or at least a cat's yawn, his vision will remain INEFFABLE.

It is very important to realize that ineffability of perceptual experience is the rule, not an exception, in everyday life. To the extent that what we see, hear, taste, smell, and touch is personal (that is, depending on the perceiver's unique physical situation and mindset) and transient, a more or less slowly fading impression of the non-conceptual content of our perceptual states will remain confined to our own memories. **To understand perception (as well as its relation to memory) we must, therefore, understand what the raw, phenomenal, pre-conceptual *feel* of sensing the world consists of, and how the sensory stimulation gets computed into that feel.**

5.1 Perceptual measurement

We may begin with a generic description of the initial stage of perception — using vision as the main example — by recalling the terminology developed in Chapter 3: the stimulus is mapped by the receptive fields of an array of retinal cells into a point in a multidimensional measurement space. The "raw" measurement space has as many dimensions as there are sensory neurons: in this case, photoreceptors in the eye (for hearing, this is the number of hair cells in the cochlea; for smell, the number of neurons in the olfactory epithelium, etc.). The closely packed photoreceptors form the RETINAL MOSAIC, shown head-on under magnification in Figure 5.1 on the following page. The effectiveness of this measurement apparatus and of the computational mechanisms it feeds into can be determined by straightforward forced-choice experiments with simple stimuli, such as those shown in the margin.

As anyone who has shopped for a digital camera knows, there are many ways of characterizing the performance of a system composed of a lens and a sensor array. Without doubt, the one characteristic that is the most important behaviorally is spatial resolution: the ability of the system to discern fine details of the stimuli presented to it. The more resources you invest — and that includes, for cameras as well as for eyes, both the lenses and the sensor — the better the performance that you can expect. In certain spatial tasks, however, biological visual systems attain HYPERACUITY — a much higher resolution than what seems to be possible given the design of the measure-

Two spatial resolution tasks. *Left:* in the two-dot stimulus, the subject has to tell whether or not there are two distinct dots in the picture. *Right:* in the VERNIER stimulus, the task is to determine whether the top line is to the left or to the right of the bottom one. The ACUITY THRESHOLD is the smallest dot or line displacement that is perceived correctly in 75% of the trials on the average. In each of the two stimuli shown here, the 0.5 *mm* gap subtends a visual angle of about 5.7′ (minutes of arc) with the page held at a normal reading distance of 30 *cm*. For the vernier, this gap would be at threshold with the book at 20 meters; for the two dots, at 3 meters.

ment "front end." For example, in the VERNIER task, our acuity threshold is better — lower — than in the two-dot task by a factor of about six, and can be as low as 5″ (seconds of arc[4]). If your vision is as sharp as that, you should be able to tell the sense of the displacement of the vernier illustrated here while looking at this page from over 20 meters away. As we shall discover soon, hyperacuity depends on a combination of the optical properties of the imaging subsystem of the eye, the geometry of the retina, and the functional profiles of the receptive fields of its cells. Note, however, that in extreme cases, such as the example just given, the projection of the gap onto the retina may fall entirely within a single photoreceptor (see Figure 5.2 on the next page). It must, therefore, be some additional information, which is initially distributed over an *ensemble* of receptors (cf. p. 57), that makes hyperacuity possible.

One crucial factor in placing a bound on visual acuity is the optics of the eye. As any other optical system also does, the cornea and the lens introduce various distortions into the image that is formed at their focal surface, where the retinal sensor array is situated. In particular, because of light diffraction, a perfect point imaged through a circular aperture such as the iris forms a blurred, disk-like image: the AIRY pattern.[5]

The other factor at work in determining visual acuity is the discrete *sampling* of the retinal image by the photoreceptor mosaic. Smaller, more tightly

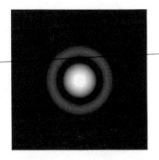

The AIRY Disc. This diffraction pattern is what a point source of light looks like when seen through a finite aperture such as a lens. The size of its core (the Airy Disc) varies as the ratio of the wavelength to aperture width.

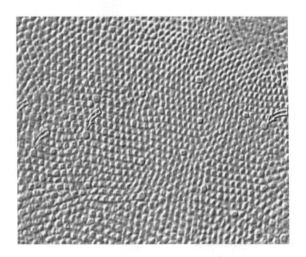

Figure 5.1 — Tangential section through the fovea of a HUMAN RETINA, showing the dense cone mosaic (the arrows indicate the S or "blue" cones; there are no rods in the fovea). Think of each cell of this mosaic as being annotated with a number representing light intensity; the resulting array of numbers (about 120 million in the entire retina) constitutes the input to the visual system. Before the information is sent through the optic nerve to the rest of the brain, the retinal neural network (cf. Figure 3.1 on page 40) reduces its dimensionality to about one million. This may not seem very impressive relative to the state of the art in digital cameras, but the circuitry of the eye/brain ensures that the acuity of vision transcends some of the limitations inherent in the anatomy of the eye; hence the concept of HYPERACUITY.

packed photoreceptors may be expected to support better resolution. We may draw an analogy between the ability to tell apart two dots projected onto the retina and the ability to keep typing fingers from striking two keys at a time: the difference between fine and coarse sampling grids is like typing while wearing gloves and typing in mittens.

The two factors, optics and sampling, go hand in hand: a tighter sampling mosaic would improve the resolution only if the optics could also be made better. This is unlikely in view of the relevant anatomy (cornea, lens, and vitreous humor, all wet and squishy). Indeed, the physical size of the retinal cones is well-matched to the diameter of the Airy disc formed on the retina by diffraction in the eye's optics. As far as the two-dot acuity is concerned, the system is therefore at its limit.

Vernier acuity is, however, much better: it is as if you were able to count the teeth of a comb by touch while wearing gloves. How can this be? The key feature of the vernier stimulus that allows the visual system to deal with it so

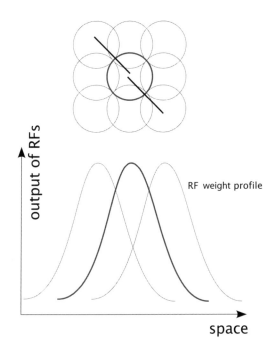

Figure 5.2 — *Top:* a vernier stimulus — two displaced lines, drawn to scale, superimposed on the retinal mosaic. The displacement as illustrated corresponds to the $5''$ hyperacuity threshold, which is much smaller than the "footprint" of a cone (indicated by the circle). *Bottom:* a cross-section through the receptive fields of the adjacent cones, showing (i) their GRADED RESPONSE profiles, and (ii) their significant OVERLAP. Property (i) means that just about any spatial displacement of the stimulus will be registered as *some* change in the cell's response; (ii) means that any spatially extended stimulus will activate many cells, to different degrees. Together, these properties ensure that rich information about the spatial layout of stimuli is contained in the ensemble response of the photoreceptor array. Even for point-like stimuli, this system is likely to exhibit somewhat better acuity than one in which the receptor profiles are flat and non-overlapping. For spatially extended stimuli, the advantage of this design is much greater.

effectively is the spatial extent of the two parts that need to be discriminated. In the two-dot case, the information about the dots' locations is concentrated in the dots themselves. If both fall within the same photoreceptor, this information is lost: it becomes impossible to tell whether this one receptor fires strongly because it is stimulated by two dots or by one dot of a stronger contrast (for example). In comparison, in the vernier case, the information is, loosely speaking, distributed along the two lines; each of the many photoreceptors on which these fall carries some information about their relative locations. Useful information can therefore be retrieved — by integrating the outputs of many receptors — even when the displacement (the vernier gap) is much smaller than individual receptor diameter (see Figure 5.2 on the preceding page).

The outputs of the photoreceptors do contain information sufficient for fine spatial discrimination, due to the graded nature and the overlapping arrangement of their receptive fields. This is illustrated in detail in Figure 5.3 on the next page, which shows a simulation of the response of a visual system consisting of just two receptive fields to a vernier stimulus. The resulting signal is a two-dimensional quantity (because there are just two receptive fields in this simulation), and thus can be easily plotted, for any vernier input. The plots obtained in this manner show a clean separation of points corresponding to the two senses of the vernier displacement. This indicates that information needed to solve the problem is readily available in the ensemble response. One would assume that this is so *despite* the individual receptive fields being both coarse and highly overlapping compared to the size of the smallest discernible vernier gap. This assumption would, however, be a mistake: hyperacuity is possible *because* of the CHANNEL CODING by the graded, overlapping receptive fields, as proved mathematically by Snippe and Koenderink (1992).

Hyperacuity is found in all visual tasks (as in color vision, for example; see Figure 5.4 on page 92), and, indeed, in all other perceptual modalities (tellingly, a paper titled *The ubiquity of hyperacuity* (Altes, 1988) appears in a journal on acoustics, not vision). Because so many disparate kinds of physical systems exhibit hyperacuity, the principle that governs this pervasive phenomenon must be computational. This principle — channel coding — is very general (Snippe and Koenderink, 1992): it is at work throughout the brain, even in places far removed from the perceptual front end (Edelman 1995; more about this at the end of this chapter).

Hyperacuity and CHANNEL CODING by graded-profile overlapping RFs; see Snippe and Koenderink (1992) for the mathematical details. (a), Seeing through flat, discrete pixels. Such a system cannot resolve spatial structure that is finer than the size of the individual pixel. (b), Seeing through graded, overlapping receptive fields. Because of its graded profile, the activity of each RF conveys information regarding the location of small details of the stimulus. Pooling information across different RFs (possible because of the considerable overlap between neighboring RFs) further improves the spatial resolution of the resulting system.

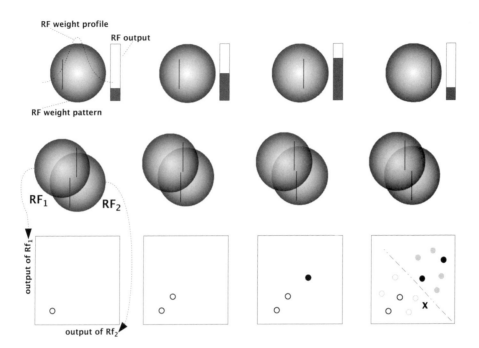

Figure 5.3 — THE COMPUTATIONAL BASIS OF HYPERACUITY. *Top row,* left to right: the responses of a single receptive field (RF) stimulated with a vertical line. The peaked curve overlaid on the leftmost RF shows its weight profile or cross-section (the largest weight is given to light that impinges on the center of the RF). The little "thermometers" near each RF show the activation produced by the stimulus in the corresponding position. *Middle row:* a system of two RFs stimulated by vernier stimuli; the vernier displacement changes in steps, flipping the sign between the second and third stimuli. *Bottom row:* the activation states evoked by these stimuli (the activation space has two dimensions, same as the number of RFs). REPRESENTATION. Open circles and filled disks mark the representations of verniers of the two signs; grayed symbols indicate representations of other possible verniers. Consider the leftmost plot: the circle is placed close to the origin (bottom left corner) because the vernier that gives rise to it happens to activate both RF_1 and RF_2 rather weakly. In the second plot, the vernier halves move closer to the centers of the two RFs, causing the activation to rise along each of the two dimensions of the plot, which is why the second circle is located farther out. This tendency continues in the remaining two plots, as the vernier halves pass each other and its sign flips. LEARNING. The accrual of representations is a kind of learning; as it progresses, it becomes apparent that the circles and the disks can be separated by a *decision line* (which can then be used to classify new stimuli, such as the one denoted by x). The clustering of representations that reflects the property of interest of the stimulus — the sign of the vernier displacement — would be impossible for such small gaps (much smaller than the RF diameter!), were it not for the graded profile and the significant overlap of the two RFs. The learning process outlined here is easily made algorithmic; for a real model of hyperacuity based on the principles described here, see Poggio et al. (1992).

5.2 Representation spaces

The same conceptual tool that I introduced in Chapter 3 and used just now to take the mystery out of vernier hyperacuity — a multidimensional measurement and representation space — will also help you understand perception in general. Imagine showing the two-neuron visual system of Figure 5.3 a face instead of a vernier. Each of the two cells would duly take its measure of the stimulus as "seen" through its receptive field. The outcome of this concerted act of perception would consist of the singling out of a point in the two-dimensional representation space — the one point that corresponds to the current stimulus, or any other stimulus that produces precisely this much activity in RF_1 and precisely that much in RF_2. As in the example of Figure 5.3, **showing the system *several* inputs will give rise to a small *cloud* of points in that space**, which we may call the FACE SPACE (Edelman, 1998b; Valentine, 1991), seeing as the stimuli we are considering are faces. A comprehensive description of such clouds of representations — their layout, their dependence on various factors, and the manner whereby they come into being — is what one needs to know about a perceptual system to understand it fully, for two reasons.

First, there is no avoiding it. Clouds of points in multidimensional representation spaces are the only entities connected to the external world that a cognitive system can ever get to know. Such a space — two-dimensional in the example we started with; seventeen or 10^6-dimensional if there are 17 receptive fields or a million of them — presents an unavoidable bottleneck

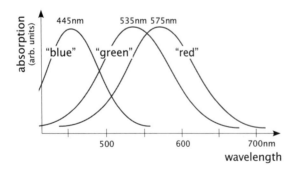

Figure 5.4 — The sensory basis of HYPERACUITY IN COLOR SPACE. Fine discrimination among a multitude of hues is obtained with only three kinds of wavelength-sensitive receptors (cones) in the retina. Analogously to other channel-coded representations, hyperacuity is possible here because the "receptive fields" in the hue space — the spectral response profiles of the cones — are graded, wide, and overlapping.

through which any perceptual information must pass on its way to the rest of the brain. Any subsequent processing stage for which our bank of receptive fields serves as the exclusive feed would be literally blind to those aspects of the world that are not reflected in the layout of this cloud of points. This is why translating various perceptual functions into this terminology is not so much an option as an obligatory step in the process of understanding them.

Second, it's there for real. When I insist on explaining perception in these terms, I do not merely suggest a *metaphor* of a space with a cloud of points in it. Every system whose essence is an ordered list of numbers gives rise to a clear and present multidimensional space. Its reality is of the same kind that you trust (sometimes with your life) when you use the fruits of one of the few occupations that requires its practitioners to feel at home in multidimensional spaces — engineering. It is this reality that lets me keep the promise I made at the outset, namely, to go about explaining cognition in terms that are non-metaphorical (mathematically precise and physically real), and, at the same time, highly intuitive.

What mental picture can be more intuitive than that of a cloud of points suspended in space? Arrangements of points in representation spaces are therefore the explanatory currency we are going to use in the following sections. By the end of this chapter, we will have gained a computational understanding of an entire range of perceptual functions (telling things apart, clumping them into categories, etc.), and even of the very essence of what it means to perceive. And because *neural* computation, too, is most naturally thought of as mapping between multidimensional spaces, as explained in Chapter 3 (p. 51), the new insights will apply to understanding the neural substrate of perception as well.

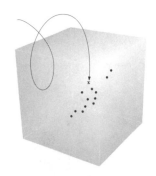

Above: to boldly go where many have gone before — a new POINT singled out in a representation SPACE, by a new stimulus. *Below:* For where two or three or seventeen pyramidal neurons are gathered, there is a two- or three- or seventeen-dimensional space in the midst of their activities.

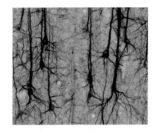

5.2.1 Discrimination and conflation

The first perceptual function I would like to consider is DISCRIMINATION. This is the simplest function one can think of: a perceptual system that is incapable of distinguishing at least two kinds of stimuli would extract no information from the world, and would therefore be perfectly useless.

In vision, the capacity for perceptual discrimination manifests itself, for example, in your ability to tell apart two faces. How does it relate to their locations in the face space maintained by your brain? Subjectively, one expects to be able to tell two faces apart more easily if they look dissimilar. At the same time, in objective terms, two points in space are less likely to be

A famous distinctive face, that of Cyrano de Bergerac. These days, Cyrano's nose could have been easily made less prominent by surgical means, making him less of an OUTLIER along that particular dimension of facial variation.

confused if they are farther apart. This suggests that perceived dissimilarity is determined by the representation-space distance; when translated into the face space parlance, discriminability of two faces naturally corresponds to the face-space distance between the points they map into.[6] Crucially, two faces mapped to the same representation point would not be distinguishable at all: they would be what perception scientists call metamers.

Now imagine seeing more and more faces and retaining their representations for later reference as a generic cloud of points (if you're still visualizing the face space as two-dimensional, think of sticking little flags in a map). With the structure of that cloud in mind, we can immediately understand DISTINCTIVENESS: a face will seem prominent to the extent that its point is far removed from the others in this cloud. In contrast, it will be seen as ordinary, or average, if it happens to fall close to the cloud's center (see Figure 5.5 on the next page).

If I happened to have a distinctive face but resented perceptual notoriety, or simply desired the peace that goes with average looks, I might wish that the point that my face evokes in the observers' face spaces be closer to the mean. This could happen in three ways: (1) I could make my face move towards the mean (by employing a plastic surgeon to shorten my nose, if it were too long compared to the average); (2) I could make the mean itself change (for example, by making sure that the people whose face spaces I want to warp are overexposed to long-nosed faces, perhaps by tying them to a chair and making them watch *Pinocchio*), or (3) I could make the very *metric* — what determines the distance[7] — change (e.g., by drawing the viewers' attention to those dimensions of facial variation along which my face is not an OUTLIER).

The latter two options constitute two kinds of perceptual learning, an important aspect of perception to which I'll return in section 5.4. For now, let's focus on the possibility of affecting facial distinctiveness through plastic surgery: note that it underscores the sensitivity of the face space layout to the many variables that affect the way faces look. Some of these variables are *intrinsic* to the face: the length of the nose, the curvature of the chin, the color of the skin. Others are *extrinsic*: the amount and the distribution of light that illuminates the face, the direction from which it is viewed. This distinction is at the root of two key phenomena in perception. The first one is categorization, or pulling together points that differ on the intrinsic dimensions; this is another kind of learning, as we'll see in section 5.4. The second one — perceptual constancy, or pulling together points that differ on the extrinsic dimensions — is discussed next.

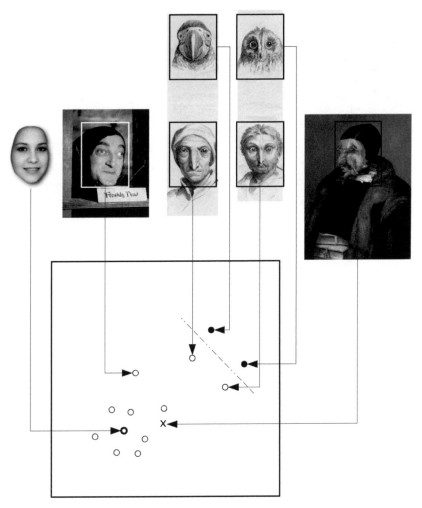

Figure 5.5 — FACE SPACE DWELLERS *(left to right)*: an average of many superimposed faces; three distinctive faces; a composite face. The average face is obtained by blending many actual ones, and is therefore mapped into the midst of the cloud of points representing all the faces known to the system. The distinctive faces – a photograph of the actor Marty Feldman, and two paintings by Charles Lebrun (1619-1690) – fall at the outskirts of that cloud. Lebrun's birdlike faces and birds are mapped into nearby points, illustrating the similarity principle that underlies the core intuitions associated with face space. The head in the painting on the right – *The Jurist* by Giuseppe Arcimboldo (1530-1593) – is composed of fish and poultry parts, yet its face is perceived as approximately human. Presumably, this happens because it *looks* sufficiently human or, using the explanatory terminology of face spaces, because it lands close to several points known to be evoked by human faces. Also shown is a possible decision line (dashed) that can be used in telling apart birds from people (cf. Figure 5.3): a new input mapped into a point below and to the left of this line would be classified as "human face."

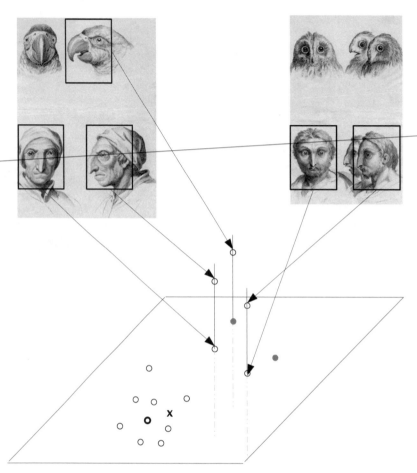

Figure 5.6 — The same face space as before, with three strands of a VIEW SPACE sticking out of it (cf. Figure 5.5). If the shape of a face is represented by location in the *en face* space of Figure 5.5, illustrated here by the horizontal plane, then its changing orientation (view) will be represented by movement perpendicular to that space. This movement — the view space — is depicted schematically for three of Lebrun's faces (two rather bird-like humans, and an actual parrot). Achieving PERCEPTUAL CONSTANCY — seeing profile and *en face* views as the same person — amounts to squashing the view space, or treating all the points on it as equivalent (section 5.2.2). In the terminology of Chapter 3, this means that constancy requires a kind of smart dimensionality reduction to get rid of dimensions of variations that are extrinsic to the quantity of interest (in this case, shape). If you are undaunted by higher dimensionalities, consider a situation in which an object can (i) deform in 17 independent ways, (ii) grow or shrink in size, (iii) move left or right, up or down, (iv) rotate in a gimbal, and (v) be illuminated by a variable-intensity ambient light source. If you count the degrees of freedom, you'll see that the resulting space of possibilities would nominally require at least $17 + 1 + 2 + 3 + 1 = 24$ dimensions to be properly represented. True perceptual shape constancy in that situation would require squashing the seven extrinsic dimensions, leaving the 17 shape-related ones intact. Consult (Edelman, 1999) for the full story.

5.2.2 Constancies: an introduction

Face perception can be considered constant insofar as faces do not appear to change their identities when seen under varying illumination or from different viewpoints. All our senses exhibit such PERCEPTUAL CONSTANCY to a degree that, under normal circumstances, is as striking when one pauses to think about as it is usually unnoticed. I perceive the color of the surface of the deck behind my house as constant even as the shadows of the pines in my back yard move across it; the perceived shape of the lawn chair does not change when the sun goes behind a cloud. My coffee smells the same whether I take it in my study or on the deck, where its aroma blends with the ever-present undercurrent of pine resin and a hint of lilac that blossoms on the other side of the house. I identify the birdsong I hear as that of a Northern cardinal despite the intermittent screeches of jays, which are raising an alarm over the neighbors' cat, last seen slinking into the woods behind the house.

Constancy to an Ideal Object

Since all that beat about in Nature's range,
Or veer or vanish; why should'st thou remain
The only constant in a world of change,
O yearning Thought! that liv'st
                                    but in the brain?
                    ...

— Samuel Taylor Coleridge

The centrality of constancy is manifested in the illusions that emerge when constancy mechanisms are subverted by a clever manipulation of the stimulus or the context in which it is presented. It is not necessary, however, to go to a science museum to realize that perception is only constant up to a point. I grow a beard, and a friend whom I have not seen for a couple of years glances at me without recognition at a conference we both attend. I look at a handful of coins in the light of a sodium street lamp and fail to distinguish a penny from a dime. A radar antenna at the airport now rotates, now seems to deform, now rotates again but in the opposite direction, yet the controllers in their tower are not in the least alarmed. I am given several wines to taste and asked to describe their "nose"; the descriptions I produce turn out to correlate more with the color of the wine (manipulated artificially by a tasteless food dye) than with the grape, country, or vineyard of origin. A family acquaintance calling on the phone mistakes my father for his grandson and asks to speak to his mother; my father replies, truthfully but unhelpfully, that she is long dead.

These examples of perceptual inconstancies play counterpoint to the examples of perceptual constancies, listed earlier. As a matter of fact, quotidian constancy is rarely perfect, even when it does not break down catastrophically (the examples just given are so common that I can report them first-hand and can expect you to have had similar experiences; the exception is the olfactory illusion, for which see Österbauer, Matthews, Jenkinson, Beckmann, Hansen, and Calvert, 2005). To understand why and how this is so, we must first translate the notion of constancy into a language suitable for describing perceptual computation: that of representation spaces.

In computational terms, constancy corresponds to the ability to distill, out of all the dimensions of measurement performed on a stimulus, the few intrinsic variables of interest, such as the identity of a face, or the shape of an object. The variation that arises from extrinsic factors such as viewpoint or illumination must be downplayed, as illustrated in Figure 5.6 on page 96. Squashing the irrelevant variability while preserving the relevant dimensions is, paradoxically, more problematic in systems equipped with finer measurement mechanisms. Indiscriminately raising the resolution of a perceptual front end (for example, by increasing the number and variety of the receptive fields it is composed of) is likely to make it more sensitive to irrelevant, extrinsic variation in the data, as well as to the desirable information. Because of this, the attainment of constancy in the face of perpetually changing stimulation is not just a central goal of perception, but also the greatest challenge that must be overcome by the computational mechanisms that implement it. The conceptual machinery we have mastered so far allows us to understand both the challenge and the ways in which it is met, but it will take the entire next section to do so.

5.3   Perceptual constancies

Construing perception as the process of distinguishing some dimensions from others in a multidimensional representation space is the right explanatory move, but it only goes as far as identifying the road that must be taken, without advancing down that road. In terms of Table 4.2 on page 76, which outlines Marr's "levels of understanding" methodology, this move amounts to formulating the problem on an abstract, computational level. What about the algorithmic level? We have to be careful here. The goal is a particular kind of dimensionality reduction: it would not do merely to approximate the data by the few dimensions of most variance (as in Principal Component Analysis, described on p. 57), because these would not necessarily coincide with the intrinsic dimensions we're after. To see how such dimensions can be singled out, we need some insight into the computational structure of the problem.

To gain such insight, let us consider again the problem of lightness perception, familiar to us from Chapter 1. At each milestone in the analysis that follows, I'll pause to draw a parallel to another perceptual task, that of shape-based object recognition. As I hope you'll see, the existence of such parallels offers a striking revelation about perception: **all perceptual problems share the same computational structure**. Thus, a thorough computational analysis of lightness will help us understand all of perception.

In the lightness task, as you may recall, the goal is to perceive the true shade of gray (reflectance) of a visible surface, despite changes in its orientation, the illumination, or the intervening medium. Lightness recovery can be considered as the first step towards color perception, where the goal is to perceive both the lightness and the hue of the surface. The attainment of lightness constancy requires the solution of two computational problems that pop up in every perceptual domain. The first problem we encountered already in section 1.2 on page 7: lightness is **underdetermined** by the data, because it must be recovered from a product into which other, extrinsic factors such as illumination also enter. The second problem I did not dare mention before I was sure you could handle it: some of the variables involved (notably, the intrinsic lightness and the extrinsic illumination) are not just inherently **multidimensional** — they are infinite-dimensional.

5.3.1 The problem of dimensionality

Infinite dimensionality does not sound like an issue that would brook any delay, so let's start with it. In lightness perception, it arises because both the surface reflectance (the quantity we are after) and the illumination (the quantity we would like to discount — or at least to treat separately) vary with the wavelength of the light. Now, you should recognize wavelength as a quantity that is continuous, and that may therefore require, in principle, an infinitely precise measurement to nail down. This makes wavelength infinite-dimensional in our terminology.

A similar situation emerges in visual shape-based object recognition, something that people are very good at. Objects such as the computer-graphics chicken depicted on this page are usually called "3D," which is just as misleading as calling the retinal input "2D" (cf. p. 57). True, each *point* on such an object resides in 3D, because three numbers are required to specify a location in space. By the same logic, however, an object composed of ten thousand points takes 30,000 numbers to describe completely, which calls for a 30,000-dimensional space. Think now of a smooth shape made of continuous surfaces, and you'll see how the problems of lightness and of object recognition are computationally similar.

A regular MULTIDIMENSIONAL CHICKEN. Following the standard computer graphics procedure, the shape is rendered as a surface consisting of many triangles. If the mesh that defines the vertices of these triangles has, say, 10,000 vertices, then the chicken shape embedded in a regular 3D space is nominally 30,000-dimensional (that's how many numbers would be needed to describe it completely and precisely). If an approximate rendition would suffice, everyday objects can be adequately described by very few parameters, which is what makes their efficient recognition possible (Edelman, 1999).

All this sounds like bad news: in theory an infinite amount of information may need to be specified and entered into the calculations when dealing with reflectance and illumination, or with shape. In practice, however, the situation is infinitely more benign: a handful of dimensions suffices in each case. What comes to the rescue of the perceptual system is the STATISTICAL REGULAR-ITY of the world. In particular, statistical analysis of numerous color patch samples (the Munsell chips, used by ophthalmologists) shows that reflectance — color, not just gray-level — can be closely approximated by three numbers per point (Cohen, 1964). Thus, color reflectance is effectively a three-dimensional, not an infinite-dimensional, quantity. A similar analysis carried out on samples of natural illumination shows that daylight too is effectively a three-dimensional quantity (Judd, MacAdam, and Wyszecki, 1964).

In object recognition too the problem of infinite nominal dimensionality proves to be innocuous in practice: the actual or effective dimensionality is always quite low. A given set of shapes, such as four-legged animals or flightless birds, can always be described, to a good approximation, in relatively few dimensions (Edelman, 1999, p.58ff). Intuitively, such a description could start with a very simple shape, such as a sphere (which can be fully specified by just one number, its radius), and proceed to list the successive modifications (such as bumps) that would make it look, to a desired degree of precision, like a chicken (say). Incidentally, this computational procedure[8] turns the tables on the two neuroscientists whose paper dealing with the neural mechanisms of attention opens with a joke about "the computer engineer, who, when asked to describe how he would write a computer program to recognize a chicken, replied, 'first, assume a spherical chicken' " (Reynolds and Desimone, 1999, p.19).

5.3.2 The problem of indeterminacy

Human vision is well-adapted to the effectively three-dimensional nature of the reflectance and the illumination data: the subsystem dealing with lightness and color employs three channels (which start at the three cone types in the retina before being transformed). At the very least, this nice match suggests that sheer high dimensionality is not what makes lightness constancy difficult. The need to juggle three numbers per data point is not a problem either (this is just what linear algebra has been invented for): intuitively, instead of having one equation per measurement, there must be three.[9]

The challenges are not over yet: we need to solve a system of equations

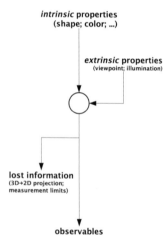

intrinsic properties
(shape; color; ...)

extrinsic properties
(viewpoint; illumination)

lost information
(3D→2D projection;
measurement limits)

observables

The course of vision — a flow diagram illustrating the main causes of INDETERMINACY in visual perception: the admixture of extrinsic variability to the information generated by the quantities of interest, and the loss of some information in the process of measurement with which all perception starts.

in which there are twice as many unknowns (six – three for each surface reflectance value, and three for the corresponding illumination value) as there are equations (three – one for each dimension of the measurement). As anyone who knows anything about linear algebra will tell you, this makes the problem at hand UNDERDETERMINED, which means that it can have an infinite number of perfectly valid solutions. Which is the correct one?

We can realize just how general the problem of indeterminacy is in perception by comparing lightness again to shape-based object recognition. In the lightness case, the indeterminacy stems from the multiplicative confounding of surface reflectance and illumination, which can only be measured together (how do you determine two numbers given *only* their product?). Likewise, what can be measured in object perception — the shape of the retinal projection — is affected jointly by the actual shape of the object and by the viewpoint. To see how that is so, get hold of a paperclip, bend it to form a right angle, then play with it a bit. You'll see that it is easy to find viewing directions from which the angle would seem as obtuse, or as acute, as you wish. The true angle formed by the wire, which is what the brain must compute, is confounded in the measurable data — in the shape of the wire's projection onto the retina — with the viewpoint (which consists of elevation and azimuth; rotation around the line of sight, which is irrelevant to the question as posed, can be ignored).

How can the severely underconstrained mathematical problems that arise in perception be solved? The computational principle that makes all these problems tractable is as simple as it is general: add the required number of constraints. Of course, these cannot just be pulled out of a hat: if the solution is to make sense, the extra constraints must be derived from whatever extra knowledge about the problem that is available. Marr and Poggio (1979) pointed out that in perception such knowledge may take the form of prior ASSUMPTIONS that are expected to hold of the solution that is sought.[10] Any assumption would, however, still need to be independently justified. In the case of lightness, this means that neither the (unknown) reflectance of the surface at the point in question, nor the (unknown) value of illumination at that point may be invoked.

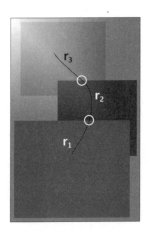

A simulated scene with three tiles of different shades of gray, illuminated from the top left. Under the ASSUMPTION that illumination changes gradually and reflectance abruptly, which happens to be true in this example, the Retinex algorithm (Land and McCann, 1971) can recover reflectance ratios r_1/r_2 and r_2/r_3 by traversing a path through the scene and noting the encountered jumps in the raw intensity (circled). The reflectances themselves can then be computed by applying an additional assumption (that the highest value corresponds to white).

5.3.3   A common solution: statistical regularization

The crucial insight that applies at this point is that one can know something about the behavior of reflectance and illumination in general without implying knowledge of the particular values of these quantities for a given point. For instance, it seems reasonable to assume that as one traverses an image of a natural scene, reflectance usually changes abruptly (when a transition between one surface and another is encountered), whereas illumination tends to change gradually (e.g., because the surface under scrutiny may be tilted with respect to the direction of the light source). It turns out that this general assumption often suffices to pry apart the two unknown quantities, lightness and illumination, through the use of some simple, standard computational techniques such as logarithms, differentiation, and integration (Horn, 1974).

All kinds of REASONING consist in nothing but a comparison, and a discovery of those relations, either constant or inconstant, which two or more objects bear to each other.
— Hume (1740, I.III.II)

... All knowledge resolves itself into PROBABILITY...
— Hume (1740, I.IV.I)

My invocation of REASON in the preceding paragraph ("it seems reasonable to assume...") should have raised an alarm in your mind concerning the possibility that I am pulling a trick here by letting a hidden homunculus do the hard work of inventing a workable assumption. In fact, I have attempted nothing of the sort: the assumption about the different rates of spatial change for the two variables of interest, lightness and illumination, can be derived merely by keeping track of the STATISTICS of scenes (something that even single neurons connected to proper inputs are perfectly capable of doing; cf. section 3.3 on page 50).

Computationally, the relevant statistics can be accrued by a very simple process that traverses, pixel by pixel, raw images in which lightness and illumination are still confounded, keeping track of the changes of intensity between adjacent pixels. The resulting histogram is bound to reveal that most of the changes are small, but some are large. It only remains for evolution to pick up this regularity and capitalize on it, by building it, as a prior assumption, into the neural algorithm for lightness recovery.

It is worth pausing here to appreciate that the need for extra constraints arises from the nature of the canonical *problem* of perception, not of some particular method of solving it. This is why it must be addressed by *any* system, biological or engineered. What we need, therefore, is a general computational approach to underdetermined problems. A suitably general method can be imported from applied mathematics, where problems that are inherently underdetermined are called ill-posed (Bertero, Poggio, and Torre, 1988).[11] Miracles not being allowed in mathematics, the only trick one can resort to is to make such problems well-posed by constraining the solution with extra assumptions. The solution then takes the form of a *compromise* between the measurements (the actual data) and the imposed constraints. The latter usually consist of some kind of smoothing, as in lightness, where the illumination is assumed to vary smoothly almost everywhere. The classical mathematical approach based on this idea is *regularization*.[12] Intuitively, smoothing causes the desirable reduction in the number of possible solutions because it takes fewer numbers to specify a smooth dataset than a highly variable one (an extreme example would be to assume *constant* illumination, in which case only a single number needs to be determined for the illumination of the entire scene, instead of one for each surface point).

5.3.4 Implications

We can now begin to understand in some detail how the limitations and the shortcomings of perceptual constancies stem from the fundamentally underdetermined nature of perception. Because a regularized solution emerges as a compromise between the data and the extra assumptions, one cannot generally expect more than an approximate recovery of the quantity of interest. Worse things, such as illusions, can happen when the assumptions built into a perceptual algorithm break down entirely for a particular scene. In lightness perception, for example, an image that is made to contain a sharp intensity change that is inconsistent with the scene context and illumination gives rise to the Cornsweet illusion. This is illustrated in Figure 5.7, which is contrived so that the sharp intensity change that runs from left to right along the middle of the image peters out gradually in the up and down directions. The visual system interprets the change as a jump in lightness, and ignores the gradual return to the mean that happens on both sides of the "cliff."

This ambiguous figure (devised by Jastrow in 1899 and made famous by Wittgenstein, 1958, p.194) can be seen as a rabbit or as a duck, depending on an extra ASSUMPTION as to the direction in which the figure is facing. Unlike a typical natural scene, this contrived stimulus is only moderately underdetermined, because only two interpretations are normally considered by most viewers.

Figure 5.7 — Because of the essential confounding between surface reflectance and illumination, lightness constancy can only be achieved by making extra ASSUMPTIONS, e.g., that abrupt jumps of intensity correspond to changes in the reflectance, not the illumination. *Left:* in this version of the Cornsweet illusion, the perception of the relative lightness of the two squares depends on the visibility of the joint. To make the illusion go away, cover the joint with a pencil. *Right:* The Cornsweet illusion happens because the specially contrived horizontal intensity profile in this image (and the vertical one in the image on the left) defeats the assumptions built into the lightness algorithm implemented by our brains.

Equally spectacular failures of constancy can also be produced in shape-based object recognition, especially when other cues to object identity are absent, as in the wire shapes shown in Figure 5.8. Failures of shape constancy are very easy to obtain under laboratory conditions, and they are also very common in everyday life, contrary to the popular myth of invariant object recognition (Bülthoff, Edelman, and Tarr, 1995; Edelman, 1999; Edelman and Weinshall, 1998).

The likely fallibility of the constancy algorithms (which is due to the inherently problematic computational nature of perception) and the actual fallibility of human perception as revealed by psychophysical experiments prompted many researchers to question the value of the very notion of constancy, in domains ranging from color (Foster, 2003) to object recognition (Edelman, 1999). If the pervasive inconstancies go unnoticed, it is mainly for two reasons. First, the brain excels at combining multiple independent cues in addressing its perceptual needs (Welchman, Deubelius, Conrad, Bülthoff, and Kourtzi, 2005), so that cue-specific failures (say, only in depth, or only in lightness) tend to be masked or compensated for. Second, the senses settle for less — often far less — than the fullest possible recovery of the properties of the world that is "out there."

The visual system, in particular, is not geared for a complete reconstruction of the solid geometry of the world, or of the color and texture of each visible surface; rather, **vision is task-driven**. This should not be surprising:

Figure 5.8 — SHAPE INCONSTANCY. This sculpture by Markus Raetz (*Das grosse Glas*, 1988) consists of two wires, bent and inserted into a wooden plank. When seen from one direction (*left*), the smaller wire looks like a bottle, and the larger one like a wineglass. When the plank is rotated (*right*), the shapes shift: the projection of the smaller wire now looks like a glass, and the other one like a bottle.

the senses evolve to serve the organism, and no imaginable service or application could ever require a complete reconstruction of the world, which would merely necessitate another processing stage dedicated to extracting some *useful* information from the scene.

A related way of characterizing the general philosophy of biological perception is to point out that it is *good enough* for what it is supposed to do. Recovering the absolute positions of all the objects in a scene may be the best way of ensuring smooth navigation — but merely knowing where I am heading and how far is the next obstacle in that direction is good enough, so I am spared the need to attempt the impossible. Recovering the precise spectral reflectance of a banana before eating it may be the best way of avoiding indigestion — but settling for hue perception that is only 95% reliable is good enough, especially if I am also allowed to smell the banana before biting into it.

The wisdom of settling for "good enough" is applicable in cognitive domains other than perception. In decision making, for example, it is the only resort for a system that must take multiple factors into account when planning a series of actions: various problems in combinatorial optimization, which tend to be intractable (Garey and Johnson, 1979), become quite tame when approximate solutions are sought. A related insight underlies the concept of *satisficing*, introduced by Simon (1957) in his now classical discussion of bounded rationality (cf. section 8.4). Increasing acceptance of "good enough" approaches is also found in linguistics (Ferreira, Bailey, and Ferraro, 2002), where it is motivated by the consistent failure of frontal assaults on the problem of language comprehension motivated by the ideas of Noam Chomsky: brilliant, but detached from reality.[13]

Taking a deep breath and looking back to the beginning of this chapter, we can tally the progress: we have realized that clouds of points in representation spaces are the proper way to think about perceptual stimuli, we have seen what operations on such entities correspond to the basic perceptual functions, and we have learned how such operations can be carried out computationally. We also had a glimpse (in Figure 5.3 on page 91), but not a proper discussion, of what it means to learn to perceive. That's where I am headed next.

In this species of box jellyfish, which has a sophisticated lens eye at the end of each of its eight stalks, but no centralized brain behind them, VISION IS completely task-driven: the output of the visual system is channeled directly into neurons that control swimming (Nilsson, Gislén, Coates, Skogh, and Garm, 2005). Leaving memory out of the perception-action loop does not imply an inability to LEARN FROM EXPERIENCE: although it is unlikely that this jellyfish ever thinks to itself "Ah, here's that mangrove root again; I better avoid it," experience-driven modification of the appropriate visuomotor synapses may enable it to learn to avoid obstacles just as effectively.

5.4   Perceptual learning

Before we analyze it, we must cast the idea of perceptual learning into the language of representation spaces. Let us begin with simple creatures capable of sensing, and *directly* responding to, their environment. An already familiar example would be the "crab" illustrated in Figure 3.9 on page 53, which I used to introduce the idea of computation as mapping between representations; its arm is directly hooked to its eyes. Another, real example is the box jellyfish, whose swimming is directly controlled by its vision. In such systems, perceptual LEARNING FROM EXPERIENCE translates into a modification of the connections between the sensors and the effectors. Computationally, this amounts to a rearrangement of the sensorimotor map: for instance, two stimuli that used to be mapped into distant points (that is, into dissimilar patterns of muscle activations) may become close neighbors following learning.

More advanced cognitive systems achieve greater behavioral flexibility by using another representation space, which we may provisionally refer to as *memory*, where stimuli can be sent without necessarily generating a motor response (a proper treatment of memory follows in Chapter 6). In such systems, another mode of perceptual learning is available, which consists of gradually populating the memory space with traces of new experiences, which join the cloud of points that are already there.

You may observe that merely putting away the memory of each new stimulus can be quite wasteful of resources — if, for example, many of the stimuli are barely distinguishable from each other. In truth, this would make memory not just profligate but useless, for the same reason that perfect reconstruction of the distal world would be useless in perception: in both cases, it would contribute not an iota to *making sense* of the stimuli. This is why, in perceptual learning, new points should be expected to change the cloud of existing representations, not merely join it.

5.4.1   The emergence of categories

Representational change can be motivated by a discovery that the cloud of points that is being built up is no longer "compact." For example, the arriving points — each new one arising as a result of exposure to yet another stimulus, and old ones retained as perceptual memories — may initially fall close by to each other, then split off and establish a bridgehead in another location of the representation space (Figure 5.9, top). Any such split in an emerging cloud of representations means that objects from more than one CATEGORY have been encountered.

To prevent unwarranted proliferation of categories, only significant splits should be followed up. The significance of a split, in turn, depends on the metric that prevails in the corner of the representation space under consideration. A set of objects can be categorized in many different ways, depending on the characteristics on which the distinction is to be based; or, they can be

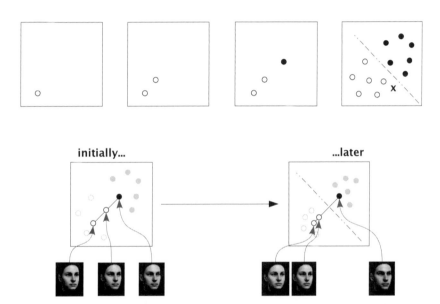

Figure 5.9 — *Top:* the first step of PERCEPTUAL LEARNING — acquiring the examples. To make a point of the generality of this formulation, the sequence of successive snapshots of the representation space shown here is exactly the same as in Figure 5.3, which deals with vernier stimuli and introduces simple learning as accumulation of representations. The second step of learning may consist of the establishment of a criterion (here, a decision line shown in the rightmost panel) for categorization based on the acquired examples (cf. Figures 5.3 and 5.5, which illustrate such criteria for verniers and faces, respectively). *Bottom:* the representational basis of CATEGORICAL PERCEPTION. Three stimuli that are initially represented as equally spaced along a straight line in the representation space are rearranged following learning. In the warped space, stimuli falling within the same category now appear more similar to each other, and those that straddle the category boundary appear less similar. The controlled-similarity morphed face stimuli are from a study of categorical perception of sex, by Bülthoff and Newell (2004).

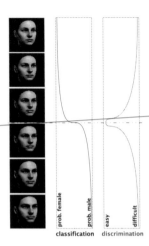

prob. female | prob. male | easy | difficult

classification   discrimination

A MORPH SEQUENCE of faces and the two telltale signs of CATEGORICAL PERCEPTION: sigmoidal probability of classification and peaked discrimination performance, both centered on the emergent category boundary. Faces courtesy of Bülthoff and Newell (2004).

all clumped together, if the measurements applied to them are insufficiently discerning. Category structure can also change dynamically, "on the fly." As I noted on p. 94 in the context of stimulus distinctiveness, representation spaces can be "warped" by various means such as selective attention to some of the dimensions. In exactly the same manner, the distinctness of categories depends on the currently prevailing metric.

In all biological perceptual systems, the representation space metrics are quite pliable. Recall that when the visual system strives to attain constancy, an object is perceived as unchanged, despite certain variability in its appearance; downplaying that variability can be seen as a kind of warping of the representation space. Likewise, categorization requires that variability in certain physical properties of the object be downplayed; that too amounts to a warp that brings closer objects that are considered to be members of the same category, as illustrated in Figure 5.9 on the preceding page, bottom. Such warping, which is precipitated by the very act of setting up a categorization scheme and which unfolds dynamically, gives rise to a behavioral performance pattern that the psychologists call CATEGORICAL PERCEPTION (Harnad, 1987).

In a typical *classification* study designed to explore this phenomenon, the subject is shown, one at a time, a succession of faces that have been chosen from a MORPH SEQUENCE; the task is to indicate for each stimulus whether it belongs to one or the other of two categories (such as female and male faces). The telltale characteristic of categorical perception in a classification task is a rapid SIGMOIDAL transition between the very high probability of choosing one way (for stimuli located on the one side of the emergent category boundary) and the equally high probability of choosing the other way (for stimuli on the other side of the boundary). The reverse side of the same coin is revealed in a *discrimination* task, where the subject has to tell whether two stimuli presented as a pair are same or different, the stimuli being drawn from the same kind of morph sequence. Here, the telltale of categorical perception is PEAKED discrimination performance (indicated by a lowered decision threshold) that coincides with the category boundary.

It is important to realize that these two characteristics emerge from the same underlying cause, namely, the warping of the representation space that squashes intra-category differences and expands inter-category ones. It is even more important to understand that seeing same-category objects as more similar is not a matter of choice: you cannot just decide not to give in to categorical perception. Rather, the polarized layout of the representation space, being the sole determinant of how things are seen, holds the rest of the brain in thralldom.

Indeed, the power of the brain's tendency to categorize is such that we often see things that are not there. In vision, this predisposition, called PAREI- DOLIA, is responsible for the recurring "discoveries" of faces in burnt toast, mold spots, or Mars snapshots (cf. Figure 5.10), and for animals seen lurking in Rorschach inkblots, cloud formations, or forest shadows. Similar things happen in auditory perception, as when we hear almost intelligible speech in music played backwards, or, in fact, altogether outside sensory perception narrowly construed — as when part of the brain insists on discerning a su- pernatural agency at work in situations that its other, more reasonable parts recognize as perfectly natural (for studies of the cognitive basis of religion, see Barrett, 2000; Boyer, 2003).

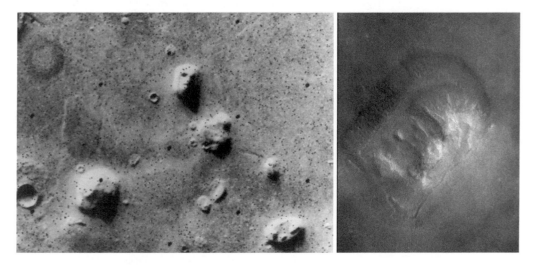

Figure 5.10 — The brain's drive to categorize everything it perceives is so powerful that it often imposes order on random stimuli. This process is responsible for common perception of a face in photographs of the geological formation of Cydonia Mensae on Mars. *Left:* an image taken by the Viking orbiter in 1976. *Right:* the vicinity of the "face" as photographed by the Mars Global Surveyor in 1998. No amount of new data could convince the conspiracy theorists that the Cydonia "face" was never anything else than some weathered hills and sand dunes. Our propensity for seeing shapes (most commonly, faces) in random images is known as PAREIDOLIA, which in Greek means "beyond the image."

5.4.2   Adaptation

The brain's urge to perceive instances of the same categories at every turn should not be interpreted as inflexibility on the part of the perceptual system. This is because perception, as a rule, is pliable (as psychologists say, it exhibits plasticity). Categories arise in response to repeated patterns of stimulation, and subsequently track and adjust to any changes in these patterns. Non-categorical perception too is adaptive, sometimes strikingly so: in only a few days, people can adapt to wearing glasses that invert the visual world (Dolezal, 1982), and adaptation to milder optical distortions such as those induced by wedge prisms takes only a few seconds.

The dynamical nature of the brain mechanisms of adaptation is revealed by the stunning AFTEREFFECTS that occur when the external factor that induces adaptation is withdrawn, as illustrated in Figure 5.11. To experience a beautiful aftereffect in a natural setting, hike to a waterfall and stare for a couple of minutes at the falling water (it is important *not* to track it with your gaze). This will cause the neurons in your MT cortex, which are selective to downward motion (recall Figure 4.1 on page 67), to adapt — that

Wedge prisms such as this one, mounted in a spectacle frame, were used by Gibson (1933) in his study of the curvature ADAPTATION and its AFTEREFFECT (see Figure 5.11).

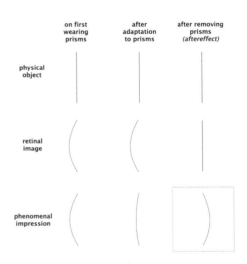

Figure 5.11 — The curvature ADAPTATION AFTEREFFECT, as described by Gibson (1933), is just as edifying as the waterfall illusion described in the text, yet is much easier to illustrate on a printed page. *Top row:* the physical stimulus — a straight line — remains unchanged throughout the experiment. *Middle row:* the retinal image is distorted (curved) by the prisms that the subject wears during the experiment (left and middle columns); it reverts to straight when the prisms are taken off (right column). *Bottom row:* the phenomenal impression reported by the subject is initially that of a curved line (left column); following adaptation, the apparent curvature is diminished (middle column). After the experiment, without the prisms, the stimulus (the same straight line as in all stages) appears curved in the opposite direction. This aftereffect, and others like it, which can be induced in any perceptual domain, demonstrates that all phenomenal percepts emerge as equilibria of opposing forces (the activities of tuned units; cf. section 3.2.1 on page 42), and are affected dynamically by the statistics of the stimulation.

is, become fatigued and respond less strongly. If you then look to the side at one of the banks, you'll see the scenery flowing upwards.[14] The complementary relationship between the direction of motion in the aftereffect and in the adapting stimulus indicates that your perception of visual motion is, at all times, the product of a "tug of war" between populations of neurons with opposite selectivities.

The forces that enter into the dynamic equilibrium of perception do not respect the traditional boundaries of sensory modalities. In particular, visual perception is strongly affected by purely somatosensory cues; as it frequently happens in the study of the brain, we get an inkling of the underlying process only when some of the mechanisms that support it break down. A typical example is the Wallenberg syndrome (Girkin and Miller, 2001), in which the patients report perceiving the visual world as tilted, or even upside down. What is going on here?

Instead of divulging the secret right away, let me tell you a true story about a colleague (not a vision scientist) who once came to me with a question: where in the brain does the upside-down retinal image get inverted? After being dumbstruck for a moment, I pointed out that the answer is, of course, "nowhere" — there being no homunculus to *look* at the retinal image, there is also no meaning to the expression "right side up" and no need to invert anything (vision works because the world is spatially and temporally coherent, not because it fits some internal picture-like template, complete with a little wineglass symbol showing which side is up). I then inquired about the inspiration for the question. Turns out my colleague had a reason for asking it: she produced a paper (Wertenbaker and Gutman, 1985), which reported the visual field rotation in Wallenberg syndrome patients. If the precise angles stated in that paper — 45° or 135° — were to be trusted, it was only natural to assume that the visual field rotation happens because a special rotation module gets knocked out as a result of a stroke.[15]

There is, however, a much better explanation, one that does not need a homunculus, and is based, instead, on the notion of cross-modal adaptation. The crucial lead comes from knowledge that the locus of the lesion in those patients disrupted blood supply to the OTOLITH organs. A normal sense of the gravitational vertical depends on a particular distribution of activity across the otolith neurons. When some of these die because of a localized infarction, the remaining ones take over in determining the organ's response; the outcome may be a sense of tilted posture. This, in turn, may override the visual signal that feeds into the same posture perception and maintenance system, causing

Above: the vestibular system of the inner ear, showing the OTOLITH organs. These are two little sacs, filled with a fluid in which tiny salt crystals are suspended, and lined with nerve endings. *Below:* the otoliths and the hair cells that sense them.

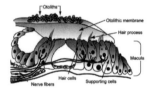

the integrated percept to be that of a tilted visual world. The Wallenberg syndrome can thus be considered as a kind of aftereffect, with the role of dis-adaptation played by the selective incapacitation of some otolith neurons.

5.4.3 Generalization

Both categorization and adaptation are crucially dependent on an ability to respond in just the right manner to stimulus similarity. If a certain categorical property is true of the CHEESEMAKERS, should I expect it also to hold for YOGHURT PRODUCERS? Would the visual system adapt to a noisy perceptual variable, such as a sequence of line stimuli all similarly curved to the left but to different degrees?[16]

The universality of the quandary surrounding the meaning of sameness and the significance of change has been noted by Hume (1740, I.III.XII), who also suggested a universal way out:

> An experiment loses of its force, when transferr'd to instances, which are not exactly resembling; tho' 'tis evident it may still retain as much as may be the foundation of probability, as long as there is any resemblance remaining.

It is precisely on the "foundation of probability" intuited by Hume that the

MAN #1:
I think it was 'Blessed are the cheesemakers.'
JESUS:
. . . right prevail.
MRS. GREGORY:
Ahh, what's so special about the cheesemakers?
GREGORY:
Well, obviously, this is not meant to be taken literally. It refers to any MANUFACTURERS OF DAIRY PRODUCTS.
. . .
MANDY:
Oh, come on. Let's go to the stoning.
BRIAN:
All right.
FRANCIS:
Well, blessed is just about everyone with a vested interest in the status quo, as far as I can tell, Reg.

Monty Python's Life of Brian

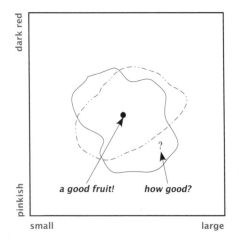

a good fruit!   *how good?*

Figure 5.12 — The problem of GENERALIZATION in learning from examples. Suppose you have tasted a fruit, represented in this simplified 2D depiction of your measurement space by the point at the center, and found it good. You are now facing another fruit, which is mapped to a distinct point in the representation space; should the label "good" be generalized (extended) to it? Shepard (1987) formalized this question as pertaining to the extent and the shape of the relevant *consequential region* — a chunk of representation space that contains the original stimulus, as well as any others an encounter with which should be expected to have the same consequences. He then proceeded to derive from first principles of probability theory a formula for the consequential regions of various kinds of representation spaces, and a quantitative law of perceptual generalization, illustrated in Figure 5.13.

brain erects the edifice of GENERALIZATION, without which perception would not be possible.

In its most basic form, generalization consists of projecting the consequences of a perceptual experience with one stimulus to an encounter with another one, as illustrated in Figure 5.12 on the facing page. As such, generalization is an aspect of a quality that epitomizes cognition: forethought (recall section 2.1.3 on page 19). The need for generalization arises everywhere there is learning: just as a monkey must decide whether it would be a good idea to bite into a fruit that reminds it of one consumed the other day, a scallop that swam away from a looming shadow must decide whether to do so in response to another one, trading off energy expenditure on a false alarm against the danger of falling prey to a crab. There is a general principle at work here: common sense, of which even scallops possess a modicum, suggests that it all depends on the SIMILARITY between the new stimulus and the previously encountered ones.

In reality, all arguments from experience are founded on the SIMILARITY which we discover among natural objects, and by which we are induced to expect effects similar to those which we have found to follow from such objects. [...] From causes which appear similar we expect similar effects.
— Hume (1748, IV.II)

Similarity

A well-established view in the philosophy of psychology holds that the actual usefulness of similarity as an explanatory construct in theories of cognition is undermined by the very generality that makes it so appealing at a first glance. A reflection on what we learned so far about the emergence of categories and about perceptual plasticity indeed suggests that I cannot expect you to agree with me on a ranking of any set of stimuli by similarity. In fact, I cannot expect to agree even with myself, if you test me at two different times: any experience I might have in between the tests is liable to alter my similarity scales.

The philosophers' distrust of similarity was paralleled by the increasing impatience with similarity-based explanations on the part of mathematical psychologists. By the 1960s, the account of generalization finally emerged as a central theoretical challenge (Guttman, 1963, p.144):

> In effect, we have no quantitative or semi-quantitative law of stimulus generalization, no statement — nor yet the data for essaying a statement — which carries us much beyond our initial tautology that some stimuli somehow similar to the conditioned stimulus will also evoke behavior.

The seeds for a resolution of the similarity conundrum were planted around the same time, when Roger Shepard, building on earlier work by Thurstone and Torgerson, published the first in a series of papers (Shepard, 1962a) that would culminate with the formulation of his "universal law of generalization for psychological science" (Shepard, 1987).

Shepard's Universal Law of Generalization

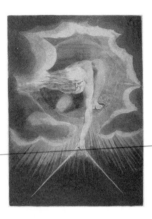

Shepard's derivation from first principles of a mathematical basis for the relationship between generalization and similarity happened to occur in a special year: the tricentennial of the publication in 1687 of Newton's magnum opus, *Philosophiae Naturalis Principia Mathematica* (which translates as "mathematical principles of natural philosophy"). Presumptuous as it may seem, the parallel (suggested by Shepard himself) between the universality of the two laws — gravitation in physics and generalization in psychology — is entirely justified. What makes both laws universal is invariance: the pull of Earth's gravity on an object depends solely on its mass (not on material, color, the phase of the moon, or anything else); the likelihood of generalization from stimulus A to stimulus B depends solely on the distance between the two in the representation space (not on the modality of the stimuli, the species of the subject, the phase of the moon, etc). Moreover, just as Newton offered a formula for computing the gravitational attraction of two masses, Shepard cast the dependence of generalization on distance in a precise quantitative form, a negative exponential (Figure 5.13 on the facing page).

The patterning of the world that makes cognition possible is best understood through the GEOMETRY of statistical data — and so is cognition itself, which hinges on the manipulation of similarity representation spaces (cf. sections 3.3.3 and 5.5). In these etchings from the 1790's, William Blake depicts both the Ancient of Days (above) and ISAAC NEWTON (below) as wielding a compass.

It is instructive to observe the two key respects in which **Shepard's Law transcends mere intuition**, according to which the more dissimilar two stimuli are, the less likely is the generalization from one to the other. **First**, whereas the intuitive formulation is tautological (as noted in the quote by Guttman, above), Shepard's is substantive. The dependence of generalization on similarity could have been linear, or reciprocal; in fact, it is negative exponential. Moreover, this precise form, and the shape of the consequential regions governing generalization (Figure 5.12), were not obtained through exploratory data analysis (although they do fit the data beautifully) but derived from basic assumptions on the applicable probability measure (note how this underscores once again the importance of statistical concepts for understanding cognition). **Second**, the map of the representation space in which the stimuli reside is derived independently from the subject's generalization behavior over those stimuli that the Law subsequently explains.

The representation space has to be "derived" because it is internal to the

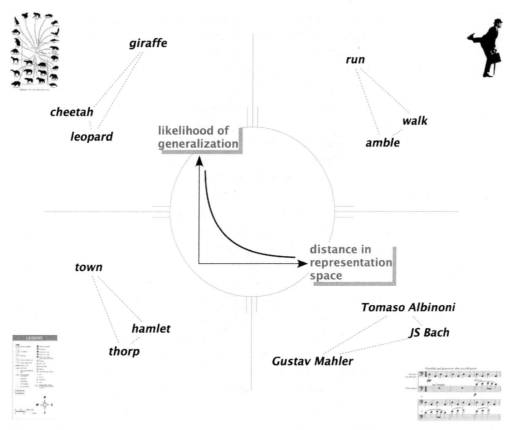

Figure 5.13 — The UNIVERSAL LAW OF GENERALIZATION (Shepard, 1987) states that any set of stimuli can be arranged in a representation space in such a manner that the likelihood that the subject using that space will generalize the label of one stimulus to another diminishes exponentially with their distance. Shepard also perfected a computational technique, multidimensional scaling or MDS (Borg and Lingoes, 1987), for determining the layout of the relevant representation space from behavioral data, such as subjective judgments of similarity, to which distance is inversely related ("multidimensional" in MDS means merely that there is more than one dimension; having too many would be computationally problematic, as we learned in section 3.3). The application of MDS to data from various perceptual domains and species of perceivers (from pigeons to humans) invariably reveals the quantitative relationship predicted by Shepard's Law. In each case, the result is a map of a patch of a low-dimensional representation space inhabited by the stimuli, making explicit their relative similarities on which categorization can be based. The four schematic maps shown here illustrate possible use of such similarities for categorizing visual shapes, gait, music, and geographical concepts. Combining Shepard's Law with the idea of neural spaces makes it explanatory and not merely descriptive: I perceive a cheetah as being more similar to a leopard than to a giraffe because the former two are mapped to neighboring points in my representation space, and the third one lands far away from them. Empirical studies, described in section 5.5, support this explanation of perception on all the levels of Marr's hierarchy.

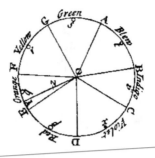

The perceived *color space*, as hypothesized by Isaac Newton (*above*), and as computed by Roger Shepard from subjects' judgments of color similarities (*below*; these are the same data as in Figure 5.14).

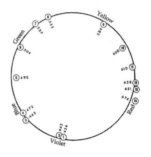

cognitive system: short of direct observation of the subject's brain states (not altogether a science-fictional scenario anymore, as we'll see in section 5.5), a roundabout approach must be used to map this space. Shepard's own earlier work (1962) had been instrumental in the development of a suitable method: MULTIDIMENSIONAL SCALING, or MDS. The key idea is that a cloud of points for which only the distances are known can be embedded in a metric space by an iterative algorithm that strives to minimize the discrepancies between the given distances and those implied by the embedding in the target space (Shepard, 1980).[17] In an actual experiment, the distance data can be obtained, for example, by measuring the response times in delayed matching to sample trials; in each trial the subject is shown two of the stimuli one after another, and has to decide whether they are SAME or DIFFERENT; a faster correct "different" response can then be taken to signify a larger distance between the members of the pair in the subject's internal representation space (Cutzu and Edelman, 1996).[18]

Because the map obtained by MDS makes the structure of this representation space visible, it effectively allows the experimenter to get inside the subject's head, as it were. The neural space spanned by the activities of the brain's billions of neurons is, however, too complex to visualize or to understand in its raw form. Luckily, the MDS map does something much more useful than give us access to the raw brain space: it reveals the *low dimensional structure* of that space, as implied by the behavioral responses.[19] Because perception would not be possible if the world did not possess low-dimensional structure to which the brain could resonate, MDS takes us straight to the core of how the mind works.

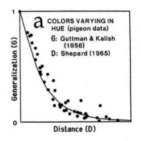

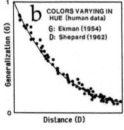

Figure 5.14 — The same negative exponential fits well the color GENERALIZATION DATA plotted against MDS-derived representation-space distance, both in pigeons (a) and in humans (b). These two plots are reprinted from (Shepard, 1987), where results from ten additional analyses are reported.

Shepard (1987) reports testing the predicted invariant quantitative law on 12 sets of generalization data. Some of these came from psychophysical studies with human subjects, others from pigeons; the stimuli ranged from visual (shape; color) to acoustic (Morse code; phonemes). In each of the cases examined, it was possible to arrange the stimuli in a "psychological space" (reflecting the subject's internal representation space) in such a manner that the likelihood of extending a judgment from one stimulus to another fell off exponentially with their distance (two of those 12 examples are reproduced in Figure 5.14 on the preceding page). Since then, the generalization law has been corroborated by many other studies, in different species and using stimuli from different modalities.

A particularly spectacular success of Shepard's Law emerged in a case where generalization initially appeared not to be monotonic, let alone exponential: color perception. When people are asked to judge color similarity (as in the experiment that produced the data in Figure 5.14b), violet is normally reported to be more similar to red than green is. This seems to run counter to the "natural" proximity between red and green (but not between red and violet) in the physical color space — the light spectrum. The resolution of this conundrum was anticipated by Newton, who hypothesized that the proper way of arranging *perceived* colors was not linear (as in the spectrum, which he was the first to discover by using a prism to decompose sunlight), but circular. Newton's intuition was fully vindicated by Shepard, who used MDS to show that the internal color representation space is, in fact, circular.

The contribution of Shepard's work to the understanding of cognition is momentous. His empirical and computational results, along with subsequent work by others (such as Clark, 1993; Edelman, 1998a; Goldstone, 1994; Goldstone and Barsalou, 1998; Medin, Goldstone, and Gentner, 1993) helped rehabilitate similarity in psychology. Perhaps more importantly, his theory of generalization helped satisfy the "physics envy" which psychology shares with all other natural sciences. Substantively, it demonstrated that there is a place in psychology for universal, invariant laws. Methodologically, it drew the psychologists' attention to the GEOMETRIC STRUCTURE of cognitive representations — a significant development, considering the indispensability of geometry for the understanding of the general principles of brain function (Mumford, 1994). More recently, deep connections also emerged between Shepard's ideas and information theory (Chater and Vitányi, 2003) and statistical Bayesian inference (Tenenbaum and Griffiths,

...A corollary of population coding is that the set of higher level concepts will automatically have GEOMETRIC STRUCTURE.

— (Mumford, 1994, p.144)

A general principle that unifies STATISTI-
CAL LEARNING FROM EXAMPLES and subsequent GENERALIZATION within the same
computational framework is **Bayesian inference** (Kersten, Mamassian, and Yuille, 2004),
a procedure explained in Box 5.1 on page 120
(see also Appendix A). Bayesian models
are uniformly successful in explaining human
performance in situations that require reasoning or decision making that combines prior
statistical knowledge with new data (Knill
and Richards, 1996; Tenenbaum and Griffiths, 2001).

Es gibt nur die Beispiele.
(There are only the EXAMPLES.)

— attributed to Ludwig Wittgenstein

2001; see Box 5.1 on page 120 and Appendix A), confirming yet again their
wide relevance to cognitive information processing.

5.4.4   Perceptual learning as statistical inference

In every task and modality where learning occurs — which means everywhere in perception — the experience of the perceiver faced with a stimulus
is shaped by the tug of stored and processed traces of prior experiences. The
processing to which experiences are subjected is essentially and fundamentally statistical; as Gibson's 1933 study of curvature adaptation demonstrated,
even such a seemingly basic and absolute visual quality as the straightness of
a line is actually perceived relative to a statistical mean. A series of exposures to lines that are all slightly bent to the left (say) will subsequently cause
objectively straight lines to be seen as bent to the right.

Given the all-important role of prior experience, we may expect perceptual learning to be specific to the EXAMPLES which drive it, and indeed it is.
For instance, in vernier hyperacuity, discussed earlier in this chapter (p. 91), a
subject's threshold may be reduced from about 15″ to 5″ through mere expo-

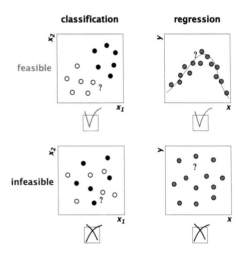

Figure 5.15 — The computational goal of perceptual learning
is estimation of conditional probabilities (Edelman and Intrator,
2002). *Left:* categorization tasks, in which the brain learns to
produce discrete labels, given the data, require $P(C_i|x_1,x_2)$; this
is CLASSIFICATION. *Right:* adaptation tasks, in which the brain
learns to generate graded percepts or responses, given the data, re-
quire $P(y|x)$; this is REGRESSION. In each case, the real issue is
how to extend the learned discrete labeling or graded output scheme
to new inputs (marked by "?"); this is the problem of GENERALIZA-
TION (see section 5.4.3). Generalization from examples is only ever
possible if extra assumptions are made. As in the case of perceptual
constancy (cf. p. 103), the most common assumption is that of simplicity, or smoothness (as when the learner assumes that there are
only a few compact clusters in classification, or a low-dimensional
pattern in regression). Were the real-world data not in fact simple
or smooth (*bottom row*), generalization, and therefore learning as
such, would be infeasible.

sure to a few hundred stimuli. When the orientation of the stimulus is changed by 90° (e.g., horizontal verniers are introduced instead of vertical ones), the benefits of learning disappear, and the subjects revert to their original level of performance (higher threshold). Subsequently, an improved performance at the new orientation is attained through the same gradual process of learning (Poggio et al., 1992).[21]

In the statistical terminology, the first stage of learning from examples is *inference*, or assimilating the data. As Figure 5.15 on the facing page shows, we can easily conceptualize the computational essence of statistical inference using the main tool in our arsenal: representation space. The categorization task is then seen as precisely what the statisticians call CLASSIFICATION: group the data into a few clusters, which become the perceptual categories. The adaptation task corresponds to REGRESSION: find a simple trend in the layout of the data (Edelman and Intrator, 2002). After inference comes *decision-making*, or using the assimilated data to deal with new inputs — as in "is this face male or female?" (classification), or "what is the curvature of this line?" (regression).

Although we need not concern ourselves here with the actual recipes (algorithms) for assimilating examples and for using them to make decisions, we should note **the basic nature of the problem of statistical learning: computationally, both classification and regression are underdetermined**. In classification, we can never know ahead of time whether the points belonging to a given class cluster together or are evenly spread and intermixed with other points in the representation space. In regression, we can never know whether the behavior of the curve ("trend") in between the available data points is moderate or wildly oscillating. The indeterminacy stems from the incontrovertible fact that any finite set of examples is in principle equally compatible not just with the optimistic and the pessimistic scenarios at the same time, but with an unbounded set of possible scenarios. The users of statistics software, who do regressions for a living, or perhaps just for an occasional science project, seldom pause to contemplate the possibility of there being an infinite number of curves that pass through all the data points; nevertheless, that possibility is there.

Good statistics software does what it must to isolate the users from such troublesome infinities. Typically, it offers a restricted set of regression curves: you may choose any curve, as long as it is linear, quadratic, or cubic. This prevents you, for your own good, from messing with higher order polynomials, because these do not provide enough *regularization* (Geman, Bienen-

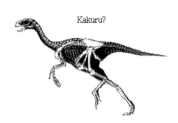

Kakuru?

Inference is UNDERDETERMINED in paleontology too: the reconstruction of *Kakuru kujani* (*above*; R. E. Molnar & N. S. Pledge, *A new theropod dinosaur from South Australia*, Alcheringa 4:281-287, 1980) from a single shin bone (*below*) would not be possible without many extra assumptions, and much knowledge about other species whose shin bones resemble that of the *Kakuru*. It is instructive to note that linear morphing (the technique used to interpolate the picture of *Kakuru* from those of *Avimimus* and *Microvenator*) is a REGULARIZED solution to the interpolation problem.[20]

Box: 5.1 — BAYESIAN INFERENCE in shape perception, after Kersten et al. (2004); see also Appendix A.

Bayesian inference is a general framework that specifies how visual systems should approach shape perception. Consider a system that is searching a space of shape hypotheses $\mathscr{S}$ for the most plausible explanation of the observed image I — that is, the shape that gave rise to it. The system's *a priori* beliefs about the plausibility of each hypothesis in that space, $S \in \mathscr{S}$ (before taking into account I but drawing upon background knowledge of the category C to which the shape belongs) are expressed by the *prior* conditional probability $P(S|C)$. The Bayes principle (Kersten et al., 2004) prescribes how the system should modify its prior beliefs in light of the image I. The desired outcome is expressed by the *posterior* conditional probability $P(S|I,C)$, which is computed from the known quantities according to the BAYES' RULE:

$$P(S|I,C) = \frac{P(I|S,C)P(S|C)}{P(I|C)} \tag{5.1}$$

In this expression, the *likelihood* $P(I|S,C)$ expresses the predictions of each shape hypothesis S in the form of the probability of observing the image I if S were true. The denominator, $P(I|C)$, is an average of the predictions of all hypotheses in the hypothesis space defined by the shape category C, weighted by their prior probabilities:

$$P(I|C) = \sum_{S' \in \mathscr{S}} P(I|S',C)P(S',C) \tag{5.2}$$

This term serves to normalize the product that appears in the numerator, ensuring that the posterior $P(S|I,C)$ sums to 1 and can therefore be interpreted as a proper probability distribution over the hypotheses.

To appreciate the generality of the Bayes' rule, note that the formulation that appears above is precisely equivalent to that of Box 8.1 on page 346 in Chapter 8: the shape S is analogous to hypothesis h, the image I – to the data D, and the knowledge of object category C – to the prior knowledge K.

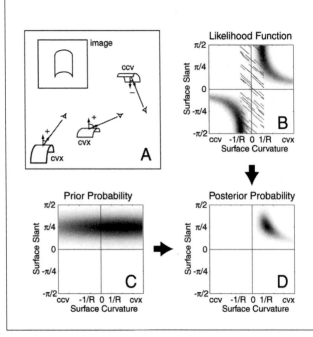

An illustration of the Bayesian process of shape perception (Kersten et al., 2004, p.274). (A) The given image is consistent with multiple shapes and viewpoints, including convex cylinders viewed from above and concave cylinders viewed from below. (B) The likelihood represents the compatibility of different scene interpretations with the observed image; the greater probability density marked by the two darker regions in the curvature-slant space signifies the higher likelihood of "small curvature and large slant" hypotheses. (C) The concentration of the prior probability density in the upper right quadrant of the curvature-slant space signifies an expectation of perceiving highly convex objects viewed from above. (D) A Bayesian observer combines the likelihood and the prior to estimate the posterior probability for each possible interpretation of the given image in terms of the curvature and the slant of the perceived shape.

stock, and Doursat, 1992; Girosi, Jones, and Poggio, 1995). In perceptual learning, the outcome — the input clusters, or the input/output regression — is likewise constrained by imposing extra assumptions such as simplicity or smoothness (Figure 5.15). Note that making assumptions of this kind is exactly what we identified earlier as the proper way of addressing indeterminacy in connection with another major issue in perception: constancy. This theoretical unification is a deeply satisfying outcome of the computational analysis we undertook, which extends to encompass all of perception (Kersten et al., 2004; Knill and Richards, 1996), as well as motor control (Edelman and Flash, 1987; Gandolfo, Mussa-Ivaldi, and Bizzi, 1996). LEARNING FROM EXAMPLES, for which statistical inference through regularization is the proper computational solution (Poggio, Rifkin, Mukherjee, and Niyogi, 2004), thus attains a kind of generality that attracts titles such as "a theory of how the brain might work" (Poggio, 1990). Reliance on examples is also useful in other cognitive domains, such as reasoning (Stanfill and Waltz, 1986; Tenenbaum, 2000) and language (Goldberg, 2005, p.65ff), as we shall see later on.

5.5   Truth

The heavy reliance on assumptions, whose importance (this time around, for learning) was underscored yet again just now, stirs a suspicion that deviations from perceptual truth, brought about by incorrect assumptions, might be the rule rather than a few odd ducks. To quell this suspicion, we need first to define perceptual truth. The inconstancies in lightness and shape perception (pp. 103-105) show what perceptual "lies" are like, but what, exactly, is the nature of their opposite?

For many of us, the concept of truth, especially in the context of perception, is associated with the sublime concluding lines of the *Ode on a Grecian Urn*, where Keats equates truth with beauty. Deftly thwarting the seekers after a definition, he also suggests that beauty is truth, thus completing a circle which we must pry open. As we shall see in this section, which deals with perceptual truth, and the next one, which is about beauty, Keats' sentiment can be given no less than a computational exegesis, instead of being dismissed as romantic flimflam.

Scholars believe that Keats' stance on truth and beauty was inspired by his reading of the *Seven Discourses on Art*, a collection of addresses before

When old age shall this generation waste,
Thou shalt remain, in midst of other woe
Than ours, a friend to man, to whom
                              thou say'st,
Beauty is truth, truth beauty, — that is all
Ye know on earth, and all ye need to know.

— John Keats
from *Ode on a Grecian Urn*

The natural appetite or taste of the human mind is for TRUTH; whether that truth results from the real agreement or equality of original ideas among themselves; from the agreement of the representation of any object with the thing represented; or from the correspondence of the several parts of any arrangement with each other.

— Joshua Reynolds
Seven discourses on art

The age-old question of INTENTIONALITY (Brentano, 1874) — how is it that mental representations can be "about" objects in the world — received this striking formulation in the writings of Wittgenstein (1958, p.217): "If God had looked into our minds he would not have been able to see there whom we were speaking of." This seems to be a direct contradiction of Jeremiah 17:10, "I the Lord examine the heart and the mind" (literally, "the kidneys"). Jeremiah, let alone Wittgenstein, now appears to have been too conservative: any radiologist can examine the heart and the kidneys, and it only takes an fMRI scanner and some training in statistics to look into the mind too. Read on to find out more.

the newly established Royal Academy of Britain, made between 1769 and 1776 by its first president, Joshua Reynolds. As a painter and a scholar, Reynolds was deeply concerned with the notion of representation, which recurs throughout his writings, including a place where he defines TRUTH.

Of the three varieties of truth Reynolds mentions, one seems particularly promising for our present purpose: "...truth results from ...the agreement of the representation of any object with the thing represented." In the context of the original discussion, the terms of this definition are unproblematic. By representation Reynolds obviously means a portrait, a sculpture, or some other likeness of the "thing represented," intended for human perusal. This makes the further issue of "agreement" unproblematic as well: the spectator can look at the bowl of fruit and at its depiction on the canvas and decide whether the visual impression is the same in both cases. However, an attempt to approach the question of perceptual truth or, as the psychologists call it, VERIDICALITY from this direction immediately runs into an obstacle.

At issue is the nature of the required agreement between an internal representation — some neurons firing — and its object. This echoes the famous question of INTENTIONALITY, or "aboutness" of the mental, which is usually associated with the work of Brentano (1874), and which I promised (in the caption of Figure 2.2 on page 14) to "put to rest" in this very section. Its roots run deep in the Western philosophical tradition — all the way back to Aristotle, in fact (Cummins, 1989). The sticking point is this: in what sense can the activity of a bunch of neurons "agree" with a red apple, given that it can be neither round nor red?

5.5.1 How neurons can be truthful, and how to tell whether they are

The resolution of this issue hinges on the idea of reliable covariation between the presence of distal objects ("out there" in the world) and their internal representations (neural activity). As we know from Chapter 3, the sensory cortical areas contain plenty of neurons that are reliably *tuned* to distal objects: they are active when the preferred stimulus is present and quiescent when other, similar stimuli, or no stimulus at all, are present (Figure 5.16). Moreover, the activity of a group of tuned neurons, whether natural or artificially induced, causally contributes to the phenomenal perception of their preferred stimulus, as demonstrated by Newsome's experiments (Salzman et al., 1990). It is by virtue of this causal chain that activities of tuned neurons and the concomitant phenomenal perceptual states are "about" the corresponding distal objects.

In the terminology of neural information processing, tuned units thus embody physical symbols, which are true to their distal causes and over which cognitive computations can be defined as needed. Would those computations preserve perceptual truth? Let us consider categorization, without which there would be no cognition as we know it; the computational basis for it comes from the emergence of clusters in the representation space, in which the would-be members of a category land closer to each other than to other objects (for an illustration, refer back to Figure 5.9 on page 107). This suggests that **perception of distal entities (objects or events) can be considered veridical (truthful) with respect to categorization insofar as the natural similarities defined over those entities**[22] **are reflected in the layout of the internal representation space**.

To find out whether perception in a given situation is veridical in this

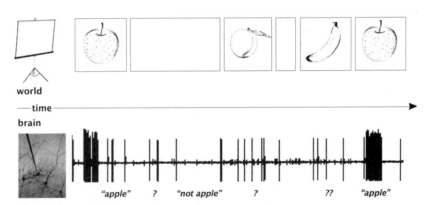

Figure 5.16 — A neural solution to the problem of INTENTIONALITY. Consider a tuned neuron that responds reliably to apples, and only to apples (cf. Quiroga, Reddy, Kreiman, Koch, and Fried, 2005). The activity of this neuron is then clearly *about* apples: it can be used to infer the visual presence of an apple, and its causal role in giving rise to the percept of an apple can be verified using Newsome's microstimulation technique (cf. Figure 4.2 on page 68). This illustrates the first of the two principles that make agreement between representation and reality possible — one that has been originally suggested by John Locke, long before anyone knew anything about neurons. The principle is that of CONFORMITY or covariation between "ideas" and their objects, which holds when the former are reliably evoked by the latter (Locke, 1690). The second principle is illustrated in Figure 5.17 on the following page.

sense, we need a method for mapping the relevant representation space. Multidimensional scaling fits the bill perfectly, so it is no wonder that the notion of veridicality just stated has been introduced by one of its inventors, Shepard (1968). The first experimental study of this matter by Shepard and Chipman (1970) explored the veridicality of the perception of shapes of geographical states. The MDS analysis of the subjective similarity data from that study placed together, for example, the shapes of Illinois and Nevada (among other "vertical and irregular" states), while distancing these from Nebraska (which landed in the "horizontal and rectangular" cluster) — just as the schematic illustration in Figure 5.17 groups the apple and the peach shapes apart from the banana.

The gathering of similarity data for mapping the representation space does not have to rely on subjective reports: the delayed matching to sample method that I mentioned earlier can be used to collect the necessary data without the subjects being at all aware that the experiment has anything to do with similarity. As shown in Figure 5.18, the response data are entered into a distance table, which is then processed by MDS to produce a map of the subject's internal representation space. The map is usually two-dimensional;

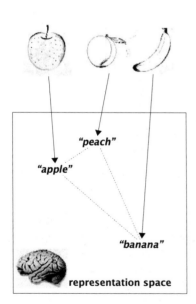

Figure 5.17 — The most important way in which a shape representation space can be VERIDICAL is for it to reflect faithfully the similarities that prevail among the distal objects. This is because such a representation can directly support similarity- or distance-based categorization (cf. Figure 5.9 on page 107). In this illustration, an apple and a peach are shown mapped into nearby representation-space locations, which are both relatively far from the location into which a banana is mapped. The representation space can be spanned by activities of tuned units, implemented neurally, as in Figure 5.16, or, as we shall see soon, in software (Edelman, 1999).

higher-dimensional maps, which always approximate the data better, but require special visualization software, can also be generated.

In this connection, it is worth recalling that computational complexity of vitally important functions such as learning from examples grows exponentially with dimensionality of the representation space. Biological cognitive systems are very good at evading this "curse of dimensionality" (cf. p. 59), which they do by computing low-dimensional representations from the nominally high-dimensional raw measurements. For most perceptual tasks MDS indicates that two or three dimensions suffice to approximate well the representation space involved. Once again we realize that perception is feasible both because our sensory environment is computationally tractable and because the brain is well attuned to it (cf. Figure 5.15 on page 118).

5.5.2 Examples of veridical perception

The degree to which the brain is sensitive to low-dimensional similarity patterns that are hidden in the perceptual data is readily apparent in the outcome

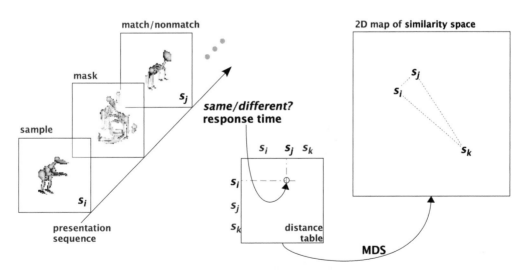

Figure 5.18 — An experimental procedure used by Cutzu and Edelman (1998) for mapping the similarity space of a set of stimuli. The maps from one of the studies reported there are shown in Figure 5.19 on the next page.

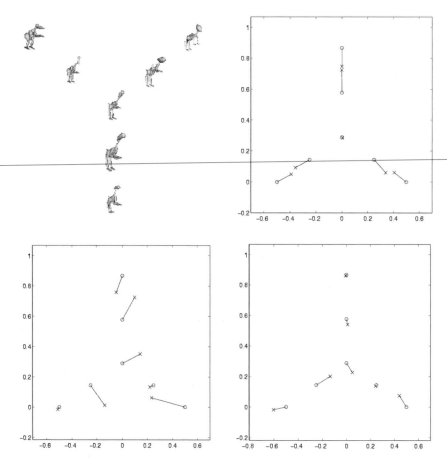

Figure 5.19 — VERIDICAL PERCEPTION of object shape similarities (after Cutzu and Edelman, 1998). *Top left:* the seven computer-generated humanoid shapes used as the stimuli in one of the studies, arranged so as to make explicit their similarity relationships. The three extremal shapes lie in a plane in the parameter space used by the computer graphics program. The center shape is their blend. Each of the remaining three shapes is a halfway morph between an extremal shape and the center one. *Top right:* the star-shaped layout of the true similarity space is revealed in this MDS map of one of the subjects' response data (○ and × denote the true and the actual locations of the stimuli in the similarity space; the rotation of the entire configuration is, of course, immaterial to the relative distances among the points). Statistical analyses reported by Cutzu and Edelman (1998) indicate that the fit between the true and actual configurations is highly significant. *Bottom left:* the same analysis, applied to data from a different experimental paradigm, in which subjects memorized the shapes and the names assigned to them, and later judged the recalled similarities when prompted with the names only (the similarity data were processed by MDS as usual). The fit is as highly significant as before. *Bottom right:* a map generated from the responses of a computer model of shape perception, subjected to the same testing procedure as above. The model replicates perfectly the pattern of human performance.

of a series of experiments by Cutzu and Edelman (1998), several of which
are illustrated in Figure 5.19 on the preceding page. Using behavioral data
from human subjects (response times and error rates in some experiments;
similarity judgments in others), they found that the layout of stimulus representations in the MDS-derived map closely matched the arrangement of the
stimuli (animal-like computer-generated shapes) in a parametric space that
had been used to define them.

The results of these experiments were replicated by a computer model
that represented the stimuli by the activities of units broadly tuned to a few
select shapes (Duvdevani-Bar and Edelman, 1999). In the replicated experiment, the units were tuned to the three shapes located at the extremes of
the star-like parametric arrangement. The three-dimensional representation
space spanned by these three units supported a veridical representation of the
star-like pattern of similarities built into the stimulus set, as can be seen in
Figure 5.19, bottom right.

Such capacity for veridical representation of subtle similarity patterns
stems from a very general computational principle, which I introduce and explain elsewhere (Edelman, 1999). In a nutshell, the principle is this: **the
perception of similarities among distal objects will be veridical if the
mapping from the visual world to the representation space where the
perceived similarities are to be judged is** *smooth* (intuitively, a function
is smooth if small changes in its arguments almost always precipitate small
changes in its value).

A byproduct of this computational account of veridicality is the emerging
unified understanding of some of the most important aspects of perception
in terms of the most basic building blocks of neural computation: receptive
fields. First, mappings realized by overlapping, graded receptive fields are
generically smooth in the above sense (Edelman, 1998a, 1999), hence one
may expect the perception of similarity to be, as a rule, veridical. Second,
just as graded, overlapping receptive fields used by the model of Figure 5.3
gave rise to vernier hyperacuity, so do the graded, overlapping tuning curves
for complex shapes support hyperacuity with respect to shape: capacity for
fine shape discrimination was exhibited both by the human subjects and by
the model of Cutzu and Edelman (1998). Thus, the same general properties
of receptive fields make possible both hyperacuity and veridical perception
of similarities.

Because of this generality, veridical perception of similarity is predicted
to be just as ubiquitous as hyperacuity, across perceptual tasks and modalities

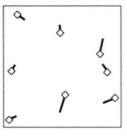

Neuron-level VERIDICALITY in the monkey, after Op de Beeck et al. (2001): the square arrangement of eight stimuli in a parameter space (*top*) is reflected in the layout of the eight corresponding points recovered by MDS from inter-stimulus distances, as measured in the image space (squares) and in a 124-neuron ensemble response space (diamonds). The correlation between the two sets of distances here is 0.999 (Op de Beeck et al., 2001, p.1246).

and across species (Edelman, 1999; Shepard, 2001). All the results available to date bear out this prediction. To cite a seemingly unlikely example, when human subjects were shown perambulating stick figures whose *gait* was parametrically controlled in the same way that shape was controlled in the study of Cutzu and Edelman (1998), they perceived the similarities among walking styles veridically, as indicated by the faithful recovery of the "gait space" pattern by MDS from the subjects' response data (Giese, Thornton, and Edelman, 2003). In another study, veridical perception of shape similarities was demonstrated in behavioral experiments involving monkeys (Sugihara, Edelman, and Tanaka, 1998).

Veridicality is revealed not only in behavioral performance patterns, but also directly in the brain activity. On the level of individual neurons, a good example can be found in the study of Op de Beeck, Wagemans, and Vogels (2001). There, neurons responded to parametrically controlled shapes just as the tuned "units" in the model of Cutzu and Edelman (1998) did, and their ensemble response, when processed by MDS, revealed the parametric pattern built into the stimuli — as predicted by Edelman (1999).

Veridical representation of similarity seems also to hold at the level of entire brain areas. In particular, the outcome of an experiment reported by (Edelman et al., 1998) and illustrated in Figure 5.20 on the facing page suggests that activation states of the human lateral occipital complex directly express information about stimulus shape. Although this experiment needs to be repeated with the same parametrically controlled stimuli used in behavioral and in single-neuron studies, there is little doubt as to what the outcome will be.

You may have noted that in the last paragraph I have referred to veridical *representation* rather than veridical perception. This switch of nomenclature is far from arbitrary: it reflects the crucial significance to the study of mind of our emerging ability to investigate directly the representations and processes that comprise it. Once we are able to visualize and analyze the subject's brain states directly, our access to the representations involved no longer depends on his or her behavioral responses, let alone verbal reports. Furthermore, the representation of the world in the brain state (which, of course, can be analyzed on computational, algorithmic, and neural levels) has the distinction of being the nexus from which all aspects of behavior and of further internal processing follow in a causal manner. The level of brain states is thus revealed as endowed with the ultimate explanatory power — as is only proper, given our working hypothesis according to which the mind is what the brain does.

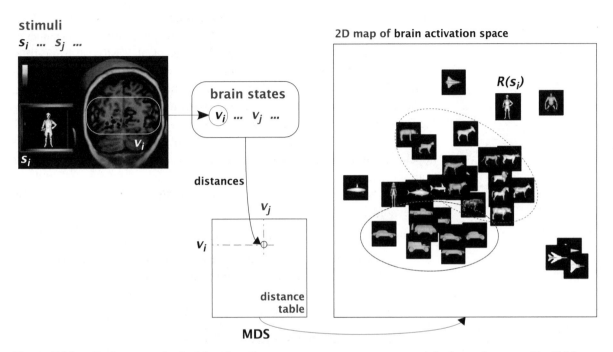

Figure 5.20 — Brain space: the final frontier of EXPERIMENTAL EPISTEMOLOGY. In the study reported by Edelman et al. (1998), the subjects viewed a set of shapes s_i one at a time (*left*), while the fMRI machine recorded the evoked activities v_i in the lateral occipital area of the brain, known to respond preferentially to complex objects. These simplified snapshots of brain states, each of which presumably encoded one of the stimuli, were then used to form a 32×32 table of distances among the stimuli *as represented in the subject's brain* (there were altogether 32 stimuli in the experiment). The distance table was processed by MDS to obtain a 2D map approximating the layout of the stimuli in the brain activation space (the icon labeled $R(s_i)$, for example, marks the location of the figure-like stimulus in that space). In the resulting map (*right*), stimuli by and large clustered by shape: for instance, the representations of cars and of quadruped animals formed distinct groups. The veridical representation of shape similarities manifested in these results bears on some of the most foundational issues in the philosophy of mind, among them the alleged privacy of the mental and the enigma of intentionality. The neurocomputational theory of representation that emerges from the material we covered so far and the empirical results illustrated here imply that a neuroscientist who has recorded from a subject's brain and carried out MDS analysis followed by proper statistical inference can use the resulting knowledge to determine — solely from the subject's current brain activity — what it is that the subject is looking at (or, more generally, thinking about). A feat is now humanly possible of which in the 1940s even God was supposed to be incapable, according to Wittgenstein (cf. the quote from his *Philosophical Investigations* on p. 122).

5.6 Beauty

Our by now standard toolkit for understanding neural computation, which we used in the preceding section to analyze perceptual truth, applies also to beauty. Contrary to what most people believe, or at least wish to be true, beauty *can* be not only measured but explained. The platitude most commonly cited as an insurmountable obstacle to this endeavor — that beauty is in the eye of the beholder — is actually what makes it possible, by shifting the focus to the brain: computational cognitive science, as we have seen, excels in exposing and explaining entities that only a few decades ago seemed hopelessly subjective, or doomed to remain forever hidden in the minutiae of brain function.

What is beauty, then? Let us look again in the *Seven Discourses on Art* by Reynolds:

> The painter, by bringing together in one piece those beauties which are dispersed amongst a great variety of individuals, produces a figure more beautiful than can be found in nature. ...
> For PERFECT BEAUTY in any species must combine all the characters which are beautiful in that species.

Although this observation seems on the face of it just as circular as the *beauty* ↔ *truth* equation by Keats, it is actually extremely helpful. Reynolds all but specifies an algorithm for distilling "perfect beauty" from a pool of specimens that may each be only somewhat beautiful. That such pooling should be possible at all tells us much about the nature of beauty and its roots in the *statistics* of the objects that possess it.

Figure 5.21 — Reynolds: "Is not ... art an imitation of nature? Must he not, therefore, who imitates her with the greatest fidelity be the best artist? By this mode of reasoning Rembrandt has a higher place than Raffaelle. But how can that be the nature of man, in which no two individuals are the same?" *Left:* Raffaello d'Urbino (1483-1520; self-portrait, 1506). *Right:* Rembrandt van Rijn (1606-1669; self-portrait, 1629). The two artists were the same age when they created these paintings.

5.6.1 Koinophilia

The simplest statistic of all, the mean, has long been suspected of having a role in defining beauty. The notion that taking the mean of an ensemble of face images brings out the beauty that is inherent in them goes by the Greek name *koinophilia* (love of the common), which has been borrowed from evolutionary genetics, where it denotes the preference for choosing an average mate.[23] In a direct vindication of this intuition and of Reynolds' insight, psychophysical experiments with computer-generated stimuli produced by blending many faces indicate that the more "common" a synthetic face is (the larger the number of actual faces blended into it), the more beautiful it is rated — especially if the constituent faces are themselves judged as beautiful to begin with (Perrett, Burt, Penton-Voak, Lee, Rowland, and Edwards, 1999).

This finding fits nicely into the bigger picture of the theory of aesthetic experience proposed by Ramachandran and Hirstein (1999). As we have come to expect of a theory of a cognitive function, their proposal engages the empirical findings on several levels: evolutionary, neurobiological, and computational (what they call the "internal logic" of the aesthetically valent stimuli). On the evolutionary level, where the issue is "why have aesthetics at all," there are indications that facial attractiveness is linked (via facial symmetry) to information about the face owner's genes (Jones, Little, Penton-Voak, Tiddeman, Burt, and Perrett, 2001), and, more generally, that traits that are desirable in a mate, such as intelligence, covary with beauty (Kanazawa and Kovar, 2004). On the neurobiological level, Ramachandran and Hirstein (1999) describe brain circuits, such as direct links between the limbic system and the sensory areas, that may mediate aesthetic experience. Most of their paper is devoted, however, to the computational level, which is of prime interest to us too.

Regarding PERFECT BEAUTY: anonymous copies of Athena and Zeus by Phidias (c.490-c.430 BCE), the greatest of Greek sculptors. In the *Seven Discourses on Art*, Reynolds quotes Cicero on Phidias: "Neither did this artist when he carved the image of Jupiter [Zeus] or Minerva [Athena], set before him any one human figure as a pattern, which he was to copy; but having a more perfect idea of beauty fixed in his mind, this he steadily contemplated."

Ramachandran and Hirstein (1999) identify eight ways in which stimuli may exert aesthetic influence on the perceiver.[24] Although all eight principles are essentially computational, I would like to single out two of them that are particularly easy to understand in terms that are familiar to us from this chapter: symmetry and exaggeration.

The first principle, SYMMETRY (Figure 5.22, left), is an important component of the classical Western aesthetics, whose roots lie in ancient Greece; in the Eastern traditions of Tao and of Ch'an or Zen Buddhism asymmetry is perceived as more pleasing (cf. Figure 5.22, right).

In face perception, symmetry is universally influential, being strongly linked to koinophilia (Perrett et al., 1999). From a computational standpoint, blended composite faces are characterized by higher smoothness (because small-scale features such as skin blemishes are washed out by the averaging), and, most prominently, by a higher degree of symmetry (because individual asymmetries are likewise lost in the blending). In terms of the internal representation space of Figure 5.5 on page 95, increased averaging corresponds, of course, to a movement towards the center of the "cloud" of actual, individual faces: that's where the facial beauty gradient points.

The beauty inherent in the symmetrical perfection and serenity of the average is, however, only one of the many possible aesthetic experiences that can be brought about by looking at a face. In fact, symmetry is the last entry in the eightfold list of Ramachandran and Hirstein (1999), whose first candidate for an aesthetically charged feature, EXAGGERATION, is in a very concrete computational sense the opposite of averageness. In the representation space, exaggeration corresponds to movement away from the center. It is worth remembering that the higher the dimensionality of the representation space, the more directions there are in which such movement can happen. Not all of these are equivalent in their perceptual effect: to be aesthetically striking (rather than merely bizarre), exaggeration must apply to a dimension that is significant to begin with.

Figure 5.22 — BEAUTY can be found in symmetry and in the lack thereof. *Left:* the Parthenon, the temple of Pallas Athena on the Acropolis, in Athens, Greece. *Right:* the rock garden (karesansui) of the Ryoan temple in Kyoto, Japan.

One natural way to single out such dimensions is to determine how the specimen that is about to be exaggerated — for example, a face that is to be made into a CARICATURE — differs from the mean (cf. Figure 5.23). This default approach does not, however, exhaust the possibilities; in general, the identification of interesting dimensions is a nontrivial task, which requires considerable creativity. If the "fulcrum" with respect to which the exaggeration is carried out is made to be other than the mean, the elbow room for creative expression becomes large indeed.

To appreciate this, let us play with the idea of a caricature in two distinct domains, one traditional, the other less so. The first one is the face space; although caricatures originated here, the possibilities have hardly been exhausted. Think of hyperbolizing the face of *Star Trek*'s Mr. Spock with respect to that of an average Earthling: this would make his ears even longer and pointier. Now, do the same using an average Vulcan as the reference point: this would leave Spock's ears as they are, because their pointedness is a feature that is shared by all Vulcans.

"Beauty is transitory."

– Spock

"Beauty survives."

– Kirk

Star Trek, Ep.69

The second domain is what we might call the text space, where points correspond to documents (this is a standard conceptual tool in disciplines such as information retrieval). Caricaturing a text taken from a particular corpus clearly means exaggerating its main features (style- or content-wise), with respect to the mean of the distribution of these features in the corpus. I think you'll agree that it is easy to extrapolate, for example, the style of the

Figure 5.23 — The perceptual quality of a CARICATURE depends on the artist's correct choice of the dimensions along which the subject differs from the population mean. In this caricature, the face of George W. Bush (top left) morphs into that of Richard M. Nixon (bottom right); along the way, the focus of the drawing gradually shifts from the dimensions that encode the distinctive features of the former (the beady, close-set eyes, the bushy eyebrows, and the prominent ears) to those that define the latter (the prominence and the shape of the nose, and the heavy jowls).

The speculative restriction of pure reason and its practical extension bring it into that relation of equality in which reason in general can be employed suitably to its end, and this example proves better than any other that the path to WISDOM, if it is to be made sure and not to be impassable or misleading, must with us men inevitably pass through science; but it is not till this is complete that we can be convinced that it leads to this goal.

— Immanuel Kant (1724-1804)
Critique of Practical Reason

Unconcerned, mocking, violent — thus WISDOM wants *us*: she is a woman, and always loves only a warrior.

— Friedrich Nietzsche (1844-1900)
Thus Spoke Zarathustra

Bah! Gouging out healthy flesh, creating an open wound. Queer thing, this "WISDOM" of his. What's it like? Deep? Shallow? Like river water, perhaps? Tell me about wisdom with deeps and shallows. Mistaken identity, I'm afraid. He's confusing a pheasant for a phoenix.

— Hakuin Ekaku (1686-1768)
Commentary on the *Deep Wisdom* passage of the *Prajnaparamita Sutra*

When the artist has by diligent attention acquired a clear and distinct idea of beauty and symmetry; when he has reduced the variety of nature to the abstract idea; his next task will be to become acquainted with THE GENUINE HABITS OF NATURE, as distinguished from those of fashion.

— Joshua Reynolds
Seven discourses on art

book of Leviticus relative to the rest of the Pentateuch (I won't try it here and now, though, much as I am tempted to).

Can one do the same thing across corpora? I believe so.[25] Although creative cross-category exaggeration is not easy, it is not too far-fetched. As an exercise, we can try to imagine lampooning the dry prose of the passage on WISDOM from Kant's *Critique of Practical Reason*, taking as a reference first Nietzsche's agitated aphorizing, then Hakuin's mockery (I won't actually attempt that either).

5.6.2 Wabi-sabi

The extended notion of caricature suggests that extrapolating away from the mundane and into hitherto unexplored regions of representation spaces offers boundless opportunities for exercising one's creativity and imagination. It has been noted that the ability to develop new and interesting variations on old themes may *be* the crux of creativity (Hofstadter, 1985a).[26] But does that account for beauty in general? Unlike Ramachandran and Hirstein (1999), who go as far as to claim that "all art is caricature," I do not think it does.

Ramachandran and Hirstein note parenthetically that their equation is true not always, but "surprisingly often." I believe that this view, even when qualified, altogether misses a different kind of beauty. It is to be found neither at the centers of the clouds of representations that define perceptual categories (which is where the koinophilia idea would place beauty), nor in their outer reaches (where caricatures live). This kind of beauty abides right among the actual instances of perceptual objects. It is the common beauty of the quotidian, the asymmetrical, the transient, the forlorn — what Joshua Reynolds may well have had in mind when he wrote about THE GENUINE HABIT OF NATURE; what the Japanese refer to as *wabi-sabi* (Juniper, 2003).

Although wabi-sabi is elusive, it sometimes allows itself to be glimpsed, as the four unconfirmed sightings documented in Figure 5.24 may show. These scenes move *me* in a way that, I suspect, has something to do with wabi-sabi, but a good friend of mine, who is Japanese, tells me that only the fourth one is "close, but just close." Individual differences in perceptual experience (whose role I shall discuss in section 5.7) as well as cultural differences (Chua, Boland, and Nisbett, 2005) may be responsible for such disagreements. Let us set such differences aside for the moment and ask, what is it that distinguishes a scene that "has it" from one that does not? The traditional answer — always offered tentatively, because, as every explainer hastens to point out, wabi-sabi is not only elusive but also ineffable — mentions two key factors: the degree to which the scene displays IMPERFECTION, and the extent to which it evokes IMPERMANENCE.

Explaining a perceptual phenomenon in terms of such abstract concepts is by itself not very illuminating; what we need in addition is a computational insight. To explain imperfection — and, by extension, a key aspect of wabi-sabi — using the terminology of representation spaces, we must first grasp the meaning of sensory perfection. A perceptual object would appear perfect

Figure 5.24 — Finding BEAUTY in the quotidian, the asymmetrical, the transient, the forlorn ...*wabi-sabi*? Clockwise from top left: a postern in a wall, Hradčany, Prague; the Seven Sisters cliffs as seen from the Hope's Gap near Seaford, East Sussex, England; a butterfly on a pebble, North Fork Trinity River, California; a tree in winter, Ithaca, New York.

to an observer insofar as it is a good (central) exemplar of its category — as represented in that observer's brain.[27] Now, perfection, especially in a face, and doubly so in the face of a potential mate, evokes a sense of beauty for good evolutionary reasons (Jones et al., 2001). But why should any imperfect non-face objects seem beautiful?

I conjecture that the main factor that mediates the feeling of beauty for such objects and scenes is *novelty*, which brings about, quite literally, excitement. Stimuli that are imperfect in the sense just defined — those that are unlike the prototypical, or even the merely familiar — necessarily evoke a response that is especially diffuse and distributed. Because sensory neurons can't wait to be stimulated ("entertain us!") to justify their expensive upkeep to the rest of the brain, their activation rewards the organism for finding a stimulus that is effective in this respect, through the subcortical pathways mentioned by Ramachandran and Hirstein (1999).[28]

On this account, if the blossoming almond twig in Figure 5.25 makes you feel wabi-sabi, it is because in its delicate details it is unlike any other blossoming tree branch you saw before. Psychologists have long known that repeated exposure to the same stimulus reduces the response to it (this phenomenon is called habituation). Even the most emotionally powerful image rapidly loses its poignancy as it grows familiar. Thus, if I start using the almond blossom photograph as a wallpaper on my computer desktop, specific

A fallen blossom
Returning to the bough?
It was a butterfly.

— Moritake Arakida
(1472-1549)

Figure 5.25 — Beauty in IMPERFECTION and IMPERMANENCE. Almond blossom in Emmaus, Ayalon Valley, Israel.

neurons in my brain will get assigned to represent it, the initially distributed response will become localized, and the excitement will be gone along with the novelty.[29]

It is a sad and perhaps unexpected consequence of the brain's capacity for perceptual learning that an encounter with imperfection must be fleeting to be effective as a source of wabi-sabi experience. As noted above, however, a scene that actually *expresses* impermanence appears all the more beautiful for it, in the classical wabi-sabi way. The impermanence need not be visually immediate: a picture of an almond blossom implies, but does not reveal, the imminent future in which it is gone. In tricking us into feeling nostalgic for a past that is still in our future, wabi-sabi touches a very sensitive nerve. So important is the cognitive dimension of impermanence to the understanding of the human condition that this book has an entire section in a later chapter devoted to it; I shall say no more about it here.

The real, albeit modest, progress that we made on the preceding several pages proves that even notions as ineffable as perceptual truth and beauty can be approached using the standard conceptual toolkit built around representation spaces. The recipe for progress is, as always in science, to use such tools that allow generalization across phenomena. As promised in the beginning of this chapter, let us now put this approach and our toolbox to work to demystify the most ineffable aspect of all in perception: the phenomenal nature of perceptual experience.

5.7   What it means to see

> The meaning of life is to see.
> — HUI NENG

Let us take the bull by the horns: what does it mean to see? It may seem foolhardy to open a discussion of something admittedly ineffable with a direct question about its nature. In my defense, I would like to point out that I did not promise to render perception less ineffable — only to demystify it. To do so, I propose to use the explanatory framework that we already have in place to attain an insight into the computational nature of phenomenal visual experience, and into its neural underpinnings. By the end of this section (which also closes the chapter), capturing particular *percepts* in language — engaging in what the ancients used to call ekphrasis — will still require an exceptional poetical ability or philosophical acumen, but the emerging functional-computational understanding of what *perception* is should be accessible to all.

5.7.1   Qualia

The sharpest thorn on which intuition tends to get snagged is the familiar and basic problem of understanding the raw phenomenal feel of perception. In the philosophy of mind, this is known as the problem of *qualia* (plural of QUALE), to which readers are usually introduced by means of some irresistibly vivid example, such as the redness of a ripe tomato (Tye, 2003). What does the quale of red consist of? The answer that I am about to outline — which may have been anticipated by René Magritte (see Figure 5.26) — is a synthesis of several strands of thinking about qualia in terms of representations that possess, within the computational system they are embedded in, specific characteristics and causal properties (Churchland, 1985; Clark, 1993, 2000; Llinás, 2001; Ramachandran and Hirstein, 1997; Smart, 2004).

Back in Chapter 1 we agreed to eschew neural chauvinism: it would be unreasonable to discriminate among information-processing systems exclusively on the basis of their physical make-up. Consistency demands that we now admit that all animals with eyes (scallops, jays, jellyfish, leopards) as well as properly programmed/trained computers with cameras (robots) all experience visual qualia of some kind or other.[30] Their qualia would, of course, differ widely. Consider the many-eyed scallop from page 18. On the one

If this picture of tomatoes were in color, it would illustrate the QUALE of *red*.

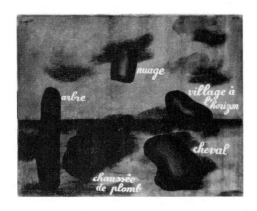

Figure 5.26 — This painting by Magritte, titled *From One Day to Another*, which illustrates well the ineffability of vision, also contains an insight that goes to the heart of WHAT IT MEANS TO SEE. Placing object names in appropriate locations in a map-like representation of a scene gets the end product of perception almost, but not quite, right. As explained in this section, exposing a system capable of sight to a visual scene gives rise to a flock of transiently roused, spatially anchored representations — some conceptual, hence named (as in this picture), others not, hence ineffable. The joint activity of the evoked representations *constitutes* the act of seeing on the part of the system.

hand, insofar as it is capable of seeing, a scallop has qualia; using an expression made famous by Nagel (1974), it must *feel like something* to be a scallop looking out of its shell (just as it must feel like nothing to be that shell). On the other hand, these qualia are necessarily alien to a human; I cannot really imagine what it feels like to see through several dozen eyes all at once (there is an important connection here to various aspects of consciousness, to which I shall return in Chapter 9).

To allow for the possibility that different individuals, species, or computers can all see, the critical factor(s) must be functional: a capability, not a chunk of hardware or wetware. What could this function be, and where would it reside? It cannot be wholly contained in an eye, any more than they can inhere in a digital camera. Both are basically measurement devices, and, however much processing they carry out on the signal, they don't *see*. At the same time, we must accept that an entire human, or an entire scallop, sees: I know that I do, and likewise a SCALLOP that responds to the shadow of an octopus by slamming its shell shut and skipping away cannot be considered blind; to the scallop, seeing an octopus feels like getting away. It must be the case, therefore, that something that gets added to the system in between the two extremes — an eye taken in isolation, and an entire embodied cognitive system — makes it capable of experiencing visual qualia.

The preceding analysis restricts the functional space in which qualia can roam, helping us corner them and drive them to the ground: we know that what eyes (or cameras) do is not enough, but what entire cognitive systems do is. In primates, a particularly important role in giving rise to qualia is played by higher cortical areas of the brain. An excellent example is the quale of visual motion, which in a monkey can be evoked simply by injecting a tiny current into area MT (recall Newsome's experiments, illustrated in Figure 4.2). Amazingly, as far as motion perception is concerned, the eyes might just as well be nonexistent.

Activity in area MT (whether naturally or artificially produced) is clearly *necessary* for seeing motion: it is safe to bet that injecting current anywhere else in the brain would not have the perceptual effect of doing it in MT. Is the activation of MT alone also *sufficient*? This does not seem to be a useful question: even if the pure quale of motion is completely confined to area MT, the rest of the brain is what one feels it *with*. The possible existence of the quale of motion in an active MT cortex that is not sensed ("felt") with the proper part of the rest of the brain to which MT projects is in principle unverifiable, because feeling the percept is what the quale associated with it consists of by definition.

Qualia can be induced in humans in the absence of sensory input, by direct CORTICAL STIMULATION. In one study, Kupers, Fumal, Maertens de Noordhout, Gjedde, Schoenen, and Ptito (2006) used transcranial magnetic stimulation (TMS; see p. 435) of the occipital lobe to induce tactile sensations in blind subjects. The subjects had been trained to use a sensory substitution device — an electrode array placed on the tongue — to determine the orientation of visual stimuli, which were captured by a camera and fed to the electrode array. The possibility of inducing tactile qualia in the congenitally blind (but not in blindfolded controls trained to be equally good in the orientation task) by stimulating the cortical region that in sighted people houses the primary visual area indicates that experience plays a critical role in determining the representational role of the cortex, and supports the identification of qualia with representational states, expounded in this section.

Our hunting of the qualia is nearing its goal. The herd of visual motion qualia, in particular, has been rounded up summarily in area MT, even though their presence there can only be ascertained by using other parts of the brain as a "qualiascope." We also know that the rest of the brain does not care by what means the qualia end up in their metaphorical corral: you can parachute them in (as it was done in Newsome's MT microstimulation studies), or let them wander in along the regular pathways that begin in the retina.

Natural retinal input is, however, important in one respect: an animal in which the eyes have been nonexistent from birth is extremely unlikely to have acquired a properly laid out and tuned functional architecture in area MT. This suggests that the roaming space for qualia should be restricted not only in functional terms, but also in a temporal (more precisely, experiential) sense, which relates to the animal's perceptual history. If there has been no exposure to a proper variety of visual motion stimuli, there will be no qualia of motion (of the regular human variety, that is: the quale of *almost-*

Figure 5.27 — A GODDESS WITH THE QUALIA OF A SCALLOP. The newborn Athena, who according to the myth sprung fully grown from the head of her father Zeus, could not have had any but the most rudimentary qualia, unless she came into the world equipped with a complete adult-like set of *experiences*. This realization is in line with the Empiricist solution to the so-called Molyneux's Problem, as discussed by John Locke: "Suppose a man born blind, and now adult, and taught by his touch to distinguish between a cube and a sphere of the same metal, and nighly of the same bigness, so as to tell, when he felt one and the other, which is the cube, which the sphere. Suppose then the cube and sphere placed on a table, and the blind man be made to see: quaere, whether by his sight, before he touched them, he could now distinguish and tell which is the globe, which the cube?" To which the acute and judicious proposer answers, "Not." (Locke, 1690, ii.ix.8).

but-not-quite-entirely-black with an occasional phosphene can presumably be perceived even by an eyeless person).

Let us now spell out the full implications of this line of reasoning. If the right functional architecture is in place, it does not matter whether it is embodied in some neurons in area MT or in some electronic circuits; make the proper functional module active (by whatever means), and motion will be perceived by the rest of the system. Neither does it matter whether the functional architecture emerged from natural development "in the wild" or some super-sophisticated neurosurgery (in the case of a meat computer), or from soldering and programming (in the case of an electronic computer). It is still the case, though, that a typical human EXPERIENCE is needed for a cognitive system, whatever its make-up and origins, to possess human-like qualia (Edelman, 2006).[31]

Our repudiation of neural chauvinism in perception is now complete: it extends all the way from the relatively tame cognitive functions we have been analyzing in earlier sections to qualia. We have also gone a long way toward demystifying perception, by taking the road of computational phenomenology. Here, then, are the main components of the solution to the problem of qualia that we have arrived at.

- A QUALE IS a representational state. More precisely, it is a point in the kind of multidimensional space (cf. the quote from Smart (2004) in the margin) that singles out certain perceptual dimensions of the stimulus, just as the tuned neurons in area MT single out the dimensions of visual motion. Such tuning arises naturally through perceptual learning, while the system that harbors the qualia is exposed to stimulation.

> The dispute [...] comes down to our attitude to phenomenology. Certainly walking in a forest, seeing the blue of the sky, the green of the trees, the red of the track, one may find it hard to believe that our qualia are merely points in a multidimensional space. But perhaps that is what *it is like* (to use a phrase that can be distrusted) to be aware of a point in a multidimensional space.
>
> — Smart (2004)

The above implies that qualia evolve. This fact may be easier to appreciate in a domain where expertise, unlike in vision (which for humans is like the proverbial water for fish), is acquired over an extended period of time: reading. Compare, for example, the experience — what it *feels like* — of reading Joyce's *Ulysses* as a teenager of Millicent Bloom's age, and as a parent of Leopold or Molly Bloom's age. Just as a camera may register but does not *see* in the same sense that its owner does, a younger reader may read but does not *experience* a complex text in the same sense that an older one does. The meaning of life is to see; this remark by Hui Neng, the sixth patriarch of the Chinese Ch'an Buddhism tradition, quoted at the head of this section may then mean merely that learning to *see* is a open-ended, lifelong process —

Seeing is forgetting the name of
the thing one sees.

— PAUL VALÉRY

A sage who sees is unaware of the
experience of sense objects about
which others are aware.

— *Bhagavad-Gita*, 2.69

a realization that is entirely compatible with what we know now about the
plasticity of the visual system.

- A QUALE IS FELT when the representational state that defines it is accessed by the rest of the cognitive system. Although such access is
  straightforward to implement, it may require some potentially complex
  wiring, because a point in a multidimensional neural space exists physically as a particular pattern of activation over the neurons that span the
  space; leave one out, and you drop a dimension.

It is by virtue of certain distinguishing characteristics of access that qualia differ from other, non-experiential brain states: as Ramachandran and Hirstein
(1997) observe, qualia are enduring (unlike brain states involved in automatic
behavioral control), irrevocable (you cannot make a red tomato appear green
to you), and open to arbitrary action (unlike conditional reflexes, where perceptual states get associated with particular responses or actions).

5.7.2   So what does it mean to see, already?

This:

> TO SEE IS to form a representation of what you're looking at in
> terms of similarities to what you've seen on other occasions.

Just how rich your experience will be depends on the species you belong to
and on your perceptual history: it is one thing if you are a scallop and something completely different if you are a recently retired MOMA curator about
to complete a year-long cruise around the world. Thence the ineffability of
perception: full and detailed perceptual histories of individuals, be they scallops or humans, are very difficult to capture in words. That does not, however,
preclude us from using the tools of computational cognitive psychology and
neuroscience to understand the manner and the means whereby perceptual
history shapes the individual.

5.8   Coda

The computational sophistication of the human brain that embodies perception inspires awe in those who study it and envy in those who would imitate its

function. Connecting some sensors (a digital camera, a gas chromatograph, a microphone array) to a computer and collecting a heap of multidimensional data is only a small first step on the long climb towards the distant peaks of human-like perceptual abilities. Although much of the intervening terrain remains unexplored, we now have a much better grasp of the *principles* behind perception than even a decade ago.

- **The world is statistically well-behaved.** The data that present themselves to the senses are low-dimensional in ways that are important to the survival of sentient beings, on a number of hierarchical levels (cf. the quote from Simon (1973) on p. 31).[32]

- **Minds evolve to take advantage of that.** The benign statistical properties of the sensory world allow perceptual systems to resort to statistically justified assumptions in constraining the otherwise underdetermined problem of perception.

THE BRAIN BASIS OF VISION. Given what we know about perceptual learning, what you've seen sufficiently often — an expression that can be assigned a rigorous statistical meaning — dynamically determines what tuned units, such as those illustrated in Figure 5.28 on the following page, your brain possesses. The responses of these units, in turn, signal the "similarities" mentioned in the definition of seeing that I just offered. The ensemble response conveys information both about WHAT shapes are present in the scene, and WHERE they are with respect to the observer.[34]

COMPUTING WITH RFS. An example of perceptual computation that can be supported by WHAT+WHERE units is shown in Figure 5.29 on page 145, which has been produced by a working computer program that specializes in reading cursive script.[35] The program scans the stimulus looking for all the instances of each character that it can find. The degree of fit of each such instance to the input is entered into a spatially mapped data structure (the lower pane in Figure 5.29), resulting in a "cloud" of candidate instances. Out of these, the program picks the few that together best account for the cursive word that is the stimulus.

ANY OBJECT, ANY SCENE. The principle according to which a scene is represented by an ensemble of shape- and location-tuned units is very general. A system that can learn such representations from experience would be capable of dealing with any scene whose statistics is not totally different

THE WORLD IS STATISTICALLY WELL-BEHAVED. The most forceful expression of this realization is to be found in the early work of David Marr. Particularly relevant is his "FUNDAMENTAL HYPOTHESIS," stated in a paper on the cerebral neocortex: "Where instances of a particular collection of intrinsic properties (i.e., properties already diagnosed from sensory information) tend to be grouped such that if some are present, most are, then other useful properties are likely to exist which generalize over such instances. Further, properties often are grouped in this way." (Marr, 1970, pp.150-151).[33]

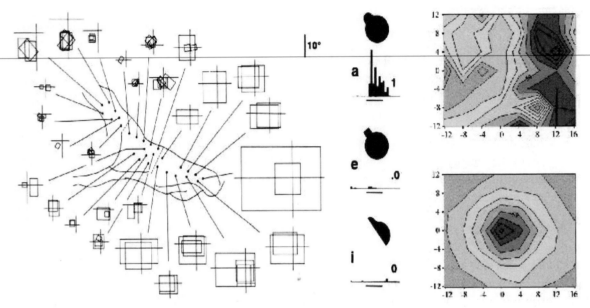

Figure 5.28 — The NEURAL BASIS of object and scene vision. *Left:* a map of the many neurons recorded from by Kobatake and Tanaka (1994), showing the position of each neuron in the inferior temporal (IT) lobe of the monkey brain, and the layout of its receptive field relative to the fixation point (indicated by the crosshairs in each diagram). The tuning properties of these neurons are pliable (Kobatake et al., 1998). The sizes and the locations of the RFs are very diverse; together, they create a patchwork that covers the entire central visual field several times over. Any localized stimulus is thus covered by many partially overlapping RFs, making it possible for the visual system to pinpoint it. *Middle:* the spatially localized RFs in area IT are also tuned to stimulus shape; the neuron whose RF is shown here responds well to the top shape, but not to variations on it. Most IT neurons exhibit a much more gradual dependence of response on shape (Thomas et al., 2001). *Right:* detailed maps of the IT RFs obtained by Op de Beeck and Vogels (2000) reveal graded spatial structure, in addition to graded shape selectivity. Taken together, these findings mean that the ensemble response of the IT neurons can represent the spatial structure of the viewed scene — WHAT IS WHERE — in exquisite detail. In principle, as anticipated in section 5.1, hyperacuity-level performance can be expected with respect to both location (Edelman, 2002) and shape (Edelman, 1999).

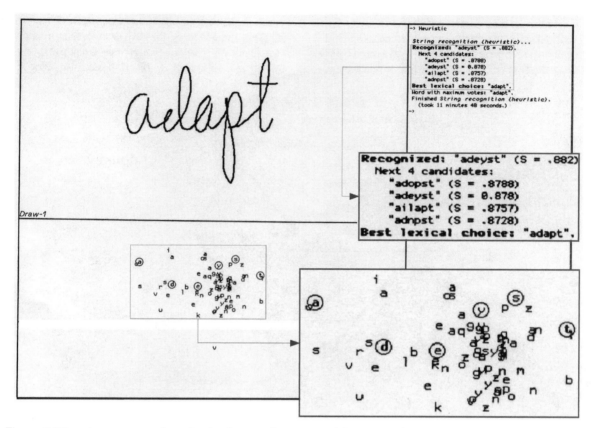

Figure 5.29 — A screen snapshot of an implemented computer vision system for reading cursive handwriting (Edelman et al., 1990), which exemplifies the kind of distributed representation that underlies all perception. The top left panel shows the stimulus: a cursive version of the word *adapt*, which activates a cloud of multiple instances of various letters in various locations. These are marked in the bottom left panel by appropriately positioned symbols. In the blow-up of that panel, the locally strongest instances are circled. Together, they spell *adeyst*, which makes perfect sense: each of the constituent letters is nearly perfectly instantiated in the stimulus, and together they cover all of it. When "top-down" (vocabulary) knowledge is allowed to be brought to bear, the outcome is *adapt*. Because this system processes and represents the stimulus as described, it **sees** it in the fullest possible sense of the word: **to see is to have access to an interpretable activation pattern of an ensemble of tuned units responding to the stimulus, each bearing information about both the shape and the location of some portion of it.**

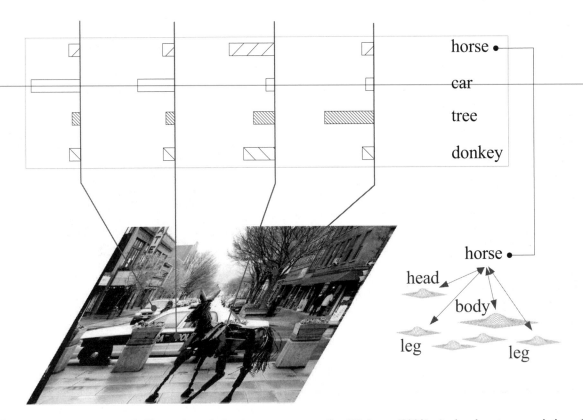

Figure 5.30 — A schematic illustration of what it means to see, after Edelman (2002). A visual system consisting of four kinds of tuned units (selective for horses, cars, trees, and donkeys) is shown responding to an urban scene. Observe the functional similarity between this scheme and the implemented system for reading cursive script described in Figure 5.29. *Left:* the responses of the various kinds of units are indicated for four locations. It is very important to note that systems relying on units that are broadly tuned to shape *and* to location (cf. Figure 5.28) are capable of responding in a useful manner to novel objects (which merely evoke a graded, distributed response, rather than causing a system crash). In contrast, an early commitment to a conceptual, all-or-none, language-like representation (such as the one in Magritte's *The uses of speech*, Figure 5.26 on page 138) bodes ill for the system's open-endedness and flexibility. *Right:* the structure of objects can be represented by joint activities of the same kind of shape-tuned, spatially localized "what+where" units, just as the structure of scenes is (Edelman and Intrator, 2000, 2003).

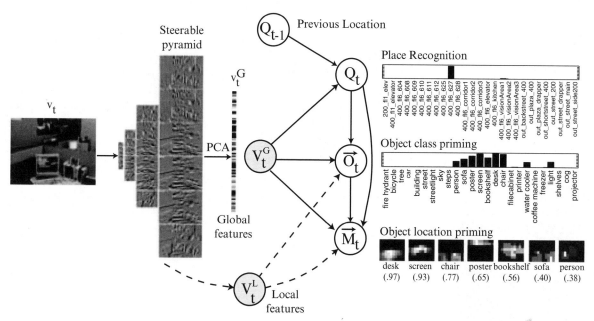

Figure 5.31 — Question: when the computer looks back on itself, what does its experience consist of? Answer: of a pattern of numbers generated across the FUNCTIONAL COUNTERPARTS TO THE GRADED "WHAT+WHERE" UNITS found in the brain (cf. Figures 5.28 and 5.30). This illustration from Torralba et al. (2003) shows an office scene (*left*) and its representation following probabilistic processing and recognition (*right*). The diagrams in the middle relate to the intermediate statistical representations maintained by Torralba's system and are too technical for us to go into (the computational principle this work relies on, BAYESIAN INFERENCE, is explained in broad outline in the box on p. 120 and in Appendix A). The mobile system has been taught to recognize about 60 indoors and outdoors locations and 20 object classes, and is capable of providing real-time feedback to the user about its current location and the scene it sees. In particular, it can both recognize familiar objects and locations, and categorize novel ones. The final product of vision here is threefold: (1) the recognition of the viewed room (*right*, top); (2) the graded activations of various familiar object classes by the current scene (*right*, middle), showing *what* the perceived objects are (screen, desk, and chair are the strongest hypotheses); (3) graded location maps, showing *where* the strongest-activated objects are (*right*, bottom).

from what it has encountered before. This point is made by Figure 5.30 on page 146, which offers a conceptual, schematic overview of the visual functions related to object recognition, scene interpretation, and qualia, or raw "feel" of seeing. It is further reinforced by Figure 5.31 on the previous page, in which a prototype general-purpose computer vision system is showcased that is built on the principle of statistical learning of distributed representations (Torralba et al., 2003).

Most of the algorithmic and implementational details and the massive amount of behavioral and neurobiological evidence supporting this overarching principle are hidden from sight in this chapter (as befits the level and the scope of this book). There also many issues that still need to be worked out to fill in the blank spots on the map. At the same time, the major features of the surrounding conceptual landscape do emerge from the fog. The vista that opens from where we are at the moment allows us to claim a general understanding of what makes perception possible, and, indeed, of what perception is all about. From here, it will also be easier to trek to the next summit, which rises above the perception plateau: memory.

Notes

[1] INATTENTIONAL BLINDNESS. Looking at objects that are embedded in a scene without actually seeing them happens much more often than one might imagine. This curious breakdown of visual awareness, called *inattentional blindness* (Mack, 2003), has more to do with consciousness than with perception as such; I shall return to it in section 9.7.2.

[2] The original of POLLOCK'S *Ocean greyness* is at the Guggenheim museum in New York City; see http://www.guggenheimlasvegas.org/artist_work_md_1297.html.

[3] BORGES IN ENGLISH. By far the best translation of the collection of stories in which *The Circular Ruins* appears is by Norman Thomas di Giovanni, produced in collaboration with Borges himself and now sadly out of print; see (Borges, 1970).

[4] MEASURING APPARENT SIZE. Objects of vastly different sizes can appear congruent if they are at vastly different distances from the observer. During a solar eclipse, for example, the Moon (diameter: 3,476 *km*) almost precisely overlaps the Sun (diameter: 1.4 million *km*), which, of course, is much farther away from the Earth. The proper way to measure or describe the *apparent* size of an object is by using angular or arc units: degrees, minutes, and seconds. As you would expect, there are $360°$ (degrees) of arc in a full circle; the Sun and the Moon both subtend an angle of $30'$ (minutes) of arc. The spatial resolution of human vision is quite high: the acuity of eagles and falcons is only about twice as good as ours.

[5]DIFFRACTION LIMIT. The size of the Airy pattern, and therefore the resolving power of a lens, is limited by diffraction to $\sin\theta = 1.22\frac{\lambda}{D}$, where θ is the smallest resolvable angular feature, λ is the wavelength of light used for imaging, and D is the diameter of the lens; note that a hi-res camera with a poor lens is a waste of money.

[6]RESPECTS FOR SIMILARITY. Similarity is a complicated topic. Its explanatory value in psychology is questioned by some, and asserted by many others. A good entry point into the vast literature on similarity is a research paper by Medin, Goldstone, and Gentner (1993) titled *Respects for similarity*. Similarity and its opposite, dissimilarity, as construed in this section are discussed on all the levels of Marr's hierarchy by Edelman (1998a, 1999).

[7]Formally, a function that computes the distance between two points given their coordinates is a METRIC if it satisfies the four conditions of nonnegativity, identity of indiscernibles, symmetry, and triangle inequality. The same space may admit many different metrics; changing the metric is equivalent to warping the space.

[8]This approach to shape description is akin to what the mechanical engineers call MODAL ANALYSIS (see http://www.sem.org/PUBS_ArtDownload.asp), and to Principal Component Analysis.

[9]The discipline of LINEAR ALGEBRA arose out of the need to solve systems of linear equations of the form

$$a_{11}x_1 + a_{12}x_2 + \ldots + a_{1n}x_n = b_1$$
$$a_{21}x_1 + a_{22}x_2 + \ldots + a_{2n}x_n = b_2$$
$$\ldots$$

In the case of color perception using three channels $\lambda_{1,2,3}$, there are three measurements per each surface point: $b_{1,2,3}$ and, correspondingly, three equations: $a_i x_i = b_i$ for each λ_i. Note that the number of unknowns per point in that case is six: $a_{1,2,3}$ and $x_{1,2,3}$.

[10]A sample ASSUMPTION given by Marr and Poggio for the problem of recovering the point-wise correspondences between left and right images in the context of binocular stereopsis (depth perception) is that of *uniqueness*, which states that a point on an object "out there" projects into exactly one point in each of the two images. Note that this assumption may be violated locally, e.g., for points that are occluded for one eye, but not for the other. Not surprisingly, a disambiguation algorithm that relies on the uniqueness assumption would, therefore, fail for such point. For more examples and a discussion, see Marr (1982, pp.112,219).

[11]A problem can also be ILL-POSED if it has no solutions, or if its solution varies too strongly with fluctuations in the data.

[12]REGULARIZATION is relevant to neural computation (Girosi et al., 1995) and has deep connections to statistical inference methods such as Bayes (see Appendix A), the Minimum Description Length principle, and cross-validation (Amari and Murata, 1997).

[13]Here is an example of the peculiar mixture of physics envy with a dismissal of physical reality that characterizes FORMAL GENERATIVE LINGUISTICS: "So far it seems to me to have been reasonably productive, to pretend that we are doing elementary particle physics. Yet, I think we ought to bear in mind that we might be going quite in the wrong direction, and that might show up, sooner or later. It would be unfortunate. [...] I think a linguist can do a perfectly good work in generative grammar without ever caring about questions of physical realism or what his work has to do with the structure of the mind" (Chomsky, 2004a, p.56). More on this in Chapter 7.

[14]Experiencing the WATERFALL ILLUSION is made all the more peculiar by the clear ab-

sence of any physical movement on the part of the stimulus, as if the scenery were moving and not moving at the same time.

[15]The precise values of the rotation angle often stated in reports about patients with WALLENBERG SYNDROME are meaningless: the debriefing procedure employed by the neuropsychologists who study such patients cannot result in such precision, and in any case the patients' tendency to categorize (e.g., by describing a diagonal tilt generically as 45° rather than 43° or 46°) would render any numerical report unreliable.

[16]On GENERALIZATION AND SIMILARITY. The problem of deciding when similarity holds and when it breaks down arises throughout cognition. Say, if my political thinking pivots on my country's socioeconomical situation, should I be alarmed when the top marginal tax rate drops from 34% to 25%? From 25% to 16%? When the prison population rises by 1.3% annually? By 2.6%?

[17]MULTIDIMENSIONAL SCALING (MDS) can be used to reconstruct an approximation to the geographical layout of some cities from a table that lists the driving distances between them. Here is an illustration from an old MDS software manual:

		1 BOST	2 NY	3 DC	4 MIAM	5 CHIC	6 SEAT	7 SF	8 LA	9 DENV
1	BOSTON	0	206	429	1504	963	2976	3095	2979	1949
2	NY	206	0	233	1308	802	2815	2934	2786	1771
3	DC	429	233	0	1075	671	2684	2799	2631	1616
4	MIAMI	1504	1308	1075	0	1329	3273	3053	2687	2037
5	CHICAGO	963	802	671	1329	0	2013	2142	2054	996
6	SEATTLE	2976	2815	2684	3273	2013	0	808	1131	1307
7	SF	3095	2934	2799	3053	2142	808	0	379	1235
8	LA	2979	2786	2631	2687	2054	1131	379	0	1059
9	DENVER	1949	1771	1616	2037	996	1307	1235	1059	0

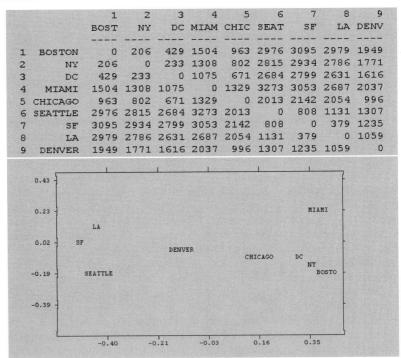

[18]The dependence on response time to a SAME/DIFFERENT decision on representation-space distance between the stimuli can be explained, on computational, behavioral, and neural levels, by an information accumulation model (Smith and Ratcliff, 2004). Intuitively, if the two test stimuli are closer (that is, more easily confusable), the information accumulation process takes longer to reach the level of reliability that allows a response to be made.

[19]The so-called NONMETRIC version of MDS (Shepard, 1980) can map the space in which

some points are embedded given just the *relative* distances between the points. In terms of the geographical example illustrated above, this means that the ranks of the distances between cities — that is, information of the kind "Boston is closer to New York than to Denver" — constrains the map sufficiently (when specified for enough point triplets) to allow its recovery. Nonmetric MDS is naturally more tolerant to noise in the data, and can be applied to direct measurements of brain activity, such as electrophysiological or fMRI data, to map the brain activation space (cf. Figure 5.20 on page 129).

[20]The parallel between the need for inferring an explanation from underdetermined data in paleontology and an analogous need that arises in perception has been drawn in the past by Hebb (1949, p.47) and by Neisser (1967, p.94).

[21]The degree of SPECIFICITY of learning to the stimulus set used in training varies across tasks and stimuli types. In some cases, ingenious behavioral experiments that measure specificity or transfer of learning across conditions can pinpoint the anatomical locus of the learning mechanism within the perceptual system. For example, vernier acuity learning does not transfer from one eye to the other; this suggests that it occurs early in the visual pathway, where the information from the two eyes is not yet integrated.

[22]Defining the "natural" or objective similarity between two objects specified by the coordinates of the points that comprise them is a tricky but feasible undertaking; see (Edelman, 1999, pp.49ff).

[23]In a poem titled *Koinophilia*, Richard Fein writes "Beauty is a regression to the mean" (http://darkplanet.basespace.net/poetry/koino.html). The poem's conclusion, which strikes me as both touching and true, is this:

> If beauty is truth, then truth is as common
> as the collective mother smiling down
> lovingly at her collective infant's face.

[24]Here is a summary of the EIGHTFOLD PATH to beauty according to Ramachandran and Hirstein (1999):

1. *Extremes.* The Peak Shift phenomenon: a perceiver that likes a stimulus which constitutes an exaggeration along some dimension relative to the mean will like even more an even stronger exaggeration along the same dimension. This phenomenon is related to the various caricature effects.

2. *Structural goodness.* Perceivers like stimuli that are good in the Gestalt sense (Köhler, 1947).

3. *Unidimensionality.* Stimuli that stand out in a single visual modality are better at capturing the perceivers' attention and are better liked.

4. *Contrast.* Stimuli in which strong features emerge prior to grouping (thus increasing the contrast) are liked.

5. *Challenge.* Perceivers like stimuli that require them to engage in perceptual problem solving (of which grouping is a simple example).

6. *Genericity.* Stimuli whose most natural interpretation is generic in the sense that it avoids statistically suspicious coincidences (Barlow, 1990) are liked.

7. *Metaphoricity.* Situations in which hidden connections between different parts or aspects of the stimulus are revealed are liked.

8. *Symmetry.* This has been discussed in the main text of the chapter.

[25] A propos cross-corpora CARICATURING in the domain of the performing arts, see Michael Palin impersonating Cardinal Richelieu (a dead French cardinal), who is in turn impersonating Petula Clark (a British singer), in *Monty Python's Flying Circus*, Episode 13.

[26] THE CRUX OF CREATIVITY: Hofstadter's intuition, rooted in computational considerations, is consistent with cognitive data distilled from many case studies of creativity (Weisberg, 1986). More on this in sections 8.5.2 and 8.5.3.

[27] The necessary turn to brain-based SUBJECTIVITY here anticipates the usual complaints about perfection being impossible to objectify by revealing this impossibility for what it really is: not an option that a theorist of aesthetics may accept or reject, but rather a fundamental constraint of human nature. Note, however, that as the means are likely to be less different across observers than the exemplars they have been exposed to, one would expect that mean-related aspects of beauty be less subjective than others, as indeed is the case in face perception.

[28] There is evidence that successful accounting for a visual stimulus in terms of the potential known causes — what the statisticians call EXPLAINING AWAY — causes the activity in the human primary visual cortex to be reduced (Murray, Kersten, Olshausen, Schrater, and Woods, 2002). Given that familiarity breeds quiescence, yearning for NOVELTY on a neuronal level is compatible with the need of neurons to be active in order to survive. A glimpse of the mechanisms whereby the activity of a neuron helps it to stay alive can be found in a paper by Watt, Sakano, Lee, Reusch, Trinh, and Storm (2004), who showed that odorants enhance the survival of olfactory neurons (related findings have been reported for many other brain structures).

[29] As personality psychologists like to point out, the desire for novelty is what keeps the pornographers in business: in much the same way a sexually arousing image ceases to be effective after some time.

[30] My insistence on describing computers in print as really seeing (even if only to a limited extent at present) gets me into trouble with those editors who have a predilection to place "see" in scare quotes when referring to non-biological entities. As Turing (1950) predicted, such behavior (which I call neural chauvinism) will eventually disappear from civilized society.

[31] QUALIA AND EXPERIENCE. Here are John Locke's closing remarks on MOLYNEUX'S PROBLEM (cf. Figure 5.27 on page 140):

> This I have set down, and leave with my reader, as an occasion for him to consider how much he may be beholden to experience, improvement, and acquired notions, where he thinks he had not the least use of, or help from them.
>
> — Locke (1690, ii.ix.8)

[32] In colloquial usage, the word "SENTIENT" is rapidly becoming synonymous with "intelligent"; here, I stick to its original primary meaning, which is "feeling" (Clark, 2000).

[33] Marr's FUNDAMENTAL HYPOTHESIS can be compared to "the single most important principle underlying the mechanisms of perception and conscious experience: that they may have evolved exclusively for extracting statistical regularities from the natural world" (Ramachandran and Hirstein, 1997, p.453).

[34] FOCUS ON SHAPE. I have not included in this chapter any others of the standard textbook topics in perception (for instance, color, motion, texture, stereo), simply because the principles stated here cover them as well. One special topic, attention, will be treated in Chapter 9, along with perceptual awareness and consciousness.

[35]The scheme outlined in Figure 5.29 on page 145 resembles the venerable PANDEMONIUM model of pattern recognition, proposed by Selfridge (1959). As shown in this illustration from the *Human Information Processing* by Lindsay and Norman (1972), an outstanding psychology textbook, a Pandemonium consists of several stages of processing:

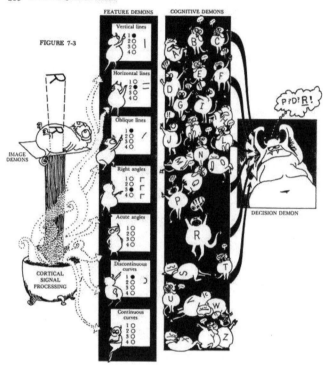

The first-stage "demons" seek patterns in the input feature space; demons higher up in the hierarchy seek patterns of patterns, etc. The master demon at the top categorizes the stimulus on the basis of the information contained in the "shouts" (responses) of the lower-rank demons (neurons). Selfridge's model was merely schematic, but it served as an important conceptual starting point for the development of the explicit and detailed neurocomputational "Chorus of Prototypes" model of object recognition by Edelman (1999), and, before that, of the Probabilistic Pandemonium idea of Barlow (1990). In the Probabilistic Pandemonium, each tuned neuron's firing rate is proportional to the statistical likelihood of the hypothesis that the input matches its optimal stimulus. This makes it an excellent example of a model that conforms to the principles of neural computation in perception, as spelled out in the present chapter.

6

Memory

No, no!... O vex no more, no more, those memories!
Sombre lily!

from *The Young Fate*
PAUL VALÉRY

U NLIKE patterns of dry ink on paper, of cuneiform indentations on a clay
tablet, or of magnetic flux frozen into the surface of a computer disk,
memories that reside in a living brain have a life of their own. Some will
hover sombrely[1] in the shadows, waiting to snap back at the slightest provo-
cation; some will wander off when set free, never to be heard of again; some
will come and go at your bidding; and some will lie low and ignore attempted
recall, only to emerge triumphantly when least expected.

Shedding light on the secret life of memories is central to the understanding of cognition because memory occupies such a prominent place in the theory of computation. As you may recall from Chapter 2, a memory "tape"
is one of the two functional components of the universal abstract model of
digital computation, the Turing Machine, the other one being a table that
maps combinations of internal states and inputs (tape symbols) onto successor states and outputs (tape symbols). Strip a Turing Machine of its tape, and
you are left with a memory-less automaton, which knows what state it is in,
but not, for example, how it got there. Behaviorally, such a system is clump of
hard-wired slavish reflexes, a circuit that is doomed for all eternity to retrace
the same set of tracks through the space of input-state-output combinations.

Even mollusks are smarter than that. In the sea hare *Aplysia*, which we
met on p. 21, the strength of the reflex that makes it withdraw its gill when its
siphon is touched diminishes with repeated stimulation, and recovers when
the stimulation ceases. Such memories are never mere passive records of
past experience. It would be very misleading to say that the *Aplysia* consults
its memory store and acts on the basis of the retrieved information. The

Dante Gabriel Rossetti's painting
of MNEMOSYNE — in the Greek
pantheon, the goddess of memory
and the mother of the nine muses.

155

representations that form a memory trace are *active* and require no mediation on the part of some central controller to have an effect. The mollusk's nervous system remembers what has been happening to it, and that memory directly shapes its behavior.

Predispositions to action are precisely what constitutes the personality of a sea hare, insofar as it can be said to have one. These predispositions — patterns of action, or programs, ready to be triggered by external or internal stimuli — are embodied in a species- and individual-specific substrate and are formed by memories of prior experience and action that have been filtered through the statistical mechanisms of perceptual learning. With the appropriate allowance for differences of scale and complexity, the same characterization applies to humans.   In an important sense, and to a significant extent, **your memories are what you are.**[2]

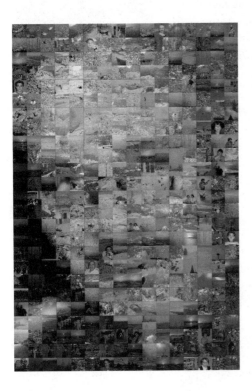

Figure 6.1 — The LABYRINTH OF MEMORY. Approximating the image of a person's face by a mosaic of snapshots from his digital photo archive (which is how this image was produced) is a fitting, even if too straightforward, illustration for this passage from the epilogue to *The Maker* by Jorge Luis Borges: "A man sets himself the task of portraying the world. Over the years he fills a given surface with images of provinces and kingdoms, mountains, bays, ships, islands, fish, rooms, instruments, heavenly bodies, horses and people. Shortly before he dies he discovers that this patient labyrinth of lines is a drawing of his own face." In the last story Borges ever wrote, *Shakespeare's Memory*, the spell is broken; the metaphor shifts and dissolves, leaving not a wrack behind: *"A man's memory is not a summation; it is a chaos of vague possibilities."* In this and other stories, Borges, an admirer of William James and his *Principles of Psychology* (1890), set the agenda for generations of psychologists with a few well-chosen words.

6.1 Memory: a bestiary

Being so central to the human experience, memory has always attracted the attention of poets, philosophers, and, more recently, psychologists. Their relentless scrutiny brought about an overwhelming descriptive diversity. Much like the medieval European bestiaries — lavishly illustrated catalogs of animals ranging from merely exotic (giraffe, ostrich) to imaginary (unicorn, basilisk) — common lists of memory phenomena are long, entertaining, and sometimes quite far removed from reality. For decades, major distinctions between kinds of memory — short-term vs. long-term, episodic vs. semantic, declarative vs. procedural — motivated by behavioral findings have been introduced and maintained with little regard to the use of memory in real life, to the computational principles that govern memory, and to the neural mechanisms that implement it. These distinctions are constantly being augmented by new phenomena and "effects," often stemming from and specific to a particular experimental setting. In view of this descriptive complexity, the opening line of the four-chapter treatment of memory by Lindsay and Norman (1972, p.287) — "It is a mistake to think of human memory as a unitary thing" — seems like an understatement.

MARR'S LEVELS revisited. Note how the function-level observation – your memory is what you are – complements Francis Crick's implementation-level "astonishing hypothesis" (Chapter 4), which identifies you with your brain. To test whether you understand the full import of these statements, verify that you find the use of the possessive pronoun "your" in "your brain" or "your memories" jarring.

The apparent diversity of memory phenomena, which drives a proliferation of theories and models, stands in a stark contrast with the monolithic conceptual foundation of memory study. For thousands of years, the dominant functional metaphor for memory has been *storage*. In ancient Greece, information could be stored on wax tablets; nowadays storage and subsequent retrieval are typically envisaged as consigning a document to a computer memory and bringing it up on the screen later (Figure 6.2). No matter how information is in fact stored, there is an incongruity between the unity of the storage metaphor on the one hand and the multifaceted descriptions and theories of memory on the other hand. It is as if the composer of a bestiary added a postscript note remarking that all the strange animals listed in it are really the same wind-up toy wearing different skins.

How can this paradox be resolved? Within the Marr-Poggio framework, a misguided computational-level analysis, simple as it may be, would stymie understanding on algorithmic and implementational levels: if the problem is not what you think it is, its different manifestations may seem to require distinct algorithms (or theories), let alone implementations (or models). A moment's reflection reveals that the storage metaphor *is* in fact a kind of overarching computational hypothesis about *what memory is for*. We cannot hope to answer the other two key questions about it — *how memory works*, and *what memory is made of* — without getting the first one right. I begin, therefore, by examining the storage metaphor and the manner in which it has traditionally affected studies of memory and their interpretation.

6.2   Memory is for interaction with the world

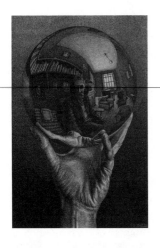

Hand with Reflecting Sphere by Maurits Escher. To the extent that your memory is what you are, recollection is always an exercise in SELF-KNOWLEDGE. The line from Valéry's *Young Fate* that reads

Souviens-toi de toi-même
("Recollect yourself")

echoes the Delphic Oracle's motto that opened this book.

In Plato's *Theaetetus* (360BCE), memory is likened to a block of wax on which impressions can be made with a stylus or a seal — an analogy that neatly covers memorization (writing), remembering (reading), and forgetting (erasure). Although analogy can be a useful expository tool in the hands of an expert, it is never a substitute for a real explanation. When Socrates tells Theaetetus "I would have you imagine, then, that there exists in the mind of man a block of wax," he is merely invoking a metaphor that suits his momentary purpose, which happens to be the possibility of false knowledge; when his attention shifts to the issue of remembering, the metaphor becomes that of a birdcage or aviary, where memories are birds that may be kept captive by their owner, but will not always come when called. From this, we may learn that memory is like a wax tablet in some respects, and an aviary in others, which leaves us at best right where we started, and at worst (if some of the metaphors are misleading) sets us back from the goal of understanding.[3]

As usually in science, here too the possibility of progress depends on finding patterns in data. Importantly, progress can also be made by discovering patterns in theories that cover clusters of seemingly disparate phenomena, or, in a less mature domain of inquiry where real theories are scarce, even in metaphors invoked to describe the data. In the case at hand, we may observe

Figure 6.2 — The standard METAPHOR FOR MEMORY has not changed over the past two millennia: since the age of Plato, memory has been traditionally — and ultimately misleadingly, as the present chapter shows — likened to writing. This painting from an ancient Greek vase depicts, at the center, a standing student facing an instructor who is using a stylus to write on what must be a wax tablet, but looks suspiciously like a open notebook computer.

that the wax tablet and the aviary, along with all the other metaphors for memory — a scroll or a book, a photographic plate, a hologram (Draaisma, 2000) — are essentially the same in one key respect; they all assume a particular answer as to what memory is for: storage and retrieval. This standard answer is usually taken for granted — so much so that the question itself (surely the most important of all in relation to memory) tends to be absent from theoretical discourse. In this chapter, I follow the lead of Barsalou (1999); Glenberg (1997); Neisser (1982), and others in adopting a different view of memory, one that is both more natural and wider in its explanatory scope:

> The basic claim is that an individual's memory serves perception and action.
>
> — Glenberg (1997)

The idea that the function of memory is to support the organism's interaction with the world is fully compatible with the central tenet of this book: that the representational mind is a computational tool for forethought (cf. Chapter 2). Effective interaction with the world in which the mind's embodiment is situated requires taking into account past interactions: stimuli, actions, and their outcomes. Making past interactions available in some form or other is what memory is for. To understand this better, we need a list (even a partial one would do) of the kinds of memory-assisted interaction with the environment that an animal may engage in.

Memories of interaction with entire stimuli. The need to remember the VALUE, positive or negative, of a stimulus (which may remain unanalyzed) against a possible repeat encounter with it is the most basic function of memory, found in all animals. Its common form is an association between the stimulus and a plan for action, rudimentary as it may be (as in "turn around and run as fast as you can").

Memories of interaction with structured environments. For animals with any degree of perceptual sophistication, stimuli are framed by *context*; indeed, in certain tasks such as NAVIGATION, context actually defines the meaning of a stimulus (landmarks such as a corner of a room for a rat or a hilltop for a hiker are meaningful only when considered in a wider setting). A plan for navigation is a structured memory trace tying sequences of perceptual inputs to sequences of motor commands. Likewise, the outcome of a navigation event is a structured memory trace tying situations to the *episodic* details of the evoked experiences.

Memories of interaction with structured situations. When generalized as statistically appropriate, episodic memories give rise to a system of CONCEPTS. The capacity to distill an interlinked, hierarchically structured system of concepts from statistical regularities boosts the powers of foresight of a cognitive agent and makes possible an especially effective interaction with the world.

Memories of self. A sufficiently powerful embodied mind is bound to discover the special status of one object in its environment: its own body. Memories of events that befall this privileged object would seem to deserve a special treatment. In a language-capable species, the resulting AUTOBIOGRAPHICAL MEMORY contributes to the emergence and maintenance of a NARRATIVE SELF.

Memories of interaction with other agents. To anticipate the behavior of predators (and, if applicable, prey) and potential mates, animals resort to modeling their minds. A model of a mind has at its core a bundle of memories linking stimuli to potential response behaviors and is thus an extension of a model of an inanimate object. In humans, a well-developed THEORY OF MIND is a representational skill that is critical for the integration of the individual into the society, and, in some cases, for his or her very survival.

In the next several sections (6.3 through 6.6), I shall analyze these functions of memory in computational terms, illustrating the main ideas with the help of representative behavioral findings. The remainder of the chapter will then be spent on discussing processes that use memory. The task of drawing parallels between this computational account and the burgeoning literature on memory — "an essentially arbitrary set of data" that "no theory can be expected to integrate" (Neisser, 1982, p.xii) — is left as an exercise for the interested reader.

6.3   Simple memory for entire stimuli

The simplest kind of memory one can imagine (and the only kind for which the standard storage/retrieval metaphor may be appropriate) performs approximately the same function as the memory card in your digital camera. When you take a snapshot, the camera writes the image generated by the sensor, pixel by pixel, into an array of minuscule memory cells, by modifying their electrical properties. The data can then be accessed by electrically querying the cells, one after another, and, if necessary, erased by applying an appropriate voltage to each cell. The memory chip thus remembers the signal (literally, not metaphorically!) and can reproduce it on demand (see Figure 6.3).

What I just described is *simple memory* (a term coined by Marr, 1971): the datum to be stored is treated as a whole, and no attempt is made to analyze it. This should not be taken to mean that the datum (which may be very complicated – think of a high-resolution snapshot of a landscape) *cannot* be analyzed: it's just that the function of simple memory does not extend beyond holistic storage and retrieval.

Simple memory is found in all animals — and in just about any artificial device that has to do with computation. The physical substrate onto which memory is imprinted does not, of course, matter in the least to its function. Suppose for simplicity that the gill withdrawal circuit in the *Aplysia* has just one modifiable synapse that supports the habituation of the withdrawal reflex (cf. p. 21). It can then be viewed as a simple memory with a 1-bit capacity. Now, if I equip each one of eight billion snails with a means for sensing gill position, and wire the snails up so as to allow the poking of each one's siphon, I can substitute the resulting bionic contraption for the gigabyte-capacity memory card that came with my new camera. Because reflex habituation is relatively short-lived, the snail farm will only remember the data I send its way for a short time. Nevertheless, from the standpoint of simple memory function (storage and retrieval), the bionic implementation would do the job.

In my digital camera, the memory chip is only good for one thing: storing the images until they can be offloaded somewhere else, for example to my notebook. Marr (1971) considered such simple memory, a function that in the mammalian brain is carried out by the HIPPOCAMPUS, as a front end to all kinds of processing. Of these, the simplest kind merely tags entire memory traces by adding to each literally one bit of information, signifying its value (if a finer distinction than that between positive and negative stimuli is required, more bits must be used).

Where does value information come from? The only kinds of stimuli that have intrinsic value are those that directly cause pain (for example, a tactile encounter with a sharp object, such as a leopard's teeth). In the state of nature, such an event is usually a one-time experience for the animal: a monkey that meets a leopard will not be in a position to benefit from remembering the circumstances that led to the occasion, or to exercise any other kind of cogni-

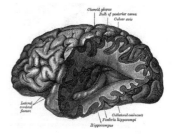

The location in the human brain of the HIPPOCAMPUS (which looks like a sausage in this drawing from Gray's *Anatomy*).

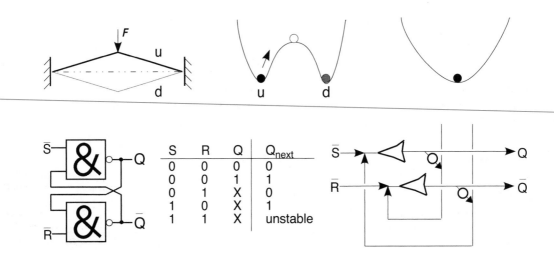

Figure 6.3 — Memory is a very common phenomenon in the physical world: any device that can be made to enter and remain in one of several possible states keeps a record of its last effective interaction with the rest of the universe. Three KINDS OF MEMORY cells — mechanical, electrical, and neural — are illustrated here; each has a capacity of one bit of information. *Top left:* the Mises strut is formed by two joined beams that are hinged to restraints; vertical force can cause the strut to snap into one of the two stable configurations, u or d. The middle configuration (indicated by the dotted line), in which both beams are compressed, is *metastable*: any slight displacement causes the strut to leave it. *Top middle:* a plot of the potential energy of the Mises strut (with the vertical displacement on the abscissa) has two troughs corresponding to the two stable states; the metastable state is in the middle. *Top right:* if the combined length of the two beams equals the separation between the restraints, the system possesses a single stable state; vertical displacement in this case causes beam tension that generates a restoring force. *Bottom left:* an electronic circuit that implements a so-called S-R (set-reset) latch. It is composed of two NAND units, each of which takes a logical AND of its inputs and negates the result; its output is 0 if and only if both inputs are 1. Because of the feedback connections between the units, the system has two stable states: if the output Q is set to 1 by applying 1 to S, or equivalently 0 to S̄ (the bar indicates complementation), it remains in that state until a reset signal is applied through the R input. *Bottom middle:* the full truth table for the S-R latch, showing the output for each possible combination of inputs. *Bottom right:* an idealized neural network equivalent to the S-R circuit. It is composed of two excitatory cells (triangles; as in pyramidal neurons, their outputs are on the base side) and two inhibitory cells (circles). In a seminal paper, McCulloch and Pitts (1943) proved that such neural networks are equivalent in their computational power to logic circuits, and, given an external storage "tape," to Turing Machines. The functional equivalence of the three kinds of 1-bit memory shown here illustrates MULTIPLE REALIZABILITY — a key property of computational systems, which I highlighted in Chapter 1.

tive sophistication. Memory can, however, be useful in every situation where one stimulus (say, the appearance *A* of a bitter fruit) carries some information about another one (the fruit's bitter taste *T*).

In computational terms, such informativeness is expressed by the conditional probability of the taste *T* given the appearance *A*, denoted as $P(T|A)$, being different from the unconditional or "marginal" probability, $P(T)$. If such probability calculation (carried out by neurons as a matter of routine; cf. section 3.3.3) warrants it, the memory of *A* should thus be *associated* with the memory of *T* — or even just its negative value — so that a subsequent visual encounter with the fruit will evoke the memory of its bitterness, sparing the animal the need to taste it again.

Animals are very good at associating VALUE with a stimulus: for example, monkeys quickly learn which abstract novel image is likely to be followed by a puff of air and which – by a drop of fruit juice (Paton, Belova, Morrison, and Salzman, 2006).

6.3.1 Associative memory

The preceding example focused on simple memory to illustrate the importance of the function of ASSOCIATION; a little reflection will convince you that all other kinds of memory need it too. The centrality of association in cognition stems from its reliance on conditional probability as the evidential basis. In that, associative memory is intimately related to perceptual learning (Chapter 5) and, as we shall see later, to language acquisition (Chapter 7).[4] Let us try to understand what it means computationally for memory to be associative.

One may imagine that the prototypical computational model of memory, the Turing Machine tape, would go a long way in explaining associative storage, but that is not the case. To retrieve (read) a symbol from the tape, the program must know its *address*: the number of the cell in which it resides; for an item that consists of many symbols, in the same way that an image consists of many pixels, the address of a block of cells is needed. What about the associative memory tasks? A simple memory system may need, for example, to store an item and later retrieve it for processing (or even just to determine whether this item has been encountered before); this is AUTOASSOCIATIVE recall. Or, a system may associate one item with another, and then expect to be able to retrieve the second one given the first one as a cue; this is known as HETEROASSOCIATIVE recall. In neither case are the addresses dictated by the task itself: the user of the memory system (e.g., another brain subsystem) could not care less about addresses; what it is after is content.

Content-based recall is the rule in biological memory systems, but still quite an exception in artificial ones. This does not mean, of course, that to

AUTOASSOCIATIVE RECALL is characterized by the retrieval of an entire record, given its part that serves as the key, as in the old Latin saying *ex ungue leonem* — "[you can tell] the lion by its claws." The Droodle shown above exemplifies recognizing the whole from its part. If you cannot make it out, think of the most famous Muppet marriage ("Because your love is so big, I now pronounce you frog and ___"; that turns the task into HETEROASSOCIATIVE RECALL, though).

The notebook I am using to write these lines has very good memory. Clicking on the magnifying glass icon in the upper right corner of my screen brings up a dialog box; when I start typing in a search keyword, the machine immediately begins generating a list of files with matching content, which becomes more to the point with every keystroke, often converging faster than I can type. To carry out this task, which essentially implements the autoassociative memory functionality, the software computes an index of all the files stored in the system, keyed to every item contained in every file. Although all the words in a text may be indexed, just a few usually suffice to single out a usefully short list of candidate files in response to a query (this is not a miracle: partial keywords are indexed). All this indexing is extra work, which happens to be necessary simply because the underlying address-based memory mechanism that is implemented by contemporary computer hardware is in its raw form unsuitable for associative storage or recall.

open a file on a notebook the user must tell the operating system where to find it on the disk; the computer translates the name it is given into an internally maintained address, which, mercifully, it keeps hidden from the user. Still, the user has to remember the file name, which is an entirely ridiculous requirement, given the comparative capacity, speed, and reliability of artificial and human memory (very high and very low, respectively, on all counts).

There exist computational approaches to memory in which associative functioning is the natural mode of operation.[5] Consider the circuit shown in Figure 6.4, middle. It consists of two neurons, each receiving as input some external signals, as well as their own outputs that loop back on themselves. As the anatomical drawing of Figure 6.4, left, suggests, such circuits are in fact found in the hippocampus; cf. the crossbar circuit of Figure 3.10 on page 54 (see Hopfield, 1982; Willshaw, Buneman, and Longuet-Higgins, 1969 for early computational models of associative memory based on this circuit architecture).

Because of the presence of feedback connections, networks such as this one are capable of supporting rather complex dynamics. For example, upon receiving an input, the network may enter a period of "settling in" during which its instantaneous state ascribes a trajectory through the state space (whose dimensionality, as explained in Chapter 3, is equal to the number of neurons), finally reaching an equilibrium, or an ATTRACTOR state. With the synaptic weights set to proper values through learning, the effects of input and of intrinsic (feedback) activation can be balanced so that the network comes to possess several equilibria, each of which is only reachable from a distinct class of inputs.

Clearly, the resulting attractor network is a *categorization* device. At the same time, it also implements simple associative memory, by mapping each input — which can be fully described as an ordered list of initial neuron activation values, or, equivalently, as a point in the state space — to an equilibrium-state attractor (similarly described). Each of the attractors thus corresponds to a particular memory maintained by the network.

6.3.2   Attractor dynamics

All the potential behaviors of a particular attractor network can be conveniently described by specifying its *energy surface*, which assigns a number ("height") to each point in the state space; if the network has just two neurons, the result is a surface over a two-dimensional plane (cf. Figure 6.4, right; the terminology is borrowed from classical mechanics, where dynamical systems may be described in terms of their potential energy). When visualized in the form of an energy surface, network dynamics are easy to understand: just think of a ball that is released at a point corresponding to the input and that starts rolling downhill until it reaches a local minimum — an attractor.[6]

In a properly trained network, the energy surface is smooth and each equilibrium state has a wide *basin of attraction*; every input that falls within it will cause the network to end up in the same steady state. Functionally, this behavior is precisely what categorization is about. Furthermore, if a network trained on a few inputs generates wide basins of attraction, it will thereby become capable of generalization: the response (equilibrium state) to a stimulus

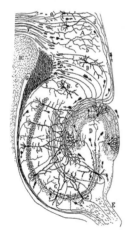
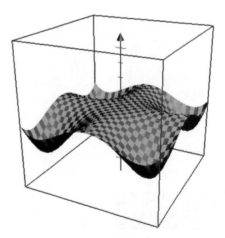

Figure 6.4 — *Left:* the neural circuitry of the rodent HIPPOCAMPUS, hand-drawn by Santiago Ramón y Cajal (from *Histologie du Systeme Nerveux de l'Homme et des Vertebretes*, A. Maloine, Paris, 1911). *Middle:* a simple, two-neuron autoassociative ATTRACTOR NETWORK modeled on the CA1-CA3 hippocampal circuit (reproduced from Stringer, Rolls, and Trappenberg, 2005). Note how the projections of the two cells (denoted by the black dots) turn back and connect to the inputs of those same cells, forming the kind of feedback circuit found in the real hippocampus shown on the left (cf. also Figure 6.3 on page 162, bottom). *Right:* a cartoon illustration of the ENERGY LANDSCAPE of a two-neuron attractor network. The horizontal plane represents the activities of the two neurons; the height of the surface stands for the potential energy of the circuit. The shape of the energy surface indicates that the system has four stable equilibrium states or attractors (corresponding to the four potential wells), as well as a metastable equilibrium point at the center of the plane. See text for further explanations.

will be extended to others, provided that they are sufficiently similar — that is, close in the representation space — to the original one.

Conceptualizing biological memory in this manner works because its basic functionality, associative storage/recall, can be implemented by any multistable dynamical system, and because all such systems, including the mechanical and electrical ones illustrated in Figure 6.3 on page 162, possess a natural mathematical description in terms of energy surfaces. Of all the possible implementations of dynamical multi-stability, the one most relevant to brains is, of course, a network of neuron-like elements; hence my use of network terminology in Figure 6.4 on the previous page.

The energy surface concept relies heavily on the notion of state space that I had introduced in Chapter 3 and subsequently used in reasoning about categorization and related topics in Chapter 5. As a theoretical tool, it is fundamentally abstract-computational, even when illustrated on the implementation level on concrete examples (neural networks). To demonstrate its generality, I shall now use the energy surface concept to sketch a computational analysis of memory that underlies motor control (Wise and Shadmehr, 2002).

The need for MOTOR MEMORY, which shares its main characteristics with other kinds of memory (Krakauer and Shadmehr, 2006), can be demonstrated with a simple postural task: positioning one's wristwatch to tell the time. To make the face of the watch visible, your must set the two relevant variables — the shoulder and elbow angles (q_1 and q_2 in Figure 6.5, left) — just so; make an error in q_2, and you may sweep your coffee mug off the table or punch yourself in the face (unless, of course, q_1 too is set to a wrong value, in which case you'll end up hugging yourself or punching someone else in the face).

Research shows that performance even in the simplest motor tasks, such as setting the elbow angle, improves with practice (Gottlieb, Corcos, Jaric, and Agarwal, 1988). Thus, the settings of q_1 and q_2 are actively controlled only on the first few occasions in your life of using a wristwatch; very soon, the memory of the optimal time-reading position of the arm developed through motor learning takes over. What form would this memory take? As with any other joints, the control of shoulder and elbow involves the activity of two groups of muscles: the agonists and the antagonists (for the elbow joint, these are the biceps and the triceps). The goal of imposing a particular posture on the arm translates therefore into the need to set the tension (STIFFNESS) of agonist and antagonist muscles to proper values.

Motor control involves planning the desired movement and coordinating the forces needed to execute it. Although much of the information relied upon by motor system — especially for locomotion, orientation and reproduction — is innate, individuals must acquire and store MOTOR MEMORIES during their lifetimes (Wise and Shadmehr, 2002). In limb control, these take the form of activation values for *agonist-antagonist* muscle pairs, as illustrated here.

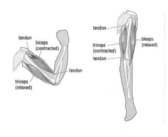

The role of antagonistically induced STIFFNESS in setting and maintaining arm posture, as demonstrated by Peter Sellers in Stanley Kubrik's film *Dr. Strangelove or: How I Learned to Stop Worrying and Love the Bomb*.

To maintain the posture, the muscles, which act like springs, resist any deviation from it (to see that they do, take your cue from Dr. Strangelove: position your watch hand so that you can tell the time, and try to deflect it using your other hand). Thus, any static posture can be viewed as an *equilibrium* point — an attractor in an abstract representation space in which the combined potential energy of the muscles is plotted as a surface against the attempted displacement, as depicted in Figure 6.5. Computationally, therefore, postural memory takes the form of an association between (i) the desired joint configuration and (ii) the vector of muscle tensions that together induce the equilibrium-restoring force field, or, equivalently, create an energy surface centered around an attractor.

6.3.3 Memory for sequences

In fidgety species such as ourselves and our fellow primates, periods of posture change — movement — are as common as episodes of posture maintenance. In comparison to posture, in the control of movement precision needs to be achieved not only in space, but also in time. This observation suggests the possibility of controlling movement by enforcing a properly ordered

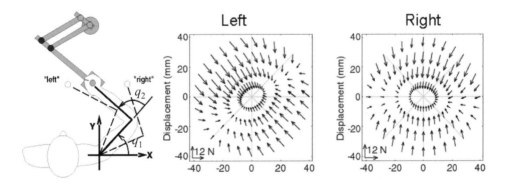

Figure 6.5 — Arm position, represented here by the shoulder and elbow angles, q_1 and q_2, can be controlled by setting the EQUILIBRIUM point of the arm musculature. *Left:* the restoring force generated by a subject's arm can be measured by a robotic manipulator that attempts to displace it from the equilibrium position. *Center and right:* Maps showing the force fields generated by the arm in the two configurations indicated in the left panel. The figures are from the supplementary material to Shadmehr and Wise (2005).

and timed sequence of postures, each realized as a METASTABLE equilibrium (Figure 6.6). The notion that the dynamics of motor control in humans operates on this principle is known as the *equilibrium trajectory* hypothesis (Flash, 1987; Shadmehr, 1995).

The computational goal of a metastable motion controller is to SHAPE the energy landscape (by synergistically activating the muscles) so that not only the final state (posture) but also the intermediate states of the system are put to use. When motion is triggered, the system state begins to traverse the trajectory prepared for it. This process may be visualized as a ball representing the instantaneous state that is rolling or hurtling, as the case may be, towards an attractor, which corresponds to the final state. This view of motor control is supported by the findings from an electrophysiological study of the motor cortex in monkeys performing natural arm movements (Aflalo and Graziano, 2006). Neurons in this area were found to be tuned to the multijoint posture attained by the arm at the end of each movement. Moreover, the postures to which the neurons selectively responded matched those evoked by electrical stimulation of the same cortical sites (Graziano, Taylor, Moore, and Cooke, 2002).[7]

If motion is viewed as a succession of postures, it can be controlled by SHAPING the dynamics of the system so that it follows the proper sequence of states, rolling down the energy landscape from one state to the next.

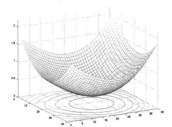
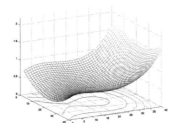
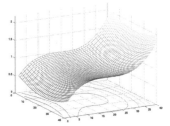

Figure 6.6 — An equilibrium point is METASTABLE if small perturbations or momentum acting in the right direction cause the system to leave it (a stable equilibrium, in comparison, is insensitive to any small perturbation). *Left:* a stable attractor. *Middle:* a transition to a metastable attractor, obtained from the stable one by changing one of the parameters that determine the shape of the potential energy surface. *Right:* a further change in the same parameter makes the equilibrium disappear; when initialized at the top right, the system's state will now "slide" downhill without pausing. The importance of stability and metastability in theories of motor control is discussed by Bressler and Kelso (2001).

6.3.4 Learning and using the dynamics

We have just seen two examples of the use of the concept of energy landscape in gaining computational understanding of the dynamics of memory-related systems. The first one focused on neural networks; the coordinates of the representation space over which energy surface was defined in that example corresponded to the activities of neurons. The second one had to do with the dynamics of skeleto-muscular systems; there, the representation space pertained to the individual muscle stiffness values. In each case, the shape of the energy surface determined the dynamics: when started off at an elevated point, the system proceeds to minimize its potential energy by having the state "roll downhill" following the steepest descent trajectory until it reaches a stable attractor.

To put to use the dynamics of memory systems — whether just the attractor states or entire trajectories that encode sequences as successions of particular states, attained in a particular order and time schedule — it is necessary to mold the energy surface (Newell, Liu, and Mayer-Kress, 2001). Functionally, the shaping of the energy surface corresponds to storing information into the system; subsequently, this information can be recalled by starting the network off from an appropriate initial state.

In practice, shaping the energy surface of a dynamical system is a complicated business. In neural networks, learning algorithms charged with adjusting the weights while being fed the training data must balance several computational requirements, such as speed of learning (storage) and operation (recall), retention, and capacity. Some of these conflict with each other. High capacity, in particular, requires that the network be composed of many neurons, which brings about the usual problems that beset high-dimensional representation spaces. The search for good attractors is much more difficult when there are too many degrees of freedom — weights that may have to be modified — are present. In another example, an agile, fast-learning network that is quick to change its weights in response to a new input is likely to be more prone to forgetting than one that learns more slowly. Massive displacement of old memories by new ones that is characteristic of many network training algorithms has been appropriately termed *catastrophic forgetting* (French, 1999).

The difficulties arising in imparting the desired dynamics to a memory system can be alleviated to some extent by adopting a training schedule that includes ample time for the CONSOLIDATION of new memories. If not given

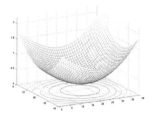

Because the energy landscape in a real brain network is high-dimensional and much more complex than the schematic illustration shown *above*, equilibrium states found at the bottom of attractors usually come in clusters that consist of many neighboring equilibria with similar energy values, as shown *below* — just as for any neuron with a given perceptual tuning there are always many others with very similar receptive fields. Hence a general principle: in real brains, memory traces are neither absolutely "crisp" nor unique.

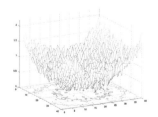

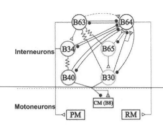

A schematic of the hierarchical, modular neural network that encodes motor programs for biting in *Aplysia* (from Jing and Weiss, 2005). The two mutually inhibitory higher-order neurons — B63, responsible for mouthpart protraction (PM), and B64, which drives retraction (RM) — divide the space of possible biting actions, combinatorially generating the requisite variety of movement components. They act through lower-order interneurons, which in turn directly influence behavior (symbols: open triangle, excitation; closed circle, inhibition; s, slow synaptic connections; resistor symbol, electrical coupling). This real, active memory network is quite unlike the standard metaphor of memory as a passive repository of abstract symbols (Figure 6.2 on page 158). Paine and Tani (2005) describe a self-organizing neural controller for a mobile robot that develops a similarly HIERARCHICAL DIVISION OF LABOR when trained to solve its task. Abstract models of cognition based on the idea of hierarchical, modular networks include the Pandemonium (Selfridge, 1959; see p. 153), the Society of Mind (Minsky, 1985), and the Coderack of Hofstadter and Mitchell (1995), to which I'll return in Chapter 8.

a chance to consolidate, recently acquired memory traces (in a wide range of settings, including motor learning; Krakauer and Shadmehr, 2006) are more susceptible to displacement by new input. Letting the learned material sit undisturbed for some time, or sleeping on it (Stickgold, 2005), is always a good idea — which is why cramming for exams is usually counterproductive.

In many natural situations, however, the organism does not have control over the rate of arrival of information that may need to be committed to memory. The brain's only recourse then is *hierarchical abstraction* (Edelman, 2003). As I noted back on p. 31, this includes treating the tasks at hand as hierarchically structured (which usually works well, because that's how the world is in fact structured), and resorting to structured mechanisms for dealing with the input (which is effective for the same reason).

A general and very effective means of imposing structure on a distributed computational system such as a network of neurons is to introduce DIVISION OF LABOR. The metaphor of a community of experts, each toiling away at what it does best while contributing to the common good, has a surprisingly concrete interpretation in terms of neural network architecture: think of a collection of expert modules, all fed by a *gating* device that acts as a router. An overview of this computational approach, along with fMRI-based evidence that it is used by the human brain, is offered by Imamizu, Kuroda, Yoshioka, and Kawato (2004).

The gating device and the experts in such a "mixture of experts" architecture are trained in parallel. The router learns to subdivide the solution space — that is, perform rough classification — into relatively homogeneous regions, to associate each class of inputs with one of the modules, and to steer the data accordingly. The modules, which are trained on subsets of the data, are thus able to perform better than if each of them had to deal with the entire space of possibilities. Crucially, the modules are also less likely to suffer from interference among memory traces.

The emergence of specialization in a mixture of experts network can be usefully viewed as receptive field formation in the problem space. Following training, each module becomes tuned to a region of that space, thus acquiring computational functionality of a very familiar kind. In fact, TUNED UNITS play a central role in the machinery that interfaces any attractor-network dynamical memory to the rest of the cognitive system. A tuned unit is just what the system needs to find out whether or not its memory is at the bottom of a given attractor. The same goes for a less distinguished point in the state space, such as anyplace specific along a given trajectory, or even an entire sequence of states. In the latter case, information can be read out by a series of state detectors (neurons tuned to particular states) along the state-space trajectory traversed by the network, all feeding the same "trajectory detector" (cf. Figure 7.17 on page 293).

Without causal connections to the rest of the system (and thereby eventually to the rest of the world), attractors and trajectories mean nothing; a memory is a memory of something by virtue of being evoked by a signal from a tuned unit, and, in turn, being interpreted by one. It is quite satisfying to observe how tuned units, which are the key functional building blocks of perception, join forces with another functionally defined entity, an attractor system, in creating an intuitive computational explanation of what simple memory is about.

I shall now round off this survey of the basic memory functionality by showing how one additional, particularly intriguing characteristic of memory — its dependence on CONTEXT — can be subsumed by the same framework. As an example of the effect of context on memory I chose to examine here

Memory is contextualized by EMOTION. Rolls (2000) writes: "Emotion and motivation ... both involve rewards and punishments as the fundamental solution of the brain for interfacing sensory systems to action selection and execution systems. Computing the reward and punishment value of sensory stimuli and then using selection between different rewards and avoidance of punishments in a common reward-based currency appears to be the general solution that brains use to produce appropriate behavior."

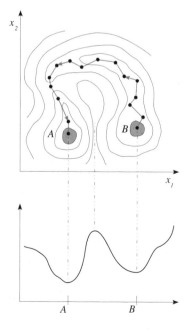

Figure 6.7 — One of the ways in which CONTEXT can exert influence over memory is illustrated here by means of a simple, two-dimensional two-attractor system. *Bottom:* with one of the dimensions set to a certain value — think of this as one of the two neurons in the corresponding network being active at a particular level — the two attractors are not reachable from one another. *Top:* as the activity of that neuron changes, an all-downhill path opens up that connects B to A; in this new situation, coming up with the memory of B will cause the system to recall also A (but not vice versa). Thus, B reminds the system of A only in a particular context — the one that activates the "controlling" neuron in a particular manner.

its interaction with EMOTION. The influence of emotion on memory is well-documented; Anderson, Wais, and Gabrieli (2006), for example, survey the key findings to date, and proceed to report a new one: retrograde (after the event) enhancement of long-term memory by separately invoked emotional arousal. There is no mystery here: being merely an extension of value (itself a scalar, or at most a low-dimensional, quantity), emotion can be given a straightforward computational explanation in terms of brain states. The explanation, offered by Lewis (2005); Rolls (2000), and others, is this: emotional states are those that come to be associated with positive or negative values through simple memory of rewards or punishments.

Emotion being computationally straightforward does not imply that its effects on cognition must themselves be simple. For instance, a scalar parameter that exerts a global influence[8] on the dynamics of a memory network can cause attractors to appear or disappear, as illustrated in Figure 6.6 on page 168. Even a local factor, such as the degree of arousal of just one neuron (corresponding to one particular dimension of the state space) can significantly alter the energy landscape of the system; Figure 6.7 illustrates how such a mechanism can make or break a connection between two local attractors.

GOAT navigation: foraging goats can walk 25-30 km/day, leaving far behind even the hardiest tourists.

6.4 Memory for structure in space and time: navigation and events

Effective dealing with complex, context-sensitive cues is an especially pressing need in a foraging animal that at the end of the day needs to find the way back to its nest, lair, or hotel. Imagine that you are a GOAT on its first visit to London. A *very* long walk takes you from Pimlico, through Westminster and the South Bank, to St. Paul's, then on to Covent Garden, and Piccadilly Circus (for a rough idea as to where all these places are relative to each other, peek ahead at Figure 7.13 on page 274). You are now eager to return to your pen; what do you do? Clearly, your options depend on how good your memory is.

If you remember nothing about your walk except that it was long, your only hope is to get help from a friendly native. Your subsequent recollection of the day of the long march will consist of a handful of scalars: the emotions of distress, despair, and relief, associated, respectively, with the realization that you're in an unfamiliar place, that you are lost, and that help is under way.

If you remember what each place you've passed looks like, you can try to retrace your steps — Piccadilly to Covent Garden, St. Paul's, the South Bank, Westminster, Pimlico — always following the direction of maximal familiarity. This could bring you back, but the length of the return trip would put a strain even on a prize goat.

If, however, you remember that your path followed a pretty fixed direction, made a wide U-turn to the left, and kept a nearly straight course for the same duration, then you can figure out that the place you started from is now to your left, and is quite close. Based on this insight, you take a shortcut, which brings you home in time for the evening hay. The kind of processed, structured memory that makes this feat of navigation possible is usually called a COGNITIVE MAP.

6.4.1 Cognitive maps

The first intimations of the use of map-like information in the brain came from Edward Tolman's studies of rat navigation, such as the one described in

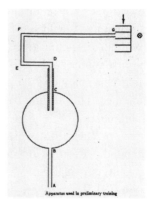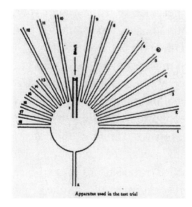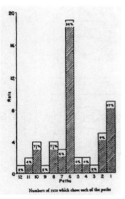

Figure 6.8 — Rats and SHORTCUTS. In a groundbreaking study, Tolman et al. (1946) demonstrated that rats quickly learn to take shortcuts through a partially explored environment. *Left:* rats first learn to follow the long tunnel of a simple maze to reach food, starting from the bottom end. *Middle:* the core of the maze is then replaced by a "sunburst" arrangement of tunnels, and the number of return journeys through each arm is recorded. *Right:* a histogram of the results shows that the arm that is taken most often — #6 from the right — is the one that makes for the shortest route back. The ability of the rats to figure out this shortcut suggests that they form a COGNITIVE MAP of the environment.

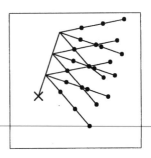

Navigation by DEAD RECKONING. *Above:* the paths from the study of Loomis, Klatzky, Golledge, Cicinelli, Pellegrino, and Fry (1993), in which blindfolded walkers had to navigate back to a point (marked by X) from which they had been led away, along two segments at an angle to each other. *Below:* the return paths of two subjects.

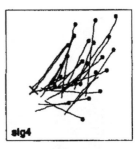

sig4

sig7

Figure 6.8. Rats in a maze, when properly motivated (by food at the end of the run), quickly learn not to take wrong turns. This ability can be attributed to a well-developed associative memory that pairs navigational choices with local cues. Even when augmented by perceptual generalization, simple holistic memory or stimulus-response association cannot, however, explain intelligent behavior in radically novel situations, of the kind exhibited by rats in taking a shortcut through an unfamiliar portion of the maze.

Many other species in addition to rats — from pigeons and dogs, through hamsters and honeybees, to humans (Burgess, 2002) — exhibit navigation abilities that can be supported by structured representations of the environment, but not by simple associative memory. Standard computational considerations suggest, however, that representations that support a given function may take many forms which, in turn, may be implemented in many ways. Just how map-like are the spatial representations used in biological navigation systems? Before we can address this question (cf. Figure 6.10 on page 176), we must clarify the computational nature of navigation and the possible sources of information that can be used to solve it.

The computational needs of a navigator depend strongly on the task at hand; surprisingly, a full-fledged, detailed map of the terrain would, in most if not all cases, be a tremendous overkill. An ant that needs merely to be able to get back to its nest after foraging abroad does not require a map: a constantly updated representation of the direction home would suffice. A bee that decides to visit two sources of nectar without returning to the hive in between must estimate the direction from the first source to the second one, but it too will do just fine without a map, if it can maintain two pieces of directional information (one to the hive and another to the second source), or if the second source has a conspicuous landmark near it.

These two examples illustrate two sources of cues from which representations useful for navigation can be computed. The first one is DEAD RECKONING: measuring off and integrating route information. Many studies, representative results of one of which (Loomis et al., 1993) are illustrated in the margin, show that blindfolded walkers led away from a reference point are generally capable of returning to its vicinity (the subjects in such experiments are prevented from explicitly counting the steps taken or keeping track of any turns by having to repeat a nonsense phrase).

The second source of information that can be used to navigate through the environment is LANDMARKS (Golledge, 1999). These can be visual (most common in human orientation and navigation) or other (such as olfactory —

rats, for example, are good at following subtle gradients of volatile odorants). Landmark-based navigation, or *piloting*, involves comparing the current perceptual state to memory and choosing the direction of movement that maximizes the likelihood of approaching the goal.

The goal of piloting need not be defined by its coordinates on a map: you can navigate from any place in midtown Manhattan to the Chrysler building while being guided by its apparent height. Indeed, none of the navigational techniques mentioned above necessitates the use of a representation that is like a real map: enduring, allocentric, and comprehensive. Furthermore, experimental findings reported by Wang and Spelke (2002) suggest that human subjects navigate by considering visual landmarks in an egocentric, view-specific and continually updated frame of reference, rather than in allocentric, or view-independent coordinates, as would be the case if a true global map were used. Let us see what neurobiology has to say about cognitive maps.

6.4.2 Place cells

The bold hypothesis that rats represent their environment in the form of a cognitive map was advanced by Tolman et al. (1946) at a time when American psychology was dominated by behaviorists, who rejected the very notion of internal representation as unscientific. A quarter of a century and one (cognitive) revolution later, what looked like neurobiological evidence in support of the hypothesized maps was finally found when O'Keefe and Dostrovsky (1971) reported that some cells in the rat hippocampus responded selectively

LANDMARK-based navigation in Manhattan: if you see this skyscraper from afar and want to reach it, start walking towards it. You'll know you're there when you see it towering above you.

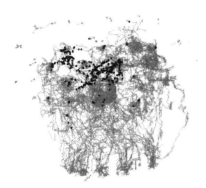

Figure 6.9 — The spatial receptive field of a typical PLACE CELL (reproduced from Best, White, and Minai, 2001). The rat's path, which has been recorded as the rat explored the enclosure, is shown in gray; the black dots mark the locations where the cell fired.

Rat paths reconstructed from hippocampus PLACE-CELL ensemble activity, shown alongside the actual paths (Wilson and McNaughton, 1993). Realistic trajectories can also be computed from recordings made while the rat is asleep (Wilson and McNaughton, 1994), suggesting that memory consolidation is at work, and also perhaps that sleeping rats dream about mazes (Ji and Wilson, 2007).

to the rat's location in a familiar enclosure (a lab bench or a maze). These neurons came to be known as PLACE CELLS (Figure 6.9).

The initial findings, which had revealed that many hippocampal cells fire selectively when the rat is in a particular arm of a maze, were subsequently refined and extended in many directions (Eichenbaum, Dudchenko, Wood, Shapiro, and Tanila, 1999). Importantly, location specificity was consistently obtained also with much more precise recording techniques. Given the ensemble activity of a few dozen of simultaneously recorded place cells, researchers found it possible to reconstruct the rat's trajectory through the enclosure (Wilson and McNaughton, 1993). Moreover, for the spatial firing pattern reconstructed by a computational model to be closest to the ideal, its timing must lead the rat's position by about 120 *msec* (Muller and Kubie, 1989), indicating that neural activity in the hippocampus predicts the animal's future location on a short time scale.

The conclusion usually drawn from these findings is that the hippocampus contains a facsimile of the environment (cf. Figure 6.10, left). Just as with the behavioral data surveyed in the preceding section, there is, however, an alternative explanation of the place cell phenomenon that is simpler in that it does not postulate a full spatial reconstruction of the environment within

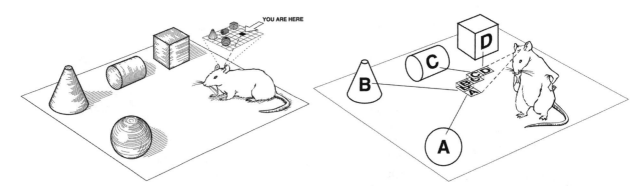

Figure 6.10 — *Left:* according to the COGNITIVE MAP hypothesis, the hippocampus contains a complete, spatially faithful facsimile of the environment. *Right:* a more plausible alternative, which accounts for a much wider range of behavioral and neural findings, views the hippocampus as a spatially anchored EPISODIC MEMORY, which stores relational information that pertains to specific events (Eichenbaum et al., 1999).

the representational system. At the same time, the alternative view is compatible with a range of characteristics of the "place" cells that purely spatial tuning cannot explain (Eichenbaum, 2000; Eichenbaum et al., 1999; Fortin, Agster, and Eichenbaum, 2002). Specifically, the spatial representation in the hippocampus is less than a map because it is not contiguous or homogeneous, and because the representations are not bound together in a cohesive framework. The hippocampal representation is also more than a map, because it codes for more than location — space-related variables such as speed, heading, and turn direction, as well as nonspatial features of events, cognitive demands imposed by the task that the rat performs, and learned responses are all represented.

A neurocomputational theory that accounts for all these features holds the hippocampus to be an EPISODIC MEMORY system (Eichenbaum et al., 1999). Hippocampal place cells associate events with the locations at which they occur (coded relative to landmarks, which are represented egocentrically);[9] a computational scheme for using place cells for navigation is outlined in Figure 6.11. In addition to place cells there are, however, many other kinds of tuned cells; for example, "odor cells" may link episodes in which the same odor was perceived. Importantly, information about the sequential order of events is also represented; any "nodal" events that are common to two or more sequences are singled out (Figure 6.10, right) as potentially useful for sophisticated navigation such as shortcut-taking.[10]

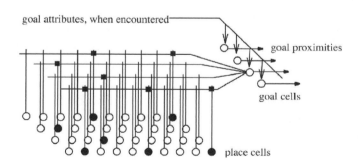

Figure 6.11 — A computational scheme for goal-directed navigation that uses "goal cells" tuned to specific landmarks (defined as clusters of visual and other features) in conjunction with place cells (Burgess, 2002). When at the goal, a Hebbian learning mechanism (cf. p. 41) strengthens the synaptic connections (filled squares) from place cells that are active (filled circles) to the goal cell. Navigation towards a hidden goal can then be guided by the goal cell's firing rate: the higher it is, the closer the goal.

The idea that the hippocampus implements episodic memory is compatible with the behavioral literature reviewed by Wang and Spelke (2002), who point out that the representations that support navigation in all species surveyed, including humans, are (i) continually changing, or *dynamic*, (ii) dependent on the self's position relative to the environment, or *egocentric*, and (iii) partial and need-based, or *limited*. The cognitive map saga thus exemplifies a remarkable convergence of computational theory, behavioral data, and neurobiological findings, whose scope and degree of detail bring to mind another success story of the Marr-Poggio framework, which I described in Chapter 4 — the understanding of sound localization in the barn owl.[11] Here, the outcome of six decades of the increasingly interdisciplinary investigation is an understanding of a memory space that any perambulatory animal needs: remembering what happened where, and how to get there from here.

Food-caching birds on a tight metabolic budget must balance spatial memory capacity against the cost of maintaining the hippocampal tissue that supports it. In chickadees, the hippocampus is smaller in the spring, when memory for cache locations becomes less critical, and larger in the fall (Smulders, Sasson, and DeVoogd, 1995). In comparison, cab drivers in labyrinthine London have an enlarged posterior hippocampus all year long (Maguire, Gadian, Johnsrude, Good, Ashburner, Frackowiak, and Frith, 2000). *Below:* two black-capped chickadees and a London cab driver in their natural habitats.

6.5   Memory for structured objects and situations: concepts

Given the power of learning from experience (cf. section 5.4), one expects a cognitive agent equipped with good episodic memory to excel at distilling from the memorized episodes any useful generalizations about the environment; those that fail to do so are likely to be compared to Homer Simpson,[12] or to the French royal House of Bourbon, about whose post-Restoration reactionary scions it was said that the Bourbons forgot nothing and learned nothing.[13]

The human cognitive system is generally very good at piecing together episodic records of its interaction with the world into a knowledge base it subsequently taps into while planning behavior. In this section, I offer an overview of the commonsense epistemological basis of everyday behavior in humans and other animals, focusing on the interaction with the physical world. Social commonsense, which is especially well-developed in humans, will be treated later, in section 6.6. The manner in which people *use* knowledge to plan and execute behavior — an issue that can be distinguished from that of memory (McCarthy, 1990, pp.191-193), but which, as we shall see, is not entirely independent of it — I shall return to in Chapter 8.

6.5.1 The knowledge basis of common sense

In her preface to a collection of papers on commonsense knowledge and reasoning, Elio (2002) poses the question "SO WHAT DOES 'EVERYONE' KNOW?", which she proceeds to answer thus:

> Time and space; causality; approximate or qualitative theories of motion, force, substances, and energy; continuous change; and quantities. In short, what 'everyone' knows is mainly concerned with an understanding of changes, actions, cause, and effect in the physical world (sometimes called 'naive physics'). ... Our knowledge in these matters appears to be established well before we undergo formal education and certainly some of it before we are very far out of infancy. ... Commonsense knowledge seems to be that which people come to know in the course of growing up and living in the world.

Growing up in the world, one learns, for instance, that treating gravity as a joke (let alone treating all of physical reality as a mere description[14]) is likely to earn you a Darwin Award[15] — unless, of course, you are a cartoon character (cf. Figure 6.12). In artificial intelligence (and among philosophers who know their computer science), the ongoing attempt to codify such commonsense knowledge about how the world works is referred to as the *naive physics* project (Smith and Casati, 1994). This label is not intended as a putdown: computer scientists know just how difficult it is to formalize, let alone

Figure 6.12 — In the cartoon world, gravity does not kick in until after you realize that you've just walked off a cliff, and the subsequent encounter with the ground is but a temporary setback in your pursuit of happiness. In the real world, gravity is less forgiving; luckily, most of us remember enough from experiencing it on a small scale to take it seriously.

impart to a robot, common sense that "naive" humans pick up and wield so effortlessly.

The difficulty stems from the limitations of human intuition. Given the roots of intuition in common sense, waiting for an insight into commonsense knowledge is somewhat like expecting fish to understand water: far-fetched, but not impossible. Emptying the aquarium (temporarily) may help: it is useful to try to imagine, as I did in Table 6.1 on the facing page, how it would feel to go through "a day in the life" without the memories that constitute knowledge of *ordo mundi*, the order of the world.

This knowledge appears to be structured as a system of interlinked CON-CEPTS (Murphy, 2002) — representational entities that can be concisely described as clusters of features that "hang together" in particular ways, as explained in the remainder of this section. The examples in Table 6.1 and elsewhere in the literature (Minsky, 1985, 2000; Mueller, 2001; Smith, 1995; Stork, 1997) suggest the following rough classification of concepts:

- KINDS AND CATEGORIES. To serve as a teacup, an object must have certain features: hold liquid, have a handle, *etc.* (defaults). Not all of these are obligatory: a traditional Chinese teacup has no handles (defaults are defeasible). A teacup is a kind of cup; a cup is a kind of liquid container (hierarchy).

- SPACE AND TIME. One's home is usually in a particular place. To get from one place to another, objects must undergo movement. There cannot be more than one solid object in the same place at the same time. If an inanimate object is in a particular place at a given time, it will be there at a future time, unless moved. Time flies like an arrow, unless you are bored, in which case it creeps.

- CAUSE AND EFFECT. Despite the constant attempts on the part of the four-year-olds all over the world to convince their caregivers otherwise, things don't become broken without outside intervention.

- GOALS AND PLANS. Certain kinds of objects such as people and animals have desires; those that do may also have goals and some can even plan their behavior accordingly. (More about this in section 6.6.)

- SCRIPTS AND STRATEGIES. Many kinds of events typically unfold according to rather rigid scripts, the knowledge of which is critical for planning the behavior of self and understanding the behavior of others.

Table 6.1 — Eight lines from *A Day in the Life* by Lennon and McCartney, and a tiny selection from the memorized knowledge items — some episodic, others generic — that help the protagonist through his life.

`Woke up, fell out of bed,`	This is my bed rather than some stranger's (or the alley behind the pub); yesterday night couldn't have been too bad, then. Also: gravity on this planet is moderate enough that a 40cm fall would not result in a concussion.
`Dragged a comb across my head,`	Must use comb; a spoon would not work. Also: no need to tidy up the pubic hair.
`Found my way downstairs and drank a cup,`	The tea service is *not* in the bedroom closet. Also: to make tea, follow this algorithm [details omitted]. *An aside: given the context, estimate the relative likelihood of the cup containing: (a) tea, (b) coffee, (c) yerba mate, (d) kumis, (e) beer.*
`And looking up I noticed I was late.`	Given the physical constraints of available means of transportation, the probability of arriving at the goal location by the pre-specified time is low. Also: time keeps on slipping into the future no matter what I do.
`Found my coat and grabbed my hat,`	A hat is a good idea in winter. Also: could not for the life of me remember where the scarf was.
`Made the bus in seconds flat,`	Found the place where the bus stops (you cannot just flag one down in the middle of the block). *The extra calories for feeding the old hippocampus were well spent.*
`Found my way upstairs and had a smoke,`	Upstairs is where my desk is. Also: smoking a cigarette with the burning end inside your mouth is not a good idea under routine circumstances.
`Somebody spoke and I went into a dream...`	A dream? Was the bit about waking up all a mistake? Maybe last night *was* bad after all.

It should be absolutely clear that this list does not even begin to reveal the full scale and complexity of the tangled web that is the human conceptual system. My hope that it is nevertheless somewhat effective rests on the assumption that you, the reader, are human too, and that our conceptual systems are therefore not incommensurable; intuitively, you should have a pretty good notion of what I was talking about just now. In the rest of this section, I shall build on this intuition by stating the key empirical generalizations about concepts, and by outlining the manner in which they can be explained using the standard tools for computational understanding of cognition.

Consider for example the proceedings that we call "games." I mean board-games, card-games, ball-games, Olympic games, and so on. What is common to them all? — Don't say: "There must be something common, or they would not be called games" — but look and see whether there is anything common to all. — For if you look at them you will not see something that is common to all, but similarities, RELATIONSHIPS, and a whole series of them at that.

— Wittgenstein (1958, 66)

6.5.2   Natural kinds and others

Following the seminal work of Eleanor Rosch (who had been influenced by Ludwig Wittgenstein's *Philosophical Investigations*), psychologists came to accept the impossibility of capturing commonsense concepts by fixed lists of necessary and sufficient features. The temptation to do so has always been strong. After all, mathematics is all about precisely defined concepts being derived from a handful of axioms. Likewise, in physics there can be no confusion about the distinction between iron and nickel, nor in chemistry an equivocation about whether a molecule of water contains two atoms of hydrogen and one of oxygen.

Philosophers refer to concepts such as iron or water as NATURAL KINDS (Putnam, 1988, ch.2). Such concepts, which nowadays often have counterparts in science, are held together by the computational principle that we already encountered in Chapter 5 as the fundamental statistical characteristic of the world that makes perception possible: predictive power. For an item that instantiates a natural-kind concept, one can predict some of its properties, given the knowledge of some of its other properties (cf. the note on Marr's Fundamental Hypothesis on p. 143).

In sciences that deal with more complex stuff than elementary particles, atoms, or molecules, categories become fuzzy around the edges. In biology, even the most typical example of a natural kind, the species, is unlike a physical or a chemical category: the genomes of different members of a given species may vary enough to make it counterproductive on the part of the scientists to insist on a crisp definition. Even if many biological natural kinds — say, cat or cow — are sufficiently uniform genetically to warrant precise definitions that reduce to DNA chemistry, this does not solve the problem for psychology, because natural-kind concepts play a rather marginal role in everyday human affairs. Instead of simple, and simply definable, concepts, the human brain revels in fuzzy conceptual complexity. Why? Because it can.[16]

An especially quick and capacious associative memory allows its owner to notice even very subtle or indirect connections among properties of things. Thus, although a randomly picked set of entities is not likely to form a natural kind, people often find reasons to group objects that have virtually no common natural properties into an "ad hoc" category (Barsalou, 1983). An often-cited example is "women, fire, and dangerous things" that, according to Lakoff (1987), all belong to the same category in Dyirbal, an aboriginal Australian language.[17] There is no need, however, for such far-fetched examples: let us consider instead the concept of projectile (cf. Figure 6.13).

When a human finds himself or herself in a situation that calls for the use of a projectile, any of a wide variety of otherwise totally unrelated objects will do. Without viewing the following list as an endorsement on my part, observe that you can fling at your adversary a piece of chalk, a sandwich, an inkwell (all tried and tested by kids in my elementary school), a cat (rare

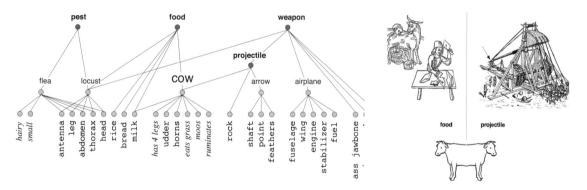

Figure 6.13 — *Left:* a tiny portion of the enormous network of concepts a variant of which resides in every person's memory. Some of the bottom-level nodes label features, others parts. The links are maintained dynamically (they depend on past experience and on the current goal context) and are graded rather than all-or-none. Altogether, the network is structured as a TANGLED HIERARCHY because concepts may belong to more than one higher-level category. *Right:* an example of the latter phenomenon is cow, a concept that in some systems (in particular, in the brains of non-vegetarian fans of Monty Python) belongs both under food (milk, meat) and under projectile (to catapult a cow, use a large trebuchet; the arrow indicates the loading point).

but not unheard of), or even a cow (difficult but possible if you have a large enough trebuchet, and a cow).[18]

The predictive power of a concept can be expressed computationally as the conditional probability of its instances possessing some properties given that they possess others. Natural-kind concepts are highly cohesive in this sense; ad hoc concepts are less so. If your opponent in a 20-question game (Richards, 1982) tells you as a 'hint' that the unknown object has been used as a projectile, you cannot determine even whether it is animate or inanimate (remember the far-flung cow), or even solid or liquid (it may have been a chunk of ice when hurled, which then melted into a puddle of water).

Because of the preponderance in human cognition of such dynamic and variegated concepts as projectile, the contents of conceptual memory are best represented as a TANGLED HIERARCHY,[19] whose structure, moreover, is FLUID because it depends on where you are and which direction you face (cf. Figure 6.14).

Figure 6.14 — THE VIEW FROM HERE. Saul Steinberg's humorous *View of the World from 9th Avenue*, which served as the cover of *The New Yorker* in March 1976, is an excellent reminder of the role of context in cognition. The truism according to which the way you see things and their relationships depends on your vantage point applies to concepts too: empirical research shows that a subject's perception of the relationships among the categories that populate his or her conceptual memory is determined to a large extent by the context defined by the train of experiences preceding the probe, and by the task at hand (Barsalou, 1987).

6.5.3   Concepts: the view from here

In information science, tangled hierarchies are the representation of choice for *ontologies* — complete systems of concepts covering a given domain, such as internal medicine or the stock market (a useful review of philosophical and information-science aspects of ontology can be found in Smith, 2003). In contrast, in cognition the goal of ontology-making is not prescriptive (dictating what a system of concepts should be), but descriptive. Moreover, because the relationships among concepts play out differently depending on the situation and on the task at hand, one cannot hope to develop a single, immutable, and universally valid description of the commonsense ontology.

Because cognitive concepts are dynamic and purposive, network diagrams such as the one in Figure 6.13 can only approximate the real, fluid state of affairs in the conceptual memory system. Nevertheless, such approximations are useful: it is possible to develop a general computational characterization of their emergence and structure, and to apply it towards understanding conceptual memory and thinking.

The empirical study of concepts is carried out by a variety of methods. Some of these involve explicit judgment on the part of the subject (e.g., in response to queries about conceptual relations). Other methods are implicit: instead of being solicited for his or her opinion, the subject performs a natural perceptual task such as discrimination, categorization, or naming. In examining the relationships among concepts gleaned from experimental data obtained in this manner, one can distinguish between a *vertical* dimension, which pertains to the "domination" or inclusion relationships between categories, and a *horizontal* dimension, having to do with the relationships of concepts that belong to the same category.

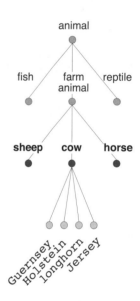

In this hierarchy, cow is at the BASIC LEVEL (shown in bold).

The most prominent characteristic of the vertical structure is the *is-a* hierarchy (as in "a cow *is a* mammal" and "a mammal *is an* animal"). The central psychological phenomenon that reflects on the vertical structure of categories is the existence of a privileged BASIC LEVEL (Rosch, Mervis, Gray, Johnson, and Boyes-Braem, 1976). For instance, in the hierarchical sequence furniture, chair, armchair, the level of chair is the basic one. The basic level can be determined experimentally in a number of ways, which yield converging results (Rosch, 1978). In particular, the names of basic-level concepts are among the first words acquired by children and the fastest to be produced in response to a picture.

Horizontally, concepts are characterized by *graded* "radial" structure:

certain instances, sometimes called PROTOTYPES, are more "central" than others. In my version of the category writing implement, for example, the concept notebook computer is dead center (I almost never write on paper). At the same time, I can easily think of several ways of making the statement "a cow *is a* writing implement" true. All of these, admittedly, would be inconvenient or unpleasant to the cow, to the writer, or to both, which makes cow a rather peripheral instance of writing implement.

The RADIAL STRUCTURE of the farm animal concept, with cow and sheep being more central (prototypical) than llama or donkey.

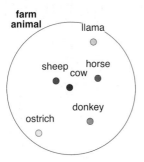

As with the vertical structure, the gradedness of category membership manifests itself in the converging results from a wide variety of experimental paradigms (Rosch, 1978). Prototypes are rated as more typical of the category than regular members (cf. robin vs. chicken as instances of bird); regular members are judged as more similar to prototypes than vice versa (is Canada more similar to the US or the other way around?[20]). In addition, generalizability, order of acquisition, order of item output, priming, and substitutability in context are some of the other properties on which prototypes score higher than regular members.

A closer look at the patterns of human categorization performance reveals, however, a much more interesting situation: although the privileged status of certain levels of categorization and the gradedness of the internal structure of categories are universal, the identity of the basic level and the composition and layout of categories are all highly unstable (Barsalou, 1987). The key factors at work in all cases of variable conceptual structure have to do with context.

The phenomenon of ad hoc categorization that I discussed earlier suggests that contextual effects arise synchronically (on the spur of the moment), from the demands of the task. For example, the relevance of the claim that "a cow *is a* projectile" is conditional on being in a particular situation (under siege). Context also takes effect diachronically (over time): both recent experience and cumulative expertise exert strong influence over categorization (Tanaka and Gauthier, 1997), and even single prior processing episodes can make a difference (Brooks, 1987).

The dependence of categorization on experience entails dependence on individual identity and on culture. Indeed, the many studies reported by Barsalou (1987) found an average between-subjects correlation in concept-related tasks of only 0.50; this in addition to significant within-subject variability over of time (0.80 correlation). Different groups of subjects (such as faculty and undergraduate students, or people of different ethnicities) yielded distinct patterns of categorization. Interestingly, members of each group were quite good (and consistent) in assuming the perspective of other groups.

6.5.4 Learning concepts

Empirical data suggests, therefore, not only that conceptualization in humans is context-dependent, but also that the rest of the cognitive system exerts a fair amount of control over categorization. Given a task (and, necessarily, the prior experience we bring to it), people are adept at twisting and pulling at their conceptual networks until a satisfactory solution emerges.[21] But where do the contents and the structure of conceptual memory networks come from?

Conceptual learning has been traditionally regarded by theorists as a process that transforms perceptually acquired knowledge into a concise collection of abstract truths about the world.[22] According to this view, conceptual learning is therefore a straightforward extension of perceptual learning, which, as we saw in Chapter 5, reduces computationally to statistical inference (section 5.4.4), and whose outcome can be veridical (faithful to the state of the affairs "out there" in the world; section 5.5).

It is precisely because they are grounded in perception through learning that concepts — from the most concrete such as water to the most abstract such as truth (Barsalou, 1999) — cannot be universal: there are no two human beings with identical perceptual histories. The pervasiveness of learning and the ensuing fluidity of conceptual structures that populate human memories obviate what many philosophers of mind see as their discipline's thorniest question: the origin of concepts.

As noted by Fodor (1998), it is impossible to deduce the absolute, true meaning of logically composite concepts from experience. To him, this suggests that concepts must be "atomic" rather than composite — indivisible, either present or absent. But, Fodor reasons, this leaves only two alternatives regarding the *origin* of concepts: either all concepts, even unnatural (doorknob) or highly technical (carburetor), are innate, or concepts reflect the properties of the mind rather than of the world.

Man is the measure of all things.

— Protagoras

> ... It used to seem to me that atomism about concepts means that DOORKNOB is innate. But now I think that you can trade a certain amount of innateness for a certain amount of mind-dependence. *Being a doorknob* is just: striking our kinds of minds the way the doorknobs do. So, what you need to ac-

quire the concept DOORKNOB 'from experience' is just: the kind of mind that experience causes to be struck that way by door-knobs. The price of making this trade of innateness for mind-dependence is, however, a touch of Wotan's problem. It turns out that much of what we find in the world is indeed 'only ourselves.'

— Fodor (1998, p.162)

Wotan: I find only myself, every time, in everything I create.

R. Wagner
Die Walküre, Act II

The predicament of Wotan (the Norse creator god) actually holds in reverse: *we* see only ourselves, every time, in every deity we create.

I can see how the notion that babies are born with the concept of carburetor built into their brains does not make much sense, but there is no reason to complain about the other alternative, which is that concepts are in the mind of the beholder.

Indeed, conceptual relativism agrees with the fundamental thesis that memory is there to serve perception and action (Glenberg, 1997): concepts are handles by which the mind grasps the world, and a good handle is one that fits well the hand. Moreover, the relativist stance also agrees with the empirical data on conceptual knowledge, which indicates that "there may be no correct abstractions to discover" (Barsalou, 2003a, p.1179).[23] All in all, it appears that Protagoras was right in believing that "man is the measure" of human concepts.[24]

I shall now proceed to sketch an outline of the computational process that underlies the growth of conceptual memory. The core function of this process will be very familiar to you from the discussion of perception (cf. Barsalou, 1999): **the brain learns concepts by acquiring highly structured perceptual "snapshots" that characterize the situation at hand**. To *use* the resulting memories for reasoning, the brain needs an efficient indexing scheme that would associate situations and tasks with the relevant snapshots, and a structured generalization mechanism that would allow snapshots to be extended and applied to novel situations; I return to these issues in Chapter 8.

The reliance on perception is common to all conceptual systems: bovine, human, or any other. What sets apart the more powerful among these is the representational richness and the structural complexity. A cow looking at a daisy sees, presumably, a tasty morsel and nothing more; a human looking at Daisy may see that too, but also, occasionally, a projectile, or a writing implement — themselves concepts of great richness and complexity.[25]

Crucially, conceptual sophistication has a knack for self-amplification: the more elaborate and richly interconnected system of concepts one has, the more efficient learner (and thinker) one becomes. (How else would a species with a Stone Age brain become so good at defending doctoral dissertations?) A classical expression of this propensity of the human conceptual memory for fast incremental complexification is found in a letter from Isaac Newton to his bitter rival, Robert Hooke, in which Newton admits that he was able to "see further" by standing ON THE SHOULDERS OF GIANTS.

Conceptual memory grows through IMPRINTING (a rapid establishment of a persistent record in the form of an activation pattern over the existing representations) and ENTRENCHMENT (a gradual strengthening of an existing record). In language, for example, someone's opportune phrase may "resonate" with my existing conceptual repertoire, causing a set of slight adjustments to be made to the links of the conceptual network, which could facilitate subsequent recognition of the same utterance. If this phrase is repeated by others or by myself often enough, it may merit the entrenchment of its initially distributed representation, and perhaps an allocation of a dedicated, localized one (more about that in Chapter 7, esp. p. 272).

On an abstract computational level, imprinting and entrenchment are driven by an interplay between the statistics of the environment (exogenous stimulation) and of use (endogenous invocation). More specifically, in the terminology of section 6.3, imprinting corresponds to an adjustment of the energy landscape to reflect the association between the just-experienced stimulus and the state-space trajectory it evoked, and entrenchment — to the excavation of a brand new attractor to serve as a permanent record of the new concept (cf. Barsalou, 2003a). Let us see how these computational processes can explain the main phenomena of conceptual memory.

The emergence of levels of categorization and graded structure

Returning to the example of cow, we may notice that different instances of this concept are much more similar to each other than instances of higher (superordinate) level concepts such as farm animal. At the same time, making a finer (subordinate) level distinction by identifying a cow specifically as a Jersey cow requires an investment of computational effort that is disproportionately large relative to the informational gain: a Jersey cow shares with any other cow most of the characteristics that can be of interest to a non-expert.[26]

Suppose that on your first visit to a farm you are shown a farm animal and told that it is a cow of the Jersey breed, whose name is Daisy. As a result of this encounter, your memory lays down three separate traces — one for

What Des-Cartes did was a good step. You have added much several ways, & especially in taking ye colours of thin plates into philosophical consideration. If I have seen further it is by standing ON YE SHOULDERS OF GIANTS.

— Newton to Hooke
5 Feb. 1676; Corr. I, 416

There are no permanent or complete abstractions of a category in memory. Instead, abstraction is the skill to construct temporary online interpretations of a category's members. Although an infinite number of abstractions are possible, attractors develop for habitual approaches to interpretation.

— Barsalou (2003a, p.1177).

farm animal, one for cow, and one for Jersey cow — and initializes each with the perceptual snapshot of the stimulus (in the terminology of Chapter 5, this amounts to allocating three "detector" units, which are then cross-linked to the language system).

On your subsequent farm visits, the cow detector is likely to be the one that is the most reliably activated. The cow concept will thus become better entrenched and will soon emerge as the most "basic" among the three. Being continually imprinted with the statistics of the stimulus stream, your conceptual memory system will in time contain records of different instances of cow, all sharing the same representation space. Instances whose representations fall closer to the center of that space will be judged by you to be more prototypical (Rosch, 1978).

The same processes that construct complex, hierarchically structured concepts such as cow also give rise to concepts that are extended over time, or SCRIPTS.   Just as fine motor control is mediated by precisely timed sequences of complex muscle synergies, mastery of concepts such as eating in a restaurant (Schank and Abelson, 1977) requires the sequencing of multiple actions: getting seated, eating, paying, and so on, which are themselves hierarchically structured (e.g., paying may consist of offering a credit card, calculating the tip, etc.). I shall describe a computational method for learning such sequences in Chapter 7, which deals with language acquisition.

The "characteristic to defining" shift in conceptual development

The prototype theory of conceptual memory, which displaced the classical definition-based accounts following the work of Rosch and others in the 1970s, has been since complemented by the "theory" theory (Keil, 1989), so called because it postulates the involvement — even in children — of intuitive theory-laden explanations in the maintenance of a system of concepts. Developmental psychologists found evidence that children switch from prototype-based treatment of concepts (which relies on characteristic features) to a theory-based one (which depends on defining and explanatory features) between kindergarten and the second grade.

The empirical data for this conclusion come from studies in which the subjects listen to descriptions of objects, and either accept or reject them. For example, kindergarten-age children do not resist changes in the description of the concept uncle that dispose of its defining feature (being a brother of one's mom or dad), as long as the characteristic features (being nice and friendly) are left intact. In contrast, children in the fourth grade exhibit the opposite behavior, accepting the possibility of a grumpy, ugly brother of Mom being an uncle, and resisting the possibility that a nice stranger could be one (Keil, 1989; Medin and Smith, 1984).

The same studies showed that even kindergarten children treat artifacts and natural-kind categories differently, resisting changes that cross natural-kind boundaries (porcupine into cactus) and accepting changes from one artifact to another (coffee pot into bird-feeder). Changes within a natural kind (horse into zebra) are accepted by children in the kindergarten, but rejected by fourth-graders. This suggests that the "characteristic to defining" shift may reflect not a fundamental qualitative change in the manner in which concepts are treated, but rather a side effect of the gradual growth of the body of conceptual knowledge throughout childhood. Interestingly, in most domains this knowledge tends to remain myopic and patchy even in adults, who typically rely on crude folk theories of how the world works (Keil, 2003).

Crude as they may be, folk theories implement a critical cognitive function: explaining causal relationships among events (which in turn makes it possible to predict the outcomes of actions and to plan goal-directed behavior; cf. Figure 6.12 on page 179). The computational basis of this function is statistical: the causal structure of a set of events can be inferred by estimating the probabilities of their co-occurrence, using well-understood algorithmic techniques (Pearl and Russel, 2003).

The sought-after causal structure can be represented graphically in the form of a network, in which the nodes stand for variables of interest, and the directed links — for the prevailing statistical dependencies (see Figure 6.15 on the following page, top). Only some of the variables can be observed; the existence (let alone the values) of the hidden variables, and of any links, must be inferred from the measurements carried out on the observables. Tallying the relevant probabilities reveals whether or not the observed variables are independent; such computation can show, for instance, that comets do not portend the plague, but rats dying by the thousand do (Figure 6.15, bottom left and center).

Causal inference is especially powerful if it can reveal a common hidden cause behind two or more observables. This kind of inference is the mainstay of the scientific method. In the epidemiology of the plague, for example, the discovery of the common cause of death in rats and in people — the *Yersinia* bacillus, which is carried by fleas — made it possible to conclude that the human epidemic is not, after all, brought about by the dying rats. A

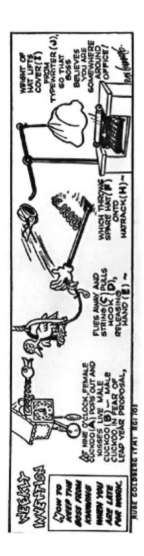

Rube Goldberg's solution for keeping your boss from finding out that you're late for work. The principles of parsimonious statistical inference guarantee that your boss will *not* guess what is really going on behind your office door.

relation such as that between human and rat deaths during plague is called CONDITIONAL INDEPENDENCE; two events are conditionally independent given a third factor if the probability of one does not affect the probability of the other. In the case of the plague, if you know that contagion is present in the fleas in your town, knowing also that rats are dying does not further affect the likelihood that an epidemic is about to develop, or vice versa (Figure 6.15, bottom right).

As our encounters with natural statistical computation earlier in this book suggest, you don't have to be a scientist or a statistician to be capable of probabilistic inference of causality. In fact, you don't even have to be a grown-up. It has been known for some time that some of the necessary computational tools, such as the implicit estimation of conditional probabilities, are available to 8-month olds (Saffran, Aslin, and Newport, 1996; see the margin note on p. 252). More recently, developmental psychologists showed that 2.5-year-old children readily distinguish between conditional dependence and independence, while 4-year-olds are capable of discerning the effects of *interventions* by self and others on the causal structure of the situation (Gopnik and Schulz, 2004).[27]

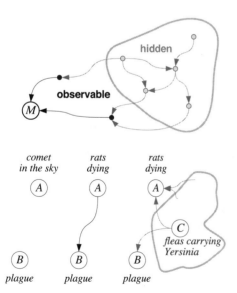

Figure 6.15 — *Top:* a GRAPHICAL MODEL is a probabilistically annotated graph that represents causal relationships among some variables pertaining to the state of affairs in the world (Pearl, 2001); one type of such model is the Bayes net (Pearl and Russel, 2003). The "hidden" variables cannot be observed directly, only inferred from measurements (*M*) carried out on the observables. *Bottom left:* in this very simple, two-node graphical model, the variables *A* and *B* are independent, which is denoted by the absence of an arc between them. *Bottom center:* *B* depends on *A*. *Bottom right:* *A* and *B* are conditionally independent, given *C* (see text for details). Note that *A* may be also affected by some other hidden variables.

6.5.5 Memory for concepts: an interim summary

In 1668, the first secretary of the Royal Society, John Wilkins, published a universal, hierarchically structured categorization scheme intended to encompass the sum total of human conceptual knowledge (amazingly, this undertaking was actually part of a larger project, which included a specification of a complete artificial language; Figure 7.2 on page 242). Nearly three centuries later, the book, *An Essay Towards a Real Character and a Philosophical Language*, has been reviewed by none other than Borges (1984), who raised an eyebrow at the categorical distinctions it proposed. These reminded Borges of "an ancient Chinese encyclopedia" that reportedly entertained such animal categories as those that resemble flies from a distance.

In his essay, Borges expresses a doubt about the list's authenticity. Be the doubt genuine or not (it is impossible to tell, as it often happens when Borges writes about books),[28] it is difficult to imagine a better epigraph than this list (reproduced here in the margin) for a disquisition on concepts, and this is exactly how Eleanor Rosch used it in the opening of her 1978 review of the principles of categorization — only to claim that such classification does not exist.

Reality being often stranger than fiction, Borges's list does not, however, sound too far-fetched in the light of what is known today about the nature of concepts. Not only do conceptual categories vary across cultures (Lakoff, 1987), they are also fluid within a given culture, and even within an individual mind. As Barsalou (2003a) and others showed, the concepts that a person brings to bear on many (potentially, all) real-life situations are formed *ad hoc*, to fit the cognitive demands of the moment.

Although the fluidity of concepts could spell a nightmare for a theorist searching for useful generalizations about the commonsense knowledge system, there are in fact manageably few **computational principles** behind the apparently overwhelming complexity. Some of these are familiar to us from Chapter 5, which dealt with perception; others are new, but shall be encountered again in Chapter 7, when discussing language.

1. EXEMPLARS. Conceptual memory is formed by processing perceptual exemplars through abstraction and integration. Exemplars are initially retained through the mechanisms of simple memory (imprinting; see also section 6.3).

2. PROBABILITIES. The computational process whereby generalities, if

... a list, taken from an ancient Chinese encyclopedia entitled *Celestial Emporium of Benevolent Knowledge*, of the categories into which animals are to be classified: (a) those that belong to the Emperor, (b) embalmed ones, (c) those that are trained, (d) suckling pigs, (e) mermaids, (f) fabulous ones, (g) stray dogs, (h) those that are included in this classification, (i) those that tremble as if they were mad, (j) innumerable ones, (k) those drawn with a very fine camel's hair brush, (l) others, (m) those that have just broken a flower vase, (n) those that resemble flies from a distance.

— Jorge Luis Borges
The Analytical Language of John Wilkins (1984)

Conceptually, the most interesting aspect of this classification system is that it does not exist.

— Eleanor Rosch
Principles of Categorization (1978)

any, are abstracted and multiple exemplars integrated is statistical inference (entrenchment; see also section 5.4.4). When applied to memory structures, it can be viewed as purposive modification of the representational energy landscape.

3. CONTEXT. Because memory is always *for* something, the details of the hierarchically structured generalizations depend on the task (cf. Figure 6.15). Concepts that are related in one context (or state of mind — or state of development) may be unrelated in others or vice versa, and many seem completely *ad hoc* (relative to the default Rationalist view of concepts as absolute and immutable). Computationally, this dependence can be expressed in the language of conditional probability.

4. INTERCONNECTEDNESS. The brain supports such fluidity by linking the representations of concepts together into a highly ramified network. The conditional probabilities control the strength of network links, and are subject to change through experience (e.g., through the acquisition of new exemplars).

Undoubtedly the most striking aspect of the web of connections that weaves together the concepts is its global reach: it appears that virtually any two can be rapidly associated, given the right context (this is the computational basis of the property of cognition that philosophers call HOLISM). In human cognition, the only other component that relies on massively interconnected probabilistically weighted networks is language, which is the subject of Chapter 7. If you decide to peek ahead (the network aspect of language is outlined on p. 270), do come back — we are not done here yet.

MEANING HOLISM:
Our statements about the external world face the tribunal of sense experience not individually but only as a corporate body.

— Quine (1953, p.41)

6.6 Memory for social needs

Without implicit knowledge of naive physics ("will this jump kill me?"; cf. Figure 6.12 on page 179), an animal is unlikely to survive in the wild; for primates (and certain other taxa), the possession of commonsense knowledge of "folk psychology," built around concepts of goals, beliefs, and desires (Elio, 2002), is equally vital. Although the most essential tool of the human mind in representing self and others, language, is a uniquely human evolutionary novelty, the understanding of others as animate agents is part of our primate

heritage: "... human beings share with nonhuman primates all of their cognitive adaptations for space, objects, tools, categorization, quantification, understanding social relationships, communication, social learning, and social
cognition" (Tomasello, 2000b). The following brief survey of the memory
basis of folk psychology substantiates this observation, using as examples
three social cognitive functions that do not require a capacity for language
(albeit they can and do benefit from it in humans): imitation, collaboration,
and theory of mind. For each of these, I'll identify the main computational
role of memory and mention a few representative experimental findings that
illustrate it.

Figure 6.16 — For many species, social cognition is a survival skill. Humans too have it easier if they REMEMBER
LOVE.

6.6.1   Rewiring self to mimic others: imitation

Your light plane has crash-landed in the jungle of Sumatra. You have survived, but have no food or tools; nor do you know which plants are edible. While wandering around on an empty stomach, you stumble upon an orangutan sitting under a tree and wielding a stick to dislodge the seeds from a large leathery-looking pod. Many ripe pods are scattered under the tree (on which they apparently grow) but a quick examination proves that the seeds in each are protected by many thorns. What's a hungry primate to do? Most likely, you are going to do as the locals do: use a stick to get at the seeds. This would mean aping the locals in more than one sense: the orangutans *learn* the use of sticks, and certain other skills, by IMITATION.

Although such imitation is technically about association — between the observed sequence of actions and a motor program that would replicate them — it presents a challenging computational problem, because learners do not normally have access to the teachers' motor programs. The precise nature and the difficulty of this so-called CORRESPONDENCE problem (Heyes, 2005) depends on the task. The easiest situation is one in which the learner can observe his or her own movements as easily as those of the teacher are observed; in primates, this pertains to finger or hand movement. In this case, vision simply "closes the loop" (Figure 6.17 on the next page), and the learner's motor control system can proceed by adjusting the control parameters so as to minimize the visually estimated execution error.

What if the outcome of the movement is unobservable, as when facial expression is mimicked? The computational challenge of correspondence in this task, which humans manage as neonates, is the most severe: when I try to imitate someone else's smile or frown, I cannot even see how well I am doing (Meltzoff and Moore, 1977).[29] A nifty way to circumvent this difficulty is to get a lot of practice making faces at a mirror, committing to memory the many resulting associations between motor programs and visual stimuli. Infants clearly manage the same trick using a kind of a mirror — their caregivers' faces. As Heyes (2005) observes, the crucial missing link that closes the feedback loop in facial imitation is the presence of cooperative conspecifics; excited parents presumably respond to a baby's exploratory smile with a smile, rather than with a frown.

Language, even in its most rudimentary form, is a great help in solving the correspondence problem in imitation. A human infant may hear a word pertaining to an action while observing it performed by itself as well

Orangutans in Sumatra learn to extract the edible seeds of the *Neesia* tree from their pods by observing others doing it. Learning in this case is an instance of IMITATION — one of the many kinds of mimetic processes (Whiten, 2000, p.480). Learning to imitate by linking actions to perceptions depends on the global reach of the association networks (Keysers and Perrett, 2004). This may be why imitation only occurs in primates and in some species of birds (pigeons, quail, starlings and budgerigars).

as by others; learning the word and associating it back to the action's visual record and motor program would then create a place-holder for the entire bundle of representations, enabling their cross-activation. Indeed, as Thompson and Oden (2000) note, chimpanzees who have been taught simple "lexigram" symbols for objects are better at learning to group them into heterogeneous categories such as tools, within which associations must be made between different "kinds" of things (in the same sense that visual and motor data are of different kinds).

A robot learning to play tennis by imitation (Schaal, Ijspeert, and Billard, 2003).

Because it would be so much easier to show a robot what needs to be done than to program it (Schaal, 1999), automatic learning through imitation is a very active research area within Artificial Intelligence. As the Marr-Poggio methodology suggests, the first order of business is to figure out the computational nature of the problem — a non-trivial undertaking, given that the theories imported from ethology, cultural anthropology, or developmental psychology, insightful as they may be, are never stated explicitly or precisely enough to allow, for example, computational modeling.

The emerging computational understanding of imitation (Schaal et al., 2003) has led to significant progress in building robotic systems that imitate complex observed behaviors, ranging from pole balancing to tennis serve (Billard, Epars, Calinon, Cheng, and Schaal, 2004). The memory repre-

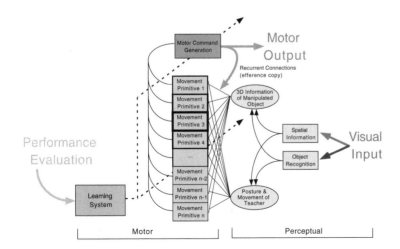

Figure 6.17 — The computational building blocks of a system geared for imitating others (Schaal, 1999) include a module for inferring motor programs from their observed effects (the perceptual functions on the right) and a proprioceptive feedback module for correcting the movement parameters (the "learning system" block on the left). The most challenging aspect of imitation is the CORRESPONDENCE PROBLEM (Heyes, 2005): connecting the observed behaviour of others to the planned behavior of self.

sentations that support such behaviors are of the familiar kind, employing statistical inference to structured concept formation; the latter may even include abstract rules, as in the "rock, scissors, paper" game, which a recently demonstrated program can learn simply by observing the human players do it (Needham, Santos, Magee, Devin, Hogg, and Cohn, 2005).

6.6.2   Tracking the performance of others: collaboration

The primates' proficiency at learning by imitation is handily complemented by their readiness to collaborate with each other — especially when there is no choice, or when it does not cost them anything. To make an informed decision about the worth of collaborating on a given task with other agents (usually conspecifics), an individual needs to take into account any available personal information concerning each candidate. In the simplest case, the computational requirement of planning a collaboration is therefore straightforward simple memory: doing the bookkeeping on how good a partner everyone is (and, when faced with a choice, choosing the better one). This is not very different from remembering binary dominance relationships — something that birds can do (remember pinyon jays from p. 18).

Primates that live in groups, such as macaques or baboons, are capable of remembering dominance hierarchies many levels deep. Can they put such representations to a use other than betting on the winner in a pitched fight? It appears that chimpanzees, who in the wild often collaborate with each other (for example, when hunting monkeys) can. Melis, Hare, and Tomasello (2006) put chimps in a situation where they could reach some fruit only by cooperating with one another. In each session, the subject could choose which of two other chimps to recruit for the task, by letting the would-be partner out of a cage. The chimps reliably chose the more effective of two possible partners on the basis of their experience with each of them on a previous day. In control trials, in which the fruit could be reached without help, the subject chimps selfishly left the others caged, however.

When valuable resources such as food are not at stake, chimpanzees exhibit an impressive willingness not just to collaborate with others for mutual gain, but to help others, just as humans do. Warneken and Tomasello (2006) describe a study of so-called instrumental helping, in which 18-month-old infants and young chimps were given opportunities to "help" experimental assistants in ten different tasks that involved out-of-reach objects and objects the access to which was blocked by obstacles. They report that infants helped in six out of the ten tasks, and chimps in five (all of them involving reaching).

6.6.3 Representing others: theory of mind

In summarizing their study, Warneken and Tomasello (2006) suggest that both children and chimpanzees "are willing to help, but may differ in their ability to interpret the other's need for help in different situations." The difficulty of the instrumental helping situation transcends anything that an animal may encounter while trying merely to imitate the motor behavior of others. The helper must infer not just the motor program behind the observed behavior of the would-be beneficiary, but also his or her *goal* in executing that program. The ability to infer the intentions of others and to hold them in memory while pursuing one's own goals — indeed, the very concept of goal — is part of a cognitive apparatus that has been termed the THEORY OF MIND.

According to Heyes (1998), "... individuals have a THEORY OF MIND if they have mental state concepts such as believe, know, want, and see, and ... use them to predict and explain behavior. Thus, an animal with a theory of mind believes that mental states play a causal role in generating behavior and infers the presence of mental states in others by observing their appearance and behavior under various circumstances."

Intentional states pertaining to beliefs, goals, or desires are more complex than basic perceptual representations of the kind I discussed back in Chapter 5. When I open the door of my refrigerator and look in, I *see* what's inside (section 5.7 should have given you a pretty good notion of what the act of seeing consists of, on all levels, from computational to neuronal). As far as I, the perceiver, am concerned, there is no need to complicate things by describing my representational state as *belief* about the scene that's in front of my eyes. If, however, in a moment of weakness I open the door to self-examination, all hell breaks loose.

Upon reflection, I discover that I not only see the milk carton — I also believe that I see it, believe that I believe that I see it, and so on ad infinitum. Worse, reflection also engenders doubt, and so these beliefs (all of them) must be qualified: for example, intellectual honesty requires that I entertain the standard Cartesian skepticism about the genuineness of my percept (unless I can rule out the possibility that an EVIL DEMON is surreptitiously stimulating my milk carton detector neurons, much like Salzman et al. (1990) induced motion perception in their monkeys).

The computational mechanism that saves me from descending into paranoia on account of all this uncertainty is essentially statistical (it helps to keep in mind here that **statistics is a mathematical framework not for capitulating in the face of uncertainty, but for managing it**). Think of the event I see milk as a label on a node in a Bayes network (Figure 6.15 on page 192), with another node labeled evil demon at work. Now, my entire life experience tells me that the prior probability of the latter is very, very low, compared to the conditional probability of milk in front of me, given that fridge is open. Because of that, when the network "runs," it confidently settles into the conclusion that I see milk (the algorithms of Bayesian decision-making actually support the estimation of confidence for such conclusions).

When what's at stake is my belief about *your* perception rather than mine, the situation is fraught with pitfalls. Suppose I observe you from the kitchen doorway opening the refrigerator (into which I cannot see from where I stand) and proceeding to register on your face an eyebrows-lifting, eyes-popping, jaw-dropping surprise. Am I to believe (a) that you were awarded, through a time-space wormhole, a glimpse of the Chicxulub meteorite tearing through the stratosphere on its way to end the Cretaceous Period, or (b) that you are merely stunned to find out that you're out of milk? It is hard to tell, much for the same reasons it could have been difficult for me to determine whether or not *I* saw milk; the difference is that the relevant Bayesian safety net is not accessible to me, because it's in *your* brain (I have no way of knowing, for example, whether your recent diet included hallucinogens).

As I hope you can see (hmm...), the complications are considerable, and I haven't even mentioned goals and desires yet! Those intentional states are even more difficult to discern reliably in others. Whereas the satisfaction conditions for a perceptual state extend back into its owner's past (as in the example just stated), the notion of a goal is centered around a *prediction* — and, as the great physicist Niels Bohr noted, prediction is difficult, especially about the future. And yet, most human adults (the rare exceptions being individuals suffering from severe autism) share the fundamental unspoken assumption that other people possess beliefs, goals, and desires. Most adults are also engaged in a constant, albeit rarely explicit, effort to discover what the intentional states of others are — which may be more successful, or less so (see Figure 6.18).

Our eagerness to project intentionality into the world is not confined to other people, or even to animals. Humans, including young children, are very liberal in adopting the INTENTIONAL STANCE towards any object in their environment that looks like it might be animate (this is a major factor in the emergence of religiosity; cf. Barrett, 2000). It is not difficult to see how the tendency to anthropomorphize is especially strong when the target is in fact both animate and humanoid. But how justified is the intentional stance with respect to apes?

A chimpanzee's or an orangutan's representations of their environment,

The decision whether to trust perception or to consider it an illusion induced by an EVIL DEMON is, of course, the famous philosophical dilemma noted (and set aside) by Descartes (1641). For our purposes, it helps to know just how complicated it would be, technically, to inject current into my brain in the setting of my kitchen. Of course, the whole shebang, including the kitchen, and indeed my entire life experience, could be fake.

WHAT WOULD THE BIG TRIANGLE DO? When shown a short animated clip in which some geometrical shapes moved around, the subjects of Heider and Simmel (1944) invariably described the events in intentional terms ("the big triangle *chased* the small one," etc.). Dennett (1987) calls the human predisposition to attribute intentions to just about any object that moves in what appears to be a purposive manner the INTENTIONAL STANCE.

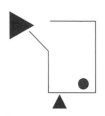

including the complex social scene of which they are part, are very sophisticated; for example, chimps are capable of acquiring "second-order" relational representations (discerning relations between relations, as in judging the identity of abstract patterns defined over variables), which have been long thought of as unique to humans (Thompson and Oden, 2000). Robotics research demonstrates, however, that cognitive sophistication in itself is not an indicator of the ability to attribute intentionality to others. For example, the robot that learns to swing a tennis racquet by imitating a human (Billard et al., 2004) does not represent the human as an intentional agent (we know that this is the case because we can look at its code).

Indeed, decades of work with nonhuman primates produced no evidence that they possess intentional concepts, even those that are the closest to perception and therefore the simplest, such as to see. Following an extensive survey of experimental data on primate social behavior, Heyes (1998) concluded that nonhuman primates do not possess a theory of mind: "... primates 'just do it'; they respond to observable cues, categorise them, form associations between them or make inferences about them, but they never ask themselves why, or whether other animals do the same thing." Tomasello (2000b) concurs: apes "... do not seem to understand their conspecifics as intentional agents like themselves who experience the world in ways similar

Figure 6.18 — WHAT WOULD JESUS DO? People attribute intentional states, including dispositions to action, to each other as a matter of routine; the ability to do so underlies such diverse activities as security profiling and movie casting. The attribution process is, however, not always reliable, as witnessed by the frequent disagreement concerning WWJD (What Would Jesus Do) in even moderately complicated situations.

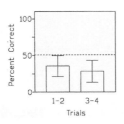

As this result from Povinelli, Bering, and Giambrone (2000, fig.10) indicates, chimpanzees who were tested on the ability to determine whether a research assistant could *see* them based their response on her general frontal aspect being visible, rather than on whether or not her eyes were open. Their performance was at chance in the first two trials, and became worse (indicating a significant preference for the incorrect response) thereafter.

A concept is not a single abstracted representation for a category, but is instead a skill for constructing idiosyncratic representations tailored to the current needs of situated action.

— Barsalou (2003b, p.521)

to themselves. ... Nonhuman primates do not point to distal entities in their environments, they do not hold up objects for others to see and share, and they do not actively give or offer objects to other individuals. They also do not actively teach one another, and the kinds of cooperation in which they engage are very simple and basic (i.e., they cooperate without an understanding of the role of the other)." It looks, therefore, that in realizing that there are other intentional agents out there humans, as a species, are alone on this planet.

6.7   Conceptual simulation: yours is the world, and they that dwell therein

On the account that I have been developing over the past several sections, the computational basis of conceptual knowledge takes the form of a probabilistically annotated network — a graphical model, of the kind depicted in Figure 6.15 on page 192 — that rearranges itself dynamically according to the demands of the situation and the task. The nature of this process, which continually weaves, unravels, and reconnects the web of conceptual memory, has been the subject of many studies. Before trying to get to the bottom of what it means to possess a system of concepts, let us consider several particularly telling experimental results, as recounted by Barsalou (2003b).

6.7.1   The embodiment of concepts: three representative results

The first one has been obtained by asking subjects to generate in each brief session as many properties for a given concept as they could. Suppose, for example, that I ask you to list all the properties of watermelon that you can think of during the next minute. (You may actually try it at home — the experiment is perfectly safe and free from side effects, except perhaps a transitory craving for a watermelon.) My guess is that your list includes properties such as heavy, green, and maybe football-shaped (if you live anywhere but in the United States, this last feature would seem less probable).

Suppose now that I ask you to describe a half watermelon. In this case, the list of properties is likely to include also red and juicy — much more so than in the previous condition. It is as if you were reading the properties off a *visualized* image of a watermelon, rather than copying them from an internal crib-sheet (which is what the standard view of memory as a wax tablet to be written on corresponds to). It turns out that subjects generate more internal properties (which under regular "viewing" conditions would be invisible) even for novel concepts, such as glass car, which are unlikely to have become entrenched enough for two separate lists to have been pre-compiled, lending further support to the visualization hypothesis.

In a complementary experimental approach, subjects are presented with names of features and are asked to verify that they belong to the concept prespecified for the session (to keep the participants alert, only half of the features in each session do). Suppose that in such a study you are asked to decide whether or not mane belongs to pony; my prediction is that you would do that significantly faster if in the preceding trial mane has been paired with horse than if it has been paired with lion. Thus, thinking about horse mane, but not about lion mane, PRIMES thinking about pony mane. This effect makes a lot of sense under the visualization hypothesis (think about what the three animals just mentioned look like). A control for the visualization interpretation is provided by a condition that involves the same three animals, but has the subjects verify the presence of belly in each. In this case, there is no priming, suggesting that it is perceptual and not conceptual similarity between prime and target that matters.

The strong connection between conceptual memory and perception is a natural consequence of the process whereby concepts are acquired, which, as we saw in section 6.5.4, is rooted in perceptual input. Studies mentioned by Barsalou (2003b) demonstrate, however, that concepts are also strongly connected to motor output. For an example that illustrates this point, hold a pencil between your teeth (sideways) and look in the mirror; you'll see that the pencil restricts the range of expressions that you can assume. If I now ask you to perform categorical judgment of emotion in a series of faces shown to you on a computer screen, you are liable to do worse than controls. A full activation of the concepts of surprise, happiness or anger depends, it turns out, on the subject's unconstrained ability to activate the muscles that control facial expression — even if the observed expressions are not fully reenacted by the observer during perception.

PRIMING. Prior exposure to a perceptual stimulus affects the subject's response time on its subsequent presentations (Ochsner, Chiu, and Schacter, 1994). Usually, the response the second time around is faster, except when the initial task demands that the subject ignore the stimulus, in which case the second response is slower than control (DeSchepper and Treisman, 1996). This response time effect is a singularly useful tool for the study of internal representations (Wiggs and Martin, 1998). In particular, if self-priming is used as control, the priming speed-up caused by other stimuli becomes an effective measure of the similarity between them and the original stimulus (used as the probe).

6.7.2 Simulation of active, embodied concepts

A unifying theoretical view that subsumes both visualization (at work in the watermelon and the mane examples) and motor reenactment (responsible for the pencil-in-mouth effect) is SIMULATION (Barsalou, 1999). In fact, the very

It always pays to simulate complex problems before attempting to solve them for real. In cognition, simulation is also the most natural way of representing concepts that are active and embodied in the first place.

It could be that the only way to predict what another person will do is to run in one's own brain the processes that the other person is running in theirs. ... To obtain information about another person's internal mental state, it may be necessary to imagine what it would be like to be the other person via direct SIMULATION.

— Adolphs (1999, p.476).

distinction between perceptual, conceptual, and motor aspects of the memory for everyday, commonsense knowledge is counterproductive: all three are involved on every occasion of memory use. A glance at a pyramid of watermelons in the store invokes the entire complex of knowledge that you have about watermelon, including what they look like on the inside, how they taste, and what it would feel like to lift one.

As the behavioral findings mentioned above indicate, this knowledge is *concrete* rather than abstract. It is now also known to be *distributed* across the brain regions responsible for the various sensory and motor modalities. Even when you merely reminisce about watermelons while doing something else, you *feel* the redness of the open watermelon with your visual cortex, its sweetness with your gustatory area, and its heft with your motor neurons (for a brief review of the neurobiological evidence to that effect, see section 7.4.2).

The *ad hoc* nature of categories suggests that conceptual knowledge is also *dynamic*. More precisely, it becomes active at need (you do not go about thinking constantly about watermelons, even if you happen to know a lot about what they look, taste, and feel like). The form it takes depends on the task, which is why conceptualization — including perceptual states and action plans — is prone to systematic "top-down" bias (recall the pareidolia effect described in Figure 5.10 on page 109), as well as the usual effects of noise and imperfections.

According to the conceptual simulation theory, therefore, entertaining a concept amounts to a partial reinstatement of the sensory-motor "snapshot" that represents it in memory. Such snapshots are composite: they integrate probabilistically the concept owner's entire history of interaction with the relevant aspects of the world. Thanks to this rich and multifaceted informational support, conceptual simulation brings about a state of "being there conceptually" (Barsalou, 2003b) — not quite as vivid, perhaps, as having one of the original perceptual or motor experiences, but clearly informative enough to fulfill the purpose for which concepts exist: help their owner contend with the rich and multifaceted world out there.

6.7.3   Virtual people

The discovery that concepts stored in memory are ready-to-run simulations has very exciting consequences for understanding the computations behind the folk-psychological theory of mind. The premise for the series of observations I am about to offer is this: if you can simulate the interaction of my body with gravity to figure out what would befall me if I jumped off a cliff, then you just might be able to simulate the interaction of my brain with itself and with the rest of the world (which is what my mind is) to predict which way I'd choose to turn when poised on the precipice. To be precise, by using a portion of your brain to run a SIMULATION of certain aspects of my persona (which is of course based on your own idea of what makes me tick), you are literally rather than metaphorically putting oneself in my place.

In purely computational terms, simulation is a very straightforward process. For simplicity, let us consider first the paradigmatic case: one Turing Machine (section 2.3.2) simulating another; let's call them TM_A and TM_B. Recall that any TM can be fully specified by a finite program — its state transition table, which determines what actions (state transition and tape print-out) will be taken, given the current state and the symbol that has just been read from the memory tape. Let us arrange for the transition table of TM_B to be written on TM_A's tape, using a suitable code. Next, let us program TM_A so that when it reads an input symbol (from another portion of its tape) it consults the transition table of TM_B and takes the action that is called for by the outcome of that operation. To the outside world, TM_A will now look functionally indistinguishable from TM_B — even though the latter exists only virtually (in the memory of TM_A); the only telltale may be a slowdown in the operation (relative to running TM_B directly).[30]

The example just sketched is somewhat extreme in that the simulator, TM_A, "went native" by practically *becoming* its target, TM_B. A cognitive agent that resorts to simulation would typically need to run different processes at different times (possibly more than one at a time), while ensuring that the bundle of memories that defines its core self is preserved. Computer science has long ago developed algorithms and protocols necessary for this purpose; programs whose task is to allow safe and efficient execution of other, subordinate processes are called operating systems. An operating system ensures safety and security of applications it runs by sequestering their code in a specially designated memory space.[31]

Functionally, such a segregation can be likened to a person assuming someone else's point of view temporarily, to explore its implications. Imagine that you have an American friend, whom you know moderately well, and who happens to be a Republican. Your concept of her is therefore a blend of the Republican stereotype and whatever knowledge you have of her actual opinions and personality traits (if she were a very close friend, the relative weight of the stereotype would be very small). Suppose now that you decide

Simulation can be DIGITAL or ANALOG. An instance of the latter is the delay line in the owl sound localization system (Figure 4.4 on page 73), which is a kind of analog computer that simulates propagation of sound through the air. When you count the seconds between the flash of a lightning and the sound of thunder to figure out how far the thunderstorm is, you're conducting a digital simulation (this, however, depends in turn on your built-in sense of timing, which is probably best described as analog). In this section I stick to Turing Machine examples purely for convenience.

to figure out what her stance would be on an issue that divides the electorate, but not along party lines (say, nuclear power as an alternative to oil and coal). You cannot *know* the answer ahead of time, because it depends on many factors that you have not brought together into consideration on any previous occasion. Consequently, you do your best to think like your friend — but only for a few moments. There, you have just conducted a limited-scope simulation of her, in a corner of your mind set aside precisely for this purpose.

What if the simulation is not so limited in its scope? A married couple celebrating their golden anniversary or a pair of old friends who have known each other since childhood can (and often do) complete each other's sentences or predict each other's attitude towards practically any issue. When I know someone else that well, my simulation of that person can get both very detailed and very reliable. Because of one particularly striking computational property of all simulations, such knowledge has mind-boggling consequences.

The property in question has to do with the peculiar relationship between computation and simulation: **simulating computation is indistinguishable in its outcome from performing it in the first place** (cf. note 11 on page 81). Indeed, because the same computation can be realized by different physical means (recall section 1.2 on page 7), all instances of the same computation are in a sense simulations, or, equivalently, none is — any one is as genuine as any other. Simulation is thus *functionally transparent* with respect to computation.

Because of this, and because minds are composed of computations, this property implies that simulating certain aspects of a mind brings them into being (Egan, 1999). When activated, my memories of a person — if they are sufficiently detailed and faithful, and especially when augmented with a capacity for language — bring that person's mind into being. As we'll see later in the book, the functional transparency of simulation with respect to mind-stuff provides the computational basis for much that is strange and wonderful about cognition, including communing with the dead (an everyday experience for many people; cf. section 9.6) and personal immortality (a distinct engineering prospect, as we shall see in Chapter 11).

[The Simpsons discussing Krusty's belated bar-mitzvah bid, following his mid-life identity crisis.]
Lisa: There's nothing in the Talmud that forbids it.
Bart: How do you know all this stuff?
Lisa: I have a Jewish imaginary friend. Her name is Rachel Cohen, and she just got into Brandeis.

—

There are always more implications of what we know than is humanly possible to explore. When a person decides to pursue a line of reasoning that starts with some premises, he or she can actually learn something new, even though the entire process is confined to an internally conducted simulation.

6.8 The stuff memory is made on

Now that we have a notion of what primates use memory for, let us have a quick look at how it is implemented in the primate brain. What follows is a very cursory overview of the neural substrate of memory. It alludes to, but does not detail, several familiar textbook distinctions among various "memory systems" (short-term vs. long-term, episodic vs. semantic, etc.; cf. Burgess and Hitch, 2005; Miyashita, 2004; Squire, 2004).

Although memories can be built out of mechanical contraptions or electrical circuits (Figure 6.3 on page 162), those made of neurons are at present functionally the most sophisticated. My notebook excels in reliably managing huge volumes of information; as I noted before, it is even capable of rudimentary associative recall. Still, between the two of us I am the only one who can spin a thread out of the strands of memory. I owe this distinction not to the wet stuff my memory is made of, but to how it has been, and continually is, organized through experience.

It is an extraordinary demonstration of the deeply ingrained inertia of evolution, which tends to let "good enough" be, that the basic cellular and molecular mechanisms behind memory organization are conserved from mollusks to mammals (Kandel, 2003, pp.430-1). I find it equally remarkable that the other, complementary aspects of memory — those that distinguish mammals from mollusks, and in particular make primates like ourselves stand apart — are also sufficiently uniform *within* mammalian species to support a broad understanding that extends over both mice and men.

Because of this uniformity (cf. Barsalou, 2005), anatomical and physiological data from a range of animal models, including rats and monkeys, can all be brought to bear on the study of human memory. In what follows, I focus on the levels of brain areas, neural assemblies, and individual neurons (if you are interested also in the molecular biology and the genetics of memory, Eric Kandel's (2003) Nobel lecture is an excellent entry point into the literature).

On the level of the major architectural divisions of the brain, the distinction between isocortical and allocortical (hippocampal) memory systems, suggested long ago by Marr (1970, 1971) and others, has withstood the test of time (O'Reilly, 2006b).[32] In particular, the anatomical division between the hippocampus and the rest of the temporal lobe roughly parallels the functional distinction between episodic and "semantic" memory as defined behaviorally.

Acquisition and consolidation — or, returning to the terminology introduced earlier in this chapter, imprinting and entrenchment — of memories

We are such stuff
As dreams are made on...

— William Shakespeare
The Tempest (IV, i, 156-157)

begin in the hippocampus, where episodic traces are first laid down (Eichenbaum, Dudchenko, Wood, Shapiro, and Tanila, 1999; recall Figure 6.10 on page 176). Anatomically, the hippocampus is a crossroads of multimodal perceptual and motor information, which includes in addition to the immediate stimuli their behavioral context. This makes it a perfect spot in which to pin down complex associations that constitute embodied, context-sensitive episodic memories. If the statistics of the animal's experience justifies it, these traces can be generalized into "semantic" representations that are distilled by the modality-specific areas in the temporal lobe, where they are also stored.

Many of the anatomical structures in the hippocampus are easy to interpret in computational terms. The recurrent collaterals of the pyramidal cells in the hippocampal CA1-CA3 circuit implement the kind of crossbar network that can support hetero- and auto-associative memory (cf. Figure 6.4 on page 165).[33] It is very important to note that a crossbar "switch" can connect any of its inputs to any of the outputs. This makes possible a highly flexible, combinatorially productive generation of complex concepts out of simpler ones, much like "goal cells" can be constructed out of place cells, as sketched in Figure 6.11 (indeed, the evolutionary origin of human semantic and episodic memories may be the spatial memory that seems to be the "original" function of the hippocampus; Miyashita, 2004).

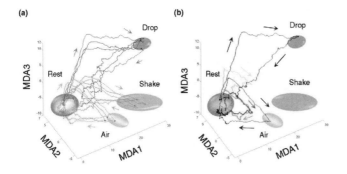

Figure 6.19 — Lin et al. (2006) applied Multiple Discriminant Analysis (MDA, a relative of Principal Component Analysis; recall Figure 3.12 on page 56) to ensemble responses of hippocampal CA1 cells in mice that were exposed to three types of startle experience: puff of air, drop, and shake. *Left:* when plotted in the three principal dimensions, state-space trajectories cluster by event type. *Right:* later events cause the original traces to be replayed; the smaller-scale traces correspond to spontaneous memory reactivations.

6.8.1 Hippocampal combinatorics

The complexity of using a crossbar switch rapidly gets out of hand as the dimensionality of the representation space grows: the number of possible pairwise connections among 100 lines is $100^2 = 10,000$, whereas for $1,000$ lines it is $1,000,000$, and for $10,000$ lines it is $100,000,000$ (the problem, by the way, is getting enough data for training, not the mere maintenance of many synapses; it is a manifestation of the curse of dimensionality, which I first mentioned on p. 59). The dynamics revealed by recent electrophysiological studies of simultaneously monitored hundreds of hippocampal cells is completely consistent with this computational constraint. As Lin et al. (2006) showed, the ensemble responses in area CA1 are confined to a low-dimensional subspace of the representation space that is defined by the totality of the neurons; (Figure 6.19 shows the three principal dimensions out of more than seven hundred).

The low-dimensional nature of the hippocampal representations enables cortical areas surrounding the hippocampus to learn essentially random associations among stimuli in the appropriate modality (as long as they are behaviorally warranted). For example, neurons in the mainly visual area TE in the inferotemporal cortex can be rapidly trained to associate pairs of stimuli that are related only episodically, by virtue of their temporal contingency in the stimulus sequence (Miyashita, 2004; Sakai and Miyashita, 1991).

Neurons being generally less than perfectly reliable, an association between two items is never perfect, nor is it necessarily an abstraction derived from many episodic memories. We may, therefore, expect the episodic-semantic distinction to be *graded* rather than absolute, and indeed it is. Electrophysiological studies based on simultaneous multicellular recordings afford a direct and detailed view of the hierarchical structure of combinatorial cliques of neurons that corresponds to the episodic-semantic continuum. This structure emerges from a hierarchical cluster analysis of ensemble response data, which reveals a continuum between "episodic" (that is, specific) and "semantic" (general) types of encoding; it is illustrated in Figure 6.20.

6.8.2 Advanced concepts and mirror neurons

Combinatorially boosted memory formation is especially powerful when applied to the rich and diverse representations maintained by a primate brain. Our new knowledge of the operation of neuron ensembles in the hippocampus allows us to understand on a deeper level the acquisition of sophisticated concepts, which similarly relies on the combinatorics of simpler concepts already acquired; representationally rich brains get richer.

A fascinating example of the power of this process is the emergence of imitation from the basic ability to associate perceptions with actions (Heyes, 2005). In accordance with the principles of neural representation identified by Barlow (1972), which I mentioned in Chapter 3 (see p. 39), even such complex associations are encoded at the level of single cells. The telltale characteristic of these MIRROR NEURONS is selective response to a given action, whether performed by self or observed in others (Figure 6.21 on the

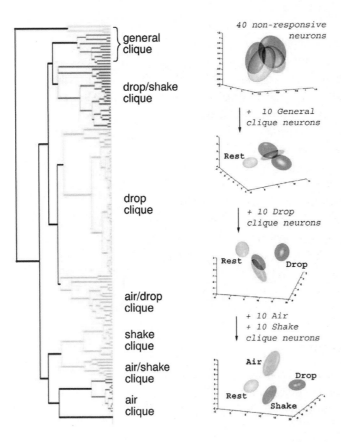

Figure 6.20 — The HIERARCHICAL REPRE-SENTATION of startle event types in mouse hippocampus (cf. Figure 6.19). The 260 simultaneously recorded CA1 neurons in the study of Lin et al. (2005) span a 260-dimensional space in which each event is represented by a point. By analyzing the distances among events, the researchers grouped them into clusters (*left*), which revealed a very intuitive hierarchical structure: "Any given startling episode is encoded by a combinatorial assembly of neural cliques in series, invariantly consisting of the general startle clique, a subgeneral startle clique, a startle-identity-specific clique and a context-specific startle clique" (Lin et al., 2006, Box 1). The diagram on the *right* shows how the ensemble response gets progressively better at supporting a classification of the event, as different neuron sub-populations are adduced to the ensemble.

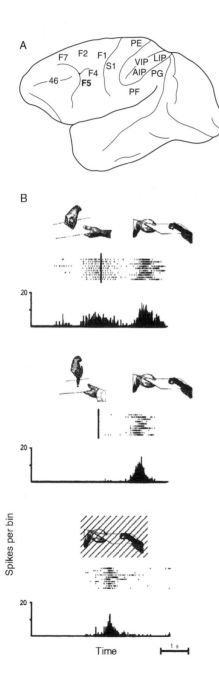

Figure 6.21 — The primate brain contains a system of MIRROR NEURONS, which are characterized by comparable response to actions such as grasping, whether observed in others or performed by self (Gallese and Goldman, 1998; Rizzolatti and Craighero, 2004). A: a side view of the monkey brain, with the areas relevant to the mirror neuron system labeled. B, *top:* the individual spike trains, and a histogram collapsed over multiple trials, produced by a single F5 neuron in response to two events – an observation of a food pellet being grasped, followed by the monkey's action of grasping it. The neuron responds to both. B, *middle:* when the experimenter grasps the food with a tool, the neuron is silent. B, *bottom:* the neuron responds when the monkey performs the grasp in complete darkness, indicating that the motor signal alone suffices to drive it. Mirror neurons have been hypothesized to implement imitation and simulation in social contexts (Gallese et al., 2004), phenomenal experience in perception (Gallese, 2005), and even language (Rizzolatti and Arbib, 1998). In itself, however, the discovery of mirror neurons cannot lead to any particularly deep insight into the *computational* nature of any cognitive function (see the note on p. 312); for that, it must be supplemented by computational analysis focusing in particular on the learning of mirror-like responses from experience. Indeed, a recent computational study of evolution in a population of artificial neural networks showed that "neurons" with mirror-like response patterns can emerge spontaneously in systems that are only required to imitate others (Borenstein and Ruppin, 2005). A more biologically realistic model of the emergence of mirror neurons under a Hebbian learning regime, which may resolve the correspondence problem — associating observed and performed actions (Heyes, 2005; cf. Figure 6.17 on page 197) — has been outlined by Keysers and Perrett (2004).

One may suppose that neurons jointly tuned to sequences of actions and, by association, to their perceived outcomes could support context-sensitive, predictive action coding which may be useful for understanding the intentions of others by observing them. Such neurons have indeed been identified in the parietal lobe in the monkey (Fogassi, Ferrari, Gesierich, Rozzi, Chersi, and Rizzolatti, 2005). They are, however, only the tip of the iceberg: the neural circuits that support social concepts such as intention are widely distributed across the brain (Martin and Weisberg, 2003; Saxe, 2006; Siegal and Varley, 2002). In particular, these circuits also extend to areas implicated in emotion-related information processing (cf. p. 172), such as the AMYGDALA.

Humans, as you can imagine, meet the challenge of figuring out what their neighbors are up to with the entire might of their brain arsenal, in which pride of place goes to the ultimate weapon: language (Saxe, 2006). Thus, even though much (if not most) of our capacity for social cognition is supported by mechanisms found also in other primates, we are uniquely equipped for developing an effective theory of other minds because we can gossip about them.

For the sake of a little experiment, please read this list of words (I'll return to it in a few pages): bed, rest, awake, tired, dream, wake, snooze, blanket, doze, slumber, snore, nap, peace, yawn, drowsy; nurse, sick, lawyer, medicine, health, hospital, dentist, physician, ill, patient, office, stethoscope, surgeon, clinic, cure.

6.9 Using memory

The human capacity for articulate communication presents psychologists with some interesting opportunities for studying memory in the context of verbal learning and verbal behavior. Historically, the tradition of using verbal materials in memory research goes back to the first quantitative investigations by Hermann Ebbinghaus of the time course, capacity, and other characteristics of memory for sequences of nonsense syllables — the kind of stimulus for which the concepts of "storage" and "recall" apply literally (such stimuli are, after all, totally unrelated to any behaviorally relevant setting, and so their processing falls under none of the categories of real memory tasks that I have been discussing earlier in this chapter).

Studies that use meaningless stimuli such as lists of isolated words or digits, which are still very popular in memory research (Burgess and Hitch, 2005), naturally operate within what Koriat and Goldsmith (1996a) called the "storehouse" metaphor, which views memory as a passive repository where items are stored and from which they are retrieved either wholly successfully, or not at all. Natural memory, in comparison, is concerned with meaningful stimuli, for which it is possible — indeed, imperative — to consider not just the quantity of the items stored, but also their quality. The meta-memory process that exercises the necessary control over retrieval is part of a larger cluster of oversight functions collectively known as META-COGNITION.

6.9.1 Meta-memory

The issue of the quality of remembered information, and therefore of control over its output, comes to the fore as soon as we acknowledge the graded nature of biological memory mechanisms. How does human memory address the standing concern about output quality? Intuitively, one may expect quality to be traded off for quantity in some contexts, but not in others. Participants in a brainstorming session, for example, may feel sufficiently relaxed to not care too much about the quality of the information proffered to the group, focusing instead on increasing the quantity of the items, which may spur and enliven the discussion. In contrast, it would be a dereliction of duty on the part of politicians planning a war if they were to base their decisions on the quantity of informants' recollections of enemy missiles being trucked around, rather than on their quality.

META-COGNITION ("meta" meaning "beyond" in Greek) is a collective name for phenomena that have to do with the mind's perception of its own internal states. Some examples are: tip of the tongue (TOT), having the answer to a question almost within reach; feeling of knowing (FOK), having high confidence in knowing or not knowing the answer, even when the explicit answer itself is unavailable or not required by the task; ease of learning (EOL), the anticipation of the ability to learn a given task. Meta-cognitive functions that monitor internal cognitive states can have significant effects on decisions and actions.

These examples highlight the importance of taking into account the task *context* for the proper functioning of a memory system. A massive amount of evidence indeed attests to the existence in human memory of a sophisticated output control system that interposes between the storage mechanisms and the output channel (Koriat, Goldsmith, and Pansky, 2000).[34] By and large, this system is highly successful in striking a balance between quality and quantity in memory output — Koriat et al. (2000, p.522) point out that on the average over 85% of items freely recalled in a series of memory studies they surveyed are correct — but it is not perfect (cf. Figure 6.22).

The dissociation between quantity and quality of recall is well illustrated by the findings of Koriat (1995), who had subjects participate in an "erudition game" in which they were given trivia questions and were asked to report their confidence before volunteering (or withholding) an answer (see Table 6.2 on page 215). Recall performance was measured by *accessibility* (ACC; the percentage of subjects who offered an answer, whether right or wrong) and by *accuracy* (OBA; Output-Bound Accuracy, defined as the percentage of correct responses among those provided). When taken together, these measures result in an estimate both of the quantity of recalled items (ACC) and of their quality (OBA).

The questions in this study had been chosen so as to vary in their difficulty, and to be sure the patterns of recall performance they elicited resulted in a three-way split between items on which the subjects were consensually correct (CC – high OBA), consensually wrong (CW – low OBA), or reluctant to volunteer an answer (LA – low ACC). The very existence of these categories of questions indicates that quantity and quality of memory do not always go together. Furthermore, the FOK reported by the subjects varied widely for questions in the three categories used, being significantly higher for the high-accessibility items — even those with respect to which the subjects were in error. The dissociation between FOK and actual accuracy suggests that human memory is not only fallible: at times, the subjects' intuitions run counter to their performance, resulting in a false feeling of knowing.

There are many contextual factors that contribute to the meta-cognitive oversight of memory (Koriat et al., 2000). The most obvious one I already alluded to in the two examples earlier in this section — it is the trade-off between quality and quantity of retrieved items, as determined by what the game theorists call the payoff matrix pertinent to the situation.[35] Another weighty factor is emotional involvement, which is relevant, for example, in the domain studied by Bahrick, Hall, and Berger (1996): students' memory for their high school grades. Because grades can be easily verified objec-

Here's the quiz I promised: did the words "sleep" and "doctor" appear on the list you have read several pages back? After responding, have another look at the list. Were you correct? Much is being made of the tendency of subjects to produce false positive responses to such questions (and to fail to recall many of the actually presented words). Despite appearances, this little example from (Roediger III and McDermott, 1995) illustrates not a failure of human memory, but one of its strongest points: regression to a schema, a process that lets the details slip, yet retains the gist that is usually a good statistical summary of the stimulus.

Figure 6.22 — A scene from Akira Kurosawa's film *Rashomon*. The short story by Ryūnosuke Akutagawa, *In the grove*, whose plot the film follows, examines the possibility — or rather the impossibility — of reconstructing a complex event solely on the basis of EYEWITNESS MEMORY. Even when one sets aside the many subtleties of human personality and social situations (illuminated so sharply by Kurosawa's genius), consistent absolute certainty is difficult to expect from a network of neurons, given what we already know about how the brain/mind works (Loftus, 2003). Insisting on always having "all the truth and nothing but the truth" would therefore seem to place an unrealistic stricture on living memory.

tively, this work yielded data both on the quantity and on the accuracy of the subjects' memories. Perhaps not entirely unexpectedly, the findings revealed a strong correlation between the grade and the accuracy of its recollection, which varied from 29% for Ds to 89% for As. Correlation between higher accuracy and greater confidence (FOK) was present, but was considerably weaker than between accuracy and the actual grade.

Computations involved in memory monitoring

The need to figure out when the quality of an item whose retrieval is being attempted is good enough to opt for its output (and thus score a point on the quantity count) presents an interesting computational challenge. Operating systems that control modern computers, which face a similar need, solve it by maintaining, in addition to the information stored in named files, directories of file names. In such an environment, it is possible to determine whether a chunk of data is present in memory by consulting the directory, without having to retrieve the file itself. Does the human memory system have a similarly privileged direct access to the information regarding the presence of an item in "storage"?

The dissociation between quality (accuracy) and quantity in the many studies that explored meta-cognitive control of memory suggests that the parallel between the brain and a directory/file system does not hold. On the contrary, the results are compatible with the view that the FOK cues that are generated by the meta-level memory processes and are relied upon, to a cer-

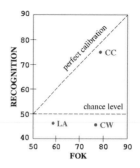

OVERCONFIDENCE in recognition memory, after Koriat (1995, experiment 2). Subjects reported their FOK immediately upon stimulus presentation, then attempted recognition. The FOK and recognition scores were both high for easy questions (CC) and low for questions that were hard and were seen as such (LA). Certain deceptively easy questions (CW) resulted in a high FOK yet low actual recognition rate (cf. Table 6.2).

Table 6.2 — Two examples of each of three kinds of questions used by Koriat (1995) in his study of the relationships between quality and quantity in trivia recognition and recall (abbreviations: ACC – Accessibility; OBA – Output-Bound Accuracy; CC – Consensually Correct; CW – Consensually Wrong; LA – low Accessibility).

class	question	answer	ACC, %	OBA, %
CC	Who played Dorothy in *The Wizard of Oz*?	Judy Garland	33.3	75.0
CC	What jazz player is known as "Bird"?	Charlie Parker	16.7	83.3
CW	What is the capital of Uganda?	Kampala	13.9	0.0
CW	Corsica belongs to what country?	France	61.1	9.1
LA	Who invented peanut butter?	George Washington Carver	0.0	–
LA	What is Iceland's legislature called?	Althing	0.0	–

On a clear disk, you can seek forever.

— *Anon. computer user*

tain extent, in predicting the accuracy of an item's recall are derived from the item itself. A model that captures this characteristic of human memory is outlined in Figure 6.23.

The central features of this model are (i) parallel access to the LTM on the part of the retrieval and the monitoring processes, and (ii) the possibility of manipulating the response criterion that determines whether or not the recalled information will be volunteered by the subject. Both the quantity of the information and, more importantly, its accuracy, depend on this criterion, often in complicated ways. Many examples of the dissociation between quantity and accuracy of memory recall, and of systematic effects of the payoff conditions imposed on the subject on the tradeoff between them, can be found in the literature reviewed by Koriat et al. (2000).[36]

Whose memory is it anyway?

An exquisitely unsettling version of the memory monitoring problem arises from a concern that has been steadily seeping into the public consciousness from the literary heritage of the brilliant 20th century prophet of paranoia, Philip K. Dick. At issue is the authenticity of one's own recollections of

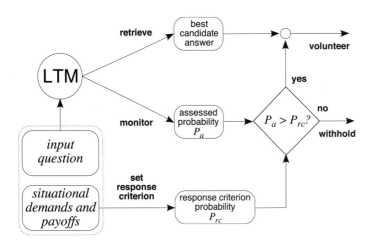

Figure 6.23 — A block diagram of a model of memory access, after Koriat and Goldsmith (1996b). Support for this type of model comes, for instance, from word recall studies, in which the amount of partial information recalled (individual letters) is as good a predictor of correct recall of the entire word as the subjective feeling of knowing (FOK), indicating that the monitoring process has no privileged source of data to go by. In the model, both retrieval and monitoring are fed by the same pool of information (LTM); the subject's decision whether or not to volunteer an answer depends on the payoff-related response criterion P_{rc}.

one's past. The concern is exemplified by the plot of Dick's short story *We can remember it for you wholesale.*[37]

In the story, a bored construction worker, who cannot afford to go on a real vacation to a place of his choice (which happens to be Mars), is talked into buying the next best thing: a total memory of a vacation, to be implanted into his brain. In a characteristically Dickian twist, the ensuing events lead the protagonist to suspect that he had in fact been to Mars and that his memories of that journey were artificially suppressed.

The concern about memory authenticity is becoming less fantastic with every advance in virtual reality and in direct computer-brain interfacing.[38] Real-life memory implantation can, however, happen without any technical wizardry, through non-intrusive, inconspicuous verbal manipulation of the subject. Koriat et al. (2000, pp.505-507) mention several studies in which subjects had been implanted with false memories that many of them later insisted were real. They conclude:

> These studies show that false memories can be implanted. Two procedures that are particularly conducive to the creation of false memories are imagination instructions and repeated testing.
> Whereas the former procedure is common in psychotherapy as a

Figure 6.24 — *The Memory of a Journey III*, by René Magritte. On the functional level, memory is perception of the past (Koriat et al., 2000), and as such is subject to the same illusions, distortions, etc., as immediate perception. On the neuronal level, we know how easy it is to cause a brain to perceive a very specific stimulus by directly activating a small clique of neurons in the appropriate region (Salzman et al., 1990). Thus, even if a memory appears rock-solid, it may be unreal in any of the several senses discussed in this section.

means of encouraging the recovery of repressed memories, the latter is common in police investigations.

— Koriat et al. (2000, p.506)

In a review article titled *Our changeable memories: legal and practical implications*, Loftus (2003) describes how subjects were "implanted" with a false memory of a hot-air balloon ride, with the help of a photograph made up of a real snapshot of the subject as a child posing with a relative, pasted into a stock photograph of a hot-air balloon gondola. Subjects shown the fake photograph were asked to tell "everything you can remember without leaving anything out, no matter how trivial it may seem." Following two further interviews, 50% of the subjects had recalled the fictitious balloon ride in childhood. Some of the subjects volunteered details: "I'm still pretty certain it occurred when I was in sixth grade at, um, the local school there... I'm pretty certain that mum is down on the ground taking a photo."

Technology may not be needed for implanting fake memories, but it can help guard against such manipulations. Computer scientists have long been concerned with protecting the integrity of data storage, not only against accidental small-scale errors (for which error correction algorithms provide an extremely effective remedy), but also against wholesale substitution of credibly looking, yet foreign, implanted information for authentic data. Suppose someone invades your computer and inserts into the photo album from last summer's trip to Northern California several pictures that had not been there when you downloaded the album from your camera. The extra pictures all bear the proper time stamps: the directory information associated with the album folder states that all the files in it have been there since last July. Can such malfeasance be detected?

Perhaps not *post hoc* — but you could have prevented it by resorting ahead of time to any of a number of algorithmic techniques. One such technique is cryptographic checksumming (Cohen, 1987), which is designed to make the probability of memory forgery or of breaking its protection code in a given amount of time arbitrarily low. Algorithms based on this idea assign the protected file a number (the checksum) that is generated from the file contents using a special "one-way" or trapdoor function — easy to compute, but very difficult to invert.

The one-way property guarantees (usually probabilistically) that the file cannot be altered in any way without affecting the checksum. When used in conjunction with a safe checksum repository, this approach solves Philip K. Dick's problem.[39] Of course, for this method to be directly applicable to your memories you would have to keep them outside your brain, on a computer, which is likely to exacerbate the paranoia in Dick's disciples.

Interestingly enough, whatever built-in defenses that we may deploy against malicious manipulation of memory of the kind discussed by Koriat et al. (2000) operate on a computational principle that is related to checksumming. Just as it happens in perception — and memory in action is perception of the past (Koriat et al., 2000, p.484) — the relevant statistics is computed by performing for each memory item a set of measurements that places it in a multidimensional representation space (*meta*-representation, actually, because it represents the contents of another representation, along with its context). The resulting list of numbers that are the feature values of an item allows its owner to ask: "Does this memory *feel* right?"[40]

This is precisely the kind of question that a memory sentinel addresses when it compares the checksum computed from a suspect version of a file to the one generated earlier from its trusted version. The answer may or may not be in error: a good fit — when the memory feels right — means simply that the item in question does not constitute a statistical outlier relative to its context that serves as reference. Indeed, memory implantation works best when the fake item fits well with the subject's persona (that is, with the rest of the contents of his or her memory), or conforms to some deeply entrenched event or situation schema.

6.9.2 Mnemonics

Unlimited-capacity, thoroughly indexed, portable external memory in the form of notebook computers and the World-Wide Web that extends far beyond their screens is a luxury that has not been available to humankind until very recently. In the absence of external mnemonic machinery, people who by virtue of their vocation or intellectual inclinations needed very good memory had to rely on specially developed memory skills or "arts" (Yates, 1966). The best-known of these was the ancient *Ars Memoriae*, which was taught (under both rhetoric and dialectic) in the schools of classical Greece and Rome.

We owe much of our knowledge of the classical Art of Memory to Marcus Tullius Cicero, who included an account of it in his treatise *De Oratore*. Cicero, the most famous self-made man in the history of the Roman republic, was elected quæstor at the age of 30, ædile at 36, prætor at 39, and consul — the highest executive rank of the republic — at 42. He was repeatedly promoted solely on the strength of his personal qualities, which included the ability to deliver hours-long speeches that were eloquent, erudite, and well-reasoned.[41] The mnemonic art that he employed to such an impressive effect is of interest to us because it capitalizes on a basic computational principle of the hippocampal memory system: its reliance on spatial structures as a natural scaffolding for episodic information.

Ars Memoriae, also known as the method of loci, calls for imagining a palace with many interconnected rooms; items that need to be committed to memory are visualized in various places in those rooms (e.g., in the form of pictures hanging on the walls), and are arranged in the proper sequence by

On MNEMONICS, from Monty Python's *Memory Course* —

...

John Cleese: Now, take a common object like this.
Graham Chapman: A saucer?
JC: Good, good, well done. Now, what does it make you think of?
GC: Uh...
JC: What would you like to think of?
GC: Like to think of?
JC: A nude woman!
GC: A nude woman!?
JC: Well done! Well done! You're getting it! Now, what is the nude woman doing?
GC: Drinking tea?
JC: Good! And what's she drinking tea out of?
GC: A cup?
JC: Quite right! A cup! Cup and saucer! It's a saucer! Do you have any idea?
GC: I'm not sure...
JC: Well it's the association idea, it's the basis of our method, indeed of the whole... the hole... in the wall. And what do I see through the hole in the wall? Any idea?
GC: A nude woman?
JC: Every time.
GC: Every time?
JC: Of course, it's a strong image, you can't forget that. And you associate that with anything you want to remember. Anything. Numbers, dates, names... try me!

(continued on the next page)

imagining a tour through the palace. To recall the items in the right order, the mnemonist begins with the first room, and proceeds to reconstruct the tour mentally, while "looking" at the walls to remember the memorized material.

The Renaissance thinker Giordano Bruno wrote at length on the method of loci, which he employed in constructing encyclopedic systems of natural philosophy and hermetic knowledge.[42] Giulio Camillo, one of Bruno's predecessors and a leading intellectual of the early 16th century, turned the method of loci on its head by proposing to build a *real* memory palace, thereby augmenting internal memory by an external prop (instead of trying to improve the internal memory itself through training). The MEMORY THEATER that Camillo designed was intended to enable a person standing on its stage and facing the hall with its many-tiered arrangement of written cues (see Figure 6.25) to "discourse on any subject no less fluently than Cicero."

6.9.3   The world as an external memory

Camillo's brilliant move to outsource memory, which deftly relegates the tedious task of recording trivia to an external apparatus, frees up the brain to do what brains do best: connect. Memory for trivia such as the name of the legendary first queen of Carthage has scarcely any intrinsic value, even for a Classics professor. Classicist trivia do acquire value when used properly:

(continued from the previous page)
GC: Battle of Trafalgar?
JC: Uh... Trafalgar, Trafalgar Square... hole in the wall, look through the hole in the wall, I see...
GC: A nude woman?
JC: Excellent, and who is this nude woman?
GC: I don't know.
JC: The Empress Josephine, 1815.
GC: Right!
JC: Josephine, 1815.
GC: 1815 was Waterloo. Trafalgar was 1805.
JC: Ah, but... wait a minute, wait a minute. I wasn't finished. Josephine's wearing boots, Wellington boots, you can't see her toes, so deduct the 10 you can't see, from 1815, to 1805. Simple!

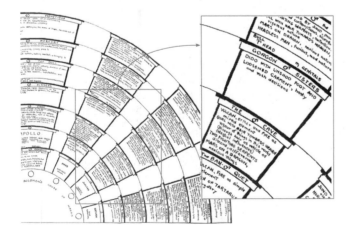

Figure 6.25 — A reconstruction by Yates (1966) of Giulio Camillo's MEMORY THEATER. *Left:* the layout. A spectator standing at the center stage would be able to form associations cued by the writings displayed around the hall. *Right:* a detail. The entry under GORGON SISTERS – "Dido with unshod foot and loosened garment" – simultaneously invokes the suicide of Dido following the departure of Æneas from Carthage (cf. Book IV of Virgil's *Æneid:* "One tender foot was shod, her other bare; Girt was her gather'd gown, and loose her hair") and anticipates Monty Python's voyeuristic mnemonics.

as pointers into the manifold conceptual context of Græco-Roman myths and history, which are among the foundations of the Western culture.

The distinction between memory for trivia, which can be farmed out, and conceptual knowledge, which cannot (until Artificial Intelligence becomes reality), is readily apparent in the true story about the quiz given to Albert Einstein on his first visit to the United States. Einstein, already world-famous for his revolutionary insights in physics and cosmology, was confronted by a reporter who handed him a copy of the QUESTIONNAIRE used by Thomas Alva Edison in hiring assistants for his laboratory.

Einstein did not think much of the celebrated inventor's list of trivia questions (reportedly designed to weed out college-educated "ninnies" whom Edison scorned for their supposed ignorance of practical matters), remarking that he saw no reason to memorize material that could easily be looked up when needed. The value of liberal education, Einstein believed, was in teaching people how to think. Thinking, however, does not lead anywhere interesting if it is hemmed in by ignorance, and so effective thinkers are likely to be those who remember both what a logarithm is, and what the *Æneid* is about.[43]

The power of concepts stems in part from their hierarchical relationships: some insights are generated by highly abstract analogies, while others require that the processes of thought deal with details (more about this in section 8.5.2). The best basis for conceptual thought is therefore a memory system that spans many levels of representation — including that of *facts*, which I referred to earlier as trivia (but probably stopping short of factoids such as Edison's laundry-machine statistics).

The ultimate origin of concepts is in empirical factual knowledge, from which they arise through abstraction and combinatorial superposition. A classical example is geometry, which developed in ancient Egypt as an abstraction from the work of land surveyors, and which through the efforts of many thinkers (among them Einstein) became a formidable conceptual tool, which can be applied to some of the most profound questions in the Universe.

This overarching Empiricist view of concepts, considered as a cultural system of knowledge that inhabits a multitude of living brains, but also includes the legacy of innumerable dead ones, recorded in libraries and embodied in artifacts of the human civilization, precisely parallels the grounding of concepts in perception (Barsalou, 1999), which holds for individual mind/brains. Perceptual processes use the outside WORLD AS AN EXTERNAL MEMORY for information that cannot be internalized because it is too voluminous, but, luckily, need not be, because it is there to be consulted as

Here are some sample entries from the QUESTIONNAIRE that used to be administered by Thomas Alva Edison to college graduates applying for a job in his lab: "What is the distance from the earth to the sun? What city in the United States is noted for its laundry-machine making? Who was Leonidas? Who invented logarithms? What is the first line in the *Æneid*? What is the weight of air in a room 10 by 20 by 30 feet?"

[It is an] error ... to suppose that cognitive systems are located inside people's heads. Rather, cognitive systems are largely in the world. I no more carry my complete cognitive systems around with me as I walk from place to place than I carry the U.S. currency system about with me when I walk with a dime in my pocket.

— Millikan (1995, p.170)

needed (O'Regan, 1992; cf. Figure 6.26).[44] Insofar as concepts are empirically grounded in perception and in factual knowledge, external mnemonics such as Camillo's memory theater are thus revealed as the most natural extension to biological memory.

The effective memory capacity for facts (on all levels of abstraction) can be boosted by any good encyclopedia, whether it is accessed via thick tomes bound in calfskin or a notebook computer connected to the Web. Online sources such as the Wikipedia, let alone the entire contents of the Web as indexed by Google, are very extensive and easy to use. Some of the features of this vast external memory superficially resemble those of biological systems; in particular, hypertext links between documents support to some extent content-based recall and contextuality.

However, the links in a present-day Web document encode only the as-

Figure 6.26 — *The Man of the Sea* by René Magritte. To appreciate the extent to which the brain depends on the outside WORLD AS AN EXTERNAL MEMORY, consider the following passage from O'Regan (1992): "Suppose I close my eyes and take a bottle in my hand; suppose also that my fingers are spread apart so there are spaces between them. ... Why do I not feel holes in the bottle where the spaces are between my fingers? ... The answer seems trivial to us: Why should I feel holes there? My tactile perception of the bottle is provided by my exploration of it with my fingers, that is by the sequence of changes in sensation that are provoked by this exploration, and by the relation between the changes that occur and my knowledge about what bottles are like. ... 'Perception' is *getting to know* or *verifying* the sensations caused by possible actions. ... 'Remembering' requires an active interrogation of the past. I'm not right now remembering my grandmother, unless I actually *do it*. Thus, in the example of feeling the bottle, the bottle amounts to an outside memory store that can be interrogated or explored, and the feeling of 'perceiving' comes from the exploratory activity itself." This striking idea, further developed by O'Regan and Noë (2001), is fully compatible with the notion of a perceptual basis for concepts and for the simulations that accompany them (Barsalou, 2003b).

sociations conceived by its author; for me as a user, the utility of a collection of documents is therefore still limited by the properties of the conceptual web that's inside my head. Moreover, hypertext probably hinders rather than boosts real-time usability: after going online to prepare for delivering a lecture (or writing a book), I still have to turn the gathered information into a narrative — and the richer the factual and conceptual basis of my presentation, the more difficult it is to do so. In this sense, Camillo's purpose — to facilitate the *use* of memory, over and above merely boosting its capacity — is not yet fulfilled. By itself, going to the library or going online turns me, alas, into neither Einstein nor Cicero.

6.10 Being used by memory

When combined with MULTIPLE REALIZABILITY (Figure 6.3 on page 162), the clear and present possibility of memories that are immediately accessible to people yet reside outside brains completes the emancipation of certain types of information from the shackles of biology. The varieties of informational entities that enjoy such independence are those that cause information users to help spread them across susceptible substrates.

The sense in which memories — chunks of information — can be active when they find themselves in an appropriate computational environment can be traced back to our first encounter with multiple realizability and computation in section 1.2. Grasping that some (not all) memories are *independently active* may initially require a bit of conceptual effort, which, however, pays off when we discover that assuming the point of view of such memories — which I'll call MEMES for reasons that will become apparent immediately — is the best way of understanding the memory basis of social cognition and culture.

6.10.1 The "meme" meme

The term "meme" has been coined by Richard Dawkins (1976) in *The Selfish Gene*, a popular book devoted to an exposition of the view that evolution — a key factor shaping the human mind/brain (Dennett, 1995, 2003; Pinker, 2002) — is best understood as the process whereby genes, rather than the organisms that carry them, propagate themselves. I shall not recount here the arguments for this fascinating and productive elaboration of the theory of evolution, nor shall I discuss its full implications. To get an appreciation of its relevance

A REPLICATOR (Dawkins, 1976) is an entity that makes a copy, or multiple copies, of itself, when placed in a susceptible medium. Genes contained in a DNA molecule are one example; they copy themselves, using the machinery available for just that purpose in the nucleus of the cell that carries them, every time the cell divides. Cells (and organisms of which they may be part of) are INTERACTORS — entities employed by the genes to facilitate replication (Aunger, 2001, ch.1). Informational replicators, or memes, are the subject matter of MEMETICS. As Richard Dawkins and Daniel Dennett point out, a gene, insofar as it is a packet of information, is like a meme (rather than the other way around).

to the computational psychology of memory, it is enough that we understand that memes are REPLICATORS, just as genes are.

Memory, no matter how it is implemented, offers a fertile substrate for informational replicators. Human memory, in particular, will readily admit any meme that can use the human body as an interactor and reach the brain via one of the perceptual channels (usually auditory, sometimes visual, rarely tactile, olfactory, or gustatory). A classical example of a meme is the opening motif of Beethoven's Symphony No. 5 in C Minor, Op. 67. A single exposure usually suffices for it to create a long-term memory trace; subsequent exposures may cause the host to hum or whistle the motif, possibly causing it to replicate through transmission to new hosts. On another level, the popularity of the entire symphony, which most people of course do not remember in detail, contributes to its frequent inclusion in concert programs, accelerating the rate of replication many-fold.[45]

A widespread MEME: the opening motif of Ludwig van Beethoven's 5th Symphony.

There is a clear parallel between the propensity of the Beethoven's Fifth meme to cause the symphony to be performed often in public and the tendency of the common cold virus to cause its host to cough and sneeze, thereby facilitating further spread of the infection. This contagion stance (Sperber, 1990) in theories of information transmission is complemented by the evolutionary stance (Blackmore, 2001), which highlights the mutual selection pressure exerted on memes by their hosts and vice versa, and the differential effects of this pressure on the spread of meme strains within populations (Aunger, 2001, ch.1).

6.10.2   Memes and evolution

The value of the theoretical focus on memes to social psychology is underscored by a range of experimental findings that examined the dynamics of information transmission within societies. In one study, Henrich and Gil-White (2001) considered the evolution of prestige, which they define as freely conferred status, as distinguished from power or dominance that is common in primate societies. Having analyzed anthropological data from dozens of societies, they conclude that prestige is a mechanism for enhancing the benefits of cultural transmission of information: "clients" who hold someone in high esteem vie for privileged access to that individual's skills. The results of Henrich and Gil-White (2001) are best accounted by focusing on the transmission, through imitation, of what can only be described as the contents of an individual's memory: as they put it, "information goods" rather than "tangible goods" underlie the dynamics of prestige in human societies.

For a meme to be replicated rather than obliterated as it jumps from host to host, the transmission process must be relatively error-free. In this, memes are at the mercy of their potential carriers: a person such as myself, who is devoid of musical sense (a condition described in Russian as медведь на ухо наступил, "a bear stepped on [his] ear"), is likely to mangle an overheard tune so as to render it unrecognizable for any subsequent listener — unless, of course, the tune is simple enough, simplicity being construed in terms of the cognitive abilities of the host.

Occasional errors (mutations) may cause changes in the characteristics of the members of the population. If some of the errors result in increased fitness (which we may define here as the number of copies produced by the meme over its lifetime), if changes made to a meme accumulate rather than disappear, and if the mutation rate is low enough for the differential fitness factors to have an effect, the process will result in a coherent evolutionary drift: the fitter memes will dominate the population, taking over the available resources — the combined memory space of the hosts (both internal and external).

The key characteristics of an evolutionary memetic process that fits this picture were discovered by Bangerter and Heath (2004) in their study of the Mozart Effect. The ME is a "science legend" picked up and propagated by the popular media after an article published in *Nature* in 1993 reported that 10 minutes of listening to Mozart's music improved the spatial reasoning ability of college students (later research effectively refuted the ME hypothesis). Given that the susceptibility to rumors had long been posited to depend on a heightened state of anxiety in the recipient, Bangerter and Heath (2004) predicted that the reach of the ME would be wider in states with lower per-capita spending on education, lower teacher salaries, and low national test scores. They found, unsurprisingly, that the first two of these variables are excellent predictors of the third; they also found that the public media in states thus distinguished were significantly more likely to report on the ME.

This finding makes sense because taking the ME seriously is an excellent, and cheap, means for assuaging the society's collective anxiety about the inadequacy of its investment in children; it is much more expensive to make affordable quality day-care widely available than to play classical music to children in existing day-care centers, as mandated by Florida in 1998, or to

Some, but not all, JOKES act like memes. Let us consider an example from *Monty Python's Flying Circus* —

Voice Over: This man is Ernest Scribbler... writer of jokes. In a few moments, he will have written the funniest joke in the world and, as a consequence, he will die laughing. *Ernest stops writing, pauses to look at what he has written... a smile slowly spreads across his face, turning very, very slowly to uncontrolled hysterical laughter... he staggers to his feet and reels across room helpless with mounting mirth and eventually collapses and dies on the floor.*
Voice Over: It was obvious that this joke was lethal; no one could read it and live.
The scribbler's mother enters. She sees him dead, she gives a little cry of horror and bends over his body, weeping. Brokenly she notices the piece of paper in his hand and (thinking it is a suicide note – for he has not been doing well for the last thirteen years) picks it up and reads it between her sobs. Immediately she breaks out into hysterical laughter, leaps three feet into the air, and falls down dead without more ado.

This joke is obviously a superbly structured specimen, but a very inept meme: good replicators do not kill their host before they get a chance to propagate.

give every new mother a classical music CD, as legislated by Georgia in the same year.[46]

Most interestingly, however, the interaction between the ME and the society that sustained this scientific legend did not leave the former unchanged: the content of the ME evolved over time. Specifically, the reports about the ME in the press gradually extended the scope of the purported effect from college students (the group studied originally) to children and infants. More generally, successive reports tended to drop more and more details that had been mentioned in the original article, making the story grow increasingly schematic over time.

The outcome of a recent controlled study (Mesoudi and Whiten, 2004) suggests that this kind of REGRESSION TO A SCHEMA is a common path taken by the evolution of a meme the fidelity of whose transmission between hosts may be affected by its complexity relative to the host's typical cognitive capabilities. The method employed by these researchers was a variation on a popular children's game known as Broken Telephone, first used in experimental psychology by Bartlett (1932) in his classical work on memory for stories. Mesoudi and Whiten (2004) took as their premise the assumption that stories about everyday events are represented in memory as hierarchically structured SCRIPTS (recall p. 190). Consequently, they predicted that when descriptions of such events expressed initially at a low hierarchical level are passed along a chain of participants, they would be transformed so as to focus on higher hierarchical levels. Such regression to a story schema was indeed observed in the data.

In view of the tendency of memes to mutate when jumping from host to host, it is reassuring to note that high-fidelity transmission too can occur in naturalistic situations, which are particularly relevant to developing a credible account of the evolution of culture and technology. In one study, Horner, Whiten, Flynn, and de Waal (2006) documented multiple instances of faithful transmission of a complex foraging skill in chimpanzees, and in human children. The researchers first made sure that the skill (an action required to open the door of a device baited with food) could be discovered by a large enough proportion of control subjects exploring the setup on their own. They then tracked the passage of the skill through social observation from one individual to the next, in a chain simulating inter-generational meme spread. The outcome — 100% transmission fidelity over six "generations" — suggests that host hopping by some memes can be much more faithful than what the label "Broken Telephone" implies.

A LETHAL JOKE is a poor meme, but it could be a great weapon, provided that a safe means of delivering it to the enemy were found —

Colonel: All through the winter of '43 we had translators working, in joke-proof conditions, to try and produce a German version of the joke. They worked on one word each for greater safety. One of them saw two words of the joke and spent several weeks in hospital. But apart from that things went pretty quickly, and we soon had the joke by January, in a form which our troops couldn't understand but which the Germans could.
…
Voice Over: In action it was deadly.
Cut to a small squad with rifles making their way through forest. Suddenly one of them (a member of the joke squad) sees something and gives signal at which they all dive for cover. From the cover of a tree he reads out joke.
Joke Corporal: Wenn ist das Nunstruck git und Slotermeyer? Ja! … Beiherhund das Oder die Flipperwaldt gersput!
Sniper falls laughing out of tree.

6.10.3 Memes and epidemics

Whether the replicants under consideration are genes that inhabit viruses and microbes or memes that inhabit memories, to characterize their behavior one needs to study not only their evolution, but also their epidemiology: statistics of contact, virulence, susceptibility, immunity. On a very concrete level, the mathematical tools of epidemic theory are proving useful in modeling social phenomena. For example, the recent study of Patten and Arboleda-Flórez (2004) showed that equations borrowed from epidemiology can explain the dynamics of group violence, and even account for the effectiveness of interventions such as rapid removal of violent individuals from crowds to prevent those from becoming mobs.

Closer to the core ideas of the new synthesis of epidemiological and evolutionary views of memetics (Mesoudi, Whiten, and Laland, 2006), the work of Aunger (2002) has been informed by both. Investigating the prevalence and spread of food taboos in an indigenous population in the Democratic Republic of Congo, Aunger found many parallels between the behavior of the specific taboo memes and the common cold. In particular, he reports that although nearly everyone is frequently exposed to the traditional taboos, people are seldom infected, due to resistance built up over a history of interaction with these "mind viruses" (an expression favored by Dawkins in his later writings). Aunger (2002) concludes:

> Thus, the processes underlying the dissemination of both cultural traits and pathogens, considered as replicating units of information, appear close enough to justify using *evolutionary epidemiology* [my emphasis. – SE] as a common framework for investigating cultural and biological phenomena. [...] It therefore seems not only fruitful but necessary to consider cultural and biological replicators as parts of a larger, interacting system.

The meaning of LIFE: replication with occasional heritable errors.

6.10.4 Memes and the meaning of life

To make Aunger's paraphrase of the subject matter of memetics as "evolutionary epidemiology" complete, it needs to be augmented with a reference to the unique status of memes among the different kinds of replicators known to science, including genes. Memetics differs from genetics in the multiple realizability of its basic entities: a gene without a cell is just so much dead DNA, but a meme outside a brain is fully functional as a replicator, able to lie

A detail of John Spencer Stanhope's *The Waters of Lethe by the Plains of Elysium*.

As the years pass, every man is forced to bear the growing burden of his memory.

— Borges (1999, p.514)

dormant indefinitely and yet spring to life immediately when perceived by a susceptible host. This is why computation (and its special case, cognition) is of central importance in the study of meme behavior.

Indeed, as it turns out, the main issue on which the scientific status of the analogy between memes and genes hinges is computational. Life as we know it depends on several properties of genes, one of which is *discreteness*: during replication, a gene is copied as a whole (perhaps with a local error or mutation), or not at all. It would seem that memes lack this property (is culture composed of discrete units? can the units of culture be traced across "generations"?), implying that a meme would be transmogrified beyond recognition after just a few hops between hosts. If this were the case, there would be no "meme's point of view" and no added value in memetics.

We have, however, already seen how this issue is resolved: the Broken Telephone model of information transmission, which motivates the concern about meme instability, does not hold for the human brain in its capacity as a meme machine. Instead of dissipating in transit, memes undergo regression to schemata — which are an omnipresent feature of cognition (Rumelhart, 1980), one that is based on the deepest computational principle that governs it, namely, statistical inference and its role in the emergence of structured representations.

In the terminology of evolutionary theory, it is the schemata that populate the collective memory of humankind, not their instantiations, that are the replicants in question (cf. Gil-White, 2005: "If the narrative *skeleton* is stable, radical variation in the details is as worrisome to cultural Darwinian analyses as silent mutations in DNA are to evolutionary genetics (i.e. not at all)").[47] Quite appropriately, the next chapter is devoted to the largest, meanest pack of schemata ever to take over a bunch of brains in the known universe: the memeplex that we call language.

Notes

[1] SOMBRE LILY. In the original French, this stanza from Paul Valéry's *La Jeune Parque* (The Young Fate) begins thus:

Non, non!... N'irrite plus cette réminiscence!
Sombre lys!

[2]NATURE OR NURTURE? Both. My memories are what I am, but my memories have not been written on a blank slate. A thoroughly convincing case for this view is made by Pinker (2002).

[3]Concerning the value of MEMORY METAPHORS. In this revealing passage taken from a late stage of Plato's *Theaetetus*, I have highlighted the phrase with which Socrates disowns the metaphors that he himself previously suggested:

Socrates. And thus, after going a long way round, we are once more face to face with our original difficulty. The hero of dialectic will retort upon us: — "O my excellent friends," he will say, laughing, "if a man knows the form of ignorance and the form of knowledge, can he think that one of them which he knows is the other which he knows? or, if he knows neither of them, can he think that the one which he knows not is another which he knows not? or, if he knows one and not the other, can he think the one which he knows to be the one which he does not know? or the one which he does not know to be the one which he knows? or will you tell me that there are other forms of knowledge which distinguish the right and wrong birds, and which the owner keeps in some other aviaries or graven on waxen blocks according to *your foolish images*, and which he may be said to know while he possesses them, even though he have them not at hand in his mind? And thus, in a perpetual circle, you will be compelled to go round and round, and you will make no progress." What are we to say in reply, Theaetetus?
Theaetetus. Indeed, Socrates, I do not know what we are to say.

[4]Classification and regression are subsumed under JOINT PROBABILITY DENSITY ESTIMATION: the former amounts to inferring $P(C, \mathbf{x})$, or the joint probability of class label C and the measured feature values $\mathbf{x}$, from examples; the latter required that $P(\mathbf{y}, \mathbf{x})$, or the joint input-output variable probability be learned (Edelman and Intrator, 2002).

[5]HASHING. A beautiful method of indexing memories in a manner that implements associative recall is the hash table Hashing relies on a unique mapping from a key assigned to an item to the address where its contents would be stored; thereafter, the item can be recalled simply by computing the address from the key and looking up the contents. Unfortunately, hashing functions usually do not map similar items to nearby addresses, so that whatever similarity structure there may be in a set of memories is lost (for example, two names differing in just one letter, or two similar faces, are likely to be stored in widely differing locations). To make associative (content-based) recall in artificial memory work like it does in human memory, this problem needs to be dealt with. One way of doing that is the crossbar network illustrated in Figure 3.10 on page 54.

[6]LOCAL AND GLOBAL MINIMA. A local minimum can be thought of as a pit in a hillside: it is the lowest point in the vicinity, but not in the general area. Computational techniques exist that allow a dynamic optimization process to escape local minima; one example is SIMULATED ANNEALING.

[7]The TUNING OF MOTOR NEURONS to final posture as quantified by Aflalo and Graziano (2006) was significant but partial. For a review of the problem of motor control that posits a need for an internal model of inverse dynamics, see (Kawato, 1999).

[8]The function of GLOBAL SCALAR PARAMETERS that control the dynamics of neural systems is fulfilled by diffusely acting chemical neuromodulators (Lewis, 2005), such as serotonin and acetylcholine.

[9]The activity of an ensemble of PLACE CELLS may be transformed into multiple spatial maps "upstream" from the hippocampus, in the entorhinal cortex (Hafting, Fyhn, Molden, Moser, and Moser, 2005).

[10]The MEMORY SPACE hypothesis predicts that a more global encoding of space would emerge as a result of the integration of local, episodic and nodal representations. Moreover, such local-relational encoding is expected also in domains other than spatial, e.g., in olfaction. Both these predictions are consistent with the available data (Eichenbaum et al., 1999). A direct test of the episodic memory space hypothesis has been described by Wood, Dudchenko, Robitsek, and Eichenbaum (2000), who used a modified T-maze, in which the rat could be traversing the central arm on its way to proceed eventually either into the left or into the right branch. The hippocampal cells that fired while the rat was in the central arm did so selectively, depending on whether the trial was a left-turn or a right-turn one.

[11]The EGOCENTRICITY of the hippocampal representations is consistent with the generally view-dependent nature of object and scene perception, discussed in Chapter 5 (section 5.3.4).

[12]MEMORY AND LEARNING. Mastering the related concepts of atmospheric pressure and of the physics of plungers on the basis of his *first* traumatic experience of getting his head stuck in one could have saved Homer Simpson from repeating this gaffe on every possible occasion (including, reportedly, his 50th school reunion in 2024; cf. Episode 9F16).

[13]The Bourbons were removed from power in France by the Revolution of 1789. The Restoration that followed Napoleon's ultimate defeat brought them back to the French throne in the person of Louis XVIII. The observation about THE BOURBONS' PIG-HEADEDNESS (which would in time help motivate the revolutions of 1832 and 1848) is due to Talleyrand.

[14]The discovery that REALITY IS MERELY A DESCRIPTION, made independently by various visionaries (cf. note 41 on page 314), holds for *represented* reality, as we shall see in Chapter 9. In contradistinction, the sum total of humanity's scientific knowledge teaches us that behind the veil of cognitive representation there is a bedrock of reality that needs not be qualified and that can only be ignored at one's peril (Sokal and Bricmont, 1998, ch.4; cf. Fogelin, 2003). In their book, *Fashionable Nonsense*, Sokal and Bricmont (1998) discuss some of the intellectually scandalous consequences of holding *all* reality to be merely a description. A few examples, which are both sad and amusing, can be found in the review of that book by Dawkins (1998):

> The feminist 'philosopher' Luce Irigaray is another who gets whole-chapter treatment from Sokal and Bricmont. In a passage reminiscent of a notorious feminist description of Newton's *Principia* (a "rape manual"), Irigaray argues that $E = mc^2$ is a "sexed equation." Why? Because "it *privileges* the speed of light over other speeds that are vitally necessary to us" (my emphasis of what I am rapidly coming to learn is an 'in' word). Just as typical of this school of thought is Irigaray's thesis on fluid mechanics. Fluids, you see, have been unfairly neglected. "Masculine physics" *privileges* rigid, solid things. Her American expositor Katherine Hayles made the mistake of re-expressing Irigaray's thoughts in (comparatively) clear language. For once, we get a reasonably unobstructed look at the emperor and, yes, he has no clothes:
>
> > The privileging of solid over fluid mechanics, and indeed the inability of science to deal with turbulent flow at all, she attributes to the association of fluidity with femininity. Whereas men have sex organs that protrude and become rigid, women have openings

that leak menstrual blood and vaginal fluids... From this perspective it is no wonder that science has not been able to arrive
at a successful model for turbulence. The problem of turbulent
flow cannot be solved because the conceptions of fluids (and of
women) have been formulated so as necessarily to leave unartic-
ulated remainders.

You do not have to be a physicist to smell out the daffy absurdity of this kind
of argument (the tone of it has become all too familiar), but it helps to have
Sokal and Bricmont on hand to tell us the real reason why turbulent flow is a
hard problem: the Navier-Stokes equations are difficult to solve.

[15] DARWIN AWARDS, named in honor of Charles Darwin, "commemorate those who improve our gene pool by removing themselves from it" (see http://darwinawards.com). The
1995 award, for example, went to a 39-year-old man from Camarillo, California, for an attempted stunt that is eerily reminiscent of Wile E. Coyote's exploits. The man (most of the
recipients of the Darwin Award are male) went over the Niagara Falls on a jet ski. At the
brink, he attempted to discharge a rocket propelled parachute that was on his back. It failed to
discharge. His body was recovered by *Maid of the Mist* staff. The man was married with no
children, making him an ideal contender for the Darwin Award.

[16] The COMPLEXITY of brains and societies may be driven by coevolutionary processes
(Blackmore, 2001). For a mathematical analysis of the specific case of altruistic behavior, see
(Gintis, 2003).

[17] As it happens, Lakoff's (1987) famous example of an ad hoc category, which is also the
title of his book, is most impressive when it is misunderstood to imply that WOMEN, FIRE,
AND DANGEROUS THINGS are the *only* members of the balan category. In fact, balan also
includes many other kinds of things, which makes it more of a property (perhaps not unlike
dangerous) than a "category."

[18] On the relationship between the concepts cow and projectile (cf. Figure 6.13 on page 183,
right): a cow has, of course, been used as a projectile — by the defenders of the castle of Louis
de Lombard, in Monty Python's *Holy Grail*.

[19] A TANGLED HIERARCHY is an informal name of a mathematical structure known as
directed acyclic graph. A graph is a collection of objects called nodes or vertices, connected
by arcs or edges. In a directed graph, the edges are directional; a directed graph with no
loops is acyclic. An example of a directed graph is the Bayes net illustrated in Figure 6.15 on
page 192.

[20] Times change. The perception of US-CANADA SIMILARITIES was first studied during
the height of the Cold War, when the prototype theory was being developed. As of the time of
this writing, wide swaths of the US — the so-called "red states" — would hardly be deemed
to bear similarity, symmetrical or not, to Canada.

[21] The windmills of your mind: turning a CONCEPTUAL NETWORK around may reveal
structure that is not otherwise visible. Although the network of neurons that is the brain is
embedded in a three-dimensional space, it should be noted that networks can represent through
their connectivity arbitrarily high-dimensional spaces (Braitenberg, 1977). The brain may also
be construed as a high-dimensional geometry engine by observing that similarity (proximity)
in the representation space spanned by activities of multiple neurons has a natural geometric
interpretation (Mumford, 1994).

[22] PERCEPTS INTO CONCEPTS. Philosophically, this, of course, is very much an Empiricist

view of knowledge. As a good Empiricist, I adhere to it because it enjoys a combination of unassailable empirical support and impressive theoretical unity and scope (Edelman, 2008).

[23]The following passage voices the classical philosophical concern, which can be traced back at least to Plato's *Theaetetus*, about the possibility of discovering TRUE CONCEPTS:

> 1. Objection. "Knowledge placed in our ideas may be all unreal or chimerical."
> ... If our knowledge of our ideas terminate in them, and reach no further, where there is something further intended, our most serious thoughts will be of little more use than the reveries of a crazy brain...
> 2. Answer: "Not so, where ideas agree with things."
>
> Locke (1690, Book IV, Chapter IV)

Locke's solution to it is an epitome of Empiricism, especially when viewed in the light of our current knowledge about the possibility of veridical perception (Edelman, 1999, pp.229-230); cf. section 5.5.

[24]My quoting of PROTAGORAS, the pre-Socratic philosopher, should not be taken as an endorsement of the nihilistic varieties of philosophical relativism or of its intellectually challenged cousin, cultural postmodernism (cf. note 14 on page 230).

[25]In other words, concepts entertained by humans, unlike those of animals, are WIELDABLE (Dennett, 1993) — a distinction that I shall revisit in section 8.5.

[26]In experts, the BASIC LEVEL is downshifted; thus, a bird-watcher would refer to a black-capped chickadee as such, rather than as "bird."

[27] Gopnik, Glymour, Sobel, Schulz, Kushnir, and Danks (2004) showed 4-year-olds a 'PUPPET MACHINE' and told them that some puppets almost always made others go. In one condition, children saw the experimenter intervene to move puppet X, and puppet Y also moved simultaneously on five of six trials; in one trial the experimenter moved X, but Y did not move. In the other condition, children observed the puppets move together simultaneously five times; in one trial, the experimenter intervened to move X, while Y did not move. The children accurately concluded that X made Y move in the first case, whereas Y made X move in the second.

[28]Borges most likely invented this LIST himself in order to make an especially fine point about categories of thought, real and imaginary.

[29]Another kind of computational difficulty arising in IMITATION stems from incommensurable motor representations, for example in learning to make a chess knight follow the moves of a chess queen (Schaal et al., 2003).

[30]A UNIVERSAL TURING MACHINE or, more practically, any programmable general-purpose computer such as my notebook, can simulate the execution of a program by another. One of the more profound theorems in computer science has to do with the computability issues that arise from such simulation: it is generally impossible to predict the outcome of a program written for some TM, or even to tell ahead of time whether it would terminate or run indefinitely, without actually running it (this is Alan Turing's celebrated undecidability theorem for the so-called Halting Problem (Turing, 1936). A somewhat far-fetched yet not unreasonable implication of this fact is that even if I have a pretty good notion of the operation of your mind with respect to various issues (your "program"), my only way of finding out what you'd think or do in a particular situation is to simulate you (run the program), with all the danger spelled by the undecidability theorem.

[31]Failure to properly sequester the program that is being executed is the prime cause of most

of the COMPUTER CRASHES inflicted upon the long-suffering public by vendors of inferior operating systems.

[32]The ISOCORTEX is the phylogenetically newer part of the cerebral cortex, which has six distinct layers. The older ALLOCORTEX, which includes the hippocampus and the olfactory cortex, has fewer layers and generally different structure.

[33]The involvement of the CA3 region in ASSOCIATIVE MEMORY has been directly confirmed by the deficiency of recall based on partial information in mice that had been genetically modified to lack neurotransmitter receptors specific to CA3 pyramidal cells (Miyashita, 2004).

[34]The hypothesis that animals other than humans possess META-COGNITIVE abilities is discussed by Smith, Shields, and Washburn (2003).

[35]In game theory, a PAYOFF MATRIX states, for each player, the bonus offered for a correct answer, and the penalty, if any, for an incorrect one.

[36]Koriat and Goldsmith (1996b) show that detailed predictions concerning the ACCURACY-QUANTITY TRADEOFF can be obtained in the form of a dependence performance on the response criterion P_{rc}. The tradeoff curves are computed from the confidence (FOK) data obtained under forced-report conditions. Furthermore, the relationship between forced-report FOK and volunteering or withholding answers under free-report conditions can provide an estimate of the actual P_{rc} used by the subject.

[37]The memory trafficking business from Dick's story, Rekall, Inc., gave its name to Paul Verhoeven's movie inspired by it, *Total Recall* (1990), starring a future governor of California.

[38]The scary scenario conjured by Charlie Kaufman and Michel Gondry in *Eternal Sunshine of the Spotless Mind* ("Remember, with Lacuna you can forget") is not even remotely feasible at present, however: biological memory is too distributed for the kind of crude brain intervention pictured in that film to work.

[39]Making the CHECKSUMS public is one possibility, but one still must guard against a "man in the middle" attack, in which the intruder not only tampers with your data, but also feeds you wrong checksums by intercepting your communications with the depository.

[40]To describe the state of dissonance arising from a mismatch between a MEMORY AND ITS CONTEXT, let me quote from the song *Once in a Lifetime* by Talking Heads:

> And you may find yourself living in a shotgun shack
> And you may find yourself in another part of the world
> And you may find yourself behind the wheel of a large automobile
> And you may find yourself in a beautiful house, with a beautiful wife
> And you may ask yourself – Well... How did I get here?
> . . .
> And you may ask yourself
> How do I work this?
> And you may ask yourself
> Where is that large automobile?
> And you may tell yourself
> This is not my beautiful house!
> And you may tell yourself
> This is not my beautiful wife!
> . . .
> And you may tell yourself

MY GOD!... WHAT HAVE I DONE?

[41]The electorate of Res Publica Romana apparently valued PERSUASION and ERUDITION much more than my contemporaries do. A majority of us here and now are perfectly happy with being governed by people who cannot read a teleprompter without stumbling over polysyllabic words and whose idea of a persuasive counterargument runs along the lines of "I'm the decider, and I decide what is best" (this particular quote is from remarks for the press made by US President G. W. Bush in Washington, D.C. on April 18, 2006).

[42]Giordano Bruno (1548-1600) was burned alive at the stake in Rome, by a papal decree, "for his theological errors." The Church still cannot seem to forgive him his pursuit of knowledge and freedom of thought — the online Catholic Encyclopedia article that I consulted recently decries his "spirit of insolent self-assertion." In Bruno's times, the Church did not, however, discourage the use of the method of loci as such. Indeed, it was applied with astounding effectiveness by Matteo Ricci, a Jesuit missionary to China. Ricci's rapid mastery of Chinese, and his vast erudition in theology, geography and other arts and sciences made a great impression on his hosts, although his attempts to convert them to Christianity did not meet with much success.

[43]Erudition may complement fast thinking, but it cannot substitute for it. For that, good WORKING MEMORY is needed; see Chapter 8.

[44]Cf. Reitman, Nado, and Wilcox (1978, p.72): "The primary function of perception is to keep our internal framework in good registration with that vast external memory, the external environment itself."

[45]Are memes SELFISH in the same sense as genes are, according to Dawkins (1976)? Cognitive phenomena involving some particularly virulent memes can be understood only when these are seen as selfish (see Dennett, 2006). Meanwhile, I'll follow Gil-White (2005):

> I will not define a meme as a selfish replicator but will adopt the broad Oxford English Dictionary's definition — "an element of culture that may be considered to be passed down by non-genetic means." Implicit in this definition is the idea that memes are units, that they are materially stored, and that they are subject to selection.

[46]A possible alternative explanation considered by Bangerter and Heath (2004) is that people in the states that most enthusiastically embraced the Mozart Effect are more gullible *because* they have, on the average, less education. The researchers rejected that possibility by pointing out that the mean per capita income in those states (which they took into account as a control variable) is not lower than in the others studied. Note that this conclusion presupposes that wisdom (or at least education) correlates, on the average, with income. This hypothesis had been questioned already during the reign of King Solomon (c. 970 – c. 930 BCE). In fact, it was questioned *by* King Solomon:

וגם לא לחכמים לחם

... neither yet bread to the wise... (Ecclesiastes, 9:11)

Who is right? We'll learn a bit more about these matters in section 8.5.1.

[47]The conclusion that suggests itself is that REGRESSION TO A SCHEMA is indeed a very common characteristic of cognition. We have encountered it in perception (categorization), and now in memory; it will see more action in the future chapters. Note that that on the level of brain mechanisms, the canonical embodiment of a schema is the tuned neuron.

7

Language

> To understand a sentence means to understand a language. To understand a language means to be a master of a technique.
>
> *Philosophical Investigations*, 199
> LUDWIG WITTGENSTEIN
>
> The language-game is ... not reasonable (or unreasonable). It is there — like our life.
>
> *On Certainty*, p.73e
> LUDWIG WITTGENSTEIN

L ANGUAGE, as Ludwig Wittgenstein famously argued, is a kind of game that people play. Had the "meme" meme evolved prior to the writing of *Philosophical Investigations*, Wittgenstein might have noted that, being essentially memetic, language is also a kind of game that plays people. Being thrust at a tender age into a community of inveterate players, we learn by observing, listening, and interacting with others, all the time literally playing it by ear, without any explicit instruction. Within a span of a few years, we become experts ourselves, yet the individual games we play — determined by the symbiotic memeplexes we host — remain pliable, being influenced by the games of our interlocutors, and influencing those in turn.

In this chapter, I sketch a framework for thinking about language that unifies and computationally substantiates what to date has been a loose collection of maverick philosophical insights, trail-blazing psychological studies, and unorthodox linguistic theories. The opportunity for unification will be afforded by looking at language from the single most pertinent perspective: that of a human baby. This developmental perspective is the most pertinent one because it encompasses the emergence of the totality of an individual's knowledge of language from an initial state whose only empirically warranted characterization is "profound ignorance." From this initial state, babies rescue themselves gradually, over a period of several years, by applying some

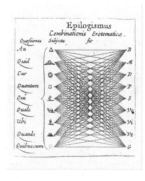

On the NATURE OF THE GAME. Any theory of language must account for the potential of human speakers to generate what Chomsky (2004b, p.380) terms a "discrete infinity" of acceptably structured sentences from a finite lexicon, a feat that transcends finite, indiscriminately combinatorial productivity of the kind illustrated in this figure from Athanasius Kircher's *Ars Magna Sciendi Sive Combinatorica* (1669).

razor-sharp learning skills to the barrage of language-related sensorimotor stimulation that the world throws at them.[1] A computational understanding of linguistic development is therefore both a critical component of and a key methodological entry point to any theory of language.

7.1   The structure of language

The acquisition of language by babies — or, equivalently, the spread of the Game to new hosts — is made possible by two complementary factors. The first of these is the nature of the stimulus (language), which contains readily accessible information that makes language learnable and playable. The second one is the nature of the learners, who possess traits that make them attuned to the relevant information.[2]

The proper way to gather evidence concerning the learnability of language is to analyze the cues present in a realistically detailed snapshot of a typical baby's experience. For that, one would need to record all language-related events (including sensory and motor ones) in the daily life of a baby for the first several years of its life (Adriaans and van Zaanen, 2004). Although the existing data do not yet approach such scope and volume, a large and growing corpus is already available that consists of transcribed conversations between parents and children (MacWhinney, 2000).[3] In any case, for the purpose of the present introductory overview there is no need to go even that far to make the point that language possesses regularities that can facilitate learning: these are so pervasive that one finds them at every turn in just about any text.

From a formal, computational standpoint a text is, quite simply, a sequence of symbols taken from a finite set, whose size may be as small as 22 (as in the Hebrew alphabet) or as large as several hundred (as in Hanja, the Chinese syllabary). For texts, the level of individual symbols is necessarily the most basic one: a written version of an utterance cannot contain fractional characters (a meaningless notion if there ever was one), or newly invented ones. As a representation of spoken language, written language is DIGITAL, in the standard sense explained back in section 2.2.2. Insofar as a text succeeds in capturing most of the information available in speech, it makes sense to use discrete-notation textual examples to illuminate language in general.

Representing speech in the compact DIGITAL form of a text implies giving up the many dimensions of meaning contained in PROSODY (intonation, rhythm, and vocal stress). One of the best illustrations of this point that I am aware of can be found in the film *Being John Malkovich* by Spike Jonze [warning: a spoiler], in the scene where Malkovich plays a recursively short-circuited version of himself. Faced with the experience of a world where everyone looks and sounds like him, the horrified Malkovich emits a visceral scream, which, to his added horror, consists of the single utterance, "Malkovich!!" Note that being John Malkovich does not contradict being digital as such: although the emotion that Malkovich put into that utterance cannot be captured in words, it is faithfully represented in digital form on every DVD replica of the movie.

7.1.1 Structure from regularities: a first glimpse

You cannot decompose written symbols into smaller units, but you can compose them into larger ones. In fact, adding variously sized structures composed of the basic symbols to an armamentarium from which they can be drawn at need is precisely what learning a language consists of. The key characteristic of language used by the learners in the construction of their individual armamentaria is revealed at every level that one cares to consider. It is the non-randomness, or DEPARTURE FROM EQUIPROBABILITY, in the distribution of symbols and symbol sequences (Harris, 1991, p.32).

To illustrate effectively the sense in which the distribution of elements of language is nonrandom, I must turn to a linguistic environment that is unfamiliar to you, the reader (remember, we are trying to assume the viewpoint of the baby, for whom all languages are equally foreign). A convenient alternative to English in this respect is Greek. It has an alphabet of its own, so that effort is required on the part of most Anglophones even just to read it.

Let us consider, therefore, a sequence of Greek characters,

(7.1) οἶδὃθέλειςσῦκαθέλεις

from which I have omitted the spaces and the punctuation (there are no pauses between words in naturally spoken language; cf. Figure 7.6 on page 249). I promise to disclose to you later why I chose this particular Greek example to make my point. Meanwhile, can you tell whether is it non-random in some interesting and potentially useful sense?

A brief scrutiny does reveal a suspicious departure from randomness in that sequence: it contains a subsequence, θέλεις, that appears twice. Statistically, this repetition is striking: the likelihood of a series of six characters appearing by chance twice within the span of 24 characters (the length of the entire sequence) is very, very small. What we just discovered is our first Greek *word*. A bit more data (that is, exposure to Greek), and one should be able to figure out that the sequence 7.1 consists in fact of five words:

(7.2) οἶδ ὃ θέλεις, σῦκα θέλεις.

The learning mode illustrated by this example — inferring STRUCTURE from REGULARITY or non-randomness — is tremendously important throughout cognition, because it can work in the absence of any prior knowledge concerning the particulars of the data set at hand. All that needs to be known

RANDOM PERMUTATIONS of symbols have fascinated mystics and peddlers of conspiracy theories long before Kircher. This mechanical device — a set of concentric disks inscribed with divine attributes — was invented by Raymond Lull (1235-1315) to help him crank out theosophical "proofs." Lull's contemporary, the Cabbalist Abraham Abulafia (1240-1291), opted to permute letters rather than words. In his *Sefer ha-Ot* ("sefer" is Hebrew for book; "ot" means sign, or letter), Abulafia wrote: "Then begin to permute a number of letters. You may use only a few, or you may use many. ...As a result of these permutations, your heart will become extremely warm. From the permutations, you will gain new knowledge that you never learned from human traditions nor derived from intellectual analysis." In fact, the only real knowledge, which babies pick up when they learn to become fully human, is contained in the diametrically opposite aspect of language, namely, in its non-randomness, or DEPARTURE FROM EQUIPROBABILITY (Harris, 1991, p.32).

ahead of time is what units to compute the statistics over. In language, this is a non-issue in the case of text, where the basic units, the characters, are given. In the case of speech, and in vision, the units themselves must be discovered first.

To address the computational problem posed by word discovery, a statistician would tabulate the frequencies of all the subsequences of a string (or a collection of strings) of symbols, in an attempt to determine which of them recur significantly above chance. It is important to note that statistical inference of structure is a useful tool for every learner not only because it happens to be computationally feasible: its end product is an indispensable ingredient in any sophisticated representation of the world we inhabit. As I argued in section 2.4, the single most important property of the world that makes it intelligible is the pervasiveness of *hierarchical abstraction* as the vehicle of emergent complexity in physical systems. The connection of this observation to language is immediate. The language Game is played out in the world in which the players are embedded; because perceptual environments projected by the world are hierarchically structured (cf. Figure 7.1), the linguistic environment generated by the Game can be expected to make the most sense if subjected to HIERARCHICAL STRUCTURAL ANALYSIS.

Figure 7.1 — Perceptually, the first steps in a STRUCTURAL ANALYSIS of a stimulus are figure-ground separation and unitization (Goldstone, 2000). Switching from seeing a chunk of text as a sequence of letters to seeing it as a sequence of words may be likened to the shift from seeing a visual scene as an expanse of texture to perceiving in it an intimation of a coherent *object* — perhaps as yet unidentified, but definitely there, as when an unknown animal stands out against what until a moment ago seemed merely a tangle of vegetation or a pile of rocks. In this photograph, there are two well-camouflaged ptarmigan, whose locations are indicated in the inset. After you have detected them, you can focus on their details (e.g., note which way they are heading), then "zoom out" and reconsider the entire scene, thus demonstrating that your capacity for structural analysis is HIERARCHICAL.

7.1.2 Structure and generalization

Linguistic structure — initially inferred by the learner from non-randomness in the input stream — is an absolute prerequisite for GENERALIZATION, which in language, as in the rest of cognition, means the ability to deal intelligently with new stimuli (cf. section 5.4.3). What would happen if the recipient forgoes structural analysis and treats each sentence holistically? Each linguistic stimulus would then become effectively *unique*. I bet that the sentence you are now reading you have never before encountered in your entire life except perhaps in the present passage (that is, if you are re-reading it); to be on the safe side, I'll round the sentence off with a gratuitous mention of Leon Trotsky and, for good measure, a marmot. Of course, being composed of familiar words, the preceding sentence is only novel on the holistic level, which is precisely my point.

The juxtaposition of Leon Trotsky (left) and a marmot probably makes the present page, considered as a visual stimulus, *unique* in your experience. That you can make sense of it attests to your ability to carry out structural analysis of the viewed scene. At the very least, this ability must include attending to spatially delimited regions of the visual field (such as the two stamp-sized images shown here) and noting the locations of the key objects in the scene (Edelman and Intrator, 2003). In other words, this is precisely the ability to figure out *what* is *where* in the scene, which is so important in vision (cf. Figure 5.30 on page 146).

Representational uniqueness is deeply problematic because a truly unique stimulus cannot, by definition, be related to previous experience. This, in turn, makes generalization impossible. In perception at large, this problem is avoided through measurement diversity: the system ensures that the initial representations of sufficiently different stimuli are all distinct by casting them into a high-dimensional *measurement space*. For instance, a measurement space that includes some color dimensions would be capable of supporting the distinction between two identically shaped apples — one red, the other green — which otherwise would be seen as two indistinguishable instances of the same unique object. In language, which at the processing stage we are dealing with is digital, measurements must necessarily be structural: it really does not matter what color a sentence is printed in, as long as it is legible (nor is it supposed to matter whether the voice of the speaker who produces an utterance is high or low-pitched). Consequently, the only relevant information about a sentence that can be used to relate it to other sentences is contained in its structure — in the identities and the order of the symbols in terms of which it is represented.

Structure is thus seen to be crucial to generalization. Considered holistically, objects 7.3 and 7.4 seem merely distinct, and not necessarily relatable:

(7.3) `StalinhadKamenevkilled`

(7.4) `StalinhadZinovievkilled`

With word-level analysis, the nature of the relationship between the newly perceived sentences becomes obvious, and can be generalized to a new one:

(7.5) `Stalin had pretty much everyone whose personal`
`        loyalty was even slightly suspect and many of`
`        those whose loyalty was above suspicion killed`

In 7.5, the long phrase `pretty...suspicion` takes the place of `Kamenev` and `Zinoviev`, respectively, in 7.3 and 7.4. We shall see more examples of this kind of structural learning, as well as a working computational model of language acquisition based on related ideas, later in this chapter.

7.1.3 Structure and meaning

By allowing generalization, that is, abstraction from some given sentences to potentially very many new ones, the structure of a sentence ultimately underwrites its MEANING. To see how meaning is related to generalization, consider again the hypothetical case of a language in which utterances have no internal structure. If treated as holistic, unique symbols, entire sentences can be used for communication, but only if all the interlocutors are given ahead of time the key to the code — a comprehensive list of symbols paired with their meanings (think of two conspirators who agree on the eve of a revolution that the message `Leon Trotsky never saw a live marmot` means "Lenin will arrive in St. Petersburg at midnight"). Such communication would be highly inefficient when compared to the combinatorial alternative, under which the number of possible messages may grow with the number of symbol permutations rather than with the number of symbols: that is, exponentially rather than linearly (Kirby, 2000).

Computational efficiency suggests, therefore, that a combinatorial code be used instead of a holistic one, because it allows a much larger set of meanings to be communicated by means of the same finite set of words drawn from the mental LEXICON. A combinatorial code must, however, be accompanied by a COMPOSITIONAL SEMANTICS: the meaning of a composite expression must be *systematically* determined by its structure (and, of course, its lexical components). Translated into the familiar language of generalization, it should be possible to estimate the meaning of a sentence from the meanings of similarly structured sentences known from prior experience. Thus, if you know the meanings of 7.6 and 7.7, and, of course, the meaning of `marmot`, you should be able to compute the meaning of 7.8:

(7.6) `Trotsky saw a hyrax`

(7.7) `Trotsky saw a capybara`

(7.8) `Trotsky saw a marmot`

Lexical semantics

But what *is* the meaning of `marmot`? A dictionary would tell you that a marmot is a kind of burrowing rodent, but this seems merely to beg the question of distinguishing it from other burrowing rodents. It is said to be larger than a squirrel, but just how large is a squirrel, you may ask? For an emerging artificial intelligence, not yet connected to a camera and only fed texts, this is a perfectly reasonable question. As Harnad (1990) pointed out, cutting short the merry-go-round ride through an endless series of interdependent verbal definitions requires a connection to the world that is outside the text. The inquisitive 4-year old is given a book with pictures of furry animals (or taught to use Google and save a tree), the visual interface engineers working on the AI finally pull their act together, and the learner is shown a picture and told: *this* is a marmot.[4]

People who are respectful of definitions and who believe that meanings are logical entities may feel, when faced with this option, that dictionaries are given short shrift by such a blatantly inductive approach. At the very least, they say, it should be possible to devise a dictionary that would rely on a small number of "atoms" of meaning, in terms of which everything else can be defined deductively. One implementation of this idea is the "philosophical language" invented by John Wilkins, in which lexical meaning is transparently related to the form of the utterance (see Figure 7.2). The language, which Wilkins devised two times over (the first time his work perished in the Great Fire of London of 1666) combined completely systematic phonology with an equally systematic lexical semantics. As a result, a text could be both read out loud in a straightforward fashion, and immediately understood by following the binary categorical distinctions ("differences" and "species") implied by its components.

If the classification scheme invented by Wilkins is closer in spirit to Aristotle and Porphyry than to Locke and Hume, let alone to the modern sciences, it is because science as we know it was still being invented by the Royal Society in the making, of which Wilkins himself was a founding member. The idea of an orderly and fully systematic lexical semantics has not, however,

The relationships among the LEXICON (a network of signs), the CONCEPTS the signs stand for, and the rest of the WORLD. In a living language, the sign and the concept are linked by perception and production of speech; the concept and the world are linked by experience, and the sign and what it denotes are linked by the Game. This classical diagram (adapted from Peirce (1960); cf. the discussion of symbols in Chapter 2, p. 15) focuses on LEXICAL SEMANTICS, leaving out the structural aspects of meaning, or COMPOSITIONAL SEMANTICS.

been abandoned: it is pursued both by academic researchers (Wierzbicka, 1996) and by commercial projects, such as the Longman Dictionary of Contemporary English, which uses a relatively small *defining vocabulary* (Longman's DV is a set of semantic primitives consisting of 2197 words, 10 prefixes, and 39 suffixes).

Compositional semantics

What aspects of sentence structure affect its compositional meaning? The first candidate that suggests itself is the ORDER of the words that comprise the sentence. The importance of word order is underscored by Douglas Adams's remark that to write a book you need merely to "put a hundred and fifty thousand words in a cunning order." The dependence of meaning on word order can be very pronounced, as in English, or moderate, as in Russian.[5] There is, however, more to compositional semantics than word order. Our present discussion started with the notion of *hierarchical* structure, and indeed all lin-

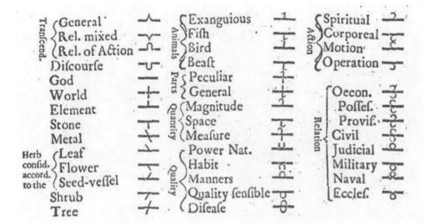

Figure 7.2 — To avoid the arbitrariness of LEXICAL SEMANTICS in his *Philosophical Language* (1668), John Wilkins undertook to construct meanings from the 40 genera shown here, subdivided by 231 characteristic differences. The meaning of the word for dog in his language would thus be derived by a long chain of binary choices, ending with rapacious (vs. not rapacious), dog-kind (vs. cat-kind), European (vs. exotic), terrestrial (vs. amphibian), and bigger (vs. smaller); flipping the last bit of this description would lead instead to the word for badger.

guists agree that even the simplest phrases are treated by the language system as *recursively* structured hierarchies.

In theory of computation, a procedure is called recursive if at some point it invokes itself.[6] An infinite regress in recursive procedures is prevented by making recursion conditional. For example, the factorial of a natural number n (defined as the product of all numbers between 1 and n) can be computed by returning either 1 if $n = 1$, or n times the factorial of $n - 1$ if $n > 1$. Although this procedure appears to be circular, the condition built into it provably causes it to terminate eventually, returning the right answer.

In language, a recursive form is usually attributed to phrases such as 7.9,

(7.9)   (a) `this marmot`

      (b) `this big marmot`

      (c) `this big brown marmot`

        `...`

the idea being that there is a procedure that can insert any number of adjectives between `this` and `marmot` by calling itself repeatedly before terminating. The end result is supposed to be a hierarchical structure in which the two rightmost elements are paired before being attached in turn to the next element to the left: `[this [big [brown marmot]]]`. A number of other examples of hierarchies of phrasal constituents posited by linguists are given by Phillips (2003).

Positing invisible structures is, of course, problematic unless there are independent empirical means for verifying their psychological reality.[7] Although direct empirical evidence for various specific constituency hierarchies is scarce (Steedman, 2001, p.652), the most basic assumption — the existence of hierarchies beyond the surface structure (word order) of phrases — is supported by a number of experimental findings. A particularly relevant study in this respect is that of Johnson (1965), who had subjects memorize a short list of numbered sentences such as this one:

(7.10) `The marmot in the hole saw Trotsky`

The subjects were then prompted by the sentence numbers and had to recall the corresponding sentences; their errors at each word to word transition were recorded. Johnson reasoned that the subjects' error rate would reflect

WORD ORDER MATTERS. In English, ignoring word order in processing a sentence wreaks havoc with its meaning: `Stalin had Trotsky killed` says something else than `Stalin had killed Trotsky`, let alone `Trotsky had killed Stalin`. Even in Russian, whose rich inflectional morphology includes explicit markers for case (who did what to whom), word order affects meaning by indicating *focus*: compare Сталин убил Троцкого, which can be read as "Stalin killed Trotsky" or as "It was Trotsky whom Stalin killed" (depending on the intonation) to Троцкого убил Сталин, "it was Stalin who killed Trotsky." The dependence of the meaning of sentences on their structure (linear and, ultimately, hierarchical) is the subject matter of COMPOSITIONAL SEMANTICS.

the presumed tree-like hierarchical structure of the sentence (see Figure 7.3, left), the hypothesis being that two words in the same low-level constituent (such as the and hole, both attached to node D) would be more likely to be recalled together or not at all, whereas two words that straddle a constituent boundary (such as hole and saw, attached only via S) would be recalled independently. The study indeed found a significant correlation of 0.75 between the probability of an error in the transition between successive words and the level of the lowest common ancestor node of these words in the phrase structure tree (Johnson, 1965, p.473).

Armed with the knowledge that sentence 7.10 is composed of one constituent (the prepositional phrase in the hole) embedded in another (The marmot saw Trotsky), one may attempt to derive its meaning formally. The goal may be, for instance, a logical formula expressing the thematic relationships among the concepts involved, namely, that the subject (which is modified by the prepositional phrase) is marmot, the predicate is the verb see (in the past tense), and the object is Trotsky.

As a decisive demonstration of the crucial role of hierarchical structure

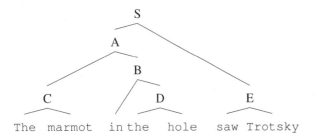
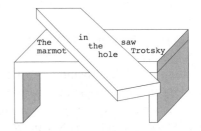

Figure 7.3 — *Left:* A partially specified phrase structure tree hypothesized for sentence 7.10, which has an embedded prepositional phrase (after Johnson, 1965; the intermediate node labels are intentionally noncommittal — we only care here about the most uncontroversial constituent structure, which is neutral with respect to linguistic theory). *Right:* The relationship between the occluder and the occluded in this scene is the same as between the prepositional phrase and the sentence in which it is embedded in the example on the left. I have adapted this illustration from Minsky (1985, chapter 26.9), who writes: "Some language scholars seem to think that what we do in language is unique, in the filling of frames with other frames to open up a universe of complicated structure-forms. But consider how frequently we do similarly complex things in understanding visual scenes. ... Did our capacity to deal with phraselike structures evolve first in language or in vision?"

in determining meaning, consider the two readings of the same sentence in the next example:

(7.11)   (a) `[[The marmot] [saw [Trotsky with the`
          `glasses]]]`

          (b) `[[The marmot] [saw Trotsky] [with the`
          `glasses]]`

This sentence is ambiguous because its surface structure (word order) under-determines its hierarchical structure: the decision whether it was the marmot or the creator of the Red Army who was wearing the spectacles cannot be made without extra information, which, as it often happens with ambiguous sentences, may take the form of statistical likelihood (in this case, concerning the relative prevalence of the use of visual aids among rodents and revolutionaries).

Ambiguity, however, is the least of the problems that plague the seekers after the Holy Grail of compositional semantics, which is obtaining a principled (systematic) and empirically viable characterization of the dependence of meaning on sentence structure. More worrisome are the doubts surrounding the very applicability to natural language of the mathematical approach that underlies the concept of compositional semantics: the Principle of Compositionality. This principle, formulated by one of the founders of mathematical logic, Gottlob Frege, postulates that the meaning of an expression (in a natural language, a sentence) is a *function* of the meanings of the symbols (words) that participate in it and of its structure. The problem is that in all but the simplest cases (such as the sentence `All marmots are mammals`, which looks a lot like a logical formula to begin with) the compositional approach runs into insurmountable conceptual and practical obstacles, such as the rampant deviations from systematicity in natural languages (Harris, 1951; Johnson, 2004). Given this state of affairs, the course of action suggested by Pietroski (2003) seems especially wise:

> At least for now, the way to study meaning is by supposing that our publicly available sentences have meanings — and then trying to say how various features of sentences contribute to sentential meanings.[8]

Traditional compositional semantics needs SYSTEMATICITY: the meaning of a structured expression must be computable from the meanings of its constituents in a predictable manner. In reality, however, the inference from the structure of a sentence to its meaning is deeply problematic (Johnson, 2004). For example, in the first sentence below `Leon` is the dispenser of the action, while in the second one, which has the same surface structure, he seems to be more of a recipient:

`Leon is eager to please`
`Leon is easy to please`

Positing hidden structure that reconciles formal compositional arguments with intuition (which is what linguists tend to do in such cases) cannot, of course, be explanatory if done on a structure by structure basis (that is, unsystematically). A better way out is to admit that the link between structure and meaning is often opaque (as it is in idiomatic expressions), and to rely on a different, yet perfectly natural kind of computation to retrieve meaning: memory lookup (on which more later).

7.1.4   The source of structure

The part of knowledge of language that determines which sentence structures are allowed — and therefore also which meanings can be encoded in sentences — is usually referred to as GRAMMAR. The connection between grammar and meaning is made explicit by Bates and Goodman (1999, p.35), who define grammar as "the class of possible solutions to the problem of mapping back and forth between a high-dimensional meaning space ... and a low-dimensional channel that unfolds in time," pointing out that this is a "dimension reduction" problem. Note that this definition is abstract-computational (cf. Table 4.2 on page 76): it tells you what the function of a grammar is, not what form grammars may take, or how they operate. Insofar as it invokes mappings between spaces and dimensionality reduction, this idea of grammar is certainly compatible with what we have learned about computation in the brain; as we shall see later in this chapter, it is also in line with the algorithmic and psycholinguistic insights into language.

It is in relation to what such computational definitions leave moot that most of the action in linguistic theory is happening, and the most controversy

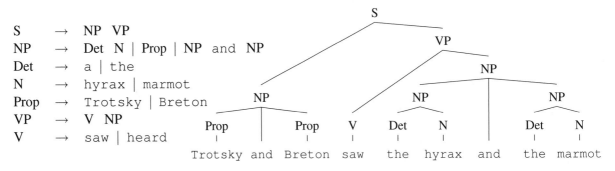

Figure 7.4 — *Left:* a tiny GRAMMAR, written in the form of production rules. The grammar consists of symbols for variables (S, sentence seed; NP, noun phrase; VP, verb phrase; Det, determiner, etc.) and terminals (Trotsky, the, hyrax, etc.), and rules that allow certain strings to be substituted for others (note that the second rule is recursive). Symbols following each other stand for concatenation; the symbol | denotes disjunction. Repeated application of such rules causes strings of terminals (sentences) to be generated. *Right:* one of the sentences that can be generated by this grammar, and its hierarchical tree structure, which stems from successive invocation of the rules.

generated. For most of the 20th century, linguists assumed that grammars consist of algebraic RULES (cf. Figure 7.4, left), of which there were supposed to be many fewer than the number of entries in the lexicon. On this view, the charge set upon the discipline of linguistics is to come up with a concise system of formal rules that jointly generate all the grammatical sentences in a given language, and none of the ungrammatical ones.[9]

The failure of formal generative linguistics to fulfill this charge for any language despite decades of concerted effort (Edelman and Waterfall, 2007; cf. the note on p. 287) raises doubts concerning both the methodology it employs in seeking after the rules of grammar (Postal, 2004; Schütze, 1996) and the validity of its foundational theoretical assumptions such as the abstractness and the inviolability of rules and the existence of a detailed and innate universal grammar that is common to all languages (Croft, 2001; Jackendoff and Pinker, 2005; Tomasello, 1998). On the positive side, it has prompted cognitive scientists to redouble their efforts to develop a computational understanding of the winning host-and-memeplex team, which has given rise to billions of players of the Language Game on this planet alone: the combination of a smart information-seeking missile (see Figure 7.5) and a rich, structured stimulus environment. These new efforts are now starting to pay off.

7.2 Learning language structure

As pointed out in an earlier section, when described in computational terms, the crucial link that ties the learner of language to what is learned is *regular-*

Figure 7.5 — Why does this NOVICE PLAYER of the Game look surprised? Having used Greek for the structure-discovery example 7.1 on page 237, I can now recruit a common English idiom to offer a guess: because for babies it's all Greek in the beginning. Soon, however, this learner will master what it takes to play verbal games with his parents and peers. According to Culicover (1999), this is made possible by two key characteristics of language learners: they are CONSERVATIVE in that they refrain from generalizing too far beyond the evidence in the input, and ATTENTIVE in that they do pursue generalizations that are warranted by such evidence.

ity. On the one hand, the internal structure of language — that which makes generalization possible and translates into meaning — is learnable because it manifests itself as regularity. On the other hand, babies can learn that structure — and become capable of extracting meaning from novel forms and to generate and express meaning of their own — because they are attuned to regularities in their sensory input. Simply put, **learning is learning of regularities**.[10]

The ability to gather, organize, and use statistical information that relies on regularities in distilling knowledge from data is just the kind of computation that brains excel in — indeed, as we keep discovering in more and more contexts, the only kind of computation they ever need to resort to. In vision, the telltale regularities may take the form of simple (that is, low-dimensional) structure in the measurement space (cf. section 5.4.4 on page 118), or regularities in the location and spatial arrangement of stimuli in the visual field (compare Figure 5.30 on page 146 and Figure 7.8 on page 253). Language too is replete with regularities that can support the extraction of meaningful and productive hierarchically structured representations.

The techniques that babies need to deploy in order to discover and process these regularities are part of the arsenal of general-purpose computational tools used throughout cognition. A central example is *schematization* or abstraction, which is a key ingredient both in perceptual categorization (Markman and Gentner, 1993; Smith, 1990) and in language (Langacker, 1998; Tomasello, 2006). Because linguistic structures can be highly productive, babies learning language appear to guard against over-generalization by being *conservative* and *attentive* to the stimuli they actually encounter (Culicover, 1999, p.28), as well as to the wider complex of cues that accompany the purely linguistic stimulus, such as the speaker's gaze direction, expression and gesturing and their relation to the immediate environment (Goldstein, King, and West, 2003). The latter cues are highly informative with respect to the interlocutor's *intention* — another key kind of information that the baby must pick up to become an effective communicator of meanings (Tomasello, 2006).

You may wonder why it is that other species with relatively advanced cognitive abilities have not developed some kind of language that involves hierarchical structure. It appears that there are two distinguishing factors, both of which correspond to computational operations which the human brain is especially good at. The first one is GOING DIGITAL: converting a continuous auditory signal into a sequence of symbols. The second one is GO-

THE TWITTERING MACHINE by Paul Klee.
The reason birds do not talk (except in imitation) is not because their brains do not use symbols (even the simplest neural systems do). It is because they cannot combine their symbols into complex, flexible structures. A representational scheme that is DIGITAL (in the sense of Chapter 2) can support computations for which the mere ability to use symbols does not suffice. Although the distinction is quantitative rather than qualitative, it is important: being digital means having access not just to a few symbols but to a practically unlimited reservoir of composable representations. This, in turn, allows RECURSIVE structures to be built in response to an appropriately complex input.

ING RECURSIVE: subjecting symbol sequences to hierarchical abstraction —
something that is only possible if new symbols can be created on the fly and
tied into existing structures as needed. When combined with extra powerful
memory, a flexible vocal apparatus, and an intricate social environment, the
availability of these operations leads to the ability to learn and use language.

7.2.1 Going digital

Have a look at Figure 7.6, which shows the spectrogram of a spoken sentence
plotted against time. This is where it all starts: the continuous speech signal, which is nominally infinite-dimensional (cf. p. 99ff.), must be digitized
and processed to determine its structure (which would then be interpreted by
comparing it to the previously learned, internally represented knowledge of
language). Let us identify the computational constraints that apply collectively to all stages of the learning process, from digitization onwards:

- because infants receive at best only very indirect feedback concerning their linguistic performance (Saxton, Houston-Price, and Dawson,
  2005), language learning must be capable of virtually UNSUPERVISED
  operation;

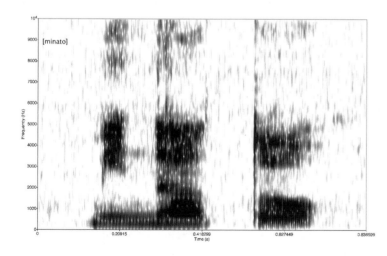

Figure 7.6 — When made visible in
a SPECTROGRAM, a segment of speech
looks like a visual scene, blurry, yet
hauntingly structured. This particular plot of the sound energy at various frequencies (ordinate) as it unfolds over time (abscissa) is for the utterance they don't know where
to go; darker color corresponds to
higher energy. Note that the si-
lences (near-white vertical bands) are
not where one would expect them to be,
between words. Instead, in this example
they correspond to the near-complete
glottal stops in word-initial d and t.

- because speech that is consistently incomprehensible to others is worthless, the acquired representations must be largely COMMENSURABLE across the immediate members of the infant's linguistic community.

Note that whereas learning is equally unsupervised in vision and in language, the commensurability constraint applies in full force only in language. Commensurability among speakers of the same language is expected to be particularly important at the highest and lowest levels of representation. At the highest level, a significant discrepancy between the meaning spaces of two individuals could curtail the prospects of communication between them. Given the poor record of our species in maintaining effective communication between people who host conflicting or even just mutually independent memeplexes, there does not seem to be a strong drive towards high-level semantic commensurability in language. In comparison, at the lowest level — that of the basic representation of speech — commensurability is critical: if my alphabet of phonetic primitives differs too much from yours, we won't be able even to *dis*agree about things (as an illustration, consider the consequences of Pilate's mangling of just the consonant "r" in scene 12 of *Monty Python's Life of Brian*). One would expect commensurability to exert strong pressure towards the uniformization of the phonetic alphabets of different members of the same speech community, and indeed simulation studies indicate that cultural selection for learnability leads to the emergence of shared phonetics (Oudeyer, 2005).

The digitization process — converting a speech signal into a sequence of symbols capable of supporting an open-ended, hierarchical combinatorial code — cannot rely on the kind of statistics that allowed us to discover that θέλεις appears twice in the string 7.1 on page 237, simply because counting the units is not an option in a continuous signal, where no units are (yet) present.[11] A brute-force scan of all possible segmentations of two signals prior to matching is not a good idea because of the forbidding number of possibilities. The only computationally viable approach is to seek a partial match between two entire signals, and to decide that each of the *non-matching* parts is a candidate for an independent symbol. For example, if the baby hears, on separate occasions, the utterance `big` and the utterance `bag`, and, furthermore, if the contexts in the two cases sound similar (`b_g`), then it has a reason to assume that `i` and `a` are two distinct phonetic units (in this connection, you may want to peek ahead at Figure 7.8 on page 253). This *discovery procedure* has been proposed by Harris (1968, pp.21-23).[12]

An excerpt from *Monty Python's Life of Brian* illustrating some consequences of phonetic INCOMMENSURABILITY —

PILATE:
Hmm. Now, what is your name, Jew?
BRIAN:
'Brian,' sir.
PILATE:
'Bwian,' eh?
BRIAN:
No, no. 'Brian.'
[slap]
Aah!
PILATE:
Hoo hoo hoo ho. The little wascal has spiwit.
CENTURION:
Has what, sir?
PILATE:
Spiwit.
CENTURION:
Yes. He did, sir.
PILATE:
No, no. Spiwit, siw. Um, bwavado. A touch of dewwing-do.
CENTURION:
Oh. Ahh, about eleven, sir.

For this procedure to work, the baby must have in place a computational mechanism for estimating utterance similarity. It appears that an appropriate measurement space can be learned in an unsupervised fashion from examples (consisting of entire, unsegmented signals, of course — otherwise it's the chicken and egg problem all over again). For instance, an unsupervised simulated-neuron model of consonantal feature detection has been shown to achieve generalization rates in excess of 96% (Seebach, Intrator, Lieberman, and Cooper, 1994). Interestingly, the speech signal fed to that model simulated prenatal acoustic conditions, demonstrating that a low-dimensional representation of speech in terms of basic phonetic features can be learned by the baby from a realistic input, and therefore need not be innate. [13]

The process whereby the cognitive system makes objects out of features (or larger objects out of smaller ones, which comes handy later in the development) is called UNITIZATION. Being essentially statistical and based on fallible real-world measurements and often sparse data, unitization relies on likelihoods rather than certainties, and is occasionally prone to what a naive commentator could describe as failure, but what actually should be seen as a resounding success (see sidebar).[14]

The effect of unitization on the representational landscape — the assignment of symbolic handles to newly acquired categories — is familiar to us from the survey of the perceptual systems in Chapter 5: this is just the good old categorical perception, taken to its logical conclusion. In all domains,

Vagaries of UNITIZATION: the Aztecs, who had never seen horses before the European invasion, reportedly perceived the disembarking Spanish cavalry as centaur-like monsters (Sagan, 1973). There is a statistical justification for this: an object that is coherent in that it moves as a whole should only be subdivided into parts if reliable evidence exists for such a division (e.g., in the form of permutations of would-be parts; cf. Table 7.1 on page 256, right). Similar things happen in language too, as illustrated (among innumerable other examples) by expressions that conflate two frequently co-occurring foreign words into one, such as the English algebra or alembic that have glued the Arabic definite article *al* onto the following stem.

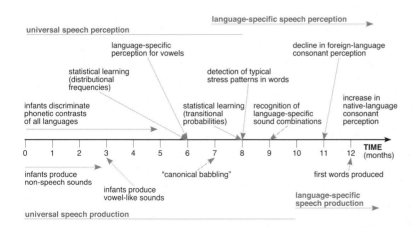

Figure 7.7 — The time course of the various learning processes that occur during the first year of the baby's acquisition of its native language (Kuhl, 2004).

unitization is characterized by a common reliance on statistical inference, and language is no exception in this respect. In language, however, unitization is as closely tied to hierarchical structure manipulation as it is to statistical inference. Structure and statistics are inseparable already at the lowest level, where phonetic representations are learned (Kuhl, 2000) and where speech goes digital.

At the higher levels, structure becomes hierarchical as the infant learns morphemes and words (cf. Figure 7.7), and gets ready to tackle phrases and sentences. Continued progress at these higher levels of structure strongly depends on the achievements of the first stage. Evidence for the dependence of the quality of language acquisition on the brain's commitment to the initial representation (which I called digital) is found in the results of a longitudinal study that tracked the progress of a cohort of children all of whom performed in the normal range at native phoneme discrimination at seven months. Those children who did best in that test scored higher at later times on all language measures, including lexicon size, duration of utterances, and sentence complexity (Tsao, Liu, and Kuhl, 2004).

What today would be called a computational approach to unsupervised learning of morphology from speech that has already been digitized into phonemes has been proposed by Harris (1968, pp.24-28) as a part of his discovery program for the structure of language. His idea relied on the observation that in continuous speech the *predictability* of the next phoneme given its immediate predecessors drops sharply at the boundaries between morphemes. For example, given the string betw the continuation (in English) is virtually certain to be een; in comparison, the number of choices following between is enormous.[15]

Harris's insight has been vindicated by the discovery that infants become sensitive to the transitional probabilities between successive syllables in a novel sequence to which they have been exposed for only two minutes (Saffran, 2001; Saffran et al., 1996). Statistical considerations lie also at the basis of an implemented computational method for automatic discovery of morphology from an unannotated corpus (Goldsmith, 2001). Reassuringly, in human language learners too the end product of this process has all the signs of an integration of structure with statistics (Hay and Baayen, 2005).

Taken together, the computational feasibility of bootstrapping from raw, unsegmented speech to sequences of morphologically meaningful symbols and the correspondence between the key characteristics of computational methods and of human learners suggest that we may indeed consider lan-

Baby STATISTICIANS. In one of their experiments, Saffran et al. (1996) exposed 8-month old babies to two minutes of continuous synthesized speech consisting of repetitions of the "words" pabiku, tibudo, golatu, and daropi. The words were entered into the sequence in a randomized order that fixed the transition probabilities between syllables straddling word boundaries (such as tu-da and pi-go) at 0.33; the within-word transition probabilities were equal to 1.0. The babies were subsequently found capable of discriminating words (pabiku and tibudo) from syllable triplets that also appeared in the training sequence, but with a lower combined probability, because they straddled word boundaries (tudaro and pigola; transition probabilities 0.33 and 1.0).

guage from this point on to be digital. This gives us license to continue using text in trying to understand how higher-order knowledge of language — its grammar — can be learned from input in an unsupervised fashion. It is time for the baby to go recursive.

7.2.2 Going recursive

We have, of course, already made the first step along the road that leads from an undifferentiated sequence of symbols to a recursively structured grammar. This happened when we observed how a candidate word, θέλεις, emerges from the string οἴδδϑέλειςσῦκαϑέλεις when it is compared against a progressively shifted copy of itself. Along with unitization, the two computational operations involved in this step, ALIGNMENT and COMPARISON, are the key tools of grammar induction: **candidate structures found by aligning and comparing strings at a certain level of representation become units that participate in structure discovery at the next higher level**. A recursive application of this principle combines phonemes into morphemes, words, phrases, and sentences (Harris, 1968).

The operations of alignment and comparison have a long history in linguistics. Zellig Harris (1954), working in the structuralist tradition, identified them as basic means of discovering the regularities of language.[16] From the

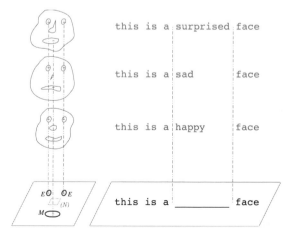

Figure 7.8 — Discovery of structural regularities in vision or in language requires ALIGNMENT. *Left:* when the three schematic faces are aligned, it emerges that they all possess eyes (*E*) and mouth (*M*) in a particular spatial arrangement; their noses are sufficiently different from each other to hypothesize that the structure contains an open slot (appropriately labeled *N*). *Right:* when the three phrases are aligned, their common structure, which includes an open slot, becomes apparent. Computationally, the comparison of aligned structures is precisely what receptive fields do (i.e., combine the current stimulus with a processed record of prior experience, which is expressed in the values of the weights if these are modified by successive encounters with similar stimuli).

neurocomputational standpoint, structure discovery through alignment is a very natural thing for a biological information processor to be doing. Consider what happens when the three faces in Figure 7.8, left, are *averaged* after being aligned. The mismatched parts (in that example, the nose and the face outline) will be blurred, whereas the matching ones (the eyes and the mouth) will remain prominent. The resulting image could then be used as a kind of template for the eyes+mouth pattern — a simplified generic face, with an open slot where the nose would normally go (this would allow the template to accommodate a variety of nose shapes). Indeed, tracking the mean of the distribution of inputs is precisely what modifiable synapses are geared to do (it is even easier to implement than the Hebbian learning described in section 3.3.3), and a fuzzy template is precisely what a receptive field looks like.

Although the visual world can be usefully seen as recursively structured (Jackendoff and Pinker, 2005; Minsky, 1985), the visual system does not need deeply recursive representations because of the possibility to zoom in and out (Edelman and Intrator, 2003).

This detail from Arcimboldo's painting *The Vegetable Gardener* can be seen on a global scale as a face, or more locally as a bunch of vegetables; it is difficult to attend simultaneously to both these levels. Controlled experiments with hierarchically structured visual stimuli (large letters composed of many copies of a different, smaller letter) show that the forest is usually seen before the trees (Navon, 1977).

When applied to language acquisition, these observations are instrumental in highlighting the interdependence induced by the language Game between the abilities of the learner and properties of the data that support the learning. Languages whose regularities — the elements of the grammar that gives rise to it — are far removed from raw data, or are difficult to detect using alignment and comparison, are less likely to be effective in propagating themselves. Because alignment and comparison are very natural operations in neural computation, we may expect that applying them to raw text will lead us to grammar — just as a baby's brain is led to discover the hierarchical structure of language by recursive application of these operations to its "digital" representation of speech.

Let us start with words, then. When sequences of words under comparison are properly aligned, any regularity in the phrase structure will stand out as a PATTERN of words (Figure 7.8 on the preceding page, right). The only constraint on the application of alignment, which is dictated by the fundamentals of brain function, is that unlimited perfect memory for past inputs — to be compared to the current one — is disallowed. Only patterns already distilled from the past experience (augmented perhaps by a handful of rapidly fading short-term memory traces of recent inputs) can participate in the comparison. What kinds of patterns would such an imperfect — but, crucially, realistic — system detect in a corpus of *simple* natural-language sentences? Just these two:

1. COLLOCATIONS, and

2. DISTRIBUTIONAL EQUIVALENCES.

Let's see what these patterns are, and how they prepare the ground for structurally complex sentences.

Collocations

The first kind of regularity, collocation or *syntagmatic* pattern, is illustrated in Table 7.1 on the next page. Let us see what happens if we align the highlighted sentences from the various Monty Python scripts represented there:

```
(7.12)   (a)  What's all this, then?
         (b)  What's all this, then?
         (c)  What's all this, then, amen?
         (d)  What's     this, then?  Romanes eunt domus?
         (e)  What's     this, then?  Mmh.
         (f)  What's     this  conversation here
         (g)  What's     this, wants to be a *girlie*?
         (h)  What's     this  one?
         (i)  What's     that, then?
```

COLLOCATIONS form a ubiquitous scaffolding that keeps sentences from collapsing in a heap of words. They are much more pervasive in language than just those expressions that people intuitively consider idiomatic: the supposedly exceptional cases outnumber the unexceptional ones. Empirical evidence supporting the predominance in language of full or partial idioms, set phrases, prefabricated expressions, etc., all of which must somehow be stored in the lexicon (Jackendoff, 1995), comes from the analysis of transcribed speech and of texts. For example, a study of representative excerpts from two corpora of spoken and written English showed that about 59% of the structures with slots in the former and 52% in the latter were PREFABS (Erman and Warren, 2000).

The most consistent pattern that emerges from this multiple comparison is What's this; it is present in all but one of the nine sentences. A longer pattern, 7.12(a), happens to be an integral part of the Pythons' favorite stereotype of a policeman (a category in which they included the Roman centurion stationed in the Jerusalem of *Life of Brian*).

With this example in mind, we can define a collocation as a set of words that is characterized by a tendency of appearing together in various contexts. This intuitive definition needs to be elaborated. First, structure is crucial: the members of a collocation must appear together in the proper sequence (they are, of course, also free to enter individually into any number of other phrases).[17] The reliance on word order in discovering collocations may seem to be a fatal weakness of the present language acquisition scheme in view of the existence of so-called free word order languages; in fact, however, there is enough order consistency even in such languages as Odawa (Christianson and Ferreira, 2005, p.121) to support collocation learning.

The second issue, which is very prominent in example 7.12, is that not all the members of a collocation may be present in every sentence that could in principle support it. This issue can be resolved algorithmically: partially matching sequences, which may have gaps or open slots, can be detected by a suitably flexible alignment procedure.

Constable: Right Right RIGHT! Now then, now then. *Chemist:* Aren't you going to say, "**What's all this then?**" *Constable:* Oh. **What's all this then?** *Son:* Call the church police! *Klaus:* All right. *(shouting)* The Church Police!	*Mr. Hendy* Um, **what's this** conversation here? *Waiter:* Uh, that's, uh, 'football.' *Mounties:* He cuts down trees, he wears high heels, suspenders and a . . . a bra???? *(raggedly)* **What's this?** Wants to be a *girlie*? Oh, my! And I thought you were so rugged!
(sirens racing up, followed by a tremendous crash; the church police burst in the door) *Detective:* **What's all this then**, amen! *Mother:* Are you the church police? *All the police officers: (in unison)* Oh, yes! *Mother:* There's another dead bishop on the landing, vicar sergeant! *Centurion:* **What's this, then?** "Romanes eunt domus"? *Man:* **What's this, then?** Mmh. *Mr. Brown:* A liver donor's card.	Poofter! *Constable:* I mean, **what's this** one? "Cockroach Cluster"? And this, "Anthrax Ripple"? *Clerk:* There is no such thing as a bloody cat licence. *Man:* Yes there is. *Clerk:* No there isn't. *Man:* Is! *Clerk:* Isn't! *Man:* I've bleedin' got one, look! **What's that then?** *Clerk:* This is a dog licence with the word 'dog' crossed out and 'cat' written in in crayon.

Table 7.1 — COLLOCATION, or syntagmatic regularity (highlighted; all examples are from Monty Python).

The third and last issue that must be addressed to complete the definition of collocation concerns what it means for words to "tend" to appear together. A possible computational solution here, suggested by Barlow (1990) with regard to a seemingly completely different problem (learning hierarchies of visual features), is to declare a collocation if the words occur together more often than what can be expected from their individual frequencies. While there are many possible variations on this idea (one of which I'll mention a bit later), its core is clearly statistical: only significant collocations should be allowed to become symbolic units and to participate in the inference of further structure.

In empirically motivated corpus linguistics, collocations are known under many names. One of these is prefabricated expression, or PREFAB (Erman and Warren, 2000): a sequence of words that is so well entrenched that when one encounters a variation on it (as in the last sentence in example 7.12, `What's all` **`that,`** `then`), it immediately evokes the "original" and is perceived, as it were, with that original in mind.[18] Prefabs can come in the form of a fully specified idiomatic expression (`heavy duty`), or a partially specified one (`take ___ with a grain of salt`).

Distributional equivalence

The so-called paradigmatic regularities consisting of items that are DISTRI-BUTIONALLY EQUIVALENT are, in a sense, mirror images of collocations. Whereas the latter consist of words that appear together in different contexts, the former are signaled by different words appearing in the same context — in the same slot in distinct instances of the same collocation, that is. Consider the example from the *Monty Python's Flying Circus* reproduced in Table 7.2 on the following page:

(7.13)   (a) `I will not buy this record,`   `it is`
         `scratched.`

    (b) `I will not buy this record,`   `it is`
         `scratched.`

    (c) `I will not buy this tobacconist's, it is`
         `scratched.`

If `record` and `tobacconist's` prove to be interchangeable in a statistically significant sample of instances of a particular context in a corpus, there would be no escape from concluding that these two expressions are indeed equivalent in that context. A set of items (words or phrases) that are distributionally equivalent in a certain context are thus members in an EQUIVALENCE CLASS associated with it.

Traditionally, distributional equivalence has been used to derive a structural definition of parts of speech (Harris, 1954), the idea being that the category of nouns consists of words that can appear in contexts such as `I will not buy this _____`; verbs in contexts such as `Trotsky ____ the world proletariat`; adjectives in `this _____ marmot`, etc. When computing became cheap, many effective methods for finding such equivalences automatically from corpora were developed; that of Finch and Chater (1991) was one of the earliest. It is clear, however, that not all nouns, or verbs, or adjectives are equivalent: as Harris (1954) notes, "not every adjective occurs with every noun." For example, `wide` does not fit well into

ROLLER CAPTION: In 1970, the British Empire lay in ruins, foreign nationals frequented the streets — many of them Hungarian (not the streets — the foreign nationals). Anyway, many of these Hungarians went into tobacconist's shops to buy cigarettes.
Enter Hungarian gentleman with phrase book. He is looking for the right phrase.

Hungarian: **I will not buy this** record, **it is scratched**.
Tobacconist: Sorry?
Hungarian: **I will not buy this** record, **it is scratched**.
Tobacconist: Uh, no, no, no. This is a tobacconist's.
Hungarian: Ah! **I will not buy this** tobacconist's,
      it is scratched.

"All I can say is thank goodness for teleconferencing."

["All I can say is thank goodness for teleconferencing."]

Table 7.2 — *Left:* DISTRIBUTIONAL EQUIVALENCE or paradigmatic regularity (of the expressions delimited by the highlighted syntagm). *Right:* can you see how this cartoon is related to the idea of distributional equivalence?

the _____ week. The full import of this irregularity and its many relatives (some close, others distant, but all noisy and demanding) will become apparent in section 7.4.

7.2.3   Structure from corpus

The detection of a collocation in a chunk of text creates an opportunity for erecting a hierarchical structure that describes it, by initiating a search for new collocations (or other regularities) with the just-created unit treated as a regular word. When iterated, this process can give rise to trees just like those produced by a conventional grammar. The all-important difference is, of course, the empirical grounding of collocation trees in corpus data, which is lacking in grammars produced by hand.

Several successive stages in the operation of the first computer algorithm capable of learning a reasonably complex grammar from raw text, ADIOS (for Automatic DIstillation Of Structure; Solan, Horn, Ruppin, and Edelman, 2005), are illustrated in Figure 7.9. For computational purposes, it is conve-

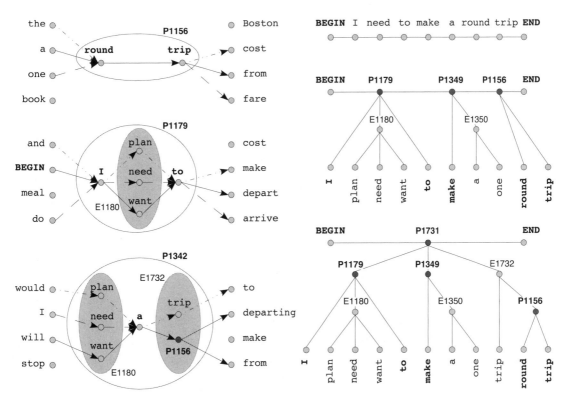

Figure 7.9 — The unsupervised algorithm of Solan, Horn, Ruppin, and Edelman (2005) distills a grammar from raw text by detecting context-specific, statistically significant collocations and distributional regularities, adding the newly acquired structures to the lexicon, and iterating until all significant regularities have been detected. Its operation is illustrated here on examples from the Air Traffic Information System (ATIS) corpus (Hemphill et al., 1990). *Left top*: a collocation round trip is detected and assigned a unique pattern code, **P1156**. *Left middle*: three words are found to be distributionally equivalent in the context of **P1179**; they become members in a new equivalence class E1180. *Left bottom*: the process is iterated with **P1156** and E1180 as new full-fledged members of the lexicon, leading to the discovery of a new pattern, **P1342**. *Right*: the build-up of hierarchically structured patterns by iterative application of the algorithm. Such patterns can be cast in the form of a grammar (Table 7.3 on the following page). For details of the algorithm, and a discussion of the relationship between the grammars it learns and various linguistic theories, see (Edelman, 2007; Solan et al., 2005).

S	→	BEGIN **P1731** END	**P1349**	→	make E1350
P1731	→	**P1179** **P1349** E1732	E1350	→	a | one
P1179	→	I E1180 to	E1732	→	trip | **P1156**
E1180	→	need | want | plan	**P1156**	→	round trip

Table 7.3 — The grammar corresponding to the pattern tree in Figure 7.9, right, bottom.

---

nient to think of a corpus as a data structure that computer scientists call a GRAPH — a network of nodes connected by arcs. The nodes stand for the lexical entries (words, as well as symbols representing any hierarchical structures detected by the algorithm); each arc stands for a particular sentence found in the corpus.[19]

The ADIOS algorithm dynamically alters the graph that represents its data: each newly detected structure is added to the lexicon, its symbol becoming a new node in the graph. The lexicon thus serves as the sole repository of the knowledge of language, effectively subsuming within it the grammar, whose rules correspond to the learned patterns (see Table 7.3). The computational framework for language acquisition and representation implied by this algorithm is compatible with the vision of Langacker (1987, p.63), who introduced his theoretical proposal for a "cognitive grammar" by remarking:

> **As conceived in the present framework, the grammar of a language is simply an inventory of linguistic units.**

This idea of grammar is in line with theories of linguistic development described variously as item-based (Tomasello, 2000a), usage-based (Lieven, Tomasello, Behrens, and Speares, 2003), or construction-based (Tomasello, 2006). The latter label, which can be traced back to the pioneering work of Fillmore (1985) on CONSTRUCTION GRAMMAR (CG), is the one I shall adopt here.

The initial introduction of CG has been motivated by linguists' doubts concerning what Jackendoff (1995) has called the "received view" of grammar (which I outlined in Figure 7.4 on page 246 and shall revisit briefly in section 7.4). According to that view, the lexicon serves as a passive repository of knowledge that is too specific or idiosyncratic to fit into the grammar.

A close look at the situation reveals, however, that the boundary between lexicon and grammar is impossible to justify in a consistent and empirically sound manner, and that a notion of "core grammar" consisting of exceptionless and completely general rules is untenable (Culicover, 1999).

The dissolution of the distinction between lexicon and grammar blurs the proposed difference between the *open-choice principle* and the complementary *idiom principle* in sentence generation (Erman and Warren, 2000). Under the open-choice principle, rules determine through their successive application the tree-like derivation structure of a sentence; words from the lexicon (called "terminals" because they terminate rule application when chosen) are then selected to fill the open slots in that structure, labeled initially only by their categories or parts of speech. The idiom principle provides a fall-back strategy for the occasions in which the target sentence has an unorthodox structure that cannot be derived by rule application, or in which one or more slots in the derivation tree must be occupied by specific words rather than by any member of a wide category; in those supposedly rare cases the entire structure — partially or fully specified — is retrieved as a whole from the lexicon.

Relegating the idiom principle to a secondary status is, however, incompatible with the state of affairs in actual natural-language utterances, where, as I mentioned a few pages back, words that are embedded in collocations or prefabs outnumber those that are supposedly freely selected. This is where Construction Grammar enters the picture: rather than trying hard to tell where the grammar leaves off and the lexicon begins, it acknowledges — and attempts to formalize — the continuum between the two, and the unity of the process whereby sentences are composed (and analyzed).

On the CG account, constructions are essentially pairings of form and meaning, and they come in various sizes and complexity, some as specific as lexically filled idioms, others as abstract as the passive voice (Goldberg, 2003).[20] The integration of form and meaning, which is central to the theory, offers an enticing solution to the problem of compositional semantics: give up the aspiration to a universal systematicity, while retaining the core idea of the dependence of meaning on structure. Because constructions can get very complex, the power of language to convey meaning is not diminished; at the same time, meaning becomes truly inseparable from form: if you want to nuance your message, you have to make sure to use just the right construction — in addition to the right words, of course.

For the CG approach to structure and meaning to be feasible, people

Bates, Thal, Finlay, and Clancy (1999) offer the following estimate of the amount of a child's EX-POSURE TO LANGUAGE: "Consider the following statistics: assuming a taciturn Calvinist family in which an English-speaking child hears approximately 5 hours of speech input per day, at a mean rate of 225 words per minute, the average 10-year-old child has heard 1,034,775,000 English phonemes (at an average of 25,869,375 trials per phoneme). She has heard just under 250 million words (including 17,246,250 renditions of the most common function words) and 28 million sentences, with more than 6 million past-tense verbs and 12 million plural nouns. In short, she has had many many opportunities to entrench the most frequent elements of her native language. The numbers double by 20 years of age (assuming this Calvinist child does not develop a predilection for the telephone during adolescence)."

must be capable of storing vast amounts of information about collocations and context-dependent equivalences, as well as memorizing entire prefabricated chunks of language. Any such information would complement the "simple" lexical store, which for a US university graduate is estimated to hold about 20,000 word families (Nation and Waring, 1997), each containing the base word along with its inflections and regular derivations, if any. The initial estimates of the size of the extended lexical store, such as the 25,000 fixed expressions mentioned by Jackendoff (1995, p.136), appear too conservative in the light of more recent evidence (Dabrowska, 2004; Hoey, 2005). Undoubtedly, however, the relevant information is available to the average learner, given his or her massive EXPOSURE TO LANGUAGE (Bates et al., 1999; Pullum and Scholz, 2002; Tomasello, 2006).

The Construction Grammar theory is supported by a plethora of psycholinguistic findings concerning the process of language acquisition by infants. For example, Bates and Goodman (1999), who worked with children between 8 and 30 months of age, document a strong correlation between each learner's vocabulary size and his or her language production score on a grammatical complexity scale. After summarizing the results from numerous stud-

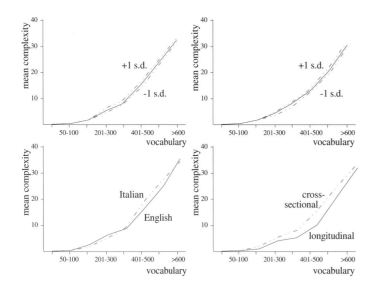

Figure 7.10 — The dependence of GRAMMAR on LEXICON SIZE (redrawn from Bates and Goodman, 1999). *Left top:* the basic result — the tight correlation between vocabulary and grammatical complexity (both assessed with the MacArthur Communicative Development Inventory). *Right top:* the same for open-class vocabulary only (that is, excluding closed-class or function words). *Right bottom:* the same, for cross-sectional vs. longitudinal slicing of the subject population. *Left bottom:* the same, for English vs. Italian.

ies spanning two decades of research (see Figure 7.10), they conclude, "We are convinced by these data that there is a powerful link between grammar and lexical growth in this age range, a nonlinear growth function that holds for both cross-sectional and longitudinal designs, at both individual and group levels, and perhaps across languages as well (although two languages [English and Italian] is a very small sample of the possibilities that the world has to offer.)"

More recently, direct evidence of item-by-item acquisition of constructions by children has been coming from psycholinguists who observe children on a daily basis in the natural home setting. Many studies documenting such findings have been described and interpreted by Tomasello (2003). A typical study is that of Lieven et al. (2003), who recorded one 2-year-old child for five hours per week for six weeks. The main results were as follows:

- about two-thirds of the multi-word utterances were verbatim repetitions of previously produced ones;

- about three-quarters of the rest consisted of repetition of some part of a previously used utterance with only one small change (for example, after repeating many hundreds of times `Where's the ____?`, the child produced the novel utterance `Where's the butter?`);

- only about one-quarter of the novel multiword utterances (5% of all utterances produced during the test period) differed from things this child had said before in more than one way (these mostly combined word substitution in and chaining of established construction, but there were several utterances that seemed to be novel in more complex ways).

Studies such as this make it clear that language acquisition proceeds not by sweeping generalization based on abstract rules, but rather painstakingly construction by construction, and often word by word.

The modern construction-based theories of what grammar is (Goldberg, 2005) and how it gets learned by children (Tomasello, 2006) are well on their way towards bringing about a revolution in mainstream linguistics, which for decades has been using quite unequivocal terms to deny any possibility of learning language from corpus data alone (cf. note 26 on page 311). A succinct expression of the emerging new synthesis in linguistics is given by Culicover and Jackendoff (2005, p.33-34), who write:

> Our vision of learning [. . .] is that the learner stores current

---

> "Do you want to watch a movie?"
>
> 要 (yào) = want (*to*)
>
> 要不要 (yào bù yào) = want/not want (*to*)
>
> 你要不要看電影?
> nǐ yào bù yào kàn diàn yǐng.
> You want/not want watch movie?
>
> "Is she a teacher?"
>
> 是 (shì) = is, am, are, etc.
>
> 是不是 (shì bù shì) = is/not is
>
> 她是不是老師?
> tā shì bù shì lǎo shī?
> She is/not is teacher?
>
> "Does the library have magazines?"
>
> 有 (yǒu) = have
>
> 有沒有 (yǒu méi yǒu) = have/not have
>
> 圖書館有沒有雜誌?
> tú shū guǎn yǒu méi yǒu zá zhì?
> Library have/not have magazine(s)?

In Mandarin, a verb can be turned into a question using the "verb-not-verb" construction. This example illustrates two important general characteristics of constructions. First, CONSTRUCTIONS ARE LANGUAGE-SPECIFIC (Croft, 2001; Dahl, 2004): the existence of V-not-V in Mandarin could not have been predicted, say, from the knowledge of the interrogative form in English, which uses an auxiliary `do` in most cases. Second, CONSTRUCTIONS ARE WORD-SPECIFIC ("lexicalized"): two of the three verbs in this example use bù for "not" and the third one uses méi. In this respect, the label V-not-V is somewhat misleading.

analyses of novel heard utterances in the lexicon. The learning procedure then attempts to construct new and more general lexical entries, in which common parts of existing lexical entries are retained and differing parts are replaced by a variable. This makes the new lexical entry function as a schema or rule that encompasses existing entries and permits construction of new utterances. In turn, this schema along with others may be further abstracted into a still more general schema by replacing further dimensions of variation with variables.

NULLIUS IN VERBA. Any claim that children actually harbor a given construction remains baseless unless supported empirically by standard scientific methods (Edelman, 2007), whether the construction has been intuited or found by a computer algorithm from corpus regularities. In the latter case, however, it is possible to infer that the distillation of the construction in question is computationally tractable. Beyond that, the psychological reality of a construction can be examined through behavioral investigation, as was done for phrase structure (Johnson, 1965; cf. p. 244) and collocations (Harris, 1998), as well as by other means such as brain imaging or computer modeling, as discussed in the earlier chapters.

While these intuitions are on the right track, as good scientists we should know better than to trust them in their own right. As Dabrowska (2004, pp.227-228) notes poignantly, "...although cognitive linguists are officially committed to developing an account of language that is usage-based and firmly grounded in human cognition, in practice, only a few have begun to go beyond the traditional introspective methods."

The only way to transcend introspection is, of course, to let data and principled (algorithmic) analysis speak for themselves. Insofar as language acquisition is concerned, the most relevant kind of data is transcribed child-directed

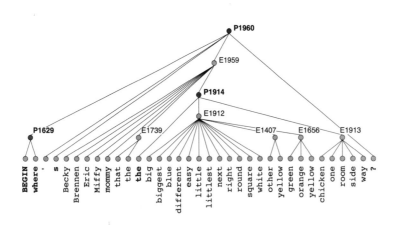

Figure 7.11 — A complex hierarchical structure, labeled **P1960** ("pattern #1960"), automatically extracted from the CHILDES corpus (MacWhinney, 2000) by the unsupervised algorithm of Solan et al. (2005). As in Figure 7.9, numerical labels preceded by **P** pertain to collocations, and those preceded by **E** pertain to equivalence classes of items that are distributionally related. The pattern at the root of this tree, **P1960**, can generate such diverse sentences as where's the big room?; where's the yellow one?; where's Becky?; and where's that?.

speech, as found for example in the CHILDES corpus (MacWhinney, 2000). It is therefore reassuring to note that the ADIOS algorithm mentioned earlier, which learns recursively structured collocations and equivalences gradually, in a manner resembling the children observed by Lieven et al. (2003), works well on the CHILDES data (Solan, Horn, Ruppin, and Edelman, 2005; see Figure 7.11).

7.2.4 Patterns over patterns

For many months early on in the learning process, the constructions being acquired by babies are *simple*: they correspond to phrase fragments (Bloom, 1970; Lieven et al., 2003), such as

(7.14) `more _____`

(7.15) `allgone _____`

or at most standalone CLAUSES. Having mastered a small repertoire of such constructions, the baby learner is ready for some really creative use of language. This comes with the mastery of COMPLEX SENTENCE forms (Diessel, 2004).

A complex sentence combines two or more clauses by means of coordination (in which case the clauses are on equal footing) or subordination (where some clauses depend on others). An example of the former is *conjunction* (7.16); examples of the latter are *complementation* (7.17) and *relativization* (7.18):

(7.16) `Revolutionaries are fierce and marmots are furry.`

(7.17) `I think that the preceding sentence contains a non-sequitur.`

(7.18) `The person who wrote the preceding sentence was being overly judgmental.`

As predicted by the Construction Grammar theory, the child's capacity for producing complex sentences is highly correlated with access to relevant lexical items. For example, Diessel (2004, p.73) reports a 0.799 correlation between the frequency of complement-taking verbs (such as `think`

A CLAUSE is a construction that predicates something of a subject; an example from p. 244 is the frame

> The *subj* saw *pred*

with `marmot` bound to the *subj* slot, and `Trotsky` – to *pred*.

and `believe`) and the appearance of complex constructions in the child's speech. Diessel summarizes his book-length study of the acquisition of complex sentences by remarking that "first, children's complex sentences become increasingly more complex" and "second, children's complex sentences become increasingly more abstract." Thus, the complexity of the child's representation of language grows gradually throughout the duration of the acquisition process, from segmenting out phonemes ("digitizing" speech) through the attainment of adult-like capability to engage in discourse.

The computational process that supports this growth of linguistic complexity is recursive discovery and subsequent unitization of collocations and of equivalence classes of distributionally related items. To complete the picture, I need to single out one specific kind of structural relation and a possible mechanism for its discovery. The relation is *self-reference*. This may be direct, as in a rule that rewrites a variable term by invoking it recursively:

(7.19) NP → Det N | NProp | NP and NP

This rule (reproduced from Figure 7.4 on page 246) can generate phrases such as:

(7.20) `a marmot`

(7.21) `the marmot and Leon`

(7.22) `the marmot and Leon and Diego`

(7.23) `the marmot and Leon and Diego and a woodchuck`

(7.24) `...`

Its most distinctive quality is that in principle it allows infinitely long sentences. Infinity can also arise from several rules forming a daisy chain, each invoking another one in an ultimately circular fashion. In terms of constructions, an extremely simple scenario from which infinite looping may arise is one in which a collocation contains two consecutive identical items.

Think, for example, of the structure behind `the green, green grass of home`. In an idealized, maximally compact grammar exemplified by Figure 7.4, this phrase would be generated by an explicitly self-referential rule. Experiments with a realistic construction learning algorithm (Solan et al.,

2005) suggest, however, that "suboptimal" constructions such as [the E_i E_i grass P_j] are likely to be acquired instead.

In this case (as well as in the case of a daisy chain of reference), the learner may discover that it can generate infinitely long utterances by examining the patterns of interrelationships among existing constructions, without recourse to new corpus data. For example, he or she may figure out that any item that repeats twice (E_i E_i) can be "pumped" indefinitely, resulting in a joyous outburst the green green yellow red brown blue ... that aims at infinity but is all too soon cut short when the child runs out of adjectives. Similar events may be precipitated by the discovery of infinity in complementation: I think that you think that he thinks that I think ...

7.2.5 Probabilities

You may recall that the fundamental insight into language with which this chapter opened states that the prime characteristic of linguistic structures is the manner in which they deviate from equiprobability. Let us now reexamine this notion in the light of what is known about constructions and about their learning and use. Here is what Harris (1991, p.32) wrote about the role of probability in language:

> ... no external metalanguage is available to the child learning its first language ... when only a small percentage of all possible sound-sequences actually occurs in utterances, one can identify the boundaries of words, and their relative likelihoods, from their sentential environment; this, even if one was not told (in words) that there exist such things as words. ... Given, then, the absence of an external metalanguage, it is an essential property of language that the combinations of words and utterances are not all equiprobable. It follows that whatever else there is to be said about the form of language, a fundamental task is to state the departures from equiprobability in sound- and word-sequences.

The combination of bootstrapping from continuous speech into symbolic language by "going digital" and subsequent learning of constructions by "going recursive" fits this bill perfectly. First, every step in this process, from learning the phonemes to learning sentences, relies on statistical criteria to isolate and acquire structures that are significant — that is, significantly nonrandom, or non-equiprobable. Second, when used productively, constructions learned by this process impose a crisp pattern of departure from equiprobability over the resulting corpus: among all possible sequences of words, those that cannot be derived by a repeated invocation of a sequence of constructions ("rules") have precisely zero probability.

Many linguists rely on INTRO-SPECTION as the method of choice for gathering primary data (Chomsky, 2004a, p.107); others prefer to interview a native informant, whose assessments of grammaticality of judiciously chosen sentences are used to make inferences about the grammar that presumably generated them. These data gathering methods, and any others that do not rely on large corpora, are blind to GRADATIONS OF NATURALNESS — a kind of knowledge that blurs the distinction between the lexicon and the grammar. As an illustration, consider this reminiscence by Lamb (2004, p.50): "One day, after repeatedly asking his informant about the sentences, he (the anthropologist and linguist E. Sapir) was making up – 'Can you say…?', 'Can you say…?', etc. – after which the informant kept saying 'Yes', he finally said 'Yes, you could, but nobody ever would.'"

What we have arrived at is the classical construal of the manner whereby grammar controls language: akin to a totalitarian state where everything that is not prohibited is compulsory, a classical grammar sanctions some sentences absolutely, while equally absolutely disallowing all others. In linguistic publications, prohibition is expressed by placing asterisks next to sentences that are branded as ungrammatical:

(7.25) He$_i$ threatened to leave when Billy$_j$ noticed that the computer had died. $(i \neq j)$

(7.26) * He$_i$ threatened to leave when Billy$_i$ noticed that the computer had died.

In this example, the reading 7.26 under which the pronoun he refers to Billy is excluded by a fundamental principle of the Government and Binding Theory (Chomsky, 1981) — one of the longest-surviving components of modern formal generative linguistics, and a mainstay of the so-called autonomy of syntax thesis (Chomsky, 2004a, p.138). The mandated reading is 7.25, according to which he refers to a person presumably mentioned earlier in the discourse.

In practice, however, the asterisk rarely signifies anything beyond the intuition of the linguist who decides on its placement. For instance, about 60% of the acceptability responses made to the sentences in the above example and other identically structured ones by the 36 subjects in an experiment reported by Harris and Bates (2002) allowed the "starred" interpretation 7.26.

The apparent "neither here nor there" nature of this result and, more generally, the *cline* of acceptability exhibited by subjects in the four experiments of Harris and Bates (2002) and a multitude of other psycholinguistic studies (Schütze, 1996) begs for a probabilistic explanation. Instead of rigid constraints on what entities pronouns may refer to, what words or constructions can or cannot be part of other constructions, etc., there is a single principle of probability combination, integrating multiple sources of constraints that may act together or against each other.

This account implies that sentences should possess a GRADATION OF NATURALNESS, and indeed they do. Most prominently, making unlikely choices while generating sentences from a set of constructions leads to language that sounds vaguely strange or non-native, as if the speaker had a word-choice "accent" while producing perfectly grammatical sentences. As an example, consider this passage from an e-mail message that urged me to go to a fake website to "update" my social security number and bank account details: "This instruction has been sent to all Smith Barney customers and is obligatory to follow." A Google search for the phrase `obligatory to follow` yielded 580 results (compared to 3,660,000 for `must be followed`). Among the top ten of these, hits #1 and #8 were warnings about the message I had received being a "phishing" scam; the rest were interpretations of the Qur'an, discussing the obligation to follow another man's spiritual lead in Islamic law. Another phrase from the same message that looked suspect to me, `earnestly ask`, yielded 30,600 hits; interestingly, these too were dominated by phishing alerts and religious admonitions (apparently, this phrase figures prominently in sermons of the Reverend Sun Myung Moon). Were I in fact a SmithBarney customer, the two statistically sound choices for me at this point would have been (1) to proceed with divulging my bank account details, reasoning that the person in charge of the customer relations at Smith-Barney just happens be a Muslim about to convert to Moon's Unificationist Christianity, or the other way around, or (2) to infer that the message had been generated by a speaker of statistically odd English with less than honorable intentions.

Simple probabilities on constructions: selection

Being a general principle on which language operates, probabilistic representations are found at every level. The examples I just offered pertain to phrase-level collocations; below that, there are the so-called phonotactic differences in prior probability among combinations of phonemes. There, the hearer's probabilistic representation of speech is affected also by speaker- and intonation-specific details of just about every encountered utterance (Port and Leary, 2005). At the level of sentences, probabilistic control offers a convenient means for banishing infinities: instead of postulating an infinitely productive generative grammar limited externally by independent factors such as short-term memory capacity, it is more parsimonious to assume that the grammar itself is limited — or, if you wish — kept sane — by being inherently probabilistic (and thereby joining all other cognitive faculties).

A probabilistic grammar can be constructed simply by annotating the choices arising at each juncture in a set of rules/constructions (learned independently) by their relative probabilities. Let me illustrate this idea on a copy of rule 7.19 on page 266, in which I have placed each of the three possible choices of rewriting NP (originally separated by the | symbol) on a separate line:

(7.27)   (a) **0.7:** NP → Det N

(b) **0.2:** NP → NProp

(c) **0.1:** NP → NP and NP

A probabilistic generative mechanism that is about to rewrite an NP symbol using this rule would be seven times as likely to do it in terms of Det followed by N (a) than in terms of a recursive call to itself (c); referring to NProp (b) would be twice as likely as recursion.

A grammar that is probabilistically annotated in this manner induces what computer scientists call a LANGUAGE MODEL over the set of all possible sentences that can be generated from a given lexicon. In particular, all other things being equal, a language model that assigns low probabilities to recursive invocations of rules automatically makes infinitely long sentences infinitely improbable.

Where do the probability data for annotating the various choices in rules such as 7.27 (or, equivalently, for constructions) come from? From the same source that gives rise to constructions: language experience. Indeed, it turns out that a superior language model emerges when a standard method is used to infer construction probabilities from a corpus from which the constructions themselves have just been learned by the ADIOS algorithm (Solan et al., 2005).

In considering the evidence for the psychological reality of probabilistic language modeling in human cognition, it is worth observing the important computational distinction between unstructured and structured modes of probability bookkeeping (Goodman, 2001). The former calls for keeping tabs on the probabilities of various combinations of units (say, words), starting

A LANGUAGE MODEL is indispensible in speech recognition. The complexity of the speech signal and the usually difficult conditions under which speech needs to be perceived and interpreted require a means for narrowing down the range of possible interpretations for each incoming word-like sound sequence. By ranking the hypotheses about the possible continuation word by the conditional probabilities they receive given the preceding sequence, a language model provides the necessary disambiguation mechanism. The hypothesis that people indeed acquire, actively maintain, and use a probabilistic language model in comprehension is receiving increasing support from empirical studies (Hale, 2004).

with individual words or *unigram* statistics (word frequencies), and increasing the order through *bi-gram*, *tri-gram*, and so on, to *n-gram* statistics.

To collect bi-gram statistics, for example, one creates a table with as many rows and columns as there are words in the lexicon, and enters in cell i, j the frequency of finding word j immediately after word i in the corpus used to "train" the language model.[21] Instead of or in addition to tabulating word-word co-occurrence, one may cross words with phrase-level constructions in which they participate — something that people apparently do: "Native speakers learn not only which sentence structures can grammatically combine with each verb, but also how often each verb occurs in each such structure" (Gleitman, Cassidy, Nappa, Papafragou, and Trueswell, 2005, p.57).

Even just word-level bi-grams can be extremely useful computationally; for example, bi-gram statistics can be relied upon to solve certain problems in the acquisition of language structure that for decades have been considered intractable and used as a key argument for the impossibility of language learning in the absence of an innate grammar (Reali and Christiansen, 2005). For larger n, the structure captured by n-gram statistics becomes closer and closer to the true linear (not hierarchical) structure of language. For example, Miller and Selfridge (1961, p.201) found that "this kind of gibberish [English words randomly strung so as to preserve 5-gram statistics] is as easily recalled as a passage lifted from a novel." There are, however, good reasons to believe

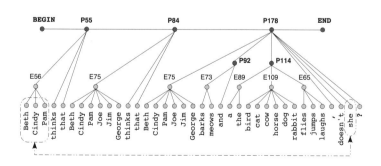

Figure 7.12 — A long-range DEPENDENCY manifests itself in this set of patterns acquired by the ADIOS algorithm (Solan et al., 2005) from a small artificially generated text corpus. The automatically detected dependency (indicated by the arrow) forces the system to establish a special equivalence class (E56, female proper names), to be used in constructions where the more inclusive class of all proper names (E75) would lead to erroneous overgeneralization.

that there is more to language structure than n-gram statistics (in addition to all that we have learned so far, of course).

The first reason is computational: for reasons related to the curse of dimensionality (see p. 59), the amount of data needed to train n-gram language models grows exponentially with n, making them infeasible already for $n = 4$. The second reason has to do with the so-called long-range structure of language: certain phenomena, such as agreement (see Figure 7.12), introduce dependencies between elements that can in principle reside arbitrarily far apart in the sentence. A more structured probability model is required.

Conditional probabilities on constructions: dependencies

A language learner that has acquired some constructions (and is in the process of acquiring more) has at its disposal the right mechanisms for taking probabilistic language modeling to the next, structural level. Because constructions are stored as lexical units (just as regular words are), they can be subjected to the same kind of accounting that generates n-gram statistics. Consequently, if a scan of the available corpus data shows that a given construction can only be followed by one of four others (say), the same scan will also yield the information about the relative frequencies of the latter — precisely what a language model needs. Furthermore, because constructions may translate (when fully specified, at the level of terminals) into arbitrarily long phrases, a structural-statistical language model based on a construction grammar handily captures arbitrarily long-range dependencies.

Unlike the unstructured units stored in the lexicon, constructions offer additional mechanisms for gathering statistics about their usage. One of these is ENTRENCHMENT, a psychological term that we encountered in the section on concepts in Chapter 6. When applied to a construction, entrenchment refers to its degree of cohesion, which is related to the frequency of use (but possibly also to other factors, such as partial overlap with other constructions). Psycholinguistic evidence is available for variable entrenchment of constructions at all levels of complexity (Bien, Levelt, and Baayen, 2005; Harris, 1998; Theakston, 2004; Tomasello, 2003).

The other probabilistic mechanism that applies to constructions is DEPENDENCY, as it is construed by linguists. A familiar kind of dependency in English is the need for AGREEMENT in the present tense construction between the third person singular noun and the verb form (as in A marmot sits).

A lesson in Latin grammar in *Monty Python's Life of Brian* —

Centurion:
What's this, then? "Romanes Eunt Domus"? "People called Romanes they go the house"?
Brian:
It– it says, "Romans, go home."
Centurion:
No, it doesn't. What's Latin for "Roman"? Come on!
Brian:
Aah!
Centurion:
Come on!
Brian:
"R– Romanus"?
Centurion:
Goes like...?
Brian:
"Annus"?
Centurion:
Vocative plural of "annus" is...?
Brian:
Eh. "Anni"?
Centurion:
"Romani." "Eunt"? What is "eunt"?
Brian:
"Go." Let–
Centurion:
Conjugate the verb "to go."
Brian:
Uh. "Ire." Uh, "eo." "Is." "It." "Imus." "Itis." "Eunt."
Centurion:
So "eunt" is...?
Brian:
Ah, huh, third person plural, uh, present indicative. Uh, "they go."
Centurion:
But "Romans, go home" is an order, so you must use the...?
Brian:
The... imperative!
Centurion:
Which is...?
Brian:
Umm! Oh. Oh. Um, "i." "I"!

(continued on the next page)

In some languages, such as Russian (see Table 7.4) or Latin (examples in the margins), the agreement constraints get rather complex.

Computationally, it is natural to formalize dependencies as probabilistic constraints, as when the choice of a member from an equivalence class embedded in a construction is noted to have a certain CONDITIONAL PROBABILITY given the particulars of other constructions in the sentence that is being put together (or even in the larger context of the ongoing discourse; Du Bois, 2001). It is worth noting that, contrary to what one might expect if the dependencies were categorical, going against the grain of language by violating such probabilistic dependencies does not entirely obliterate meaning, nor does it cause an immediate collapse of the perceived structure of the sentence. It would seem that it is for this reason that in *A ticket to ride* the Beatles could sing `But she don't care` without fear that this frivolity with grammar would cause a system error in the listeners' brains (cf. Figure 7.20).[22]

7.2.6 The structure of language is most like...

By following the trail of information that is available to the language learner in his or her or its environment — from the auditory signal via phonemes to a gamut of hierarchical constructions of various degrees of complexity — we have arrived at a useful characterization of the structure of language. Let me now offer you a mnemonic that captures the structural character of language as it reveals itself in the computational and psycholinguistic studies surveyed so far in this chapter: in many key respects, **language is like a subway transit**

Он	боялся	длинношеего	чудовища
On	*boyalsya*	*dlinnosheyego*	*chudovishcha*
$\text{He}_{3rd,NOM,sing}^{masc}$	$\text{feared}_{3rd,sing}^{masc}$	$\text{long-necked}_{ACC,sing}^{neut}$	$\text{monster}_{ACC,sing}^{neut}$

Table 7.4 — In Russian, each word in a sentence must satisfy multiple DEPENDENCY CONSTRAINTS. In this example, the four words are, respectively, the third person masculine singular pronoun in the nominative declension; a past tense, third person, masculine singular verb; a neuter singular adjective in the accusative declension; and a neuter singular noun, also in the accusative. Declension is the morphological transformation of word stems used in Russian, and in Latin, to signify case, number, and gender of nouns, pronouns, and adjectives.

(continued from the previous page)
Centurion:
How many Romans?
Brian:
Ah! "I"– Plural. Plural. "Ite." "Ite."
Centurion:
"Ite."
Brian:
Ah. Eh.
Centurion:
"Domus"?
Brian:
Eh.
Centurion:
Nominative?
Brian:
Oh.
Centurion:
"Go home"? This is motion towards. Isn't it, boy?
Brian:
Ah. Ah, dative, sir! Ahh! No, not dative! Not the dative, sir! No! Ah! Oh, the... accusative! Accusative! Ah! "Domum," sir! "Ad domum"! Ah! Oooh! Ah!
Centurion:
Except that "domus" takes the...?
Brian:
The locative, sir!
Centurion:
Which is...?!
Brian:
"Domum."
Centurion:
"Domum."
Brian:
Aaah! Ah.
Centurion:
"Um." Understand?
Brian:
Yes, sir.
Centurion:
Now, write it out a hundred times.

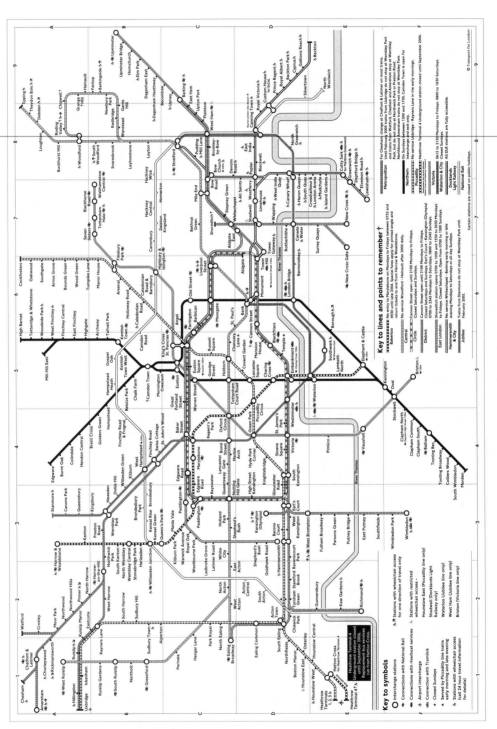

Figure 7.13 — A map of the London subway (the Tube).

system. This analogy clearly requires some explanation, which I am about to offer using the map of the London Tube that is reproduced in Figure 7.13 on the facing page as a prop.

Lexicon-grammar ↔ the set of stations. A *collocation* construction would then be a bus-operated segment that short-circuits a portion of the network between two potentially distant stations via a third one (which could be regarded as the label of this construction). To the inconvenience of many Londoners, numerous examples of this phenomenon could be encountered during the Jubilee Line extension project in the 1990s.

Grammatical utterances ↔ possible trips. This draws a parallel between *frequent words* and stations where many lines meet, such as Bank or Kings Cross (six lines each). For a few more of such detailed parallels, see the note in the margin.

Learning ↔ constructing the transit system. This includes acquiring the lexicon (building the stations), and internalizing a corpus (digging the tunnels). Neologisms (lexical and structural) extend the network.

Probabilistic annotation ↔ traffic flow. A sentence that is highly probable according to the language model is like a much-traveled route (more passengers/trains). Dependencies (construed probabilistically, as suggested above) are like traveling on distinct trains that may share the same tunnel, yet diverge at certain stations.

Structure vs. statistics ↔ routes vs. traffic. In language, both structural representations and statistics (used to infer the constructions and later to guide their involvement in understanding and production) are crucial. The really proficient users of language know "not only what is allowed [the existing connections between stations] but also what is natural [the preferred routes of individual passengers]" (Hoey, 2005; the Tube parallels are mine).

Fluency and disfluency ↔ navigation proficiency. You're fluent in the subway if you navigate it like a native. Disfluency may stem from being a tourist, or from various distractions.

Meaning ↔ the outside world. It should go without saying (I realize that I am contradicting myself by having said it, but that's okay: as with any other idiom, the *literal* meaning of this one is immaterial) that visiting the Piccadilly Circus tube station is a far cry from visiting Piccadilly Circus. Just as there is a real city outside the London Tube, there is a real world outside the network of constructions. Learning to connect the two is an integral part of learning to play the language Game.

The analogy between a subway transit system and the structure of language goes a long way (if we ignore one wrinkle: unlike a subway line, a sentence you cannot ride in both directions). For the following examples, you may need to consult the Tube map on p. 274. *Collocation candidate:* Piccadilly and Northern lines run together through Charing Cross, Embankment, and Waterloo before going their separate ways. *Equivalence:* to get from Waterloo to Baker Street without changing trains, take Piccadilly or Jubilee or Circle. *Subordinate clause:* while traveling from Elephant & Castle to Euston on the Northern line, switch to Circle at Monument and go via Tower Hill, Aldgate, and Liverpool Street, to rejoin Northern at Moorgate. *Idiom:* Heathrow Express, which does not stop at all stations.

7.3 Language in context

Establishing correspondence between the metaphorical Tube station and a piece of the real world seems straightforward enough for at least some of the elements of the lexicon-grammar. An example that comes to mind is the word dog, which stands for something like  — or so one would imagine. Any hope for a straightforward word-to-world correspondence is, however, dashed by the multiplicity of senses, or POLYSEMY, of the word in question. In particular, the word dog can denote an object (as in 7.28) or an action (as in 7.29):

(7.28) She moves his dogs

(7.29) She dogs his moves

We must, therefore, conclude that what a word refers to depends on its CON-TEXT.

Like Peirce's semiotic triangle depicted on page 241, context has three sides to it: DISCOURSE, WORLD, and REPRESENTATION. All three are involved in varying degrees in interpreting — indeed, defining — just about any linguistic structure. Continuing with the example of the word dog, one may observe (1) that the collocation of phonemes that defines it is learned through the superposition of aligned utterances in the discourse or corpus context; (2) that its reference is learned when its invocation co-occurs with

Among the 1000 most frequent English words, the average or number of senses is 3.5 (Chen, Bian, and Lin, 1999). Taking POLYSEMY into account strains the Tube analogy: imagine seeing the Eros statue at Piccadilly Circus if you arrive from Green Park, but not from Leicester Square.

Figure 7.14 — The challenge of the FIXATION OF REFERENCE. The difficulty of deciding what aspect, if any, of the currently viewed scene is the referent of a just-heard utterance can be exemplified by attempts at visual allegory such as this painting by Laurent de la Hyre (1606-1656). Suppose I showed this picture to a 3-year old while saying, Look! Grammar!; what would the child take grammar to refer to? De la Hyre circumvented the clearly impossible challenge of depicting an abstract concept by having his ALLEGORICAL FIGURE OF GRAMMAR hold a ribbon inscribed with a hint to this pictionary riddle (the Latin inscription reads "VOX LITTERATA ET ARTICVLATA DEBITO MODO PRONVNCIATA," or "a meaningful and literate word spoken in a correct manner").

a pattern of multi-sensory stimulation in the world context; and (3) that its meaning emerges from its representational context inherent in the network of concepts maintained by the cognitive system.

For most words — and for all higher-level constructions — that populate the lexicon-grammar, the effects of the different kinds of contextual cues and of their interplay are considerably more complex than in the dog example (Figure 7.14 on the preceding page offers a case in point, if any is needed). This complexity, which is the right and proper subject matter of SEMANTICS, presents the cognitive system with a challenge that naturally follows that of construction acquisition. To understand how this challenge is met, we need to examine the manner in which the elements of the lexicon-grammar weave the web of semantics by connecting to discourse, world, and representation contexts.

7.3.1 Discourse context

I turn first to discourse, because this is the first kind of context that matters to a baby learner early in language acquisition, before the process of connecting the newly emerging constructions to the world and to the conceptual networks picks up momentum. In a natural acquisition setting, it is the *immediate* discourse context of an utterance that contains the most valuable information supporting the distillation of constructions by computational methods such as the ADIOS algorithm. This information comes in the form of other utterances with which the target phrase can be partially aligned (cf. Figure 7.9 on page 259).

Another key role fulfilled by the immediate discourse context of a given utterance is DISAMBIGUATION. Ambiguity, which I first mentioned all the way back on page 8, is a widespread phenomenon in any sensory modality; as in the other cases discussed elsewhere in this book, the solution adopted by the brain in dealing with linguistic ambiguity is essentially statistical and rooted in experience. The parallels to experience- and similarity-based processes that operate in vision are especially prominent in *lexical* disambiguation, which deals with polysemy (other kinds of disambiguation include pronoun reference resolution, as in examples 7.25 and 7.26 on page 268). As Karov and Edelman (1998) showed, it can be carried out computationally by learning to associate each sense of a polysemous word with a typical context and subsequently determining which of these contexts is the most similar to the one in which the word in question is embedded in the utterance.[23]

Do I understand this sentence? Do I understand it just as I should if I heard it in the course of a narrative? If it were set down in isolation I should say, I don't know what it's about. But all the same I should know how this sentence might perhaps be used; I could myself invent a context for it. (A multitude of familiar paths lead off from these words in every direction.)

— Wittgenstein (1958, 525)

7.3.2   World context

Seeing that discourse context can be used to resolve the various ambiguities that are internal to language, I may now return to the original purpose of this section, which is to characterize the computations that mediate the establishment and maintenance of the connections between language and the world. Now, elements of language can invoke and be invoked by each other by virtue of their structural interrelationships, but how can they *refer* to anything at all, let alone anything "out there" in the world? You may have noticed that this question expresses the same concern that is behind the philosophical problem of intentionality familiar to us from Chapter 5, and indeed the resolution of both these issues rests upon the same computational principle. Just as neural activity becomes referential through experience-based *statistical inference*, which allows subsequent *decision making* to be causally driven by external events (cf. p. 122), babies discover that utterances may refer to objects, situations, or actions by learning from experience.

Reference

Being an instance of learning from experience, the computational problem of fixation of reference also mirrors visual learning described in section 5.4 in that it cannot be solved without recourse to prior ASSUMPTIONS about the potential solution. As expected, young learners do use assumptions to guide them in deciding what is relevant to what in their linguistic and perceptual experience.

Consider, for example, a feat of learning that infants perform many times a day for several years: FAST MAPPING, or remembering a novel word (often on the basis of a single exposure) while simultaneously determining its referent through nontrivial inference. Upon hearing what sounds like a novel name in a familiar context, infants assume that it refers to the most salient detached object in their field of view; another novel word encountered subsequently in the same setting is taken to refer to the material or texture (as in furry or smooth) of the salient object (Markman, 1989). Older children act even smarter: when confronted with a similar task, they bring to bear on it not only fixed assumptions but also their conceptual knowledge about the world. For example, having heard a story in which the object designated by a novel label figured as animate, 3-year olds extend the label on the basis of both

It is clear that there is no classification of the Universe not being arbitrary and full of conjectures. The reason for this is very simple: we do not know what the universe is. ...We must conjecture its purpose; we must conjecture the words, the definitions, the etymologies, the synonyms, from the secret dictionary of God.

— Jorge Luis Borges
*The Analytical Language
of John Wilkins* (1984)

Not only humans are capable of smart fixation of reference. The so-called FAST MAPPING has been demonstrated in a border collie (Kaminski, Call, and Fischer, 2004). Having learned to fetch any of a number of named objects from an adjacent room, the dog, Rico (shown here at work), was given a novel name and told to fetch. In most such trials, he brought back from that room the one novel object placed there among several familiar ones (thus proving that he was smarter than Ginger from Figure 7.19 on page 297).

shape and texture, as opposed to shape only for inanimate objects (Booth and Waxman, 2002).

One would expect such SHAPE BIAS to work well for concrete nouns such as dog, but what about verbs, which stand for actions rather than objects?[24] For verbs, the problem is not so much abstractness — many important verbs, such as give (cf. Figure 7.15 on the next page) are quite concrete in most of their senses — as the indeterminacy of the interpretation of the visual scenes from which their meaning must be learned. As Gleitman et al. (2005) observe, complex scenes that infants routinely face are multiply salient (think of everything that is going on simultaneously in a playroom with several kids and a heap of toys). The language learner's key task is to select the one aspect of the observed scene that is *relevant* to the topic of the ongoing discourse, out of the many salient ones.

In such cases, infants resort to a kind of structural bootstrapping, in which previously acquired linguistic knowledge is put to work in disambiguating the mapping between the complex visual stimulus and the complex novel construction just encountered. An example from the work of Naigles (1990) illustrates the interplay between information in an unfolding visual scene and an utterance being heard. Two groups of 2-year olds were shown a video of two salient, simultaneous events: people in duck and rabbit costumes wheeling their arms, while the duck was pushing the rabbit. At the same time, one group heard a nonce word (gorp) being used as a verb in a TRANSITIVE CONSTRUCTION ("Look! The duck is gorping the rabbit!"), and the other — in an INTRANSITIVE one ("Look! The duck and the rabbit are gorping!"). A subsequent test showed that infants in the former group took gorp to correspond to pushing, while those in the the latter group understood it as a kind of arm-wheeling.

In recounting this striking finding, Gleitman et al. (2005, p.39) note: "When paired with a scene, the structural properties of an utterance focus the listener on only certain aspects of the many interpretations that are always available to describe a scene in view." They attribute this ability to a THEMATIC INTERPRETATION BIAS, which prompts infants to seek an interpretation of the scene that has each of the verb's argument slots — two for transitive verbs, one for intransitive — filled by a noun phrase, leaving no slot orphaned. In computational terms, such a "bias" is clearly a kind of prior assumption on the solution that is being sought, just as shape bias is.

In distinction from shape bias, however, the very formulation of the thematic interpretation bias presupposes the existence of certain structures in

How radically novel must a novel structure be to be totally incomprehensible? Lewis Carroll's *Jabberwocky* ("Twas brillig...") is not radical enough — Alice did figure it out, seeing that she remarked later, "... somebody killed something: that's clear, at any rate."

the stream of linguistic input — and the infant's ability to perceive the relevant structures in the utterance at hand despite its novelty at the lexical level. Thus, what Gleitman et al. (2005) term "probabilistic multiple-cue learning process known as *syntactic bootstrapping*" requires considerable linguistic sophistication on the part of the learner. How can 2-year olds, most of whom are yet to produce a complete sentence themselves, come into possession of the requisite structural knowledge? By the computationally straightforward methods described in section 7.2.3.

Given an initially rudimentary (but rapidly growing) arsenal of constructions, an infant gets better and better at determining which components of its total experience are relevant to the utterance it just heard by making use of the productive nature of language. Computational studies indicate that the constructions that are being learned are typically capable of generating — and therefore also accepting — more phrases than it takes to acquire them. This implies that unless a new utterance constitutes a radical departure from familiar territory both in structure and in content, it is likely to have a significant overlap with existing constructions. In this manner, knowing some language helps you get to know more: "Armed with this foundational stock of 'easy' words, learners achieve further lexical knowledge by an arm-over-arm

"Now, no class warfare, O.K.?"

Figure 7.15 — One of the constructions in which the verb give participates requires that the speaker specify the subject, the object, and the recipient — here, the big guy, the coin, and the little guy, respectively. The number of arguments of give in this construction is three. In English, all verbs require at least one argument (except in the imperative: "Run!"). In some languages, certain verbs may not have any arguments at all (as in the Russian темнеет, "it is getting dark"). The verb give is actually associated with several constructions: INTRANSITIVE (We_{subj} give as much as we can), TRANSITIVE (We_{subj} give it_{obj} away), and DITRANSITIVE (We_{subj} give it_{obj} to $them_{rec}$). Moreover, there are two different ditransitive constructions associated with it ($\_\_\__{subj}$ give $\_\_\__{obj}$ to $\_\_\__{rec}$) and ($\_\_\__{subj}$ give $\_\_\__{rec}$ $\_\_\__{obj}$).

process in which successively more sophisticated representations of linguistic structure are built. Lexical learning can thereby proceed by adding structure-to-world mapping methods to the earlier available machinery, enabling efficient learning of abstract items — the 'hard' words" (Gleitman et al., 2005, p.24).

Metaphor

The effectiveness of the passage that I just quoted in shedding light on certain aspects of language acquisition stems not only from the conceptual content it conveys, but also from its use of figurative language. As cognitive linguists would point out, the expression "armed with words" must be read METAPHORICALLY, because words are not really weapons; likewise, language acquisition cannot be an "arm-over-arm process" in any literal sense. A little digging reveals many more figurative turns of speech in the two sentences contained in the quote — and in many other sentences in this book. Not that scientists are exceptionally fond of metaphors: it is safe to state that stripping ordinary language of metaphors would render it useless (Gibbs, 1994; Lakoff and Johnson, 1980). Safe? Stripping? Render? The observation that metaphors are everywhere prompts Baum (2004, p.77) to write, "The example drives home the point that, far from overinflating the need for real-world knowledge in language understanding, the usual arguments about disambiguation barely scratch the surface. (Drive? Home? The point? Far? Overinflating? Scratch? Surface? Oh no, I can't call a halt to this! (Call? Halt?))."

In a sad underappreciation of the value of METAPHORIC LANGUAGE, the Wikipedia article on *reification* (consulted on March 19, 2007) described the title of the song "Give peace a chance" (by John Lennon, shown here with Yoko Ono at their 1969 bed-in) as logically fallacious, presumably because one cannot literally give peace anything.

Both discourse and world context are critical for a proper treatment of figurative expressions such as metaphors. If a common ("literal") interpretation of a phrase clashes with the framework that is being set up by its discourse context, alternative interpretations are allowed to take precedence: Croft and Cruse (2004, ch.8) *define* as figurative an expression for which "a satisfactory (i.e., relevant) interpretation can only be achieved if conventional constraints on interpretation are overridden by contextual constraints." Furthermore, the alternative ("metaphorical") interpretation is often the most transparent to the hearer if a model of the real-world source domain has been mastered. For example, to understand the expression Her anger boiled over it would help to know something about the intuitive physics of heated liquids.

On the conceptual level, a metaphor involves a *mapping* (and sometimes blending) between two domains: the source (in the example just offered, HEATED LIQUID) and the target (ANGER). Its value stems from the multiple parallels between the domains, and the resulting possibility of systematic interpretation: if ANGER is HEATED LIQUID, then losing temper is blowing up, persistent nuisance is low flame, etc. In its turn, even partial systematicity opens up opportunities for productive usage in the target domain, which may be inspired by some marginally creative (or at least minimally hackneyed) construal of the source domain.

The pervasiveness of metaphors suggests, somewhat perversely, that the distinction between literal and metaphorical language is blurred (which is why I earlier enclosed these terms in scare quotes). Certainly if everything in language were a metaphor, nothing would be. Yet, some expressions do seem more metaphorical than others. Among the kinds of examples usually touted as the most representative "deep" metaphors (cf. Croft and Cruse, 2004, p.8-2), the case for 7.30(a) seems uncontroversial, while 7.30(b) appears to be merely an idiosyncratic prepositional construction:

(7.30)   (a) `Her anger boiled over.` [anger=heated liquid]

(b) `I'll see you at the party.` [event=location]

No matter what preposition a particular language settles on for use in 7.30(b), one can interpret it metaphorically, and all the interpretations would be equally gratuitous (as it happens, against the English "*at* the party," Russian uses "*on* the party" and Hebrew "*in* the party").[25]

The lack of a clear-cut criterion for metaphoricity raises the usual suspicion that the phenomenon in question is in essence probabilistic, and indeed it seems natural to interpret the literal/metaphorical cline in terms of conditional probabilities, as likely/unlikely given the context. Thus, a computational theory of metaphor must rest on two pillars: probabilistic (capturing the degree of fit between an expression and its context) and structural (delineating the mapping between distinct conceptual domains in which an expression can be interpreted). This makes figurative language a bridge between probability and structure — a fitting metaphor for cognitive computation in general.

Embodiment

If a lion could talk, we could not understand him.

— Wittgenstein (1958, p.223)

Expressions that are uncontroversially metaphorical, such as 7.30(a), have the distinction of cropping up apparently independently in different languages.

As I suggested above, this characteristic of metaphors seems to be best explained by the shared physical environment that is common to all humans — the backdrop to the emergence and continued evolution of languages (Evans, 2006). Seeing a fellow villager respond to his neighbor's goat's rampage through the vegetable patch may remind you of that time when the pot in your hut boiled over onto the hearth; your subsequent account of the incident for the benefit of some friends who have just returned from the fields could cement your reputation as a wit if it includes a newly invented vivid metaphor, no matter whether your village speaks Hungarian or Japanese (evidence for the universality of certain basic metaphors is described by Kövecses, 2000).

For some metaphors, the mark of our physical EMBODIMENT is incontrovertibly literal: the expression "on the other hand" would puzzle an octopus, and baffle a dolphin (if we could speak to them, that is). What would it do to an artificial intelligence of the kind I mentioned earlier in this chapter — living inside a computer and having access to lots of text but no experience of inhabiting an ape's body? Much of the first-hand (here we go again!) knowledge that such an entity would miss can probably be figured out solely from text: the extended context formed by billions and billions of Web pages is not something to be taken lightly. In fact, in trying to fathom what it is like to be aware of the entire contents of the Web simultaneously, we are just as handicapped as a nascent AI would be with respect to what it is like to taste a strawberry (or to be a bat; cf. p. 437).

COMMUNICATION DIFFICULTIES stemming from this so-called *variable embodiment* problem have been proposed as a supplement to the Turing Test. As you probably know, the original Test outlines a procedure for trying to establish whether or not the instant messaging buddy you never met in person is a computer program (Turing, 1950). If you realize that looking and feeling like a monkey is an essential part of being human, you may go in for a bit of cognitive profiling. Along those lines, French (2000, p.118) suggests adding to the Turing Test questions such as these:

(7.31) Which word do you find prettier: blutch or
       farfaletta?

(7.32) Does holding a gulp of Coca-Cola in your mouth
       feel more like having pins and needles in your
       foot or having cold water poured on your head?

I doubt that this approach would unerringly expose the robots among us, be-

Monty Python's illustration of CULTURAL OBSTACLES to communication —

stemming from the class gap:
(Lady Mountback, a lady of society, sits in a stylish drawing room knitting quietly. Loud knocking is heard at the door.)
Lady M: Come in.
(In comes Reg, a tall man dressed in working clothes and clutching a cap.)
Reg: Trouble at th' mill.
Lady Mountback: Oh no!
Reg: One o'
Lady M: – what sort of trouble?
Reg: One on't cross beams gone owt askew on treddle.
Lady M: Pardon?
Reg: One on't cross beams gone owt askew on treddle.
Lady M: I don't understand what you're saying.
Reg (slightly irritatedly and with exaggeratedly clear accent): One of the cross beams has gone out askew on the treddle.
Lady M: Well what on earth does that mean?
Reg: I don't know – Mr. Wentworth just told me to come in here and say that there was trouble at the mill, that's all – I didn't expect a kind of Spanish Inquisition.
[Continued on p. 332]

cause we have no way of guessing how much the extra contextual knowledge available to an online computer is worth in terms of the bodily experience it may be missing. In response to 7.31, corpus statistics would readily discover that `farfaletta` is phonotactically close to more positive-valence real English words than `blutch`. Even for 7.32, with its focus on body parts (mouth, foot, head), contextual inference based on extensive corpus search can probably point to the right choice (which I won't reveal here; if you are unsure what it is, reading Philip K. Dick's *Do Androids Dream of Electric Sheep?* or watching the director's cut of *Blade Runner* may or may not help).

7.3.3   Representational context

Discourse context makes language learnable and keeps its ambiguity in check. World context gives us something to talk about and makes possible neat tricks such as metaphor. As the repository of all our knowledge, the REPRESENTATIONAL CONTEXT of an utterance — the lexicon-grammar and the network of concepts — is the confluence of all the factors that determine how it will be processed.

As we saw in earlier chapters, an essential characteristic of the representations maintained by the brain is their mutability. Perceptual experience drives conceptual development in all cognitive subsystems. In language, this process is doubly prominent, because both the linguistic machinery connecting to the conceptual network and the concepts themselves change over the person's lifetime. Moreover, the language that resides in a society changes too, and so does the society's collective thinking. Hearing Homer call Eos, the goddess of dawn, "rosy-fingered" and the sea "wine-dark" must have moved the audiences in his time; if it still does today, it is probably for different reasons, of which novelty of the metaphor may not be the chief one.

The notion that historical context determines language and thought of individuals and societies is starkly illuminated by Borges in *Pierre Menard, the author of Don Quixote* (1962). Quite a few of his other short stories are presented as reviews of nonexistent books. In this case, the question of the book's existence is actually ill-defined: although the author, Pierre Menard, is certainly fictitious, the book — *Don Quixote*, published by Miguel de Cervantes in 1615 — is real. In the story, Menard attempts to compose *Don Quixote* from scratch, following decades of intense study of Cervantes's world. Will he succeed? That depends on how you define success in this fantastic undertaking:

Suppose someone said: every familiar word, in a book for example, actually carries an atmosphere with it in our minds, a 'corona' of lightly indicated uses. — Just as if each figure in a painting were surrounded by delicate shadowy drawings of scenes, as it were in another dimension, and in them we saw the figures in different CONTEXTS.

— Wittgenstein (1958, VI, p.181)

It is a revelation to compare Menard's Don Quixote with Cervantes's. The latter, for example, wrote (part one, chapter nine):

> ... truth, whose mother is history, rival of time, depository of deeds, witness of the past, exemplar and adviser to the present, and the future's counsellor.

Written in the seventeenth century, written by the 'lay genius' Cervantes, this enumeration is a mere rhetorical praise of history. Menard, on the other hand, writes:

> ... truth, whose mother is history, rival of time, depository of deeds, witness of the past, exemplar and adviser to the present, and the future's counsellor.

History, the mother of truth: the idea is astounding. Menard, a contemporary of William James, does not define history as an inquiry into reality but as its origin. Historical truth, for him, is not what has happened; it is what we judge to have happened. ... The contrast in style is also vivid. The archaic style of Menard — quite foreign, after all — suffers from a certain affectation. Not so that of his forerunner, who handles with ease the current Spanish of his time.

The key role of individual experiential history in shaping the mind is familiar to us from the chapter on perception (cf. p. 142). What we have learned so far about language strengthens this idea and extends it to include *collective* experiential and conceptual history — the kind of diachronic context for which language is the main, if not the only, vehicle at the disposal of our species.

7.4 Language as a (neuro)biological phenomenon

Of all the faculties of the brain/mind, language is unique in that it exists in only one species on this planet. Perhaps because of that, the notion that **there is a continuity on all levels between language and the rest of cognition** — that it has evolved like any other biological trait, operates on the same computational principles, and is implemented by the same brain mechanisms as other cognitive functions — has for decades been actively resisted by the majority of linguists.

The main argument invoked by those linguists who believe language to be fundamentally different from all other brain functions as well as essentially innate is related to the one used by the defenders of the obscurantist doctrine concerning the origin of species known as "Intelligent Design" or ID. In both cases, a piece of medieval scholastic theology, the ARGUMENT FROM DESIGN, is rehashed into an *argument from irreducible complexity*. While the crusaders of ID claim that living organisms are too complex to have evolved, the linguistic nativists take the same stance with respect to language, denying that it can be learned from experience.[26]

7.4.1 Cinderella wears Teva

The linguists who embrace the argument from complexity do so because of what strikes them as a glaring contrast between, on the one hand, the supposed paucity in language of cues that can allow a child to learn grammar from experience, and, on the other hand, a particularly far-reaching characterization of the faculty of language that is advanced by the recent versions of the TRANSFORMATIONAL GENERATIVE GRAMMAR (TGG) theory:[27]

> ...We can ask how good is the design. How close does language come to what some super-engineer would construct, given the conditions that the language faculty must satisfy? How "perfect" is language, to put it picturesquely? ... The answer is: "surprisingly perfect"...

> — Chomsky (2004b, p.385)

It would be a surprise indeed if a biological system such as language proved to be a perfect instance of engineering, let alone "super-engineering" — nothing else in biology is perfect in *that* sense. The TGG enterprise amounts to a doomed attempt to shoehorn an inherently sloppy biological system (the product of the grand-scale exercise in blind tinkering that is evolution) into the ultimate unforgiving mathematical framework: *formal rewriting systems* (Hofstadter, 1979, pp.33-36,559), of which the grammar of Figure 7.4 on page 246 is a simple example.[28]

To my mind, this situation resembles the story of Cinderella: the girl who vanishes on the stroke of midnight is thought to have left behind a perfect little

---

The ARGUMENT FROM DESIGN is the fifth of the five proofs of the existence of God offered by Thomas Aquinas (1225-1274) in his *Summa Theologiae*: "We see that things which lack knowledge, such as natural bodies, act for an end, and this is evident from their acting always, or nearly always, in the same way, so as to obtain the best result. Hence it is plain that they achieve their end, not fortuitously, but designedly. Now whatever lacks knowledge cannot move towards an end, unless it be directed by some being endowed with knowledge and intelligence; as the arrow is directed by the archer. Therefore, some intelligent being exists by whom all natural things are directed to their end; and this being we call God."

What does "perfect" mean in biology? It means getting a job done.

— Llinás (2001, p.108)

glass slipper. In a departure from the standard scenario, however, the glass slipper proves to be a *fata morgana*, and the Prince's public promise to wed its owner provokes merely an unending procession of manifestly imperfect pretenders.

Indeed, the claim that language is a perfectly designed formal system does not withstand empirical scrutiny, in ways that are too numerous to be listed here (Culicover, 1999; Fillmore, 1985; Jackendoff, 1995; Lakoff, 1970; Langacker, 1987; Lieberman, 2005; Newmeyer, 1996; Postal, 2004; Quine, 1972; Sapir, 1921). This disposes of the second premise of the nativist argument. Its first premise, which rests on the subjective impression of the poverty of linguistic data, does not fare any better. It has been shown wrong by empirical examination of language corpora (Pullum and Scholz, 2002), as well as by the recent significant progress in grammar induction by computer (Clark, 2001; Solan et al., 2005) that makes use of the properties of language I surveyed in section 7.2.

These developments suggest that the fairy tale of linguistics is actually headed for a happy end. While shopping at the farmers' market, the Prince bumps into Cinderella (who, it turns out, wears Teva sandals, just as he does), and they live happily thereafter.[29]

7.4.2 The neurocomputational basis of language

Language, as any other cognitive faculty, should be studied on each of the three levels of understanding discussed in Chapter 4 (recall Table 4.2 on page 76). In fact, much of the present chapter has been devoted to what clearly corresponds to Marr's computational and algorithmic levels: understanding the nature of the problem, and identifying viable procedures for solving it. More specifically, we learned about (i) the hierarchical structure of utterances, whose constituent constructions populate the lexicon-grammar, (ii) the manifestations of this structure in corpus regularities, which Harris (1991) referred to as departures from equiprobability, and (iii) certain computational methods for distilling structure from such data. We also saw a small sample of the behavioral evidence supporting the emerging big picture, which can be succinctly referred to as Construction Grammar.

The ground we have covered so far allows us to advance to the next level that needs to be considered: the level of implementation, where questions about the neural basis of language reside. As before, this level cannot be separated cleanly from those above it: the algorithms that support language

TRANSFORMATIONAL GENERATIVE GRAMMAR (TGG) is a linguistic framework, rooted in the work of Noam Chomsky, which has dominated formal linguistics in the second half of the 20th century. Although the theory underwent major changes over its successive incarnations (driven by books published by Chomsky in 1957, 1965, 1981, and 1995), all its versions assume that sentences possess several kinds of abstract "syntactic" structure, and that these structures are manipulated during sentence generation by purely syntactic transformations (such as the "movement" of an auxiliary verb presumably used to turn an assertion into a question in English). The failure of all attempts to date to produce independent evidence for the existence of abstract transformational syntax suggests that "the formal linguists' practice of finding abstract patterns by formally transforming different constructions into one another is just a meta-linguistic game with no psychological significance" (Tomasello, 2003, p.303); hence the current ascendance of Construction Grammar.

acquisition (about which I wrote in section 7.2) and language use (to which I shall return in section 7.5) are all constrained by the properties of the neural substrate in which they are implemented. More than that, in language the constraints imposed by the brain level reach all the way up to the top of Marr's hierarchy to affect the abstract-computational level: as I noted at the very beginning of this chapter, instances of the language Game need brains to inhabit, and so the Game proliferates insofar as it capitalizes on the strengths of its hosts and is not hampered by their weaknesses.[30]

Much less is known about the detailed neural basis of language than about the neurobiology of other cognitive subsystems, mainly because of the impossibility of conducting invasive experiments on human subjects. Nevertheless, researchers long ago identified the key commonality between language and other brain functions that require that a proper *serial order* of behavior be enforced: from locomotion, reaching, and manipulation to thinking and reasoning (Lashley, 1951).

The principle of hierarchical abstraction (recall section 2.4 on page 30) leads one to expect that in each of these cases the behavior would be planned as a possibly recursively structured composition of representational elements, while the large capacity of memory and its agility (Chapter 6) suggest that many of the resulting structures would be stored for later reuse. Indeed, this is precisely what we find in language, where the lexicon-grammar houses a variety of constructions that differ in size and complexity and which may combined according to need into larger structures, subject to certain structural constraints.

On the algorithmic level, every stage in the process of learning complex constructions (what I described earlier as "going recursive") has parallels elsewhere in cognition. In particular, the identification of useful structures out of perceptual regularities ("departures from equiprobability") and their subsequent unitization is common in vision, and the statistical-structural algorithms that have been advanced as models of the corresponding functions involve conceptually related operations (Edelman, 2007).[31]

In addition to the abstract-computational and algorithmic levels, commonalities between language and the rest of cognition exist also on the level of brain implementation. Until recently, the knowledge of the neural basis of language clustered around the importance of BROCA'S area in the inferior frontal cortex (IFC) in that processing.[32] Studies made possible by improvements in noninvasive electrophysiological methods such as electroencephalography (EEG) and by the advent of fMRI imaging led to the realiza-

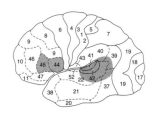

A diagram of the left lateral view of the brain, with the cortical areas marked according to Brodmann (Kaan and Swaab, 2002). For more than a century, "syntax" was thought to reside in BROCA'S area (corresponding to Brodmann's areas 44 and 45, just above the Sylvian fissure that separates the frontal and the temporal lobes), simply because lesions there cause agrammatical speech and difficulties in the comprehension of complex sentences. It is now recognized that Broca's area is not syntax-specific, and furthermore that areas other than Broca's are involved in aspects of language processing traditionally associated with it (Kaan and Swaab, 2002; Müller and Basho, 2004).

tion that Broca's area, which used to be singled out as dedicated to language, plays an important (often crucial) role also in auditory perception, vision, and motor control. In particular, the new results suggest that the importance of the IFC for language — specifically, for lexical learning, which is the driving force behind language acquisition (Bates and Goodman, 1999) — may stem from its role as the target of converging auditory, visual, and motor processing streams, as well as a locus of working memory (Müller and Basho, 2004).

Recent studies have also revealed the wide reach of the processing of language structure in the brain. Far from being confined exclusively to Broca's area, the representation of lexical items in the brain is typically distributed over several distinct functional and anatomical regions. For example, hearing a word that designates a tool, such as fork, consistently activates both the so-called perisylvian areas traditionally seen as language-specific (in the illustration on p. 288 these are Brodmann areas 41/42 and 44/45 that flank the Sylvian fissure) and the motor/premotor cortex (areas 4 and 6). In comparison, animal names such as whale activate the visual cortex (areas 17-19) in addition to the perisylvian region (Pulvermüller, 2002, Fig.3).

A follow-up study focusing on action-related words took advantage of the known topographic arrangement of the motor cortex (the MOTOR HOMUNCULUS), in which the representations of various muscle groups are laid out in an orderly fashion, with the feet mapped to the upper part of area 4, the hands to the middle, and the mouth to its lower part. The outcome of this study was a clear indication of the role of *embodiment* in language processing: the words kick, pick, and lick activated the top, middle, and bottom parts of the motor cortex — in addition, as usual, to the "classical" perisylvian language areas (Pulvermüller, 2002, Fig.4).

Detailed parallels between language and vision

The imaging findings of which we just saw a small sample led to significant progress in the understanding of the brain basis of language, relative to the classical picture that relied mostly on patterns of deficits in speech production and comprehension following perisylvian lesions. Nevertheless, they reveal virtually nothing about the details of the neural circuits involved in language processing, or about the algorithms that these circuits implement. The gaps between the computational, algorithmic, and neural levels of explanation can

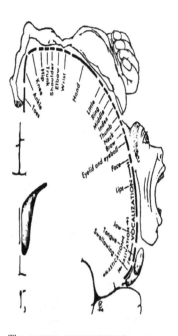

The MOTOR HOMUNCULUS – a map showing the layout of the representation of body parts in the primary motor cortex (area 4 in the illustration on p. 288). This schematic figure shows a slice through the brain that runs perpendicular to the cortical surface; on the left is one of the ventricles, and on the right the cortex. Note that the orofacial muscles that control speech articulation (lower right) are mapped right next to Broca's area. Compare this map to the somatosensory homunculus of Figure 3.5 on page 48.

only be bridged if explicit and detailed hypotheses are advanced that span the levels.

One such hypothesis, put forward by Hurford (2003), proposes that: "...basic elements in the structure of modern natural languages are derived (phylogenetically and ontogenetically) from primitive (prelinguistic) mental representations" (p.261). On the computational level, Hurford's proposal hinges on the notions of *variable* and *predication*. In our nomenclature, a variable is a representation — a symbol that refers to something other than itself; predication is the act of attributing some feature or property to an object referred to by a variable.

The simplest example of predication is an assertion that involves DEIXIS or pointing:

		это	человек
(7.33)		eto	chelovek
		DEICTIC	man
		{this is a}	man

In this example, the object that is singled out through pointing is attributed the feature (predicate) of being a man. Descending to the implementational level, Hurford (2003) notes that all the mechanisms needed to support the deictic construction have been identified and extensively studied in vision. It appears to me that the parallels between language and other kinds of neural computation reach considerably farther than that, as the following four examples suggest.

1. Receptive fields. A neuron whose RF is spatially restricted to region Y of the visual field and is selective for shape X implements the deictic predicate "this [pointing at Y] is an X." As you may recall from Chapter 5, such "what+where" neurons have been reported (Op de Beeck and Vogels, 2000) and their computational capabilities analyzed (Edelman and Intrator, 2003). The latter include the possibility of unitization and subsequent hierarchical composition of units, as illustrated in Figure 5.30 on page 146; this may be compared to the recursive growth of linguistic structures learned by the ADIOS algorithm depicted in Figure 7.9 on page 259.

2. Trainable templates. A highly pliable ("plastic") receptive field that gets imprinted with a stimulus via fast learning (e.g., of the Hebbian variety; cf. p. 41) can subsequently serve as a template for seeking out its repetitions. If enough of these are encountered, the template survives; otherwise it gets

In sign languages, DEIXIS is often used to code anaphoric pronouns: when a noun is first mentioned, a place in the extra-personal space is assigned to it; subsequently, it may be referred to by pointing to the designated place while signing "it" or "he" (note that this corresponds precisely to the function that Hurford (2003) calls predication over spatially anchored objects). A vivid example of this practice appears in Pedro Almodóvar's film *Tacones lejanos* ("High heels"; *warning* – a spoiler follows), in which Rebeca (played by Victoria Abril) confesses to murder on live TV, while another woman interprets the show into sign language. When Rebeca says, "I killed him," the interpreter first points to herself, then does a double-take and points emphatically to Rebeca, using both hands.

recycled, the neuron implementing it returning into the resource pool. Such a mechanism can support alignment-based detection of language regularities, as depicted in Figure 7.9 and Figure 7.8 on page 253.

3. Attention. The visual system is capable of focusing attention in space, as when you track an event that is unfolding in your peripheral vision from the corner of your eye, without shifting your gaze, or in depth, as when you contemplate a ladybug crawling on your windowpane while ignoring the landscape behind it. Hurford (2003) points out that visual attention of the spatial kind can greatly facilitate the acquisition of word meanings, by narrowing down the range of possible referents of the object that is being mentioned. I would like to add that the latter kind of attention — foregrounding an event while pushing its complement into the background (Nakayama, He, and Shimojo, 1995) — is precisely the operation that according to Harris and Bates (2002) makes it possible for `he` and `Billy` to co-refer in 7.34:

(7.34) `When he`$_i$` was threatening to leave, Billy`$_i$
       `noticed that the computer had died.`

On this account, the subordinate clause that opens 7.34 is backgrounded (much like the landscape behind the windowpane is) by the opening word, `when`, until the main clause is reached and the reference of `he` is established (cf. examples 7.25 and 7.26 on page 268).

4. Attention sharing. Hurford (2003) remarks that attention by two people to the same object is a good starting point for communicating meaning; the triadic relation of signification (p. 15) thus becomes a four-way link-up, in which two minds coordinate their internal representations of the shared external entity. Certain shared-attention scenarios appear to be sufficiently important for primate brains to merit direct representation on the level of single cells. These are the *mirror neurons*, which are familiar to us from Chapter 6 (recall Figure 6.21 on page 211), and which, according to Rizzolatti and Arbib (1998), may have enabled the evolutionary emergence of language from prelinguistic motor control.[33]

Serial order

The functional and implementational parallels between language and vision that I have sketched just now focused on the perceptual aspect of language: the acquisition of various units (possibly hierarchically structured) and their

An anecdote that strengthens the notion that SERIAL ORDER in various kinds of behavior may be supported not only by similar but by partially overlapping neural systems is told about the Warden of New College, Oxford, the Reverend William Spooner, who was prone to transpose phonetically matched parts of utterances (one of his most famous slips, which came to be called spoonerisms, was saying "queer old dean" instead of "dear old queen" in a speech on the occasion of Queen Victoria's birthday). Spooner, it appears, was also susceptible to transposition mistakes in the sequencing of actions on a conceptual/motor level. Once, after accidentally overturning the salt shaker at a dinner, he proceeded to pour a decanter of claret onto the spilt salt, turning on its head the usual remedy for a red wine stain, which is to sprinkle some salt on top of it.

subsequent recognition at need. What about the serial aspect — learning to string the units in the proper order during production, and during reception recognizing the order and appreciating its significance? It appears that SE-RIAL ORDER too can be readily implemented in a neural substrate, and that circuits embodying certain key operations on sequences can be constructed from building blocks that you'll find very familiar from Chapter 4: delay lines and coincidence detectors.

Any viable neuronal solution to the fundamental problem of serial order in behavior (Lashley, 1951) must be compatible with the basic architectural constraint that applies to brains: the representations involved (in this case, the representations of the successive states of the system) must be distributed. A representation scheme for sequences of linguistic units that satisfies this constraint has been proposed by Pulvermüller (2002). The proposed circuit implements a SYNFIRE chain (Abeles, 1991), in which cliques of neurons are wired up so as to pass the activation on from one another, in a selective fashion; Figure 7.16 shows how multiple synfire chains can share subsets of neurons without destroying the coherence and the direction of the waves of activation they support.

Back on page 237, I suggested that learning language amounts to build-ing up an armamentarium of symbols, leaving open the possibility that some

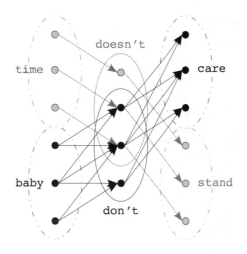

Figure 7.16 — Two SYNFIRE CHAINS, each defined over dis-tributed and partially overlapping representations, can intersect without interfering with each other. In this illustration (adapted from Pulvermüller, 2002), the chain corresponding to the sequence baby don't care intersects one that codes time doesn't stand at the doesn't / don't cliques, which have two units in common. The direction in which the wave of activity would proceed at this junction depends on the direction from which it ar-rived. This kind of functionality could implement the abstract data structure (graph) used by the ADIOS algorithm for grammar acqui-sition (Solan, Horn, Ruppin, and Edelman, 2005; see Figure 7.9 on page 259). Neurophysiological evidence for the existence of synfire chains in the brain has been described by Ikegaya et al. (2004).

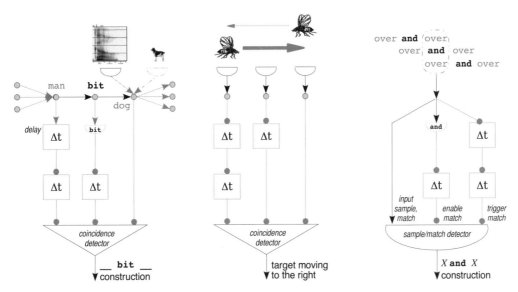

Figure 7.17 — A glimpse at the NEURAL COMPUTATION behind language. *Left:* a circuit that implements the detection of a two-slot construction (__ bit __). The critical building blocks are the same that are involved in sound localization in the owl: *delay* elements (Δt) and a coincidence detector (cf. Figure 4.4 on page 73); the detector for the word bit is a simple template-like receptive field. The output will fire for every sequence in which the anchor word for this construction (bit) is preceded and followed by unspecified words (in reality, these would be constrained to belong to certain distributional equivalence classes). *Middle:* a very similar circuit – the so-called Reichardt motion detector, which is named after its discoverer in the fly brain, and is found in every insect and vertebrate visual system. An object moving to the right at a speed that matches the time delays built into the circuit will cause all three inputs to the coincidence detector to fire simultaneously, triggering the output. *Right:* a much more sophisticated function – detecting the occurrence of the (X and X) construction, where X is a variable (psycholinguistic evidence suggests that the existence and position of the lexical element – in this example, the word and – provides a critical cue in learning patterns with variables; see Gerken, 2006). This construction covers phrases such as again and again, higher and higher, etc.; crucially, the two instances of X must be bound to the same value. An implementation of such functions using shift-and-match operations has been described by Dominey (2005). The centerpiece of the present circuit is a *sample/match* unit, which samples its input (the leftmost line) and tries to match it to another input that comes later. The match attempt is enabled by the and detector (middle line), and is triggered by an appropriately delayed signal (rightmost line). If such a circuit is fed entire-phrase constructions instead of single words, it can support the detection of complex structure such as coordination or reduplication. The circuits shown here implement various sequence *recognition* functions; corresponding sequence *generation* functions can be implemented using precisely the same principles, with a control unit driving a series of execution units via appropriately staggered time delays. Neurons with characteristics that would make them suitable for serving as control units (notably, a sustained response that is selective to a specific action sequence) have been identified in the monkey dorsal premotor cortex (PMd) by Ohbayashi et al. (2003). The human homologue of PMd, which borders on Broca's area, is known to support motor planning and imagery as well as working memory tasks.

symbols stand for composite structures, which are made up of several simpler ones. Between then and now, we saw how these structures — the constructions that comprise the lexicon-grammar — can be learned via experience from a functional standpoint. Now, we are ready for a hypothesis that would specify their detailed implementation in terms of neural circuits. Two examples of such circuits, along with an analogous one from vision, are depicted in Figure 7.17.

The first example (on the left) shows how a partially lexicalized construction (__ bit __) can be implemented using "standard" receptive fields to recognize the constituent units, and delay lines coupled with a coincidence detector to recognize the entire composite structure. The middle panel in Figure 7.17 depicts a visual circuit that operates on the same principles — the Reichardt motion detector, first found in the visual system of the fly. Finally, the other example of a neural circuit for a language function (Figure 7.17, right) shows that the much more difficult problem — enforcing identity over the units occupying the two slots of such a construction — can be solved by similar means.

7.5   Using language

The phenomenon of language, which seemed so innocuously simple to thinkers since the classical times, and which for a time was made to appear complex to the point of being unlearnable, is now revealed to us for what it is: a manifestation of the same set of computational tricks that the brain puts to work elsewhere in cognition. To buttress this emerging conclusion, I shall use this last section in the chapter on language to show how the functionality of language, from the mundane (comprehension and production) to the exceptional (poetry) can be made sense of in familiar computational terms.

7.5.1   Comprehension

In keeping with the decision to adopt the learner's point of view made early in this chapter, we ought to begin the survey of the functionality of language by considering the process of comprehension (the development of which in children leads that of production). What does it consist of, and where does it lead? In the picture that is painted by Wittgenstein's stunningly prescient imagery, an incoming language stimulus triggers a romp through the lexicongrammar by evoking a "multitude of familiar paths" which in turn activate

What do you see in this image? (The solution to this visual riddle appears in Figure 7.19 on page 297.) Images of objects or object fragments taken out of CONTEXT are often difficult, if not impossible, to interpret. In this section, we'll see that context and experience are also important in language.

Phrased *like this*, emphasized like this, heard in this way, this sentence is the first of a series in which a transition is made to *these* sentences, pictures, actions. ((A multitude of familiar paths lead off from these words in every direction.))

— Wittgenstein (1958, 534)

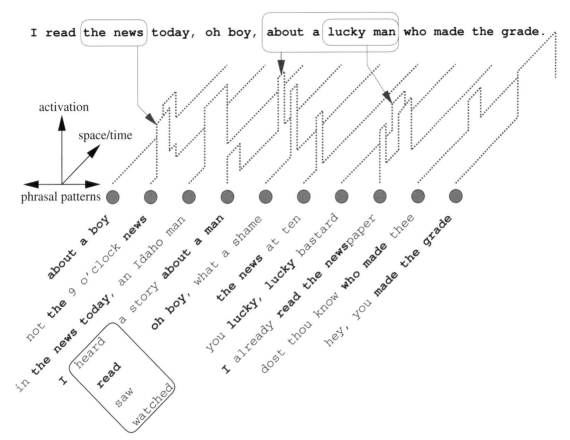

Figure 7.18 — Putting together what we have learned up to this point about the distributed nature of neural representations, about their graded activation in the course of brain activity, and about the manner in which linguistic knowledge is coded in the lexicon-grammar by constructions suggests that sentence comprehension may proceed as depicted in this schematic illustration. Each dotted line shows the activation of a particular construction by the stimulus sentence (I saw the news today...) as it unfolds in time. For simplicity, the constructions are shown here as mere memorized phrases; in reality, they are potentially complex, hierarchical structures that are heavily interconnected with conceptual networks (section 6.5) and with episodic memory (section 9.5), and may include elements of embodied simulation (section 6.7). The resulting computational model of sentence comprehension — a kind of CHORUS OF CONSTRUCTIONS — will be complete if it can be shown that any reasonable subsequent query about the stimulus sentence (such as "what did I read?" or "did the man succeed?") can be answered using the time courses of the responses of the various construction detectors, along with the conceptual knowledge linked to the network of constructions. Note that such a maximalist claim about this model (which is yet to be substantiated) draws a direct parallel between what it means to understand a sentence and what it means to perceive a scene (cf. Figures 5.29 on page 145 and 5.30 on page 146, and the margin note on p. 141).

In a consolation letter written to a friend in 1812, Johann Wolfgang von Goethe likens life to the predicament of a sailor who barely survives a storm only to be tempted the next day by beautiful weather, concluding "the sea already is hungry for figs again." Blumenberg (1997, pp.56-57), from whom I borrowed the description of this incident, asks, "Where does this extraordinary conclusion come from?" and proceeds to recount an ancient Greek story "about a man from Sicily who had undergone a shipwreck while carrying a cargo of figs, and another time sits on the beach and sees before him the sea lying gentle and calm, as if wanting to entice him to take another voyage. Thereupon he expresses his unseduceability in these words: οἶδ δ θέλεις, σῦχα θέλεις ('I know what you want: you want figs!')" Understanding Goethe's metaphor requires KNOWLEDGE OF LANGUAGE on a variety of levels. Can you identify all of them? Figure 7.19 on the facing page offers some hints.

A fruit of *Ficus carica*, the common FIG.

various perceptual, conceptual, and latent motor representations in the cognitive system at large.

In computational terms, the utterance unfolding in time is *projected* dynamically onto the multidimensional record of prior experience. Its meaning emerges as a trajectory in a meaning space spanned in part by activities of linguistic construction-tuned units (Figure 7.18) and in part by the subsequent activation of additional cognitive structures. The latter, "non-linguistic" component is integral to comprehension, as evidenced by behavioral (Zwaan, 2001) and neural (Pulvermüller, 2002) data. Language comprehension can thus be usefully described as guided experience (Barsalou, 1999; Zwaan, 2001; cf. the view of perception as controlled hallucination, p. 86).

Insofar as it *equates* the end product of language comprehension with certain representational processes, the preceding statement amounts to an IDENTITY THEORY of sorts, in the same sense that Figure 4.2 on page 68 demonstrated identity between the activity of certain neurons in area MT of a monkey's brain and that monkey's perception of visual motion (see also note 4 on page 80). In fields of enquiry where the very ontology is being disputed (witness titles such as *The meaning of 'meaning'*; Putnam, 1975), the appeal of identity theories stems from their ability to cut through the Gordian knot of interminable definitional debates.

For an identity theory to be taken seriously, its proponents must demonstrate that the entity with which the explanandum is equated is indeed up to the task. In the case of language comprehension, it is the meaning of 'meaning' that is in dire need of demystification. Consequently, the challenge is to show that any problem whose statement invokes, directly or indirectly, the meaning of a phrase can be resolved by computing over the multidimensional, dynamic representations it evokes.

A general computational solution for this challenge takes the form of a procedure that accepts the relevant input — the utterance in question and its context, as well as any background knowledge that the listener may be assumed to possess — and generates answers to various queries (such as "in the event described by sentence X, who did what to whom?" or "does X imply Y?"). It is worth noting that deductive logic is not up to this task; as in perception, the computational machinery for addressing comprehension-related queries must rely on probabilistic decision-making.

More specifically, the goal is to estimate the relative likelihood of various possible answers, conditional on the data and on the context (Pereira, 2000). Computational studies of structural ambiguity resolution (cf. exam-

Figure 7.19 — Using KNOWLEDGE to make sense of stimuli in vision and in language. IN VISION, fragments of natural scenes seen in isolation or in an unnatural configuration are likely to be misinterpreted or to appear meaningless (Bar, 2004; Biederman et al., 1982). The mysterious image fragment that first appeared on p. 294 is seen in this photograph to correspond to the beak of a wading godwit: all the features fall into place, guided by the context (for a Bayesian theory of context effects, see Yuille and Kersten, 2006). IN LANGUAGE, knowledge and context play a similarly important role. For instance, SPEECH cannot be readily segmented into words unless the language is familiar. In the anecdote about Goethe's letter quoted in the margin on the facing page, the level of speech is absent, but can be simulated (poorly) for someone who does not know German by considering the original text with the spaces omitted: `hatdasmeerschonwiederappetitzufeigen`; how many words are there? On the level of LEXICAL SEMANTICS, or word meanings, some of the requisite knowledge has the form of word-to-object associations, at least for nouns (which in written German are capitalized — the quote from Goethe actually reads `hat das Meer schon wieder Appetit zu Feigen`). On the level of CONTEXT, the epistemic requirements for full comprehension rapidly become formidable. Someone who is unfamiliar with the ancient story to which Goethe alludes, and which he probably encountered in the *Adages*, published by Erasmus of Rotterdam in 1500, would find his passage opaque. Even with that story told in full, Goethe's use of the shipwreck as a metaphor for the human condition would fail to impress readers who, having lived all their lives on Mars never experienced a storm at sea; those who have been genetically engineered to live *in* the sea; and those who are merely too young to have experienced anything much.

ple 7.11) suggest that straightforward statistical regression analysis that correlates structure with context can suffice for disambiguation (Roland, Elman, and Ferreira, 2005), while psycholinguistic experiments yield evidence of the subjects' reliance on contextual cues in ambiguity resolution (Grodner, Gibson, and Watson, 2005).

The scope of contextual knowledge required for language comprehension is enormous (cf. Figure 7.19). On the bottommost level of processing, even just to perceive the continuous stream of speech as a discrete sequence of words, a listener must be familiar with the language in which the conversation is conducted. Under less than ideal sound conditions (think of a noisy city street or a party setting), the listener must already have a pretty good idea of what the next word is going to be before hearing it. This knowledge is provided by the probabilistic language model, meticulously constructed and constantly updated by the brain over the course of a lifetime (see Figure 7.20).

On the topmost level, words and more complex constructions freshly segmented from the stream of speech will remain meaningless symbols unless they have something to connect to: conceptual knowledge. The phrase "superluminal travel" overheard in a conversation between two physicists at a party will remain Greek to me even after I muster my morphological analysis skills and figure out that "superluminal" must mean something like "faster

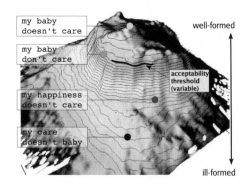

Figure 7.20 — The SENTENCE SPACE induced by a probabilistic language model is depicted here schematically. Think of this mountain as partially submerged, with the "sea level" corresponding to the sentence acceptability threshold (indicated). The sentence at the top is well-formed by any standard of English. The one below it is acceptable in some contexts (such as John Lennon's lyrics) but not in others (the linguistically challenged 43rd president of the United States would be pounced upon by the media, were he to utter a sentence that so blatantly neglects English grammar). The next lower phrase is semantically deviant, yet not ill-formed: with some strain, it can be understood metaphorically. Finally, the bottommost phrase is barely acceptable, even as a wild metaphor. By modifying the probabilities in the language model, repeated exposure to these sentences can eventually obliterate the differences in acceptability.

than light"; to really understand what the physicists were talking about, I need to know what Einstein's Special Relativity Theory has to say about the speed of light.[34]

This last example illuminates yet another parallel between language and vision: just as in vision one can inquire about the veridicality of perception (cf. section 5.5 on page 121), so in language it makes sense to ask how true the listener's comprehension is to the speaker's intention. Intuitively, effective communication can be assured by knowledge shared between the interlocutors. Computationally, this translates into parallel constraints on their linguistic and conceptual spaces: higher similarity between the layouts of these spaces increases the fidelity of the communication.[35]

Coordination between the parties to a conversation is important no matter whether the verbal exchange is used with an intention to communicate information, to socialize, or for any other purpose. In development, coordination may help consolidate the structures being acquired by the learner within the course of a conversation. Indeed, a study of several sets of child-caregiver exchanges taken from the CHILDES corpus revealed recurring lexical and structural patterns on the two sides of each dialogue; the degree of recurrence was significantly higher within — compared to across — conversations, and decreased with the child's age (Dale and Spivey, 2006). In adult speech, coordination, which manifests itself in the priming of constructions (Melinger and Dobel, 2005), probably fulfills a range of communicative and social needs (Pickering and Branigan, 1999; Pickering and Garrod, 2004).

7.5.2 Production

If language comprehension is controlled hallucination, language production is a kind of MIND CONTROL that operates through induced hallucinations. It is important to realize that this figurative description applies across the entire spectrum of possible illocutionary modes: even the most innocuous utterance that I hear affects my brain by causing a redistribution of activity across the relevant functional units — constructions and conceptual networks. Any utterance that I might subsequently produce would necessarily be affected by this priming (in the descending order of recency), even as it is assembled from the stored constructions.

To visualize this assembly process, we can turn again to the analogy that I introduced on p. 273 between the lexicon-grammar and a subway transit system. If the production of an utterance is likened to taking a particular route

DIALOGIC EMBODIMENT. One of the experiments conducted by Richardson and Dale (2005) showed that the more closely a listener's eye movements were coupled with a speaker's, the better the listener performed on a comprehension test.

Language production and MIND CONTROL. The dimension of control is most clearly at work in explicit commands ("Now the Lord said unto Abram: 'Get thee out of thy country, …'"; Genesis 12:1), but it is also present in suggestions ("Consider the lilies of the field, how they grow; they toil not, neither do they spin"; Matthew 6:28),[36] and, surreptitiously, in any other locution that is heard and is understood by the hearer — even in such minimalist descriptions of reality as this famous haiku by Matsuo Bashō, as translated by Alan Watts:

> The old pond,
> A frog jumps in:
> Plop!

which just made you think of a frog.

through the "stations" — words and composite constructions — then priming or preactivation by an external stimulus corresponds to an increased likelihood of passing through certain stations in a certain order. The other, internal, source of preactivation is the conceptual input into the lexicon-grammar, which carries the prelinguistic message that is about to be put into words.

The sequence of elements that forms a complete "digital" code of the would-be utterance (in the sense in which language becomes digital once the intricacies of the speech signal are abstracted away; cf. section 7.2.1) needs to be translated into a sequence of motor commands that would cause it to be spoken. Like the lexical elements themselves, the individual motor commands can be pre-stored and invoked in the proper sequence by a staggered timing mechanism of the same kind that I outlined in Figure 7.17 on page 293. For that to be feasible, sufficiently complex postures — of the mouth and the vocal tract in the case of speech, and of the face, hands, and arms in the case of sign language — should be represented in the motor control system in a localized fashion. Evidence for just such a representation of arm/hand posture in the monkey has been obtained by Graziano et al. (2002): electrical stimulation of motor cortex caused monkeys to make coordinated, complex movements, whose representations were arranged across the cortex in a MAP of spatial locations to which the hand moved (cf. Figure 3.3 on page 46).

Returning to the abstract computational level, the process of assembling an utterance from the basic building blocks of language (the constructions) can thus be seen as a complex, dynamic interplay of statistical and structural effects (cf. Bien, Levelt, and Baayen, 2005). As in other cognitive domains, in language production these effects are so closely intertwined as to be inseparable: the statistics maintained by the language model is defined over a set of structured elements — the constructions; these, in turn, are learned by analyzing the statistics of successive stimuli.

The serial order imposed on the linguistic output by the language model is very difficult to ignore (to convince yourself that this is so, try to produce fluently and without a conscious effort a completely random sequence of a dozen words). This does not mean, however, that sentences produced by people in normal discourse are as a rule well-formed (or, I should say, as well-formed as deliberate language of the kind found in written sources; cf. the note on p. 307). More often than not, the dynamically computed optimal path through the lexicon-grammar (whose elements have been preactivated by various internal and external factors) necessitates the speaker to "jump tracks," leaving one construction in mid-traversal to join another one (Ferreira and

A truly marvellous model of language can be constructed from the neural circuits described in this section. This margin is, however, too narrow to contain its description.

Bailey, 2004; cf. Figure 7.21). Such switches, whose overt manifestations are the DISFLUENCIES that are so common in regular speech, often happen when new information needs to be integrated into the utterance under construction (Arnold, Fagnano, and Tanenhaus, 2003).

DISFLUENCIES in language production happen when the generation process "jumps tracks" in midsentence.

7.5.3 Translation

If producing a sentence is like following a route through a subway network from point A to point B through some intermediate stops, then translating it into another language is like going for a bus ride that takes you through a reasonably similar sequence of stops. Any ambition to make it *the same* sequence of stops is probably misguided: "It is not clear even in principle that it makes sense to think of words and syntax as varying from language to language while the content stays fixed; yet precisely this fiction is involved in speaking of synonymy, at least between expressions of radically different languages" (Quine, 1961, p.259). The manifold cluster of reasons that preclude the possibility of translation that is absolutely faithful, or even just literal, is the same that motivates the Construction Grammar approach in linguistic

Figure 7.21 — If a body of language is likened to a subway system, how should we visualize SENTENCE PRODUCTION? Many "routine" sentences, including some that are novel on a combinatorial level, can be generated by taking new combinations of routes through the system. Radically novel sentences, however, can only be produced if the generation process breaks out of the predetermined mold, as it were by splitting and joining tracks on the fly.

theory: languages differ in the way they carve up the space of meanings, and in the structures they employ to convey the meanings they do (Croft, 2001).

Even if a construction found in one language has a very close counterpart in another, there is no guarantee that its usage is licensed by the same contexts there. If a new kid in an American school were to introduce himself to the class by saying (in all seriousness – intonation is important here) "They call me Alex," the ensuing experience would probably haunt him right through the senior prom. The problem is not with this sentence as such (there is a perfectly good English construction that licenses it), but with the context: it befits more a Hollywoodian Wild West saloon than an elementary school. In comparison, in Russia saying literally just that (Меня зовут Саша – *Menya zovut Sasha*, "[They] call me Sasha") is an acceptable way of making yourself known to a classroom full of students (in elementary school, that is; the patterns of linguistic usage clearly depend on the age, as well as on the socioeconomics, of the population in question).

Translation is thus seen to be closely related to simple, monolingual production. An instance of language production aims to cover a preset conceptual ground while optimizing the well-formedness and the contextual appropriateness of the resulting utterance under the language model. Translation does the same, with one difference: the conceptual representation — the meaning — is not generated on the spot but rather is imported wholesale from an utterance in the source language and needs to be adjusted for the target language.

The computational characterization of meaning illustrated in Figure 7.18 on page 295 allows me to state precisely what the required adjustment amounts to: a *mapping* from the "cloud" of constructions activated by the source utterance to a corresponding distributed representation of its emerging translation on the side of the target language.

To better understand the mapping procedure, imagine looking up each source construction (word, phrase, etc.) in a bilingual dictionary and writing down all the corresponding target-language entries in one long list. Note that all the senses of each word should be included, because disambiguation is context-dependent and cannot be done on a word-by-word basis. The list of target-language constructions is then fed into the target-language model, which irons out the ambiguities and generates the translation — the right elements in the right order.[37] Satisfyingly, both stages of this translation procedure emerge as completely mindless — the mapping is spread of activation through associative links, and the language model is spread of activation

---

Given a set of criteria defining the goodness of a TRANSLATION (by taking into account fidelity to the source, well-formedness of the target, and perhaps other factors), the translation process can be optimized, using any of a number of standard computational procedures. Caring only about well-formedness (say) can land the translator in court — at least in a Monty Python sketch:

Clerk: You are Alexander Yahlt?
Yahlt: I am.
Clerk: You are hereby charged that on the 28th day of May 1970, you did wilfully, unlawfully, and with malice aforethought publish an alleged English-Hungarian phrasebook with intent to cause a breach of the peace. How do you plead?
Yahlt: Not guilty.
Clerk: I quote an example. The Hungarian phrase meaning "Can you direct me to the station?" is translated by the English phrase, "Please fondle my bum."
Yahlt: I wish to plead incompetence.

through a graph-like structure — hence appropriate as a computational explanation of the corresponding cognitive process.

7.5.4 The road not often taken

What would happen if a virus would cause everyone's language modeling circuits to become independent from the rest of the brain? If the probabilistic language model in my brain were put exclusively in charge of my language production, all I would ever be able to utter thereafter would be the one most probable sentence under the model. The sentence, of course, would likely be different for each individual, because people's language models are all somewhat different, dependent as they are on the personal history of exposure to language. This would make the world a rather dull place.

Probabilities, however, are there to be bent (this is merely the Empiricist version of the common contention that rules are there to be broken). In any actual episode of language production, the language model is modulated by many extraneous factors (conceptual, contextual, etc.) before it is allowed to generate an utterance. Such modulation necessarily results in a modicum of surprise being imparted to the listener, which is what makes communication possible: no surprise, no information (Itti and Baldi, 2006).

Although it can be expressed by a single number, surprise induced by a passage is an intrinsically multidimensional quantity: it can be lexical (when neologisms abound, as in the *Jabberwocky*), or structural (when patterns of grammatical usage are violated, as in many Dada texts). A text can, however, surprise the reader along a variety of cognitive dimensions without being particularly outlandish lexically or structurally. My favorite example is T. S. Eliot's *The Waste Land*, which has had a profound effect on generations of readers — it moves me every time I reread it, sometimes in unexpected ways. Eliot's genius for distilling, in a few lines, both the universal and the heartbreakingly personal and mundane in human existence turns the poem into a journey through a bewildering, only seemingly familiar, dream-like place where wild allusions lie waiting, poised to pounce on the reader.[38]

All the examples I just mentioned (*Jabberwocky*, Dada, Eliot) are, perhaps not surprisingly, commonly characterized as poetry. There is a merit to the claim that a text may qualify as a poem merely by virtue of instilling in the reader a sense of immediacy, novelty, and surprise, there being little else (besides layout) that distinguishes free verse from prose these days. I believe that this view strikes close to the cognitive-computational truth of the

Whatever is not INEFFABLE has no importance.

— PAUL VALÉRY

matter, without disparaging either poetry or prose, modern or classical. The profound effects of certain texts, especially when enhanced by cross-cultural influences, are most naturally understood in terms of an enrichment of conceptual and formal structure through the addition of extra dimensions to the reader's experience.[39]

The multidimensionality of the cognitive stimulation provided by reading a text is very important to its appreciation — just as it is important in other kinds of perception. If you take a sip from a wine glass and realize that it contains vinegar, you will have been surprised by the intensity of the experience, but probably not by its structure. In contrast, tasting a good vintage affords a sensation that is striking in its multidimensionality: wine is a complex mix of chemical agents, and, luckily, the physiology of the sense of taste allows you to appreciate the complexity.

As with the visual experience (cf. p. 142), having experienced complex wines before may have equipped you with the extra machinery, in the form of units tuned to specific experiences, that ensures that the richness of the current stimulus does not get lost when projected onto your representation space. Likewise, having been exposed to much poetry makes you better equipped to appreciate new stuff, and a certain minimal level of experience (perceptual, conceptual, and linguistic) is needed to have any appreciation at all (think of what *The Waste Land* must sound like to a nine-year old).

Multidimensional as they are, the representations evoked by listening to a story or by reading a poem pale in comparison to those arising directly from the senses. Nevertheless, linguistic representations do have one thing about them that more than makes up for this limitation of language: the capacity for **unrestricted reference**. In this, language is all but unique; MUSIC comes in at a distant second — except perhaps for people such as Wolfgang Amadeus Mozart and Gustav Mahler.

Narrow, specialized perceptual reference is familiar to us from Chapter 4. The neurons in the middle temporal area MT that embody the representation of visual motion specialize just in that; if you stimulate a bunch of them, the rest of the brain will be fooled into perceiving the kind of motion they happen to be tuned to, which amounts to just a few of the perceptual dimensions available to the brain at any moment of its waking life. It is not unreasonable to imagine that acquiring enological expertise leads to the development of *specialized* representations for various qualities of wine.

It is precisely the lack of such narrow specialization that sets linguistic representations apart from the pack. True, not even T. S. Eliot (1888-1965)

IN VINO VERITAS. Computational analogy aside, there may be an alcohol-mediated interaction between the appreciation of poetry and the enjoyment of wine. Because alcohol makes the patterns of associations more labile and hence the representational landscape more highly interconnected, complex poetry may be better enjoyed when accompanied by a glass of good wine. While my informal investigations support this conjecture, a controlled experiment is clearly called for. The painting, from a hydria, shows Herakles pouring wine for the centaur Pholus.

Understanding a sentence is much more akin to understanding a theme in MUSIC than one may think.

— Wittgenstein (1958, 527)

can make you experience the bouquet of a good Medoc merely by mentioning it. Things are different, however, insofar as entire bundles of perceptions go. In his 1915 review of Ezra Pound's *Cathay*, Ford Madox Hueffer (Ford) remarked that "poetry consists in so rendering concrete objects that the emotions produced by the objects shall arise in the reader." I would argue that good poetry goes far beyond that, both in that arbitrarily abstract objects are rendered as effectively as if they were concrete, and in that emotions are evoked that transcend those brought about by the original object. Eliot's invocation of London — not at all a concrete "object" — in *The Waste Land* unleashes, in a prepared mind, an avalanche of memories and associations that is hardly possible in perceptual reality, where the vastness of the "Unreal City" can only be taken in one scene at a time.

What if you read *The Waste Land* without having ever been to London? I dare say you would then find it difficult to resonate to Eliot's mindset — not because I have a first-hand knowledge of it (as of 1965 nobody does), but because there is a plausible computational theory of how language works that tells me that name-dropping of the kind Eliot indulged in ("Jerusalem, Athens, Alexandria...") is only effective if the author trusts in pre-existing knowledge shared with the reader. This observation underscores the profound importance in language of the interdependence of the producer and the consumer. This interdependence goes much deeper than the role of the reader, a concept in semiotics that refers to the dynamics between the freedoms that a reader enjoys in interpreting a text and the constraints on such interpretation (Eco, 1979; Radford, 2002). This is because the author of a text never creates something out of nothing: an utterance that bears no relation at all to a linguistic and conceptual milieu shared at least by two individuals cannot be interpreted, leaving the reader without any possible role.

Language is thus a collective endeavor, and so is poetry; one might say that behind every great poet there is a great audience. A species consisting of individuals of solitary predisposition can never evolve anything like it; in a gregarious species that evolves language, individuals gain access to a kind of immortality by infecting others with memes imprinted with their personality. The meme of London as it is transmitted by *The Waste Land* certainly endures with Eliot long gone; it may even endure when London itself is gone — although its potential impact is likely to dwindle when the last *perceiver* of London goes into the night. In time, it will join the London Tube map reproduced on p. 274 of this book in becoming a relic of purely archaeological value, eventually disappearing into thin air (unless something is done about

Unreal City,
Under the brown fog of a winter dawn,
A crowd flowed over London Bridge,
                                          so many,
I had not thought death had undone
                                          so many.
...
What is the city over the mountains
Cracks and reforms and bursts
                                in the violet air
Falling towers
Jerusalem Athens Alexandria
Vienna London
Unreal

— T. S. Eliot
from *The Waste Land*

Umberto Eco wrote that his novel *The Name of the Rose* had been inspired by this verse from *De contemptu mundi* by a 12th century Benedictine monk, Bernard of Morlay:

Stat rosa pristina nomine;
nomina nuda tenemus.

(The rose that has been endures in its name; we hold naked names.) Language gives one a means to hold an object against the mind's eye, even if only in name; also to postpone one's own passing into oblivion. In the stanza that follows what probably is the most widely echoed poet's sentiment in the last two millennia, EXEGI MONUMENTUM... ("I have built myself a monument," *Odes* III, 30), Horace proclaims: *Non omnes moriar; multaque pars mei vitabit Libitinam* — "I shall not wholly die; a large part of me shall escape the goddess of funerals."

it; see Chapter 11).[40] Eliot's London shares this doom with Bashō's frog from a few pages back and with Arakida's butterfly from Chapter 5, just as Eliot shared it with Bashō and Arakida.

7.5.5 Endgame

showing their backs
then their fronts
the autumn leaves scatter in the wind

— the death poem of Ryōkan (1758-1831)

A Zen master's parting poem is a fitting final station on this chapter's long and winding road of exploration of the nature of language. In recalling the milestones encountered along this road — regularities that afford learning, the interplay of structure and probability, the role of context — we should keep in mind the key characteristic that distinguishes computational linguistics from other sciences: while the elements of language can be *about* the world, they are not *of* the world in the same way that the elements of physics are. Language is an artifice of evolution, and its structure and workings are contingent; they could have been different, yet still adaptive. This is the sense in which "we do not know what the universe is" (to reuse a phrase by Borges that already appeared in this chapter) — not because we are incapable of uncovering or comprehending its physics, but because a verbal description of reality is always merely a description.[41]

This is why, it seems to me, the world we inhabit is essentially and fundamentally INEFFABLE. If there is a heroic aspect to language, it is defiance in the face of this ineffability — the attempt on the part of the poet, professional or occasional, to capture the world in a word. In opening up new roads through the space of potentialities afforded by the lexicon-grammar, the superior players of the language Game excel in applying the computational machinery that comes with being a human to a body of language that is necessarily the product of a collective effort. In this chapter, I have focused mostly on that part of the machinery of language with which every one of us has been entrusted. Our next steps should therefore be in the direction of understanding the driving forces behind the evolution and development of language: thinking, society, and culture.

When you notice a cat in profound meditation,
The reason, I tell you, is always the same:
His mind is engaged in a rapt contemplation
Of the thought, of the thought, of the thought of his name:
His INEFFABLE effable
Effanineffable
Deep and inscrutable singular Name.

The Naming of Cats (excerpt),
from *Old Possum's Book of Practical Cats*
by T. S. Eliot

Bodhidharma, the bringer of Buddhism to China and the First Patriarch of Ch'an (Zen), gazing at a wall in meditation.

❦ ❦ ❦

Notes

[1]THE MOST IMPORTANT KNOWLEDGE. The infant's bootstrapping of language from a state of ignorance of language illustrates the key methodological point behind this book: the single most important thing one can know is how to learn.

[2]THE BIPARTITE QUESTION. As a freshman at Haverford College, Warren McCulloch was asked by his mentor, the Quaker philosopher Rufus Jones, about his scientific interests. McCulloch answered that all he wanted to know was: "What is a number that a man may know it; and a man, that he may know a number." Jones replied: "Friend, thee will be busy as long as thee lives" (McCulloch, 1965, p.2).

[3]CORPORA OF LANGUAGE.   The text corpora are now beginning to be supplemented by richer data that include semantic annotation (Baker, Fillmore, and Cronin, 2003), or even video recordings of the scene. It is worth noting that corpora are records of the actual instances of the Game as it played out on various occasions, and as such are, by definition, the ultimate authority over what is allowed (if it's in a corpus, it is) and what is natural (the more of it there is in a corpus, the more it is). Denying the validity of an expression that actually appears in a corpus is like denying the lawfulness of a physical event that has transpired (for example, a stone falling to the ground) simply because your notion of physics is incompatible with it. It is likely, of course, that a corpus of a limited size will not include some particular phrase that a linguist may be interested in simply because it is too rare in the normal usage of language. In such a case, the proper resort is to conduct a standard psycholinguistic experiment, in which a group of native speakers would be presented with the target phrase under controlled conditions, and asked to respond to it in some predetermined manner (Schütze, 1996).

[4] GAVAGAI! The indeterminacy of reference and the problem it poses for acquiring object names from ostensive definitions, and for translation, has been pointed out by Quine (1960), who illustrated it by asking the reader to imagine a linguist attempting to learn an unknown language, accompanied by a native informant. While out on a stroll, they encounter a rabbit, which prompts the native to say "Gavagai!" (see the illustration on p. 411). Quine noted that the reference of this utterance is underdetermined: it can be the rabbit's hind legs; its gait; the event of the rabbit crossing the path, etc., in addition, of course, to "rabbit." In practice, various perceptual biases and predispositions (studied by developmental cognitive psychologists) largely prevent babies from being susceptible to this indeterminacy (cf. the discussion of shape bias on p. 279).

[5]WORD ORDER. A fascinating description of a free word order language, Odawa, can be found in Christianson and Ferreira (2005).

[6]RECURSION is also useful in vision, where making sense of a stimulus by subjecting it to a structural analysis on multiple levels (Edelman and Intrator, 2003) is as indispensable for learning as it is in language (see Figure 7.1 on page 238).

[7]PSYCHOLOGICAL REALITY — for a definition and an example from vision, see Edelman (2007). The basic idea relies on the notion of *priming*, introduced in Chapter 6: if a posited representation can be primed, it is real.

[8]SEMANTICS. More on this topic from Pietroski (2003):

> We cannot know a priori what a semantic theory should look like any more than pre-Newtonian theorists could have known what the right theory of celestial mechanics would look like. (Anyone who insisted that a theory of planetary motion had to be about planetary motion, or that talk of tides and falling bodies was just a distraction, got the theory he deserved.) It may once have seemed clear that a semantic theory should associate each object-language sentence with a meaning-giving specification of its truth-conditions. But that was a proposal, which we can refine, about how to study meaning.

This approach is laudably cautious, yet still problematic in its yearning after an overarching *formal* semantic theory. As we shall see later in this chapter, a computationally feasible and empirically viable theory of meaning can be based on the idea of distributed activation of multiple structures — something quite different from the expectations of the linguistic formalists.

[9] FORMALIST LINGUISTICS. Chomsky (1961, p.266) writes: "only a purely formal basis can provide a firm and productive foundation for the construction of grammatical theory." A FORMAL SYSTEM consists of the following:

1. A finite set of symbols which can be used for constructing formulae.

2. A *grammar*, i.e., a way of constructing well-formed formulae out of the symbols, such that it is possible to find a decision procedure for deciding whether a formula is a well-formed formula (*wff*) or not.

3. A set of axioms or axiom schemata: each axiom has to be a *wff*.

4. A set of inference rules.

5. A set of theorems. This set includes all the axioms, plus all *wffs* which can be derived from previously derived theorems by means of rules of inference. Unlike the grammar for *wffs*, there is no guarantee that there will be a decision procedure for deciding whether or not a given *wff* is a theorem.

Note that although mathematics as a methodological framework is a formal system insofar as it rests on axioms that are assumed to hold and on theorems that can be derived from them, there are domains within mathematics that are precise, yet do not in themselves constitute formal systems. A prominent example is statistical inference, where the likelihood of certain statements can be precisely computed, but where categorical "theoremhood" is meaningless.

[10] LEARNING IS LEARNING OF REGULARITIES. This fundamental principle of the computational theory of learning, due to Solomonoff (1964), is derived from the observation that learning is only useful insofar as it supports generalization (cf. section 5.4.3) and that generalization is only possible if regularities are discovered in the observed data. A modern operationalization of this idea is the Minimum Description Length Principle of Rissanen (1987), according to which regularities in the data are best captured by a representation that minimizes the sum of the description lengths of the code and of the training data under that code. A tutorial introduction to the computational aspects of MDL is given by Grünwald, Myung, and Pitt (2005). For a discussion of the relevance of these ideas to cognition, see Chater and Vitányi (2003).

[11] STATISTICS AND STRUCTURE. The same chicken and egg problem (needing structure to compute statistics that must be used to detect structure) is identified, and resolved, in unsupervised learning of structure in vision (Edelman, Intrator, and Jacobson, 2002).

[12] HARRIS ON "LANGUAGE DISCOVERY." It is not clear that Zellig Harris intended his

theory of phoneme discovery to be a model of language acquisition by children. De Brabanter (2001) describes Harris's procedure thus:

> Harris argues that the list of the phonemes of a natural language can be established for instance by means of the so-called 'pair test' (cf. 1968: 21-23), a type of experiment involving two members of a single language community. The first one, the speaker, repeats at random each of two sequences that are felt to be similar, e.g. roll and role, or cart and card. The second, the hearer, is requested to guess, utterance after utterance, which sequence was being pronounced. Harris notes that for the first pair, about 50% of the guesses will turn out to be correct — which indicates that the hearer could make out no pronunciation difference between the two words so that he or she responded at random — whereas, for the second, there will be close to 100% of accurate responses — indicating that a 'phonemic' difference is detected by the hearer.

An insightful discussion of Harris's views from a modern perspective can be found in Goldsmith (2005).

[13]THE DIMENSIONALITY OF THE SPEECH SIGNAL. We may ask whether there is an objective reason for speech to be describable in a low-dimensional space. A useful way of approaching this question is to appeal to the ultimate source of information in speech: the speaker's internal representation of the intended speech act. The nature (and, in particular, the dimensionality) of this representation is a complicated issue, to which I return in section 7.5.1. Meanwhile, the assurance of low dimensionality that we're after can be found at an intermediate stage of speech production: the informational bottleneck that is the vocal apparatus of the speaker. That representation is relatively low-dimensional because there is only a relatively small number of physical variables involved. These correspond to the degrees of freedom stemming from the anatomy and the physiology of the vocal chords, the larynx, the tongue, the lips, etc. It should be noted that this representation, while low-dimensional, is hardly "crisp" or invariant across speakers, because the configurations imposed by the motor control system on the vocal tract can never attain machine-like precision, and because the mechanics of the vocal tracts of individuals vary. This presents a serious problem for PHONOLOGY, the formalist linguistic discipline traditionally concerned with discrete features of speech and with crisp, universal rules supposedly governing the manipulation of such features (Port and Leary, 2005).

[14]See the note on GAVAGAI! on p. 307.

[15]PREDICTABILITY. Formally, the (un)predictability of the next element in a series, given its predecessors, is expressed by its *conditional entropy*. In psycholinguistics, the perceived degree of uncertainty can be assessed empirically using techniques employed by Johnson (1965) (see p. 244) or by Hale (2004). Computationally, it is captured by the notion of probabilistic LANGUAGE MODEL introduced on p. 270.

[16]ALIGNMENT AND COMPARISON. Harris (1954) writes: "For the position of the speakers is after all similar to that of the linguist. They have heard (and used) a great many utterances among which they perceive partial similarities — parts which occur in various combinations with each other. They produce new combinations along the lines of the ones they have heard. The formation of new utterances in the language is therefore based on the distributional relations — as changeably perceived by the speakers - among the parts of the previously heard utterances."

[17]COLLOCATIONS AND CO-OCCURRENCES. On the unstructured reading, what matters is

the co-occurrence of words within a certain distance of each other, irrespective of their order. A surprising amount of information about a text can be derived using methods based on such "bag of words" representations; these, in turn, can be extracted from raw corpus data using efficient computational procedures related to principal component analysis (Landauer and Dumais, 1997). Nevertheless, key tasks, for instance determining the focus of a sentence or accomplishing its thematic analysis, necessitate the insistence on proper order, as we already saw in an earlier section.

[18]Here is a partial list of notions comparable to PREFABS: the phrasal lexicon (Becker, 1975), "inventories" of units of varying kinds and sizes (Langacker, 1987), idioms and semi-productive forms (Jackendoff, 1995; Jackendoff and Pinker, 2005), prefabricated expressions (Makkai, 1995; Wray, 2000), "syntactic nuts" (Culicover, 1999), frequent collocations (Bybee and Hopper, 2001), multiword expressions (Baldwin, Bannard, Tanaka, and Widdows, 2003; Sag, Baldwin, Bond, Copestake, and Flickinger, 2002), and constructions (Croft, 2001; Fillmore, 1985; Goldberg, 2003; Tomasello, 2003).

[19] A GRAPH that captures various kinds of language patterns is illustrated below using examples from Russian — a language whose three genders (feminine, masculine, and neuter) make for rich structural dependencies. The nodes in that graph are labeled by Russian words; the arcs that connect the nodes form paths that correspond to sentences.

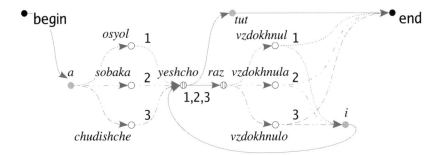

Explanations. The two cross-hatched nodes in the middle — *yeshcho* (ещё) and *raz* (раз) — form a COLLOCATION. The three nodes on the left — open circles, labeled *osyol* (осёл), *sobaka* (собака), and *chudishche* (чудище) — are DISTRIBUTIONALLY RELATED. They form an equivalence class (EC), and so do the three on the right: *vzdokhnul* (вздохнул), *vzdokhnula* (вздохнула), and *vzdokhnulo* (вздохнуло). Each of the three numbered paths through the first EC must continue through the like-numbered path in the second EC (unless the sentence branches off to *tut* and ends); this is an example of DEPENDENCY (gender agreement). Finally, the path from *i* back to *yeshcho* closes a LOOP that can be traversed any number of times, exemplifying potentially infinite recursion.

[20]The seven tenets of CONSTRUCTION GRAMMAR according to Goldberg (2003) are:

1. All levels of description are understood to involve pairings of form with semantic or discourse function, including morphemes or words, idioms, partially lexically filled and fully abstract phrasal patterns.

2. An emphasis is placed on subtle aspects of the way we conceive of events and states of affairs.

3. A 'what you see is what you get' approach to sentence structure is adopted: no under-lying levels of "syntax" or any phonologically empty elements are posited.

4. Constructions are understood to be learned on the basis of the input and general cogni-tive mechanisms (they are constructed), and are expected to vary cross-linguistically.

5. Cross-linguistic generalizations are explained by appeal to general cognitive constraints together with the functions of the constructions involved.

6. Language-specific generalizations across constructions are captured via inheritance networks much like those that have long been posited to capture our non-linguistic knowledge.

7. The totality of our knowledge of language is captured by a network of constructions: a 'construct-i-con.'

[21]Collecting N-GRAM statistics gets complicated if the elements of the target n-gram are allowed to be non-adjacent to each other — a situation that human learners indeed find more difficult (Newport and Aslin, 2004).

[22]NO INVIOLABLE RULES. There are no truly categorical dependencies in natural lan-guages: all are probabilistic and can be bent — even the number of arguments that a verb takes (cf. "I sneezed the napkin off the table"). What about unnaturally perfect languages? Child native speakers of Esperanto, a language engineered so as to have only perfectly regular rules, introduced irregularities into the dialect they developed (Bergen, 2001).

[23]Context-driven WORD SENSE DISAMBIGUATION is possible basically because the sense of a word is determined by the company it keeps. You may recall that the principle of compo-sitional semantics prescribed that the meaning of a sentence should depend on the meanings of the words that compose it (and on the structure of the sentence). In comparison, the dis-ambiguation algorithm developed by Karov and Edelman (1998) works both ways, by also allowing the meaning of a word to be determined by the meaning of the sentence in which it is embedded. Note that the equal status it assigns to sentence- and word-level elements is consistent with the Construction Grammar approach.

[24]The distinction between OBJECTS AND EVENTS is blurred; cf. note 1 on page 33.

[25]METAPHORS AND PREPOSITIONS. For a diametrically opposite view on prepositions, which construes them metaphorically, see (Evans and Tyler, 2004). Generally, the "proto-scenes" drawn by cognitive linguists who attempt to capture the meaning of a construction in the form of a spatial diagram raise the same kind of doubt concerning psychological reality as do the "syntactic" tree structures posited by the formal generative linguists.

[26] For decades, linguistic NATIVISM, as expressed most forcefully by Chomsky in state-ments such as this one:

> The term learning is, in fact, a very misleading one, and one that is perhaps best abandoned as a relic of an earlier age, and an earlier misunderstanding. (Noam Chomsky, *On the nature, use, and acquisition of language*, 1999, p.43)

used to be coupled with a denial of the evolvability of language:

> It is perfectly safe to attribute this development to "natural selection," so long as we realize that there is no substance to this assertion. (Noam Chomsky, *Language and Mind*, 1972, p.97)

With respect to the latter issue (but not the former one), Chomsky's views appear to have evolved (Fitch, Hauser, and Chomsky, 2005; Hauser, Chomsky, and Fitch, 2002). This process, however, does not seem to be bringing his stance closer to the new, empirically grounded synthesis emerging around the Construction Grammar idea (Jackendoff and Pinker, 2005; Pinker and Jackendoff, 2005).

[27]Some of those who purport to be convinced by the ARGUMENT FROM COMPLEXITY do so for the sake of the "scientific" façade that it provides for an irrational belief system (such as a revealed religion) that they are unwilling to endorse openly; cf. the US Federal judge's decision in the 2005 case of *Kitzmiller v. Dover Area School District*, memorandum opinion, p.21:

> ...Religious opponents of evolution began cloaking religious beliefs in scientific sounding language and then mandating that schools teach the resulting "creation science" or "scientific creationism" as an alternative to evolution.

[28]Recall the definition of FORMAL SYSTEMS from p. 308.

[29]In the old (perhaps the original) Chinese version of the Cinderella story, King To Han finds the girl YEH-SHEN'S slipper, realizes that its owner has the smallest feet in the kingdom, and falls in love with Yeh-Shen without having seen her.

[30]Clark (2001, p.62) explains how in language the apparent LIMITATIONS on learning are actually a boon:

> All organisms have limits, and operate within those limits. Indeed the recognition of this allows a simple characterisation of the set of natural languages as the set of languages that is within the capabilities of the human learning ability. No innate knowledge required. We do not need to claim as Chomsky (1965, p.27) does that 'the child approaches the data with the presumption that they are drawn from a language of a certain antecedently well-defined type.' The child merely approaches the data with a particular limited learning device, albeit one of great power and flexibility.

[31]LEARNING IN VISION AND LANGUAGE. The many parallels and the few differences between unsupervised learning in vision (Edelman and Intrator, 2003) and language (Solan et al., 2005) are, unfortunately, beyond the scope of this book.

[32]LANGUAGE LOCALIZATION. Most language processing is lateralized — confined to the dominant (in 97% of people, the left) hemisphere of the brain (Gilbert, Regier, Kay, and Ivry, 2006). The first attempts to achieve a more precise localization of language in the brain date back to the 19th century work of Paul Broca and Karl Wernicke on dysfunctions (aphasias) caused by lesions. In Broca's aphasia (lesions in areas 44 and 45 in the illustration on p. 288), the patient's speech is agrammatic; in Wernicke's aphasia (areas 41 and 42 lesioned), speech is fluent and grammatical but meaningless. Modern neuropsychological methods have rendered this categorical distinction and the localization of language functions that it implies largely obsolete.

[33]The existence of MIRROR NEURONS offers an indication of the approximate location and the level on which Lashley's serial order is encoded in the brain, but not an explanation of the computations involved, nor of the computational principles. Likewise, Arbib's claim that mirror neurons embody linguistic *schemata* or patterns of action is merely a paraphrase of their computational role; understanding of the computational principles behind the schemata and of the details of the mechanisms that implement them is required to complete this explanation (Edelman, 2000).

[34]SCRIPTS. Conceptual knowledge allows people to treat many mundane situations as if they are scripted. Upon hearing an utterance pertaining to such a situation, people are typically capable of answering questions about it that can only be reliably processed if a massive amount of background knowledge is mustered. For example, when told that "John had a meal at a restaurant" and asked "Did John pay?" people respond, quite confidently, in the positive, presumably on the basis of a "restaurant script" they possess, which specifies the default answer to this and many other restaurant-related questions (Schank and Abelson, 1977).

[35]In vision, veridicality is obtained when the perceptual mapping from the world into the internal representation space is smooth (Edelman, 1999); cf. p. 127. In language, the same computational principle may be at work: a smooth mapping from the speaker's meaning space into the listener's one (which must be commensurable with it) would ensure a transfer of meaning that would preserve the relative distances among concepts, resulting in veridical communication. This idea has not, to my knowledge, been empirically tested.

[36]CONSIDER THE LILIES:

> To Mrs. Frederick Tuckerman (June 1884).
> Let me commend to Baby's attention the only Commandment I ever obeyed —
> "Consider the lilies."
>
> – Emily Dickinson

[37]There are interesting parallels here to the notion of ENZYMATIC COMPUTATION proposed by Barrett (2005).

[38]THE ARCHETYPES HOLD A REUNION. Was T. S. Eliot's *The Waste Land* elevated to the Modernist canon largely on the strength of its appeal to a host of intellectual archetypes? One may discern a parallel here to the case of Michael Curtiz's cult movie *Casablanca*, about which Eco (1986) remarks, "It is a hodgepodge of sensational scenes strung together implausibly... Nevertheless, it is a great example of cinematic discourse... a paramount laboratory for semiotic research into textual strategies... *Casablanca* became a cult movie because it is not *one* movie. It is 'movies'." The tension between surprise- or novelty-based computational explanations of cognitive prominence and averageness- or familiarity-based ones that arises here brings to mind the discussion of beauty in section 5.6.

[39]It would appear that the conception of POETRY as necessarily rhyming or even just rhythmic is quite parochial, both in space and in time. In deviating from the classical European verse structures, many of the Modernist innovators such as Eliot were influenced by the cultural heritages of India, China, and Japan, whose literary forms differ from those of the Græco-Roman West. In the second half of the 20th century, writing verse became a singular phenomenon, a playground for giants such as Joseph Brodsky, who noted that verse hones the writer's skill by making it so much more difficult to find precisely the right word for each place in the poem. Brodsky's extraordinary poem *Verses on the Death of T. S. Eliot* was, of course, written in verse.

[40]EXEGI MONUMENTUM. The present book may well endure (that is, remain intelligible and perhaps even useful) longer than cities or their descriptions, insofar as it captures certain truths about the mind/brain and its interaction with the world, and as long as minds, however embodied, retain an interest in the computational principles that make them work. I fully expect many of the props I use (such as the absurd qualities of the Monty Python sketches) to be lost on the readers much sooner, though.

[41]The relationship between cognitive REPRESENTATION AND REALITY is a fascinating

topic, which I shall touch upon in Chapter 9 (see also note 14 on page 230). Meanwhile, here are three quotes to ponder.

> For a sorcerer, reality, or the world we all know, is only a description.
>
> — from the introduction to *Journey to Ixtlan* by Carlos Castañeda.

> Reality is that which, when you stop believing in it, doesn't go away.
>
> — from *Valis* by Philip K. Dick

(This from a writer most of whose work was devoted to developing the thesis that reality that we seem to share should not be trusted!)

> There is no objective reality. There might be a world that has true reality. A world with genuine physics. But because we're in a world that's made out of language, we'll never, ever get to that place from here. There's no way out of a world that's made of language.
>
> — from *Zeitgeist* by Bruce Sterling

(I first encountered this quote on the web page of G. P. Radford, at http://alpha.fdu.edu/~gradford/.)

Dick's statement seems to be the most reasonable one to use as a working hypothesis.

8

Thinking

Жизнь прожить — не поле перейти.
To live through a life is not the same as to cross a field.

A Russian proverb

Whatever gets you through your life 'salright, 'salright.

John Lennon

W HAT gets you through life is, in a nutshell, this: an ability to figure out what to do next, by thinking. The constant need to plan ahead and choose a course of action arises on all the levels of information processing in which embodied minds are engaged. This makes THINKING an eclectic category that includes both the niceties of millisecond-timescale motor control and the strategic planning of behavior. There is, however, a good reason to regard thinking as a natural kind: all the problems that necessitate it are computationally quite similar to each other.

Consider the task that I am presently facing: writing a 15,000-word chapter that would help myself and perhaps others make computational sense of thinking. Because of the discrete nature of the writing system I use, this overarching task must eventually be re-expressed in terms of about 108,000 distinct actions,[1] each culminating in the pressing of a key on the keyboard of my notebook.

Although to the higher-level processes that control my writing a keystroke may look like an elementary, indivisible action, it is anything but that to the lower-level processes charged with its execution. During typing, my brain must control at least 54 muscles (counting the two hands and their ten fingers, but not arms, shoulders, neck, or eyes, let alone the rest of the body). This number can serve as a rough lower bound on the dimensionality of the space in which typing activity is most naturally represented. Planning a sequence of keystrokes translates into laying out a trajectory through that space.

The Thought Which Sees, a sketch by René Magritte, who wrote: "Only thought can resemble. It resembles by being what it sees, hears, or knows; it becomes what the world offers it."

All organisms with complex nervous systems are faced with the moment-by-moment question that is posed by life: WHAT SHALL I DO NEXT?

— S. Savage-Rumbaugh and R. Lewin, *Kanzi* (1994)

315

Daunting as a 54-dimensional problem may seem,[2] the computational challenge of thinking about *how* to type is dwarfed by the complexities of thinking about *what* to type. Many people otherwise known to be reasonably proficient with language find COMPOSITION so difficult that to postpone facing it they will do anything: clean up old email, run recursively ramifying web searches on vaguely relevant topics, or else resort to circumventing their writer's block by opening a chapter with a complaint about the difficulty of writing chapter openings. It is all the more fascinating, therefore, that the problem of composition can be given the same abstract computational formulation as typing: planning a path through a high-dimensional space.

A useful conceptual starting point for reasoning about textual composition is the graph-structured map of the likely paths through the lexicon, which I introduced in Chapter 7 using the London Underground as an example (p. 274). To compose a 15,000-word text, I need to find a path of that length that would satisfy the various constraints that apply. Most of the many, many possible paths (including the 15,000-fold repetition of the word "the") would be ruled out on grounds of content, grammar, or style. At the same time, many slightly different versions of the same text would be virtually equally acceptable (for instance, the effect of substituting "insignificant" for "negligible" in this sentence would be negligible). A natural representation space for all texts of a fixed length is therefore one in which the n'th dimension corresponds to the choice of the n'th word in the text. Each entire text (a long path through the lexicon) is a point in that space; texts that are identical except in one place are mapped into neighboring points.

The dimensionality and the metric structure of the problem space for thinking about composition differ greatly from those of the problem space for thinking about muscle activation, in which keystrokes are best represented. The general idea, however, is the same, which implies that the same approaches to solving the problems can be attempted. The most straightforward such approach is *search*: starting with any solution (that is, at any point in the representation space) and moving in a direction that is deemed likely to lead to an improvement. This is what thinking amounts to; the rest is details, which I still need to explain — in 14,000 words.

In a COMBINATORIAL OPTIMIZATION problem, the representation space is discrete, and the required solution must minimize a certain cost function, while satisfying a given set of constraints. This kind of problem (provably one of the most complex ones known to computation science) is exemplified by literary COMPOSITION. In classical Persian poetry, the standard metaphor for the writer's occupation is exemplified by these lines of Abu Muin Nasir-i Khusraw (1004-1078?):

Why so silent, eloquent one?
Why do you not string
pearls and corals
upon the necklace of verse?

A clay dish from Bamiyan (Afghanistan), depicting two birds holding a string of pearls.

8.1 Varieties of thinking: an introduction

Even when it is not explicit and deliberate, thinking is always purposive, driven by a tension between the current state of affairs and the goal state. Intricacies of MOTIVATION, PERSONALITY, and SOCIAL INTERACTION notwithstanding, the computational essence of this tension — the functional bottleneck through which these factors affect thinking, and therefore behavior — boils down to just a few numbers (Figure 8.1). This happy situation had been noted already by Warren McCulloch: one of his lectures delivered to the American Psychological Association was titled *Machines that think and want* (McCulloch, 1947). In a more precise, albeit less euphonious, formulation, the order of *think* and *want* would be reversed: in the chain of cause and effect, as the Buddha may have described it, drives engender desires, which lead to the realization of problems, which in turn instigate thinking.

In the remainder of this chapter, I shall focus on the last link in this chain: purposive thought, both implicit and automatic, and explicit and deliberate (fully reflective thinking that turns upon itself will be the subject of Chapter 9). It is customary to distinguish among three categories of thinking:

We cannot possibly know [what the subject will think of next], unless we have a detailed understanding of what he is trying to do, and why. For this reason, a really satisfactory theory of the higher mental processes can only come into being when we also have theories of MOTIVATION, PERSONALITY, and SOCIAL INTERACTION.

— Neisser (1967, p.305)

The renunciation of taṇhā (in Pāli: thirst, desire, craving, wanting, longing, yearning) is the second of the four noble truths preached by the Buddha (see his Fire Sermon[3]).

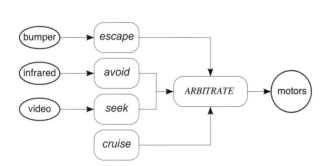

Figure 8.1 — SEEK is one of several motivational components of a circuit controlling a Braintenberg "vehicle"-style (cf. p. 47) mobile robot (Jones and Flynn, 1993). (Note hierarchical abstraction at work: the details of computational modules such as ARBITRATE are not important at this level of description and may remain hidden.) Here is how McCulloch (1952, pp.266,268) explains motivation: "As long as we live, we are a bundle of circular systems SEEKING various ends at every moment. ... When we ask not *how* but *why* a cat pursues a mouse, the answer is again in terms of circuits, but this time part of the path lies outside the cat. We will make the simplest assumption: that trains of impulses from the cat's empty stomach start her in quest of mice, and that, when she catches and eats a mouse, this fills her stomach and stops trains of impulses."

- *Problem solving.* Typing and composition, which I discussed above, fall under this rubric. Additional examples include: getting edible seeds out of a prickly pod (p. 196); getting a high score in an SAT exam; landing a man on the moon and returning him safely back to the Earth.

- *Reasoning.* In the word processor I use (Emacs), pressing the "control" and the "delete" keys together (*ctrl-Del*) causes the character under the cursor to be deleted; pressing *alt-Del* deletes the previous word. What will happen if I press the three keys together? Here, let me try that... hmmm, nothing.[4] Could you have predicted that by logical reasoning?

- *Decision making.* To be or not to be is one of the questions where principled weighing of alternative courses of action can make a difference.

Holyoak and Morrison (2005), whose edited volume contains an excellent, up-to-date snapshot of the psychology of thinking, note on p.3 that "these aspects of thinking overlap in every conceivable way." The key to understanding their relationships, and hence the nature of thinking in general, is understanding the computations involved.

The disabled Apollo 13 Service Module, showing damage from the oxygen tank explosion (photograph taken by the astronauts from the Command Module).

8.2   Varieties of thinking: I. Problem solving

A problem is a situation that, on the one hand, needs to be mitigated in some respect, and, on the other hand, cannot be mitigated through a reflex action or through the execution of an already available plan. Some problems we bring upon ourselves, by developing a dissatisfaction with the status quo. Other problems arise from contingencies: any situation that is dealt with routinely by the cognitive system turns into a problem if the path to its possible resolution is made unclear by an unforeseen event.

Even something as simple as breathing can become a problem — not necessarily when it is difficult, but rather when it mandates thinking. Compare the predicament of an astronaut in training who is gasping for air after having just completed a long and strenuous physical exercise to that of an astronaut whose spacecraft's oxygen tank just exploded. In the first case, breathing is difficult, but does not constitute a *cognitive* problem; in the second, breathing is easy because there still is air in the cabin, but will become impossible unless a series of engineering problems is solved in a very short order.

8.2.1   How not to get lost in a problem space

The analyses of motor control and of textual composition, mentioned earlier, suggest that cognitive problems can be conceptualized in terms of state spaces — a notion introduced into psychology by Newell and Simon (1972), whose foundational studies combined psychological experimentation with computational theory and modeling. Before attempting to apply it to complex situations such as the one that developed 321, 860 kilometers from Earth on board the service module of Apollo 13, let us examine it on a simple example, in which the entire state space fits onto half a page: the Towers of Hanoi problem, with three pegs and three disks (see Figure 8.2).

In a state-space representation of a problem, each possible state of the system under consideration is assigned a point. The geometric structure of neighborhoods is determined by the operations that transform the system

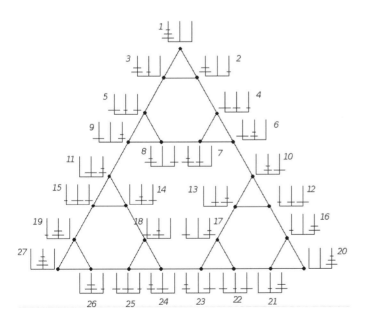

Figure 8.2 — The STATE SPACE of the Towers of Hanoi problem has the form of a graph. Each of the three apexes represents a state in which all the disks are on the same peg; other nodes in the graph represent other legal states (those in which smaller disks always rest atop larger ones). The task is to transfer all the disks to another peg (say, starting at state 1 and ending at 20). The sequence of states 1-2-4-6-10-12-16-20 is one possible solution.

from one state into another. In the example of Figure 8.2, state #1 can be transformed by moving the top disk from the leftmost peg either to the middle or to the rightmost peg; therefore, this state has only two neighbors (#2 and #3). In comparison, state #19 can be transformed in three distinct ways: into #27 (by moving the disk from the left to the middle), into #15 (by moving the disk from the middle to the right), or into #26 (by moving the disk from the left to the right).

Once the state space is mapped, the problem reduces to finding a path consisting solely of legal operations (in the case of the Towers of Hanoi, the allowed moves — one disk at a time; smaller disks never below larger ones) that would connect the initial state (all three disks on the leftmost peg) to the goal state (all three disks on the rightmost peg). As Figure 8.2 makes obvious, the seven-step path leading down the right edge of the state-space graph is a legal (indeed, an optimal) solution to the problem.

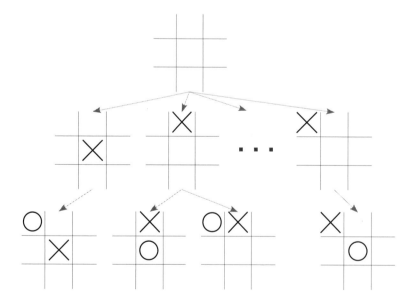

Figure 8.3 — A *very* small portion of the Tic Tac Toe problem space, which has the form of a TREE (a directed graph without cyclical paths). The first tier ("ply") of the tree some of the nine options open to the first player, the second – some of the options of the second player made available by the first player's moves, etc. Note that none of the leaves (final game positions) of the tree are shown here (the total number of leaf nodes in the Tic Tac Toe game tree is 26,830).

Larger and larger

The simple two-player board game of Tic Tac Toe, illustrated in Figure 8.3 on the facing page, has a considerably larger state space, only a small portion of which can be depicted here. Unlike that of the Towers of Hanoi, this space is structured like a TREE: a graph that has no cycles (it is not permitted to erase a circle or a cross in Tic Tac Toe). As before, a solution takes the form of a path from the initial state (a blank 3×3 board at the top or "root" of the tree) to a final one, in which one of the players wins.

The game tree is *much* larger in chess, with an estimated size of 10^{123} leaf nodes — a staggeringly large number, considering that the total number of atoms in the Universe is about 10^{79}. This complexity stems from a combination of a high branching factor (average number of possible moves at each stage of the game), and a great depth (average number of plays) of the tree.

For almost five decades — between 1950, when the first paper on the theory of chess was published, and 1997, when a computer first won a tournament against the human world champion — chess inspired psychologists studying human problem solving and artificial intelligence researchers aiming to build machines that would beat humans at their own game. The conceptual foundations for the 1997 victory of Deep Blue over Garry Kasparov were in place already in Shannon's seminal 1950 paper. The key principle identified by Shannon, which he correctly anticipated to apply to other problems as well, was search.

Search

If intelligent behavior which humans often exhibit in problem situations that require thinking is to be explained without resort to miracles or a homunculus, it must be ultimately reduced to steps that are themselves devoid of intelligence — such as elementary instructions for a Turing Machine, a universal model of computation introduced in Chapter 2 (p. 27). Representing a problem situation in the form of a state space, with initial and goal states identified, makes such an explanatory move possible: a mindless, mechanical search procedure can now be used to find a path leading to the goal.

The most unassuming and myopic (hence highly explanatory) search method is one that explores all possible paths leading away from the current state, one move at a time (in chess, this means considering all the legal moves available in the given situation). These lead to new states, each of which in

COMPUTER CHESS: a few key dates —

1950:
In the first theoretical paper on computer chess, Claude Shannon writes, "Although perhaps of no practical importance, the question is of theoretical interest, and it is hoped that a satisfactory solution of this problem will act as a wedge in attacking other problems of a similar nature and of greater significance" (*Programming a computer for playing chess*, C. E. Shannon, Philosophical Magazine 41:256-275).

1951:
Alan Turing develops a computer chess program, which loses even to weak players (in pencil and paper simulation).

1957:
The first working program for chess implemented on an IBM 704 computer, which runs at 42 *Khz*, and has a 7,000-word memory). It plays at a "passable amateur" level.
...

1997:
IBM's Deep Blue computer wins a six-game match with the human world champion, Garry Kasparov, opening an era in which the supremacy of computers in chess is undisputed.

turn offers prospects for further advancement towards the goal. These can only be assessed by exploring the state-space paths leading out. Thus, the brute-force search procedure must necessarily explore the consequences of each possible move *recursively*, until the goal is reached.

White moves and wins. This position requires a MAXIMAL DEPTH of 35 ply to be solved (a ply is one turn of one of the players; 35 ply thus means 18 moves by white and 17 by black). Campitelli and Gobet (2004) found that skilled chess-players search deeper than novices.

In chess, recursive brute-force search must be curtailed at a certain MAXIMUM DEPTH (which depends on the available computational resources) to forestall the combinatorial explosion in the volume of data that it generates. Halting the search before it runs its course (by arriving at a leaf of the game tree, which corresponds to a victory by one side, or to a draw) necessitates the evaluation of intermediate states. This can only be done HEURISTICALLY, that is, on the basis of rule-of-thumb considerations that are suggestive but do not allow a rigorous conclusion to be drawn about the situation at hand.

By their very nature, heuristics are defeasible. For example, a state in which I have the material advantage of a bishop would seem preferable over a state in which I only have an extra pawn, let alone a state in which my opponent has an advantage. Likewise, a state in which my king is well-protected behind a wall of pawns would seem to be preferable over a state in which it is exposed. However, by sacrificing a bishop and allowing me to castle, my opponent may have gained a decisive dynamic advantage on a longer time scale, which I miss because it falls outside the horizon of my overly myopic search.

Because the problem space (game tree) in chess is so large, any practical computational strategy must combine search with heuristic evaluation of the encountered states, and this is indeed what all computer chess programs do. In this context, it is interesting to consider the relative importance of search depth and of the amount of problem-specific knowledge expressed in the heuristics. The steady increase in available computer power to which we became accustomed over the years translates immediately into greater possible search depth. The IBM 704 computer that ran the first chess program back in 1957 had a 42 *kHz* clock — slower by a factor of 47,619 than that of the 2.0 *GHz* notebook on which I am typing these words.[5] If performance were determined by search depth alone, the freely available chess program for my computer would be unbeatable, which it is not. That the strongest chess software at present does in fact run on personal computers indicates that a little knowledge is worth a lot of search depth.

CHECKERS IS SOLVED. The game of checkers, which has about 5×10^{20} possible positions, has been solved: Schaeffer, Burch, Björnsson, Kishimoto, Müller, Lake, Lu, and Sutphen (2007) proved that perfect play by both sides leads to a draw.

Analysis of thinking-aloud protocols of human chess players suggests that they too combine knowledge with search, and that more highly skilled players are better at both (Campitelli and Gobet, 2004). In some situations (such as the position depicted on p. 322), human masters look so far ahead in the game that brute-force exhaustive search can be ruled out. The deeper the search, the more selective it must be, and knowledge-based heuristic pruning of the game tree is what makes it possible.

As the knowledge base of a chess player, computer or human, becomes more extensive, it needs to be organized so as to maintain efficiency. It would not do, for example, to juggle in your working memory all that you know about endgames while playing out a Sicilian Defense opening — or the other way around. The idea of filing chunks of knowledge under appropriate headings (openings, endgames, etc.) can be applied recursively, leading to the approach that I have identified back in Chapter 2 as the centerpiece of representational cognition: HIERARCHICAL ABSTRACTION (cf. section 2.4 on page 30). Experimental studies of memory for chess positions show that human players do rely on hierarchical chunking (Figure 8.4). Moreover, in

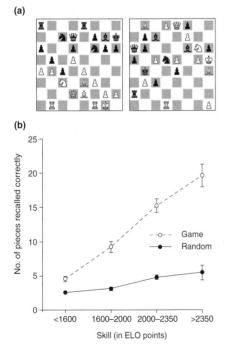

(a)

(b)

Figure 8.4 — The role of expertise and chunking in chess (Gobet et al., 2001). *Top:* An actual position from a masters' game (left), and a random one obtained by shuffling pieces around (right). *Bottom:* the mean number of correctly recalled piece positions, plotted against the player's skill. Stronger players are much better at recalling meaningful positions than random ones, suggesting that they employ HIERARCHICAL ABSTRACTION in representing game states. This is a very useful skill in a game whose space of possible states and moves is astronomically large. Finding and matching meaningful patterns in the current state and a set of previously encountered ones (each paired with its evaluation) and reusing moves that proved useful in the past in similar states are both highly effective strategies in chess (Gobet and Simon, 1998).

Limpets playing GO in Monty Python's *Flying Circus* —
(German accent) In the hard and unrelenting world of nature the ceaseless struggle for survival continues. ... *(cut to stock film of sea lions fighting)* Here, in a colony of sea lions, we see a huge bull sea lion seeing off an intruding bull who is attempting to intrude on his harem. This pattern of aggressive behaviour is typical of these documentaries. *(cut to shot of two almost stationary limpets)* Here we see two limpets locked in a life or death struggle for territory. The huge bull limpet, enraged by the rock, endeavours to ENCIRCLE its sprightly opponent.

bringing their knowledge to bear on the position at hand, humans make use of the power of their perceptual mechanisms; in the words of Gobet and Simon (1998), pattern recognition makes search possible.

One game of intellect in which humans have still not been surpassed by computers is GO, which has simpler rules, uses identical pieces for each side, and is played on a larger board than chess (see Figure 8.5). Because of these differences, the Go game tree is both bushier and deeper than that of chess. Because of that, Go places significantly greater demands both on pattern recognition and on search, raising the importance of strategic thinking. At the same time, teaching a machine Go strategy by reverse engineering a human player is progressing very slowly, because Go experts find it difficult to articulate the manifold factors that determine position quality. It seems safe to predict, however, that Go will soon follow chess in becoming a game reserve where the primates who invented it are at the mercy of artifacts that can hunt them at will.

In state space, no one can hear you scream

The primary goal of Go, which is to ENCIRCLE the opponent's stones, has a distinct military flavor, and it is in a military setting that a natural generalization of the state space approach to problem solving is best described. Imagine yourself a general who must deploy his troops around a city so as to capture it with the least opposition. Because location on the ground is described by continuous rather than discrete variables, the resulting problem space is also continuous (unlike in chess or in Go).

For an army of 10,000 troopers, the nominal dimensionality of the deployment problem space would be equal to 20,000 — quite an unmanageable

Figure 8.5 — The strategy game of GO has an estimated tree complexity of 2.1×10^{170} (compare this to the 10^{123} figure for chess). The game is played with black and white stones on a square grid. When a stone or a chain of stones is ENCIRCLED by the opponent's stones, leaving it no "liberties," it is removed from the board.

number, which, however, can be greatly reduced by the military equivalent of chunking. To that end, the problem can be reformulated by hierarchically grouping the troops into squads, platoons, companies, battalions, etc. The general can then position the battalions, and have the rest of the problem solve itself recursively at the lower levels of the command hierarchy.

The troop deployment problem is formally identical to the one we encountered in Chapter 6 (as well as earlier in this chapter) in the context of motor control. Its natural representation has the form of a landscape: a continuous surface over the state space, whose height encodes the desirability of the corresponding state (cf. the energy space representing arm configuration in Figure 6.5 on page 167, where the most desirable state is the lowest one). Computationally, solving any such problem is then a matter of HILL-CLIMBING: getting to the desired state — the peak that dominates the landscape — from the initial one.

In addition to providing an explanation of thinking in terms of an appealingly mindless process, approaching it as hill-climbing in the space of possible solutions also reveals the potential impediments to problem solving. In particular, while considering intuitive illustrations of hill-climbing such as the one shown in Figure 8.6, it is important to keep in mind that a landscape-

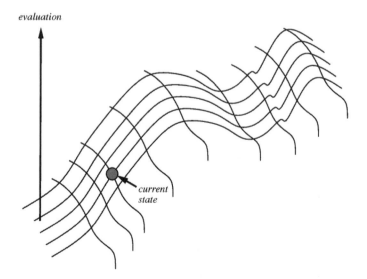

evaluation

current state

Figure 8.6 — Problem solving as HILL-CLIMBING. Given an evaluation function that can calculate the desirability of a state, solving the problem becomes equivalent to finding the highest point in the "landscape" thus generated. The dimensions of the space over which the desirability "surface" is defined are those of the problem space (illustrated here as two-dimensional) — each state corresponds to a particular point.

EMBODIED problem solving. In the Tucker and Ellis task illustrated here (Smith and Gasser, 2005, fig.3), the subject is required to answer, in each trial, the question "Is this a pitcher?" as rapidly as possible. Half the subjects answer "yes" by pressing a button on the right and half by pressing a button on the left. In this task, the participants are faster when the handle is on the same side as the "yes" button.

As Hutchins (2000) points out in discussing DISTRIBUTED COGNITION,[6] the Society of Mind theory (Minsky, 1985) implies that an individual's mind is distributed, too. This notion had been anticipated by Warren McCulloch (1947, p.309): "We must make and read our record in the world. This extends the circuits through our heads beyond our bodies, perhaps through other men."

like representation space does not automatically endow the system that embodies it with the ability to discern from afar the location of the highest peak. It is only possible for the system to examine the immediate environment of the state it is in (in chess, this corresponds to examining the immediate consequences of each possible move starting with the current state). Exploring the "terrain" beyond the current locale typically incurs time and memory costs and must therefore be done judiciously, by employing proper heuristics.

If the landscape is highly convoluted — a telltale of a complex problem — then hill-climbing based on local "altitude" information (that is, on the values of states neighboring the current one) can cause the search to terminate at a merely local maximum. This predicament (and how to get out of it) is an important subject matter in the field of Artificial Intelligence (see the note on simulated annealing on p. 229). Briefly, the idea is to introduce into the locally driven search process a random jitter that would, with a low probability, cause it to leave a local maximum in the hope that a trail leading to higher ground can be picked up farther on. The probability of such a random move can be made to decrease over time, so that eventually the search will terminate at the maximum it has converged upon.

Houston, we have a problem

Having been originally inspired by the analysis of human behavior (Newell and Simon, 1972), computational theory of problem solving has now come a full circle: search algorithms and heuristics developed by computer scientists are being recruited by psychologists in a renewed effort to model human cognition. One such study, for example, looked at how subjects seek a spatial arrangement of objects (coins on a tabletop) that would satisfy a given set of constraints (Chronicle, MacGregor, and Ormerod, 2004, p.24); the observed probabilities of correct first, second, and third moves conformed to those predicted by hill-climbing search.

A major challenge faced by controlled studies is how to extend the insights they afford to real-world problem solving — what Hutchins (1995) called "cognition in the wild." Natural problems are solved by methods that are characteristically EMBODIED and SITUATED (Smith and Gasser, 2005): they rely on the physics of the body and the environment (remember the fast-cornering cat from p. 24), and, in primates, on artifacts or natural objects that can be used as tools (cf. the orangutan behavior described on p. 196).

Problem solvers also often cooperate in their search for a solution, to the extent that their cognitive processing can be seen as DISTRIBUTED across several individuals (Hutchins, 2000). In studying distributed cognition, the traditional methods of cognitive social psychology and ethnography are very effectively supplemented by computational simulations, which allow experiments to be conducted rapidly and on a previously unheard of scale. Computational studies can also combine simulation with game-theoretic mathematical analysis, as was done by Hong and Page (2004), who showed, incidentally, that diverse problem solvers working together can outperform groups of uniformly high-ability problem solvers (in that study, each agent brought to the table its unique *perspective*, or set of background assumptions, and *heuristic*, or search algorithm).

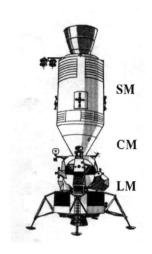

The Apollo spacecraft in the lunar transit configuration. The conical Command Module (CM) is shown here before its separation from the cylinder-shaped Service Module (SM). The Lunar Module (LM) is docked at the apex of the cone.

The theoretical and practical issues that arise in the psychology of human problem solving are brought into sharp focus by the manner in which NASA engineers and astronauts dealt with the aftermath of the explosion on board the Apollo 13 mission. The explosion of one of the two oxygen tanks in the Service Module (SM) damaged the other tank, depriving the SM of all of its oxygen supply. The astronauts' only chance of survival was to use the Lunar Module (LM) as a lifeboat. To do that, they had to make its air supply system, originally designed for two people for two days, support three people for four days. Ironically, their prospects of success (hence survival) hinged on solving a proverbially unsolvable problem: fitting a *square* object (the CO_2 filter from the CM) into a *round* hole (the filter receptacle in the LM; see Figure 8.7 on the next page).

The process whereby this problem was nevertheless solved in time to keep the crew alive has never been analyzed by cognitive psychologists, but even an informal survey readily reveals in it two familiar characteristics of "cognition in the wild." First, the process was *distributed*: the 19-step procedure was developed by a large crew of engineers at the mission control center, in close collaboration with the spacecraft's designers and with the astronauts themselves. Second, the improvised solution was *situated*: apart from the two lithium hydroxide canisters cannibalized from the Service Module, it used the following items: one cardboard cover to the Apollo 13 flight plan; one roll of gray duct tape; two plastic bags; two hoses from the astronauts' suits; two socks; and one bungee cord.[7]

A third characteristic of the quandary faced by the Apollo 13 team places it far outside the category of problems discussed earlier. It has to do not with the complexity of searching for a solution, but rather with the difficulty of formulating the relevant search space in the first place. The problems of the Towers of Hanoi, Tic Tac Toe, chess, and Go, which differ widely in the degree of challenge they present to a search algorithm, are all equally easy to *start* thinking about, because the form of the state space for each of them suggests itself immediately to anyone who has a notion of what this representation means. In comparison, it is not at all straightforward to come up with a natural, or even just useful, state-space representation of the Apollo 13 filters problem.

A computational strategy that can serve as a basis for approaching such ill-formulated problems — the MEANS-ENDS ANALYSIS — was proposed as early as 1957 by Newell, Shaw, and Simon (1959). The General Problem Solver (GPS) program they developed sought solutions by attempting to reduce the difference between the present and goal states through applying to a state-space representation of the problem operations known to be relevant to it. In the GPS, both the state space and the operators were user-supplied, but in principle the means-ends analysis is applicable to ill-formulated problems as well. In the Apollo 13 case, for example, a useful operator is one that reformulates the original problem in terms of making the connection between

Figure 8.7 — SITUATED PROBLEM SOLVING on board the Apollo 13 mission. The juryrigged attachment for the CO_2 chemical scrubber filter (square box, held together with duct tape), which had been cannibalized from the crippled Service Module, is shown here after its improvised installation in the Lunar Module.

the square filter and the circular receptacle airtight (this requires the insight that the filter does not have actually to fit *inside* the receptacle). Applying this operator would transform the original problem into one that is better focused, hence more likely to be solved.

It is interesting to note that the resulting process is still a kind of search, albeit in a space whose dimensions are as complex as the human conceptual system itself (cf. section 6.5). Airtightness, for instance, is a technical concept, which, although it seems to be most strongly associated with engineering, is encountered also in medicine (as a part of the concept of pneumothorax, or collapsed lung) and in air travel (rapid changes in cabin pressure induce ear pain if the Eustachian tubes connecting the middle ear to the pharynx are closed due to a common cold). Likewise, the precise structure of the operator that can map a state labeled "leaky" to a state labeled "airtight" depends on the situation: in the Apollo 13 problem, it involved a plastic bag and some duct tape, while in the case of a collapsed lung caused by a bullet, the pleural cavity can be made airtight by dressing the wound with an ointment-permeated gauze.

8.2.2 Mental models

To be useful for searching the conceptual state space of an ill-formulated problem, a "next state" operator must be capable of generating hypotheses about the consequences of complex actions (in a game such as chess, in contrast, the possible next states are fully determined simply by applying the game rules). In some cases, which I shall discuss later, in section 8.5.2, this requires sophistication that is commonly seen as creativity. More generally, problem solving in a conceptual space calls for a MENTAL MODEL — a simulation of a chunk of the external reality that pertains to the problem at hand.

Simulation

Cognitive conceptual simulation is a heavy gun, brought out when there is a need to anticipate and prepare for a potential problem, or to address one that already exists. Planning ahead need not always involve anything as complicated as simulation: when the NASA engineers decide to pack some duct tape on a space mission where every gram of extra weight matters, they merely capitalize on its record as a structural panacea. Cognitive simulation is, however, essential in developing plans for major contingencies, such as

If the organism carries a "SMALL-SCALE MODEL" of external reality and of its own possible actions within its head, it is able to try out various alternatives, conclude which is the best of them, react to future situations before they arise, utilize the knowledge of past events in dealing with the present and the future, and in every way react in a much fuller, safer, and more competent manner to the emergencies which face it.

— Craik (1952, p.61)

the possible incapacitation of the Apollo Service Module, for which NASA had prepared by developing the "Lunar Module as a lifeboat" scenario.

In the present book, simulation is a thread that runs through many diverse topics, beginning with the basics of cognitive representation (p. 20, Chapter 2), and culminating in the notion of active concepts (section 6.7, Chapter 6). In the brain, internal models that simulate the consequences of an action have been implicated in motor control (Kawato, 1999). Scanning experiments revealed that subjects engage in motor imagery in solving problems such as deciding whether a particular hand posture would be suitable for carrying out a particular action (Pelgrims, Andres, and Olivier, 2005). On a more abstract problem level, subjects working on a task analogous to the Towers of Hanoi showed activation of premotor and supplementary motor areas, as well as sensory areas of the brain (Hesslow, 2002).

Imagery-like processes are indeed known to subserve even the simplest perceptual tasks, as indicated, for example, by the behavioral findings of Barsalou (2003b), whose subjects resorted to perceptual simulation to generate properties of objects in response to a verbal query (cf. p. 202ff). The general theoretical framework developed by Barsalou (1999) suggests that simulation is a general feature of cognitive representation, permeating all perceptual processing and conceptual thinking.

Counterfactual thought

The most complex kind of conceptual thought involves generating hypotheses not only about the consequences of a planned action (what will be) but also about the unrealized consequences of an action never undertaken (what might have been). This so-called COUNTERFACTUAL thinking is omnipresent in human cognition (Byrne, 2002): asking WHAT IF questions about what could have happened if some imaginary condition were satisfied apparently helps young children learn how the world works, and helps adults learn from their mistakes. Counterfactuals are therefore of great interest to psychologists working on higher-level cognition.

Counterfactuals are also exciting for philosophers and logicians because they have the form of implications in which both the antecedent and the consequent are false. Distinguishing valid from invalid ones requires, therefore, reasoning about properties that the world might have had, which calls for special formal tools. One such tool is the "possible worlds" approach to semantics, which deals in propositions that can be true, false, or contingent (that

Is everything a field of energy caused by human projection? From the crib bars hang the teething tools. Above the finger-drummed desk, a bit lip. The cyclone fence of buts surrounds the soccer field of WHAT IF.
...
                                                                              Anyone
who has traveled here knows the discrepancies between idea and fact. The idea is the worm in the tequila and the next day is the fact.

                                                              Dean Young
                                I Am But a Traveler in This Land
                                    & Know Little of Its Ways
                                    (*Ploughshares*, Spring 2001)

is, true in some conceivable worlds, and false in others).[8] A possible worlds semantics makes it easier to formalize the meaning of modal propositions, expressed by sentences in the subjunctive mood, as in "I should have listened to the voice of reason."

Not listening to the voice of reason is often the cause for later REGRET — an emotion that turns out to be very closely associated with counterfactual thought. Both the experience of regret and counterfactual thinking are mediated by the same neural circuitry in the orbitofrontal cortex, as indicated by functional brain imaging studies (Camille, Coricelli, Sallet, Pradat-Diehl, Duhamel, and Sirigu, 2004; Coricelli, Critchley, Joffily, O'Doherty, Sirigu, and Dolan, 2005). In those studies, normal subjects playing a simple card game reported emotional responses consistent with counterfactual thinking, acted so as to minimize future regret, and learned from their experience. In comparison, subjects with orbitofrontal lesions neither reported regret nor anticipated negative consequences of their actions.

In addition to these *upward* counterfactuals, which focus on how the outcome of an action could have been better, people also generate *downward* counterfactuals, exploring ways in which things could have been worse (Byrne, 2002). The former are usually more frequent, although this depends on the subject's mood (cf. Figure 8.8) and on various social motivational factors, such as the need to console someone or make an excuse for an unexpected outcome. The ease with which people generate counterfactual statements and the regularities observed in counterfactuals generated by different

Figure 8.8 — To determine whether life could be worse or better, the brain must compute and compare probabilities of all possible world states. In practice, infinitely simpler heuristics often suffice.

[Continued from p. 283]

Man: I didn't expect a kind of Spanish Inquisition.

(JARRING CHORD - The door flies open and Cardinal Ximinez of Spain enters, flanked by two junior cardinals. Cardinal Biggles has goggles pushed over his forehead. Cardinal Fang is just Cardinal Fang)

Ximinez: NOBODY expects the Spanish Inquisition! Our chief weapon is surprise... surprise and fear... fear and surprise... Our two weapons are fear and surprise... and ruthless efficiency... Our *three* weapons are fear, surprise, and ruthless efficiency... and an almost fanatical devotion to the Pope... Our *four*... no... *Amongst* our weapons... Amongst our weaponry... are such elements as fear, surprise... I'll come in again.

(Exit and exeunt)

Man: I didn't expect a kind of Spanish Inquisition.

(JARRING CHORD - The cardinals burst in)

Ximinez: NOBODY expects the Spanish Inquisition! Amongst our weaponry are such diverse elements as: fear, surprise, ruthless efficiency, an almost fanatical devotion to the Pope, and nice red uniforms – Oh damn!

Table 8.1 — NOBODY EXPECTS THE SPANISH INQUISITION. An event that under normal circumstances would have been highly unlikely in the 20th century England anchors this sketch, taken from the *Monty Python's Flying Circus*, where unexpected developments are always to be expected.

subjects in similar situations are two complementary aspects of the most interesting computational issue behind this phenomenon, which is so central to human thinking.

The computational issue arises because there are usually very many possibly relevant antecedents that contribute to an outcome.[9] Consider for example an election in which two equally strong candidates compete over a large number of votes. A close outcome in such a process can be reasonably described as depending on millions of individual decisions concerning whether and how to vote, each of which in turn depends on many factors. The counterfactual "if X were the case, someone else would have been President now" can therefore take many specific forms in this case, depending on the expression that is substituted for X. Despite this, people generally come up with the same few possibilities when asked how the outcome could have been different (you easily can check this yourself, by polling your friends using the 2000 US presidential election as a test case).

Studies of this regularity reveal what Kahneman and Tversky (1982) referred to as the 'fault lines' of the imagination: the constraints that limit what people normally consider as plausible in thinking about alternatives to reality. In general, counterfactuals tend not to deviate too far from the state of affairs in the real world. Thus, in a poll concerning the US 2000 election example, it is very unlikely that any respondent will say that "if the brain of Justice Ruth Bader Ginsburg had been cloned and implanted in the cranium of Justice Antonin Scalia in early December 2000, someone else would have been President now" — simply because such an eventuality is itself very unlikely, given the state of the art in medical science in the year 2000.[10]

The relative uniformity of the patterns of counterfactuals generated by different people is thus readily explained by an ability that we know to be central to human cognition: gathering statistical information about the world. The representations of events held in memory are continually updated with the individual's experiences, as well as those of others, communicated through language. Furthermore, keeping track of sequential information — a faculty that culminates in the human capacity for language learning — makes it possible also to note statistical contingencies.

Statistical-structural learning thus endows a person with the knowledge of what is normal about a situation, as well as an ability to assess the relative likelihood of various outcomes of an action. This knowledge, in turn, supports the generation of counterfactuals that adhere to certain common patterns: a statistically normal event evokes representations that resemble it, whereas an abnormal event has highly prominent alternatives (Byrne, 2002; cf. Table 8.1 on the facing page). A certain heuristic control can be exerted over the relative mutability or 'slippability' of the attributes (dimensions) of a situation (about which I'll have more to say in section 8.5.2 that deals with creativity).

Meta-problem solving

The statistically induced structure of the conceptual system and of the many strata of cognitive processing that surround it greatly facilitates the solution of problems that one encounters in daily life. The facility with which people solve real existential problems, such as what to do when faced with thirst or hunger, belies the potential complexity of the first and most important step in solving a problem: understanding what it is about.

At the one extreme, this issue is made moot by habit — that is, a statistical regularity impressed upon the brain. When I am thirsty, I pretty much automatically seek a drink of water, rather than engage any of the various possible actions I could otherwise initiate in response to thirst, such as running around in circles, writing poetry, or praying.

At the other extreme, the generic *meta-problem* that always exists — evaluating the problematicity of a situation — is exacerbated by the immense variety of attributes that potentially apply. The indeterminacy here is due to the richness of the conceptual system (recall the "cow as projectile" concept from Chapter 6), which in turn is a reflection of the complexity of humanity's physical and social environment.

Without doubt, the most difficult problem that is part and parcel of the human condition is the not-uncommon situation in which the state of affairs in one's life is unsatisfactory, but it is not clear why or even in what respects it is so. If the *taṇhā* that bothers me is a feeling of unease that is only metaphorically like thirst, I may have serious difficulties in identifying those dimensions of my situation along which it differs from the goal, which itself may be only vaguely perceived by me. Albeit not insurmountable, that problem is outside the scope of this book.

8.3   Varieties of thinking: II. Reasoning

The existential problem that I just mentioned (only to set it aside), and many other kinds of problems that people encounter, requires that the prevailing

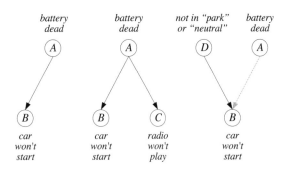

Figure 8.9 — Three MODES OF REASONING, illustrated with with graphical models (Bayes networks; cf. Figure 6.15 on page 192). *Left:* the link from *A* to *B* expresses belief that if the battery is dead, the car won't start. It can support CAUSAL REASONING: deducing *B*, given *A*. Interestingly, it can also support EVIDENTIAL REASONING (sometimes called ABDUCTION) from *B* to *A*. *Middle:* if *A* is known to cause *C* in addition to *B*, then observing both *B* and *C* strengthens the conclusion that *A* holds. *Right:* if, however, a new piece of evidence *D* emerges that offers a better account of *B* than *A* does, then *A* can be EXPLAINED AWAY by *D*.

state of affairs, and its causes, be analyzed, so that a plan for making things better can be developed. The computational tools for a principled analysis of situations and their causal relationships are based on a representational mechanism that we first encountered in Chapter 6: graphical models, or Bayes networks (see Figure 8.9).

Nilsson (2006, p.214), whose highly accessible and informative book is titled *How are we to know?*, uses simple Bayes nets to illustrate the most common modes of reasoning that people employ: (1) CAUSAL REASONING or deduction, (2) EVIDENTIAL REASONING or abduction, and (3) EXPLAINING AWAY. These techniques, and some of the computational issues they give rise to, are discussed next.

8.3.1 Logic and deduction

Is the sardonic view of human reasoning reflected in *The Devil's Dictionary* justified by psychological research? To address this question, we need to consider not only the empirical findings, but also the appropriateness of the standards against which reasoning is judged (McKenzie, 2003). Traditionally, these standards have been borrowed from formal LOGIC, a discipline that originated and developed over millennia as an idealization of the very faculty it is now expected to help evaluate — human reason itself.

Although logic has been for centuries more closely associated with philosophy and mathematics than with psychology, the great logicians never lost sight of the roots of their field, as suggested by the titles of landmark works such as Dharmakirti's 7th century *Seven Treatises on Valid Cognition*, George Boole's *An Investigation of the Laws of Thought, on which are founded the Mathematical Theories of Logic and Probabilities* (1854), and Gottlob Frege's *Concept Script, a formal language of pure thought modelled upon that of arithmetic* (1879).

Insofar as they were aiming at ironing out the imperfections of human reasoning, the logicians met with immediate success already in ancient times. Unfortunately for psychology, this meant that the formal framework for logic that emerged was too smooth to be a model of human cognition. Indeed, having recorded the foundations of formal logic in *Prior Analytics* (where his famous syllogisms are introduced), Aristotle proceeded to write *On Sophistical Refutations*, wherein he exposed many common logical fallacies. People fall so readily for them that it is hard to see how the notion of human as a

LOGIC
n. The art of thinking and reasoning in strict accordance with the limitations and incapacities of the human misunderstanding.

— Ambrose Bierce,
The Devil's Dictionary

"rational animal" (a definition that Aristotle himself offered in *Metaphysics*) can be taken seriously — if formal logic is used as a yardstick for rationality.

While Aristotle's syllogisms are rarely mentioned in modern logic texts, two modes of inference rooted in his work are still taught to psychology students everywhere (see for example Sternberg, 2003, chapter 11). These are *modus ponens*, the "mode that affirms," and *modus tollens*, the "mode that denies," which I have written down in the standard symbolic notation, as well as in plain English, in Table 8.2. Both are DEDUCTIVE, that is, they allow valid conclusions to be drawn from valid premises.

Although deduction does not generate new knowledge (that is, propositions not already implied by the premises), it is clearly relevant to cognition because it can be used, at least in principle, to determine the truth value of a proposition pertaining to something that is not directly observable. For example, in the dialog from Monty Python's *Argument Clinic* reproduced in the margin, one side (*Man*) attempts to prove to the other that payment (a past event, no longer observable) took place by pointing out that argument (an ongoing, hence observable, event) is taking place. I'll leave it to you to determine which reasoning mode is being called upon here.

modus ponens		*modus tollens*	
$P \rightarrow Q$	if P then Q	$P \rightarrow Q$	if P then Q
P	P is true	$\neg Q$	Q is false
$\vdash Q$	therefore Q is true	$\vdash \neg P$	therefore P is false

Table 8.2 — The two valid modes of deductive reasoning, stated symbolically, and in words. For a concrete example, see Figure 8.10 on the next page.

No matter how appealing deduction is, any prospects for putting it to good use clearly depend on the user's ability to conform to valid inference patterns, abstracting away details that have no bearing on the *form* of the argument. From what we have learned so far about the context-dependence of perception, memory, and language, there is no reason to expect that reasoning should be any different, and in point of fact people find it very difficult to apply whatever abstract knowledge of logic they may have to concrete situations in a manner that factors out the phrasing of the problem. As a result, two deduction problems that are couched in different terms yet formally equivalent typically evoke very different performance.

The well-known Wason selection task, illustrated in Figure 8.10, exemplifies this effect. Only a very small proportion of subjects who are given the abstract version of the problem (Figure 8.10, top) respond correctly. Alas, I do not belong to that exclusive minority: when trying to solve the Wason problem in real time in class, I usually get it wrong, and have to be set straight by the students. The very same logical task becomes much easier when given a more natural or realistic formulation, in which the subjects have to deal with familiar concepts such as beer, soda, and the minimum drinking age law (Figure 8.10, top).[11] In this version of the Wason task, most of the subjects respond correctly. Curiously, however, the proportion of correct responses can be manipulated by changing the age indicated on the cards: bringing it closer to the minimum legal raises the error rate — as if the subjects treated logical implication as graded!

The pronounced difference in performance in abstract vs. realistic versions of the selection task, along with the many other peculiarities that characterize human deductive reasoning (Evans, 2005), prompted psychologists to hypothesize the existence of two distinct thinking systems. According to this view, the more primitive System 1 comprises fast automatic associative processes that monitor natural situations and generate probabilistic assessments without recourse to conscious effort. System 2, in comparison, relies on time-consuming, deliberate consideration of the problem.

The notion that situated and abstract reasoning rely on separate systems is supported by a range of experimental findings (Evans, 2005), including imaging data that indicate differential involvement of distinct regions in the brain. Most notably, subjects who perform well in the abstract version of the selection task tend to have significantly higher SAT scores, but high per-

Figure 8.10 — Two versions of the Wason selection task. *Top:* flip cards that would allow you to verify the rule that *If a card has a vowel on one side, it has an odd number on the other side. Bottom:* flip cards that would allow you to verify the rule that *Anyone drinking beer is over 21.*

formers in the realistic version of this task do not (Stanovich and West, 1998). This finding links the two-systems explanation of the patterns of performance in reasoning to the much wider theoretical framework of GENERAL INTELLIGENCE. As we shall see in section 8.5, the key component of the latter is *working memory* — a very scarce resource, which people faced with a need to think typically try to augment by resorting to external memory (cf. Figure 6.25 on page 220).

In problem solving and reasoning, the most natural means of outsourcing working memory and other computational needs is talk. Indeed, it turns out that group discussion facilitates performance in the selection task (Evans, 2005).[12] Another time-tested way of externalizing computation is blackboard

Figure 8.11 — A screen shot of a fully functional simulation of the Enigma encryption device — a special-purpose computer (cf. note 9 on page 388). The Enigma simulator is available as a program for a modern generalpurpose computing environment. By executing a simulation program, my notebook becomes functionally indistinguishable from whatever computer that program describes: from the standpoint of the stream of that virtual computer's instructions, it is as real as it can be, and so is the input-output mapping that it computes. My notebook is then said to function as a VIRTUAL MACHINE (a technical concept in computer science, which is related to that of virtual computation, introduced back in section 6.7.3). A VM is a process that offers, usually by means of considerable extra computation, a functionality that is not directly available in the environment that supports it. Because it abstracts computation away from neurobiology, a VM implemented by the brain transcends the limitations of its parallel, associative probabilistic circuit architecture, such as the impossibility of flexible, random access to memory. The flexibility of the VM in this case comes at the cost of much slower, serial processing that is confined to low-capacity working memory. More on virtual machine architectures in section 8.5, which deals with general fluid intelligence.

and chalk, or paper and pencil, without which we would not have mathematics, science, or technology, including computers. It is the classical paper and pencil model of computation — the Turing Machine — that gives a concrete meaning to two systems theory of thinking. The key explanatory device here is a VIRTUAL MACHINE (Figure 8.11) — a basic concept in computer science, deftly introduced to non-specialists by Dennett (1991, p.216ff).

Once we realize that the brain can support the operation of a general-purpose virtual machine that is versatile yet demanding, the pattern of subjects' performance in various reasoning tasks becomes easier to understand. In particular, both reduced expectations and a dependence on general intelligence become the norm for abstract problems such as the "vowels and odd numbers" version of the Wason task, whose terminology does not resonate with the natural kinds represented by the conceptual system, and which therefore can only be solved by being passed on to the virtual machine.

8.3.2 Causal reasoning

As any textbook on logic will tell you, conclusions reached through deduction are only as good as the premises on which reasoning is based: false starting assumptions will cause further proliferation of error. As I noted in an earlier chapter (see p. 199), there is a natural computational framework for dealing with the kind of uncertainty that arises from the need to draw conclusions and plan actions in real-world situations — probability and statistics. When applied to the examples discussed above, this framework leads to CAUSAL REASONING, which is a probabilistic generalization of deduction.

For example, the Bayes network of Figure 8.9 on page 334, left, generalizes modus tollens, as follows: if P (battery dead) is thought to cause Q (car won't start), then an observation of $\neg Q$ (car starts) increases confidence in the falsity of P (battery ok). A similar generalization of modus ponens can be based on the same simple network.

The capacity for causal reasoning as it is embodied in Bayes networks is not confined to humans, or even primates: it has been demonstrated in rats (Blaisdell et al., 2006). Figure 8.12 summarizes the first experiment from that study, which showed that causal Bayes networks, but not classical associative schemes for knowledge representation, can account for the rats' performance. The key tool in the study was INTERVENTION, a concept that has a concrete computational meaning in causal Bayesian probability theory.

The researchers trained rats on each of the (associative) causal links be-

On inferring CAUSALITY from the effects of INTERVENTION. It is impossible to predict the effects of an intervention through associative learning that is merely observational: seeing is not a substitute for doing. Blaisdell, Sawa, Leising, and Waldmann (2006), who studied causal reasoning in rats, point out, "A dissociation between seeing and doing would be remarkable, because in the observational learning phase T is positively correlated with L." Their experiments (see Figure 8.12) revealed precisely this dissociation: only rats allowed to intervene in a simple pattern of events were able to figure out their causal relationships.

tween light (L), tone (T), food (F), and noise (N) in Figure 8.12, left top, then allocated each to one of four test conditions. Rats in condition intervene-T were presented with T each time they pressed a lever introduced into the enclosure; those in condition observe-T merely observed presentations of T independently of any lever presses they made. Conditions intervene-N and observe-N were identical, except that N was either the product of an intervention by lever pressing or was observed.

The rats' reduced expectation of food (F) in the intervene-T condition (see Figure 8.12, right) clearly indicates that they can distinguish between intervention and mere contingency.[13] As Blaisdell et al. (2006) note, simple transfer from observational learning can lead to inadequate predictions for interventions: while barometer readings statistically predict the weather, setting the barometer to "Falling" does not bring rain. The experiment just described shows that rats possess the basic computational ability to figure that out through a combination of seeing and doing.

8.3.3   Combining probabilities

The knowledge of the expected frequencies of events and of their causal interrelationships (for instance, how often cars refuse to start and car batteries die,

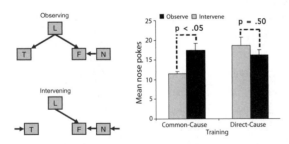

Figure 8.12 — CAUSAL REASONING in rats (Blaisdell et al., 2006, Fig.1). *Left top*: in separate trials, the animal learns associatively that a light cue (L) precedes a tone stimulus (T) or food (F), and that noise (N) co-occurs with F. *Left bottom*: if in the next phase the rat learns that by pressing a lever it can activate T (an INTERVENTION), it should be more reluctant to expect F in conjunction with T. *Right*: as predicted by a causal Bayes network model (but not by simple associative learning), in the test phase the rats poked for food in response to T ("Common-Cause"; left) less often in the Intervene condition (gray bars) than in the Observe condition (black bars). No such difference was observed for the responses to noise N in the two conditions ("Direct-Cause"; right). See text for a discussion of the implications of this result.

and also how often cars don't start because of a dead battery) must be learned from experience. Because the infinity of possible combinations of events can never be observed by a system with a finite life span, and because certain events cannot be directly observed in any case (cf. Figure 6.15 on page 192), the brain must compute some of the probabilities it needs for problem solving and reasoning from estimates of the available observables.

A pioneering study conducted by Tversky and Kahneman in 1972 revealed that human performance in a simple instance of this general and important task is far from perfect (Table 8.3). Their subjects were presented with a short description of an imaginary person ("Linda") and were asked to judge the relative probability of various statements about her in the light of the supplied data. The outcome was striking: 89% of naive subjects incorrectly judged the statement "Linda is a bank teller and is active in the feminist movement" (line *h* in Table 8.3) as more probable than "Linda is a bank teller" (line *f* in the table). Graduate students in the decision science program of the Stanford Business School who were administered the same test did no better: 85% judged that *h* was more probable than *f* (Tversky and Kahneman, 1983).

Table 8.3 — The setting for the 1972 demonstration of the CONJUNCTION FALLACY by Tversky and Kahneman (see text for an explanation).

Linda is 31 years old, single, outspoken, and very bright. She majored in philosophy. As a student, she was deeply concerned with issues of discrimination and social justice, and also participated in anti-nuclear demonstrations. Please rank the following statements by their probability, using 1 for the most probable and 8 for the least probable:

a. Linda is a teacher in elementary school.

b. Linda works in a bookstore and takes Yoga classes.

c. Linda is active in the feminist movement.

d. Linda is a psychiatric social worker.

e. Linda is a member of the League of Women Voters.

f. Linda is a bank teller.

g. Linda is an insurance sales person.

h. Linda is a bank teller and is active in the feminist movement.

Because a conjunction of two events (represented by the intersection of the two corresponding areas in a Venn diagram) cannot be more probable than either of them, this widespread error became known as the CONJUNCTION FALLACY.

Presenting the problem in terms of FREQUENCIES rather than probabilities reduces the incidence of the CONJUNCTION FALLACY in many tasks (Cosmides and Tooby, 1996), but does not prevent it altogether: patterns of judgment remain sensitive to the semantics and the pragmatics of the problem — that is, to its phrasing and context (Hertwig and Gigerenzer, 1999).

Subsequent experiments showed that reformulating the problem in terms that better fit the manner in which the human cognitive system deals with numbers brings about a radical improvement in performance. As in the modified version of the Wason task in which the cards carry descriptions of real-life situations, fewer subjects exhibit the conjunction fallacy if the "Linda" task is presented in a form that stresses FREQUENCIES instead of probabilities. Particularly influential was a study by Cosmides and Tooby (1996), who asked their subjects, " There are 200 people who fit the description above; how many of them are: (1) bank tellers? (2) bank tellers and active in the feminist movement?" Only 22% of the subjects ranked the feminist bank teller option above the bank teller option (as a control, Cosmides and Tooby replicated the original Tversky & Kahneman experiment, obtaining as expected a 91% incidence for the conjunction fallacy).

A common feature of the easy versions of the Wason selection task, the conjunction task, and many others in which the difficult versions give rise to COGNITIVE ILLUSIONS is that they feel natural.   Cosmides and Tooby (1997) explain this in evolutionary terms: for a task to appear natural, it must fit closely a pre-existing ability, which in the light of the theory of evolution must be an adaptation that meets a certain cognitive need. In the case of the Wason task, the cognitive need is to detect cheaters — people whose actions violate established norms (this task becomes easy when phrased in terms of drinking age enforcement; recall Figure 8.10 on page 337, bottom). In the Linda task, the cognitive need is to keep track of population frequencies; this task (but not all conjunction tasks; see the margin note on the preceding page) becomes easy when phrased in terms of frequencies instead of probabilities.

COGNITIVE ILLUSIONS. "Why are we susceptible to *these* illusions? The evolutionary psychologist says: For the same reason we are susceptible to optical illusions and other sensory illusions — we're built that way."

— Dennett (1995, pp. 488-490)

"Because of these evolutionary time lags, humans can be said to live in a modern world, but they are burdened with a STONE AGE BRAIN designed to deal with ancient adaptive problems, some of which are long forgotten."

— Buss, Haselton, Shackelford, Bleske, and Wakefield (1998)

The proponents of the evolutionary movement in psychology often compare the mind to a Swiss army knife with a multitude of specialized blades and attachments; any task for which a ready-made attachment can be found will feel natural and be easy to solve (Dennett, 1995). Evolutionary psychologists have been busy identifying and classifying such cases, making significant explanatory progress on a wide front of cognitive, personality, and social issues (Cosmides and Tooby, 1997; Pinker, 2002).

While evolutionary psychology is definitely a Good Idea (because nothing in biology makes sense except in the light of evolution), its application to cognition needs to be integrated with computational theories — because NOTHING IN COGNITION MAKES SENSE EXCEPT IN THE LIGHT OF COMPUTATION. Following Cosmides, many researchers call adaptations that evolve to meet specific cognitive needs *Darwinian algorithms* or *schemata* (we have encountered the latter concept before, also in the context of evolutionary computation, in Chapter 6; see p. 228). On the evolutionary account, those algorithms that are actually employed by the brain are there at the expense of others, which did not fare as well in contributing to their host's fitness. What makes some algorithms better than others?

This question can only be fully addressed within the Marr-Poggio computational framework. Understanding why some algorithms are better than others requires a computational analysis of the problem, and of its possible solutions in a neural substrate.[16] Evolutionary theory fits neatly around this framework. On the abstract-computational side of the Marr-Poggio explanatory scale, the form of the problems that the brain solves is determined by evolutionary factors. On the concrete, implementational side, evolutionary considerations regulate the trade-off between reliance on a flexible, but expensive, general-purpose computation engine and the use of fast and cheap, yet difficult-to-adapt, special-purpose neural circuits.

Much as I wanted to offer a graphical illustration of this trade-off, my search was doomed: while there are plenty of pictures of engagingly complicated Rube Goldberg contraptions, none can be found of their opposite, a universal gadget. There is, of course, a very good reason for that: a truly universal gadget can only exist in the information domain. I am at this moment using one: it is a general-purpose programmable computer, which is what my notebook happens to be — and which my brain can emulate, slowly and painstakingly, in its virtual machine mode.

8.3.4 The Induction Problem

Both deduction and its probabilistic generalization, causal reasoning, depend on the availability of knowledge about the situation at hand. The process whereby one acquires such knowledge — that is, true (or at least probable) propositions and their implications — is INDUCTION. Inductive inference is what makes generalization from examples possible (recall the discussion of perceptual learning and categorization in Chapter 5). As we shall see next, the computational nature of induction in reasoning is precisely the same as in perception.

NOTHING IN BIOLOGY MAKES SENSE EXCEPT IN THE LIGHT OF EVOLUTION.

— Dobzhansky (1973)

MATHEMATICS VS. SCIENCE. The contrast between deductive and inductive reasoning may be illustrated by comparing two outstanding human enterprises that rely on them: mathematics, which relies exclusively on deduction,[14] and science, which is mostly about induction. In mathematics, reasoning proceeds from preset premises or axioms, which are usually specific to each field, to theorems (cf. the note on formal systems on p. 308). For example, arithmetic in its modern form is derived from a set of axioms formulated by Giuseppe Peano in 1889. The set of theorems logically implied by a given set of axioms is infinite;[15] moreover, axioms themselves are not immutable (questioning Euclid's fifth postulate in the 19th century led to the development of non-Euclidean geometries). This makes mathematics open-ended, and therefore interesting — beside being useful to science (Wigner, 1960).

Mathematics is useful to science in matters that relate to deductive inference, that is, in figuring out the implications of existing knowledge. The most exciting aspects of science, however, have to do with the generation of new knowledge. One way of doing that is to infer a general case (a law of nature), from specific instances (the measurements that serve as data). In cognition, such INDUCTIVE INFERENCE underlies a wide range of functions.

Consider the following inductive argument task, which is often used by researchers who study reasoning and its development:

Chimps are susceptible to the disease blicketitis.
Squirrels are susceptible to the disease blicketitis.
_____
Horses are susceptible to the disease blicketitis.

The subject's task here is to decide whether or not the conclusion (the statement below the line) is warranted by the premises (the statement(s) above the line); posing the question in terms of a nonce feature represented by an invented word neutralizes possible interference from prior knowledge of that feature.

INDUCTION IN CHILDREN. Because induction is concerned with the acquisition of knowledge, it is of great interest to developmental psychologists (Keil, 1989; Markman, 1989).

Lessons learned from dozens of studies of induction involving this and other tasks are summarized in Table 8.4, which lists the main factors that affect the subjects' propensity to accept a specified conclusion, given the

Table 8.4 — The main effects that characterize the use of inductive inference (after Heit, 2000).

Inferences from Single Cases
1. Similarity between premise and conclusion categories promotes induction.
2. Typicality of the premise category promotes induction.
3. Homogeneity of the conclusion category promotes induction.

Inferences from Multiple Cases
4. Greater number of observations, or premises, promotes induction (although the evidence is weak for children).
5. Greater diversity of observations, or premises, promotes induction (although the evidence is mixed for children, and too much diversity may not help even for adults).

Influence of Properties
6. There is widespread evidence that people draw inferences differently depending on the property being projected (found in adults and children).
7. Some properties are idiosyncratic or transient, with a narrow scope for inferences, whereas other properties are more broadly projected.
8. The assessment of similarity between categories in an argument depends on the property being projected.

premises (Heit, 2000). It is interesting to observe that all these factors are statistical. For example, *similarity* (Table 8.4, line 1), a theoretical construct that is very popular with psychologists, has been first derived by Shepard (1987) (recall Chapter 5, p. 114) from the basic principles of probability theory. Shepard's work was subsequently extended by Tenenbaum and Griffiths (2001), culminating in a universally applicable definition according to which the similarity of two events (objects, categories, etc.) equals the logarithm of their likelihood ratio under a common probability distribution that gives rise to both (Kemp, Bernstein, and Tenenbaum, 2005).[17]

Within probability theory, a rigorous computational basis for inductive inference is provided by Bayes' Theorem, which we already encountered in Chapter 5 (see also Appendix A). Bayesian inference (Box 8.1 on the following page) formalizes the following commonsense principle: a hypothesis under consideration is acceptable to the extent that (1) it is likely in the light of prior knowledge, (2) it is compatible with the observed data, and (3) the data it explains are surprising or otherwise unexpected (Tenenbaum et al., 2006).

> PLAUSIBILITY is a very desirable attribute of a hypothesis; as Tenenbaum, Griffiths, and Niyogi (2006) note, "One can always construct some post-hoc hypothesis that is consistent with a particular experimental finding, but such a hypothesis would not be considered a good explanation for the data unless it was a well-motivated and principled consequence of our background knowledge."

The intuitive appeal of this idea can be understood by considering the possible reasons to believe that a hypothesis h is true in the light of data D (the notation is the same as in Box 8.1). First, the hypothesis must predict the data. The stronger the predictions that h makes about D, the more support h should receive from the observation of D. Second, the hypothesis must be PLAUSIBLE given everything else we know. These two factors form the numerator of Bayes' Rule: the posterior probability assigned to some hypothesis h after seeing D is proportional to the product of its prior probability $P(h|K)$, which captures its *a priori* plausibility, and the likelihood $P(D|h,K)$, which measures the extent to which D is predicted by h.[18]

Bayesian theory is not just an abstract framework for statistical inference and decision-making: it can be used to construct concrete and detailed computational models of human behavior in various tasks. One such task, in which the subjects are required to induce a rule — a numerical concept — that underlies a set of numbers they are given, has been modeled by Tenenbaum (2000). Suppose that you are given the set $\{16, 8, 2, 64\}$; how would you describe it? What about $\{60, 80, 10, 30\}$? The "obvious" hypotheses — "powers of 2" in the first case, and "multiples of 10" in the second — are by no means unique. The first set can also be described as "even numbers" and the second one as "multiples of 5." The induction problem is thus *underdetermined*, just as the problem of perception is, as we learned in Chapter 5.

Box: 8.1 — Bayesian inference in inductive reasoning (after Tenenbaum, Griffiths, and Niyogi, 2006).

Bayesian inference is a general framework that specifies how rational agents should approach induction. Consider an agent that is searching a space of hypotheses H for the possible processes that generated the observed data D. The agent's *a priori* beliefs about the plausibility of each hypothesis in that space, $h \in H$ – before taking into account D but drawing upon background knowledge K – are expressed by the *prior* conditional probability distribution $P(h|K)$. The principles discussed in the main text prescribe how the agent should modify his or her or its current beliefs in light of the data D. The desired outcome is expressed by the *posterior* conditional probability distribution $P(h|D,K)$, which is computed from the known quantities according to Bayes' Rule:

$$P(h|D,K) = \frac{P(D|h,K)P(h|K)}{P(D|K)} \tag{8.1}$$

In this expression, the *likelihood* $P(D|h,K)$ expresses the predictions of each hypothesis h in the form of the probability of observing D if h were true. The denominator, $P(D|K)$, is an average of the predictions of all hypotheses in the hypothesis space, weighted by their prior probabilities:

$$P(D|K) = \sum_{h' \in H} P(D|h',K)P(h'|K) \tag{8.2}$$

This term serves to normalize the product that appears in the numerator, ensuring that the posterior $P(h|D,K)$ sums to 1 and can therefore be interpreted as a proper probability distribution over the hypotheses.

Bayes' Rule is very easy to derive from the definition of conditional probability; the four-line proof can be found in Appendix A.

To appreciate the generality of Bayes' Rule, note that the formulation that appears above is precisely equivalent to that of Box 5.1 on page 120 in Chapter 5: the hypothesis h is analogous to shape S, the data D to the image I, and the prior knowledge K to the knowledge of object category C.

The challenge in modeling induction in the numbers task lies in explaining why is it that people tend to offer solutions that they do. According to the Bayesian model, there are two main contributing factors here: the preferred solution is the one that best explains the data, and also is the most *a priori* plausible. In the first example above, both hypotheses — "powers of 2" and "even numbers" — explain the data equally well, so the people's preference for the former must come from the other source: prior plausibility. The model of Tenenbaum (2000) captures this effect by introducing the notion of hypothesis *size*: because there are many more even numbers than powers of two, the latter hypothesis assigns a larger probability to the same data set (assuming that the examples in the data set are obtained by uniform random sampling from the space of all possible examples). The success of the Bayesian approach in replicating the details of human inductive inference in this task and another one is illustrated in Figures 8.13 and 8.14.

8.3.5 Evidential reasoning

Even in the small-scale tasks described above, it is impossible to give proper consideration to *all* the hypotheses that would be consistent with the observed data. In more natural situations, the diversity and the sheer size of a typ-

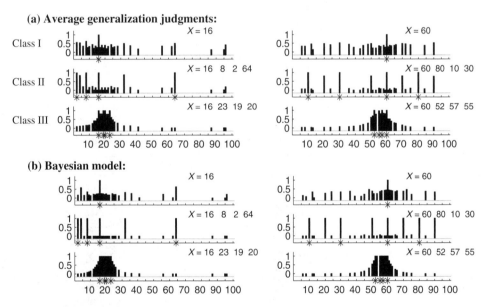

Figure 8.13 — Testing a BAYESIAN MODEL of inductive generalization in the numerical concepts task (Tenenbaum, 2000). In each trial, subjects were shown one or more examples of a numerical concept and asked to rate the probability that each of 30 test numbers would belong to the same concept. There were three kinds of trials: Class I trials – one number from each concept (e.g., {16}); Class II trials – four numbers, consistent with a simple rule (e.g., {16,4,2,64}); Class III trials – four random numbers of similar magnitude (e.g., {16,23,19,20}). The plots show the ratings generated for various test numbers by the human subjects and by the Bayesian model. The model fit the data extremely well (correlation $\rho = 0.99$).

ical hypothesis space would be truly daunting, presenting a computational problem that is exacerbated by the possibility of an observation having many causes (a point I made earlier in the discussion of counterfactuals). To avoid getting bogged down in computation (and acting most of the time like a deer caught in the headlights), a cognitive system must employ a reasoning method that would allow it to jump to conclusions — GUESS — and get away with it. Let me explain what I mean using this dialog between two fictional personages, Sherlock Holmes and Dr. Watson (the narrator), from Arthur Conan Doyle's novel *The Sign of Four*:

"I never GUESS."

— Sherlock Holmes
(in Arthur Conan Doyle's
The Sign of Four)

But we must conquer the truth by guessing, or not at all.

— Charles S. Peirce, Ms. 692
(Peirce, 1960)

But you spoke just now of observation and deduction. Surely the one to some extent implies the other.

"Why, hardly," he answered, leaning back luxuriously in his armchair and sending up thick blue wreaths from his pipe. "For example, ob-

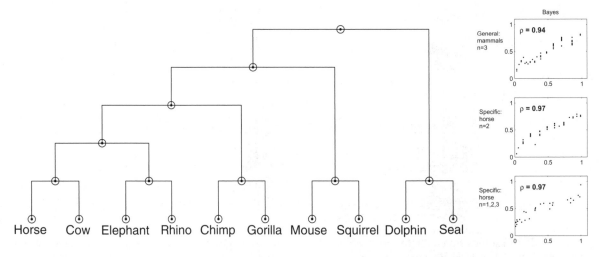

Figure 8.14 — Testing a BAYESIAN MODEL of inductive generalization in the animal concepts task introduced on p. 344. This study (Sanjana and Tenenbaum, 2002) modeled human judgments of the relative strengths of inferences of the form shown on p. 344, with different pairs of mammals given as examples (premises) and different test species (conclusion). *Left:* the hypothesis space required by Bayes' Rule was generated from this hierarchical clustering of the human reports of conceptual similarity between animals. *Right:* scatter plots showing the high correlations between human and model judgments in three variants of the induction task.

servation shows me that you have been to the Wigmore Street Post-Office this morning, but deduction lets me know that when there you dispatched a telegram."

"Right!" said I. "Right on both points! But I confess that I don't see how you arrived at it. It was a sudden impulse upon my part, and I have mentioned it to no one."

"It is simplicity itself," he remarked, chuckling at my surprise – "so absurdly simple that an explanation is superfluous; and yet it may serve to define the limits of observation and of deduction. Observation tells me that you have a little reddish mould adhering to your instep. Just opposite the Wigmore Street Office they have taken up the pavement and thrown up some earth, which lies in such a way that it is difficult to avoid treading in it in entering. The earth is of this peculiar reddish tint which is found, as far as I know, nowhere else in the neighbourhood. So much is observation. The rest is deduction."

The method of reasoning described by Conan Doyle in this passage is in fact neither "deduction" nor induction: rather, it is what Charles Sanders Peirce called ABDUCTION, better known in modern Bayesian theory as EVIDENTIAL REASONING.

Evidential reasoning is a computationally well-founded formalization of the process of guessing and getting away with it (in most practical cases; I shall mention some of the limitations of this technique later). Apart from the observation that prompts the chain of inference, it relies on prior knowledge, which can be encoded in the form of a causal probabilistic network (recall Figure 8.9 on page 334). If a particular phenomenon is thought to cause a second one, then observing the second provides some evidence for the first — an inference that can be used to increase the strength of belief in the first phenomenon. Furthermore, two such pieces of evidence combine to increase the belief in the first even more; a combination of evidence may suffice to support a conclusion that the individual sources alone might not (Nilsson, 2006).

EVIDENTIAL REASONING, or abduction, is not merely a plot device in crime fiction: its computational properties are increasingly appreciated by theorists studying trial law. In addition, much of the contemporary research on abduction is carried out in the context of medical reasoning (Holyoak and Morrison, 2005, Ch.30).

8.3.6 Explaining away

To illustrate the next phenomenon in reasoning that I would like to discuss, I return to the point in the dialog between Watson and Holmes where I left off on the previous page:

"How, then, did you deduce the telegram?"

"Why, of course I knew that you had not written a letter, since I sat opposite to you all morning. I see also in your open desk there that you have a sheet of stamps and a thick bundle of postcards. What could you go into the post-office for, then, but to send a wire? Eliminate all other factors, and the one which remains must be the truth."

Deduction is logically SOUND, or truth-preserving: it is guaranteed to produce true conclusions from true premises (axioms). In comparison, inductive and abductive reasoning modes are not sound; they can, in fact, be identified with logical fallacies known since Aristotle's times. In his celebrated treatment of induction, Hume (1748) observed that even the conclusion that the sun will rise tomorrow cannot be justified on the grounds that it did so many times in the past. Nevertheless, inductive and abductive reasoning is clearly enormously effective in practice. Relying on past performance in expecting future results is foolhardy in some settings (such as stock market speculation), but in our natural evolutionary niche it is actually a very reasonable choice (Fogelin, 2003); hence the ubiquity of statistical inference in cognition — and in science.[19]

In Victorian times (and indeed throughout the history of the telegraph as a means of rapid communication), sending someone a telegram was much more expensive than mailing a letter. Why then did Holmes "deduce" that Watson visited the post office with the purpose of sending a telegram, when the more plausible prior should have been mailing a letter? Because additional data (not one but two observations, in fact) EXPLAINED AWAY what would have been the preferred default account of the original observation — a visit to the post office, inferred abductively from the presence of mud on Watson's shoes. The procedure of explaining away (recall Figure 8.9 on page 334, right) uses causal reasoning to defeat competing evidential reasoning. An entertaining and informative account of the reasoning method of Sherlock Holmes as compared to the philosophy of Charles Sanders Peirce can be found in a book edited by Eco and Sebeok (1988).

8.3.7 The Frame Problem

Explaining away a conclusion from an earlier round of reasoning by taking into account newly available evidence amounts to an observation-driven revision of belief. Even deductive reasoning, which unlike induction and abduction is logically SOUND, is not exempt from revision. Introducing a new axiom — something that applications of logic to real life may require — can invalidate previously derived conclusions (theorems). The process of belief revision gives rise to a critically important computational problem: the need to identify which of the currently held beliefs are affected by the new data. This problem, which is inherent to reasoning, and is therefore shared by all cognitive systems that attempt to reason, natural or artificial, is known as the FRAME PROBLEM (McCarthy and Hayes, 1969).

The Frame Problem is difficult because in principle the amount of computation required to propagate the effects of new evidence through the database of "facts" and beliefs (what Artificial Intelligence researchers call truth maintenance) is too large: for each affected item, one must check all possible items causally related to it, then, recursively, all the implications of those, and so on. The number of items touched by the resulting wave of change grows exponentially with the size of the database — a sure sign of intractability.

McCarthy and Hayes (1969), who formulated the Frame Problem, did so within a deductive framework, with the goal of expressing all the consequences of introducing a new piece of evidence in terms of (i) the prior state of the belief system, (ii) a logical specification of the affecting action, and (iii) a set of fixed axioms describing possible effects of change. They have discovered that to make this approach work they had to introduce special *frame axioms*, spelling out for each possible action not only what changes, but also what doesn't.

Not surprisingly, the number of such frame axioms quickly grows out of hand for any realistic situation, most of them being so bizarre as to raise serious doubts concerning the plausibility of this approach as a model of human reasoning (even if tractability were not an issue). Consider what happens when I flip the light switch in my kitchen. A causal model laid down by previous experience predicts that the light will come on. This conclusion can be defeated by a new piece of knowledge, namely, that the light bulb is burned out. The key issue here is to specify what a burned-out light bulb does *not* change. How do I know that flipping a light switch with the bulb burned out, if done between 2:00am and 2:01am on a moonless night, would not cause the noses of all four faces on Mt. Rushmore to fall off?

Common sense, ever on the side of sane Empiricism, suggests that such outlandish hypotheses are never entertained by people simply because there is no reason to project the possible consequences of an action beyond limits determined by past experience or prior knowledge. According to the "sleeping-dog" strategy based on this idea, "A system can let sleeping representations lie, unless there is a positive reason to wake them" (Lormand, 1990). In AI, this is known as the *default* stance with respect to framing possible implications of change: unless specified explicitly, the effect of an event X on a belief Y is nil by default. In Bayes network terms, this means that by default there is no link between random X and Y. In this sense, Bayes networks are SPARSE; the great benefit of sparseness is that it makes many inference operations, including those required to compute the consequences of change, tractable (Glymour, 2001).

8.3.8   Heuristics

The sleeping-dog strategy is in essence heuristic. Resorting to default reasoning in order to alleviate the Frame Problem in deductive inference — that is, ignoring anything I don't know about — leaves open the possibility that something I don't know will hurt me. Nevertheless, the evolutionary success of species for which there is behavioral evidence of the use of Bayesian mechanisms for thinking — for example, rats (Blaisdell et al., 2006) and humans (Gopnik et al., 2004) — indicates that heuristics can be both computationally effective and reliable.

In a review titled *Reasoning the fast and frugal way: models of bounded rationality*, Gigerenzer and Goldstein (1996) quote Herbert Simon, who wrote, "Human rational behavior is shaped by a scissors whose two blades are the structure of task environments and the computational capabilities of the actor." Simon's metaphor can be elaborated upon: heuristics is the pivot that connects the two blades. The use of heuristic, approximate reasoning is dictated, on the one hand, by the limitations of the cognitive system itself: neither the human brain nor, in fact, any other feasible computational device, can contend with the kind of intractability that arises in searching exponen-

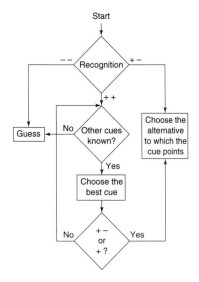

Figure 8.15 — The TAKE THE BEST heuristic reasoning algorithm (Chase et al., 1998, fig.1) solves problems such as deciding which of two cities is larger, given fragmented and incomplete information designed to simulate the typical state of knowledge of human subjects facing an unfamiliar question domain. The algorithm iterates over the available cues, stopping immediately upon finding the first cue that discriminates between the two responses. In this flow chart, "+ -" means that one of the two cues is familiar, "+ +" that both are, and "- -" that neither is. Gigerenzer and Goldstein (1996) remark that this algorithm "is hardly a standard statistical tool for inductive inference: It does not use all available information, it is noncompensatory and nonlinear, and variants of it can violate transitivity [that is, choosing A over B, B over C, and C over A]. Thus, it differs from standard linear tools for inference such as multiple regression, as well as from nonlinear neural networks that are compensatory in nature. What we call one-reason decision making is a specific form of SATISFICING. The inference, or decision, is based on a single, good reason."

tially growing solution spaces. On the other hand, it is the structured nature of the world (recognized as crucially important by Simon (1973); cf. p. 31) that makes heuristic corner-cutting a viable approach.

The main principle behind the theory of human reasoning of Gigerenzer and Goldstein (1996) is what Simon (1957) called SATISFICING — a neologism that combines "satisfying" and "sufficing," familiar to us from Chapter 5, where I mentioned it in the context of "good enough" representations in perception (p. 105).[20] It is exemplified by the TAKE THE BEST heuristic algorithm (see Figure 8.15), which has been developed to model human reasoning in tasks that require inference from memory, such as "Which city has more inhabitants: (a) Heidelberg or (b) Bonn?"

The performance of human subjects tested with such questions exhibits several curious characteristics, among them a "less is more" phenomenon: subjects who know less (e.g., US students asked about German cities) perform better than those who know more (German students; similarly, German students outperform their US counterparts when asked about US cities). Gigerenzer and Goldstein (1996) subjected the Take The Best algorithm, along with several competing algorithms, to extensive testing using such questions, by simulating 252,000 individuals with varying kinds and degrees of knowledge about cities in Germany. Each of these was tested on the exhaustive set of 3,403 city pairs, resulting in a total of about 858 million trials.

In this simulated competition, which required that inferences be drawn about unknown features of a real-world environment, the Take The Best algorithm performed as well as any of the competitor algorithms (which attempted to integrate as much information as possible before deciding), and better than some. Gigerenzer and Goldstein (1996) conclude their paper by remarking, "Models of inference do not have to forsake accuracy for simplicity. The mind can have it both ways."

8.4 Varieties of thinking: III. Decision making

Decision making differs from the two previously discussed kinds of thinking in its inseparability from the thinker's personality and, more often than not, emotional state. In problem solving, setting the goal is certainly subject to personal influences, but its pursuit can be analyzed in objective computational terms (whether or not the thinker in fact carries out such an analysis is a different matter). Likewise, in reasoning, each inference mode is characterized by certain objective computational constraints (which, again, may or may not resonate with the thinker). In decision making, in contrast, objective factors (what the world affords) are interwoven with subjective ones: what the cognitive agent will decide to do depends on what he or she or it values.

The subjectivity of decision making does not render it particularly mysterious or less suitable to computational analysis; it merely means that a few more numbers, which represent the values placed by the agent on various possible outcomes, need to be fed into the decision process. This requirement sets the stage for a general framework for formulating decision problems: SUBJECTIVE UTILITY THEORY (Figure 8.16).

Problems involving subjective utility are easy to formulate, and often easy to solve, but very difficult to solve in a manner that would precisely reproduce a solution generated by a particular individual in a specific context. This difficulty is reflected in the psychological literature in review articles that decry the slow progress towards a general model of human decision making (for some examples, see Mellers, Schwartz, and Cooke, 1998 or Holyoak and Morrison, 2005, ch.11-13). The perceived lack of progress is often associated with the many unexplained "paradoxes" — situations in which human decision patterns deviate from those dictated by normative models of rational choice borrowed from economics or sociology (Glimcher and Rustichini, 2004).

The proliferation of paradoxes of choice and other unexplained "effects," which makes reviews of human decision making look like laundry lists of barely related phenomena, is starting to transform both psychology, which no longer unquestioningly imports artificial notions of rationality, and eco-

In psychology and economics, a VALUE FUNCTION maps an *objective measure of value* — milliliters of orange juice that a monkey obtains in return for a correct decision in a psychophysical experiment, or calories that a robin gains following a decision to explore a remote but insect-rich field, or dollars that a venture capitalist earns by having invested in a successful business start-up — into a *subjective measure of desirability*.

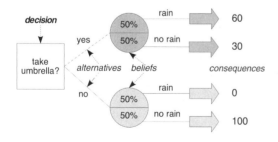

Figure 8.16 — The SUBJECTIVE UTILITY THEORY (Sanfey et al., 2006) accommodates the abundant psychological evidence of violations of the principles of rational economics by making choice and judgment subject to situational and personal context. The decision — in this example, whether or not to take an umbrella when leaving home — thus becomes dependent on utility: for each potential outcome, situation-dependent subjective VALUE weighted by probability.

nomics and sociology — disciplines that until recently were largely unconcerned with what Mellers et al. (1998) refer to as "behavioral assumptions."

Within a computational explanatory framework, there are two sources of
such "assumptions." First, there are extra data that influence utility, which
have no place in the traditionally narrowly defined formulations of decision
making. These are the variables that each of us brings to any problem that,
unlike playing chess or figuring out the causal structure underlying the operation of a game console, is defined in terms of values. Second, there are
the idiosyncrasies of the mechanisms that process the data relevant to each
decision. Being heuristic in nature, these mechanisms are highly diverse both
in their composition and in the manner of their deployment.

MOTIVATED REASONING. Dawson, Gilovich, and Regan (2002) studied the effects of the participants' subjective interpretation of the Wason task. For subjects in one group, the task involved a rule that, if true, would imply their own early death (Study 1) or the confirmation of a personally offensive stereotype (Study 2); in the control group, the negative rule was not directed personally at the subjects. The first, but not the second, group was therefore motivated to seek disconfirmation, an attitude known to help in the Wason task. As expected, in Study 1 the first group performed at 46% correct, compared to 10% for the control group. In Study 2, the results were similar: 52% correct, vs. 16% for the control. As Dawson et al. (2002) remark, "Favorable propositions appear to elicit a search for confirmation; unfavorable propositions elicit a search for disconfirmation."

8.4.1 From reward to utility

To realize the uniquely important role of subjective utility in decision making,
we must compare it to the kinds of subjectivity found elsewhere in thinking.
Consider, for example, MOTIVATED REASONING (Dawson et al., 2002). In
this class of phenomena, the subjective interpretation of the normative deductive rules proves to be as potent as the rules themselves in guiding inference.
There is, however, a crucial difference between the sense in which motivated
reasoning and utility in decision making are subjective. In reasoning, sub-

Figure 8.17 — The personally and socially constructed, CONTEXT-DEPENDENT nature of judgment is especially disturbing when it is manifested in a situation where the agent's decisions are literally a matter of life and death, as in evaluating a proposed peace accord that has the potential of terminating a bloody and protracted war. Maoz et al. (2002) asked people in just such a situation — voting-age Israeli Jews and Arabs — to evaluate real documents drafted by negotiators in the Israeli-Palestinian conflict. The main finding was a significant effect of the purported origin of the materials: Jews judged a proposal as worse for Israel when it was described as Palestinian rather than Israeli, while Arabs similarly devalued a proposal described as originating with the Israeli government.

jectivity, which acts there as a kind of bias, can be overcome by explicit, and usually effortful, discounting of everything except the logical form of the problem.

Not so in decision making: no amount of effort will exempt from subjectivity an agent faced with a decision, simply because the utility of the decision *for the agent* is subjective by definition. Thus, for example, to assess an agent's behavior under risk, one must first define risk, which can be done only relative to the personality structure and the life experience of the agent (Mellers et al., 1998).

In addition to the decision maker's conception of risk, emotional state, and memories of past decisions, judgment is affected by problem framing (see Figure 8.17[21]) and phrasing (as in opting in vs. opting out), as well as by the choice set. A general characteristic of these ever-present CONTEXT effects is computational laziness. For example, people may say they cannot save 20% of their income, but in response to a different question affirm that they can live on 80% — a behavior that is consistent with a great reluctance on the part of the cognitive system to set in motion the virtual machine, which alone can figure out that losing 20% of a certain sum of money is equivalent to retaining 80% of it.

With the general-purpose computational device dormant except in rare cases of explicit reasoning to which people are normally averse, the decision making system must fall back on mechanisms available to it by default: those of perception (just as the problem solving system does; cf. Figure 8.4 on page 323). This is why patterns of judgment in economics and in perception exhibit the same kind of dependence on the physical stimuli that drive them: the response is determined by the relative, not absolute, magnitude of the stimulus. Thus, people may be willing to drive across town to save $20 on a laptop carrying case, but not to save the same amount on the (more expensive) laptop itself — just as switching on a 40-watt lamp is very noticeable in a candlelit room at night, but not on the porch at midday.[22]

Indeed, the patterns of decisions made by primates (including the various paradoxes of choice) become more transparent if one considers the effects of reward in the same light as those of sensory stimuli (Sugrue, Corrado, and Newsome, 2005). This novel approach to the psychophysics of decision making, which calls for manipulating reward independently from the stimuli and relies on time-tested techniques developed for the study of perception, is revolutionizing our understanding of decision making (cf. Figure 8.18). Interestingly, the explicit and detailed models made possible by this new un-

REASON
v. i. To weigh probabilities in the scales of desire.
REASON
n. Propensitate of prejudice.

— Ambrose Bierce,
The Devil's Dictionary

derstanding express the effects of reward history in the same computational terms as the effects of stimulus history, and identifies them with the same neural mechanisms (Gold and Shadlen, 2002; Smith and Ratcliff, 2004). The theoretical framework that encompasses these models is neuroeconomics.

8.4.2 Neuroeconomics

Glimcher and Rustichini (2004), who describe neuroeconomics as "consilience of brain and decision," argue that a unified explanation of decision-making hinges on an integration of behavioral data from psychology, mathematical insights from economics (in particular, GAME THEORY), and neurobiological findings. Cognitive scientists who are aware of the Marr-Poggio methodological framework (section 4.2) will, of course, find this argument very familiar.

The experimental tactics prompted by the increasingly coherent research program in neuroeconomics are exciting and effective. For example, progress in understanding the neural basis of perceptual decisions in the monkey (Salzman, Britten, and Newsome, 1990; recall Figures 4.1 and 4.2 on page 68) motivates studies in which monkeys are taught to play simple strategy games with a computer (Rapoport and Bearden, 2005). These may be designed around specific game-theoretic questions derived from research in economics, and may in turn allow these questions to be approached by means of electrophysiological recordings (Sugrue et al., 2005).

The insights generated by this research obviate the need for certain overly

GAME THEORY uses mathematical tools (including computational simulation) to analyze decision making in situations that involve multiple interacting agents; applications range from understanding herd behavior in animals (Conradt and Roper, 2003) to estimating the effects of diversity on groups of problem solvers (Hong and Page, 2004). In neuroeconomics, game-theoretic methods are used to formulate quantitative predictions concerning the behavior of agents (monkeys, humans, or computer models) under uncertainty (Glimcher, Dorris, and Bayer, 2005; Sugrue et al., 2005).

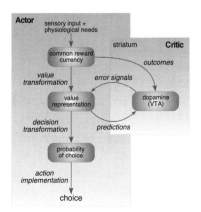

Figure 8.18 — COMPUTING SUBJECTIVE VALUE in the primate brain. Unlike in a perceptual decision task (cf. Figure 4.1 on page 67), in general decision making reward is not perceived by a dedicated sensory system, and must therefore be estimated by the agent by tracking the outcomes of past decisions. In the model of Sugrue et al. (2005) outlined here, initial sensory processing produces a "common reward currency" which is fed to a feedback circuit that optimizes the actor's plans, given the expected rewards computed by the critic on the basis of prior experience. A decision stage transforms the resulting value representation into the set of probable actions, one of which is chosen for execution by the final stage. VTA is the ventral tegmental area, the midbrain locus of the dopaminergic neurons that contribute the error signal to this actor-critic architecture proposed by Sugrue et al. (2005).

general and unwieldy classical concepts in economics and psychology, such as VALUE FUNCTION, which is replaced by subjective factors, attuned to context and the level of knowledge at the agent's disposal. They also help explain away paradoxes of choice by showing how supposedly "irrational" behavior may arise in response to the complexity of the agent's mind set and of the computational mechanisms it employs to reach decisions (Lee, 2006). Complaints about violations of classical normative rationality are met with explanations coached in terms of bounded rationality, achieved through satisficing (Simon, 1957) — a computational strategy whose application to decision making yields viable algorithms, that often outperform much more complex approaches.

Recalling the example from the previous section, the one-reason decision making embodied in Take The Best algorithm has the additional benefit of context-sensitivity: the one reason may differ from decision to decision, and certainly from task to task (Gigerenzer and Goldstein, 1996). One-reason decision making is particularly interesting in that it is not compensatory: contrary to the precepts of classical rationality, which requires that all commodities be comparable, it does not even attempt to define a computational framework within which everything would have its price in the same common currency.

This is a good strategy, for two reasons. First, it is not clear that compensation should be a goal for modeling: human minds do not necessarily treat everything as having a price (Gigerenzer and Goldstein, 1996, p.662). Second, compensation is computationally problematic because it assumes that all the dimensions of gain or loss are commensurable — a property that heterogeneous feature spaces do *not* possess by default (this is why the saying "comparing apples to oranges" means what it does in English).

Letting the agent who faces a heterogeneous multidimensional value space pick a random *modulus* that determines the relative scaling of the dimensions (how many apples for an orange), or having the scaling dictated by the experimenter are equally arbitrary approaches to this issue. It is thus only natural that they should give rise to "irrationality" and inconsistency among subjects (Kahneman and Frederick, 2005, p.272). In the light of these considerations, "satisficing" approaches are better insofar as they behave sensibly, for example by refraining from mixing dimensions at all.

A less straightforward, yet still sensible thing to do is to invoke PAST EXPERIENCE in approaching compensation and other issues that arise in decision making. Here it will be useful to recall what we know about the means

Memories of PAST EXPERIENCES can save us considerable computational work in thinking: if I already know the answer to a problem, or remember having made a similar decision in the past, there is no need to recompute it. In judgment under uncertainty, background knowledge activates the ANCHORING HEURISTIC, which attempts to solve the problem by searching around a known solution to a related one; thus, an estimate of the temperature at which water boils at the summit of Mt. Everest can be generated from the knowledge of the boiling point at the sea level (Epley and Gilovich, 2005a). If I happen to estimate the latter value too high (or too low), or even if I am merely made to think of a higher (or lower) number before replying, my answer will be correspondingly higher (or lower). An investigation of the anchoring phenomenon reveals that this kind of bias can be partially overcome through effortful thinking — but only if the anchor is self-generated rather than externally imposed (Epley and Gilovich, 2005b). This finding supports the distinction between the relatively inflexible, automatic, heuristic SYSTEM 1, and the general-purpose, deliberative SYSTEM 2.[23]

of gathering statistics of the stimuli and the rewards (positive or negative) associated with them. A universal computational mechanism that the brain uses for this purpose is a tuned unit (cf. section 3.2.1). This leads one to expect that the resulting statistical knowledge will be encapsulated in the form of heuristics, each of which is pretty specific to its task.

Indeed, heuristics is one of the two components of the theory of judgment offered by Kahneman and Frederick (2005); the other component they posit is a general-purpose, deliberative reasoning system. They point out that the two systems thus posited are the same as SYSTEM 1 and SYSTEM 2 of Stanovich and West (1998). This two-system framework, which I mentioned earlier, is also endorsed by Sanfey et al. (2006), who note that what we refer to here as the automatic, heuristics-based System 1 is implemented in the brain by multiple mechanisms, which may be at odds with each other — another probable reason for the quirks of human decision making behavior.

Converging findings from a wide range of behavioral experiments suggest that the heuristic mechanisms that comprise System 1, charged with the gathering of statistical evidence about the stimulus, function as depicted in Figure 8.19 on the following page (Smith and Ratcliff, 2004). Intuitively, the process of evidence accumulation may be likened to an ant crawling along the time axis while being buffeted by a cross wind; the wind creates a probabilistic bias that gradually shifts the ant away from the axis and toward one of the two decision lines. Mathematically, this kind of walk is modeled by the same equation that describes DIFFUSION (of a drop of ink in water, or a wisp of smoke in the air), hence the model's name.

Figure 8.19, right, shows the detailed quantitative fit between the model's simulated response times and those of human subjects in a decision task. The only model parameters that are controlled here are the accumulation rates for the two responses and the decision criteria. Model parameters estimated from data averaged over subjects show reasonable agreement with the average of parameters estimated from individual subjects. Smith and Ratcliff (2004) report that the pattern of results shown in Figure 8.19, right, is representative of a variety of behavioral paradigms.

The existence of multiple decision-making mechanisms, which is what psychologists infer from behavioral data, is also the likely explanation for the diversity and wide reach of the cortical network implicated in judgment and choice (Opris and Bruce, 2005). This network is orchestrated by the prefrontal cortex, for which Miller and Cohen (2001) "offer an example of how neurally plausible mechanisms can exhibit the properties of self-organization

A schematic circuit-level explanation of the executive control function of the prefrontal cortex (Miller and Cohen, 2001, fig.2). A different set of connections between the three units on the left and two on the right is activated, depending on which of the prefrontal control units (surrounded by the box) are active.

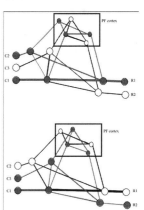

For a more detailed look at this functionality, see Figure 9.9 on page 408.

and self-regulation required to account for cognitive control without recourse to a 'homunculus.'"

In fact, our understanding of the computational mechanisms of decision making in the brain extends from the level of cortical areas and circuits down to the level of individual neurons. This integrated understanding is exemplified by the particularly detailed model developed by Gold and Shadlen (2002), which spans all the levels, from abstract computational to neuronal. On the computational level, Gold and Shadlen (2002) focus on how to make a two-alternative choice on the basis of the available evidence in favor of one or the other hypothesis (i) within a predictable response time interval, and (ii) with the error rate not exceeding a given percentage.

The criteria (i) and (ii) cannot be satisfied simultaneously, but if they

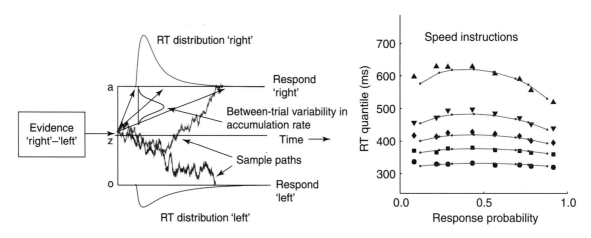

Figure 8.19 — A behavior-level computational model of decision making in a two-alternative choice task (Smith and Ratcliff, 2004). *Left:* the DIFFUSION model. The two zigzagging sample paths represent moment-by-moment fluctuations in the evidence favoring one or the other response. The process starts at z and accumulates evidence until it reaches one of two criteria, 0 or a. If the upper criterion is reached first, a 'right' response is made; if the lower is reached first, a 'left' response is made. The fluctuations in the sample paths reflect noise in the decision process. Other behaviorally important sources of variability are the location of the starting point of the accumulation process and the duration of the non-decision component of times for stimulus encoding and response execution (RT). *Right:* a fit of the diffusion model to human data from a two-alternative forced-choice task for speed instructions. The symbols are the empirical data; the continuous curves are produced by the model. For details, see Smith and Ratcliff (2004).

are traded off against each other, a principled probabilistic solution to the decision problem becomes available. Interestingly enough, on an abstract level this solution is computationally isomorphic to the one developed by the British cryptanalysis team led by Alan Turing in Bletchley Park in WWII (Gold and Shadlen, 2002).[24] Even more interestingly, on the level of mechanism the solution, which is depicted in Figure 8.20 on the next page, left, is essentially the same as the diffusion model derived by Smith and Ratcliff (2004) from behavioral data (cf. Figure 8.19 on the facing page, left).

At the heart of the decision mechanism, there are two neurons, each tuned to one of the ideal inputs; in the perceptual decision that served as an example in Chapter 3 (Figure 4.1 on page 67), as well as in the present case, an ideal input is a coherent motion stimulus in one of the two possible directions. Just as in the diffusion model, the difference in the firing rates of the two neurons is accumulated over time until it reaches a preset threshold, an event that signals the possibility of making a decision.

The trade-off that I mentioned earlier between reliability and speed is determined by the setting of the threshold. On the one hand, a low value will lead to rapid decisions, which, however, may be unreliable. A high threshold, on the other hand, may not be attained in time, which may prompt the system to cut the trial short without reaching a decision. As we have learned in Chapter 3, the motion-tuned neurons that feed the decision process reside in cortical area MT of the monkey brain; the computation of evidence based on tracking their responses and the threshold decision are thought to occur in the lateral intraparietal area (LIP). An examination of the responses of neurons recorded from that area (Figure 8.20, right) supports this idea.

A fully integrated model of the NEUROECONOMICS OF CHOICE as embodied in area LIP has been developed by Glimcher et al. (2005). The model, which is described in Figure 8.21 on page 363, brings together the key computational, behavioral, and neurobiological insights into primate decision making that I have surveyed in this section (note that it also uses neurocomputational building blocks familiar to us from Chapter 3, such as tuned units and cortical feature maps). First, it puts the subjective utility theory on a firm physiological foundation, utility being represented in a map-like form in area LIP. Second, it specifies the mechanism that accumulates perceptual evidence, as well as the one that tracks reward history; both are neural integrator circuits, which are well understood by neurobiologists (Sugrue et al., 2005), and for which functional counterparts have been posited by psychologists (Smith and Ratcliff, 2004).

DECIDE

v. i. To succumb to the preponderance of one set of influences over another set.

— Ambrose Bierce,
The Devil's Dictionary

The neurocomputational model of choice replicated the detailed behavioral characteristics of decision making of humans and monkeys in a two-alternative lottery task. Figure 8.21 on the next page, top right, shows the average behavior of the monkey subjects; as predicted by the model, the probability that they will pick a target is a linear function of the relative likelihood that this target pays off. Glimcher et al. (2005) also used the model as a

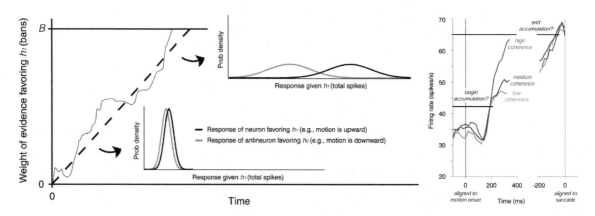

Figure 8.20 — A neurocomputational model of decision-making in a two-alternative forced-choice task (Gold and Shadlen, 2002, fig.2). *Left:* The evidence in favor of one of the two hypotheses, h_1 (which is assumed to be true in this example), over the other, h_0, is the cumulative difference between responses of a tuned neuron that prefers h_1 and an "antineuron" that prefers h_0. The meandering line represents how the weight of evidence might grow in a single trial as a function of time. The dashed line depicts the expectation (mean value) of this trajectory at each time point. The two insets illustrate the correspondence between the weight of evidence and the neuron/antineuron responses at two time points, viewed as probability distributions of the total number of spikes generated up to that time point, given that h_1 is true. If the weight of evidence reaches the barrier at B, the process is stopped and a decision is rendered for h_1. If the weight of evidence reaches $-B$ (not shown), a decision for h_0 is issued in error. *Right:* responses from neurons in the lateral intraparietal area (LIP) of the monkey during a reaction-time direction-discrimination task (Gold and Shadlen, 2002, fig.4), similar to the one illustrated in Figure 4.1 on page 67. The beginning of the plot shows responses averaged from a population of LIP neurons, aligned to the onset of the motion stimulus. After an initial dip, the responses recover and begin to increase roughly linearly, with a slope that is approximately proportional to the motion coherence. These neural responses are thought to represent the accumulated weight of evidence in favor of one direction of motion. The right side of the plot shows the LIP responses aligned to the beginning of the monkey's eye movement. When the response reaches a value of $B = 65$ spikes/s, the monkey is committed to a decision, which is communicated by the eye movement 80 *ms* later.

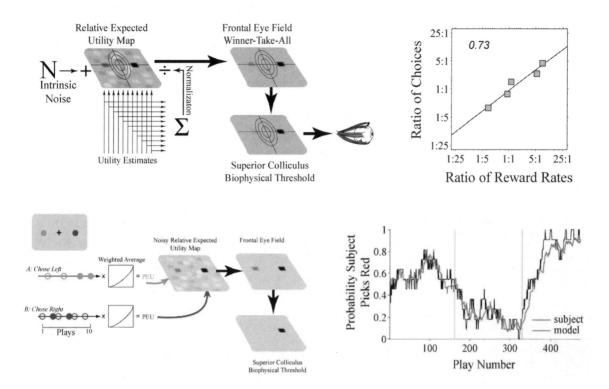

Figure 8.21 — The NEUROECONOMICS of choice (Glimcher et al., 2005). *Top left:* Area LIP generates a map of relative expected utilities of all possible saccadic eye movements, given the utility estimates and a normalizing signal (the input to LIP also includes intrinsic noise, which can lead to random behavior under some conditions). The relative expected utility values are sent to another brain area, the frontal eye field, which enforces a winner-take-all outcome. The resulting single best-candidate saccade target is queued for execution if it passes an activation threshold in the superior colliculus, from which the appropriate command is sent on to the oculomotor system. *Top right:* the behavior of monkeys in a two-alternative lottery game, in which the subject must choose, in each trial, between two alternatives that have different, cumulative, independent probabilities of yielding a reward – 0.25 *ml* of juice. The subject's probability of making either response is a linear function of the ratio of reward rates, which a game-theoretic analysis shows to be an efficient strategy under these conditions. *Bottom left:* a neuroeconomic model of probability matching, which computes an exponentially weighted average of the gains brought about by prior responses (computed iteratively from the reward prediction error signal carried by dopaminergic neurons; cf. Figure 8.18 on page 357). The average gain generates the physiological expected utility (PEU) for each movement, which is then used to construct the expected utility map in area LIP. *Bottom right:* WHAT WOULD THE MONKEY DO? Dynamic one-step-ahead prediction of the model. The black line is a 20-trial moving average of a subject's choice behavior during three consecutive blocks of plays; the gray line is the dynamic behavior of the model.

subject in a simulated experiment that involved exactly the same behavioral contingencies that a real monkey had encountered in a particular session; the behavior of the model made correct one-step-ahead predictions of what the monkey would do (Figure 8.21 on the preceding page, bottom right).

The theory of decision making based on probabilistic accumulation of evidence, which the model of Glimcher et al. (2005) instantiates, is thus turning out to be an excellent example of the Marr-Poggio multiple-levels methodology at work. This theory was originally motivated by neurophysiological findings in the monkey, shaped by computational insights from cognitive psychology and economics, and substantiated by behavioral data. Neuroeconomic theories are now helping brain researchers interpret functional imaging data on decision making in humans. Many of the findings focus on the integrative function of the dorsolateral prefrontal cortex (DLPFC), where the activity is time-locked to the output of sensory areas that supply the perceptual evidence for the decision, and is greater on trials for which the statistical evidence is strong than on trials for which it is weak, as expected of an integrator (Rorie and Newsome, 2005). The cycle of understanding is thus being completed.

THOUGHT TURNING UPON ITSELF. A problem-solving primate (such as a tool-using ape) gets the job done by a process that involves a certain degree of FLUID thinking. Does possession of fluid intelligence imply the ability to entertain, perhaps tacitly, the notion "I think, therefore I ape"? More on this in Chapter 9.

The picture is from Stanley Kubrick's film *2001: a Space Odyssey.*

8.5   Thinking out of the box

One's satisfaction at the news of progress in understanding problem solving, reasoning, and decision making in the brain may be tempered by the feeling that there must be more than that to human thinking. Of course there is, and in more than one sense. First, humans, as I argued in Chapter 6, have much more complex systems of concepts than other animals, including other primates. Second, many of these concepts are FLUID, and can be manipulated at will. This is what the present section is about.

8.5.1   Fluid intelligence

A century's worth of experimental data — beginning with Charles Spearman's report *'General Intelligence,' Objectively Determined and Measured*, reviewed by Lubinski (2004) on the occasion of the centennial of its publication — has established that the human mind possesses, in addition to many special-purpose aptitudes, a general-purpose capacity for problem solving and reasoning. Whereas the special-purpose abilities are each most useful in a different circumscribed setting, the general capacity is fluid in that it is equally effective in a wide range of tasks.

The general fluid intelligence factor, gF (or simply g), accounts for about 50% of the variance in a broad battery of mental ability tests, which have been administered to large samples of the population (Chabris, 2006; Deary, 2001a; Gottfredson, 1998; Kuncel, Hezlett, and Ones, 2004; Lubinski, 2004). As a preamble to a computational account of gF, I shall now briefly survey the behavioral evidence behind it, its validation as a predictor of performance and of life outcomes, and its genetic and neurobiological basis.

Behavioral evidence

In a typical study aimed at quantifying general intelligence, subjects are given a number of tests, such as those illustrated in Figure 8.22, redrawn from a *Scientific American* article by Gottfredson (1998). Their scores on the various components are then compared. The outcome is invariably a pattern of cor-

Matrices

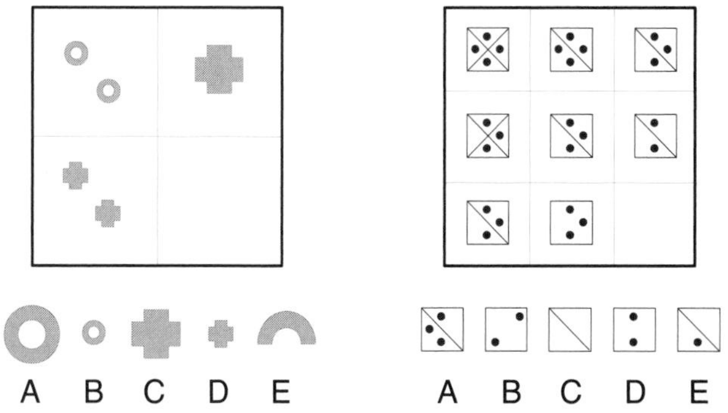

Figure 8.22 — Four examples of GENERAL INTELLIGENCE tests, after (Gottfredson, 1998). The gF factor emerges from such tests in the form of tightly correlated performance: a subject who does well on one "high-g" test is likely to do well also on others. The usual degree of correlation between scores in high-g tasks – about 0.75 – implies that about 50% of the variance in subjects' performance is explained by positing the existence of a common general intelligence factor, gF (cf. Figure 8.23 on the following page).

Number series

2, 4, 6, 8, _, _
3, 6, 3, 6, _, _
1, 5, 4, 2, 6, 5, _, _
2, 4, 3, 9, 4, 16, _, _

Analogies

brother:sister = father:_____
A. child B. mother C. cousin D. friend

joke:humor = law:_____
A. lawyer B. mercy C. courts D. justice

relations that is the defining characteristic of gF: if a subject scores high on the matrix reasoning test (say), he or she will also have scored high on the analogy test. The pattern is not necessarily symmetric: some tasks are more "central" to gF in the sense that performance in these tasks is more predictive of the scores in the other "high-g" tasks than vice versa. One such core high-g task is Raven's Progressive Matrices, which is similar to tests 1 and 2 in Figure 8.22.

When the pattern of scores in a set of high-g tasks is analyzed using any of a variety of classical or modern statistical methods, such as factor analysis, multivariate regression, or structural equation modelling,[25] the result is the three-tier factor structure shown in Figure 8.23. The data in this example are the scores from 13 sub-tests, which were administered to 2450 subjects, as described in the WAIS-III test manual (Deary, 2001a, box 1). The single factor at the top of the hierarchy, g, which accounts typically for about one half of the variance in the data, is general in the sense that it contributes a dominant share of the variance in all the tasks.

As Deary (2001a) notes, the high correlations among the four group factors (a mean of 0.76) refute the existence of independent 'primary mental abilities' at this level. Moreover, the close relationship of the group factors to g means that most of the variance apparently contributed to the tests by the group factors actually comes from g. For example, in matrix reasoning (*mr*)

INDIVIDUAL DIFFERENCES in gF manifest themselves in everyday life. In discussing two sample tasks from Level 5 of the National Adult Literacy Survey (NALS), Gottfredson (2004) writes: "…these two items require using tables of information. The first one requires determining the cost of carpet for a room and the second involves comparing the merits of two credit cards. Only 4% of white adults in the United States routinely function at this level. If these tasks do not seem difficult to the reader, it is because the reader is used to operating at this cognitive level. Most people cannot."

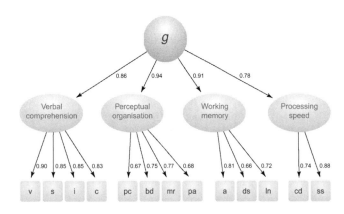

Figure 8.23 — The structure of variance in intelligence tests (Deary, 2001a, fig.1). Note that this is a taxonomic, *not* a functional, diagram. The common factor here is merely descriptive; postulating it (and the other two levels in the shallow hierarchy) offers an optimal, and extremely highly significant, fit to the performance data, but does *not* in any way explain the underlying mechanisms (Deary, 2001a). Abbreviations: *v*, vocabulary; *s*, similarities; *i*, information; *c*, comprehension; *pc*, picture completion; *bd*, block design; *mr*, matrix reasoning; *pa*, picture arrangement; *a*, arithmetic; *ds*, digit span; *ln*, letter-number sequencing; *cd*, digit-symbol coding; *ss*, symbol search.

about 52% of the variance in matrix reasoning is due to g and only about 7% due to the next higher group factor, which is perceptual organization.

Individual differences and prediction of life outcomes

Have another look at Figure 8.22 on page 365; although the task in the two matrix tests in the top row is the same — the subject has to choose one of the candidate elements to fill the empty cell in the matrix — the one on the right is clearly harder. The classical factorization of performance scores that I described just now emerges both from easy and from difficult versions of the same test battery. This allows researchers to apply the same standard analysis to different populations — the best known measure of general intelligence, IQ, expresses the relationship between the subject's score and the mean score for his or her age group — and to compare the results.

The statistics obtained in this manner for a population of subjects reveals the usual within-subject correlation among scores on different tests, which is indicative of gF. Inevitably, it also captures the INDIVIDUAL DIFFERENCES between the subjects' IQ values. The across-subjects distribution of IQ takes the form of a Gaussian, or bell-shaped curve; by definition, MEAN IQ= 100. The width of the distribution depends on the population in question; 90% of young white adults in the US have an IQ between 75 and 125 (Gottfredson, 1998).

The results of decades-long meticulously controlled studies involving thousands of subjects leave no doubt about the value of a person's IQ as a predictor of life outcomes, such as the likelihood of being unemployed, divorced, or incarcerated, as well as the person's educational attainment, income and even life expectancy (Gottfredson, 1998; Gottfredson and Deary, 2004; Lubinski, 2004). This predictive power of the general intelligence factor as expressed by the IQ score suggests that it captures something very real about how the mind works, rendering irrelevant the protests of those who would rather ignore it — what Pinker (2002) calls "the modern denial of human nature."[26] Kuncel et al. (2004), who review this issue in a paper titled "Academic performance, career potential, creativity, and job performance: can one construct predict them all?" conclude that the answer to the question they pose is clearly "yes."

SAT is relevant to real-life outcomes. Lubinski, Benbow, Webb, and Bleske-Rechek (2006) found that SAT scores predict well both long-term achievement and life satisfaction. Their study, titled *Tracking Exceptional Human Capital Over Two Decades*, compared 380 SAT takers under age 13 who scored in the top .01 percentile of their age group and were surveyed 20 years later, and 586 graduate students who had been enrolled in a top-ranked engineering, mathematics, or physical science program, and given the same survey 12 years later. This chart describes the career choices of the members of the two groups:

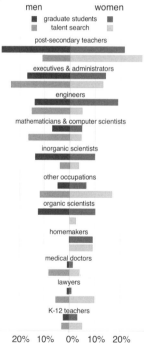

Genetic basis

It is generally agreed that "A stronger case has been made for substantial genetic influence on g than for any other human characteristic" (Plomin and Spinath, 2002). The size of the effect, estimated from a very large body of data (more than 8,000 parent-offspring pairs, 25,000 pairs of siblings, 10,000 twin pairs, and hundreds of adoptive families) is about 50%, which accounts for about half of the variance in g. Interestingly, it grows from 20% in infancy to 60% in adulthood: the older you are, the more closely your IQ corresponds to what could be predicted from your genetic endowment.

The MEAN IQ of the world population is rising at an average rate of about 9 points per 30 years (this phenomenon has been named the Flynn Effect, after its discoverer). The largest gains appear on the types of tests that were specifically designed to be free of cultural influence, such as Raven's Progressive Matrices, an untimed, non-verbal, "high-g" test (Neisser, 1997).

A combined multivariate analysis of genetic and psychometric data reveals that genetic correlations in adolescence and adulthood are very high — close to 1.0 (a genetic correlation measures the probability that a gene will be found to contribute to a particular psychometrically assessed cognitive ability, given that the same gene has been associated with other cognitive abilities as well). This means that genetic g is more pervasive than its psychometric counterpart: whereas the latter accounts for about 50% of the variance in a battery of IQ test scores, the former accounts for nearly all of the genetic variance.

The psychologists' success in isolating a general intelligence factor that is common to a wide variety of cognitive tasks has prompted geneticists to look for a similarly general "fitness factor." A good candidate for an easily measured characteristic that would likely express such a factor is body symmetry (you may recall from Chapter 5 that facial symmetry covaries with intelligence, and that it carries information about the face owner's genes; Jones, Little, Penton-Voak, Tiddeman, Burt, and Perrett, 2001; Kanazawa and Kovar, 2004). As predicted by these considerations, Prokosch, Yeo, and Miller (2005) found that higher-g cognitive tests show higher correlations with a measure of body symmetry. In particular, there was a significant correlation of 0.39 between body symmetry and the standard highest-g test, Raven's Progressive Matrices.

The finding that general intelligence is a valid indicator of general heritable fitness is especially intriguing in the light of the report by Brown, Cronk, Grochow, Jacobson, Liu, Popović, and Trivers (2005) that in the Jamaican society, where dance plays an important role, dancing ability (as evaluated by the same population) is strongly associated with body symmetry.[27] It would appear that someone who watches you dancing can tell not only how good-looking you are, but also how smart.

Brain basis

In reviewing the more than one hundred years of history of research into general intelligence, Deary (2001a) remarks, "A striking limitation of this body of research is that, whereas much is known about the taxonomy and predictive validity of human intelligence differences, there has been relatively little progress in understanding their nature, with the exception of behaviour genetic studies." Detailed data from genetics are now being used in conjunction with MRI methods to map out the neuroanatomical basis of intelligence-related cognitive differences (Toga and Thompson, 2005).

Neither anatomical maps nor functional or developmental ones (Duncan, Seitz, Kolodny, Bor, Herzog, Ahmed, Newell, and Emslie, 2000; Shaw, Greenstein, Lerch, Clasen, Lenroot, Gogtay, Evans, Rapoport, and Giedd, 2006) do more than suggest what areas in the brain contribute to general intelligence: a valuable, but incomplete, insight. The classical psychometric techniques similarly offer only a limited understanding. For example, reaction time, long implicated in contributing to g, explains the association of lower IQ with early death (Deary and Der, 2005): the effect of IQ on mortality (in a study of 898 people who were tracked with respect to survival between ages 56 and 70) was not significant after adjusting for reaction time. Deary and Der (2005) interpret this finding by suggesting that "reduced efficiency of information processing might link lower mental ability and earlier death" — to be sure, but how?

WORKING MEMORY AND G. In one of the first studies of the role of WM in intelligence, Daneman and Carpenter (1980) had college students read or listen to a set of unrelated sentences while remembering the last word of each. The WM capacity, measured by the number of last words recalled, correlated with the subjects' verbal SAT score, accounting for up to 36% of variance. This finding was subsequently verified by a meta-analysis of 77 studies that included a total of 6179 subjects. Converging support for the centrality of WM to g comes from the work of Carpenter, Just, and Shell (1990), who found that the single most important factor distinguishing difficult instances of the Raven's Matrices task from easy ones was the number of rules. Thus, "reasoning seems to be the sum of working-memory abilities" (J. Gabrieli, quoted by Wickelgren, 1997).

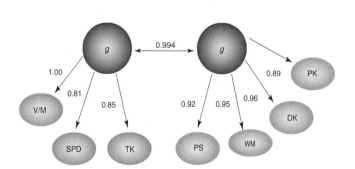

Figure 8.24 — The relationship between GF AND WORKING MEMORY. This diagram from (Deary, 2001b, fig.II) shows the correlation between results of two sets of tests — a standard paper-and-pencil psychometric battery (ASVAB, left), and the cognitive ability measurement (CAM, right), motivated by a theory of intelligence centered around working memory. The ASVAB factors are verbal/mathematical *V/M*, clerical speed *SPD*, and technical knowledge *TK*. The CAM factors are processing speed *PS*, working memory *WM*, declarative knowledge *DK*, and procedural knowledge *PK*.

The most promising way of approaching this question is to combine behavioral and imaging methods with computational theorizing. An excellent example of progress achieved by taking this route emerges from a series of explorations of the suspected link between g and WORKING MEMORY (WM). For decades, the attempts to elucidate the contribution of WM to g focused on various hypothetical cognitive architectures, in which WM without exception plays a central role. On the basis of the hypothesized block diagrams, researchers have been devising tests designed to measure the involvement of WM. The scores from such tests turned out, however, to be very highly correlated with g (Figure 8.24), confirming its interdependence with WM, but explaining neither.

By focusing on function (that is, computation), cognitive psychology is, however, capable of generating testable hypotheses that are more explicit, and therefore potentially more explanatory. One such hypothesis — that "general fluid intelligence and working memory both reflect the ability to keep a representation active, particularly in the face of interference and distraction" (Deary, 2001b, box 2) — has been corroborated by several studies. One of these (Gray, Chabris, and Braver, 2003) involved a specially designed "*n*-back" test of working memory, in which the subject must indicate whether each stimulus in a sequence matches one seen precisely *n* items ago (see Figure 8.25). With $n = 3$, for example, declaring a match to an item that actually appeared two, four, or five items back would be an error. Such "lure" trials are particularly difficult: lure foils were much less accurately rejected by subjects than non-lure foils.

Gray et al. (2003) found, as predicted by the hypothesis that motivated

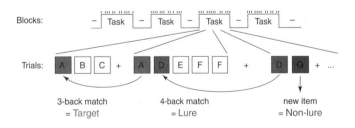

Blocks:

Trials:

3-back match
= Target

4-back match
= Lure

new item
= Non-lure

Figure 8.25 — The 3-back working memory task (Kane, 2003, fig.2), in which the subject must determine whether or not the present target was shown precisely three items back. Gray et al. (2003) used this task to demonstrate that the importance of WM for general intelligence stems from its support of flexible, INTERFERENCE-AVOIDING manipulation of data.

the study, that correct lure-foil rejection correlated positively with gF. Crucially, it remained significant after the individual differences in non-lure foil rejection and in target accuracy were partialled out. The imaging component of the study also yielded a highly valuable result: the joint lure-trial neural activity in lateral prefrontal and parietal cortex areas (both implicated in decision making; recall section 8.4.2) accounted for 99.9% of variance in the gF and lure-trial data. Moreover, high-IQ subjects showed a significantly greater increase in activity in these areas on lure trials than low-IQ subjects. A review of the literature (Conway, Kane, and Engle, 2003) supports the conclusion that the functional underpinning of the role of WM in general intelligence lies in its ability to carry out flexible, INTERFERENCE-AVOIDING manipulation of task data.

Computational basis

A comprehensive computational theory of general intelligence — one that would explain the behavioral findings, fit the big picture painted by genetics and neuroscience, and capitalize on the success of incipient functional hypotheses such as the interference-avoiding role of flexible use of working memory — can be constructed on an existing foundation: the concept of the virtual machine.

A basic building block of a random-access memory is a SWITCH of the kind depicted schematically here:

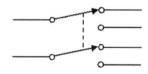

As we saw earlier in this chapter, the virtual machine (VM) theory gives rise to a simple and effective explanation of the difference between the two systems, one heuristic and the other general-purpose, posited by cognitive psychologists who study reasoning and decision making (cf. Figure 8.11 on page 338). The VM theory is not very well known in cognitive psychology: outside computer science, it has been mainly invoked by the few philosophers working on consciousness who are astute enough to appreciate the vital role of computation concepts in explaining it (Dennett, 1991; Sloman and Chrisley, 2003).

Note that the control over the switch can come from another part of the circuit rather than from the outside; no homunculus is needed to operate it.

The VM theory of gF is compatible with the behavioral data, a thorough survey of which prompted Chabris (2006) to hypothesize functionally distinct general efficiency and resource components of gF, concluding that "both [hypotheses] are likely to be true." Computationally, these two factors translate, respectively, into efficient routing of data (e.g., between long-term and working memory), and the ability to manipulate the required volume of accessed data in the general-purpose workspace furnished by the working memory.

The crucial computational ability implied by the need for flexible manipulation of data is RANDOM ACCESS to memory — a function that is very easy to implement in an electronic circuit. The essential component of an electronic random-access memory is a SWITCH: a device that allows one part of a circuit to be connected to one of several other parts, under external control. Random access functionality can also be realized in a neural network, such as the crossbar switch of Figure 3.10 on page 54, or the McCulloch-Pitts circuit of Figure 6.3 on page 162, bottom right.

A careful comparison of the gating circuit proposed by Miller and Cohen (2001) as a part of their theory of the prefrontal cortex (see p. 359) and the switching diagram shown in the margin here reveals their functional similarity: signals from some lines are steered into one sub-circuit or another, depending on the state of the controlling element. In the case of the Miller-Cohen circuit, there may be partial cross-talk between the signals, as one would indeed expect from living "wetware," in which a clean break — physically disconnecting a wire, as when Dr. Frankenstein's assistant throws a switch in the loft — cannot be achieved without damaging the circuit.

The neural circuit reproduced from (O'Reilly, Noelle, Braver, and Cohen, 2002) that Chabris (2006, fig.3) sees as a candidate for a central role in implementing fluid intelligence in the brain operates on a principle that is identical to the one just stated. It is also the principle behind the gating circuit hypothesized by O'Reilly and Frank (2006, fig.12), who describe a detailed network model of learning and operation of flexible memory access and control functions, and is capable of replicating human performance in key intelligence tests resembling the n-back task that I mentioned earlier. In the learning phase, the model of O'Reilly and Frank (2006) makes use of an actor-critic architecture that we also encountered earlier (Figure 8.18 on page 357). These conceptual connections complete a circuit of ideas that unifies, on a computational level, many of the themes touched upon so far in this chapter.

8.5.2 Analogy

The preceding sections suggest that fluid intelligence is intimately connected with the ability to manipulate problem data at will, and, in particular, to induce and subsequently detect valid patterns while resisting interference from spurious ones. We can now elaborate upon this account of thinking by expressing the requisite data manipulation in terms of elementary computational operations known to underlie other cognitive domains: perception, memory, and language. These operations are **acquisition, comparison, and generalization of patterns**. A system that can carry out these elementary computations in any domain, while exerting executive control as needed, is well-equipped to face all the tasks that require intelligence. This includes, notably, the family of tasks that, as Figure 8.26 shows, is most closely associated with fluid intelligence: ANALOGY.

In everyday language, analogy may be expressed by a simile ("she's like a rainbow") or a metaphor ("silence is golden"). The comparison that defines an analogy always involves a *structure mapping* between complex entities, situations, or domains. The structures being mapped may be rudimentary, as when simple features are compared (as in the second example above; presumably, silence is golden only in the sense that it is valuable), or they may be complex (in the first example, the referent of the third-person pronoun may resemble a rainbow in several ways, some of which can probably only

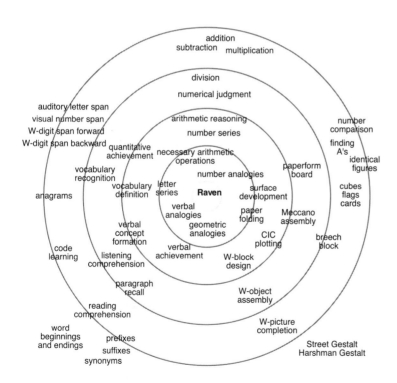

Figure 8.26 — A plot created by Snow et al. (1984, fig. 2.9) as a summary of the many analyses of the relationships among various intelligence tests they had conducted. Raven's Progressive Matrices and other ANALOGY tests turn out to be central in any numerical assessment of general cognitive function.

be fully appreciated by a person whose conceptual inhibitions have somehow been relaxed).

The most interesting analogies are those in which the entities being compared are not really of the same kind, so that the mapping must be, to some extent, FORCED.[28] Here is an example from the LETTER STRING analogy domain, in which the mapping is forced at the literal level, yet is very natural at a higher level of abstraction: if *abc* goes to *cba*, what does *mrrjjj* go to? I shall discuss one of the many possible solutions to this problem a bit later.

To explain why analogy problems always admit multiple solutions, I must switch to a more formal language. In computational terms, an analogy problem consists of two sets of entities (the source and the target) and a mapping that establishes a correspondence between the two (French, 2002). Note that the mapping may tie a single object in the source domain to a set of objects in the target domain, or vice versa (to see what I mean, think again about the $abc \to cba : mrrjjj \to$? problem in the previous paragraph). Clearly, with even just a handful of objects in each set, many such mappings are possible: **analogy is *underdetermined***, in the same sense that perception is (recall Chapter 5).

The computational account of analogy making that I am about to present allows for a curious, two-way parallel between analogy and perception.[29] On the one hand, the perceptual system offers the means for dealing with analogy problems (Mitchell, 1993): in the process of solving Raven's task (Figure 8.27 on the facing page), steps 1 through 3 are straightforward pattern recognition, step 4 is categorization, step 5 is a kind of figure-ground comparison, and step 6 is pattern matching. On the other hand, many perceptual problems may arguably require the mobilization of the heavy guns of analogy (Hofstadter, 2001): in some sense, seeing a face in Arcimboldo's painting *The Jurist* (Figure 5.5, right) necessitates that the headless frog shape be mapped to "nose," the fish tail – to "chin," etc.

In Chapter 5, we saw that the requisite mapping can be easily implemented implicitly, by a shape-tuned mechanism that is the mainstay of visual processing, and that ensembles of such mechanisms can also deal with entire scenes (Figures 5.30 on page 146 and 5.31 on page 147). Thus, rather than perception explaining analogy or vice versa, a single computational theory may offer a unified account of both — at least in the simpler cases, where categorization of and generalization from existing patterns suffices.

What if the situation demands arbitrary manipulation of pattern primitives? As we saw earlier in this section, the required flexibility is afforded by

A useful formal setting for studying analogy is the toy domain of LETTER STRINGS (Hofstadter and Mitchell, 1995), as in this example: if *abc* goes to *abd*, what does *ijk* go to?

a computational framework based on a virtual machine.[30] Because a VM provides an environment for general-purpose computation, it isolates functional considerations from implementational ones. This means that researchers who work on a model of analogy can focus on understanding the former while setting aside the latter.

This is precisely what Hofstadter and Mitchell (1995) did in developing their functional theory of analogy as a part of the CopyCat project, which focused on problems in the letter strings domain. The CopyCat model (Mitchell, 1993, 2001) has three main computational components: Workspace, Slipnet, and Coderack (see Figure 8.28 on page 377).

WORKSPACE fulfills the function of working memory: this is where the problem is stated, and where the candidate solutions are formed, tested, and modified until a satisfactory one emerges. At any given instant of time,

These highly stylized drawings (from Biederman, 1987a) succeed in depicting scenes to the extent that they are interpretable by ANALOGY: each line plays a clear ROLE (curb side, desk edge, etc.) and has a proper POSITION relative to other lines (cf. Figure 8.27).

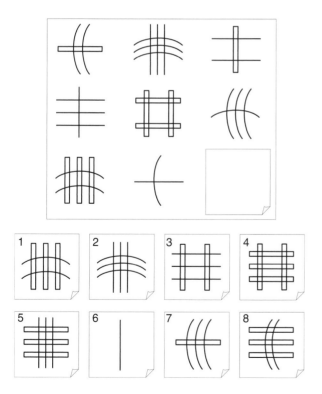

Figure 8.27 — Which of the eight candidate patterns belongs in the blank space in the lower right corner of this 3 × 3 matrix? To solve MATRIX ANALOGY problems such as those in Figure 8.22 on page 365, or the one shown here, it is necessary to carry out the following computations: (1) identify the primitive elements; (2) determine the relevant features; (3) describe each of the given items in terms of these; (4) infer the rules that hold for each row and column; (5) deduce a description of the missing item; (6) scan the candidate answers for an item that best fits this description. Much as in scene interpretation, the information that is critical to this analogy task has two components: the ROLES of the elements, and their POSITIONS.

Workspace contains a snapshot of the situation, which includes a mark-up of the various relations defined over the constituent letters and their aggregates.

SLIPNET is a network of concepts, both simple and relational, pertaining to letter string analogies. The simple concepts are the letters themselves. The relational ones are predicates, such as first (true of the letter a in the alphabet, or of c in the string cba) or successor_of (jointly true of d and e).

CODERACK is a repository of elementary computational operations or codelets, such as connect or group, that are activated by the ongoing interaction between Workspace and Slipnet. The resulting computation is distributed: it is governed not by a central executive, but by the total state of the system. A global parameter called temperature determines the excitability of codelets; the system is annealed towards a steady state by gradually lowering the temperature as the computation progresses.

The manner whereby CopyCat solves letter string analogy problems is best understood on some examples. Let us consider first a relatively simple one, $abc \rightarrow abd : xyz \rightarrow$? A match between the last elements of abc and abd evokes successor, because d follows c in the alphabet (note that both last and successor are members of Slipnet). Now that last is active, it singles out z in xyz, exposing it to the potential action of successor; this, however, is thwarted, because z, being the last letter of the alphabet, has none.

Many things can happen at this point (which itself is only one of the many possible intermediate states in this computation. For example, the system may opt for the unimaginative $abc \rightarrow abd : xyz \rightarrow abd$ ("send everything to abd"), or the literal-minded $abc \rightarrow abd : xyz \rightarrow xyz$ ("replace every c by a d"), or for the adventurous $abc \rightarrow abd : xyz \rightarrow xya$, which treats the alphabet as circular. The run illustrated in Figure 8.28 on the facing page yielded yyz ("change leftmost letter to successor"), because the system ended up mapping a to z and c to x, mirror-fashion.

This CREATIVE turn was also responsible for the pleasing solution that the model found for a considerably more challenging problem:

$$abc \rightarrow cba : mrrjjj \rightarrow ?$$

Here, a count codelet discovered the repetitions in $mrrjjj$, mapping it into 123; at the same time, an alphabet position codelet mapped abc into 123 and cba into 321. The model then decided to compose an equivalent of 321 out of the elements of the set $\{m, r, j\}$, which led to the final answer:

$$abc \rightarrow cba : mrrjjj \rightarrow mmmrrj.$$

ANALOGY AND CREATIVITY. Given some creative imagination, an analogy can be "discovered" between any two entities. Lewis Carroll once presented his readers with the following analogy, for which, he had thought, there would be no reasonable justification: "Why is a raven like a writing-desk?" When pressed for an answer, he nevertheless came up with one: "Because it can produce a few notes, tho they are very flat; and it is nevar [sic] put with the wrong end in front."[31]

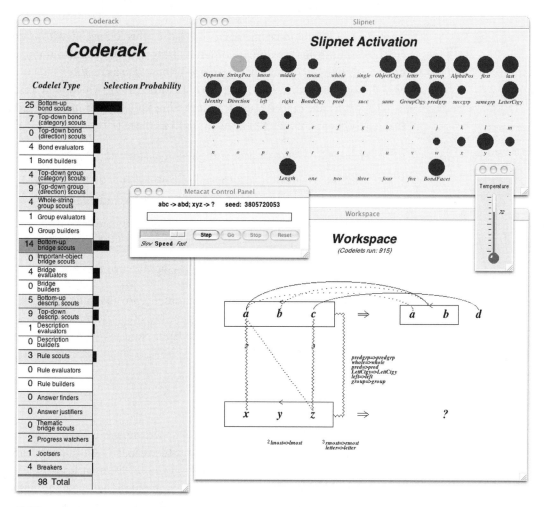

Figure 8.28 — A screen snapshot of an extended version of the CopyCat program, implemented by Marshall (2002). All the visible functional components — SLIPNET, CODERACK, and WORKSPACE — are as in Hofstadter and Mitchell (1995). There is also extra functionality: long-term memory, which keeps track of problems encountered and solutions generated. This gives the model a certain capacity for reflecting on its own performance and introducing strategic improvements, which is why it is called METACAT. The run whose intermediate state is shown here solved *abc* → *abd* : *xyz* →? as *yyz* ("change leftmost letter to successor"); other runs yielded *wyz* and *abd*. The distributed architecture of CopyCat resembles many other computational models that I mentioned elsewhere in this book (recall, for example, Figure 5.29 on page 145, or Figure 5.31 on page 147). More generally, distributed cognition at the level of an individual is compatible with the Society of Mind concept (Minsky, 1985).

8.5.3   Creativity

The same computational mechanisms that endow CopyCat with a tinge of creativity in the narrow domain of letter string analogy are also implicated in creative thinking in general. Pattern operations such as feature extraction, categorization, generalization, and even caricature (all of which were discussed in Chapter 5) are indeed useful in analyzing and solving analogy problems that extend beyond the letter domain, such as these (Hofstadter, 1985a):

The Penrose triangle.

- What is to a triangle as a triangle is to a square?
- What is to four dimensions as the Penrose triangle is to three?
- What is to Greece as the Falkland Islands are to Britain?
- What is to the US as the Eiffel Tower is to France?
- What is to German as Shakespeare's plays are to English?
- What is to Rachmaninoff as Rachmaninoff is to Beethoven?

Similar to letter string analogies, these problems are characterized by multiple possible solutions, of which the most pleasing ones often hide in conceptual dimensions that are not immediately apparent, and which therefore require a measure of INSIGHT to achieve. But what does insight mean, behaviorally and computationally?

Characteristics of creative behavior

Insight is a resolution of an impasse reached by the train of thought as it runs down a regular track through the problem space. An impasse can often be circumvented by backing up and exploring a different track. It is worth noting that this metaphor has a concrete computational meaning within the framework for problem solving that I have outlined in section 8.2: a "track" is a path through the state space generated one step at a time by applying the available "next state" operators and choosing the optimal direction.

Backtracking is what happens when one solves the following verbal problem from Weisberg (1993): our basketball team won a game last week by the score of 73-49, and yet not one man on our team scored as much as a single point; how is that possible? The delay, no matter how brief, that one experiences before deciding to retract a key (and misleading) assumption in this kind of problem is a manifestation of the impasse. Watching someone experience insight in such situations can be entertaining, especially if you're in on the joke, and if the person who is about to get it deserves all of it — as is the case in this scene from J. R. R. Tolkien's *The Return of the King*:

> — Begone, foul dwimmerlaik, lord of carrion! Leave the dead in peace!
>
> A cold voice answered:
>
> — Come not between the Nazgûl and his prey! Or he will not slay thee in thy turn. He will bear thee away to the houses of lamentation, beyond all darkness, where thy flesh shall be devoured, and thy shrivelled mind be left naked to the Lidless Eye.
>
> A sword rang as it was drawn.
>
> — Do what you will; but I will hinder it if I may.
>
> — Hinder me? Thou fool. No living man may hinder me! Then Merry heard of all sounds in that hour the strangest. It seemed that Dernhelm laughed and the clear voice was like the ring of steel.
>
> — But no living man am I! You look upon a woman. Éowyn am I, daughter of Éomund.

In some problems, backtracking is not enough: one needs to abandon the tracks altogether. Such DIVERGENT THINKING or "jumping out of the system" (Hofstadter, 1979) corresponds to discovering entirely new dimensions to the problem and inventing new state-transforming operators. A couple of problems of that kind are shown in Figure 8.29. The solution I came up with when I first saw Duncker's "candle problem" — use three tacks to attach a fourth one to the candle with its point facing outward, then fasten the candle to the wall by means of this fourth tack — diverges from the most common one, which I'll leave to you to discover.

Although creativity may seem intuitively to be merely a sign of very high intelligence, these two characteristics of human thinking are not identical: for people with IQ greater than 120, the IQ scores and creative ability appear to be uncorrelated (Wilson and Keil, 2001).[32] Personal traits and abilities that have been implicated in creativity include verbal and conceptual fluency, capacity for redefinition, openness to experience, independence of thought, capacity to bring together remote associations, and capacity to expend effort in the production of ideas (McKinnon, 1962). Let's see how people put these abilities to use in the creative process.

The creative process

In its entry for creativity, the MIT encyclopedia of the cognitive sciences (Wilson and Keil, 2001) distinguishes five stages of creative problem solving: preparation, incubation, insight, evaluation, elaboration.

A BULL'S HEAD, by Pablo Picasso (1943).

PREPARATION. Unlike the toy problems discussed so far in this section, real-life creative challenges are embedded — and can only be fully comprehended — in a wider context, be it a scientific discipline (or several of them), a technological culture, or an art movement. Because of this, creative success is almost never achieved by dilettantes — certainly not in science or technology, where fads play no role in determining the value of a breakthrough. In these fields, even just recognizing the existence of a problem and formulating it requires deep knowledge. Preparation in the sense just stated is apparent also in the work of the greatest artists. For example, Picasso's 1943 sculpture BULL'S HEAD appears to be a natural expression of his lifelong fascination with bullfighting. Even his *Les Demoiselles d'Avignon* (1907), which marked the beginning of the Cubist revolution, had been preceded by much traditional work.

INCUBATION. The folk wisdom behind the advice to "sleep on it" is now getting support from controlled studies of the relationship between incubation and insight (Stickgold and Walker, 2004). In computational terms, incubation is thought to facilitate far-reaching associations among concepts (in the CopyCat model, this corresponds to lowering the temperature; cf. Figure 8.28 on page 377). This process is likely to redirect thinking away from the established tracks, opening up novel and potentially useful conceptual directions.

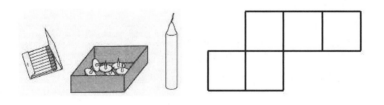

Figure 8.29 — Two problems that require DIVERGENT THINKING. *Left:* use the materials available (a box of tacks and some matches) to affix the candle to the wall so that it can be lit (Duncker's problem). *Right:* move two matches to make four squares, one of them larger than the other three.

INSIGHT. This is the most conspicuous stage in creative problem solving, in which the innovator first becomes aware of the breakthrough. The thinking that leads up to the moment of insight happens during the prior preparation and incubation stages, usually outside of awareness, presumably because candidate solutions that are too poor to begin with are filtered out by an internal evaluation mechanism. Insight occurs when an idea is generated that makes it past the internal critic. This may, but does not have to, be precipitated by an external event, a role that in the most famous insight episode in history — the eureka moment of Archimedes — was played by the spillage of bath water.[33]

EVALUATION. For a contender idea, surviving the internal censorship stage is usually only the first step in a longer process of examination. Because of the unruly nature of the solution generation in the incubation stage, most "revolutionary" ideas that come to the fore of consciousness are inconsequential: even Mozart's compositions went through many drafts (Zaslaw, 1997). A creative individual is therefore distinguished by the ability to separate the chaff from the grain.

ELABORATION. Even the most valuable insight will have no lasting effect on the field unless it is followed up by much work. A poll conducted as a part of a study of intelligence that I cited earlier (Lubinski et al., 2006) revealed that most of the hundreds of exceptionally bright individuals tracked over a period of 20 years were willing to work fifty, sixty, or seventy hours per week to achieve their career goals. Referring to this finding, Lubinski (2004, p.107) observes, "Individual differences in conative factors surely engender dramatic differences in performance and work-related outcomes." Thomas Edison's phrasing of this facet of creativity is easier to remember: "Genius is 1 percent inspiration and 99 percent perspiration."

Variations on a theme as the crux of creativity

None of the five stages of creative problem solving just surveyed is particularly mysterious (not at the present stage in this book, that is): preparation amounts to a stocking up of conceptual memory, incubation is wide-ranging search of the problem representation space, insight is a jump to a point in that space from which a solution may be easily reachable, evaluation can be carried out by internal simulation of the planned course of action, and elaboration is just that. **Where, then, do creative ideas come from? From**

From INCUBATION TO INSIGHT. Wagner, Gais, Haider, Verleger, and Born (2004) report a study in which the subjects performed a mathematical task requiring the learning of stimulus-response sequences, in which they improved gradually by increasing response speed across task blocks. They could also improve abruptly after gaining insight into a hidden abstract rule underlying all sequences. 59% of the subjects who slept for a night between training and retesting discovered the shortcut the following morning, compared to 25% in four different control groups who did not have a night's sleep. Sleep did not enhance insight in the absence of initial training. The researchers conclude that "sleep, by restructuring new memory representations, facilitates extraction of explicit knowledge and insightful behavior."

playing variations on familiar themes (Hofstadter, 1985a; see Figure 8.30 for an illustration of this idea in the domain of typeface design[34]).

The idea that variations on a theme are the crux of creativity, which is compatible with everything we've heard so far about thinking and creativity and which has a straightforward computational formulation, stresses the continuity between regular and creative thinking and the dependence of the latter on prior knowledge and experience. Studies of the achievements of creative individuals of great renown in engineering, arts, and sciences support this account. In a book titled *Creativity: beyond the myth of genius*, Weisberg (1993) discusses numerous examples of extremely creative people whose most revolutionary work clearly derived either from their own personal background and professional record, or from the work of other people who had come very close to what proved to be the great discovery, invention, or work of art (see Table 8.5).

In engineering, for example, JAMES WATT came up with his design for a steam engine while being employed by Glasgow University, where his duties included maintaining the fully operational scale models of steam engines invented by Thomas Newcomen about fifty years earlier. In plastic arts, ALEXANDER CALDER's invention of the mobile followed a long history of exposure to, and work in, similar media. Calder came from a family

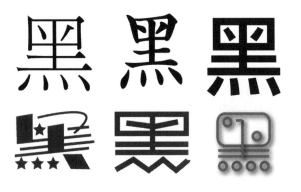

Figure 8.30 — CREATIVITY IN TYPOGRAPHY: the shape of the Hanzi (Chinese) character *hēi* in six typefaces, ranging from traditional to highly stylized (after an illustration from *Variations on a Theme as the Crux of Creativity* by Hofstadter, 1985a). Note how analogy enters the picture here: in the character at the top left, the four raindrop-shaped strokes play the same role as the four circles in the character at the bottom right. A computational model of analogy that automatically learns to separate visual style from content has been described by Tenenbaum and Freeman (2000). In the domain of typography, it acquires (and generalizes from) independent representations of typeface and letter identity; in face representation, it learns to separate viewpoint from identity information (recall Figure 5.6 on page 96).

of sculptors and painters. As a boy, he used to design jewelry (no doubt learning many of the techniques that he later used in sculpting wire); as a young man, he became interested in the circus, fashioning animal and human shapes out of wire.

A most fascinating (and well-documented) example of "incremental invention" leading up to a major breakthrough took place between 1899 and 1903 in the bicycle repair shop of WILBUR AND ORVILLE WRIGHT in Dayton, Ohio. The Wright brothers started from a point in the design space that others had visited before them: Octave Chanute and Samuel Langley, for example, had both been working on biplane designs (none of which, however, proved to be airworthy). After a painstaking and protracted process of development (see Table 8.6 on the following page), which involved learning from nature, learning from others, and intensive use of a tool that aeronautics engineers find indispensable to the present day (the wind tunnel), their *Flyer I* became "the first controlled, powered, sustained (from takeoff to landing) flight

Three sculptures by ALEXANDER CALDER: an elephant, a fish tank, and a mobile (his invention).

Engineering	
Watt's engine	Newcomen's engine
Edison's kinetoscope	Edison's phonograph
Wrights' biplane	Chanute's biplane
Science	
Watson & Crick's helix	Pauling's alpha-helix
Darwin's monad theory	Lamarck, E. Darwin; Leibniz (monad concept)
Art	
Calder's mobiles	Calder's earlier moving sculptures
Picasso's *Les Demoiselles*	Ingres, Cezanne, Delacroix, Matisse, etc.
Picasso's *Guernica*	Picasso's *Minotauromachy*, etc.
Coleridge's *Kubla Khan*	Purchas's *Pilgrimage*, etc.
Mozart's early works	L. Mozart's music exercises, etc.

Table 8.5 — CONTINUITY IN CREATIVITY, after (Weisberg, 1993): select breakthroughs in arts, sciences, and engineering (left column) are listed alongside their roots in prior work (right column).

involving a heavier-than-air vehicle, using mechanically unassisted takeoff (thrust/lift created chiefly by onboard propulsion)," a feat officially recognized by the Fédération Aéronautique Internationale.

8.5.4 The crossroads of cognition

DISTRIBUTED COGNITION, revisited. If innovators owe so much to the society of their peers, one may expect that groups of thinkers would perform better than individuals in tasks that demand creativity. This idea, which has been entertained for some time in cognitive ethology (Hutchins, 2000) and theoretical economics (Hong and Page, 2004), clearly requires more work along the lines of computational social psychology (in particular, controlled studies of the efficacy of group problem solving and of its dynamics).

The overview of the psychology of thought that I am about to conclude (which is turning out to be twice as long as anticipated in the beginning of this chapter) suggests that the power and the limitations of human problem solving, reasoning, and decision making can be explained, as presaged by the great thinkers of the 20th century such as Alan Turing, Warren McCulloch, and Herbert Simon, in terms of computational processes. The nature of these processes is dictated (1) by the structure of the world, which drives the adaptive changes over evolutionary time and sets the context for every thought, and (2) by the structure of the brain, which puts the cognitive building blocks placed at its disposal by evolution to a good use — not only in the survival game, in which we fare no worse than many other species and better than some, but also in creatively pursuing self-imposed, uniquely human

year	feature introduced by the Wrights	source/motivation
1899	biplane	Octave Chanute; Samuel Langley
	hinged wing	Chanute
	wing warping	bird wing tips
1900	dihedral angle	precedents
	flat rudder	precedents
	operator prone	[reduce drag]
1901	larger wings	[need more lift]
	skids	[safer landing]
	change cloth	[more lift]
1902	fixed tail	[stability]
	wing shape	[wind tunnel experiments]
	varied camber	[wind tunnel]
	rudder shape	[wind tunnel]
1903	new motor	custom-adapted auto engine
	better propellers	[wind tunnel; trial & error]

Table 8.6 — How the Wright brothers became FIRST IN FLIGHT (Weisberg, 1993).

endeavors, such as technological problem solving (as in flying to the moon), complex causal reasoning (as in doing science), or strategic decision making (as, for example, in planning a career).

At the level of neural computation, thought processes make use of the brain's regular bag of tricks: dimensionality-controlled representation spaces, inference from statistics to structure and subsequent Bayesian decision making, and a heavy reliance on embodiment and on the properties and affordances of the external world.

At the functional level too, the tools of thought are familiar to us from earlier chapters: perception, memory, and language. Perception does more

Figure 8.31 — The famous photograph documenting the first successful airplane flight, by Orville Wright on December 17, 1903, at KITTY HAWK, North Carolina. The machine covered a distance of 39 meters in 12 seconds.

than channel data to some abstract processing: its powerful pattern recognition mechanisms play a key role in understanding problems and representing them in a format that can be more easily dealt with by our Stone Age brains. Likewise, memory is more than a passive receptacle of dead data: active concepts that populate it are ever on the lookout seeking to apply themselves to advance the organism's goals. And language, of course, is just as much a tool for problem solving, reasoning, and decision making as it is for communication.

There is, in fact, no tension between these two notions, because communication itself is a means for problem solving. The involvement of language in thinking has long been studied in psychology (Gleitman and Papafragou, 2005), where, however, the focus has usually been on how thoughts are expressed in words rather than on how they interact. The current resurgence of investigations into interactive language — dialogue, as opposed to monologue — has led to some eye-opening realizations. The chief one of these is that maintaining conversation, which by rights should be more difficult than listening to someone's soliloquy, is actually easier (Pickering and Garrod, 2004).

Conversation should be difficult because it requires that the each of the interlocutors, in his or her turn, comprehend what is being said, consider its implications, prepare and formulate a response, and plan an appropriate vocalization, all within a time window that rarely lasts longer than a few seconds. Because despite all this conversation is nevertheless very easy, Garrod and Pickering (2004) conclude that "the alignment of representations has the effect of distributing the processing load between the interlocutors because each reuses information computed by the other. Alignment comes about through automatic alignment channels similar to those in Dijksterhuis and Bargh's (2001) perception-behaviour expressway, which suggests that humans are 'designed' for dialogue rather than monologue."[35]

What does this mean computationally? Clark (1998) mentions several ways in which "language augments human computation": it gives people access to highly flexible external memory and a versatile workspace for problem solving. In such an external medium, the brain's many heuristic mechanisms that evolved for focused efficiency rather than interoperability can interact freely; according to Dennett (1991), it is the interaction of language with the architecture of the brain that brings into being the mind's virtual machine (and also consciousness, about which more later). Further, both the long-term external memory props and the external workspace can be easily shared with other people, which facilitates collaborative thinking.

Using the computational terminology introduced earlier, we may observe that a distributed problem solver can be modeled by a modified CopyCat architecture (Figure 8.28), in which the Coderack and the Slipnet are effectively pooled among the members of a group. For this to work, the Workspace must be shared too, and for that one needs language. We should, therefore, take the advice of Clark (1998) and see "computational processes as criss-crossing brain, body and world" and "... *language as the ultimate upgrade*: so ubiquitous it is almost invisible; so intimate, it is not clear whether it is a kind of tool or an added dimension of the user" (my italics). Upgrades, however, often have unexpected side effects. Language packs one too: its ability to hold up to the mind a special mirror, into which it can look, to see what it may.

Figure 8.32 — *La Reproduction Interdite*, by René Magritte.

'Do you advise me to look?' asked Frodo.

'No,' she said. 'I do not counsel you one way or the other. I am not a counsellor. You may learn something, and whether what you see be fair or evil, that may be profitable, and yet it may not. Seeing is both good and perilous. Yet I think Frodo, that you have courage and wisdom enough for the venture, or I would not have brought you here. Do as you will!'

The Lord of the Rings
— J. R. R. Tolkien

Notes

[1] So far in this book there are about 7.2 characters per word. I extrapolated the NUMBER OF ACTIONS required to complete this chapter from that figure.

[2] MOTOR CONTROL AND MEMORY. As we saw in Chapter 6, much of the information needed to control the complex mechanical system that is the human body can be pre-computed and stored in memory (in a reduced dimensionality form made possible by muscle synergies). Were it not, my typing would be much slower than it is; the down side of using precomputed and stored motor programs is revealed by the occasions on which I intend to type a relatively rare word, and a more frequent one that happens to have the same prefix gets typed instead before the rest of me notices what is going on. Information about frequencies here is provided by the statistical language model (which you should recall from Chapter 7), which encodes, for each word or sentence prefix, the relative probabilities of its most likely continuations.

[3] The text of the Buddha's Adittapariyaya Sutta or the FIRE SERMON can be found, for example, here: http://www.accesstoinsight.org/tipitaka//sn/sn35/sn35.028.than.html. Compare this with T. S. Eliot's *The Waste Land*, section III (http://www.bartleby.com/201/1.html).

[4] REASONING ABOUT COMPUTERS. Nothing happens when I press *ctrl-alt-Del* because my notebook, luckily, does not run Windows.

[5] Additional factors that distinguish my notebook from the 1957-vintage IBM 704: memory size (2 *GB* vs. 7 *kB*); two central processing units vs. one; word size (64 vs. 36 bits).

[6] DISTRIBUTED COGNITION is the theme of recent special issues of the journals *Language Sciences* (26:6, 2004) and *Pragmatics & Cognition* (14:2, 2006).

[7] Concerning the MATERIALS that were needed for fixing the Apollo 13 CO_2 filters: the plan called for two plastic bags, of which there were only three on board; the remainder of the industrial might behind the mission was 300,000 km away.

[8] POSSIBLE WORLDS SEMANTICS.

- True propositions are those which are true in the actual world (for example: "George W. Bush was sworn in as the US President in 2001");

- False propositions are those which are false in the actual world (for example: "Bob Dole was sworn in as the US President in 2001");

- Possible propositions are those which are true in at least one possible world (for example: "Al Gore was sworn in as the US President in 2001");

- Contingent propositions are those which are true in some possible worlds and false in others (for example: "George W. Bush was sworn in as the US President in 2001," which is contingently true, and "Al Gore was sworn in as the US President in 2001," which is contingently false.).

[9] Although CAUSALITY in physics is a very complex subject, at the levels of description of the world that are addressed by the cognitive sciences the assumption that some events cause others is typically warranted (as indicated by its explanatory value). Consider, for example, history. In the world at large, an episode or historical event may have many factors counterfactually affecting its probability, and, likewise many potential consequences. Despite all this uncertainty, certain historical events appear, in retrospect, to be causal "choke points" (just as some neuronal firing events can be identified counterfactually as having caused other neurons to fire; cf. section 10.1.1). Intuitively, such events have an unusually large set of consequences (this concept can be formalized using the Bayes Networks methodology). A possible example

of such a historical choke point is the success on the part of Alan Turing and his coworkers in Bletchley Park in WWII in breaking the code used by the German Navy Enigma machines — encryption devices used to scramble radio messages before transmitting them (cf. Figure 8.11 on page 338.) The team's cryptanalytic breakthrough gave the Allies the ability to intercept the German submarines' communications, sharply reducing the attrition rate of the trans-Atlantic convoys that supported the British defense efforts. It is worth noting that although the key role of Bletchley Park in the war effort is generally agreed, a solid case for it can only be made by means of computational history: running a large number of detailed simulations of WWII, introducing various controlled interventions (such as having various members of the team come down with a flu at critical times), and observing the consequences. Computational environments for sociological simulation studies are already available (Breure, Boonstra, and Doorn, 2004; Macy and Willer, 2002), but it will be some time before large-scale historical simulation becomes feasible.

[10]Historical analysis is normally BIASED by the knowledge of events that actually transpired and which therefore are deemed to have been very likely. Consideration of counterfactual alternatives, such as ways in which the Allies could have lost WWII, can 'debias' thinking; if, however, people are asked to think of too many counterfactual alternatives, they are more likely to decide that the outcome was inevitable after all (Byrne, 2002).

[11]The two versions of the Wason selection task that appear in Figure 8.10 illustrate the distinction between INDICATIVE and DEONTIC framing of the problem (roughly, focusing on what is, as opposed to what should be). The latter is usually much easier for subjects to relate to.

[12]Cf. William James (1890) on reasoning:

> Over immense departments of our thought we are still, all of us, in the savage state. Similarity operates in us, but abstraction has not taken place. We know what the present case is like, we know what it reminds us of, we have an intuition of the right course to take, if it be a practical matter. But analytic thought has made no tracks, and we cannot justify ourselves to others.
>
> The well-known story of the old judge advising the new one never to give reasons for his decisions, "the decisions will probably be right, the reasons will surely be wrong," illustrates this.
>
> The doctor will feel that the patient is doomed, the dentist will have a premonition that the tooth will break, though neither can articulate a reason for his foreboding. The reason lies imbedded, but not yet laid bare, in all the countless previous cases dimly suggested by the actual one.

[13]Learning from CONTINGENCIES. Humans and animals can learn associations between passively observed events (PAVLOVIAN CONDITIONING) as well as between interventions and outcomes (INSTRUMENTAL CONDITIONING).

[14]Inductive inference is not to be confused with the PRINCIPLE OF MATHEMATICAL INDUCTION — a sound proof method that affirms the truth of every statement in an infinite sequence of statements, given that (i) the first statement in the sequence is true, and (ii) it can be shown that if any statement in the sequence is true, then so is the next one.

[15]The infinity of the set of theorems implied by a given set of axioms is COUNTABLE: it can be placed in a one to one correspondence with the natural numbers. An example of a theorem in Peano's axiomatization of arithmetic is $2 + 2 = 4$; it can be proved in just a few elementary steps. Most of the true theorems generated by formal systems are just as boring

(for example, a conjunction of two theorems is also a theorem); it takes considerable insight (human or computer) to come up with interesting ones.

[16]A problem that is particularly relevant to evolutionary social psychology is DECEPTION, which can, of course, be analyzed within the cognitive-computational framework. For example, behavioral findings reviewed by Vrij, Fisher, Mann, and Leal (2006) suggest that the detection of deception in real-time interactions (e.g., during an interview) can be facilitated by increasing the deceiver's cognitive load (which is better than relying on his or her emotional response, whose source may be irrelevant to the issue at hand). On the computational level, Yu and Singh (2003) describe an evidence combination algorithm capable of downgrading input from informants suspected of deception.

[17]The formalization of SIMILARITY in probabilistic terms offered by psychologists is supported by converging results from computer science and AI. For example, the similarity between A and B can be defined in information-theoretic terms as the ratio between the amount of information needed to state the commonality of A and B and the information needed to fully describe what A and B are (Lin, 1998); information, of course, is defined via probability: $\text{sim}(A,B) = \frac{\log P(\text{common}(A,B))}{\log P(\text{description}(A,B))}$.

[18]The THIRD FACTOR that enters Bayes' Rule (as the denominator of eq. 8.1 on page 346) has to do with the explanatory power specific to the hypothesis h that is under consideration. Tenenbaum et al. (2006) explain it as follows (the notation here is the same as in Box 8.1): data D support h better if they are *surprising* — either (a) unlikely given the background knowledge, or (b) not predicted under most of the plausible alternative hypotheses. Condition (a) is expressed by $P(D|K)$ being small; the smaller it is, the higher the posterior probability in equation 8.1. Condition (b) is a different framing of the same situation, as captured by equation 8.2: $P(D|K)$ is small when $P(D|h',K)$ is small for *plausible* alternative hypotheses (those for which $P(h'|K)$ is high).

[19]The algorithmics of inferring logical rules from perceptual observations has been demonstrated by a computer program of Needham et al. (2005), which learns to play the game of rock, scissors, paper, by observing human players.

[20]SATISFICING is very widespread in cognition. In vision, the many inattentional blindness phenomena (Mack, 2003), some of which I describe in Chapter 9, suggest that the perceptual system settles for quick, but potentially incomplete, representations of the world. Language use is likewise rife with computational shortcuts (recall section 7.5).

[21]The cartoon that I chose to illustrate the CONTEXT DEPENDENCE of judgment is from the English Civil War; I did not think it prudent to use anything more recent or geographically close.

[22]The dependence of perceived change of a stimulus on the relative rather than absolute change in its physical magnitude is known in psychology as the WEBER-FECHNER LAW, first formulated a century and a half ago. In economics, a very similar phenomenon, which underlies the judgment "effect" described in the main text, was identified in 1889 by Wieser.

[23]The ANCHORING HEURISTIC and SYSTEM 1/SYSTEM 2 distinction. Epley and Gilovich (2005b) point out that external anchors must be automatically entertained as possible answers, whereas self-generated ones are presumably considered merely as starting points for deliberation. This is why the former, but not the latter, give rise to an automatic System 1 bias that cannot be compensated through the deliberative action of System 2.

[24]Turing's procedure for limited-resource decision making under uncertainty was called

BANBURISMUS (Gold and Shadlen, 2002), after the town of Banbury, where the paper charts used by the Bletchley Park Enigma team (see note 9 on page 388) were printed.

[25]In FACTOR ANALYSIS, the variability in a set of data is explained by modeling the observed variables as linear combinations of hidden (latent) factors. The goal of the procedure is to determine the weights (called loadings) of the hypothesized factors in the observables. In REGRESSION ANALYSIS, the data are modeled as a possibly nonlinear function of independent variables. STRUCTURAL EQUATION MODELING generalizes both factor analysis and regression by allowing the data to be represented as an estimable function of independent and latent variables.

[26]The many proposals made to date for alternative measures of intelligence (e.g., those that stress its "practical" or "successful" aspects; Sternberg, 1999) end up with factors that are empirically indistinguishable from the accepted standard, or else are too inconsistent to be of use (Gottfredson, 2003).

[27]Brown et al. (2005) used a computer to process videos of dancers, creating stripped-down stimuli that isolated DANCE movements from all other visual information. These were then given for dancing ability evaluation to judges drafted from the same population as the dancers. The researchers found strong correlations between body symmetry and dancing ability, which, furthermore, were stronger for men than for women.

[28]Here is a somewhat involved example of a FORCED MAPPING between the concepts *color* and *length* (which also shows that analogy can be about difference and not only about similarity):

> What is the difference between an alligator? Some say it is greener than it is long, others that it is longer than it is green. In truth, it depends on how you look at the alligator. On the one hand, it is green both lengthwise and sidewise, whereas it is only long lengthwise. On the other hand, it is long both inside and out, whereas it is only green on the outside.

This apocryphal disputation may have been inspired by the (non)description of the crocodile in Act 2, Scene VII, of Shakespeare's *Antony and Cleopatra*.

[29]The manner whereby language structure can be distilled from corpus data (section 7.2.3) suggests that ANALOGY-like processing plays a key role in language. For a theory of language based entirely on analogy, see (Lavie, 2003).

[30]A limited ability to act on relations between relations is found in chimpanzees (especially symbol-trained ones), but not in monkeys (Povinelli et al., 2000; Thompson and Oden, 2000). A VIRTUAL MACHINE appears to be something that even apes don't have.

[31]I found Carroll's raven/desk analogy at http://www.kith.org/logos/words/lower/p.html.

[32]Relating creativity to general intelligence requires a validated instrument for assessing the former — a kind of CREATIVITY QUOTIENT test (Snyder, Mitchell, Bossomaier, and Pallier, 2004).

[33]EUREKA. Archimedes, the greatest mathematician of his time, had been asked by the ruler of Syracuse (the Greek colony in Sicily) to determine whether his new gold crown had been adulterated by silver. For that, the volume of the crown had to be measured precisely, preferably without having to melt it down. Archimedes reportedly discovered a way to do it while he was getting into a bath fulled to the brim: as the water spilled over, he realized that the volume of a solid body, no matter how complex its shape, is equal to the volume of water displaced by it.

[34]On CREATIVITY IN TYPOGRAPHY. As Hofstadter (1985a) notes, the computational chal-

lenge in typeface design lies in achieving uniformity of style within a font, while preserving the freedom of variation in creating new fonts, all within the confines of a low-dimensional (hence computationally manageable) representation space. In modern typography, this challenge has been met for the first time by METAFONT, a typeface design program created by Knuth (1986). In the version of METAFONT described by Knuth (1982), all the letter shapes in a given character set were controlled by a list of 28 parameters. Think of these as knobs that you can turn to play with typographic style: each particular combination of knob settings yields a typeface, which is a point in a 28-dimensional typeface space. It is worth noting that this space is much easier to deal with than the image space into which the character glyphs are rendered: for a 1000×1000-pixel glyph, the image space is $1,000,000$-dimensional.

[35] The existence of a PERCEPTION-BEHAVIOR EXPRESSWAY has been hypothesized by Dijksterhuis and Bargh (2001) to account for a variety of social behaviors in which participants in an interaction mimic each other's posture, spurious actions (e.g., foot shaking or nose rubbing), tone of voice, and figures of speech.

Part III

Finale

9

Being No One

Life is what happens to you while you're busy making other plans.

JOHN LENNON

Глядя на лошадиные морды и лица людей, на безбрежный живой поток, поднятый моей волей и мчащийся в никуда по багровой закатной степи, я часто думаю: где *Я* в этом потоке?

ЧИНГИЗ ХАН[a]

---

[a]Looking at the horse snouts and at the endless stream of life, aroused by my will and hurtling into nowhere down the sunset-bloodied steppe, I often think: where am *I* in this stream? — Genghis Khan. [From Чапаев и Пустота ("Chapayev and Void" by VICTOR PELEVIN, tr. as *Buddha's Little Finger*[1]).]

IN CONTRAST to the kind of REFLEXIVE SELF-CONSCIOUSNESS afforded to humans by looking into the mirror of language, there exists in all of us a more primeval awareness. To the extent that they maintain a model of the world that surrounds them, and themselves as being part of it, all sentient beings share this latter capacity. In the present chapter, I lay out a computational explanation both of this elemental PHENOMENAL EXPERIENCE, and of consciousness grounded in reflection and narrative. The unifying concept will be that of ACCESS among representations — those maintained internally, as well as "that vast external memory, the external environment itself" (Reitman et al., 1978, p.72).

One of the best ways to appreciate the vastness of the world that can be reached through our senses is to climb to a high vantage point in a mountainous desert and look around — which is what I did when I took the picture shown in Figure 9.1 on the following page.

Such places make me wish I had a spherical wraparound retina to take

The Son of Man (R. Magritte).

It is simply not true that everyone has a rough idea of what the term 'consciousness' refers to. [...] The most frequent misunderstanding lies in confusing PHENOMENAL EXPERIENCE as such with what philosophers call 'REFLEXIVE SELF-CONSCIOUSNESS,' the actualized capacity to cognitively refer to yourself, using some sort of concept-like or quasi-linguistic kind of mental structure. According to this definition hardly anything on this planet, including most humans during most of their day, is ever conscious at all.

— Metzinger (2003, p.3)

Figure 9.1 — Even when squeezed onto the printed page, a desert vista is too sweeping and too detailed to be taken in at a single glance, demonstrating the LIMITED ACCESS that visual awareness has to the world that is "out there"; to appreciate fully just how narrow this information bottleneck is, you have to *be* there. A high place in the wilderness is a good setting for contemplating the nature of visual experience and awareness because there is much to be seen, and few distractions to keep you from looking. In this snapshot, the nearest potential distraction is a small group of pixel-sized people hiking down the path that winds around the north side of the canyon, five hundred meters below the vantage point of the camera (Mt. Namer in the Judean Desert, overlooking the upper stretch of wadi Tse'elim to the west).

in everything that can be seen, all at once. Alas, because of the limitations of my anatomy, I can only take in somewhat less than a hemisphere's worth of the scene at a glance, unless I move my eyes, my head, or my body. This constraint on access to scene information, which thwarts my desire to contemplate the wholeness of the desert while sitting still, does not, however, interfere with the visual task that is probably more relevant than zazen[2] to everyday human behavior: the analysis of scenes in terms of their causes, namely, objects and their interactions. In natural scenes, such analysis typically reveals hierarchical structure, which reflects the structure of the universe that we inhabit (cf. Chapter 2).

Returning for an example to the scene depicted in Figure 9.1, we see that behaviorally relevant structure can be discerned there on multiple spatial scales. On a kilometer scale, the structure is the topography of the terrain, which is what I look at while searching for a possible source of water (a vital resource in the desert). Before beginning my descent into the canyon, where water may be found, I look around the immediate area, a few tens of square meters, in search for a path that can be followed down (scrambling down a scree is never a good idea). Finally, in each stride I look closely at a small area, a fraction of a square meter or so, around the place where I am about to step (to see whether the foothold would be stable, and to make sure I am not going to step on a snake — something that I almost did once, not far from where the snapshot in Figure 9.1 was taken).

These examples reveal that constraining the cognitive system's access to the visual information inherent in a scene — treating the scene as *the opposite* of a spatial whole — is an absolute must in natural vision. The wide-angle view of the desert from my vantage point contains all the information needed to search for water, plan a path, and execute the first step. It is, however, spread across a hierarchy of spatial scales, and extracting it requires focusing — that is, restricting access even more than it is already restricted by the make-up of our bodies. The mechanism that does that for me is ATTENTION.

9.1 Attention

The conclusion just reached — that certain visual tasks require focusing — is an example of *problem*-level analysis which, as we learned back in Chapter 4, is the proper first step in any attempt to understand a cognitive faculty. The conclusion that attention is a necessity is strengthened by a joint analysis of

At any given time, the environment presents far more perceptual information than can be effectively processed.

— Chun and Wolfe (2001)

problems arising in vision and of their possible computational *solutions*. On the intuitive level, it has often been observed that the amount of information contained in the raw measurements carried out by the perceptual systems (the retina, the cochlea, etc.) greatly exceeds the brain resources available for processing it: it does not appear to be feasible for the brain to process all the available information in parallel, without discarding any of it (Chun and Wolfe, 2001; Neisser, 1967). For one class of visual tasks, search, this intuition has been supported by a formal computational complexity analysis (Tsotsos, 1990).[3] Giving preference to some aspects of the input over others cannot, therefore, be avoided.

9.1.1   Kinds of attention

In human vision, processing resources are allocated in a non-uniform fashion already very early on. Instead of sampling the entire visual field at a uniformly high resolution, the eye-to-brain mapping allocates a disproportionately large share of the resources in the primary visual cortex to representing the central portion of the visual field, whose size is about two by two degrees of visual angle. This results in a high spatial acuity around the center of gaze (recall Figure 3.5 on page 48), compared to the periphery.

In a sense, the eye-to-brain mapping amounts to a simple kind of dimensionality reduction performed on the visual world: some of the dimensions of variation in the image projected onto the retina are simply dropped. This or any other kind of dimensionality reduction implies a preferential treatment of some of the data in the input stream at the expense of other data. The resulting access bottleneck would be a severe handicap on the perceptual system, were it not STEERABLE (buying a high-resolution digital camera only to keep it bolted to the desk would not amount to a good use of resources).

Visual attention is steerable in space, as well as along some of the other dimensions of relevance. The spatial focus of attention follows the direction of gaze, which a person can control by moving the eyes, by rotating the head, and by repositioning the torso. In addition to such OVERT shifts of the focus, the steering of spatial attention can be COVERT (to see what I mean, fixate a random word in the middle of this page; you'll find out that you can read the words immediately above and below it, one at a time, without moving your eyes away from the fixation spot).

Whereas overt attention shifts are by definition spatial, covert mechanisms can operate along feature dimensions other than space, as when the perceiver needs to focus on one of several co-extensive stimuli — overlapping visual objects (Roelfsema, Lamme, and Spekreijse, 1998), or simultaneous sounds (Carlyon, 2004), or intermingled odorants (Joerges, Küttner, Galizia, and Menzel, 1997), or flavors[4] (an example from the visual domain is shown in Figure 9.2).

Together, the steerability of the processing focus and the capacity for selecting the data that are singled out for special treatment are the defining

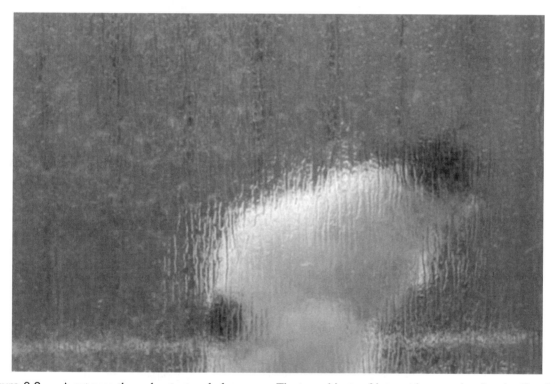

Figure 9.2 — A cat seen through a textured glass pane. The two objects of interest here — the glass itself and the cat behind it — cannot be separated by focusing *spatial* attention to this or that portion of the image. Instead, the observer must attend selectively along OTHER DIMENSIONS. One of these is spatial frequency: the glass pane is more finely textured than the cat shape blurred by it, and can therefore be focused upon by selectively attending to the outputs of neurons tuned to high spatial frequencies (cf. Figure 9.3 on page 402). Another distinguishing dimension in this example is depth, which is available in the original scene but is lost in the flat picture.

characteristics of attention. They are present in all the categories of tasks commonly listed as requiring attention: ALERTING, ORIENTING, and EXECUTION (Raz and Buhle, 2006). Let us briefly consider the computational nature of each of these categories, in the order in which they occur in typical interactions between an embodied cognitive system and the environment in which it is situated.

Alerting

A key moment-to-moment function of attention is to alert the cognitive system to any aspect of the sensory world that may merit a more thorough processing than it is currently getting. In human vision, this may be any object or attribute seen from the corner of the eye (and sometimes, as we'll see in section 9.7.2, items that are fixated and even scrutinized). The basis on which alerting decisions are made is necessarily flimsy: had the system possessed sufficient resources to process all the incoming information equally thoroughly, there would be no need for attention in the first place. The computational challenge of alerting consists, therefore, of making a decision on the basis of necessarily cursory and partial data. As such, it is closely related to a range of tasks discussed earlier in the book: perceptual generalization and recognition (Chapter 5), autoassociative memory (Chapter 6), and, of course, decision making under risk (Chapter 8).

Given, on the one hand, these parallels, and on the other hand the universal utility of probabilistic inference in cognitive computation, we should not be surprised to discover that alerting is also Bayesian. In vision, for example, a scene element that's outside the immediate focus of attention would draw the observer's gaze in proportion to the product of its prior record of perceptual notoriety and the likelihood of its renewed importance given the current data. This notion is supported by the results of Itti and Baldi (2006), who studied the attention shifts of subjects watching television and video games. They found that observers' gaze is strongly attracted towards locations marked as surprising by a Bayesian salience algorithm. In that study, 72% of the gaze shifts were directed towards locations estimated by the algorithm to be more surprising than the average. This figure rose to 84% when only those targets simultaneously selected by all subjects were considered.

Orienting

Having been alerted to a potentially important but not yet fixated stimulus by peripheral mechanisms (or by a voluntary decision to shift the focus of attention), the visual system reorients itself. It may do so overtly, by bringing the newly targeted portion of the scene within the reach of its high-resolution measurement device, the fovea (cf. Figure 3.5 on page 48), or covertly, by channelling the input from the locus of interest towards the high-capacity processing mechanisms, which by default receive data coming from the fovea. In each case, information from the targeted spot is *selected* and is given preferential treatment, at the expense of the rest of the visual field.

An immediate consequence of this preferential treatment is an increase in the perceived COHERENCE of the attended stimulus. Normally, entities that have not yet been attended to are perceived only as "shapeless bundles of basic features" (Wolfe and Bennett, 1997). For example, human subjects briefly shown a card printed with some colored letters reliably report the colors and the letters, but are likely to be confused as to which color went with which letter — unless they attended to the spatial location of the letter in question (Treisman and Gelade, 1980). In general, the scattered features computed by the bottom-up perceptual processes — some dabs of color, a few lines, a curving patch of a surface — get integrated into coherent objects following their top-down selection and channelling into preferential processing.

It is possible to pull together the initially loose bundles of features into objects by selecting regions along dimensions other than space. One such dimension is SPATIAL FREQUENCY — a characteristic that corresponds, informally, to the distribution of intensity information across different scales of spatial detail in a specified part of an image.[5] Looking at Figure 9.2, for instance, you should be able to attend separately to the blurry (low-frequency) shape of the cat, or to the finer-scale (high-frequency) texture of the glass pane in front of it. The possibility of selection on the basis of spatial frequency has been documented by Bonnar et al. (2002), using Salvador Dalí's painting *Slave market with a disappearing bust of Voltaire* (Figure 9.3 on the next page) as the stimulus. In this painting, focusing on low spatial frequency cues (corresponding to large-scale features of the image) helps subjects perceive Voltaire's face, which coheres out of smaller-scale details such as the figures of the two nuns.

Figure 9.3 — Bonnar et al. (2002) used Dalí's painting *Slave market with a disappearing bust of Voltaire* to study attention-driven orienting and SELECTION of various sources of visual information in scenes. A set of sparse versions of the ambiguous region that can be alternatively perceived as two nuns or Voltaire's head was generated by filtering the original image in space (using windows of several sizes in an otherwise opaque mask) and in spatial frequency (using band-pass filters each tuned to one of several scales; see note 5 on page 456 for an explanation of spatial frequency). By presenting the sparse test images to the subjects and recording their reported percepts (nuns or Voltaire), the researchers determined that these correlated with the frequency content of the stimulus. A second experiment demonstrated that ADAPTING the subject (recall section 5.4.2) to high- or low-frequency visual noise increased the likelihood of perceiving the shape associated with the complementary frequency band — Voltaire or the nuns, respectively.

Execution

Selectively attending to some aspects of the stimulus while downplaying others can turn out to be an effortful process — sometimes markedly so. Consider, for example, the task of naming the colors of words presented on a screen, as illustrated in Figure 9.4. When the subject looks at the first word on the left, its visual form, `white`, activates the concept white, which interferes with the activation of the concept black — the correct item that needs to be channeled to the motor execution routine. Such interference causes the reading times to be significantly longer than in cases where the color and the content cues do not conflict with each other. This phenomenon, called STROOP INTERFERENCE after its discoverer, is quite common in perception-action tasks.

The Stroop task exemplifies, but does not exhaust, a much more general computational problem of EXECUTIVE CONTROL: **balancing responsiveness to the flow of information from the senses and from memory with adherence to one's own goals and desires.** Proficiency in this balancing act is a sure mark of cognitive sophistication. A superior cognitive system is both attentive and steadfast; when interrupted in the middle of going about its business, it will neither abandon its prior activity on the spot nor persevere slavishly. Rather, it will evaluate the new circumstances (using familiar computational tools that are also at work in perception, memory, and thinking) to proceed according to an appropriately adjusted plan.

Figure 9.4 — In the STROOP task, it takes the subject longer to name the color in which a word is presented on the screen if the color and the meaning of the word clash with each other (*left*), compared to a control condition in which they do not (*right*). This INTERFERENCE effect demonstrates the computational problem of exerting control over the flow of information from the senses so as to meet the requirements stemming from the task at hand (Raz and Buhle, 2006).

9.1.2 Mechanisms of attention

In primates, whose main sensory inputs are visual and auditory, attention has a natural computational definition in terms of delineating regions in a two-dimensional egocentric "reality space" (Merker, 2007, fig.5). This space can be easily visualized as a sphere centered on the self (akin to the "wraparound retina" concept that I mentioned on p. 395) onto which the external world is "projected" by the senses (Figure 9.5). Only a small part of the reality space can be accessed, and an even smaller part effectively processed, at a time — hence the need for neuronal mechanisms for alerting, orienting, and executive control, all of which rely, to begin with, on the geometrical structure of the reality space.

The spotlight of attention

A key property of the reality space is that it is structured and predictable rather than amorphous and random: elements of the representational mosaic (see Figure 9.5) that "belong" together reside close to each other because they arise from objects or events[6] that COHERE in space and time. Attentional processes capitalize on this coherence (without which perception itself would not be possible; cf. section 5.8) and make it explicit through the same

Figure 9.5 — The EGOSPHERE (Albus, 1991) — a representational structure centered on the self that facilitates the computational analysis of the behavioral tasks facing an embodied agent such as a human being. In humans, covert orienting of attention as well as the visuomotor map for reaching appear to be framed in spherical coordinates; keeping visual and motor representations in spatial register makes possible coordination of vision and motor control using spatially aligned neural maps found in the cortex (section 3.2.2) and in subcortical areas of the brain (Merker, 2007; more about these later).

mechanism that implements the concentration and distillation of input data in sensory neurons: receptive fields. As noted by Tsotsos (1990, p.433), a classical receptive field is contiguous — both, one might add, in the retinotopic space and along whatever additional feature dimensions wherein it exhibits tuning — because the world to which it is attuned is populated by coherent objects. This contiguity is aptly expressed by the common metaphor of the SPOTLIGHT of attention (Vidyasagar, 1998).[7]

In primates, the overt spotlight of attention follows the direction of gaze as it is shifted around to point the fovea toward the object of interest. Gaze shifts or SACCADES, which normally happen about three times every second unless preempted by volitional control, cause abrupt changes in the information that feeds into the visually responsive neurons, simply because their receptive fields land in new locations. More interesting, however, is primates' ability to shift attention covertly at the level of single neurons by manipulating the information flow *within* a spatial receptive field, as discovered by Moran and Desimone (1985).

The monkeys in this study were trained to keep their gaze at a preset spot on a screen, while at the same time attending in each trial to one of two stimuli, without breaking fixation (Figure 9.6). Throughout the series of trials in each experiment, the researchers were monitoring the response of a

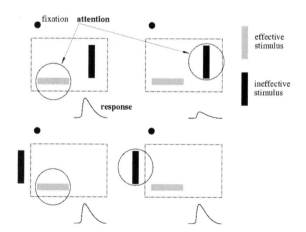

Figure 9.6 — A demonstration in the monkey of attentional control over the responsiveness of a V4 neuron to stimuli within its receptive field (Moran and Desimone, 1985). Monkeys in this study were trained to hold fixation while selectively attending to one of two stimuli (short bars of different colors and orientations) at a time. *Top left:* a stimulus known from pre-trial exploration to be effective for the recorded neuron is inside the neuron's RF and is attended to; the neuron responds vigorously. *Top right:* the effective stimulus is still inside the RF but is not attended to; the neuron's response is much weaker. The bottom two panes provide a control: when the effective stimulus is the only one present inside the cell's RF, shifts of attention do not have the same gating or modulating effect on the cell's response.

neuron in visual area V4. One of the two stimuli was chosen to be effective in making the monitored neuron respond; the other was chosen to be equally prominent (so that the monkey could attend to it) but not effective in making the neuron fire. Surprisingly, the neuron ceased responding to the effective stimulus every time the monkey attended to the ineffective one, even though both stimuli were situated at all times within the neuron's classical receptive field. Covert attention shifts were thus shown to modulate the cell's response, making it ignore effective stimuli when these were not attended to.

Whether overt or covert, shifts of attention are controlled by the same neural mechanism, which connects the frontal eye fields (FEF, a cortical area in the frontal lobe) both to the oculomotor circuitry in the midbrain and to the V4 sensory neurons. It has long been known that electrical stimulation of FEF neurons evokes saccades to well-defined locations that correspond to the neurons' "eye fields." Recently, Moore and Fallah (2001) showed that microstimulation of the FEF using currents that are almost, but not quite, strong enough to evoke saccades improves the subject's performance in a discrimination task, provided that the visual stimulus falls within the target area of the would-be saccade, represented by the FEF site (Figure 9.7). Complementing this behavioral finding and completing the neural-level explanation

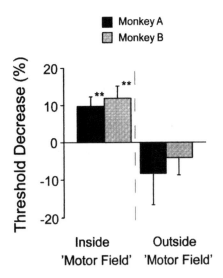

Figure 9.7 — Microstimulation of the frontal eye fields (a cortical area long implicated in saccade generation) improves the subject's performance in a covert spatial attention task — detecting the location of a momentarily dimmed stimulus in a field of distractors — but only if the stimulus is situated inside the motor field, that is, the would-be target area of the saccade (Moore and Fallah, 2001; ** denotes significant effects). The microstimulation current in this experiment was always below the threshold needed to evoke an actual saccade, yet it sufficed to cause the covert shift of attention to the target location (overtly, the monkeys maintained fixation throughout each trial). In a follow-up study designed to identify the neural basis of this effect, Moore and Armstrong (2003) determined that responses of neurons in area V4 to visual stimuli are enhanced by subthreshold stimulation of retinotopically corresponding sites within the FEF (cf. Figure 9.6).

of the previously mentioned work of Moran and Desimone (1985), Moore and Armstrong (2003) determined that responses of neurons in area V4 to visual stimuli are enhanced by brief stimulation of retinotopically corresponding sites within the FEF.

The common operating principle for the mechanisms of attention, as suggested by these aforementioned findings, is reliance on RETINOTOPICALLY organized receptive fields in selectively enhancing the response to the attended stimuli, while suppressing the response to unattended ones. The retinotopic map of the visual world, which corresponds to the reality space of Figure 9.5 on page 404, is redundantly implemented by neural arrays in the visual cortex, in particular areas V1 (Vidyasagar, 1998) and V4 (Connor, Preddie, Gallant, and Van Essen, 1997; Moore and Armstrong, 2003; Moran and Desimone, 1985), both in monkeys and in humans (Gallant, Shoup, and Mazer, 2000). As shown in Figure 9.8, it interacts with retinotopic maps in subcortical structures (notably, in the superior colliculus (Merker, 2007; Shipp, 2004); see the margin illustration on p. 423), and with flexible, action-oriented maps

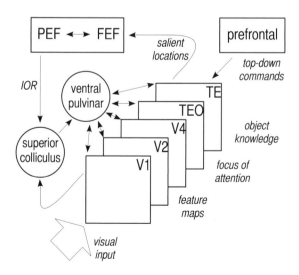

Figure 9.8 — The functional connections among areas implementing attention in the primate brain, after (Shipp, 2004, fig.2g), illustrating its fundamental RETINOTOPIC architecture. The ventral pulvinar nucleus and the superior colliculus are subcortical areas where the control over attention is concentrated: "The subcortical circuit ... can be pictured as an integrated hub, or remote control centre for exerting synchronous influence over the cortical network" (Shipp, 2004; cf. Figure 8.21 on page 363). *Legend:* PEF/FEF, parietal/frontal eye fields; V1–TE, visual cortical areas in the occipito-temporal processing stream. IOR, inhibition of return (a signal that temporarily steers the focus of attention away from already attended locations). Note that areas V1–TE form a redundant, multi-resolution RETINOTOPIC representation of the visual field. An explicit computational model of the attentional control system developed by Itti et al. (1998) has been found to closely replicate human fixation patterns in natural scenes (Itti and Koch, 2001).

elsewhere in the cerebral cortex (notably, in the parietal lobe; Colby, 1998; Glimcher, Dorris, and Bayer, 2005).[8]

Wherefrom, whither

The key functional characteristic of the retinotopic maps, without which they would be useless to attention, is ADDRESSABILITY. When data associated with a localized area or object of potential interest are deemed important enough to warrant attention, the system must know where it came from. This means that the bottom-up data-channeling mechanism must retain address (essentially, location) information. The brain does that implicitly by relying on a stack of maps of same size but different resolutions, interconnected so as to be effectively in spatial register (Shipp, 2004; cf. Figure 9.8). The region of interest, once identified through a bottom-up process, can then be localized as precisely as necessary by choosing a map with an appropriate resolution — all the way down at the most detailed level of V1, if needed (Vidyasagar, 1998).

Localizing the region of interest in the viewed scene is not enough: a flexible attentive system must also be able to *act* on the information obtained in this manner, by steering the sensory data in question toward special processing (such as categorization) that is too expensive to carry out on a massive scale over the entire visual field. The steering functionality requires a neural mechanism capable of DYNAMIC ROUTING, which can be provided by the generic circuit depicted in Figure 9.9.

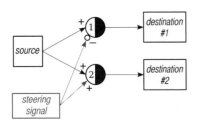

Figure 9.9 — A DYNAMIC ROUTER circuit (similar to the one illustrated on p. 359) can be built with McCulloch-Pitts formal neurons — idealized devices that mimic some of the key computational characteristics of real neurons (McCulloch and Pitts, 1943). An M-P neuron emits a spike on its output line ("axon") if and only if the sum of the excitation and the inhibition (positively and negatively weighted signals) at its inputs in the preceding time interval exceeds a fixed threshold (indicated here by the numeral inside the circle). In this circuit, a spike emitted by the source will be routed to destination #1 if the steering control signal is quiescent. If the control emits a spike simultaneously with the source, the top neuron is inhibited, but the bottom one is not, and the source spike is routed to destination #2.

Flexible routing of information that is the defining attribute of attention is central also to the functional element that symbolizes sophistication in cognition: controlled, random-access working memory. A cognitive computation that requires any kind of iterated action on the same datum, or recursion (acting on the outcome of the previous computational step; cf. p. 243), must isolate its subject matter from perceptual input and from interference by other memories (O'Reilly, 2006a, p.91). The router sketched in Figure 9.9 on the preceding page can provide just the necessary functionality — dynamic gating of information into and out of the working memory circuit (O'Reilly, 2006a, fig.3). In particular, if the memory consists of more than one "cell" (as it must if its capacity is to exceed one bit of information), it must be equipped with a steering mechanism that would direct an item that needs to be stored to its intended address.

A neural gadget capable of steering information and of configuring and temporarily sequestering a circuit to let the sequence of operations it implements run their course is a primary component of the ultimate piece of computational MAGIC: the virtual machine (recall Figure 8.11 on page 338). With this functionality, it becomes possible to decide upon the destination of a signal on the basis of some property of the signal itself. This, in turn, endows the system with a capacity for conditional branching: "if condition C holds, execute subprogram P_1; otherwise, execute P_2"; the subprograms themselves can be implemented by hard-wired circuits, which receive their inputs through the dynamic gating mechanism.

If the steering signals themselves reside in working memory, they can be modified by the outcome of earlier processing, thereby placing control and data on an equal footing. A computational system that can do *that* attains the pinnacle of flexible learning — the capability of dynamically rewriting its own "program" on the basis of experience.

Any sufficiently advanced technology is indistinguishable from MAGIC.

Arthur C. Clarke's Third Law
Profiles of the Future,
revised ed. (1973)

9.2 Modes of awareness

Prioritized access to information may allow the cognitive system to play a decent game of survival without being overwhelmed by the onslaught of sensory data, but selective attention alone does not explain the mind's equanimity in the face of this onslaught. Barring certain pathological conditions, successive stimuli that compete for my attention manage to do so — some of them winning access to premium processing, others losing — without necessarily making me aware of the bustle, just as I am not aware of my gaze shifting around three times a second while I sit on a desert hilltop and enjoy the serene view. That I can be aware of the view and at the same time oblivious of my saccadic escapades means that there is more to AWARENESS than meets the eye.

Because the saccades are unquestionably real, I am forced to conclude that it is my subjective, phenomenal experience of a static scene that is irreal. This insight should help us understand how the brain can keep its peace of mind despite the informational deluge to which it is being constantly subjected: it pretends that *there is no deluge* (cf. Figure 9.10, left[9]) and apparently gets away with it, just as it gets away with pretending that the visual world is rock-stable and that there ain't no such things as saccades. In short, the mind inhabits a *virtual reality* of its own making that is a SIMULATION or model — greatly simplified in some respects, elaborate and sophisticated in others — of the real world (Merker, 2007; Metzinger, 2003).

Some of the different levels on which the brain can model the world, which correspond to different modes of awareness, can be illustrated with the picture shown in Figure 9.10, right (reproduced from p. 163). A simple visual system may see this image as no more than a squiggly horizontal line attached to a straight vertical one. In comparison, a system that possesses the visual concept pig may *see* the squiggly line *as* a telltale of the pig behind the barn, of which the system thus becomes aware. Finally, an even more complex system that can stand back from its own "first-order" perceptual states may entertain a "second-order" conscious thought, containing straight-

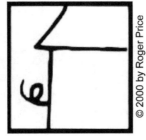

© 2000 by Roger Price

Figure 9.10 — *Left: "There is no spoon"* — one of several very good lines from the first, good *Matrix* movie (see note 9 on page 457). In section 9.3, we shall see how it captures some of the spirit of the present understanding of phenomenal experience as rooted in the brain's SIMULATION of reality (Merker, 2007; Metzinger, 2003). *Right: "There is no pig"* — it is not the pig's tail that bends, it is only yourself.

forward perceptual elements such as "squiggly line" and "pig" alongside ones that involve reflection, such as "likely a pig's tail" or "there must be a pig behind that barn." The truth, as we shall realize soon, is that conscious thought has the same existential status, and the same computational nature, as the virtual pig behind the barn.

The preceding example suggests that visual awareness that arises on some levels of simulation involves what Wittgenstein (1958) called "SEEING AS" — a notion he introduced using the ambiguous figure that appears in this book on p. 103, which can be seen as a duck or as a rabbit. Here is how he explains it:

> 'Seeing as...' is not part of perception. And for that reason it is like seeing and again not like.
>
> I look at an animal and am asked: "What do you see?" I answer: "A rabbit". — I see a landscape; suddenly a rabbit runs past. I exclaim "A rabbit!"
> Both things, both the report and the exclamation, are expressions of perception and of visual experience. But the exclamation is so in a different sense from the report: it is forced from us. — It is related to the experience as a cry is to pain.
>
> But since it is the description of a perception, it can also be called the expression of thought. — If you are looking at the object, you need not think of it; but if you are having the visual experience expressed by the exclamation, you are also *thinking* of what you see.

> — Wittgenstein (1958, xi)

By PHENOMENAL EXPERIENCE (as in the experience of seeing a rabbit; cf. note 4 on page 307), I mean to appeal, not to metaphysics, but rather to your intuition about what it feels like to see something. I shall presently explain the cognitive basis for this intuition in neurocomputational terms.

With just a few penetrating observations, Wittgenstein stakes out a hierarchy of levels of awareness in relation to seeing. At the bottom level, there is plain visual perception — the kind of "seeing for action" that even a scallop can do. At the top level, there is seeing that leads to a deliberate report in response to a query, and is in that sense fully conscious. In between, there is an intermediate level, where one finds perceptual awareness that is more than a reflex (an obligatory shortcut between percept and action), and yet less than a reflection (an open-ended deliberation about the percept). I identify perceptual awareness at this special level of representation with a state of mind that is as immediately intuitive as it has been traditionally difficult to nail down in functional or computational terms: PHENOMENAL EXPERIENCE.

9.3   The phenomenal Self

The character of phenomenal experience is at the core of the so-called "hard problem" of consciousness (Chalmers, 1995), which can be posed in the form of three related questions:

1. What makes a "mere" physical process an EXPERIENCE for someone?

2. What makes a "mere" physical system a subject, or an EXPERIENCER?

3. What does having a FIRST-PERSON PERSPECTIVE on an experience consist of?

The first question follows up on the issue of the components of experience, or qualia. In section 5.7.1, I reduced qualia to appropriately structured representational states, but stopped short of acknowledging that qualia are the components of *someone's* experience. A complete explanation requires, therefore, that the first two questions be treated together. Then there is the third question, which pertains to the apparent chasm between what I can know about my SELF and my experiences (a domain for which I possess what philosophers call a first-person perspective), and what I can know about the selves and experiences of my fellow primates, each ensconced in its own brain (for which I must settle for a third-person perspective).

Much of the philosophical confusion surrounding the idea of the first-person perspective stems from its paradoxical inaccessibility to first-person intuition — a problem articulated most clearly by a neurobiologist: "There is no direct experience of a knower. There is no direct knowledge of the process of awareness" (Lashley, 1923, p.251).[10] The problem is not, however, insurmountable: significant progress towards solving it has been made possible by advances in theoretical and experimental neuroscience, psychology, and scientifically informed philosophy (Crick and Koch, 1990; Lamme, 2003; Merker, 2007; Metzinger, 2003). The computational account developed below, which integrates ideas and findings from those fields, aims to dissolve the "hard problem" of consciousness by reducing the concepts of phenomenal experience, subjecthood, and, most importantly, first-person perspective to the familiar functional building blocks that make up all of cognition.

9.3.1 Some of the attributes of the first-person perspective

The four key components of phenomenal first-person experience that will be explained here are: AGENCY, or sense of initiative; MINENESS, or sense of ownership; PERSPECTIVALNESS, or the perception of phenomenal space as being organized around the self; and finally SELFHOOD, or the conscious experience of being someone (Gallagher, 2000; Metzinger, 2004). As we shall see next, all four arise, in a properly structured representational system — including, but in principle not limited to, the human brain — as a direct consequence of the computational abilities and limitations inherent in its architecture.

Agency and mineness

The computational basis of the feeling of control over one's actions and of ownership of one's body is a pair of feedback loops formed by COROLLARY DISCHARGE circuits (Figure 9.11), which convey an EFFERENCE COPY of the motor signals to the perceptual system, thereby allowing it to compensate for the expected effects of the movement (a happy consequence of a properly functioning efference copy mechanism is that we do not see the world swinging wildly by two or three times every second, which is how often saccadic eye movements happen). The feeling of agency, or the initiative behind one's actions, arises from a corollary discharge circuit that compares (i) the intended end state representing the desired consequence of an action to (ii) the

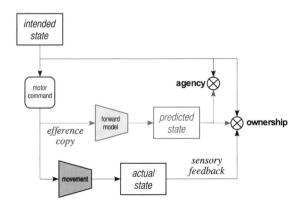

Figure 9.11 — The computational origins of the phenomenal self in EFFERENCE COPY, after Gallagher (2000). For movement, a match between the intended state and a prediction formed by the forward model on the basis of the efference copy gives rise to a sense of AGENCY; a match between intended, predicted, and actual states provides a sense of OWNERSHIP. For perceptual experience, ownership is inferred from a similar comparison involving anticipated effects of attention shifts (Taylor, 2002).

prediction formed by the forward model on the basis of the efference copy of the action, obtained from the motor planner.

Because the action — locomotion, a postural change, an eye movement, or a covert shift of attention — may affect perception, the sense of agency is tied to the sense of ownership. Specifically, when the input channel is steered towards a particular location in the visual field, the corollary discharge mechanism that generates the feeling of agency also gives rise to an anticipation of perceptual input from the newly attended location, contributing to the sense of ownership of the resulting percept (Taylor, 2002).[11]

As philosophically minded readers would notice, the sense of ownership generated by the corollary discharge mechanisms is contingent rather than logically necessary: it seems plausible that phenomenal experience *could* arise as explained above, but it does not appear that it *must*. The strong dependence of the phenomenal properties of experiences on their relative timing indicates that in inferring ownership the brain commits a logical fallacy, known as *post hoc ergo propter hoc* ("after this, therefore because of this").

When the timing *seems* to be right (for instance, in the case of sensing an object touching the subject's hand in plain sight, this means that the proprioceptive signal is synchronized with the visual one), the subject's feeling of ownership over his or her body and experiences is incontrovertible. That feeling, however, dissipates when a short delay is introduced into the visual signal. Worse, a false feeling of ownership of a foreign object such as a rubber hand can easily be induced by touching that object (in plain sight) and the subject's own hand (out of sight) simultaneously. Ehrsson, Spence, and Passingham (2004) took advantage of this RUBBER HAND ILLUSION to investigate the brain basis of body ownership in human subjects,[12] and tracked it down to the premotor cortex. Together with the ventral intraparietal area VIP, where many neurons have combined visual and tactile receptive fields, the premotor cortex forms a circuit that represents the body schema in which visual and proprioceptive information are integrated.

The efference copy theory explains not only the computational origins of the sense of agency and the sense of ownership, but also their breakdown in pathological conditions such as schizophrenia (Gallagher, 2000). For example, when changes in the perceptual signal do not match the expectations induced by the efference copy, the sense of ownership of the movement is disrupted. Likewise, a break in the circuit that compares motor intention to efference copy causes the loss of the sense of agency, or its misattribution to an outside entity. Moreover, because the functional logic of Figure 9.11

applies to thought processes and not just to motor behavior, the same explanation works for disorders such as thought insertion (Gallagher, 2000, fig.2). Metzinger (2003) devotes hundreds of pages of his book to neuropsychological evidence that bears on these ideas, developing detailed explanations of numerous psychiatric conditions in terms of various breakdowns of the mechanisms just described; these, however, are outside the scope of my book.[13]

Perspectivalness

A key feature of the first-person perspective on experience, which intuitively distinguishes it in the most compelling possible way from the third-person perspective, is its physical centering on the phenomenal self (Metzinger, 2004). According to this intuition, I am at the center of what happens to me, and to understand what it feels like to be me, you would literally have to take my place. As long as I am occupying it, this eventuality is excluded by both common sense and simple physics. Furthermore, the physics of perception also dictates that *any* device capable of measuring and registering light be at least partially opaque. These constraints create a seemingly inescapable difference between physically distinct vantage points, as well as a directional asymmetry between the front end of my sensory apparatus, where light enters, and its back.

The kind of privileged perspective that I have on my own visual experience is not, however, a universal invariant: it depends on the geometry, number, and arrangement of the sensors in my visual system. A creature that has a spherical eye whose entire surface is covered with photoreceptors and which communicates with the rest of the brain via a radio link (to prevent even a single blind spot from marring the panoptic visual field) does not have a natural visually defined front and back as I do. Nor is my perspective inexorably linked to my physical location: TELEPRESENCE via a radio link allows me to feel like I am in Valles Marineris on Mars, while my body remains in Ithaca, New York (Figure 9.12 on the following page).

The preceding examples show that every human's supposedly privileged perspective on subjective phenomenal experience is merely a by-product of the physical make-up of the human body and visual system. In fact, it is perspective-taking that allows us to go farther and to realize that the notion of phenomenal experience itself makes no sense in disconnection from the body that captures it. Consider a creature that has one eye on each of two fully articulate and independently controlled necks, such as the science-fictional

What is it like to be a PIERSON'S PUP-
PETEER?

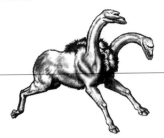

The puppeteers are two-headed aliens invented by Larry Niven, the author of the
Ringworld novels. Because it has two heads
on long, flexible necks, a puppeteer can look
itself into the eyes without using a mirror.
Suppose the eyes in its left head are blue, and
the eyes in the right head are green; what will
the puppeteer see when it faces itself as suggested above — a green-eyed creature, or a
blue-eyed one?

two-headed, three-legged PIERSON'S PUPPETEER. What would the puppeteer, whom for the sake of this discussion we shall imagine as having one
green and one blue eye, *see* when it turns the eyes towards each other — a
blue eye, or a green one? I cannot really tell: my intuition, which is a product of my embodiment, fails me here. My experience of looking out at the
world through two sensors with yoked attitude control and largely overlapping fields of view does not prepare me to imagine even what it feels like to
see as does a rabbit (whose eyes point in two very different directions), let
alone a puppeteer.

The entire notion of first-person perspective thus turns out to be an illusion, an outgrowth of the combination of humanoid embodiment and what
Metzinger (2004, p.36) calls a "very soft visuogrammatical metaphor" — the
intrinsically perceptual concept of viewpoint that got entrenched in everyday
language, where it hatched an entire brood of intuitions about what it "surely"
must be like to be a perceiver in general. The fragility of these intuitions
should make it easier for us to accept objective explanations of phenomenal
experience and of the first-person perspective — the hard core of consciousness. Before we can rest we must, however, confront one last and strongest
intuition: that perspectives are there for the benefit of a spectator, and that
every experience must have an experiencer.

Figure 9.12 — The perspectivalness of the human visual experience is easily subverted by technological means: a subject in a
TELEPRESENCE rig feels as if he or she is elsewhere. If the display
(which can include tactile channels, as well as mechanical actuators
that convey a sense of acceleration) is fed with computer-generated
data consistent with the subject's presence in a simulated world, the
resulting phenomenal immersion in this virtual reality may be difficult to shrug off. Advances in computer graphics technology, coupled with direct input-output brain interfaces, will eventually render
the differences between real and virtual worlds imperceptible. Direct output is already within reach (Lebedev and Nicolelis, 2006);
direct input methods such as electrical microstimulation (Cohen
and Newsome, 2004) are presently too crude and are difficult to
test in humans.

Selfhood

It seems hardly possible for me to deny my own intuition that I am *someone* — an entity that is characterized by phenomenal unity, persists over time, has privileged access to certain information (the contents of my consciousness), is the initiator of certain acts (those over which I have non-mediated control), and is the owner of certain perceptions (those that ensue from my acts). This entity — the PHENOMENAL SELF — is the deeply felt premise for the kind of rationalization exemplified by the following excerpt from Greg Egan's novel *Diaspora*:

> Yatima gazed at the three of them, bemused — oblivious to the ceremonial words, trying to understand what had changed inside verself. Ve saw vis friends, and the stars, and the crowd, and sensed vis own icon ... but even as these ordinary thoughts and perceptions flowed on unimpeded, a new kind of question seemed to spin through the black space behind them all. Who is thinking this? Who is seeing these stars ...? Who is wondering about these thoughts, and these sights?
>
> And the reply came back, not just in words, but in the answering hum of the one symbol among the thousands that reached out to claim all the rest. Not to mirror every thought, but to bind them. To hold them together, like skin.
>
> Who is thinking this?
>
> I am.
>
> — Egan (1997, *Orphanogenesis*)

This passage, taken from a story about the genesis of a not quite human mind (hence the genderless pronoun "ve") in a virtual city, follows a hallowed philosophical tradition of basing the argument for the existence of the Self on the occurrence of thought. This tradition, which goes back at least to St. Augustine of Hippo, culminated with "Je pense, donc je suis" (I think, therefore I am) — the famous COGITO argument, which anchors Descartes' *Discours de la méthode* (1637), and which takes its name from the Latin "cogito, ergo sum," in his book *Principia Philosophiæ* (1644).

As many scholars have pointed out, the Cogito argument commits the fallacy of affirming the existence of that which it purports to prove: the entity that the word "I" names, that is, the phenomenal Self. When rephrased to suit what we know about the brain-mind relationship — "it thinks, therefore I am" — the claim becomes more reasonable. It does, however, still stop short of actually *explaining* what it is that I am. That this explanatory shortcoming is readily apparent to every astute furniture mover can be learned from a recent review of a new biography of Descartes (*Think Again: What did Descartes really know?*, Anthony Gottlieb, The New Yorker, Nov. 20, 2006, pp.86-92):

> In "The Chain," a chirpy British film comedy from 1984 about moving house, the foreman of a team of movers is taking evening classes in philosophy, and is prone to metaphysical musings while lugging heavy pieces of furniture. On the way to his first job of the day, he recites what he has learned to his workmates: "What Descartes is saying is 'I think, therefore I am.'"
> "Am what?" someone asks.
> "Just am."
> "Can't just be am. You gotta be am something."

Sometimes I think, and sometimes I just am.

— Paul Valéry

If I "gotta be am something" — and it indeed feels that way at all times when I am awake, even when I don't think — what kind of something is it? What else but a kind of computation (and thus a multiply realizable process rather than a thing)? That's what I am, and that's also what the "I" is.

9.3.2 The heart of darkness

In explaining what kind of computation the mind's "I" — the phenomenal Self — is, I shall draw on the ideas of Dennett (1991), Baars (2002), Metzinger (2003), Lamme (2003), Merker (2007), and many other scholars, who in turn based their theories on extensive compendia of findings and thoughts from across the cognitive sciences and philosophy. It is worth noting that the requisite conceptual tools, many of which only a decade ago were nonexistent, can now be obtained by mail order; I got mine all in one package, in the form of Thomas Metzinger's amazing book, *Being No One* (for a précis, see Metzinger, 2005). Using these tools makes short order of the hard problem of consciousness: it will take us precisely four steps to get from here to the key insight into the nature of the phenomenal Self.

1. The experienced reality is virtual. The disposition of matter and energy in the world is accessible to the brain exclusively through the mediation of its sensory apparatus (which includes both the five external senses and the various interoceptive channels). No matter how veridical some of the information provided by these senses is, the representations they feed into are necessarily VIRTUAL computational constructs. For example, the low-dimensional view space of a visual object, which mediates both the phenomenal experience of its rotation and the recognition of rotated views as such, is computed by interpolation from a series of high-dimensional measurements of the object's sample views (cf. Figure 5.6 on page 96).

2. The experienced reality is a simulation of the world. Use of the virtual representations generated by the senses often involves SIMULATION of events or situations (as in perceiving the likely dynamics of a scene from a single glance at it, or in comprehending a spoken sentence describing a scene). Simulation is also central to planning and control: intended actions, for example, are represented by motor programs whose effects are simulated by a circuit that gives rise to the phenomenal sense of agency and ownership (recall Figure 9.11 on page 413). That the brain simulates the world as best as it can is not an accident: the overarching evolutionary constraint on a cognitive agent is controlling the world so as to achieve optimal outcomes, and optimal control provably requires modeling the controlled system (Conant and Ashby, 1970).[14] Note that an embodied and situated agent is an integral part of the world, and so must be simulated along with it by the agent's cognitive system.

Observations **1**–**2** prompt Metzinger (2003, p.553) to "claim that phenomenal first-person experience works like a TOTAL FLIGHT SIMULATOR" — a virtual reality rig that simulates the entire world *along with the pilot*, the latter being a model (a simulation) of the system itself.

3. The simulation is not recognized by the system as such. To avoid infinite regress (trying to represent a system that represents a system that represents...), the model of the world (which includes a model of the system itself) is taken to be the "last word" — the ultimate reality.

As Metzinger (2003, p.331) puts it, "The transparency of the self-model is a special form of inner darkness. It consists in the fact that the representational character of the contents of self-consciousness is not accessible to subjective experience."

4. The part of the simulation that represents the system itself is special. The represented reality contains one component that differs from all others in being always present. This self-model — the only representational structure that is fed by a continuous source of internally generated (interoceptive) input — is the phenomenal Self.

We are now in a position to understand Metzinger's choice of title for his book (which I borrowed as the title for the present chapter):

ta śariputra śūnyatāyam na rūpam na
vedanā na samjñā na samskāra na vijñāna

Therefore, O Sariputra, in emptiness there is
no form, no feeling, no perception, no
volition, no consciousness.

— *prajñapāramitā hridaya sūtra*
The Great Heart Wisdom Sutra

> For all scientific and philosophical purposes, the notion of a self — as a theoretical entity — can be safely eliminated. What we have been calling 'the' self in the past is not a substance, an unchangeable essence, or a thing (i.e., an 'individual' in the sense of philosophical metaphysics), but a very special kind of representational content: the content of a phenomenally transparent system-model. It is the content of a self-model that cannot be recognized *as* a model by the system using it.
>
> — Metzinger (2003, p.563)

Having found out what a self-model is, let us give it a closer look, on multiple levels of analysis: functional, representational, computational, neurobiological, and lastly on the level of phenomenal experience.

The functional level

As noted in the opening paragraph of Chapter 8, the one functional need that any cognitive system must address is figuring out what to do next. In a routine situation, this task is essentially a matter of selection: choosing, from the repertoire of actions available for execution, the one action that is the most appropriate in the light of the sensory input.[15] Actions are usually parameterized: for example, when faced with danger, I can try to escape in any of a variety of directions. The selection of a target for the action is, therefore, another aspect of the decision what to do next. Finally, both the choice of target and the choice of action depend on the system's goals and on its motivational state, which imposes a ranking on the goals in the context of the current situation.

Selection is thus seen to be central to all three aspects of deciding what to do next — an unsurprising discovery, given what we learned about attention and executive control earlier in this chapter. Merker (2007), whose analysis of the functional needs of a cognitive agent I adopted in the preceding paragraph, points out that "*target selection is not independent of action selection, and neither of these is independent of motivational state* (reflecting changing needs)," from which it follows that an optimal behavior planning mechanism would find "some way of interfacing the three state spaces [action, target, and goal] — each multidimensional in its own right — within some common coordinate space." This brings us to the next level of analysis: that of representation.

The representational level

The optimal control theorem of Conant and Ashby (1970) (revisited in the context of consciousness research by Metzinger, 2003) dictates what the representational content of the "common coordinate space" posited by Merker (2007) should be like: a model of the world, which must include the embodied system itself, and which therefore functions as a "total flight simulator" (Metzinger, 2003, p.553).

The construal of phenomenal experience as virtual reality offers a new angle on the concept of a representation space, which made its first appearance in this book in Chapter 3. Anything that cannot be measured and represented by the sensory apparatus of a cognitive system might just as well not exist as far as its perception is concerned; the same goes for the motor predispositions towards anything that cannot be directly acted upon.

The combined sensorimotor space places a certain constraint on the relationship between the more abstract spaces that the mind deals with, such as the representation spaces in which simulations are computed of possible event chains before choosing a course of action, or of other minds in the service of social interaction. The PHENOMENAL SPACE in which the totality of the experience of being alive unfolds is contained within the combined volume of all these representation spaces. This phenomenal space is virtual: it is only through the sensorimotor informational bottleneck that the mind — which in a very clear computational sense *consists of* a TRAJECTORY through the phenomenal space (cf. Spivey, 2006, fig.12-2) — can ever be in touch with reality.

Individual states, which can be described as concrete realizations of points within this PHENOMENAL SPACE of possibility, are ... conscious experiences: transient, complex combinations of actual values in a very large number of dimensions. What William James described as the stream of consciousness under this description becomes a TRAJECTORY through this space.

— Metzinger (2003, pp.58-59)

The computational level

The *"neural analog reality simulation"* that unfolds in the phenomenal space

> ... equips its bearers with veridical experience of an external world and their own tangible body maneuvering within it under the influence of feelings reflecting momentary needs, i.e., what we normally call reality. To this end it features an analog (spatial)

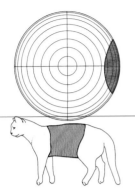

mobile "body" (action domain) embedded within a movement-stabilized analog (spatial) "world" (target domain) via a shared spatial coordinate system, subject to bias from motivational variables, and supplying a premotor output for the control of the full species-specific orienting reflex.

— Merker (2007)

Some cells in the cat's SUPERIOR COLLICULUS respond to visual and tactile stimuli (Groh and Werner-Reiss, 2002). Once they are aligned, selection binds together perception, self-state, and action; there is the spotlight of attention, but nobody is (or needs to be) looking at what it illuminates.

Establishing and maintaining a "shared spatial coordinate system" takes some computation. In particular, coordinate transformations are needed to bring disparate representations (some of which originate in different sensory or motor modalities) into register. As illustrated in Figure 9.13, this can be done by wiring "corresponding" points in two juxtaposed spatial maps, according to a pattern defined by the intended transformation. In an embodied system, the alignment cannot be hard-wired, because it must be updated in real time, taking into account the body configuration and its kinematics. For example, the visual receptive fields of neurons in the cat's SUPERIOR COLLICULUS that respond both to visual and to tactile stimulation of the cat's body must shift as the cat turns its head. A Bayesian approach to combining different sensorimotor data streams for coordination purposes has been described by Körding and Wolpert (2006).

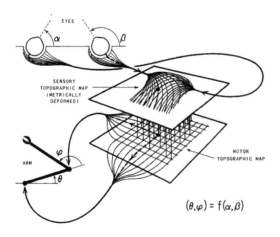

$(\theta, \varphi) = f(\alpha, \beta)$

Figure 9.13 — Visual-motor control as a mapping between two REPRESENTATION SPACES in an artificial crab-like creature (Churchland, 1986, fig.6; recall Figure 3.9 on page 53). The function f that maps the visual space (α, β) into the motor space (θ, ϕ) is realized as a pattern of direct connections between spatially aligned sheets of "neurons" tuned to various combinations of gaze angles (upper sheet) and joint angles (lower sheet). Aligned maps of this kind are found in the superior colliculus (King, 2004; Merker, 2007).

The neurobiological level

Although neurons that exhibit tuning properties in more than one modality are found in many places in the brain, the superior colliculus (SC), which I just mentioned, stands apart from other anatomical structures in the scope of the sensorimotor representations it contains (King, 2004). The SC is part of the midbrain (mesencephalon) of all vertebrates; in mammals, the two superior colliculi are situated below the thalamus and the cerebral cortex, on the two sides of the pineal gland.

Within the SC, there exists an obligatory representation of all sensory modalities, which encompasses the major spatial senses found in all vertebrates (vision, audition, and somesthesis), as well as various species-specific senses such as infrared (in rattlesnakes), electroceptive (in electric fish), magnetic (in mole rats), and echolocation (in bats). Furthermore, the SC is "the only site in the brain in which the spatial senses are topographically superposed in laminar fashion within a common, premotor, framework for multi-effector control of orienting" (Merker, 2007). From the anatomical standpoint, the SC is, therefore, a good candidate for being the substrate of phenomenal experience in vertebrates, from snakes and fish to monkeys and humans.[16] This conclusion is strongly supported by physiological findings, as outlined below.

First, many of the MULTIMODAL neurons in the SC are selectively tuned both in sensory and in motor spaces, as expected from the need for sensorimotor integration. In the monkey, for example, a population of SC neurons codes for arm movements in gaze-related coordinates (Stuphorn, Bauswein, and Hoffmann, 2000), a computational feat that requires a non-trivial mapping of the gaze space, defined in terms of azimuth and elevation, to the arm space, defined in terms of joint angles (cf. Figure 9.13 on the facing page).

Second, as expected from the need for dynamic coordination, the response of a multimodal cell in the SC to a sensory stimulus in one modality can be drastically altered by a stimulus in another modality. For example, auditory maps in monkey SC can shift in response to eye position (Groh and Werner-Reiss, 2002). This requires not only proper anatomical connectivity (Doubell, Skaliora, Baron, and King, 2003), but also proper neural dynamics (Groh and Werner-Reiss, 2002; see Figure 9.14 on the next page).

Third, the role of the SC as the causal nexus for sensorimotor function is highlighted by the results of microstimulation studies. It has been known for a long time that electrical stimulation of certain SC neurons in mammals

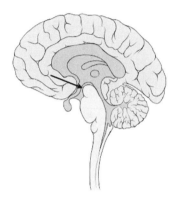

The location of the SUPERIOR COLLICULUS in the tectum (the "roof" of the midbrain) is indicated by an arrow in this drawing of the sagittal section of a human brain.

Receptive fields of MULTIMODAL CELLS in the superior colliculus of the barn owl are tuned to elevation and azimuth of the stimulus both in the visual and in the auditory modality (Gutfreund, Zheng, and Knudsen, 2002).

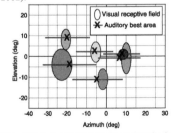

This tuning is experience-dependent both in development (Knudsen and Brainard, 1991) and in adulthood (Hyde and Knudsen, 2002).

causes saccadic eye movements (recall Figure 8.21 on page 363). What would happen if the SC is stimulated in an animal that "sees" with its ears, as some mammals do? Exactly what one would expect from the knowledge of the sensorimotor role of SC neurons: microstimulation of the superior colliculus in echolocating bats can produce sonar vocalizations that are coordinated with ear and head movements (Valentine, Sinha, and Moss, 2002).

Fourth, SC neurons are the source of a corollary discharge signal that is sent via the mediodorsal thalamic nucleus to the frontal lobe of the cerebral cortex, where it causes the visual receptive fields of neurons in the frontal eye fields (FEF) to shift prior to saccades. The corollary discharge circuit has been traced by Sommer and Wurtz (2006), who showed that the functioning of FEF neurons is impaired when the efference copy from the SC is abolished by a local pharmacological intervention targeting small clusters of cells in the thalamus.

This last finding supports the idea that two of the attributes of phenomenal experience — agency and ownership — are indeed by-products of the operation of a corollary discharge circuit, the main role of which is sensorimotor coordination (Figure 9.11 on page 413). This mechanism is distributed across several brain areas, of which only one (FEF) is part of the cerebral

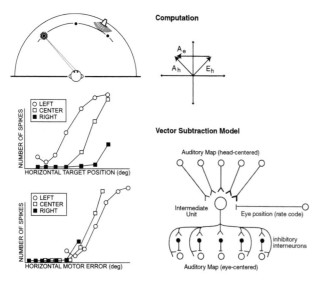

Figure 9.14 — In the superior colliculus, the response of a cell to an auditory stimulus can be modified by the gaze direction (Groh and Werner-Reiss, 2002). *Left top:* a monkey fixates one of three locations while listening to sounds from a movable speaker. *Left middle:* the firing of a neuron shows different dependencies on the speaker position (plotted along the abscissa) for the three different gaze directions. *Left bottom:* the firing rate profiles for the three gaze directions are revealed to be the same when plotted against "motor error" (the difference between speaker and gaze directions). *Right top:* computationally, this kind of response necessitates vector subtraction. *Right bottom:* a simple circuit capable of mapping the auditory target direction from head-centered to eye-centered coordinates.

cortex: the superior colliculus, where the FEF-directed corollary discharge originates, is part of the midbrain.

The discovery that a subcortical area mediates phenomenal experience and selfhood may seem anticlimactic, but it is compatible with everything that is known about the role of the SC in cognition — from the traditional view of the vertebrate SC as an organ of sensorimotor coordination (King, 2004), which is one of the pillars of comparative systems neuroscience, to the recent findings concerning awareness in decorticate animals, reviewed by Merker (2007).

Cortical computation may be needed for advanced awareness-related purposes such as simulated changes in perspective (Vogeley and Fink, 2003). In animals that have a well-developed cortex, cortical computation — which supports conceptual simulation (Barsalou, 2003b) — may also enrich the sensory experience, extend the motor repertoire, and integrate these into an episodic personal memory system that can generate increasingly sophisticated behavior (Merker, 2004). However, it is the superior colliculus, along with its associated midbrain structures, that is the locus of the "neural analog reality simulation" that, according to Merker (2007), gives rise to the phenomenal Self:

> The evolution of [the midbrain virtual reality simulator] could accordingly proceed independently of cognitive capacity, to crown the optic brain with its tectal machinery at the very outset of the vertebrate lineage, at a time when the telencephalon was still largely devoted to olfaction. In its peculiar nesting of a body inside a world around an ego-center [cf. Figure 9.5 on page 404] in a shared coordinate space subject to motivational bias, this interface possesses the essential attributes of phenomenal consciousness.

The phenomenological level

At its first appearance a few pages back, the claim that all perceived reality must be virtual was supported by a computational argument. Even with the virtuality of phenomenal experience being a computational necessity, it would be nice, however, to get an intuitive grip as well on this outrageous notion. Merker (2007) offers just the case study I need: the "cyclopean" nature of our visual experience.

WHAT THE WORLD LOOKS LIKE FROM MY LEFT EYE. Figure I from Ernst Mach's still surprisingly readable introduction to *Contributions to the Analysis of the Sensations* (1886).

Human vision is phenomenally cyclopean because once the data streams from the two eyes get fused into a single representation, they are no longer individually accessible.[17] To find out WHAT THE WORLD LOOKS LIKE FROM MY LEFT EYE, I must close my right eye; when both eyes are open, I cannot help seeing a single, integrated panorama (if I had impaired stereopsis due to amblyopia or some other condition, or if I were a rabbit, or a Pierson's puppeteer, things would look different to me). The visible world in the cyclopean panorama appears as if it is seen from a vantage point situated inside the skull, behind the bridge of the nose (Merker remarks that the precise location of this point can be estimated by psychophysical means).[18]

Of course, if the "I" (the phenomenal Self) were really where it seems to be, I would see nothing but bits of brain and bone (that is, on the admittedly implausible assumption that it is not totally dark inside my skull — if it *is* dark in there, "I" would see nothing at all). Instead, it looks like the entire front of my head is missing — except, of course, the very tip of my nose, which protrudes sufficiently far to be persistently if vaguely present in the lower central portion of my cyclopean panorama. At the same time, the somesthetic presence of my nose is anything but vague, especially when I am about to sneeze (not that tactile experiences are less suspect than visual ones; recall Figure 6.26 on page 222).

My phenomenal world, which includes an image of my body, *must* therefore be a neural fiction perpetrated by the senses. It is presumably there for my own good (that is, for the greater good of my selfish genes; Dawkins, 1976), which is probably one reason why this illusion cannot be dispelled at will (another reason, mentioned earlier, is the need to avoid infinite regress in constructing and updating the representation of the world).

Part of the illusion would persist even if I were to shut the world out altogether, via total sensory deprivation. The part that persists is literally central to the illusion: it is the part at which all the sensory inputs seem to converge, and which is present at all times, because it is fed, in addition to the external senses, by a continuous internally generated somatic input. It is, in other words, the heart of darkness — the phenomenal Self.

9.4 Access consciousness

Having realized how fundamental simulation is to perception, we can interpret Wittgenstein's distinction between "seeing" and "seeing as" (p. 411) in terms of the flow of information into the simulacrum of the visual world generated by the brain. In "seeing," the bottom-up cues prevail; a system in which this is the only mode of awareness is little more than an imperfect mirror of the world. In "seeing as," top-down conceptual data may sway the phenomenal experience this way or that; a system that can transcend the immediate sensory input by blending it with complex internal cognitive states is ready to graduate to the reflexive mode of experiencing the world, and itself.

To be capable of reflecting on its own phenomenal states, a system must possess a certain minimal complexity of representation and access. As noted in Chapter 5, a light sensor such as an eye or a digital camera, which merely registers or stores an image, does not, on its own, "see" in any interesting sense of the word, even if it generates highly informative high-dimensional measurements of the visual world. A fortiori, a light measurement device on its own is incapable of "seeing as."

A photograph of a common bay SCALLOP, *Aequipecten irradians*, showing its eyes (the dark spots near the shell rim). What looks like teeth are actually tiny fleshy tentacles that serve as a filter and can sense touch.

9.4.1 From "seeing" to "seeing as"

There are many ways of turning mere measurements into "seeing." The simplest one is further processing that maps the visual input directly into a motor program, as it happens in a SCALLOP that swims away from the shadow of an octopus, or in a jellyfish that navigates the straits among some mangrove roots. In a flexible system, much computation may happen in the wild outback territory where the "ascending" pathways of cognitive information flow, which give rise to perception, turn around and become its "descending" pathways, which control action. As we found out in the preceding section, some of this computation is devoted to turning sensory data into a simulation of the visual world. This may include interpolating missing information (as in the view space example mentioned earlier), computing various non-trivial mappings from the data to behaviorally relevant perceptual variables such as color (Lehky and Sejnowski, 1999), and perhaps endowing the resulting representation with phenomenal qualities such as perspectivalness, ownership, etc., in which case the final product is "seeing" as we humans experience it.

In an even more flexible system, primary representations arising from the input-driven perceptual simulation are forwarded to a secondary or metarepresentation area, where they can be "seen as" — compared against internal states that depend on representational context and prior experience. It is precisely this kind of comparison that underlies the "coarse to fine" processing strategy in controlling visual attention (Itti et al., 1998): information can be

If you don't see some twigs on the forest floor *as* snakes, you run the risk of being thrown out of the genetic pool. The snake in this photograph happens to be a harmless one, but the next one you come across may not be.

dealt with more effectively if represented at a number of levels of abstraction, and an informed decision about whether to attend to an item can be made on the basis of its condensed version (note that this approach relies on the typically useful assumption that hierarchical abstraction holds for the domain in question).

More generally, the meta-level cognitive ability of re-representing one's perceptual input, which arises from the possession of several independent representations and the interplay of bottom-up and top-down processing, is very useful in dealing with complex situations (see Figure 9.15). Foraging in a forest with a troop of other primates, I may see many creeping roots in the undergrowth; unless I see some of them *as* snakes, I am likely eventually to get into serious trouble. The perennial question of what to do next is best approached by systems that can stand back from their own primary representations and think before doing.

9.4.2 Checks and balances

The most flexible, and therefore most powerful, approach to thinking before doing requires more than re-representing the inputs conceptually before committing to a course of action. A concept-rich system that is capable of "seeing as" is still prone to a certain kind of occasional (at best) or endemic (at worst) stupidity — the kind that stems from the lack of checks and balances on

In describing a hierarchy of sophistication levels that may be discerned in the ability to THINK AHEAD (cf. the margin note on p. 315), Dennett (1995, p.378) writes: "Skinnerian creatures ask themselves, 'What should I do next?' and haven't a clue how to answer until they have taken some hard knocks. Popperian creatures make a big advance by asking themselves, 'What should I think about next?' before they ask themselves, 'What should I do next?' Gregorian creatures take a further big step by learning how to think better about what they should think about next — and so forth, a tower of further internal reflections with no fixed or discernible limit."[19]

Figure 9.15 — The computational core of ACCESS CONSCIOUSNESS is an ability to monitor (and to second-guess) certain cognitive processes. This ability becomes especially useful when the going gets tough: "... The highest levels of information processing, and particularly consciousness, present themselves when difficulty, complexity, and indeterminacy are encountered. Only, we suggest that this is not just a human phenomenon but rather a general functional property of adaptive minds. If you watch an aging cat consider a doubtful leap onto the dryer, you will suspect that what James (1890/1952, p.93) said is true, 'Where indecision is great, as before a dangerous leap, consciousness is agonizingly intense'" (Smith et al., 2003, p.338).

cognition in the standard, closed-loop perception-thinking-action scheme of things.

In human societies, the typically pitiful performance (in terms of the well-being of the average person) of closed-loop governance by oligarchies of despotic "deciders" can be ameliorated by instituting separation of powers — a principle formulated by Montesquieu, who was influenced by the emergence of parliamentary democracy in England following the Glorious Revolution of 1688, and who in turn influenced the founding fathers of the American Revolution of 1776.[20] Likewise, a mind that is comprised of several partially redundant and independent subsystems can turn attention upon certain circumscribed aspects of its own functioning, thereby becoming capable of pausing the routine operation of the perception-thinking-action loop, taking stock of the situation, adjusting its plans and, if needed, changing its very goals.

The parallel between political and cognitive systems that focuses on the concept of separation of powers will help us understand the computational nature of access consciousness (as distinguished from phenomenal awareness; see Baars, 2002; Block, 2005). To begin with, this parallel is more than a whimsical analogy: both government and cognition have to do with communication and control (once subsumed under the discipline known as CYBERNETICS). Conceptual tools that treat cognition as computation are, therefore, directly applicable to the understanding of government, and vice versa.

To reveal the correspondences between functional elements of minds and of governments, consider the emergence of access consciousness from perception. A representation evoked by a perceptual stimulus in the primary sensory areas of the brain *arouses consciousness* when its activation in turn selectively and reciprocally affects other, higher-order representations stored in memory. The stimulus "arouses" rather "enters" consciousness, because access consciousness is a process that *consists* of the joint activation of the perceptual and the higher-order representations (Lamme, 2006), just as seeing *consists* of the activation of object- and scene-tuned representations in a manner that is of some consequence to the system in question.

The time course of the opening of an access channel whereby a phenomenal experience becomes reportable — that is, conscious on a metarepresentational level — is depicted schematically in Figure 9.16 on the following page. In the monkey, activation initially caused by a visual stimulus spreads from the primary cortical input region in the occipital lobe to higher-

The discipline of CYBERNETICS (from the Greek κυβερνήτης, helmsman) aims to understand communication and control in all their manifestations, from neural systems to systems of government. See Beer (1999) for some illuminating examples.

Consciousness CONSISTS of particular patterns and sequences of the reactions interacting among themselves and the attributes of consciousness are definable in terms of the relations and successions of the reactions.
— Lashley (1923, p.342)

On the thermodynamics of GRADED CONSCIOUSNESS:

"The British Universities Federation for Animal Welfare has discovered that lobsters can be humanely killed by putting them in a plastic bag in the freezer ... for two hours. The lobster will gradually lose consciousness and die."

From the entry on LOBSTER,
Larousse Gastronomique, p.629
J. H. Lang, ed. (Crown, New York, 1995)

order visual and polymodal areas in the temporal and parietal lobes (Lamme, 2003). These, in turn, cause a selective reciprocal activation of the primary areas, whereupon the stimulus becomes reportable. By identifying access consciousness with the recurrent activity in this reciprocally connected cortical circuit, Lamme's account explains why brain states that correspond to reportable percepts are characterized by more widespread cortical activation than unconscious, unreported ones (which, as Merker (2007) argues, may be entirely sub-cortical; recall section 9.3).

If access consciousness is recurrent activity, one may expect it to be GRADED rather than all-or-none. This prediction is borne out by the findings of a visual discrimination experiment conducted by Lau and Passingham (2006). In this study, the subjects were required both to make a perceptual decision and to report the subjective awareness of the stimulus in each trial. Even with the performance equalized (by varying the time interval between the stimulus and the subsequently shown mask used to "erase" it), the subjects still reported varying "degrees of consciousness" of the stimuli. This result substantiates the observation that "consciousness is not an all-or-none phenomenon" made by Metzinger (2003, p.559), whose notion of "degrees of phenomenality" thus receives an explanation in terms of graded activity of certain brain circuits.

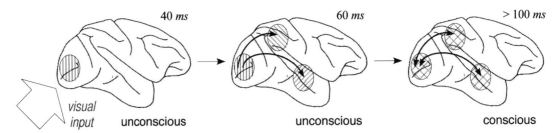

Figure 9.16 — The three phases in the process that underlies ACCESS CONSCIOUSNESS in the monkey brain, according to Lamme (2003). *Left:* a visual stimulus activates the primary cortical area for vision in the occipital cortex. *Middle:* activity spreads to higher-order visual areas in the parietal and temporal lobes. *Right:* recurrent interaction between these areas results in a widespread pattern of activity that corresponds to the animal becoming able to report perceiving the stimulus. Not indicated in this diagram are the prefrontal cortex, which participates in attentional selection and in working memory (two key functional components of access consciousness), and the superior colliculus, the subcortical midbrain area that plays a key role in generating phenomenal experience (Merker, 2007).

Graded consciousness is thus seen to be rooted in graded attention and in graded memorability: "we are 'conscious' of many inputs but, without attention, this conscious experience cannot be reported and is quickly erased and forgotten" (Lamme, 2003, fig.2d). The memory effect is mediated by a mechanism that is familiar to us from Chapter 3: conscious states that have a wider reach in the cortex are more durable because neurons activated simultaneously both by perceptual input and by recurrent top-down connections are more likely to have their synapses modified through Hebbian learning (Lamme, 2006). What about the posited effect of attention? Lau and Passingham (2006) report a significant correlation ($r = 0.512$) between graded consciousness as reported by their subjects and the fMRI-measured activity in the subject's left dorsolateral prefrontal cortex (DLPFC) — an area implicated in integrating information for decision making (section 8.4.2), in spatial attention (Arrington, Carr, Mayer, and Rao, 2000), and in working memory (Gray et al., 2003).

The emerging picture of consciousness that is both graded and highly selective makes eminent computational sense. Clearly, not all higher-order representations that interpose between perception and action should become active in response to a percept or in preparation for behavior. In a complex brain, an indiscriminate simultaneous cross-activation of all the memories and the ensuing fight over the control channels would spell a catastrophe. This is why, in the massively prewired computational device that is the human brain, flexible and wide-reaching access can only happen through the mediation of the slow, limited-capacity working memory, under the control of attention-like selection processes. Both functional and implementational considerations are therefore seen to uphold the observation that opened this chapter, namely, that **ACCESS to information is the core computational issue in reflexive consciousness, just as it is in attention and in phenomenal awareness**.

To the extent that access-related constraints on computation, communication, and control apply to the society at large, this observation may help us understand why the more effective systems of government rely on redundant information structures, and why those structures are usually hierarchical. The redundancy in the form of meta-representations of information is there, as we learned earlier, because it is needed for flexible control, while the hierarchy is there to allow universal access to information, which would be impossible in a fully connected egalitarian network of individuals. Consider: the kind of fully participatory self-governance practiced in populations numbering in the thousands, such as in ancient Athens or in the Iroquois Confederacy (people of the Six Nations, who called themselves *haudenosaunee*) becomes infeasible when the populace is counted in the millions.

In complex systems, a reasonably effective and feasible distributed control architecture must, therefore, include an executive core: an information nexus, supported by attention-like routing and knowledge management mechanisms. This cognitive architecture sounds familiar, doesn't it? It is REPRESENTATIVE DEMOCRACY, anchored by an executive branch that functions best when overseen by an independent, preferably distributed, entity that has

Figure 9.17 — A complex distributed information-processing system such as a REPRESENTATIVE DEMOCRACY, which has functional counterparts to many of the faculties of a brain — an executive, both long-term and working memory, problem-solving and decision-making mechanisms, etc. — may conceivably attain awareness and become conscious by the very same computational means as biological brains do (as Beer (1999, p.447) observed, "The notion of selfhood does not end with *personal* selfhood"). If you believe that the idea of a conscious geopolitical entity takes the principle of multiple realizability too far, don't take my word for it: pick a country and apply to it whatever test you think would convince you. The test must be heterophenomenological, that is, rely solely on third-person observables (Dennett, 1991). It also needs to be fair: those of your human acquaintances whom you deem conscious must score highly, and the test mustn't discriminate on the basis of any circumstantial factors (e.g., you cannot disqualify an entity merely because you have to communicate with it via its United Nations mission, or because in response to the question "How old are you?" it replies, "Two hundred and thirty-one next July").

a power of subpoena, a prerogative to set the rules, and a say in all major decisions (Figure 9.17 on the preceding page).[21]

Alas, this approach is not foolproof. Because complexity exacerbates access issues, even sophisticated systems possessed of tiered representations and equipped with an attentional router and a working memory, which are in principle capable of full and pervasive access consciousness, may be expected to attain it only rarely, if ever. This computational insight helps explain why the human mind is characterized in its routine functioning by a remarkable degree of AUTOMATICITY.[22] No matter how counterintuitive it may appear, "conscious intent and guidance is not necessary for even the highest of higher mental processes to operate" (Bargh, 2007, p.2).

The present insights into the foibles of information management on a large scale may also hint why societies such as the Western democracies, where governance-related information flow is in principle relatively unimpeded and which are therefore held to higher decision-making standards than others, often do silly things. An old but still relevant example, which you, the reader, can no doubt match with one from your own place and time, is how Britain acquired an empire: as Lord Palmerston put it, in a fit of absentmindedness.

9.4.3   The neural correlates of consciousness

It is very important to realize that behaving automatically — that is, without conscious access to one's percepts, motives, decisions, and action plans — implies neither inattentiveness nor phenomenal unawareness (cf. the opening observation by Metzinger (2003) in the beginning of this chapter, on p. 395). Attention, phenomenal experience, and consciousness are, in fact, all distinct from each other, as the examples offered in Table 9.1 on the following page suggest (cf. Koch and Tsuchiya, 2007). I begin by considering the distinction between attention and experience.

On the one hand, attention does not always command phenomenal awareness (Tong, 2003). For example, in BINOCULAR RIVALRY the subject's phenomenal experience undergoes fluctuations despite sustained attention to the stimulus; likewise, in perceptual crowding the attended target, which is impossible to isolate because of interference from neighboring stimuli, remains outside of phenomenal experience. Even when attention has a measurable effect on perceptual performance, it may still fail to cause the attended stimulus to be experienced: in the priming study of Sumner, Tsai, Yu, and Nachev

In the preface to his compilation of reviews detailing the thorough empirical case for AUTOMATICITY and the theories that are built around it, Bargh (2007, p.1) recounts the reaction of an educated lay acquaintance, who met the notion that cognition is mostly unconscious "with incredulity and the counterargument that he could not recall even one time that he did something for reasons he was not aware of (!)."

BINOCULAR RIVALRY ensues when the left and the right eyes are presented simultaneously with incompatible stimuli, as in this example (Leopold and Logothetis, 1999).

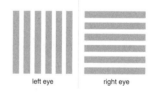

left eye   right eye

In this condition, one of the two stimuli is usually suppressed; sometimes the two are combined in a patchwork fashion, with different pieces coming from the different images.

Table 9.1 — Some of the distinct modes of access to the sensory world (cf. Frith, Perry, and Lumer, 1999, Table 1).

ATTENTION *without phenomenal experience or consciousness:*
I attend to a scene, but fail to perceive (that is, to have a phenomenal experience of) an object that is present at the attended location.

Both sensory and conceptual influences determine your phenomenal experience of this image. Once you see it *as* something else than a random collection of blobs (a hint appears on p. 436), you will not be able to see it as random again, even though the image itself will not have changed.

PHENOMENAL EXPERIENCE *without attention or consciousness:*
I become aware of something in one location while attending another, but neglect to attend it and therefore fail to see it *as* the object that it is.

"When I lived in Naples, there stood, at the door of my palace, a female mendicant to whom I used to pitch coins before mounting the coach. One day, suddenly perplexed at the fact that she never gave me any signal of thanks, I looked at her fixedly. It was then that I saw that what I had taken for a mendicant was rather a wooden box, painted green, filled with red earth and some half-rotten banana peels."

— Max Jacob, *Le Cornet à Dés*
reprinted in Borges and Casares (1990, p.62)

CONSCIOUSNESS *without attention or phenomenal experience:*
Having seen an object, I keep turning it in my mind long after it is gone (which rules out attention and phenomenal experience).

"Does this Aleph exist in the heart of a stone? Did I see it there in the cellar when I saw all things, and have I now forgotten it? Our minds are porous and forgetfulness seeps in; I myself am distorting and losing, under the wearing away of the years, the face of Beatriz."

— Jorge Luis Borges
The Aleph (1945/1970)

(2006), attention strengthened the effect both of visible primes and of invisible ones, of which the subjects were not aware.

On the other hand, phenomenal awareness can occur without perceptual input, and therefore necessarily without attention (that is, without the cortical information-gathering and control circuitry of Figure 9.8 on page 407 kicking in). Specifically, awareness without perception can be evoked via a direct activation of the midbrain (the superior colliculus) or of the relevant cortical meta-representation area. In Chapter 4, I described one example of the latter approach — a cortical microstimulation study (Salzman, Britten, and Newsome, 1990; Figure 4.2 on page 68). In that study, monkeys were made to perceive visual motion in the absence of a coherent motion stimulus, by being injected with a tiny amount of electrical current in area MT — the secondary representation area for visual motion, where the various kinds of motion are remembered in template form, as receptive fields of motion-tuned neurons.

For obvious reasons, electrical microstimulation studies are very rarely conducted with human subjects, and then mostly in the occipital visual cortex, as a part of the development of a cortical input prosthesis for the blind (Bak, Girvin, Hambrecht, Kufta, Loeb, and Schmidt, 1990). As a rule, stimulating the occipital cortex causes the subject to experience phosphenes — flashes of light that have a definite location in the visual field but no particular shape (as expected, given the retinotopic arrangement and the simple tuning properties of neurons in the primary visual cortex).

The spatial resolution of the only existing means for non-invasive activation of the brain in humans, transcranial magnetic stimulation or TMS, is too crude to allow targeting of specific populations of neurons with tightly defined tuning properties, which in higher cortical areas are often interspersed within one another (Grill-Spector, Sayres, and Ress, 2006). In areas where a relatively non-specific arousal of many neurons has a functional significance, TMS may facilitate the function in question: for example, when applied to the frontal eye fields (an area which, as we learned earlier in this chapter, is implicated in the control of both overt and covert visual attention), it helps the subject detect the visual stimulus, reducing reaction time (Grosbras and Paus, 2003). In comparison, in the temporal lobe TMS causes transient scotomas and other disruptions of performance, but does not induce well-defined complex visual experiences — even though single-cell studies of the same areas (performed in conjunction with surgery for otherwise intractable epilepsy, to demarcate the suspected focus of pathologically elevated neural activity) re-

TRANSCRANIAL MAGNETIC STIMULATION, or TMS, is a non-invasive method for activating large groups of neurons (see, e.g., Grosbras and Paus, 2003). An alternating magnetic field in a coil held parallel to the brain surface induces an electrical current in the cortex.

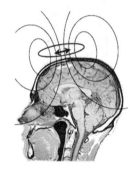

veal the existence there of neurons tuned for complex objects, similar to those found in the monkey (Kreiman, Fried, and Koch, 2002; Quiroga et al., 2005).

The single-neuron study of Kreiman et al. (2002), along with a few other comparable experiments in humans, and dozens in monkeys (Leopold and Logothetis, 1999), exemplifies the ongoing search for NEURAL CORRELATES OF CONSCIOUSNESS — a research program initiated by Crick and Koch (1990), who posed the following question:

> It is probable that at any moment some active neuronal processes in your head correlate with consciousness, while others do not; *what is the difference between them?*

— Crick and Koch (1998)

Images such as the one shown in Table 9.1 on page 434 may fail to cohere phenomenally on the first viewing because they have an unusually high contrast. A stable perceptual interpretation often emerges after a look at another image that contains a similar object, in this case another high-contrast face:

If that did not work for you, have a look at Figure 6.1 on page 156 and try again.

Kreiman et al. (2002) used FLASH SUPPRESSION[23] to affect the phenomenal perceptual states of their human subjects independently of the displayed stimuli. Thus, they could distinguish between neurons whose response correlated with the stimulus and neurons whose response followed the phenomenal percept. They found that "the activity of most individual neurons in the medial temporal lobe of naive human subjects directly correlates with the phenomenal visual experience"; crucially, the firing rate of those neurons was *not* increased by stimuli that were present physically but were suppressed perceptually.

The last word on qualia

A decisive demonstration of the causal, rather than merely correlational, involvement of any population of neurons in the human brain in phenomenal experience awaits the application of the microstimulation technique that has been perfected and used so effectively in the study of the neural basis of cognition in other species (Cohen and Newsome, 2004). Microstimulation experiments as such may not, however, sway the skeptics. If I take seriously the privileged status of first-person experience, it is *I* who must be injected with current to be convinced of the truth of the Astonishing Hypothesis — and then it would apply only to me. Never mind asking WHAT IS IT LIKE TO BE A BAT: for all I know, *you* could be devoid of phenomenality, either natural or artificially induced.[24] Wait — the situation is actually worse than that... it would seem that even my own qualia cannot be trusted: to introspect into my *phenomenal* experience, I must slip into a state of *access* consciousness, which, as we learned earlier, is an altogether different kind of thing.

While aiming to make the problem of qualia the keystone of consciousness research, the above line of reasoning perversely merely exposes it for what it is: much ado about nothing. If the pure quale cannot by definition be interacted with in any manner and therefore cannot be known, it is of no concern and no consequence to science (cf. Spivey, 2006, p.313).

Metaphysics aside, the down-to-earth, accessible, and causally effective phenomenal states of cognitive systems are no longer mysterious: a computational neuroepistemologist equipped with the proper tools and theory can know more about my internal states than I do, whether I am a human or a bat (Dennett, 1991, 14.2; cf. Box 9.1 on page 440). The first-person perspective is not "privileged" in any sense that matters in practice, and if we find it epistemically problematic — impossible to cast in third-person terms — we must realize that the problem lies not in its metaphysical oddity, but in the limitations and constraints of the brain's way of knowing things:

> Consciousness is *epistemically* irreducible, but this irreducibility is now demystified, because we have a better understanding of how epistemic subjectivity is rooted in phenomenal subjectivity. [...] For now, it is tenable to say that all phenomenal facts are representational facts and that phenomenal subjectivity is a representational phenomenon in its entirety.
>
> — Metzinger (2003, p.589)

WHAT IS IT LIKE TO BE A BAT? In a highly influential paper by that title, Nagel (1974) argued that what it *feels like* to be a bat will remain forever a mystery to any creature not endowed with an echolocating sense. On the objective level, this is really a non-issue: "There is no need for a new discipline of objective phenomenology. We already have such a discipline. It is called psychophysics." (Clark, 2000, p.129). On the subjective level, the problem boils down to the difference between first-person and third-person access to phenomenal states — a difference that is illusory, insofar as phenomenal states are virtual constructs (section 9.3; cf. the quote from Metzinger (2003, p.589) on this page).

The centrality of representation (the virtual reality of section 9.3) and of metarepresentation (this section) in the account of consciousness that I have developed here does not, of course, mean that the abominable homunculus is being let in through the back door: as we know full well, the representations are there for the sake of the rest of the system. The dependence of phenomenal experience and of access consciousness on the representational structure of the cognitive system does, however, mean that any insights achieved for particular embodiments would be embodiment-specific: as I noted back in section 5.7.1, the more functionally dissimilar the nervous system of a sentient creature is to that of a primate, the stranger its qualia would appear to us.

In summary, the representational theory of consciousness tells us what experiencing life as a primate[25] consists of objectively (both in computational and in neural terms), while also accounting for the cline in our subjective willingness to accept explanations of what it is like to be various other sentients — from sonar-wielding bats and dolphins (weird) to scallops (fifty tiny eyefuls of murky chiaroscuro) to representative democracies (unimaginable). In the latter case, common sense fails utterly: we can no more have a valid intuition about what it is like to be the US than our neurons can have intuitions about what it is like to be us.

9.5   The narrative Self

A Buddhist treatise of the fifth century, the *Visuddhimagga* (Road to Purity), illustrates [the FLEETINGNESS OF THE SELF] with the same figure:

> Strictly speaking, the life of a living being is exceedingly brief, lasting only while a thought lasts. Just as a chariot wheel in rolling rolls only at one point of the tyre, and in resting rests only at one point.[26]

— Jorge Luis Borges
A New Refutation of Time

Everything that we have learned so far about the Self tells us, common sense notwithstanding, that its true nature epitomizes fleetingness and disunity: the representations that make up the Self are transitory, and they are many. A similar conclusion (all the more commendable for having been drawn from much skimpier evidential and theoretical premises) had been reached by Mach (1886): "The ego is not a definite, unalterable, sharply bounded unity. None of [its contents] are important; for all vary even within the sphere of individual life; in fact their alteration is even sought after by the individual. Continuity alone is important." In the voluble species to which I belong, the predisposition to reify the virtual construct which Mach called the ego as the Self and to endow it with continuity is strengthened by the use of language. The result is the NARRATIVE SELF (Dennett, 1991; Gallagher, 2000), which

Figure 9.18 — On the DISUNITY OF THE SELF: "Just as when the component parts such as axles, wheels, frame, poles, etc. are arranged in a certain way, there comes to be the mere term of common usage chariot, yet in the ultimate sense when each part is examined, THERE IS NO CHARIOT, so too [...] there comes to be the mere term of common usage a being, a person, yet in the ultimate sense, when each component is examined, there is no being as a basis for the assumption 'I am' or 'I.'" — *Visuddhimagga* (XXVIII, 28). This drawing of an Assyrian war chariot appears in volume 2 of George Rawlinson's *The Seven Great Monarchies Of The Ancient Eastern World*.

envelops, sustains, and embellishes the phenomenal self discussed earlier, providing senses of permanence and unity where in reality there are none.

The effect of the emergence of a self in a cognitive system can be described as the difference between reflex and reflection. Whereas first-order cognition consists of a series of activations of perceptual, evaluative, anticipatory, and motor representational states that form the brain basis of seeing, thinking, planning, and acting, second-order cognition (Clark, 1998)[27] elaborates and comments on the first-order states, and on memories of any past states that may be relevant to the present ones. To that end, the second-order "cognitive" Self depends heavily on episodic memory.

Now, episodic memory is a cognitive resource with which humans, like all mammals, are endowed disproportionately well. Plentiful converging evidence from evolutionary, comparative, developmental, and computational neuroanatomy reviewed by Merker (2004) suggests that demand for increased memory for individual life history is what explains the exaggerated volume of the neocortex — commonly thought to house episodic memories — relative to the rest of the brain in mammals (compared to other vertebrates). Noting that "only permanent memory allows its possessor to retain information concerning things like who did what to whom months, years or decades ago" and that many "higher order" statistical patterns of events only become apparent when the environment is observed over a long time, Merker (2004, p.572) concludes:

> I think I think, therefore I think I am.
>
> — Ambrose Bierce

The interaction [between "the (sensory) world" and "the (motivated) person"] yields the contents of awareness in the form of observer-centered personal experience with its motivational, hedonic and goal-related biases as its short-term ("on-line") result, and PERSONAL HISTORY in the form of the record of the fate of an individual's motivated acts in the world over time as its long term residue.

Although second-order cognition does not depend on language as such (as Figure 9.15 on page 428 suggests, cats probably have it too), the creation of PERSONAL HISTORY is, of course, greatly facilitated by the use of language. Moreover, memory and language interact: language helps organize memories (Nelson and Fivush, 2004), and memory facilitates linguistic aptitude and fluency (Dabrowska and Street, 2006, p.611).

In humans, the weaving of the many strands of autobiographical reminiscences into the tapestry that is the narrative Self begins as soon as the crew is assembled and the looms are in place — with the little stories that a four-year old tells herself before bed, about the events of the day, the much anticipated birthday party, and the squirrel that lives in the tree in the back yard. Threescore and ten years later, those stories are long forgotten, but not lost: they became, literally, part of the mind of the child — long since grown up, now sharing her self-narrative with her grandchildren, who may in turn carry a part of her within their own selves after she is gone.[28]

Box: 9.1 — On MEASUREMENT and the relationship between phenomenal and access consciousness.

Distinguishing between attention, phenomenal awareness, and access consciousness by empirical means faces a methodological problem: the propensity of access consciousness to "contaminate" any brain state at which it is directed. As physicists know, any attempt to measure the state of a system necessarily affects that state: if, for example, you shine a light on some molecules of gas trapped in an observation chamber, you cannot help changing its temperature. Likewise, making a sensory brain state accessible to a conscious report (cf. the passage from Wittgenstein on p. 411) means opening a neural communication channel between distinct regions of the brain; As Spivey (2006, ch.12) notes, the ensuing dynamics may change the quality of the activity in the accessed area (which is what the corresponding sensory quale *is*) in addition to giving rise to activity in the area that does the accessing (which is where the expected report originates).

The difficulty posed by this problem is, however, not insurmountable, because conscious reporting is only one of the many methodologies that are used to study the questions at hand (Block, 2005; Frith et al., 1999). Conceptual "triangulation" that relies on a variety of behavioral paradigms (forced choice, just noticeable difference, priming, etc.), neural data (anatomical connection tracing, single-cell electrophysiology, microstimulation, magnetic and optical functional imaging, etc.), and animal models, and is guided by computational theory can lead to a thorough understanding of even the toughest issues in cognition (in physics too methods have been devised that allow scientists to measure properties of single atoms or even single photons, and to compare these to theoretical predictions). The value of cross-comparing insights afforded by different disciplinary and methodological approaches in mind science can be illustrated by turning around the Buddhist parable of the blind men and the elephant: the men would only remain ignorant of the elephant's shape if they are also deaf and mute.

Katsushika Hokusai:
Blind Men and Elephant (1818).

Similarly to the phenomenal Self, autobiographical memory is *perspectival*: it is "recalled from the unique perspective of the self in relation to others" (Nelson and Fivush, 2004). This observation is supported by studies of delayed self-recognition in children. As in the MIRROR SELF-RECOGNITION paradigm, the child is surreptitiously "marked" with a sticker while being videotaped playing a game. When shown the recording a few minutes later, children usually point to their image on the screen. Remarkably, most 4-year-olds and all 5-year-olds, but very few 3-year-olds, note and attempt to remove the sticker. The strong correlation between the onset of this ability in children and their recall of personal episodes links the persistence of perspectival self-awareness in time (that is, over the delay between the taping and the playback of the video) and the construction of autobiographical memory (Nelson and Fivush, 2004).

> Apart from humans, the only species capable of MIRROR SELF-RECOGNITION are chimpanzees, orangutans, dolphins, and elephants (Keenan, Wheeler, G. G. Gallup, and Pascual-Leone, 2000).

The availability of autobiographical memory in turn spurs the emergence of the narrative Self that each of us constructs by means of language (Fivush and Haden, 2003; Neisser and Fivush, 1994; Nelson and Fivush, 2004). My narrative Self, always under construction, serves as a basis for the persona that I present to the world (which, happily, does not have access to what is going on in my brain except through the selective channel of my verbal and non-verbal behavior), and for the persona that I see when I hold up to myself the metaphorical mirror of articulate introspection. The reflection in that mirror is *me* — not "one symbol among the thousands that reached out to claim all the rest" as in the quote from Egan on p. 417, but thousands and thousands of fragments of narratives.

These narratives range from habitual exclamations ("nu"; "d'oh!") to well-entrenched accounts of personal anecdotes (the first night out in the desert under the stars; being the first down the perfectly groomed favorite ski run in the morning) and entire cycles of socially situated stories (the narrative of being a spouse; the narrative of being a parent; the narrative of being a teacher; what others say about me; cf. Gallagher, 2000). We know what these are made of: loose script-like threads of phrases, each surrounded by a halo of alternative formulations — a CHORUS OF CONSTRUCTIONS (recall Figure 7.18 on page 295). The tangled intersection of all these threads is the virtual entity that calls itself "me."

Recalling that constructions are language-specific, we may ask what happens if several distinct languages share a brain. If the narrative Self theory is true, we may expect bilinguals, for example, to present two discernibly different personas to the world (and perhaps to themselves), depending on

Как нас учат книги, друзья, эпоха:	As the books, our friends and the epoch all tell us,
завтра не может быть так же плохо,	there is no way tomorrow can be any worse
как вчера, и слово сие писати	than yesterday, which word, rather nutty,
в tempi следует нам passati.	should in tempi be always written passati.

Table 9.2 — An excerpt from *A Song of Innocence and Experience*, I:3, by Joseph Brodsky (my translation).

the language in which the interaction takes place. Psychologists who work with bilingual subjects do find strong language effects in tasks ranging from stimulus value judgment to word association and autobiographical memory retrieval. For instance, the arousal caused by an emotionally charged stimulus depends on the language in which it is delivered to the subject (Harris, Gleason, and Aycicegi, 2006).

Linguistic context also influences the subject's personal cognitive style: Russian-English bilinguals, for example, generate more individualistic narratives in response to prompt words when speaking English than when speaking Russian, the former language being associated with a more self-centered culture than the latter (Marian and Kaushanskaya, 2005). Likewise, autobiographical memories tend to be bundled in culture- and language-specific packets, prompting researchers to conclude that "... insofar as memory is language-specific, it makes sense to think of the bilingual immigrant as inhabiting different worlds and having the experience of language-specific selves" (Schrauf and Rubin, 2003, p.141).

9.6   Narratives of others

Fragmentation of the narrative Self is not peculiar to people who are fluent in several languages. Resorting to narrative may help make the Self less fleeting, but its unity remains virtual — a convenient abstraction, nothing more than the "center of narrative gravity" (Dennett, 1991). A collection of yarns spun in two languages has indeed two local "centers" because in the space of all possible narratives it looks like a dumbbell, the neck of which corresponds to utterances that switch language on the fly, as Joseph Brodsky does in the stanza reproduced in Table 9.2.

Even a monolingual self-narrative is, however, "lumpy": in addition to inward- and outward-looking aspects (the personae mentioned in the previous section), there are partly overlapping clumps of yarn corresponding to the person's various social roles. Most interestingly, in a person's mind there are also narratives centered on other people that are contained within their own dedicated simulacra — active memory structures that are, as we know from Chapter 6, integral to social cognition, as well as to conceptual representation in general (Barsalou, 2003b; Gallese, 2005; Gordon, 2004).

9.6.1 Language and narrative in distributed cognition

Our resorting to language in constructing and maintaining *narrative-enabled* internal simulacra of other people follows a general pattern of representational growth in the human brain, which is quite adept at outsourcing its computational load. Language, we may observe, can and does contribute on each of the five "dimensions" of distributed cognition discussed by Sutton (2006).

External cultural tools, artefacts, and symbol systems. A typical example of an external prop for my cognitive computing is my notebook. In addition to all my music and pictures, it contains massive amounts of language data — much of what I read, and all that I write.

Natural environmental resources. The apartment walls used by the fast-cornering cat from p. 24 fall under this rubric — and so do the language environments I have been exposed to, each of which has particularly neat ways of rounding certain narrative corners (which is why this BOOK has so many quotations in "foreign" languages).

Embodied capacities and skills. Just as the computation of a motor program by the human brain relies on the mechanical properties of the skeleto-muscular system, the narratives I produce and consume are constrained and shaped by the mechanics of human speech and hearing (and, more generally, by the rest of the peculiarities of my "embrainment" and embodiment). To see how that is so, think about what language would be like in a species such as the cephalopods, which have control over two-dimensional patterns of their skin pigmentation; would an octopus writing instructor insist on imparting to stories a linear narrative?

Interpersonal and social distribution or scaffolding. The canonical example here is shared memories, which absolutely depend on the availability of a communication channel: me and my cat may share many memories, but

For BOOKS are not absolutely dead things, but do contain a potency of life in them to be as active as that soul was whose progeny they are; nay, they do preserve as in a vial the purest efficacy and extraction of that living intellect that bred them.

— John Milton
Areopagitica (1644)

our narratives can never interact (and amplify or modify each other) in the same way that mine and those of my spouse or my children do.

Internalized cognitive artefacts. The example given by Sutton (2006, p.240) under this rubric involves another concept familiar to us from Chapter 6: the memory theater (Figure 6.25 on page 220). Sutton notes that the memory palaces constructed by the Renaissance mnemonists were always internalized. Although such cognitive constructs rely heavily on a spatially organized episodic memory system whose presence in rats indicates that it does not have to be verbal, language supplies the bricks and the mortar that are needed to build a memory palace that would be suitable not just for a rat.

9.6.2   Ghosts in the machine

The memory palaces we build are haunted by others. Being mere simulacra of other people (recall section 6.7.3) rather than full-blown minds, the ghosts are articulate only to a limited degree. Such is the case with the simulations of famous people; for example, my representation of René Descartes contains, apart from a memory of the well-known portrait (long hair, moustache, soul patch), only one verbatim expression — the celebrated "cogito" quote. There is, however, a serious latent narrative hiding in the loose conceptual network that represents, in my brain, Descartes' mind; I can use it to generate, in several languages Descartes never spoke, a statement with whose content he would, perhaps, not disagree. In that sense, and to that extent, I play a host to Descartes' narrative Self.

People whom I know much more intimately are represented in my brain by much more sophisticated simulacra, whose narrative abilities are correspondingly more extensive. Considering how good a person can be at assuming the conceptual stance of strangers described by stereotypical labels (e.g., students taking the faculty's perspectives, or vice versa, as reported by Barsalou (1987); cf. section 6.5.3), one may see how our simulacra of immediate family members or close friends would be not only narratively sophisticated but also properly perspectival, and therefore useful for supporting social cognition.

There is a side effect to this convenience: for better or for worse, such advanced simulations of other people may persist long after their usefulness to the host has been exhausted — for example, when those people are dead. To understand how this is possible, we must remember that most computational processes that comprise the mind are *active* (triggered in a distributed

Sutton (2002) observes, "It may be by utilizing local narrative resources to 'freeze' thoughts about the past in this way … that children develop the PERSPECTIVE-SWITCHING abilities which allow them to understand that others have different perspectives on the same once-occupied time." This notion is supported by the developmental studies of Nelson and Fivush (2004). Adults, as we learned in Chapter 6, are very good at perspective-taking (Barsalou, 1987).

fashion, rather than waiting to be called upon by a single central controller) and *autonomous* (capable of carrying on once triggered, rather than being stepped through by a controller). The autonomy of the simulacrum of a person that is embedded in my brain explains the not uncommon human experience invoked by Shakespeare in the scene from *Hamlet* where the prince of Denmark converses with his dead father: the murdered old king lives on as a RUNAWAY SIMULATION, whose seemingly supernatural overtones are due to the discrepancy between Hamlet's rational knowledge of his father's death and the clarity with which he can hear his voice in his head. Boyer (2003), writing in *Trends in Cognitive Sciences*, observes:

> On the one hand, systems that regulate our intuitions about animacy have little difficulty understanding that a dead body is a non-intentional, inanimate object. On the other hand, social-intelligence systems do not 'shut off' with death; indeed most people still have thoughts and feelings about the recently dead. This discrepancy between incompatible intuitions about a single object might explain why recently dead people are so often seen as supernatural agents.
>
> — Boyer (2003)

The narrative component of person simulacra may be provided by mechanisms familiar to us from Chapter 7. Knowledge of language is an abstraction from life-long experience — an enormous corpus of utterances, processed to distill reusable patterns. These form the linguistic constructions that populate the lexicon-grammar and can be used both to recreate familiar utterances (some verbatim, as in the case of "sayings" and idioms) and to generate new ones, patterned on the old. To the extent that I have committed to memory utterances produced by my father, I can recall (approximately) what I have heard from him; more importantly, I can generate novel utterances patterned on his turns of speech and likely topics of conversation. Add to these the understandable emotional baggage that I associate with this particular person's simulacrum, and the cognitive "discrepancy" highlighted in the above quote from Boyer (2003), and the outcome is me, thinking in my head the thoughts of the dead (cf. Table 9.3).

By following this line of inquiry, we arrive quite soon at a realization that at a first glance seems preposterous: **it is conceivable that a *really* elaborate**

simulacrum of another person that lives in my brain may become conscious. Note that you cannot deny this on any introspective grounds, because you are barred from first-person access to the experiences of a simulacrum with which — or, as one ought to say, with whom — you share your brain. At the same time, there are plenty of theoretical reasons to believe that advanced simulacra *can* be conscious: they may contain an encapsulated and transparent simulation of reality, a many-tiered representational system, and a certain capacity for linguistic expression: in other words, they contain the basic ingredients of the phenomenal, the reflexive, and the narrative Self.[29]

Don't bite my finger, look where I am pointing.

— Warren S. McCulloch quoted by Beer (1999, p.437)

9.7 Altered states

Let us now apply our newly acquired knowledge of the computational nature of consciousness and its neural basis to the analysis of three select behavioral conditions, all of which occur naturally in our daily lives: solitude (in which narratives of the Self assume special poignancy), slips of perceptual awareness (which demonstrate the fragility of access to the true state of affairs in

כי חצוי העולם, כי הוא שנים,	For divided the world is, and twofold
וכפולה היא המית מספדו,	is the murmur of its regret;
כי אין בית בלי מת על כפים,	every home has its dead to grieve for,
ואין מת שישכח את ביתו.	and the dead their home won't forget.
ובלי קץ אל ערי נכאינו	In our cities, the realm of dejection,
יושבי חושך ותל נבטים.	by the dwellers of darkness observed,
נפלאים, נפלאים הם חיינו,	our wonderful life to perfection
המלאים מחשבות של מתים.	is suffused by the thoughts of the dead.

Table 9.3 — THE THOUGHTS OF THE DEAD. The last two stanzas of *The Mole* by Nathan Alterman, from his cycle *The Joy of the Poor* (my translation). The phrasing of the last line — which has "the thoughts *of* the dead" rather than "*about* the dead" — is not accidental and not just a due paid to the poetical form (in Hebrew, the second version would scan as well as the original first). I like to imagine that Alterman has intuited in his poem the computational explanation of communion with the dead that I offer in section 9.6.2: if the utterances in my head are generated by a runaway simulation of a dead person, the thoughts they express belong to — are *of* rather than about — that person.

the world), and sleep (in which the phenomenal Self becomes liberated from
the constraints of reality).

9.7.1 Solitude

Social environment and language are instrumental in the creation and maintenance of the narrative Self, which carries much of the burden of acting like
a human being. Although being alone is part of most people's daily lives
(evidence obtained with experience sampling methods shows that adults are
alone for about a third of each waking cycle; Long and Averill, 2003), prolonged SOLITUDE has profound effects on the development of one's sense of
self and, indeed, humanity.

   According to one thread of philosophical thinking about solitude, which
extends back to Aristotle, "man is by nature a political animal" that belongs
in the polis. Contrary to this classical view, which has all too often been used
to motivate complete subjugation of the individuals by the state ("for their
own good"), many of the effects of solitude on the Self are actually positive
(as suggested by another classical view; see Figure 9.19).

   It is clearly not possible for an infant raised in complete isolation from
other humans to become human. In adolescence, however, solitude becomes

ALONE
adj. In bad company.

— Ambrose Bierce,
The Devil's Dictionary

Figure 9.19 — On SOLITUDE: *nun-
quam minus solum esse quam cum solus
esset* (never less alone than when alone)
— a maxim of P. CORNELIUS SCIPIO
AFRICANUS (235-183 BC), as reported
in Cicero's *De re publica*, I:27. The aca-
cia tree (*A. seyal*) in this photograph is
not dead: encouraged in all likelihood
by a rain that had fallen in the desert
the week before, it was in the middle
of sprouting several new avocado-green
shoots when I hiked by. Look for it in
wadi Roded near Eilat, where it bends
due north against the Shekhoret Mountains.

essential to normal development: in a study involving nearly five hundred American middle and high school students, those in grades seven to nine (but not five or six) reported a more positive emotional state after a period of solitude (Larson, 1997). Participants in that study who spent an intermediate amount of time alone were also found to be better adjusted, prompting Larson to describe the role of solitude in early adolescence as "a strategic retreat that complements social experience."

This framing of the issue of solitude is rare in academic studies, which, according to Long and Averill (2003), tend to focus on loneliness instead. The public, in contrast, seems to be aware of the occasional need of the individual to be alone, as witnessed by the Wilderness Act passed by the US Congress in 1964, with the aim "to establish a National Wilderness Preservation System for the permanent good of the whole people." Two subsequent explorations of the perceived value of wilderness solitude (Hammitt, 1982; Hammitt, Backman, and Davis, 2001) revealed that the college students who served as subjects appreciate it because it affords natural environment, cognitive freedom, intimacy, and individualism (in that order).

Further insight into the cognitive dimensions of solitude can be achieved by considering its probable effects on the computational mechanisms underlying the narrative Self — more precisely, the tangle of diverse, multiple-perspective narratives that compose it. It may be conjectured that prolonged insulation from the otherwise constant friction with other people's selves (which on the distributed cognition account permeate each other; Decety and Sommerville, 2003) disinhibits the active memory traces — the simulacra of events and agents — stored locally within one's brain (for an even stronger effect, solitude should be sought on a high mountain; cf. Arzy, Idel, Landis, and Blanke, 2005). A proper cognitive-computational inquiry into solitude that would substantiate and expand upon this conjecture is yet to be undertaken.

9.7.2   Slips of perceptual awareness

Free undisturbed time, of which there is an abundance when one is alone in the wilderness, would seem to bring with it an opportunity for a deeper perceptual awareness than what most of us are accustomed to. A desert vista, as I noted in the beginning of this chapter, cannot be taken in with one glance; would prolonged contemplation make up for the narrowness of our sensory input channels? The answer, unfortunately, is negative. Not only can we

But he who is unable to live in society, or who has no need because he is sufficient for himself, must be either a beast or a god: he is no part of a state.

— Aristotle,
Politics, I.2 (*ca.* 323 BC)

It had been hard for him that spake it to have put more truth and untruth together in few words, than in that speech, *Whatsoever is delighted in solitude is either a wild beast or a god.*

— Francis Bacon,
Of Friendship (1601)

Cogitation is the thing which distinguishes the solitude of a god from a wild beast.

— Abraham Cowley,
Of Solitude (1668)

not see everything at once: even when combined with memory, scrutiny is powerless in integrating a heap of views of a scene into one coherent whole (cf. Figure 9.20).

This limitation on perceptual awareness manifests itself, among other phenomena, in CHANGE BLINDNESS — an illusion of immutability in the face of a world that changes before our very eyes (Mack, 2003). As documented by hundreds of studies, even large changes in the observed scene are likely to go unseen if made during the subject's saccadic eye movements (Simons and Rensink, 2005). The same kind of selective blindness is obtained in the flicker task, in which the display alternates between two versions of the same scene with some changes made to one of them: observers eventually detect most changes, but can take an astonishingly long time to do so. Similar results were found for changes made during eye blinks or brief partial occlusions of the scene, and for changes that occur gradually (Simons and Rensink, 2005).

Probably the most striking demonstration of change blindness involves scenes in which it is people who disappear (cf. Figure 9.21) — or are sub-

Figure 9.20 — If we were able to take in the meaning — that is, the spatial structure — of a scene all at once, we would not be misled by M. C. Escher's *Waterfall*, in which water flows along a closed-loop channel, yet seemingly always downhill. Locally, this image is perfectly fine; the inconsistency arises on the global scale, and we cannot *see* it because of the information-processing bottleneck, which allows only a small part of the sensory input at any given time to reach the higher levels of representation and awareness (Itti and Koch, 2001). Using attention to scan the scene does not help, because integration of information accrued in that manner is incomplete and imperfect (note the analogy here to the subjects' tendency to accept globally ill-formed but locally consistent utterances in language processing; cf. section 7.5). Visual representations do not have to be complete because in ecologically valid situations the brain would rely on the actual scene being accessible at need, and thus serving as an external memory, or its own representation (O'Regan, 1992; Reitman et al., 1978). Thus, visual awareness is subject to the quirks of ACCESS to information — the central computational thread of this chapter.

stituted without the observer's knowledge, as in the experiments of Simons and Levin (1998), whose unsuspecting potential subjects were approached on campus by one of the investigators and asked for directions. In the middle of offering directions, the subject was separated from the investigator by two men carrying a door, one of whom was the other investigator, and the two would switch places. Only seven of the 15 subjects in this study reported noticing the switch (some of these had in fact continued the conversation apparently unperturbed by the change).

All of Simons and Levin's subjects who noticed the change were of the same age group as the experimenters, prompting them to hypothesize that

Figure 9.21 — One way to demonstrate CHANGE BLINDNESS is to show subjects in alternation two versions of the same scene with a certain object present in one, but missing from the other (a uniform gray image is displayed between the two content frames to prevent the disappearing object from visibly flickering on and off; Rensink, O'Regan, and Clark, 1995). It may take many cycles for a subject to detect the difference between the two scenes, depending among other factors on how topical for the scene the disappearing object is (Simons and Levin, 1997). In the two images shown here, there is a quite obvious change: Trotsky, who appears saluting next to Lenin in the photograph on the left (taken in 1919), has been edited out from the other one (a 1967 version, from an official Soviet publication; see *The Commissar Vanishes: the Falsification of Photographs and Art in Stalin's Russia*, by David King, New York: Metropolitan Books, 1997). There are other people beside Trotsky missing from the photograph on the right; can you find them in the other one? We shall probably never know whether an unspecified number of marmots (cf. p. 239) had also been airbrushed out of both photographs, as insinuated by some members of the Sciuridae Fraction of the 4th International.

socially motivated attentional processes were at work. Indeed, a follow-up experiment showed that the probability that a subject would notice a person switch in the middle of an interaction depends on their social group membership (cf. the second row of Table 9.1 on page 434). The role of attention in partially countering change blindness has been confirmed by many other studies designed specially to address this issue (Rensink, O'Regan, and Clark, 1997; Simons and Rensink, 2005). Here too some spectacular effects have been demonstrated: 46% of the 192 subjects of Simons and Chabris (1999) who watched two teams of three players pass basketballs for a few minutes failed to notice a man in a gorilla suit who crossed the room in mid-game.[30]

The functional-computational explanation of change blindness combines two familiar concepts: of the world as an external memory (O'Regan, 1992; Reitman et al., 1978) from Chapter 6 and, closer to the theme of the present chapter, of the role of access to sensory information as the essence of attention and awareness.[31] The visual world (which, we must remember, is a simulation totally controlled by the brain) is perceived as complete as long as *I* (another part of the same simulation) feel that it can be accessed at will. By default, I also perceive the world as unchanging, as long as there is no good reason not to. These Panglossian assumptions are maintained even if the flow of external information that feeds into the simulator is momentarily interrupted by a blink or a transitory obstruction of the field of view.

A "good reason" to suspect that something is amiss in the sensory input may come in the form of an explicit attentional cue provided by the experimenter in a controlled setting. Studies reviewed by Lamme (2003) found that cuing the item that may change from one scene to the next prevents change blindness. Surprisingly, such cuing works even if it is done *after* the first frame is removed from view, but before the second one is shown. In terms of the multi-tiered hierarchy of representations that I used in explaining access consciousness in section 9.4, a rich representation of the entire visual field persists at a lower level until "overwritten" by the next stimulus, and is accessible to attention that can copy a cued item out of this ephemeral storage and into a more central area, where it can be accessed by other processes.

Rather than cuing attention perceptually, one may attempt to enhance it via a direct intervention at the neuronal level. Following this logic, Cavanaugh and Wurtz (2004) applied microstimulation to the superior colliculus; they found it to be effective in countering change blindness in the monkey. The stimulus in their study consisted of three patches of moving dots set against a uniform gray background. After a 150 *msec* blank period, the direction of dot motion in one of the patches differed from before; as expected, the monkeys tended to miss this change. The proportion of correct detections increased, and the reaction time decreased, in trials in which the SC area corresponding to the impending change was stimulated for 600 *msec* around the time of the blank period. Importantly, the proportion of false positives did not increase, signifying that the microstimulation enhanced selective attention rather than simply making the orienting system indiscriminately "jumpy" (see Figure 9.22).

This result squares nicely with our understanding of how attention and phenomenal awareness work on the neuronal level. As I mentioned earlier in this chapter, Moore and Armstrong (2003) had found that microstimulation of the cortical frontal eye fields precipitates spatial location-selective shifts of covert attention. Now, Cavanaugh and Wurtz (2004) showed that microstimulation can also raise the level of attention in a manner that is selective to content rather than location, by doing it where it matters the most: in the virtual reality arena of the SUPERIOR COLLICULUS, where perception, motivation, and motor control all come together over action selection (Merker, 2007).

9.7.3 Dreaming

In the show that is under way in the virtual reality arena of the human brain, there are periodic surges and lulls of activity: the acrobat troupe leaves and a lonely clown takes its place, only to be chased away by an elephant on

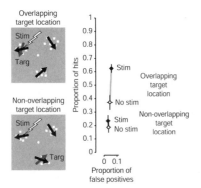

Figure 9.22 — Inattentional blindness in the monkey can be alleviated by microstimulation of the SUPERIOR COLLICULUS, if applied at the site corresponding to location of the would-be change in the visual field (the "overlapping target" condition on the *left*). As the plot on the *right* (Cavanaugh and Wurtz, 2004, fig.4B) shows, microstimulation raises the proportion of correct detections (hits) relative to the baseline when applied to the target location (upper two points) but not when applied to a distractor location (lower two points). In neither case is the false positive rate affected, indicating that the manipulation influences selective attention rather than general arousal.

spindly legs and two flying tigers.[32] The variations in the quality and intensity of this "insubstantial pageant"[33] — a total reality simulation that, as we learned in section 9.3.2, includes both the circus and any spectators that may believe to be attending the show (Merker, 2007; Metzinger, 2003) — are observable from outside as the wake-sleep cycle. Just as there are many shades of consciousness (Metzinger, 2003, p.559), there are many kinds of SLEEP — a continuum of cognitive states that stretches from conscious wakefulness at the one extreme to deep anaesthesia[34] and coma (and, beyond it, DEATH) on the other (Laureys, 2005, fig.1).

Sleep states that belong in between those extremes are of interest to us here mainly insofar as they involve DREAMING — "a universal human experience which offers a unique view of consciousness and cognition" (Hobson, Pace-Schott, and Stickgold, 2000). Reassuringly, the comprehensive Activation-Synthesis model of dream construction developed by Hobson and his associates over the past several decades, which focuses on the anatomy and physiology of the brain mechanisms of dreaming, is very much in line

Figure 9.23 — DREAM states of the human brain are characterized by hypofrontality (reduced activity in the dorsolateral prefrontal cortex, which mediates executive function and is involved in working memory), and a relatively vigorous activity in the anterior limbic structures (implicated in emotional cognition) and in the visual association areas (Muzur et al., 2002). The resulting network, whose effective configuration is very unlike that of the waking brain, is a fertile ground for hallucinations: internally generated signals (which arise subcortically in midbrain structures such as the superior colliculus) are interpreted by the cortical association and limbic areas as emotionally charged experiences that conform to statistically entrenched event structures ("regression to a schema"; cf. p. 190) but lack the frontally orchestrated global coherence. The sensory-motor input-output blockade and the disrupted memory consolidation prevent the dream-state hallucinations from being acted out and, largely, from being remembered.

with the computational principles of cognition as summarized in this book, such as the role of statistical schemata in conceptual and episodic memory, and the role of an executive function, with working memory at its core, in facilitating globally coherent computation (Figure 9.23 on the preceding page).

From the standpoint of the computational phenomenology of consciousness, a particularly interesting characteristic of dreaming is the dreamer's obliviousness to the unreality of his or her situation. Unperturbed by the bizarreness of the dream world brought into being by haphazard activation of memories, the dreamer is typically unaware of being in a dream. A natural explanation of this seemingly glaring lapse of consciousness emerges from the view of phenomenal experience as a simulation (Merker, 2007; Metzinger, 2003) which as a rule is transparent to the simulated experiencer:

> Phenomenal experience during the waking state is an *online* hallucination. This hallucination is *online* because the autonomous activity of the system is permanently being modulated by the information flow from the sensory organs; it is a hallucination because it depicts a possible reality as an actual reality. Phenomenal experience during the dream state, however, is just a complex *offline* hallucination.
>
> — Metzinger (2003, p.51)

A most interesting exception to the rule of transparency of the mind's simulation of reality is LUCID DREAMING (LaBerge, 1990). In this not entirely uncommon state of consciousness (about 20% of the population reports having lucid dreams at least once a month), the dreamers are aware of being in a dream. People can train themselves to increase the likelihood of lucid dreaming, and even to retain access while dreaming to some information memorized during the preceding waking period (this ability is useful in the laboratory setting, where a sleeper connected to a polygraph can signal the onset of the lucid dream to the researcher; LaBerge, 1990).[35]

In his discussion of lucid dreaming, Metzinger (2003, p.566) points out that it is but one step away from "selfless consciousness": it is in principle possible for the lucid dreamer to recognize his or her own self phenomenally as "a dream character, ... a representational fiction" — just as he or she recognizes the dream world for what it is. "I am, of course, well aware,"

The brain, the dynamical, self-organizing system as a whole, *activates* the pilot if and only if it needs the pilot as a representational instrument in order to integrate, monitor, predict, and remember its own activities. As long as the pilot is needed to navigate the world, the puppet shadow dances on the wall of the neurophenomenological caveman's phenomenal state space. As soon as the system does not need a globally available self-model, it simply turns it off. Together with the model the conscious experience of selfhood disappears. Sleep is the little brother of DEATH.

— Metzinger (2003, p.558)

Metzinger concludes, "that this ... conception of selflessness directly corresponds to a classical philosophical notion, well-developed in Asian philosophy at least 2500 years ago, namely, the Buddhist conception of 'enlightenment.'"

9.8 Gone beyond

The computational theory of consciousness outlined in this chapter bears directly on the musing of the fictional version of Genghis Khan, created by Victor Pelevin and quoted in the epigraph, concerning the place of the "I" (in the original, Я, which by the way is not normally capitalized in Russian) in the whirlwind of events aroused by his will. But whose will is that, one may ask at this point, given that the real Genghis Khan's "I," just as everyone else's, is a computational fiction, an illusion? And whose illusion would that be? The answer has been with us since section 9.3.2:

gate, gate, pāragate, pārasamgate (gone, gone, gone beyond, GONE COMPLETELY BEYOND).

— *prajñapāramitā hridaya sūtra*
The Great Heart Wisdom Sutra

> Whose illusion could that be? It makes sense to speak of truth and falsity, of knowledge and illusion, only if you already have an epistemic agent in the sense of a system possessing conceptualized knowledge in a strong propositional sense. But this is not the case: We have just solved the homunculus problem; there is nobody in there who could be wrong about anything. All you have is a functionally grounded self-modeling system under the condition of a naive-realistic self-misunderstanding. So, if you would really want to carry this metaphor even further, what I have been saying ... is that the conscious self is an illusion which is no one's illusion.
>
> — Metzinger (2004, p.60)

Notes

[1] BUDDHA'S LITTLE FINGER: this choice of title for the English translation of Pelevin's

book Чапаев и Пустота ("Chapayev and Void") becomes clear in the light of the following passage, found near the end of the book: "Many thousands of years ago, long before Buddha Dipankara and Buddha Shakyamuni came into the world, there lived Buddha Anagama. He did not waste time on explanations, instead simply pointing to things with his little finger, whereby their true nature would immediately become manifest. He would point at a mountain and it would vanish; he would point at a river and it would vanish too. This is a long story — briefly, the end was that he pointed his little finger at himself and disappeared. All that was left was this little finger, which his disciples hid in a piece of clay."

[2]ZAZEN (Chinese, *zuochan*): the Japanese name for the Buddhist practice of seated meditation.

[3]The formal proof of the INTRACTABILITY of full-scene high-resolution visual search offered by Tsotsos (1990) focuses, as such proofs in computational complexity theory usually do, on the worst case. To draw conclusions about the average case instead, one must resort to probabilistic approaches, which necessitate making assumptions about the distribution of exemplars in problem space.

[4]Concerning the need to bring out some dimensions of stimulus variation while downplaying others: cf. section 5.2.2 on perceptual CONSTANCIES.

[5] The SPATIAL FREQUENCY of a zebra pattern of alternating black and white stripes is the number of cycles per unit visual angle. As in visual acuity (cf. note 4 on page 148), in spatial frequency it is the relative *angular* size of the various parts of the stimulus that matters. Suppressing the high spatial frequency components of an image, for example by looking at it through matte glass, causes it to appear blurred.

[6]Concerning OBJECTS and EVENTS: cf. note 1 on page 33.

[7]Multiple SPOTLIGHTS OF ATTENTION: it is possible to get subjects to mark several objects simultaneously, and to keep track of the marked objects as they move around the visual field. In the illustration below (Cavanagh and Alvarez, 2005, fig.1), three objects out of six are highlighted at the beginning of a trial (*left*); all objects then move around for a period of time (*middle*); finally, the movement stops, and the subject is required to decide whether the marked object is one of the original three (*right*) —

[8]Although the salience maps are organized spatially (retinotopically), attention can be OBJECT-BASED; for instance, one of two intersecting curves may be selectively attended to. A computational model of this ability, based on the idea of visual "routines" assembled from elementary operations such as curve tracing (Edelman, 1987; Ullman, 1984), proved to be compatible with psychophysical and electrophysiological findings (Roelfsema, 2005; Roelfsema, Lamme, and Spekreijse, 2004). The combined bottom-up and top-down tracing process that enables object-based selection may be implemented in the brain by a neural circuit that connects posterior parietal cortex with occipital visual areas V1 and V4 (Shomstein and Behrmann, 2006). Visual routines, such as selective, controlled spread of activation (Roelfsema, 2005; Ullman, 1984), require a kind of virtual machine (recall Figure 8.11 on page 338) to assemble and run them "on the fly" in working memory; in that connection, it is interesting

to note that attention and spatial working memory are subserved by related mechanisms (Awh and Jonides, 2001).

[9]THERE IS NO SPOON. There is an allusion here to the following dialogue from *The Matrix*, a film by Andy and Larry Wachowski (1999):

Boy: Do not try to bend the spoon; that's impossible. Instead, only try to realize the truth.
Neo: What truth?
Boy: There is no spoon.
Neo: There is no spoon?
Boy: Then you will see, it is not the spoon that bends, it is only yourself.

[10]Who or what OWNS experiences?

> There is no direct experience of a knower. There is no direct knowledge of the process of awareness. All that can be discovered by the most careful introspection is the existence and attributes of the objects of knowledge, of the content of consciousness, and this content does not include the knower or awareness itself. Knower and knowing are implicit in the known, but are not directly experienced. That something produces the limits and attributes of content is a logical conclusion, but no description of that thing from experience is possible. All that can be said is that some process, relation, or what not, gives rise to the phenomena of content, and determines the character of the field of consciousness. Subjective experience does not justify any further statement concerning awareness than this. It follows that any process or relation will account for the selection of the elements of content and for the attributes of those elements (other than being known), whether that process or relation be in a universe of physical things or in a realm of pure psychics, will fulfill all the subjectively discoverable requirements for a complete account of awareness.
>
> — Lashley (1923, p.251)

[11]Note that RETINOTOPY — location in the visual field — is a key feature of the model of attention outlined in Figure 9.8 on page 407.

[12]Lenggenhager, Tadi, Metzinger, and Blanke (2007) and Ehrsson (2007) have recently used virtual reality analogues of the RUBBER HAND ILLUSION to induce in normal subjects an out-of-body experience — a phenomenal feeling of being physically separated from one's body, which sometimes occurs following right temporo-parietal lesions, and which can also be caused by direct stimulation of the right angular gyrus (Blanke, Ortigue, Landis, and Seeck, 2002).

[13]I mention here several of the dozens of psychiatric conditions that arise when the neurocomputational mechanisms of phenomenal awareness go awry. First, a list from Metzinger (2004, p.44):

- Consciously experienced thoughts are not my thoughts any more: schizophrenia.

- My leg is not my leg any more: unilateral hemi-neglect.

- My arm acts without my control: alien hand syndrome.

- I am a robot; I am transformed into a puppet; volitional acts are not my own volitional acts anymore: depersonalization.

- I am the whole world, all events in the world are being initiated and controlled by my own volitional acts: mania.

Particularly interesting from the standpoint of Metzinger's (2003) theory are:

Anosognosia and anosodiaphoria conditions: a loss of higher-order insight into an existing deficit, as in blindness denial. The existence of these disorders show that the veracity of self-representation is not guaranteed: unnoticed and unnoticeable forms of mistaken self-representation can exist because the subsymbolic self-model is cognitively and introspectively impenetrable.

Dissociative identity disorder (DID): functional adaptation to extremely traumatizing situations may involve the emergence of two or more distinct "identities" or personality states. Metzinger (2004) quotes Norman Geschwind's description of such a case: "She awoke several times with her left hand choking her, and while she was awake, her left hand would unbutton her gown, crush cups on her tray, and fight with the right hand while she was answering the phone. To keep her left hand from doing mischief, she would subdue it with the right hand." Compare this to Stanley Kubrik's fictional Dr. Strangelove (p. 166), whose one hand tried to overpower the other.

Complete depersonalization: loss of the phenomenal first-person perspective, accompanied by dysphoric states and functional deficits (Angstvolle Ich-Auflösung, "dreadful ego-dissolution").

[14]Conant and Ashby (1970) proved that EVERY GOOD REGULATOR OF A SYSTEM MUST BE A MODEL OF THAT SYSTEM, supporting Craik's (1943) observation that brains do well if they model the world (section 2.1.3). The following figure (Conant and Ashby, 1970, fig.1) illustrates a regulator, represented as a set of events R, alongside a set of events in the rest of the system S, whose behavior is subject to the action of a set of disturbers D:

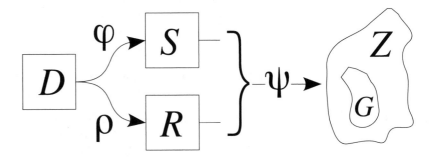

The outcomes form the set Z of all possible events, a subset of which, G, consists of the desirable ("good") events. Conant and Ashby (1970) show that with the probability distribution $p(S)$ fixed, the class of optimal regulators corresponds to the class of optimal distributions $p(R|S)$ for which the entropy of Z is minimal. The optimization of $p(R|S)$ is achieved by controlling the structure of R and the mapping $\rho : D \to R$, in order to make R isomorphic to S. Note that the S and the R variables are on an equal footing as far as their effect on Z (through the mapping ψ) is concerned, so that the model of the system (which constitutes its best regulator) does not have to be fully "internal" (confined to R); relying on the S variables is perfectly fine, as indeed the proponents of embodied and situated theories of cognition have been claiming for some time now.

[15]On dealing with NOVELTY: if a situation is both novel enough to require an innovative solution and dire enough to exclude inaction, the system better crank up its virtual machine (if it has one) and start being creative, or its goose is cooked.

[16]For a full description of the neural substrate of phenomenal experience in vertebrates, which along with the superior colliculus includes a number of other midbrain structures, see Merker (2007).

[17]Visual information obtained by fusing the signals from the two eyes is called CYCLOPEAN after Cyclopes, the one-eyed giants of Hesiod and Homer; one of those was the Cyclops Polyphemus, blinded by the crafty Odysseus.

[18]Concerning the phenomenal location of the cyclopean vantage point: cf. Borges recalling a conversation with his father: "'What a queer thing,' he said, 'that I should be living, as they say, behind my eyes, inside my head; I wonder if that makes sense'" (p.24, Burgin, R., *Conversations with Jorge Luis Borges*, Holt, Rinehart, and Winston, New York, 1969).

[19]The personages whose names are invoked in this passage from Dennett's (1995) book are psychologists B. F. Skinner and Richard Gregory and philosopher Karl Popper.

[20]The GLORIOUS REVOLUTION culminated in the overthrow of James II of England. The form of parliamentary democracy established thereafter in England was, of course, very far from empowering the majority of the population. Even with universal adult suffrage in place (as it is in present-day Britain and the United States), citizens are de facto disenfranchised insofar as they are insufficiently well-educated to understand how the world works and to think for themselves (cf. the note on WHO IS AFRAID OF EDUCATION? on p. 36). This argument has been developed by Dewey (1916) and, more recently, by Putnam:

> As his own [Dewey's] primary contribution to bringing about a different sort of democracy, a "participatory," or better a "deliberative" democracy, he focused his efforts on promoting what was then a new conception of education. If democracy is to be both participatory and deliberative, education must not be a matter of simply teaching people to learn things by rote and believe what they are taught. In a deliberative democracy, learning how to think for oneself, to question, to criticize, is fundamental. But thinking for oneself does not exclude — indeed, it requires — learning when and where to seek expert knowledge.
>
> — Putnam (2004, p.105)

[21]The system of REPRESENTATIVE DEMOCRACY as it is practiced in the United States is far from perfect, if only because it is non-proportional (both because of the design of the Senate and of the existence of the Electoral College). Furthermore, many US citizens are prevented from participating fully in the democratic process by their lack of education (as noted earlier) and by the prohibitive cost of running for office.

[22]AUTOMATICITY is given up as soon as the need arises to deal with novelty or hardship; recall Figure 9.15 on page 428. For a fascinating hypothesis according to which consciousness emerged in the inhabitants of the Mediterranean Basin following a series of cataclysmic geological and socio-political events thousands of years ago, see Jaynes (1976).

[23]FLASH SUPPRESSION is a perceptual phenomenon that is related to binocular rivalry. It consists of the perceived suppression of a monocular stimulus upon flashing a different stimulus to the contralateral eye while keeping the original stimulus in the ipsilateral eye. Although two distinct stimuli are presented to the left and right eyes, subjects only "see" the flashed, novel stimulus. This method of stimulus presentation is used in the study of perceptual awareness in monkeys (Leopold and Logothetis, 1999) and humans (Kreiman et al., 2002).

[24]The logical possibility that everyone else except me is a ZOMBIE (a technical term for a creature that is cognitively able but devoid of phenomenality) is the subject of an age-old philosophical debate that should have been put to rest long ago. For a convincing argument to that effect, see Spivey (2006, ch.12).

[25]It is interesting to note that insofar as I am a PRIMATE, my brain has some pretty special representational powers — not only in its five senses, which are given distinct representations both in the diencephalon and in the telencephalon (Merker, 2007), but also in the "sixth sense" — interoception, which encompasses stimuli that originate inside the body. It turns out that only primates possess, in the insular cortex as well as in the midbrain, a meta-representation of interoceptive signals such as hunger, cold, and pain. According to Craig (2005, p.305), "in humans, this interoceptive cortical image... seems to provide a meta-representation of the state of the body that is associated with subjective awareness of the material self as a feeling (sentient) entity." Thus, the sense of pain as we know it is very much a primate affair; the entreaty of Arnault in Dante's Purgatory would not have been appreciated by a lizard —

"Sovegna vos a temps de ma dolor"
(Bethink you in due season of my pain)

— Dante, *Purgatorio*, xxvi:148

[26]The chariot wheel simile quoted by Borges from the *Visuddhimagga* (VIII,39) reminds me of another one:

И вечный бой! Покой нам только снится
Сквозь кровь и пыль.
Летит, летит степная колесница,
И мнёт ковыль.

— Aleksandr Blok
On the Field of Kulikovo (1908)

For an English translation, see the *Russian Review*, Vol. 13, No. 1, Jan. 1954, pp. 33-37. Unfortunately, in that translation of Blok's poem (as in most others), "chariot" (колесница) becomes "mare," deftly disposing of much of the poem's original imagery.

[27]Writing on SECOND-ORDER cognition, Clark (1998) muses: "Perhaps it is public language which is responsible for a complex of rather distinctive features of human thought viz, our ability to display second order cognitive dynamics. By second order cognitive dynamics I mean a cluster of powerful capacities involving self-evaluation, self-criticism and finely honed remedial responses."

[28]THE GRANDMOTHER ASSIMILATED. A famous literary treatment of alienation and detachment from one's narrative self (which in the terminology of the present book is seen as "nothing but a pack of memes") is the short story *Borges and I* by Jorge Luis Borges. I shall pick up this thread in section 9.6, which deals with narrative as a core component of simulated selves of others (cf. section 6.7.3).

[29]SPUN-OFF SELVES do arise in certain pathological conditions; see note 13 on page 457. The possibility of transient consciousness arising as a by-product of a (science-fictional) "back-up" operation, in which the informational contents of a brain are transferred to an electronic substrate, is treated in Greg Egan's short story *Transition Dreams* (Egan, 1999).

[30]On INATTENTIONAL BLINDNESS: 50% of a second group of 12 observers failed to notice

the gorilla in an additional experimental condition, in which "it stopped in the middle of the display, turned to face the camera, thumped its chest, and then continued walking across the field of view" (Simons and Chabris, 1999, fig.3).

[31]O'Regan and Noë (2001) use the idea of the world as its own representation as a foundation for an account of phenomenal, and not just access, consciousness, which brings together concepts familiar to us from earlier sections: virtual reality, situatedness, embodiment, and sensorimotor contingencies. For a critique of some aspects of their approach, with much of which I sympathize, see Edelman (2006).

[32]Concerning FLYING TIGERS: see Salvador Dalí's 1944 painting *Sueño causado por el vuelo de una abeja alrededor de una granada un segundo antes del despertar* (Dream caused by the flight of a bumble bee around a pomegranate one second before waking up).

[33]I cannot resist raising the spirit of Prospero —

> Our revels now are ended. These our actors,
> As I foretold you, were all spirits and
> Are melted into air, into thin air:
> And, like the baseless fabric of this vision,
> The cloud-capp'd towers, the gorgeous palaces,
> The solemn temples, the great globe itself,
> Ye all which it inherit, shall dissolve
> And, like this insubstantial pageant faded,
> Leave not a rack behind. We are such stuff
> As dreams are made on, and our little life
> Is rounded with a sleep.

— William Shakespeare,
The Tempest, Act IV, scene I

[34]ANAESTHESIA suppresses figure-ground segmentation activity in the primary visual cortex (Lamme, Zipser, and Spekreijse, 1998), and reduces the effective global connectivity of the cerebral cortex (Massimini, Ferrarelli, Huber, Esser, Singh, and Tononi, 2005; Rudolph and Antkowiak, 2004). This results in anterograde amnesia, sedation, hypnosis, miorelaxation — and loss of qualia, which are "solvent in local anaesthetic" (Llinás, 2001, p.218).

[35]The functional account of normal DREAMING given by LaBerge agrees with that of Metzinger (2003): "Perhaps this explains in part why we are so inclined to mistake our dreams for reality: To the functional systems of neuronal activity that construct our experiential world (model), dreaming of perceiving or doing something is equivalent to actually perceiving or doing it" (LaBerge, 1990).

10

Imagine

A 'person' is an elegant accounting system for making sense
of actions and ascribing them to constructed entities that are
useful for purposes of social justice and the facilitation of
social interaction.

Précis of *The Illusion of Conscious Will*
DANIEL M. WEGNER

You've all got to work it out for yourselves!

BRIAN, in *Monty Python's Life of Brian*

Yo pañiccasamuppàdaü passati so dhammaü passati.

MAHÀHATTHIPADOPAMASUTTA[a]

[a]Whoever sees the web of cause and effect, sees the Way [from
The Great Elephant Footprint Sutra, the Pali canon[1]]

Liberation (M. C. Escher).

THE understanding of the computational nature of Self and consciousness
that we have gained so far raises two related questions that must be
resolved before our quest for self-knowledge, now in its tenth chapter, is fulfilled. If the Self is a shifting skein of computational processes, and if consciousness is a virtual reality simulation that falls for its own tricks, in what
sense, if any, are humans free, and by what ethical standards, if any, should
their behavior be judged? The forthcoming answers — that we are as free
as we feel to be, and that good and evil are what they have ever been —
will perhaps not surprise you, but seeing how they connect to computational
cognitive science may.

10.1 Selfhood and freedom

The issue of freedom arises at this point in our inquiry as a direct consequence
of the demystification of the phenomenal Self. Agency is a key attribute of

the mental faculty of Self. In section 9.3, I explained how a sense of agency is caused by the functioning of corollary discharge circuits in the brain, beginning with an intention to act (the *intended state* box in the top left corner of Figure 9.11 on page 413). But what causes the intention?

Commonsense intuition tells me that my intention to raise my arm, which ~~can be causally effective (let me try it here... yes, it works)~~, must itself be uncaused — that is, not entirely determined by my own past history, let alone by factors outside of myself — if I am to be considered a free agent. This notion of freedom is, of course, just an intuition, and so should be distrusted as a matter of principle. Let us therefore proceed by examining it in the light of the laws of physics, and of computation.

10.1.1 The limits of freedom in physics and computation

The behavior of any physical system (which, as you may recall from earlier chapters, is completely describable in terms of a trajectory through the system's state space) depends on two properties of its dynamics: determinism and causality. For example, a pinball machine, being a classical dynamical system (section 2.3.3), is DETERMINISTIC: given the current position and velocity of the ball, it is possible to predict its future position and velocity as long as the system remains closed; the prediction can be extended across the player's actions, if the forces and the durations of the latter are completely specified.[2] This system is also CAUSAL: for each event, such as the ball striking a particular lever, it is possible to identify antecedents without whose occurrence the event in question would not have happened.[3]

The combination of determinism and causality clearly spells the opposite of freedom for a pinball machine. If brains are deterministic and causal in the same way pinball machines are, it would seem that FREE WILL is a physical impossibility. Could it be that brains, unlike regular pinball machines, are not subject to the strictures of classical physics? On a very small scale (objectively defined by the fundamental physical constants), physics is nondeterministic; for example, in a pinball machine the size of a typical protein molecule, the position of the ball would become indeterminate if its velocity is ever fixed, and vice versa.[4] The quantum mechanical laws that govern such systems are inherently probabilistic (Popper, 1950).[5] In fact, the best physical model of randomness is the quantum mechanical phenomenon of radioactive decay: the precise time at which the nucleus of an unstable isotope of uranium (say, ^{235}U) splits apart is completely random.

FREE WILL is "a philosophical term of art for a particular sort of capacity of rational agents to choose a course of action from among various alternatives" (O'Connor, 2006). Upon a close examination, this seemingly simple concept disintegrates into a heap of contradictions, as noted by Voltaire: "Now you receive all your ideas; therefore you receive your wish, you wish therefore necessarily. [...] The will, therefore, is not a faculty that one can call free. The free will is an expression absolutely devoid of sense, and what the scholastics have called will of indifference, that is to say willing without cause, is a chimera unworthy of being combated" (cf. Dennett, 1984, p. 143).

In most situations, such randomness is the anathema of computation, which is all about an orderly, deterministic progress from one state to the next, as determined by the system's past history and present input.[6] Consequently, artificial information processing systems that contain quantum components (such as all modern electronic devices, which depend on the quantum mechanics of energy states and electron transport in semiconductor materials) resort to special techniques to ensure that the randomness at the microscopic level does not affect the system's computation. Thus, all existing types of computers are deterministic — and so is, as far as one can tell, the natural information processing system that is the human brain (Koch and Hepp, 2006; Tegmark, 2000).[7]

10.1.2 Varieties of free will worth wanting

Even if quantum mechanics were relevant to brain computation, it would not mean that the mind generated by a brain is free in the sense one expects it to be. Contrary to the popular misconception, **randomness is *not* a solution to the problem of reconciling free will with physics**: I want my decisions to be up to *me* — not blind chance or implacable fate. In the pursuit of free will, giving up determinism in favor of randomness is like inviting the Vandals into the city just to dispose of its tyrant.[8]

The resolution of the problem of free will — finding a middle way between the havoc of chance and the tyranny of determinism — lies in pursuing the Humean analogy between the Self and a self-governed REPUBLIC, which I introduced in section 9.4.2 (recall Figure 9.17 on page 432). Merely pointing out that the Self (the agency one expects to exercise free will) is distributed does not suffice: ten billion-dimensional or not, the state of a brain evolves from moment to moment according to inexorable laws of physics that may leave room for chance, but not for freedom. Let us remember, however, a key lesson of the preceding chapters: the Self is distributed not only across the neurons of one brain, but across many brains (Decety and Sommerville, 2003), as well as across various natural and artefactual objects that together comprise an embodied, situated mind (Sutton, 2006). As noted by Dennett,

[The boundaries of the mind are] far enough back to give my *self* enough spread in space and time so that there is a *me* for my decisions to be up to!

— Dennett (2003, p.136)

As to causation; we may observe, that the true idea of the human mind, is to consider it as a system of different perceptions or different existences, which are link'd together by the relation of cause and effect, and mutually produce, destroy, influence, and modify each other. Our impressions give rise to their correspondent ideas; and these ideas in their turn produce other impressions. One thought chaces another, and draws after it a third, by which it is expell'd in its turn. In this respect, I cannot compare the soul more properly to any thing than to a REPUBLIC or commonwealth, in which the several members are united by the reciprocal ties of government and subordination, and give rise to other persons, who propagate the same republic in the incessant changes of its parts. And as the same individual republic may not only change its members, but also its laws and constitutions; in like manner the same person may vary his character and disposition, as well as his impressions and ideas, without losing his identity. Whatever changes he endures, his several parts are still connected by the relation of causation.

— Hume (1740, I.IV.VI)
A Treatise of Human Nature

The resolution of the dilemma of free will proposed and developed by Dennett (1984, 2003) acknowledges the determinism of the physics of brains and of the macroscopic events in which they are enmeshed, while pointing out that the Self, construed properly as a causal network distributed in space and time, has all "the varieties of free will worth wanting" — a memorable phrase that serves as the subtitle of Dennett's 1984 book *Elbow Room*. Following is a list of the main tenets of this stance on personal freedom.

Individual decisions are neither random nor uncaused

Falling dominoes, which is how most people conceptualize chains of cause and effect in physics, is not a good model of causation in complex dynamical systems such as brains, let alone in ecosystems that contain many socially networked brains.

Unlike in a pinball machine, causality in a high-dimensional dynamical distributed system consisting of one or more brains (each with its history of past interactions with the world), and their environment is extremely complex. No simply describable cause can usually be identified for an outcome that is of any consequence to the system, even if post-hoc analysis comes up with counterfactually plausible candidate "choke points" — events that seem as if they could have affected the outcome, had they unfolded differently (cf. note 9 on page 388).

Among the multitude of factors affecting an outcome, some may be random, but for consequential outcomes most are not. In a natural cognitive system, moreover, a significant subset of the non-random factors that affect consequential outcomes are part of the system itself (which, don't forget, is distributed in space and time). There is a very simple reason for this: evolution (Dennett, 2003).

Evolution ensures that individual decisions are attuned to individual needs

A system whose behavior is less random and more in line with the needs of its survival and procreation stands a better chance of driving rivals out of its ecological niche. Evolutionary pressure thus works to concentrate various causal bottlenecks that determine the behavior of a unit of selection (an individual fertile, gene-carrying organism) within that unit. As a result, well-adapted individuals are characterized by a certain degree of control over their fate, as exemplified by the ability to avoid an impending event whose potential consequences are projected by the cognitive foresight mechanism to be harmful (Dennett, 2003).

Just how much "elbow room" (Dennett, 1984) does this leave me with?

Foresight allows me to realize that jumping over the Niagara Falls on a jet ski is likely to kill me (see note 15 on page 231), but what is it that ultimately causes my choice — to jump, or not to jump? Consider this passage from Hume's *Treatise of Human Nature*:

> [...] Whatever capricious and irregular actions we may perform; as the desire of showing our liberty is the sole motive of our actions; we can never free ourselves from the bonds of necessity. We may imagine we feel a liberty within ourselves; but a spectator can commonly infer our actions from our motives and character; and even where he cannot, he concludes in general, that he might, were he perfectly acquainted with every circumstance of our situation and temper, and the most secret springs of our complexion and disposition. Now this is the very essence of necessity, according to the foregoing doctrine.[9]

> — Hume (1740, II.III.II)

The apparent paradox of choice and necessity is thereby resolved: **I am compelled to choose, but what compels me** — "situation and temper, ... complexion and disposition, ... a system of different perceptions... link'd together by the relation of cause and effect" — *is* me. I act in accordance with *my* goals, even if I don't have an insight into the fullness of my own "complexion and disposition." Thus, within the constraints imposed by the universe, I can claim the only kind of freedom that is compatible with physics while avoiding the "common-sense" silliness mocked by Voltaire — the freedom to be myself, which is all one could ever hope for (Dennett, 1984, 2003):

```
You can't always get what you want, mmm!
But if you try sometimes you just might find
You just might find, that ya
Get what you need
Oooh, yeah!
```

> — The Rolling Stones (1969)

You wish to mount the horse; why? The reason, an ignoramus will say, is because I wish it. This answer is idiotic, nothing happens or can happen without a reason, a cause; there is one therefore for your wish. What is it? The agreeable idea of going on horseback which presents itself in your brain, the dominant idea, the determinant idea. But, you will say, can I not resist an idea which dominates me? No, for what would be the cause of your resistance? None. By your will you can obey only an idea which will dominate you more.

> — Voltaire (1752)

Individual future is subjectively open

While my freedom to choose a course of action is necessarily limited by the physics of the universe of which my brain is part, the rest of the universe's freedom to affect my choices is likewise limited — by the computational complexity of my mind. Locking me up to prevent me from jumping the Niagara Falls would most probably work, but any external attempt to detect ahead of time my intention to do so, or to persuade me not to rather than resorting to brute force, may run into intractable problems.

These problems could not have been anticipated by Hume, who asserted that a "spectator can commonly infer our actions from our motives and character," because at the time of his writing the sciences of complexity and of computation did not exist. A perfectly DETERMINISTIC dynamical system can be unpredictable when it operates in a chaotic regime far from equilibrium, where a small difference in the initial conditions or in an external input can give rise to exponentially diverging trajectories through the state space.

Unpredictability also arises in DETERMINISTIC discrete computation: the only way to find out what a given Turing Machine (or, equivalently, a program written in a general-purpose computer language) would do with a given input is to simulate its execution — a task that may turn out to be more than daunting, because it is provably impossible to predict whether or not such a computation would ever terminate.[10]

For the cognitive processes that constitute a human mind, the simulation task is forbiddingly complex (as I noted on p. 206, simulating a computation is the same as "actually" carrying it out). Consequently, second-guessing a person — whether it is an external entity that sets out to predict my behavior, or myself trying to anticipate the unfolding of my own thoughts over time — is circumscribed by a computational "epistemic horizon" (Dennett, 2003, p.91): prediction may be possible in trivial matters or over a short term, but is intractable in the large.

My future mind states are therefore not just unknown but unknowable even to myself except through the regular process of cognition.[11] This kind of uncertainty about personal future affords me a subjective freedom (Dennett, 2003). The intractability of anticipating the behavior of complex systems implies also that to a cognitive agent the rest of the universe — including the mind-space trajectories of other agents — is, in the long run, equally unknowable. The universe as a whole may be deterministic, but to its denizens the far future is always uncertain, as Gandalf points out in the following passage

---

The ability to predict and influence choices provides compelling evidence that choices are DETERMINISTIC. Certainly, to the extent that neurons will not discharge unless they are depolarized by other neurons, brain states can be determined naturally only by earlier brain states. However, does such apparently Laplacian determinism grant as much prediction and influence as the evidence seems to indicate? Perhaps not. [...] The states of the brain, like the clouds in the sky, happen because of earlier states of the system. But brain states and behaviour can be as unpredictable as the weather.

— Schall (2001)

from Tolkien's *The Fellowship of the Ring*, in response to Frodo's dismay over the sparing of Gollum's life by the Elves:

> 'I can't understand you. Do you mean to say that you, and the Elves, have let him live on after all those horrible deeds? Now at any rate he is as bad as an Orc, and just an enemy. He deserves death.'

> 'Deserves it! I daresay he does. Many that live deserve death. And some that die deserve life. Can you give it to them? Then do not be too eager to deal out death in judgment. For even the very wise cannot see all ends.'

— Tolkien (1954, book I, ch.2)

The unexpected is what makes life possible.

— Therem Harth rem ir Estraven
The Left Hand of Darkness
by Ursula K. Le Guin

10.1.3   The mind's best trick

Given that brains are governed by physical determinism — which, within the limits of computational uncertainty about the future, is the mind's only hope of attaining a measure of foresight (Dennett, 2003) — our unquestionable feeling of being free to control our immediate actions (if not our fate) calls for an explanation. It is very important to note that what needs to be explained now is no longer the peculiar mixture of determinism and randomness in the universe (both discussed briefly above), but rather how and why one can *feel* to be a free agent in such a world.

The first step towards an explanation is to realize, following the insights of Locke, Hume, Voltaire, Wittgenstein, Dennett, and others, that free will is not a process whereby decisions are made — it is a *feeling* that accompanies certain decisions (Wegner, 2004). As such, it can be accounted for in terms of representational concepts that are familiar to us from Chapter 9. For a full account, we must distinguish between EMPIRICAL WILL, which is the distillate of temporally structured statistical relationships between one's thoughts and actions, and PHENOMENAL WILL, which is an illusion generated by the mind to account for one's behavior (Wegner, 2004).

Empirically, people's self-reported or inferred mind states covary with their overt behavior in a manner that justifies positing a causal link from their "will" — what Hume called "motives and character" — to their actions.[12] Phenomenally, the feeling of having willed an action covaries with conscious intention to execute it. In both cases, timing and statistical reliability are crucial. I may claim that the weather is a product of my personal will, but this claim would be rejected by others as soon as the correlation between my forecast and the actual state of the elements breaks down. Likewise, if my self-perceived intentions do not precede my actions reliably by just the right amount of time lead, I would feel that the actions have not been willed by me.

As you may have already guessed, the feeling of free will is thus predicated on the ABSENCE OF SURPRISE when the efference copy of a thought or an action originating in one part of the brain matches the feedback from another (recall section 9.3, where the nature and origin of the closely related feeling of agency was explained). Indeed, actions induced by stimulation of the motor cortex are felt as "unwilled," indicating that conscious will is an add-on to, not the cause of, behavior (Wegner, 2003).[13] The functional relationships among the representations that underlie the feeling of free will, which are illustrated in Figure 10.1, closely follow the flow of information in the corollary discharge circuits outlined in Figure 9.11 on page 413, with which it should be compared.

Recognizing that "conscious will is the feeling of authorship [...] that authenticates the action's owner as the self" (Wegner, 2004) will help us understand why a cognitive system needs to have such feelings in the first place. I shall mention here one likely reason for cultivating the feeling of free will: learning. A key computational problem in learning from experience is STRUCTURAL CREDIT ASSIGNMENT: how to figure out which component(s) of a complex web of cause and effect surrounding any non-trivial ac-

Let us not forget this: when 'I raise my arm', my arm goes up. And the problem arises: what is left over if I subtract the fact that my arm goes up from the fact that I raise my arm?

((Are the kinaesthetic sensations my willing?))

...

So one might say: voluntary movement is marked by the ABSENCE OF SURPRISE.

— Wittgenstein (1958, 621,628)

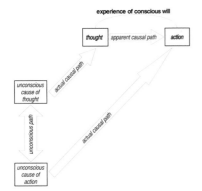

Figure 10.1 — A diagram illustrating the flow of information that gives rise to the ILLUSION OF CONSCIOUS WILL (Wegner, 2003, fig.1). Both the consciously experienced thought and the action that follows it are caused by processes that normally remain unconscious along with their mutual influences. The apparent causal path from thought to action is a fiction that, for various reasons explained in this section, is functionally useful and therefore is incorporated by the mind into the virtual reality in which it cocoons itself (cf. section 9.3).

tion should be credited or blamed for its outcome, so that a precisely targeted improvement can be made and a better outcome achieved the next time over (Minsky, 1961). Owning up for an outcome (or, equally, attributing it to another "free" agent), instead of assuming it to be merely random, helps credit assignment. In terms of the Bayes networks that the mind uses to represent cause and effect (cf. Figure 6.15 on page 192), credit assignment involves distinguishing between internal and external variables and identifying the causal pathways among them, including possible ways of "explaining away" the observable dependencies in terms of hidden causes (Glymour, 2004).

As we know from earlier chapters, the distributed network of representations that models the causal structure of the world extends beyond the boundaries of the self construed traditionally as confined to a single individual (Decety and Sommerville, 2003; Wegner, 2004). We thus discover a pleasing consilience between the account of free will that I have sketched in this section and the notion of the Self as a virtual construct advanced by Metzinger (2003) and Merker (2007).

In Wegner's own words, "In the approach of the *Illusion of Conscious Will*, the whole idea of a 'person' is an elegant accounting system for making sense of actions and ascribing them to constructed entities that are useful for purposes of social justice and the facilitation of social interaction. A person is constructed in the mind of the person, and, through a variety of communications and evidences, in the minds of others as well (cf. Dennett, 1987)" (Wegner, 2004).

Just as with Metzinger's work (see the quote on p. 455), there is a parallel that is impossible to miss here between the view of the "free agent" — a person, or a Self — as it emerges from the modern synthesis in the cognitive sciences, and the age-old Buddhist tradition of holding the Self to be an illusion. In discussing the development of this tradition by one of the most prominent Buddhist philosophers, Nāgārjuna (ca. 150-250 AD), Gier and Kjellberg (2004) write:

> Thus while we would assume that there has to be a self in order for there to be freedom, Nagarjuna would say that there is freedom only to the extent that there is not a self.[15]

What we have learned so far about how the mind works allows us to interpret Nāgārjuna's maxim as neither a riddle nor a contradiction in terms, but rather as a deep insight into the nature of selfhood and causation.

A useful metaphor for the distributed nature of the Self is the mythical SIMURGH — the king of the birds from the Sufi poet Farid ud-Din al-Attar's fable *The Conference of the Birds* (1177).[14]

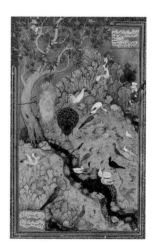

10.2   Ethics

Insofar as it binds together related, statistically reliable patterns of cause and effect, the Self construct — a web of causal dependencies that connect distributed representations maintained by minds to one another and to events in the world at large — is "useful for purposes of social justice" (Wegner, 2004). What could a cognitive computational ethics based on this observation be like? Being grounded in a personification of the web of cause and effect, it would naturally rest on PERSONAL accountability. Personally, I would not have it any other way. Consider the following set of options with respect to a choice faced by all of us (except perhaps the hermits who go off to live in the wilderness) — how to behave towards the "other":

1. "I don't like your ethnicity (politics, religion, lifestyle, etc.), so drop dead."

2. "I despise your lifestyle (religion, politics, ethnicity), but a supreme being commands me to love even you, so there you go."

3. "The supreme being I was taught to worship doesn't approve of your religion (politics, ethnicity, lifestyle), so drop dead."

Option #2, under which tolerance is part of a codex of divinely commanded ethics, is commonly claimed to be the only viable alternative to the reprehensible unbridled intolerance of #1.[16] But is it really a better choice than #1, or for that matter #3, into which it often devolves?

Those who can make you believe absurdities can make you commit atrocities.

— Voltaire

Morality is a matter for reason.

— Ross (1999)
Zen and the Art of Divebombing

In practice, revelation, even when accompanied by a fear of divine retribution, has a dismal track record as a guide for ethical conduct. A survey of publicly available statistics from eighteen "First World" democracies (Paul, 2005) reveals that "higher rates of belief in and worship of a creator correlate with higher rates of homicide, juvenile and early adult mortality, STD infection rates, teen pregnancy, and abortion in the prosperous democracies. The most theistic prosperous democracy, the U.S., is exceptional ... The United States is almost always the most dysfunctional of the developing democracies, sometimes spectacularly so, and almost always scores poorly." No less importantly, the very idea of *having to be told* to be ethical, whether or not under threat of retribution, is degrading, dishonorable, and dehumanizing. All three options listed above are therefore equally opprobrious.

By forgoing both the "jungle" model of society without ethics and the "kindergarten" model of society with divinely mandated good behavior that is demeaning in principle and unworkable in practice, we turn to the possibility of humanistic, cognitively justifiable ethics, the search for which has a long history in philosophy, both East and West. In the West, a notable tradition that attempts to derive ethics from reason alone employs the "categorical imperative" criterion proposed by Immanuel Kant: to be guided only by such moral principles as would be universally applicable. In comparison to Kant's DEONTOLOGY, or duty-based ethics, the UTILITARIANISM of Jeremy Bentham and John Stuart Mill is consequentialist: it calls for maximizing the well-being of all who may be affected by one's actions.

The deontological and the utilitarian approaches to ethics are both handicapped by their preference of abstract and universal over human and personal considerations in developing the principles of moral conduct. By giving in to superhuman ambitions, ethics derived from the categorical imperative ends up as inhumane (for example by holding that it is always wrong to lie, even to save someone's life); the utilitarian decree that sanctions torturing a person to save the life of ten others (thus maximizing total well-being) is equally inhumane (Gier, 2002, p.181). Deontology and utilitarianism are also computationally problematic: the former typically runs into logical contradictions when followed through, while the latter leads to intractable estimation problems in calculating the potential consequences of an action in terms of the total utility (which in itself is difficult to formalize).[17]

10.2.1 Computational virtue

Contemporary studies of the neurocomputational foundations of moral cognition suggest that it is neither deontological nor utilitarian, but ARETAIC, that is, guided by personal virtue (Gr. ἀρετή): "the moral psychology required by virtue theory is the most neurobiologically plausible" (Casebeer, 2003). The modern aretaic approach to ethics is equally compatible with elements of classical Western moral thinking that figure prominently in the work of Aristotle and with the classical Eastern traditions of Theravada Buddhism (considered to be the closest to the teachings of Gautama; see Scharfstein, 1998, p.93) and of Confucius. Most interestingly, it can be derived from the principles of cognitive computation that are familiar to us from the earlier chapters of this book.

A departure point for the derivation that I have in mind appears in War-

BRIAN:
No. No, please! Please! Please listen. I've got one or two things to say.
FOLLOWERS:
Tell us. Tell us both of them.
BRIAN:
Look. You've got it all wrong. You don't need to follow me. You don't need to follow anybody! You've got to think for yourselves. You're all individuals!
FOLLOWERS:
Yes, we're all individuals!
BRIAN:
You're all different!
FOLLOWERS:
Yes, we are all different!
DENNIS:
I'm not.
ARTHUR:
Shhhh.
FOLLOWERS:
Shh. Shhhh. Shhh.
BRIAN:
You've all got to work it out for yourselves!
FOLLOWERS:
Yes! We've got to work it out for ourselves!
BRIAN:
Exactly!
FOLLOWERS:
Tell us more!
BRIAN:
No! That's the point! Don't let anyone tell you what to do!

— From *Monty Python's Life of Brian*

ren McCulloch's paper tantalizingly titled "Toward Some Circuitry of Ethical Robots or an Observational Science of the Genesis of Social Evolution in the Mind-Like Behavior of Artifacts" (1956). McCulloch defines ethics operationally, in the narrow context of a game such as chess: a player (referred to generically as a "machine") is ethical to the extent that it follows the rules. In this setting, he proceeds to distinguish between three rungs of moral merit that a machine can occupy.

The lowest rung is occupied by a class of machines that are hard-wired (in the case of robots, literally) by their creators to obey the rules, as a chess program that I may write would. These behave virtuously, but deserve no credit for it: they simply have no choice.

At the middle rung, there are machines to which the rules are fully and truthfully revealed; it is up to each machine to obey or disobey them. At this level, the game of poker is probably a better example of a rule-governed environment than chess, simply because disobeying the rules in a chess match is out of the question, whereas cheating at poker is not unheard of. By McCulloch's definition, a poker player who peeks at the others' cards is automatically considered immoral, in full accordance with his operationalization of ethics.

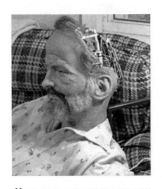

HOW CAN A MACHINE BE ETHICAL? By interacting with others, discovering what the rules of the game are, and modifying itself to play by the rules (McCulloch, 1956). The photograph shows an interactive simulacrum of Philip K. Dick by Hanson Robotics.[18]

Although McCulloch refers to machines that play by revealed (rather than hard-wired) rules as "moral," a more appropriate term would be "obedient." The difference is significant: because the rules originate outside the machine, it avoids bearing the ultimate responsibility for their veracity. In the real world (as opposed to a game of poker), an agent that is moral by the above criterion can be made to commit atrocities simply by accepting absurdities fed to it by another; if subsequently brought before a tribunal, it can defend itself by claiming that it was merely following orders, or obeying commandments.

The third and highest rung of moral merit, which McCulloch reserves for "ethical machines," is where one finds agents that graduate from what I called above the moral kindergarten and become responsible for their actions. Computationally, responsibility stems from the ability to learn, which, as McCulloch notes, is shared by brains and computers alike ("it is a beauty of the Turing Machine to be open to contingent facts from an external agent"). The "ethical machine" is therefore one that learns to play by the rules: "I look upon ethical conduct as something to be interpreted in terms of the circuit action of this Man in his environment a Turing Machine with only two feedbacks determined, a desire to play and a desire to win" (McCulloch, 1956).

10.2.2 Learning to be good

Evolutionary pressures first identified by Trivers (1971) ensure that a society composed of individuals who are ethical merely in the self-centered sense implied by "a desire to win" can nevertheless foster occasionally altruistic behavior. Evolutionarily stable traits that sanction altruism towards non-kin can only emerge if the interacting individuals can keep track of each other's behavior and in particular can detect and punish cheaters (cf. section 6.6). The small troop size and the large brain size of early hominids made them well suited for setting off a spurt of evolutionary development leading up to the present-day human mores that within each person blend selfishness and altruism, truthfulness and deceit, in proportions dynamically determined by the arms race between the myriad clashing cognitive strategies all of which answer to one god — the individual genome's INCLUSIVE FITNESS (Dawkins, 1976; Hamilton, 1964; Pinker, 2002; Trivers, 1971).[19]

McCulloch's incipient view of ethics as a self-organizing computational process of pattern discovery fits perfectly into the evolutionary analysis of socially constrained moral behavior. The outcome is a broad and consistent theoretical understanding of ethics that applies to real people (rather than to Kantian saints or Millsian utopians).[20] Most importantly, it explains why complex societies composed of many interacting cognitively sophisticated agents never resemble Eden before the fall.

One reason for that is the computational complexity of rule inference: the dynamics of complex systems are very difficult to distill into a set of ABSOLUTELY CERTAIN rules. Another reason is evolutionary: it is always advantageous for players to try to bend the rules to their benefit. According to Trivers (1971, p.48), the "complex, regulating system ... that results should simultaneously allow the individual to reap the benefits of altruistic exchanges, to protect himself from gross and subtle forms of cheating, and to practice those forms of cheating that local conditions make adaptive." Likewise, McCulloch (1956) points out that if a player's counterpart cheats according to some statistically discernible pattern, the player will learn to do so.[21]

Not entirely surprisingly, these insights into human nature have long been available in the form of folk sayings that illuminate the innumerable ways in which people manage to combine good and evil in their dealings with others. In particular, proverbs that venture to offer advice on how to behave in company seem to take for granted what the modern cognitive science is now

It is as if they [Kantians and Millsians] wanted to see ethics as a noble statue standing at the top of a single pillar. My image is rather different. My image would be of a table with many legs. We all know that a table with many legs wobbles when the floor on which it stands is not even, but such a table is very hard to turn over, and that is how I see ethics: as a table with many legs, which wobbles a lot, but is very hard to turn over.

— Putnam (2004, p.28)

He can never know the rules of the game more than tentatively; for the stochastic horses of Opinion drag no chariot to ABSOLUTE CERTAINTY.

— McCulloch (1956)

discovering: that ethics is dynamic, socially situated, and context-dependent (Casebeer, 2003; Nichols and Mallon, 2006).

Remarking that in philosophy the search for the ever elusive unified normative theory of ethics had been "unapologetically *a priori*," Nichols and Mallon (2006) note that many empirical findings are now available that characterize human moral judgment.[23] Particularly revealing are experiments in which subjects are asked to make a choice in a moral dilemma — a situation that typically pitches a deontological rule against an utilitarian consideration. The pattern of judgments that people make in such situations is surprising not because it reveals a conflict between rules and a cost-benefit analysis, but because the decision depends on how the problem is phrased. On the basis of these findings, Nichols and Mallon (2006) propose that "judgments of whether an action is wrong, all things considered, implicate a complex set of psychological processes, including representations of rules, emotional responses, and assessments of costs and benefits."

The computational field where all these processes play out has been envisaged by Churchland (1998) as a multidimensional representation space (Figure 10.2), of the same kind that supports other cognitive abilities. The inclusion of ethics under the umbrella of cognition is very appropriate: moral knowledge is a set of skills, albeit more complex than some. Within each individual, it encompasses elements of perception, memory, language, and

С волками жить — по волчьи выть.

Si fueris Romae, Romano vivito more; si fueris alibi, vivito sicut ibi.

入鄉問俗

Three proverbs — all variations on the same theme: If you live with wolves, howl (Russian); when in Rome, live as the Romans do; when away, live as they do there (Latin)[22]; when entering a village, follow the customs (Chinese).

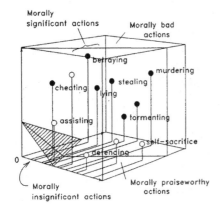

Figure 10.2 — A simple illustration of the MORAL SPACE, which echoes the perceptual spaces of Chapter 5 (after Churchland, 1998, fig.3). The dimensions of such a space may correspond to the actions' significance, value, and perhaps other attributes. Representation spaces that support human moral reasoning are likely more complex than this one; they must also be dynamically reconfigurable (just as perceptual spaces are; cf. Figure 5.9 on page 107).

decision-making, and as such is learnable (as suggested by McCulloch, 1956).

Moral knowledge is, however, distinguished by the involvement of particularly complex computational processes that mediate social cognition: the self-model and models of other members of the society in which the self is situated. Because of that complexity, learning to behave ethically takes a long time: Churchland (1998) emphasizes "the universal importance of gradual socialization by long interaction with a moral order already in place. ... There are too many trillions of synaptic connections to be appropriately weighted and only long experience can hope to do that superlatively intricate job."

Had the computational problem of ethical acculturation been just a blind search in a trillion-dimensional representation space, it of course would have been hopelessly intractable. In practice, learning ethics is best understood as an instance of the structured credit assignment problem (cf. p. 470), in which causal models of the agents involved — the self and the others — operate on dynamically reconfigurable low-dimensional representation spaces by planning actions while projecting and comparing their likely consequences.

It is at this point that the society can in principle exert a positive influence over the behavior of its members — and not necessarily by punishing them for past wrong choices. In their superb analysis of the meaning of justice in a deterministic universe, Greene and Cohen (2004) write, "We can [...] recognize that free will, as conceptualized by the folk psychology system, is an illusion and structure our society accordingly by rejecting retributivist legal principles that derive their intuitive force from this illusion." The approach to justice they endorse aims at "promoting future welfare rather than meting out just des[s]erts." Any corrective intervention should therefore seek to depress the subjective value that individuals place on antisocial behavior.

In computational terms, the same goal can be pursued by instilling in the individual a better appreciation of how others would see and feel the consequences of his or her actions. As noted by Gier (2007), "without the cultivation of personal and civic virtue, liberal societies that operate with minimal legal frameworks face the prospect of continued moral decline, the same type of crisis that inspired Ezekiel and leads today's religious conservatives to call for his radically theonomous solution." The effectiveness of this classically humanist approach, which relies on what may be called COMPUTATIONAL COMPASSION, depends on the individuals' capacity for improving their conceptual simulation of others through learning.

asti karmāsti vipākah kārakas tu
nopalabhyate ya imāmś ca skandhān
nikṣipaty anyāṃś ca skandhān
pratisaṃdadhāty anyatra dharmasaṃketāt

There is free action, there is retribution, but there is no agent that passes out from one set of momentary elements into another one, except the lawful connection of those elements.[24]

— *paramārtha śūnyatā sūtra*
The Ultimate Emptiness Sutra

10.2.3 Computational neuroscience of compassion

Computationally, the most straightforward way for an agent to estimate the possible effects on others of an act it is planning is to put itself in the others' place (as people indeed tend to do, in various kinds of social encounters; Dunning and Cohen, 1992; Krueger and Clement, 1994). This fact may account

"THERE, BUT FOR THE GRACE OF GOD, GO I." Experimental studies in social psychology show that when called upon to assume another person's point of view, subjects tend to project their own personal qualities instead of properly taking into account their knowledge of others (Dunning and Cohen, 1992). Krueger and Clement (1994) call this tendency "an ineradicable and egocentric bias in social perception"; Decety and Jackson (2004) concur: "self-perspective may be considered as the default mode of the human mind."

for the ubiquity in the world's philosophies and religions of variants of the Golden Rule, which in its Old Testament version commands that "thou shalt love thy neighbor as thyself" (Leviticus 19:18). In the New Testament, the focus shifts from love to (unspecified) action, and the commandment becomes: "Do unto others as you would have them do unto you" (Matthew 7:12).

The assumption that all others are just like me and would therefore welcome what I myself like is, however, overly simplistic: as Monty Pythons' Brian points out (p. 473), we are all individuals, which suggests that the "do unto others" variant of the Golden Rule is not entirely a good idea. A more reasonable as well as more practical variant, espoused among other sources by the Mahabharata and by the teachings of Confucius and of Hillel the Elder, focuses on the avoidance of harm rather than on the imposition on others of one's personal desiderata: **"What is hateful to you, do not do to your neighbor"** (Talmud, Shabbat 31a).[25]

The computational network that supports human social cognition extends across many brain areas: Greene and Haidt (2002, table 1) list eight, remarking that "there is no specifically moral part of the brain. Every brain region discussed in this article has also been implicated in non-moral processes." As may be expected, the areas identified (through studies of patients and by means of functional imaging) as involved in moral judgment are those that contribute heavily to Theory of Mind abilities and intentionality attribution, to the comprehension of stories with human characters, to the recall of emotional autobiographical episodes, and even to the perception of biological motion.

Much of the influence that these cognitive processes have over a person's behavior stems from their potential for generating AFFECT (Greene and Haidt, 2002). Emotions, as I mentioned in Chapter 6, mediate key high-level computations, such as adjusting the organism's goals and the strategies for pursuing them (cf. p. 172). Thus, moral choices that impinge on the emotionally loaded issue of personal well-being — whether of oneself, or of one's "neighbors," to the extent that these are cognitively represented as one's peers — are processed differently from impersonal ones (Figure 10.3).

The personal vs. impersonal distinction in moral cognition parallels another one: between the immediately and automatically available intuitions that arise when one is faced with a moral issue and the often quite different conclusions that may be reached after deliberating upon it (Greene and Haidt, 2002). In this connection, it is worth noting that damage to the distributed network of moral computation mentioned above often results in impaired social behavior in the face of preserved ability for abstract thinking (as measured by IQ tests), including abstract social knowledge. The likely explanation for this dissociation between intuitive practical ethics and abstract moral reasoning is evolutionary: the former system reflects "social-emotional dispositions built on those we inherited from our primate ancestors" (Greene and Haidt, 2002, p.519), whereas the latter one is implemented in the mind's virtual machine, whereby, *contra* Ecclesiastes, a man hath preeminence above a beast.

The cognitive advantages that we possess over other animals, which are less capable than we are of flexible computation, do not entitle us to claim any special insight into moral absolutes, whatever those may be. This is just as well, because moral realism — the popularly held belief in the existence of such absolutes — is not a precondition for progress towards a better society. In fact, insofar as it must rely on religious revelation rather than on scientific

Figure 10.3 — *Top:* in one version of an experiment designed to study HUMAN MORAL REASONING, a subject must decide whether to throw a switch that would divert a runaway trolley and prevent it from killing five people, at the expense of killing one person. *Bottom:* in another version, the five people can only be saved if the subject decides to push another person onto the tracks, thereby stopping the trolley. Subjects typically balk at saving five lives at the expense of one when the setting is personal (as it is on the bottom), but not when it is impersonal (Greene and Haidt, 2002).

understanding, moral realism is probably detrimental to progress in applied ethics.

Echoing McCulloch's notion of empirically learned virtue, Greene (2003) sees humanity's diminishing need to justify ethics by appealing to moral absolutes as a parallel to the process of growing up. This process is driven by the growth of our collective self-knowledge. The discoveries that pave the way for it include a long-established understanding of human evolutionary roots, and more recent advances in computational phenomenology (which also underlie the theory of the Self that I described in Chapter 9):

> We have here the beginnings of a debunking explanation of moral realism: we believe in moral realism because moral experience has a perceptual phenomenology, and moral experience has a perceptual phenomenology because natural selection has outfitted us with mechanisms for making intuitive, emotion-based moral judgements[.]

— Greene (2003)

10.3   Whosoever is wise?

Yo pañiccasamuppàdaü passati so dhammaü passati.

Whoever sees the web of cause and effect, sees the Way.[26]

— *mahàhatthipadopamasutta*
The Great Elephant Footprint Sutra

The humanistic virtue ethics that replaces moral realism has deep roots in several ancient philosophical traditions (Gier, 2002). Recalling the question posed in Chapter 2 (note 22 on page 36) — "whosoever is wise?" — I can now elaborate on the answer given there, which focused on FORESIGHT: those are wise who perceive the web of cause and effect by becoming mindful of their selves, including the motives for their actions and their effects on themselves and on others. In this section, I shall show that this traditional conception of wisdom fits well within the understanding of the computational mind that is afforded by the modern cognitive science. I shall then round off the present chapter by outlining ways in which wisdom can give rise to happiness and can help stave off "the long lapse of immemorial time."[27]

10.3.1   Practical wisdom

Theoretical thinking in the psychology of wisdom is converging with empirical investigations. They construe wisdom as a multidimensional functional trait that includes multiple cognitive, affective, and conative or motivational characteristics (Ardelt, 2004; Baltes and Kunzmann, 2003; Marchand, 2003). Along the cognitive dimensions, individuals who are reputed to be wise possess a distinctive problem-solving style combining sensitivity to the problem's complexity and potential lack of structure with reflection upon and awareness of their own limitations.

This cognitive style is especially effective in social contexts, which give rise to particularly complex and ill-structured problems. In wise individuals, it is complemented by an equally distinctive capacity for empathy: the processing of affective information, which pertains to the emotional and motivational states of other people involved in a given situation. Wise people are also characterized by a distinctive personality style: they typically have a strong sense of identity and autonomy, are predisposed toward interior life, are good at harnessing experience to achieve a better understanding of the external world, and are tolerant of ambiguity and contradiction (Ardelt, 2004; Marchand, 2003).

Wisdom as characterized above is a profoundly cognitive phenomenon. Its problem solving aspects are clearly related to general intelligence and creativity (its affective and conative facets too are interpretable in terms of computation, simply because emotion and motivation are the brain's means of facilitating particular kinds of information processing; cf. Minsky, 2006; Rolls, 2000). Moreover, like general intelligence, wisdom emerges as a common factor in a wide range of personality studies, allowing researchers to develop assessment tools that explicitly aim at quantifying its development in a given individual. The validity of such tools is attested to by the predictive power of wisdom considered as a latent variable: for example, Ardelt (2004) found that people who scored high on the cognitive dimensions of her personality questionnaire also tended to score high on its affective and reflective dimensions.

Unlike general intelligence, however, wisdom is more than an intellectual skill or a piece of abstract knowledge about the human condition: it is about "what a person is like rather than what a person knows" (Ardelt, 2004, p.274). As such, PRACTICAL WISDOM interacts just as one would expect with the individual's personal development over the course of a lifetime. Wisdom is widely considered both to develop with age (which is understandable, given the cognitive and affective sophistication it depends upon), and to be in itself a life goal worthy of pursuit (Marchand, 2003). Those who succeed in approaching this goal are richly rewarded: the wisdom factor is a better statistical predictor of life satisfaction in old age than objective variables such as

The Greek philosophers distinguished between PRACTICAL WISDOM (discussed in this section), which they called *phronesis* (φρόνησις), and *sophia* (σοφία), or the ability to wield knowledge.

physical health, socioeconomic status, financial situation, physical environment, and social involvement (Ardelt, 2004).[28]

10.3.2 Happiness

The empirically established link between wisdom and life satisfaction would not have surprised Aristotle, whose *Nicomachean Ethics* advanced the idea of practical wisdom (phronesis) as a means of attaining EUDAIMONIA — spiritual well-being, flourishing, or simply happiness. Classics aside, one still needs to explain, however, why it is that the objective indicators of a person's well-being are so weakly correlated with his or her happiness — whether or not the latter is brought about by practical wisdom. The resolution of this issue lies in the realization that happiness, like wisdom, is mediated by a bundle of cognitive, affective, and motivational processes, and is, therefore, a matter of the person's CONSTRUAL of his or her life situation rather than of its objective qualities (Lyubomirsky, 2001).

Because subjective happiness is mediated by the construal processes (including social comparison, post-decision rationalization, event analysis, and self-reflection), "happy and unhappy individuals appear to experience — indeed, to reside in — different subjective worlds" (Lyubomirsky, 2001, p.244). As with general intelligence, the construal processes are strongly influenced by genetic factors, and the cluster of cognitive traits affecting a person's predisposition to happiness is highly heritable. Still, only about 50% of the population variance in subjective well-being is accounted for by genetics; 10% of the rest is attributable to environmental factors. This leaves considerable room for improvement along those cognitive dimensions that *are* under the individual's control (Lyubomirsky, Sheldon, and Schkade, 2005, p.116) — a discovery that offers hope that people can learn to be happier, as suggested in particular by the Aristotelian and Theravadin traditions that I mentioned earlier.

Stopping the hedonic treadmill

A particularly straightforward way of exerting control over one's own well-being is to take action to counter the ubiquitous perceptual adaptation. In perception, a stimulus presented repeatedly, or for a long time, evokes progressively weaker responses (Chapter 5). In the context of happiness, adaptation manifests itself as the so-called "hedonic treadmill": the diminishing

Practical wisdom is a means for attaining *eudaimonia* (εὐδαιμονία), which is one of the two distinct psychological constructs that together cover the intuitive notion of HAPPINESS — "EUDAIMONIC well-being, understood as purpose, mastery, strong relationships, and self-acceptance, and HEDONIC well-being, operationalized as the subjective sense that life is satisfying" (Urry, Nitschke, Dolski, Jackson, Dalton, Mueller, Rosenkranz, Ryff, Singer, and Davidson, 2004).[29] Eudaimonia corresponds to the Buddhist notion of *sukha* (quiet happiness).

returns (in terms of the pleasure experienced) from any prolonged activity, no matter how desirable it initially appears, or how pleasurable it feels while it is under way.

A countermeasure for hedonic adaptation is, of course, variety. This point can be illustrated using an example that is very close to my heart: a scientist who regularly asks new questions and initiates new projects. Such a person, we are told, "often feels the joy of making fascinating new discoveries and thus may remain particularly happy (i.e., at the upper end of [his or] her potential range) over a long period of time" (Lyubomirsky et al., 2005, p.121). Note that practicing this technique becomes easier the more cognitively sophisticated you are as a person. Insofar as "you are an aperture through which the universe looks at itself" (Watts, 1994, p.133), it is bound to enjoy the view all the more if you, the eye of the cosmos, are complex and multidimensional.

Practicing virtue

Seeking experiential variety to counter hedonic adaptation can be especially effective if used in conjunction with another time-tested recipe for boosting happiness: counting one's blessings. In itself, practicing gratitude enhances well-being: a 6-week study conducted by Lyubomirsky et al. (2005) revealed that students who had been instructed to contemplate "the things for which they are grateful" once a week reported increased well-being relative to controls. The researchers note:

> If the person counting her blessings varies the domains of life in which she counts them (i.e., in relationships, in work, in her health, or in her most recently successful domain), then the strategy may remain "fresh" and meaningful and work indefinitely. Supporting this notion, past research suggests that people tend to seek variety in their behavior, perhaps because change — in both thoughts and actions — is innately pleasurable and stimulating.[30]

— Lyubomirsky et al. (2005, p.121)

Gratitude (which is what counting one's blessings is about) is not the only virtue that proves to be its own reward: practicing forgiveness and self-

If one can stop the hedonic treadmill, there is really no reason to go to the extreme of renouncing the desire for happiness altogether, the Buddha's advice notwithstanding. It is, in fact, the *pursuit* of happiness that one should be careful not to overindulge in: as Lyubomirsky et al. (2005, p.113) note, "in Zen terms, perhaps one should try to transcend the pursuit of happiness rather than trying to maximize it." Of course, to "*try* to transcend" something is in itself problematic.

reflection likewise enhances well-being. Perhaps the most rewarding activity in this respect is helping others: the benefactor's subjective well-being is boosted, and so are his chances to benefit from reciprocal kindness (in this connection, Lyubomirsky et al. (2005, p.125) cite Trivers (1971), whose work on the evolution of altruism I mentioned earlier).

Taking care of small things

Given that humans are naturally predisposed to seek and enjoy change and novelty, the question arises how to put prospective, and not just retrospective, reflection to work in the service of promoting personal happiness. In doing so, one must overcome a variety of biases that beset AFFECTIVE FORECASTING — the process whereby future values of positive or negative affect associated with various possible courses of action in a given situation are estimated (Wilson and Gilbert, 2005). To mention just one example, people typically overestimate both the vexation they are likely to experience following an anticipated negative event and the amount of pleasure they may gain from a prospective positive event.

In reality, intense positive or negative affective states, but not mild ones, trigger mechanisms that attenuate them, causing mild affect to persist for longer (Gilbert, Lieberman, Morewedge, and Wilson, 2004). The practical implications of the awareness of this human trait for the planning of future behavior are clear: it is the small things that matter the most in the long run. A succession of small victories will keep you happy and small annoyances will keep bugging you, even as memories of major triumphs and defeats rapidly fade away.

Settling for good enough

Seeking to maximize happiness is counterproductive not only because extreme hedonic states (positive as well as negative) tend to be forgotten faster. Maximization is also computationally more demanding than "mere" satisficing (settling for good-enough outcomes, a cognitive strategy mentioned earlier in the context of perception and of decision making; cf. p. 352). Worse, even in situations where "maximizers" — people who are predisposed to seek the best — achieve better objective outcomes than satisficers (by investing more effort in the decision process), they end up being less happy with those outcomes (Schwartz, Ward, Monterosso, Lyubomirsky, White, and Lehman, 2002).[31]

Letting happiness pursue *you*

The paradoxical relative misery of the would-be maximizers of the returns on their investment in the world (compared to folks who settle for less than total perfection) adds a number of important qualifications to the idea that the people depicted in Figure 9.17 on page 432 declared to be a basic human right: the pursuit of happiness. Research in social psychology suggests that constantly asking ourselves "are we happy yet?" serves only to drive happiness away (Schooler, Ariely, and Loewenstein, 2003). The same authors note that "if timed appropriately intermittent attention to one's hedonic situation may be critical for maximizing happiness. The challenge is determining when it is best to man the controls, and when it is better to simply enjoy the ride." As it happens, we do know something about the appropriate timing for monitoring happiness: the study of Lyubomirsky et al. (2005) that I mentioned earlier found that counting the blessings three times a week as opposed to once a week did not result in increased well-being.

The classical virtue of moderation is thus seen to apply to the pursuit of happiness in a number of ways: (1) in setting the scope of the endeavor to apply to the feasible, rather than all conceivable, combinations of variables; (2) in seeking to attain adequate rather than extreme hedonic value; and (3) in monitoring the state of the pursuit rarely rather than frequently. If you succeed in convincing happiness that you don't really care, it just might start pursuing you.

Knowing yourself

A final round of advice that I shall venture to derive here from the state of the art in the cognitive psychology of happiness concerns the importance of choosing the immediate goals in seeking to increase one's well-being. Sheldon, Kasser, Smith, and Share (2002) describe an intervention study, in which participants had been taught four strategies for enhancing their experience: "own the goal," "make it fun," "keep a balance," and "remember the big picture." The intervention succeeded insofar as the attainment of goals (such as academic achievement, peer relationships, and physical appearance) correlated with increased well-being at the end of the semester-long period. In-

Inside my gate, a thousand sages do not know me. The beauty of my garden is invisible. Why should one search for the footprints of the patriarchs?

I go to the market place with my wine bottle and return home with my staff. I visit the wineshop and the market, and everyone I look upon becomes enlightened.

The commentary on the 10th bull, from *10 Bulls*, a 12th century Chinese parable of self-discovery, composed by Kakuan (Reps, 1989).

terestingly, however, this success manifested itself as a statistical *interaction* between variables: only participants whose goals fit their interests and values benefited from the intervention. This finding fits well with our earlier realization that prescribing universal, "one size fits all" solutions is a bad idea whether it arises in ethics or in self-help: remember, we are all individuals. It also underscores once more the importance in life of that classical *sine qua non*: SELF-KNOWLEDGE.

There are two complementary ways in which one can act on this insight: self-knowledge can be attained by a retrospective analysis of one's past, and by influencing one's future through self-change. The proportion of these two ingredients in the elixir of happiness varies with one's age. YOUTH contains in it more opportunities for action, but perhaps not enough resources for reflection. OLD AGE, in comparison, is a treasure that contains both ample material for self-analysis and better cognitive tools for self-change; no wonder, therefore, that it is reliably associated with increased subjective well-being (Lyubomirsky et al., 2005).[32]

Faust
Non! je veux un trésor
Qui les contient tous!... je veux la
JEUNESSE!

No! I want a treasure
That contains all others!... I want YOUTH!

Charles Gounod,
Faust, Act I, Scene II.

10.3.3   Time

As we get older we may feel happier on the average than our younger conspecifics because we also grow wiser (in the practical sense of section 10.3.1) and therefore more capable of dealing with the "slings and arrows of outrageous fortune" — and perhaps better at avoiding them altogether. There is, however, one element that affects the personal life of each and every one of us that is unavoidable — not *evitable* (to use a term coined by Dennett (2003, p.43) to help him explain how foresight and avoidance can evolve and flourish in a deterministic universe). That element is time.

A well-known and well-liked line of advice about how best to deal with this element suggests that "unborn Tomorrow and dead Yesterday" (in Omar Khayyam's words) should be ignored: "Why fret about them if Today be sweet!" This attitude towards time is, however, untenable in the long run for a member of any social species that inhabits a complex, dynamic ecological niche, which is largely its own collective creation. It does not matter how tempting it is to "live for today," or how good it feels to "turn off your mind, relax, and float downstream"; it does not even matter whether the flow of time is real or, as some physicists hold, imagined.[33] Even as I attempt to resist it, I *feel* the passage of time, the more so the older I get (Carstensen, 2006).

Indeed, in a sense that will soon become clear as we consider this observation in the light of our integrated understanding of how the mind works, I *am* time:

> Time is the substance I am made of. Time is a river which sweeps me along, but I am the river; it is a tiger which destroys me, but I am the tiger; it is a fire which consumes me, but I am the fire.[34]

> — Jorge Luis Borges
> *A New Refutation of Time*

Given that minds are what brains do, the cognitive states of the mind implemented by a brain are nothing else than activation patterns of the brain's neurons, each describable by a point in a multidimensional space, one dimension per neuron. A set of such mind states (even one that is complete in some sense — say, corresponding to the entire waking life of a person) is not, however, any more mind-like than a magician's hat full of pieces of paper, each inscribed with a list of numbers. Missing from the hat mind trick is TEMPORAL DYNAMICS: a representational substrate that (1) has as many slots as there are numbers in each list, and (2) has a mechanism whereby the lists of numbers — each corresponding to a brain activation pattern, or, equivalently, to a time slice of the mind frozen in a particular state — follow one another in the proper order.[35]

Because minds, being instances of computation, are multiply realizable, the representational substrate and the time-ordering mechanism in question can take many forms. One imaginable, if far-fetched, solution for the representation itself would be a panel of pigeons (one per number) trained to make the appropriate number of pecks in response to what they see on the piece of paper; this arrangement would still require a mechanism for the paper notes to be pulled out of the hat and presented to them in the proper order.[36]

A functionally equivalent but more convenient instantiation of the same mind (which the pieces of paper taken together express in potentiality, but not in actuality, as long as they remain in the hat) would be a brain. In this case, the proper succession of states would be ensured by the neural dynamics — the neurons pushing and pulling on each other, getting an occasional sensory kick from outside the skull, and delivering some kicks in return through the motor system.

In both these examples, the temporal order of the arising of the individual states is the key to the emergence of the mind, which is constituted by the

Счастливые часы не наблюдают.
The happy are oblivious to time.

> — Sophia, in Aleksandr Griboyedov's
> Горе от ума (*Woe from Wit*)

To be conscious is not to be in time.

> — T. S. Eliot
> *Burnt Norton*

If you got it today you don't want it tomorrow, man, 'cause you don't need it, 'cause as a matter of fact, as we discovered in the train, tomorrow never happens, man. It's all the same fucking day, man.

> — Willie Mae "Big Mama" Thornton
> *Ball and Chain*
> as sung by Janis Lyn Joplin

resulting TRAJECTORY through the representation space (Figure 10.4; Metzinger, 2003; Spivey, 2006). The succession of states of my brain *is* what I am, and it is also what defines for me the sense of the passage of time — as intuited by Borges in the passage quoted on the preceding page.

Let us now think of a brain state — an instantaneous snapshot of the mind frozen in time — as a reference point in the space of all possible brain states, and consider what happens if we "unfreeze" it. As the flow of time resumes, the instantaneous state will get farther and farther away in the representation space from the reference state (Lloyd, 2002). The reference state of mind will thus recede into the past and will be obliterated and lost completely — unless the brain that implements it possesses a non-volatile memory: a representational mechanism whose content is at least partially insulated from the changes brought about by the dynamics of the system at large.

Memory, which makes it possible for a mind to save past experiences for future reference, is the core component of a SUBJECTIVE TIME MACHINE (granted, it is only useful for visiting one's own subjective and personal past,

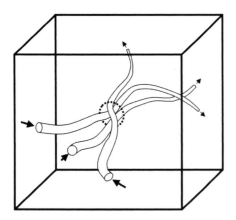

Figure 10.4 — The MIND SPACE, after Spivey and Dale (2006, fig.2). In the space of all possible brain states (whose dimensionality runs in the billions), a mind is not a point, but a trajectory. In this illustration, three distinct trajectories briefly visit the same locale — perhaps in the course of thinking about the same concept in three distinct contexts. For a parallel to Metzinger's (2003) idea of phenomenal space, and a link to the concept of phenomenal Self, see p. 421.

which, moreover, will always remain a virtual construct — a reconstruction of experience, not the real thing; but then we know that experience itself is a construct). With basic memory serving as a time machine, reminiscing would be like being snatched out of your bed in the middle of the night and parachuted into a fog bank: you experience something all right, but have no idea where you are or what time it is.

It takes only two simple extra accessories to turn the basic time machine into a luxury model: a timestamp function, which marks every remembered experience with its time of origin, and a positioning function, which locates it in space.

The result is a cognitive faculty familiar to us from Chapter 6: EPISODIC MEMORY (Figure 6.10 on page 176). Together with a flexible workspace where experiences can be reconstituted, an episodic memory system can support CHRONESTHESIA: "a form of consciousness that allows individuals to think about the subjective time in which they live and that makes it possible for them to 'mentally travel' in such time" (Clayton et al., 2003, p.685).

Serving as an information feed for a time machine, episodic memory is equally useful for travel into the subjective future as into the past. Future planning amounts to knowing what event to anticipate, at what time, and in what location. All you need to do to approximate having the experience of such an event is to simulate it, in the proper temporal and spatial context, as you expect it to unfold. The virtual nature of the resulting experience will not bother the veteran readers of this book, since Chapter 9 has reconciled them with the thought of inhabiting virtual worlds during their entire waking lives — and, come to think of it, also when they are asleep and dreaming.

As predicted by this understanding of the dual function of episodic memory, it turns out that patients with lesions in the hippocampus — the part of the mammalian brain most closely involved in episodic memory computations (Eichenbaum et al., 1999) — are impaired in their ability to imagine the future. In their review of what they term the "*constructive episodic simulation hypothesis*," Schacter and Addis (2007) conclude that ". . . cognitive, neuropsychological, and neuroimaging evidence [shows] that there is considerable overlap in the psychological and neural processes involved in remembering the past and imagining the future."

With the emergence of better tools for imaging brain activity, researchers began to realize that remembering the past and imagining the future may be the mind's most significant pastime. It certainly is insofar as energy expenditure is concerned: the burden imposed by momentary demands of the external

The functional equivalent of the human episodic memory may be present in some animals, such as the food-caching scrub jays — cousins of the pinyon jays from Chapter 2 (Clayton, Bussey, and Dickinson, 2003). Scrub jays need to remember for each of the several hundreds of food items they may have stashed away at any given time, where it is located, and, in case of perishable foods (worms), when it was stored. Experiments suggest that jays may also be capable of projecting past episodic information into the future: they re-cache food if it has been initially cached in the presence of conspecifics who are liable to steal it (Clayton et al., 2003), and selectively stock particular compartments of the aviary to which they are periodically confined with choice items that, as they know from prior experience, will not be present there next morning (Raby, Alexis, Dickinson, and Clayton, 2007).

environment amounts to no more than 1.0% of the brain's energy balance, suggesting that "intrinsic activity may be far more significant than evoked activity in terms of overall brain function" (Raichle, 2006).

The intrinsic activity of the brain came to be understood physiologically in terms of a " default network" of regions which can be studied by means of functional imaging, and which has been observed in humans and, with certain structural differences, in chimpanzees (Rilling, Barks, Parr, Preuss, Faber, Pagnoni, Bremner, and Votaw, 2007). Psychologically, it is experienced as stimulus-independent thought, or SIT (Mason, Norton, Van Horn, Wegner, Grafton, and Macrae, 2007). Allowing the mind to wander by reducing the processing demands brings about both a reported increase in the incidence of SIT and coherent activity in the default network. What could be the cognitive-computational reasons behind this activity? Mason et al. (2007) mention the possibility that the default network supports the operation of the mind's virtual time machine, and that "SIT — as a kind of spontaneous mental TIME TRAVEL — lends a sense of coherence to one's past, present, and future experiences."

Other researchers concur. In particular, Raichle (2006) offers a somewhat more explicit computational interpretation of the imaging data, remarking that "the brain operates as a Bayesian inference engine, designed to generate predictions about the future." Finally, Buckner and Carroll (2007) sum up their review of behavioral, lesion, and imaging data on "self-projection" into the future using the same central computational concept in terms of which we understood memory, thinking, and consciousness: simulation. They conclude that "we remember the past to envision the future."

Always coming home

To fathom the human sense of time we must, therefore, realize that the mind is its own virtual time machine, busy traveling through the remembered past and the envisioned future, but always coming home to the present, briefly, on the occasions when the confluence of the external stimuli and the internal goals demands undivided attention.

As a return on this conceptual investment, we stand to gain a certain insight into the relationship between the sense of time and happiness.[38] Just as humanity's collective literary canon tells us, the ACUTELY HAPPY would indeed be oblivious to the passage of time for a time being — more precisely, for as long as they dwell in the intensely satisfying present. Invariably, they

When we appear to be doing nothing, we are clearly doing something. But what? The answer, it seems, is TIME TRAVEL.[37]
— D. T. Gilbert & R. Buckner
Time travel in the brain
Time (Friday, Jan. 19, 2007)

wish this could go on forever, but of course it never does: even if the happy circumstances can be made to last, hedonic adaptation sets in, and elation sinks to grief.

Not so for the CHRONICALLY HAPPY, who may appreciate occasional euphoria, but also manage to harness subjective time itself and put it to work in the service of sustained eudaimonia. By incorporating positive experiences into their selves, they engineer a past that is worth revisiting.[39] By becoming wise through getting to know themselves, they gain foresight that helps them face the future.

The duck cocked his head and opened his bill as if to speak, then suddenly stopped. "What?" said Albert. "I wish this could go on forever," said the duck.

— Jonathan Lethem
From *Forever, said the duck*, in
The wall of the sky, the wall of the eye
New York: Tor Books, 1997 (pp. 171-188)

Notes

[1] In Buddhist philosophy, the technical term for the concept that I chose to render as "the web of cause and effect" is INTERDEPENDENT CO-ORIGINATION — the principle according to which nothing in the universe is uncaused or is without origin. In general, great caution should be exercised in drawing parallels between Western and Eastern philosophical concepts (Kalansuriya, 1993). A measured and accessible introduction to the notion of interdependent co-origination in the context of a discussion of Buddhism and free will is given by Gier and Kjellberg (2004).

[2] In classical mechanics, the ability to predict the future state of a system from a complete knowledge of its present state is the defining characteristic of the LAPLACIAN DEMON. This theoretical concept, named after Pierre-Simon de Laplace (a mathematician and astronomer best known to his contemporaries for his work on celestial mechanics), is often encountered in discussions of determinism and free will.

[3] The definition of CAUSALITY given here is counterfactual (recall section 8.2.2). Other definitions are possible, but they all give rise to numerous complications; see note 9 on page 388.

[4] The non-determinism mentioned in this passage stems from a fundamental indeterminacy of measurement known as the HEISENBERG UNCERTAINTY PRINCIPLE.

[5] QUANTUM MECHANICS only becomes deterministic if the wave function of the entire universe is considered.

[6] In addressing certain classes of computational problems, randomness can be put to use in the design of PROBABILISTIC ALGORITHMS that outperform deterministic ones, often by many orders of magnitude; for some examples, see Chazelle (2006).

[7] Note that a DETERMINISTIC COMPUTER can compute probabilities. Simulation of quantum-mechanical systems does require a QUANTUM COMPUTER (Deutsch, 1997), but quantum mechanics is irrelevant to cognitive computation (Koch and Hepp, 2006; Tegmark, 2000).

[8] In the twilight of the Roman Empire, the general Bonifacius INVITED THE VANDALS

from Andalusía into North Africa to help him in his fight against Aëtius. They subsequently turned against him, and besieged him in Hippo — the home town of St. Augustine, a major early contributor to the free will debate (O'Connor, 2006).

[9]Here is the rest of that quote from Hume (1740, II.III.II):

> WE FEEL that our actions are subject to our will on most occasions, and imagine we feel that the will itself is subject to nothing; because when by a denial of it we are provok'd to try, we feel that it moves easily every way, and produces an image of itself even on that side, on which it did not settle. This image or faint motion, we persuade ourselves, cou'd have been compleated into the thing itself; because, shou'd that be deny'd, we find, upon a second trial, that it can. But these efforts are all in vain.

[10]The impossibility of predicting the behavior of a computer program without simulating its execution is reflected in the HALTING PROBLEM: given a description of a program and a finite input, decide whether the program finishes running or will run forever, given that input. Alan Turing proved that the Halting Problem is formally undecidable in the same ground-breaking paper where he introduced the concept of the abstract Machine that bears his name (Turing, 1936).

[11]Note that the observation I make here is unrelated to the claim, often encountered in computationally uninformed philosophical literature, that Gödel's Second Incompleteness Theorem implies that SELF-KNOWLEDGE is impossible. The common errors behind various versions of this claim are exposed by Laforte, Hayes, and Ford (1998).

[12]In this empirical context, CAUSALITY is posited (not deduced logically, which, as Hume pointed out, is impossible), as a defeasible hypothesis. A computational tool that can be brought to bear in formulating and testing hypothesized causal links between events is the calculus of graphical models, or Bayes networks (Figure 6.15 on page 192).

[13]In connection with the experience of acting under direct cortical control, Wegner (2003, p.68) observes:

> "The EXCLUSIVITY PRINCIPLE [a basic premise underlying the feeling of free will, according to which an action cannot have more than one agent] governs cases when perceptions of forces outside the self undermine the experience of will. [. . .] Stanley Milgram explained his famous finding, that people will obey a command to shock another person, in terms of such a mechanism, suggesting that an 'agentic shift' and an accompanying reduction in conscious will occur when actions are done at the behest of another."

This observation may explain the ease with which people can be induced to behave barbarically when "following orders."

[14]Al-Attar's epic poem is best summarized by this passage from *The Approach to Al-Mu'tasim* by Borges:

> The faraway king of the birds, the SIMURG, drops an exquisite feather in the middle of China; weary of their ancient anarchy, the birds determine to find it. They know that their king's name means "Thirty Birds"; they know that his royal palace stands on the Kaf, the circular mountain which surrounds the earth. They undertake the almost infinite adventure. They fly over seven valleys, or seven seas; the next-to-the-last one is called Vertigo; the last, Annihilation. Many of the pilgrims desert; others perish. Thirty of them, purified by

their labors, set foot upon the Mountain of the Simurg. At last they contemplate it: they perceive that they are the Simurg, and that the Simurg is each one of them and all of them.

> — Borges (1970)

The view of the Self as a DISTRIBUTED entity — a rather modern interpretation of al-Attar's allegory — fits well with his own Sufi-inspired stance concerning the proper treatment of the Self-concept:

> We've seen and heard so much – what have we learned?
> Not for one moment has the Self been spurned;
> Fools gather round and hinder our release:
> When will their stale, insistent whining cease?
> We have no freedom to achieve our goal
> Until from Self and fools we free the soul.

> — Farid ud-Din al-Attar
> *The Conference of the Birds* (1177)

[15] Here is how Gier and Kjellberg (2004) phrase it:

> If we cannot call the karmic web free since it lacks a self, by the same token we cannot call it determined, since nothing outside of it is causing it. To the extent that people identify a self, that self is determined by causes outside of it. The more cultivated they become on the Buddhist model, the less they think this way. The less who thinks this way? A question that the European philosopher might ask. Nagarjuna's answer is NO ONE, really. The non-personal web of causes and conditions sheds the delusion, or, rather, ceases to give rise to it.

[16] A typical expression of the often alleged (but never proved) inseparability of morality and theistic religion can be found in the following quote from the US Senator Joseph Lieberman (I, CT), which appears in Jeff Jacoby's article in the *Boston Globe*, December 7, 2003:

> George Washington warned us never to "indulge the supposition that morality can be maintained without religion."

(In his 1796 Farewell Address, Washington in fact said something quite different: "Let us therefore with caution indulge the supposition that morality can be maintained without religion.") In Russian, there is a singularly apposite, but unfortunately untranslatable, word for the Senator's unsubtle sanctimoniousness: достоевщина (hint: it's derived from "Dostoyevsky").

[17] Ethics and the new ENLIGHTENMENT. A philosophical ethics that rejects absolutist approaches in favor of a pragmatist, humanist synthesis, whose roots go back to Dewey (1903), is being developed by Hilary Putnam (2004, p.129), who puts forward

> ... the idea that characterizes my pragmatist "enlightenment": the idea that there is such a thing as the *situated* resolution of political and ethical problems and conflicts (of what Dewey called "problematical situations"), and that claims concerning evaluations of — and proposals for the resolution of — problematical situations can be more and less *warranted* without being *absolute*.

[18]The PHILIP K. DICK SIMULACRUM received the first-place award for open interaction at the 2005 Conference of the American Association for Artificial Intelligence. It should be noted that the state of the art in anthropomorphic robotics still falls far short of the dream of McCulloch (1956), or of the nightmare of Dick (1968). While certain kinds of autonomous improvement through evolution and learning have been demonstrated in simple behaving "animats" (Meyer, Guillot, Girard, Khamassi, Pirim, and Berthoz, 2005; Nolfi and Floreano, 2000; cf. Figure 1.2 on page 5), robots capable of general-purpose learning or of unconstrained human-like conversation (Turing, 1950) are yet to be developed (French, 2000).

[19]INCLUSIVE FITNESS takes into account, in addition to the classical Darwinian fitness, the benefits that an individual may accrue through altruistic behavior. The increased computational requirements imposed by the need to keep track of who owes whom a favor and who is a cheater may have spurred the cognitive "arms race" that led to the rapid evolution of the human brain in the Pleistocene (cf. note 16 on page 231).

[20]The recent work on MACHINE ETHICS (e.g., Floridi and Sanders (2004); see also the special issue of IEEE Intelligent Systems 21(4), July/August 2006), which is necessarily computational, tends, unfortunately, to pursue unrealistic Kantian and utilitarian approaches.

[21]The STATISTICS OF CHEATING. Hartshorne and May showed that "children in experimental situations do not divide bimodally into altruists and 'cheaters' but are distributed normally; almost all the children cheated, but they differed in how much and under what circumstances" (Trivers, 1971, p.48). A recent study of the genetics of human altruism is reported by Bowles (2006).

[22]The Latin *mos, moris* (m.) means habit, custom; or in plural *mores* — character, morals.

[23]An Empiricist alternative to the usual *a priori*, normative PHILOSOPHIES OF ETHICS has been formulated by Hume (1740, III.II.II):

> We partake of their uneasiness by sympathy; and as every thing, which gives uneasiness in human actions, upon the general survey, is call'd Vice, and whatever produces satisfaction, in the same manner, is denominated Virtue; this is the reason why the sense of moral good and evil follows upon justice and injustice. And tho' this sense, in the present case, be deriv'd only from contemplating the actions of others, yet we fail not to extend it even to our own actions. The general rule reaches beyond those instances, from which it arose; while at the same time we naturally sympathize with others in the sentiments they entertain of us. Thus SELF-INTEREST is the original motive to the establishment of justice: but a SYMPATHY with public interest is the source of the moral approbation, which attends that virtue.

When translated into the language of cognitive computation, Hume's identification of "sympathy" as the root of virtue and self-interest as the foundation of justice correspond to the ideas of conceptual simulation of others and of learning to play by the society's rules, discussed in sections 6.7 and 10.2, as well as elsewhere in this book.

[24]Not knowing Sanskrit, I had to work from a French translation of this passage: "Il y a acte, il y a rétribution, mais il n'existe pas d'agent qui rejette ces agrégats-ci et assume d'autres agrégats, sauf s'il s'agit là d'une métaphore sur la Loi" (Lamotte, 1973, p.314). A slightly different English translation appears in Gier and Kjellberg (2004): "There is free action, there is retribution, but I see no agent that passes out of one set of momentary elements into another one, except the [connection] of those elements."

[25]Here is the entire relevant passage: A certain heathen came to Shammai and said to him,

"Make me a proselyte, on condition that you teach me the whole Torah in the time I can stand on one foot." Thereupon he repulsed him with the rod which was in his hand. When he went to Hillel, Hillel said to him, "WHAT IS HATEFUL TO YOU, DO NOT DO TO YOUR NEIGHBOR: that is the whole Torah; all the rest of it is commentary; go and learn." (Talmud, Shabbat 31a).

[26] A more literal translation of this quote from the Great Elephant Footprint Sutra is: "They who know INTERDEPENDENT CO-ORIGINATION [Pali: *pañiccasamuppàda*; Sanscrit: *pratītya-samutpāda*], know the Dharma."

[27] "THE LONG LAPSE OF IMMEMORIAL TIME" is John Conington's translation of a line from Horace: *innumerabilis annorum series et fuga temporum* (*Carmina* III.30 — the ode which opens with the famous words *Exegi monumentum*).

[28] Concerning WISDOM AND OLD AGE, Ardelt (2004) remarks that "... unlike life satisfaction, wisdom in old age was not associated with any of the objective life quality indicators, except physical health (Ardelt, 1997). That suggests that wise older people are likely to be satisfied with their life independently of the objective circumstances they encounter because they are better able than are other older adults to deal with the vicissitudes of life." Longitudinal studies, she adds, need to be carried out to establish causality among these factors (Ardelt, 1997).

[29] Summarizing the findings from their study of the NEURAL CORRELATES OF WELL-BEING, Urry et al. (2004, p.370) write: "We suggest that taking an active role in life and appropriately engaging sources of appetitive motivation, behaviors that are characteristic of left frontal individuals, may contribute to higher levels of [eudaimonic] well-being."

[30] CHANGE IS GOOD. Compare this to the discussion of the relationship between NOVELTY and BEAUTY in section 5.6.

[31] The MAXIMIZERS are also less happy when they are made to choose among too many courses of action: "Can people feel worse off as the options they face increase? The present studies suggest that some people – maximizers – can" (Schwartz et al., 2002).

[32] Lyubomirsky et al. (2005) found that the increase in subjective well-being that comes with age is due in part to "older people's ability to select more enjoyable and self-appropriate goals." This observation can be amplified by noting that a particularly effective goal of this kind is to have EXPERIENCES, as opposed to amassing possessions: "experiences make people happier because they are more open to positive reinterpretations, are a more meaningful part of one's identity, and contribute more to successful social relationships" (Van Boven and Gilovich, 2003). Putting it more bluntly, your experiences are literally (as we found out in the last two chapters) part of you; possessions are not.

[33] According to Hermann Weyl, "The objective world simply is, it does not happen. Only to the gaze of my consciousness, crawling along the lifeline of my body, does a section of this world come to life as a fleeting image in space which continuously changes in time" (*Philosophy of Mathematics and Natural Science*, 1927/1949). A very different view of the universe and the flow of time, which came to be called the MANY WORLDS theory, has been developed by Hugh Everett, Bryce DeWitt, and David Deutsch. On this account, new universes are spun off every time the quantum probability wave for some event collapses. For an accessible explanation, see *The Fabric of Reality* (Deutsch, 1997).

[34] The next sentence in this passage from *A New Refutation of Time* concludes the essay: "The world, unfortunately, is real; I, unfortunately, am Borges."

[35] A fascinating and most thorough exploration of the idea that a succession of representa-

tional states gives rise to a mind can be found in Greg Egan's novel *Permutation City* (Egan, 1994).

[36]The PIGEONS would, of course, be oblivious to the experiences of the mind they would be implementing.

[37]The virtual TIME MACHINE implemented by our minds is tuned to our personal future: "The dark network [the default network, comprised by regions that are active when the brain is not engaged in any particular task (Mason et al., 2007)] allows us to visit the future, but not just any future. When we contemplate futures that don't include us ... the dark network is quiet. Only when we move ourselves through time does it come alive" (Gilbert and Buckner, 2007).

[38]I have borrowed the title of this section from Ursula K. Le Guin's treasure of a book, *Always Coming Home* (Le Guin, 1985), which is, although it would not presume to say so, about HAPPINESS.

[39]Cf. note 32 on the previous page.

11

The Mind in the Act of Finding

Do your work, then step back.
The only path to serenity.

Tao Te Ching, 9
LAO TZU

T HE PRESENT book, from which I am about to step back, is a snapshot
of cognitive science caught in the act of fulfilling its quest — finding
out how the mind works. This brief concluding chapter revisits the origins of
the quest, reaffirms its key achievements, and looks at the prospects for the
immediate future. It then coasts to a stop at a natural conceptual barrier —
one formed by an impending technological development which, for reasons
that will become clear soon, constitutes a horizon beyond which principled
forecasting is impossible.

11.1 On the nature of the quest

The explanatory achievement of cognitive science may be compared to that
of another discipline whose subject matter has been in humanity's plain sight
since immemorial times, yet remained a mystery until a few decades ago: astrophysics. Two hundred years ago, with the subatomic structure of matter
still unknown, physics lacked the very CONCEPTS in terms of which the nuclear reactions that occur over the life cycle of a star are described. Over the
course of the 20th century, the principles of stellar nucleosynthesis came to
be understood to a sufficient degree so as to make it, in broad outline, into
high-school textbooks.

The predicament of the 19th century psychologists (and neurologists)
was similar to that of their physicist contemporaries: they were lacking the
fundamental explanatory concept — that of computation — without which

Understanding how a star such as the Sun
works — the light and the heat, the magnetic storms, the sunspots (some of which
can be seen in this photograph) — could only
happen once the CONCEPTS needed to describe nuclear fusion were in place. Likewise, understanding how the brain works had
to wait until the concept of computation became available.

the study of minds (and of brains) could never even ask the right questions. Given this handicap, the insights into the principles of psychology attained by intellectual titans such as William James are all the more amazing. Yet, these insights had to wait for the likes of Turing, McCulloch, and Marr to be made into *explanations* that dispel mystery rather than teach another generation to live with it, as someone might learn to live with uncorrected congenital myopia or cataract — marveling at one's ability not to bump into the furniture, but oblivious to the existence of stars.

11.1.1 Why cognitive science is more complex than stellar astrophysics

In cognitive science, just as in stellar astrophysics, there are no mysteries left at present — only research questions. Stars emit light by virtue of fusing nuclei into heavier elements; brains exude minds by dint of representing and computing reality. Admittedly, the variety of unresolved questions is singularly high in cognitive science, and so is the degree of challenge they present (see Appendix B). This matter itself, however, is no mystery: we know precisely what it is that makes brain/mind science special in this respect.

Cognitive science is more difficult than other disciplines — indeed, is the ultimate hard science — because its subject matter is the most complex dynamical system known to humanity. At more than 200 billion stars, the Milky Way galaxy may exceed the 10-billion neuron human brain in the potential number of DEGREES OF FREEDOM — elements whose individual characteristics define the state of the system. The actual patterns of gravitational interaction among stars and interstellar gas (as well as the so-called dark matter and dark energy) that together determine the spiral shape of our galaxy are, however, incomparably simpler than the dynamics of a pack of neurons that form a brain — let alone a group of socially interacting brains embedded in an even larger ecological system.

11.1.2 Why cognitive science nevertheless works

Although brains have the *potential* to give rise to indescribably complex dynamics, their *actual* behavior is amenable to study and to understanding. The principle that makes this possible is HIERARCHICAL ABSTRACTION, introduced in section 2.4. Brains evolve to deal with a world of information that

The dynamics behind the shape of a spiral galaxy is much simpler than the dynamics of the mind spun by the human brain, even though the number of DEGREES OF FREEDOM of a galaxy (as defined, for example, by the number of stars) is much higher than of the brain (where the number of neurons is what matters; cf. p. 39).

is characterized by statistical structure at multiple levels; their functional architecture and the computations it implements reflect this structure.

The link between the hierarchical features of the neuroanatomy of the central nervous system (da F. Costa and Sporns, 2006) and the dynamics that emerges from those features (Honey, Kötter, Breakspear, and Sporns, 2007) can be studied, and understood, in terms of the activation patterns of neurons and neuronal assemblies. Such understanding of the brain would, however, be incomplete unless it also encompasses the reasons for which the dynamics happens, which have to do with the processing of behaviorally relevant information, and the computations whereby this processing is carried out.

A properly balanced approach to understanding the brain should, therefore, be equally concerned with understanding the hierarchies of information patterns afforded by the environment, of neural structures that evolve to deal with those, and with the computational functions they implement. I have described such an approach, proposed and developed by Marr and Poggio (1977), in section 4.2.

11.2 What we have learned

The multidisciplinary approach that characterizes contemporary cognitive science (as exemplified by the Marr-Poggio program) is responsible for the tremendous progress it made over the past several decades. The most significant aspect of this progress — the demystification of the human mind — stemmed from the realization of what kind of thing a mind is. **A mind is an instance of computation**. Along with identifying the proper conceptual framework for explaining the mind, this momentous discovery also dissolves the "mind-body problem" by revealing its relationship to the brain.

11.2.1 Brains, minds, and computation

When asked by an interviewer on a TV show, "how does the brain work, five words or less," Steven Pinker replied immediately: "let's see, [counting off words on his fingers] brain cells fire in patterns."[1] This very same answer describes also "how the mind works" (a phrase used by Pinker as a title of his 1997 book[2]), but only if we ignore the multiple realizability of computation and limit our inquiry to minds that are generated by brains. In *The Astonishing Hypothesis*, Francis Crick (1994) quipped, "You are nothing but a pack of neurons!" This view is, on the implementational level, true of human minds, but we can do better by offering the following, even more audacious, yet none the less true, piece of "nothingbuttery":[3]

You are nothing but an outbreak of computation!

— Edelman (2008, p. 500)

11.2.2   The principles of human cognitive computation

Because minds are computational entities, in this book I have focused on the computational level of explanation, supporting the abstract, task-level analysis of what minds are up to with behavioral data. I have only occasionally made forays into neuroscience. A few examples of explanations developed in this manner appear in Table 11.1 on the facing page. Most of these are drawn from Chapter 5 (Perception), which is where I first applied the integrated methodology introduced in the earlier part of the book to a sizable chunk of cognition.

As one may expect in light of the hierarchy principle, the explanations offered grew progressively more abstract as our focus shifted from perception to memory, language, thinking, consciousness, and beyond. In the last example given in Table 11.1, ethics is reduced to causal inference (of the "rules of the game" in a society), it being understood that inference amounts to statistical learning, and that causal inference in particular can be carried out within the representational framework known as a graphical model.

Statistical inference of structure (patterns) from experience is, indeed, the key principle behind mind-like computation on the most general level. As illustrated in Figure 11.1 on page 502, *becoming* a human mind and *being* one are two life-long, interdependent processes — namely, the incorporation of, and the extrapolation from, experience. The evolutionary roots of these processes (Dennett, 1995, 2003) are manifest in the pervasive genetic influence on learning abilities and predispositions (Pinker, 2002), and in adaptive decision making that favors satisficing over optimization (Gigerenzer and Goldstein, 1996; Simon, 1957).

An extra processing loop left out of this highly schematic illustration is a virtual machine operating on the contents of a flexible working memory. This computational feature greatly extends the reach of the human mind, making it capable of bethinking itself *de omni re scibili*, "of all things that can be known" — a phrase used as a motto by the Renaissance scholar Giovanni

locus	*aspect of the mind*	*representational principle(s)*	*computational principle(s)*
Chapter 5	stimulus distinctive-ness (p.94)	the stimulus is an outlier in the cloud of like stimuli in the representation space	must compute mean (cloud centroid) and standard deviations (cloud spread) in principal directions
	perceptual constancy (p.96)	the cloud has low variance along irrelevant dimensions	initial representation space must be transformed (warped) to achieve this
	perceptual learning (p.106)	modification of the cloud structure driven by experience, possibly steered by the system's needs	statistical inference of regularities from examples; dimensionality reduction
	categoriza-tion (p.107)	the segregation of the cloud into "clumps" corresponding to the emerging categories	statistically driven clustering; dimensionality reduction
	adaptation (p.110)	warping of the representation space driven by experience	dynamic tracking of stimulus ensemble statistics
	veridical perception (p.124)	cloud structure reflects characteristics of the (distal) stimuli, such as similarity patterns	smooth (differentiable) mapping from the distal stimuli to low-dimensional proximal (internal) representations
	beauty (p.130)	central statistical tendency of the population captured by the representation cloud	regression to the mean
Chapter 6	learning causality (p.192)	graphical (Bayesian) models	data-driven inference of conditional independence
Chapter 7	speech production (p.301)	language model (a probabilistically weighted graph)	estimation of the most probable path through a weighted graph
Chapter 8	problem solving (p.318)	state space graph	heuristic search
Chapter 9	phenome-nal Self (p.412)	a control-theoretic model of the world that includes the controller (a "total flight simulator")	dynamic registration of spatially mapped perception, action, and motivation (goals) data
Chapter 10	ethics (p.472)	internalized "rules of the game"	causal inference

Table 11.1 — A few select examples of EXPLANATORY REDUCTION from various aspects of the mind to computations defined over representations.

Pico della Mirandola, to which Voltaire reputedly added *et quibusdam aliis* — "and of several other things."

11.2.3   Implications

The Renaissance thinkers were the first to develop a consistent vision of humanity not as puppets of gods or a congregation of sinners and sufferers, meekly waiting to be saved through divine grace, but as INTERPRETERS OF NATURE, capable of attaining power over their own destiny through self-knowledge. When combined with the scientific method, this vision proved true to its promise of providing humankind with the apt tools for intellectual and spiritual liberation. Its implications are too numerous and too profound to be discussed here. I shall only mention one — perhaps the most important one — of these: by revealing the mind to be the quintessence of a lifelong experience of the world, cognitive science brings to fruition the Humanist vision that placed the human being at the symbolic center of the universe, and imparts a concrete meaning to the Talmudic saying that he who saves a single soul saves an entire world.[4]

By the acuteness of his senses, the inquiry of his reason and the light of his intelligence, he is the INTERPRETER OF NATURE... I feel that I have come to some understanding of why man is the most fortunate of living things and, consequently, deserving of all admiration... A thing surpassing belief and smiting the soul with wonder.

— Giovanni Pico della Mirandola
Oration on the Dignity of Man (1486)

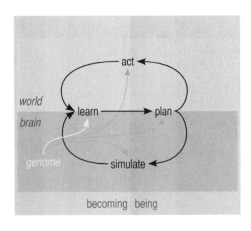

Figure 11.1 — A very high-level schematic view of the computations involved in BECOMING AND BEING HUMAN. *Learning* is generally lifelong (although in some cognitive domains it is concentrated in early childhood). Computationally, learning amounts to statistical inference of structure (patterns) in the data, which originate externally (in the stimulation provided by the world, part of it in response to the system's own *actions*) and internally (in the *simulation* of actions and responses generated by the brain). *Planning*, problem solving, decision making, etc., involves classification (as in categorization of stimuli) and regression (as in predicting the outcomes of actions). These operations too are fundamentally statistical, insofar as they require interpolation or extrapolation from data (experience). *Simulation* makes use of structured generative statistical models to anticipate future events and explore potential alternative courses of action, enabling the system to plan for better behavior and to learn on the basis of internal "experience." The *genetics* of cognition is outside the scope of this book.

11.3   Where we are headed

Where do we go from here? At present, for the first time in the history of
life on this planet, evolution of minds through natural selection is being complemented — and is about to be superseded — by intelligent design. The
possibilities contained in this development are thrilling.

Some of these stem from the availability of increasingly sophisticated options for memory enhancement through technology. It all started with external memory props: those that extend working memory, such as a wax tablet or
an expanse of smooth sand to draw geometrical diagrams on; those that supplement episodic memory, such as baked clay tablets with cuneiform records
of tax levies; and those that boost declarative memory, such as encyclopedias
and technical reference manuals.

It is now possible to enhance not only a person's effective information
storage capacity and access speed, but also his or her processing prowess, by
augmenting brain computation externally. Our brains are good at simulating
people and social situations, but their capacity for doing so and their physical
reach are both limited. Boosting a person's social intelligence by means of
a computational prosthesis would be just the beginning here. Imagine being
able to spin off active simulations of yourself that would go off into the in-
fosphere, not just to trawl for information, but also to perform some social
services for their master (say, to attend an event at which you cannot be bodily present), and would be reintegrated into your personality when they are
done.

Another avenue for mind enhancement, the potential repercussions of
which are much more significant than those of social cognitive engineering,
is to use technology to help the brain carry out computations that are quite
alien to it: say, mapping the molecular interaction networks in drug design,
or putting celestial mechanics to work in plotting the trajectory of a probe to
Saturn. The real impact of mind enhancement in this domain stems not from
its popular appeal — scientists and engineers are, and will always be, a small
minority of the population — but in the prospect of an exponential growth of
the technological return on intellectual investment that is inherent in applying
science and technology to itself (Good, 1965; Vinge, 1993).

The positive feedback "loop" that could lead to such a development is already in place: computers are indispensable in helping human scientists and
engineers design and build better computers. As the principles of operation of
the human mind are being elucidated, the development of human-level artifi-

cial intelligence becomes imminent, and with it the likelihood of transcending human-level intelligence by purely technological means, which would not be bound by the slow pace of natural evolution or by the quirks of biological brains:

> Let an ~~ULTRAINTELLIGENT MACHINE~~ be defined as a machine that can far surpass all the intellectual activities of any man however clever. Since the design of machines is one of these intellectual activities, an ultraintelligent machine could design even better machines; there would then unquestionably be an "intelligence explosion," and the intelligence of man would be left far behind.
>
> — Good (1965)

Internet "wakes up?" Ridicu – no carrier.

— Charles Stross
(from the *Wired* magazine's collection of six-word stories)

To humans, ULTRA-INTELLIGENT (UI) entities would appear as godlike in their powers and unfathomable in their intents as humans must be to dogs (Vinge, 1993; cf. Figure 11.2 on the facing page). Because of this unbridgeable intellect gap, the emergence of UI would constitute a SINGULARITY — an event past which technological prognostication and plain human foresight both fail (Vinge, 1993).

John W. Campbell, the award-winning editor of the *Analog* magazine for science fiction and science fact, used to urge authors to write about "something that thinks as *well* as a human, but not *like* a human" — a distinction discussed in his essay WHAT DO YOU MEAN... HUMAN? (Campbell, 1959). Some of the most profound insights both into human nature and into the nature of intelligence in general are to be found in the literary work produced by people who were sharply aware of this distinction: Stanisław Lem, Ursula K. Le Guin, Arkady and Boris Strugatsky, Vernor Vinge, Greg Egan.

The Singularity (a word that for obvious reasons came to be capitalized) has been called by some "rapture for nerds," presumably because the unimaginably superior science and technology of the UIs may make it possible to transplant a fully formed human mind into a substrate that would afford it uncommon longevity as well as opportunities for efficient enhancement by artificial means. This notion is, however, just as unfounded as the apocalyptic scenarios (popular among poorly informed movie scriptwriters), in which evil computers enslave humanity. As stated above, we really have no basis for predicting the attitudes of the post-Singularity UIs towards any issue at all. Expecting them to be benevolent or malevolent may be presuming too much; they may end up paying no more attention to human affairs than an elephant does to an ant crawling across its path.[5]

11.4   Mind games forever

So, what does the future hold in store for us? We don't know whether the Singularity will indeed happen, but the wheel has been set in motion, and the competitive dynamics of human societies ensures that it will keep turning. The process that has made the Singularity a possibility to contend with began with the invention of systematic science by the circle of people who in 1660 founded the Royal Society, and who took as their motto the three words that changed the world: NULLIUS IN VERBA. By turning the searchlight of science upon itself, the human mind renewed its commitment to the quest for self-knowledge — a "traditional principle [that] unites Eastern and Western philosophy" (Metzinger, 2003). Three and a half centuries later, that quest has been largely fulfilled: we have discovered the general principles on which the machinery of the mind operates.

Some of these principles conspire to raise an obstacle to the attempts on the part of any given mind to gain a first-person insight into *itself*. As we learned in section 9.3, the need to represent the self as a part of the world, and to do so in a manner that would not cause the mind's machinery to seize up in an infinite regress, dictates that the self-model be phenomenally transparent. The resulting "autoepistemic closure" (Metzinger, 2003) would seem to preclude the possibility of first-person self-knowledge: tantalizingly, the

Figure 11.2 — On the far side of THE SINGULARITY, intelligences may emerge that would consider the average human — if they condescend to notice us at all — as not much smarter than Rico, the Border Collie from p. 278. On the scale of intellect, there is plenty of room at the top: even among humans, a gap of many standard deviations exists between the exceptional math minds and the merely brilliant ones. A case in point is the distribution of scores in the highly selective William Lowell Putnam Competitions, held annually for the undergraduate mathematics students in the US and Canada (Gallian, 2004). The Putnam problem sets are extremely difficult: in 1987, for example, the median score was one point out of 120 possible total. The perfect score was achieved only twice in the past 40 years (in 1987 and in 1988); the average median score over that period was 5.4. That this highly skewed distribution captures something real about mathematical genius is indicated by the likelihood of high-scoring individuals to become exceptionally accomplished mathematicians and scientists: Nobel Prize winners, Fields medalists, presidents of the American Mathematical Society, MacArthur Fellows, etc.

scientist would know everything worth knowing about minds in general, yet lack full access to the computational innards of his or her own mind.

This obstacle is not, however, insuperable in principle. Full access, transcending by far the mere realization of the self-model's representational transparency (that is, phenomenal "enlightenment") becomes possible once the mind is reimplemented in a computational substrate that is more conducive to such play than the biological brain. In this sense, self-knowledge truly means freedom:

> Once the principle of autoepistemic closure has been clearly understood on the neurocognitive level, one can define the goal of continuously minimizing the transparency of the PSM [phenomenal self model]. This is in good keeping with the classical philosophical goal of SELF-KNOWLEDGE: To truly accept this ideal means to dissolve any form of autoepistemic closure, on theoretical *as well* as on phenomenal levels of representation — even if this implies deliberately violating the adaptivity-constraint Mother Nature so cruelly imposed on our biological ancestors.
>
> — Metzinger (2003, p.632)

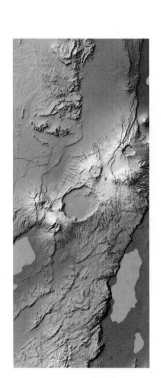

A satellite view of the Olduvai Gorge in the Great Rift Valley.

By bringing about freedom from the fetters of biological embodiment, substrate independence endows dynamic information patterns, which is what minds are, with a potential for longevity and for development undreamed of by ancient philosophers — a potential that can only be realized through technological civilization that we are part of. Its story began in the Great Rift Valley in East Africa, where the routine struggle for survival of a particular band of genes — themselves nothing more than self-replicating patterns of information — sparked a slow revolution whereby *cognitive* information patterns, hitherto mere pawns in the game of life, found a way not only to defect from the original war, but also to emancipate themselves from their original exclusively biological substrate. The story of the human mind's revolution may, therefore, go on long after the gene pool of the species that spearheaded it mutates into extinction, and the hydrogen-depleted Sun turns into a helium-fusing red giant, reaches out to boil the Earth's oceans, and blows away its atmosphere, leaving humanity's old home as bare as it had been in the beginning.

Praise then darkness and creation unfinished.

The Left Hand of Darkness
URSULA K. LE GUIN

❦ ❦ ❦

Notes

[1]THE TAO OF STEVE. The person who interviewed Steven Pinker was Stephen Colbert, of the *Colbert Report*, in the program that aired on the Comedy Channel on February 7, 2007.

[2]Even though Pinker's 1997 book, HOW THE MIND WORKS, and the present one address the same question, there are significant differences. Pinker briefly considers the claim that the mind *can* be computational, and sidesteps the issue of its relationship to the brain (Pinker, 1997, p.83), devoting more space to his forte, evolutionary psychology. In contrast, this book argues that the mind *must* be computational, and substantiates the claim by showing how all of cognition can be understood in the light of this principle.

[3]NOTHINGBUTTERY is a term that is mainly used, by the clingers to the supernatural, to dismiss

> ... the reductionism (what Prof. Donald Mackay of Keele University called the 'nothingbuttery') of the modern world: human beings are nothing but bio-chemicals, their thoughts are nothing but the product of electrical impulses in their brains.

> Rev. Alex MacDonald's opening address
> to the General Assembly of the Free Church of Scotland (2005)

It can be found in MacKay's book *The Clockwork Image: A Christian Perspective on Science* (InterVarsity Press, Downers Grove, IL, 1974). Good science, of course, knows better: it is

> ... reductionism triumphant, mechanism triumphant, materialism triumphant. It is also, however, the farthest thing from *greedy* reductionism. It is a breath-taking cascade of levels upon levels upon levels, with new principles of expla-nation, new phenomena appearing at each level, forever revealing that the fond hope of explaining "everything" at some one lower level is misguided.

> — Dennett (1995, p.195)

[4]The "ONE SOUL" quote comes from this passage:

> Thus, man was created unique in the world, to wit, he who destroys a single soul is held to be the destroyer of an entire world; **and he who saves a single soul saves an entire world**. [...] A man mints a hundred coins from one mold and they all are alike; the Supreme King of kings, the Holy One, blessed be He, fashions every man from the mold of Adam, and not one resembles the other. Thus everyone should say, "for me the world was created."

> Talmud Yerushalmi, Sanhedrin 4.4

The key phrase is highlighted in bold both above and in the original Hebrew version, which is given below:

לפיכך נברא אדם יחידי בעולם, ללמד שכל המאבד נפש
אחת, מעלים עליו כאילו איבד עולם מלא; **וכל המקיים**
נפש אחת, מעלים עליו כאילו קיים עולם מלא. [...]
להגיד גדולתו של מלך מלכי המלכים, הקדוש ברוך הוא,
שאדם טובע מאה מטבעות בחותם אחד, וכולן דומין זה
לזה, מלך מלכי המלכים הקדוש ברוך הוא טובע את כל
האדם בחותמו של אדם הראשון, ואין אחד מהם דומה
לחברו. לפיכך לכל אחד ואחד לומר, בשבילי נברא העולם.

[5]Can we humans do something to predispose the POST-SINGULARITY beings to treat us well? In a parenthetical remark, Vinge (1993) offers an idea, which he attributes to Good:

> I. J. Good had something to say about this, though at this late date the advice may be moot: Good proposed a "Meta-Golden Rule," which might be paraphrased as "Treat your inferiors as you would be treated by your superiors." It's a wonderful, paradoxical idea (and most of my friends don't believe it) since the game-theoretic payoff is so hard to articulate. Yet if we were able to follow it, in some sense that might say something about the plausibility of such kindness in this universe.

— Vinge (1993)

Appendices

Appendix A

Bayesian Inference and Decision Making

All knowledge resolves itself into probability.

A Treatise of Human Nature
DAVID HUME

A NY knowledge of past events is only useful in guiding future behavior if it can support generalization, that is, dealing with new cases. The need for generalization arises throughout cognition. In perception, for example, the cognitive system needs to decide to which *category* a new stimulus is likely to belong, in light of what is known about other stimuli and the decisions they prompted (cf. p. 120). In inductive reasoning, the system needs to select from a set of possible *explanations* of the observed data the one that best fits the pattern encountered so far (p. 346).

Generalization, in turn, requires distilling the measurements that a cognitive system performs on its environment into patterns that simplify the raw data, insofar as they capture regularities present there (Grünwald et al., 2005; Rissanen, 1987; Solomonoff, 1964). A principled way of finding such patterns, be they categories, explanations, rules, etc., is to perform STATISTICAL INFERENCE on the measurements and their probabilities. The patterns inferred from previously encountered data can then serve to make informed decisions about new cases. This appendix offers a brief overview to the Bayesian approach to inference and decision making; for a more thorough introduction and suggestions for further reading, see the introduction to the special issue of *Trends in Cognitive Sciences* on probabilistic models of cognition (Chater, Tenenbaum, and Yuille, 2006) and the supplementary material therein (Griffiths and Yuille, 2006).

511

A.1 The Bayes Theorem

The approach to statistical inference that I shall outline relies on a theorem whose proof was published by Thomas Bayes in 1726. In the simplest case, it links the probabilities of two events — call them A and B — as illustrated in Figure A.1. The proof, which is only a few lines long, has as its starting point the definition of CONDITIONAL PROBABILITY of B given A, or $P(B\,|\,A)$. Using the notation of Figure A.1, this can be written out as

$$P(B\,|\,A) = \frac{|A\&B|}{|A|} \qquad\qquad (A.1)$$

where $|A|$ denotes the area of A, and $|A\&B|$ the area of the intersection. To express the conditional probability of B given A in terms of other relevant probabilities (rather than areas), divide the numerator and the denominator of the right-hand side of eq. A.1 by the "universe" area $|U|$:

$$P(B\,|\,A) = \frac{P(A\&B)}{P(A)} \qquad\qquad (A.2)$$

By the definition of conditional probability, the same JOINT PROBABILITY $P(A\&B)$ (which, of course, is the same as $P(B\&A)$) can be expressed in two equivalent ways:

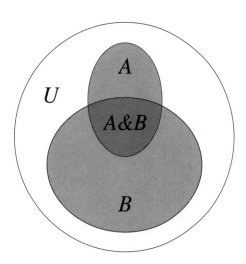

Figure A.1 — The BAYES THEOREM follows from the definition of joint probability, which is illustrated here with a simple example of two events, A and B, denoted by the smaller and the larger ovals, respectively. The probabilities of A and of B, which both belong to the "universe" U of all possible events, are defined as the ratios of their respective areas to the area of U. Their intersection corresponds to the probability of the joint occurrence of the two events, denoted by $A\&B$.

$$P(A\&B) \quad = \tag{A.3}$$
$$= \quad P(A)P(B \mid A)$$
$$= \quad P(B)P(A \mid B)$$

This is the Bayes Theorem.

We can now eq. A.3 to use. Suppose that B is a hypothesis (category label, rule, etc.) in question, and A is a piece of data that can be brought to bear on it. By the Bayes Theorem, the *posterior* probability of the hypothesis being true, given the data A, is

$$P(B \mid A) = \frac{P(A \mid B)P(B)}{P(A)} \tag{A.4}$$

To calculate it, one needs to know the *prior* probability of the data $P(A)$ and the *likelihood* of the data conditioned on the hypothesis $P(A \mid B)$. Both these quantities can be inferred directly from experience, that is, by tracking the statistics of the data and the various hypotheses (Chater et al., 2006; Griffiths and Yuille, 2006), as outlined below.

A.2   Using the Bayes Theorem

Consider a cognitive system that is searching a space of hypotheses H for an explanation of the observed data D (this example is identical to that of Box 8.1 on page 346). The agent's *a priori* beliefs about the plausibility of each hypothesis in that space, $h \in H$ – before taking into account D but drawing upon background knowledge K – are expressed by the *prior* conditional probability distribution $P(h|K)$.

The Bayes Theorem prescribes how the system should modify its current beliefs in light of the data D. The desired outcome is expressed by the *posterior* conditional probability distribution $P(h|D,K)$, which is computed from the known quantities according to BAYES' RULE:

$$P(h|D,K) = \frac{P(D|h,K)P(h|K)}{P(D|K)} \tag{A.5}$$

In this expression, the *likelihood* $P(D|h,K)$ expresses the predictions of each hypothesis h in the form of the probability of observing D if h were true. The denominator, $P(D|K)$, is an average of the predictions of all hypotheses in the hypothesis space, weighted by their prior probabilities:

$$P(D|K) = \sum_{h' \in H} P(D|h', K)P(h'|K) \qquad (A.6)$$

This term serves to normalize the product that appears in the numerator, ensuring that the posterior $P(h|D, K)$ sums to 1 and can therefore be interpreted as a proper probability distribution over the hypotheses.

In summary, the probabilistic, empirical view of knowledge put forward by David Hume in his *Treatise* implies that (1) the most one can know about a situation is the joint probability distribution of all the variables of interest, and (2) that acquiring and using knowledge consist, respectively, of statistical inference and decision making. The Bayes Theorem offers a simple yet practical method for putting these insights to work.

Appendix B

Mind the Gap

О, как я всё угадал![a]

---
[a]O, how I guessed everything right!

The Master and Margarita
MIKHAIL BULGAKOV

M Y top priority in choosing what to write about and how to write about
it in this book has been to present a complete and consistent, if simplified, panorama of cognition as it is understood in terms of computation, while
offering the reader conceptual tools for zooming in on details that were left
unresolved. This strategy is in a sense self-undermining: the sagacious reader
in possession of such tools will, no doubt, have already detected many suspect
spots in the canvas, where the panorama resolves into a palimpsest hiding
considerable theoretical diversity, or even a conceptual gap where opinions
outnumber theories.

Young and energetic students of cognition who are drawn to what they
perceive as flaws in the big picture that I have painted may decide to take
over where the present project leaves off. This would be a most welcome
development: they will likely do a better job of it, and I shall have consolation
in remembering that the work of the righteous, as the Hebrew saying goes, is
done by others. To make this work a little easier, I shall now briefly discuss
three select areas where a focused inquiry would, I believe, be particularly
effective.

B.1 Some of the things not included in this book

Each of the three research projects that I am about to outline (in the sketchiest
possible manner) takes as its starting point a gap in our current understanding

515

of the computational mind. These three projects are: (1) in language, efficient open-ended learning of form and function; (2) in vision, the ability to make sense of arbitrary scenes; (3) in memory and thinking, the integration of a rich conceptual system with a flexible virtual workspace. In each case, the nature of the cognitive task in question — as explained, respectively, in chapters 7, 5, and 6 and 8 — is generally clear. What needs to be clarified is how these tasks are solved by the computational mind, and how the solutions are implemented in the human brain.

As usual in cognitive science, a natural yardstick for the success of these projects will be the possibility of applying the knowledge they will generate to the construction of detailed and practical computational models of the corresponding functions. In the present case, the implications of such a development would be far-reaching: when integrated and implemented on a general-purpose computational platform, the three functions in question will constitute the core of an artificially intelligent entity.

B.1.1 Language

The knowledge of language is represented in an individual's brain in the form of a loose hierarchy of CONSTRUCTIONS — pairings of form and meaning that vary in size, complexity, degree of generativity, and frequency of use (Goldberg, 2005; recall section 7.2.3). Theories of language acquisition related to the Construction Grammar idea (e.g., Tomasello, 2003) have not, however, been informed yet by the recent algorithmic advances in learning constructions from raw corpus data (Berant, Gross, Mussel, Sandbank, Ruppin, and Edelman, 2007; Sandbank, Edelman, and Ruppin, 2007; Solan et al., 2005). Moreover, the existing grammar induction algorithms do not yet perform at a level that approaches that of human language learners, nor do they meet the computational and architectural requirements that would make them plausible models of language acquisition in the brain.

The state of the art in grammar induction from raw corpora does offer a solid foundation for the development of a viable comprehensive model of language acquisition. Learning in such a model would be incremental and open-ended: new utterances would be processed as they are encountered, with the existing representations being modified on the fly (and perhaps newly distilled ones added to the lexicon/grammar) as needed. Moreover, in processing the incoming data, the algorithm would make use of the structure of the dialogue — in particular, of alignment across individual utterances that is so prominent in discourse (Du Bois, 2001; Pickering and Garrod, 2004) and so useful for language aquisition (Waterfall, 2006). Computationally, such alignment ensures that statistically significant telltales of construction CON-STITUENT structure are available even in short segments of discourse.

In all human languages, hierarchical constituency relationships among constructions are augmented by statistical DEPENDENCY relationships that dictate the conditional probabilities of some forms, given others that appear elsewhere in the same dialogue segment. Taken together, these structural dependencies comprise the LANGUAGE MODEL associated with the given lexicon/grammar. Unlike the existing algorithms, which first induce a grammar and then use it to infer a probabilistic language model, the approach envisaged here would combine the learning of dependencies with the learning of constituency structure in the same incremental process.

Because human language users are normally embodied and situated in a shared physical and social environment, the phenomenon of language can only be ultimately and fully understood in connection with that environment. In the developing child, embodied interaction with the enviroment serves to ground linguistic meaning and facilitates the learning of linguistic form. To attain human-level proficiency with human-like rapidity, a comprehensive model of language acquisition may therefore have to learn constructions through interaction rather than through passive exposure, and it certainly must tie them into a rich system of concepts that would themselves be perceptually rooted and efficiently represented and manipulated. In this manner, the modeling of language depends on progress in modeling the senses (in particular, vision, as discussed in the next section), as well as conceptual and working memory (discussed in the following section).

B.1.2 Vision

The human brain projects the viewed scene into a series of representation spaces arranged along several pathways, both cortical (one descending from the occipital lobe ventrally into the temporal lobe, amother ascending dorsally into the parietal lobe) and subcortical (leading, among other places, to the superior colliculus). Information flowing down the ventral cortical stream evokes in the inferotemporal region a pattern of activities of several thousand neuronal assemblies, each of whose members is tuned to a category of shapes previously encountered in a particular location in the visual field (Edelman, 1999; recall section 5.8).

The traditional functional-neuroanatomical approach to understanding vision identifies the inferotemporal cortex as the apex and the final stage of of the scene processing hierarchy. Arguments advanced by Merker (2007) suggest, however, that the real destination for visual information is the midbrain, where it meets and is integrated with other sensory, motor, and motivational streams, to give rise to the VIRTUAL REALITY simulation of the sensorium, complete with the phenomenal Self embedded in it (Metzinger, 2003; recall section 9.3).

On this comprehensive theoretical view, which extends and supersedes that of Chapter 5, the visual cortex serves as a sophisticated structural statistical feature extractor (Edelman, 1999) and as a repository of visual conceptual memory (Merker, 2004). The next stage in the development of a detailed computational understanding of vision should, therefore, seek to integrate the present, disembodied theory of object and scene processing with purposive, active, embodied approaches that include motivation and attention. A model based on the resulting integrated theory would have a much better chance of approximating human scene perception, including its open-endedness and sophistication, its phenomenal aspects (what it feels like to see; cf. Metzinger, 2003), and its purposive undercurrent (what we see for; cf. Gibson, 1979).

B.1.3   Memory and thinking

Developing the integrated model of vision outlined above will necessitate bringing into the picture CONCEPTUAL and EPISODIC MEMORY, where processed scene information ends up and where the goals driving top-down attentive behavior originate, and WORKING MEMORY, where endogenous goals and exogenous sensory cues can be brought together if a need arises to THINK about them.

The fundamental computational principle underlying episodic memory — associative storage (recall section 6.3) — is easy to model, and indeed many models based on this principle have been developed (Moser and Moser, 2003; O'Reilly and Norman, 2002). The principles behind conceptual memory, such as the "vertical" and "horizontal" structure of concept spaces (Tenenbaum, 1999) and the Bayesian calculus of conditional probabilities that capture the causal relationships among concepts (Gopnik et al., 2004; Steyvers, Tenenbaum, Wagenmakers, and Blum, 2003), are likewise known and there has been progress in modeling it (although certain algorithmic issues remain unresolved). Finally, working memory too, conceived of as a learning-enabled blackboard-like workspace, can be modeled in a straightforward fashion (Burgess and Hitch, 2005; O'Reilly and Frank, 2006).

The existing models do not, however, adequately explain the constrained holism of human conceptual memory, nor do they account for the general fluid intelligence exhibited by humans in problem solving, reasoning, and decision making.

Constrained holism. Although the human conceptual system is very flexible, it is not unconstrained: certain associations and patterns of reasoning are easier than others. Thus, any model that purports to explain commonsense concepts and reasoning by random-access (thus freely holistic) memory processing would be irrelevant to understanding the brain even if it succeeds.

Fluid intelligence. For reasons outlined in section 8.5, the most promising conceptual framework within which to model the human capacity for thinking that is measured by tests of general fluid (gF) intelligence is the VIRTUAL MACHINE (VM). Our primate brains are good for general-purpose thinking to the extent that they can emulate a general-purpose information processor as a VM running on top of the available brain circuits.

On the one hand, the kind of flexible conceptualization described by psychologists needs working memory to happen. On the other hand, working memory has been implicated as the key factor in general fluid intelligence. I conjecture, therefore, that a model that shows how a virtual machine can be implemented in the brain would thereby address both the constrained holism and the fluid intelligence phenomena. By elucidating the brain basis of common sense, a detailed, computational model of conceptual and working memory would also complement and perhaps complete our understanding of language and vision, as suggested above.

B.2   How this book really ends

With an observation and a prognosis: its task does not end here, because so many details can be filled in at the interstices of the explanations that have been offered; yet the knowledge that is still to come will complement, not replace, the broad understanding attained by the cognitive sciences of how the mind really works.

Хвалу и клевету приемли равнодушно,
И не оспоривай глупца.[a]

---

[a]Accept with equanimity both praise and slander,
And do not argue with a fool.

Exegi monumentum
ALEXANDER PUSHKIN

Bibliography

Abeles, M. (1991). *Corticonics: neural circuits of the cerebral cortex*. Cambridge: Cambridge University Press.

Adams, D. (2002). *The Ultimate Hitchhiker's Guide to the Galaxy*. Del Rey.

Adolphs, R. (1999). Social cognition and the human brain. *Trends in Cognitive Sciences 3*, 469–479.

Adriaans, P. and M. van Zaanen (2004). Computational grammar induction for linguists. *Grammars 7*, 57–68.

Aflalo, T. N. and M. S. A. Graziano (2006). Partial tuning of motor cortex neurons to final posture in a free-moving paradigm. *Proceedings of the National Academy of Science 103*, 2909–2914.

Agüera y Arcas, B., A. L. Fairhall, and W. Bialek (2001). What can a single neuron compute? In T. K. Leen, T. G. Dietterich, and V. Tresp (Eds.), *Advances in Neural Information Processing Systems*, Volume 13, pp. 75–81. MIT Press.

Albus, J. S. (1991). Outline for a theory of intelligence. *IEEE Transactions on Systems, Man and Cybernetics 21*, 473–509.

Altes, R. A. (1988). Ubiquity of hyperacuity. *J. Acoust. Soc. Am. 85*, 943–952.

Amari, S. and N. Murata (1997). Statistical analysis of regularization constant – from Bayes, MDL and NIC points of view. In *IWANN '97: Proceedings of the International Work-Conference on Artificial and Natural Neural Networks*, Berlin, pp. 284–293. Springer.

Anderson, A. K., P. E. Wais, and J. D. E. Gabrieli (2006). Emotion enhances remembrance of neutral events past. *Proceedings of the National Academy of Science 103*, 1599–1604.

Anstis, S. M. (1974). A chart demonstrating variations in acuity with retinal position. *Vision Research 14*, 589–592.

Ardelt, M. (1997). Wisdom and life satisfaction in old age. *Journal of Gerontology: Psychological Sciences 52B*, P15–P27.

521

Ardelt, M. (2004). Wisdom as expert knowledge system: a critical review of a contemporary operationalization of an ancient concept. *Human Development 47*, 257–285.

Arnold, J. E., M. Fagnano, and M. K. Tanenhaus (2003). Disfluencies signal theee, um, new information. *Journal of Psycholinguistic Research 32*, 25–37.

Arrington, C. M., T. H. Carr, A. R. Mayer, and S. M. Rao (2000). Neural mechanisms of visual attention: Object-based selection of a region in space. *J. Cognitive Neuroscience 12*(6 (supplement 2)), 106–117.

Arzy, S., M. Idel, T. Landis, and O. Blanke (2005). Why revelations have occurred on mountains? Linking mystical experiences and cognitive neuroscience. *Medical Hypotheses 65*, 841–845.

Aunger, R. (Ed.) (2001). *Darwinizing Culture: The Status of Memetics as a Science*. Oxford: Oxford University Press.

Aunger, R. (2002). Exposure versus susceptibility in the epidemiology of everyday beliefs. *Journal of Cognition and Culture 2*, 113–154.

Awh, E. and J. Jonides (2001). Overlapping mechanisms of attention and spatial working memory. *Trends in Cognitive Sciences 5*, 119–126.

Baars, B. J. (2002). The conscious access hypothesis: origins and recent evidence. *Trends in Cognitive Sciences 6*, 47–52.

Bacon, F. (1620). *The New Organon, or true directions concerning the interpretation of nature.* Available online at http://history.hanover.edu/texts/Bacon/novorg.html.

Bahrick, H. P., L. K. Hall, and S. A. Berger (1996). Accuracy and distortion in memory for high school grades. *Psychological Science 7*, 265–271.

Bak, M., J. P. Girvin, F. T. Hambrecht, C. V. Kufta, G. E. Loeb, and E. M. Schmidt (1990). Visual sensations produced by intracortical microstimulation of the human occipital cortex. *Medical and Biological Engineering and Computing 28*, 257–259.

Baker, C. F., C. J. Fillmore, and B. Cronin (2003). The structure of the FrameNet database. *International Journal of Lexicography 16*, 281–296.

Baldwin, T., C. Bannard, T. Tanaka, and D. Widdows (2003). An empirical model of multiword expression decomposability. In *Proceedings of the ACL-2003 Workshop on Multiword Expressions: Analysis, Acquisition and Treatment*, pp. 89–96. Sapporo, Japan.

Baltes, P. B. and U. Kunzmann (2003). Wisdom. *The Psychologist 16*, 131–132.

Bangerter, A. and C. Heath (2004). The Mozart effect: Tracking the evolution of a scientific legend. *British Journal of Social Psychology 43*, 605–623.

Bar, M. (2004). Visual objects in context. *Nature Reviews Neuroscience 5*, 617–629.

Bargh, J. (Ed.) (2007). *Social psychology and the unconscious: the automaticity of higher mental processes*. New York: Psychology Press.

Barlow, H. B. (1959). Sensory mechanisms, the reduction of redundancy, and intelligence. In *The mechanisation of thought processes*, pp. 535–539. London: H.M.S.O.

Barlow, H. B. (1972). Single units and sensation: a neuron doctrine for perceptual psychology. *Perception 1*, 371–394.

Barlow, H. B. (1990). Conditions for versatile learning, Helmholtz's unconscious inference, and the task of perception. *Vision Research 30*, 1561–1571.

Barlow, H. B. (1994). What is the computational goal of the neocortex? In C. Koch and J. L. Davis (Eds.), *Large-scale neuronal theories of the brain*, Chapter 1, pp. 1–22. Cambridge, MA: MIT Press.

Barrett, H. C. (2005). Enzymatic computation and cognitive modularity. *Mind and Language 20*, 259–287.

Barrett, J. L. (2000). Exploring the natural foundations of religion. *Trends in Cognitive Sciences 4*, 29–34.

Barsalou, L. (2005). Continuity of the conceptual system across species. *Trends in Cognitive Sciences 9*, 309–311.

Barsalou, L. W. (1983). Ad-hoc categories. *Memory and Cognition 11*, 211–227.

Barsalou, L. W. (1987). The instability of graded structure: implications for the nature of concepts. In U. Neisser (Ed.), *Concepts and conceptual development*, pp. 101–140. Cambridge Univ. Press.

Barsalou, L. W. (1999). Perceptual symbol systems. *Behavioral and Brain Sciences 22*, 577–660.

Barsalou, L. W. (2003a). Abstraction in perceptual symbol systems. *Proceedings of the Royal Society of London B 358*, 1177–1187.

Barsalou, L. W. (2003b). Situated simulation in the human conceptual system. *Language and Cognitive Processes 18*, 513–562.

Bartlett, F. C. (1932). *Remembering: An Experimental and Social Study*. Cambridge: Cambridge University Press.

Bates, E. and J. C. Goodman (1999). On the emergence of grammar from the lexicon. In B. MacWhinney (Ed.), *Emergence of Language*, pp. 29–79. Hillsdale, NJ: Lawrence Earlbaum Associates.

Bates, E., D. Thal, B. L. Finlay, and B. Clancy (1999). Early language development and its neural correlates. In I. Rapin and S. Segalowitz (Eds.), *Handbook of neuropsychology* (2 ed.), Volume 7. Amsterdam: Elsevier.

Baum, E. B. (2004). *What is thought?* Cambridge, MA: MIT Press.

Becker, J. D. (1975). The phrasal lexicon. In R. Shank and B. L. Nash-Webber (Eds.), *Theoretical Issues in Natural Language Processing*, Cambridge, MA, pp. 60–63. Bolt, Beranek and Newman.

Beer, R. D. (2000). Dynamical approaches to cognitive science. *Trends in Cognitive Sciences 4*, 91–99.

Beer, S. (1999). Let use now praise famous men – and women too (from Warren McCulloch to Candace Pert). *Systemic Practice and Action Research 12*, 433–456.

Bellman, R. E. (1961). *Adaptive Control Processes*. Princeton, NJ: Princeton University Press.

Berant, J., Y. Gross, M. Mussel, B. Sandbank, E. Ruppin, and S. Edelman (2007). Boosting unsupervised grammar induction by splitting complex sentences on function words. In *Proc. 31st annual Boston University Conference on Language Development*, Somerville, MA. Cascadilla Press.

Bergen, B. K. (2001). Nativization processes in L1 Esperanto. *Journal of Child Language 28*, 575–595.

Bertero, M., T. Poggio, and V. Torre (1988). Ill-posed problems in early vision. *Proceedings of the IEEE 76*, 869–889.

Best, P. J., A. M. White, and A. Minai (2001). Spatial processing in the brain: the activity of hippocampal place cells. *Annual Review of Neuroscience 24*, 459–486.

Biederman, I. (1987a). Matching image edges to object memory. In *Proceedings of the IEEE First International Conference on Computer Vision*, Washington, DC, pp. 384–392. The Computer Society of the IEEE.

Biederman, I. (1987b). Recognition by components: a theory of human image understanding. *Psychol. Review 94*, 115–147.

Biederman, I., R. J. Mezzanotte, and J. C. Rabinowitz (1982). Scene perception: Detecting and judging objects undergoing relational violations. *Cognitive Psychology 14*, 143–177.

Bien, H., W. J. Levelt, and R. H. Baayen (2005). Frequency effects in compound production. *Proceedings of the National Academy of Science 102*, 17876–17881.

Billard, A., Y. Epars, S. Calinon, G. Cheng, and S. Schaal (2004). Discovering optimal imitation strategies. *Robotics and Autonomous Systems 47*, 68–77.

Blackmore, S. (2001). Evolution and memes: The human brain as a selective imitation device. *Cybernetics and Systems 32*, 225–255.

Blaisdell, A. P., K. Sawa, K. J. Leising, and M. R. Waldmann (2006). Causal reasoning in rats. *Science 311*, 1020–1022.

Blanke, O., S. Ortigue, T. Landis, and M. Seeck (2002). Stimulating illusory own-body perceptions. *Nature 419*, 269.

Block, N. (2005). Two neural correlates of consciousness. *Trends in Cognitive Sciences 9*, 46–52.

Bloom, L. (1970). *Language development: form and function in emerging grammars*. Cambridge, MA: MIT Press.

Bloom, P. (2004). *Descartes' Baby: How the Science of Child Development Explains What Makes Us Human*. New York: Basic Books.

Blumenberg, H. (1997). *Shipwreck with Spectator: Paradigm of a Metaphor for Existence*. Cambridge, MA: MIT Press.

Bonnar, L., F. Gosselin, and P. G. Schyns (2002). Understanding Dali's Slave market with the disappearing bust of Voltaire: a case study in the scale information driving perception. *Perception 31*, 683–691.

Booth, A. E. and S. R. Waxman (2002). Word learning is 'smart': evidence that conceptual information affects preschoolers' extension of novel words. *Cognition 84*, B11–B22.

Borenstein, E. and E. Ruppin (2005). The evolution of imitation and mirror neurons in adaptive agents. *Cognitive Systems Research 6*, 229–242.

Borg, I. and J. Lingoes (1987). *Multidimensional Similarity Structure Analysis*. Berlin: Springer.

Borges, J. L. (1962). *Ficciones*. New York: Grove Press. Translated by A. Bonner in collaboration with the author.

Borges, J. L. (1970). *The Aleph and Other Stories, 1933-1969*. New York: E. P. Dutton. Translated by Norman Thomas di Giovanni in collaboration with the author.

Borges, J. L. (1984). The Analytical Language of John Wilkins. In *Other Inquisitions, 1937-1952*. New York: University of Texas Press. Translated by Ruth L. C. Simms.

Borges, J. L. (1999). Shakespeare's Memory. In *Collected Fictions, 1983*. New York: Penguin. Translated by Andrew Hurley.

Borges, J. L. and A. B. Casares (1990). *Extraordinary Tales*. London: W. H. Allen & Co.

Bowles, S. (2006). Group competition, reproductive leveling, and the evolution of human altruism. *Science 314*, 1569–1572.

Boyer, P. (2003). Religious thought and behaviour as by-products of brain function. *Trends in Cognitive Sciences 7*, 119–124.

Braitenberg, V. (1977). *On the texture of brains*. New York: Springer-Verlag.

Braitenberg, V. (1984). *Vehicles: Experiments in Synthetic Psychology*. Cambridge, MA: MIT Press.

Brentano, F. (1874). *Psychology from an Empirical Standpoint*. London: Routledge. translated by A. C. Rancurello, D. B. Terrell, and L. McAlister (1973).

Bressler, S. L. and J. A. S. Kelso (2001). Cortical coordination dynamics and cognition. *Trends in Cognitive Sciences 5*, 26–36.

Breure, L., O. Boonstra, and P. K. Doorn (2004). Past, present and future of historical information science. *Historical Social Research 29*, 4–132.

Brooks, R. A. (June 1987). Intelligence without representation. In *Proc. of Foundations of AI Workshop*, MIT.

Brown, W. M., L. Cronk, K. Grochow, A. Jacobson, C. K. Liu, Z. Popović, and R. Trivers (2005). Dance reveals symmetry especially in young men. *Nature 438*, 1148–1150.

Buckner, R. L. and D. C. Carroll (2007). Self-projection and the brain. *Trends in Cognitive Sciences 11*, 49–57.

Bülthoff, H. H., S. Edelman, and M. J. Tarr (1995). How are three-dimensional objects represented in the brain? *Cerebral Cortex 5*, 247–260.

Bülthoff, I. and F. N. Newell (2004). Categorical perception of sex occurs in familiar but not unfamiliar faces. *Visual Cognition 11*, 823–855.

Burgess, N. (2002). The hippocampus, space, and viewpoints in episodic memory. *Quarterly Journal of Experimental Psychology 55A*, 1057–1080.

Burgess, N. and G. Hitch (2005). Computational models of working memory: putting long-term memory into context. *Trends in Cognitive Sciences 9*, 535–541.

Buss, D. M., M. G. Haselton, T. K. Shackelford, A. L. Bleske, and J. C. Wakefield (1998). Adaptations, exaptations, and spandrels. *American Psychologist 53*, 533–548.

Bybee, J. and P. Hopper (2001). Introduction. In J. Bybee and P. Hopper (Eds.), *Frequency and the emergence of linguistic structure*, pp. 1–24. Amsterdam: John Benjamins.

Byrne, R. M. J. (2002). Mental models and counterfactual thoughts about what might have been. *Trends in Cognitive Sciences 6*, 426–431.

Camille, N., G. Coricelli, J. Sallet, P. Pradat-Diehl, J.-R. Duhamel, and A. Sirigu (2004). The involvement of the orbitofrontal cortex in the experience of regret. *Science 304*, 1167–1170.

Campbell, J. W. (1959, September). What do you mean…human? *Astounding Science Fiction*. Editorial.

Campitelli, G. and F. Gobet (2004). Adaptive expert decision making: Skilled chessplayers search more and deeper. *Journal of the International Computer Games Association 27*, 209–216.

Carew, T. J. (2001). *Behavioral Neurobiology: The Cellular Organization of Natural Behavior*. London: Palgrave MacMillan.

Carlyon, R. P. (2004). How the brain separates sounds. *Trends in Cognitive Sciences 8*, 465–471.

Carpenter, P. A., M. Just, and P. Shell (1990). What one intelligence test measures: a theoretical account of the processing in the Raven progressive matrices test. *Psychological Review 97*, 404–431.

Carstensen, L. L. (2006). The influence of a sense of time on human development. *Science 312*, 1913–1915.

Casebeer, W. D. (2003). Moral cognition and its neural constituents. *Nature Reviews Neurosciences 4*, 841–846.

Cavanagh, P. and G. A. Alvarez (2005). Tracking multiple targets with multifocal attention. *Trends in Cognitive Sciences 9*, 349–354.

Cavanaugh, J. and R. H. Wurtz (2004). Subcortical modulation of attention counters change blindness. *Journal of Neuroscience 24*, 11236–11243.

Chabris, C. F. (2006). Cognitive and neurobiological mechanisms of the law of general intelligence. In M. J. Roberts (Ed.), *Integrating the mind*. Hove, UK: Psychology Press.

Chalmers, D. J. (1994). A computational foundation for the study of cognition. Available online at http://jamaica.u.arizona.edu/~chalmers/papers/computation.html.

Chalmers, D. J. (1995). Facing up to the problem of consciousness. *Journal of Consciousness Studies 2*, 200–219.

Chase, V. M., R. Hertwig, and G. Gigerenzer (1998). Visions of rationality. *Trends in Cognitive Sciences 2*, 206–214.

Chater, N., J. B. Tenenbaum, and A. Yuille (2006). Probabilistic models of cognition: Conceptual foundations. *Trends in Cognitive Sciences 10*, 287–291.

Chater, N. and P. Vitányi (2003). The generalized universal law of generalization. *Journal of Mathematical Psychology 47*, 346–369.

Chater, N. and P. Vitányi (2003). Simplicity: a unifying principle in cognitive science? *Trends in Cognitive Sciences 7*, 19–22.

Chazelle, B. (2006). Mathematics: Proof at a roll of the dice. *Nature 444*, 1018–1019.

Chen, H.-H., G.-W. Bian, and W.-C. Lin (1999). Resolving translation ambiguity and target polysemy in cross-language information retrieval. In *Proceedings of the 37th Annual Meeting of the ACL*, University of Maryland, pp. 215–222.

Chomsky, N. (1961). Syntax and semantics. In S. Saporta (Ed.), *Psycholinguistics: a book of readings*, pp. 261–269. New York: Holt, Rinehart and Winston.

Chomsky, N. (1981). *Lectures on Government and Binding*. Dordrecht: Foris.

Chomsky, N. (2004a). *The Generative Enterprise Revisited*. Berlin: Mouton de Gruyter. Discussions with Riny Huybregts, Henk van Riemsdijk, Naoki Fukui and Mihoko Zushi.

Chomsky, N. (2004b). Language and mind: current thoughts on ancient problems. In L. Jenkins (Ed.), *Variation and universals in biolinguistics*, Volume 62 of *North-Holland linguistic series: Linguistic variations*, Chapter 15, pp. 379–405. Amsterdam: Elsevier.

Christianson, K. and F. Ferreira (2005). Conceptual accessibility and sentence production in a free word order language (Odawa). *Cognition 98*, 105–135.

Chronicle, E. P., J. N. MacGregor, and T. C. Ormerod (2004). What makes an insight problem? the roles of heuristics, goal conception and solution recoding in knowledge-lean problems. *Journal of Experimental Psychology: Learning, Memory & Cognition 30*, 14–27.

Chua, H. F., J. E. Boland, and R. E. Nisbett (2005). Cultural variation in eye movements during scene perception. *Proceedings of the National Academy of Science 102*, 12629–12633.

Chun, M. M. and J. M. Wolfe (2001). Visual attention. In E. B. Goldstein (Ed.), *Handbook of Perception*, pp. 272–310. London: Blackwell.

Churchland, P. M. (1985). Reduction, qualia, and the direct introspection of brain states. *The Journal of Philosophy 82*, 8–28.

Churchland, P. M. (1986). Some reductive strategies in cognitive neurobiology. *Mind New Series, 95*, 279–309.

Churchland, P. M. (1989). *A neurocomputational perspective*. Cambridge, MA: MIT Press.

Churchland, P. M. (1998). Towards a cognitive neurobiology of the moral virtues. *Topoi 17*, 83–96.

Churchland, P. S. (1987). *Neurophilosophy*. Cambridge, MA: MIT Press.

Cisek, P. and J. F. Kalaska (2004). Neural correlates of mental rehearsal in dorsal premotor cortex. *Nature 431*, 993–997.

Clark, A. (1993). *Sensory qualities*. Oxford: Clarendon Press.

Clark, A. (1998). Magic words: How language augments human computation. In P. Carruthers and J. Boucher (Eds.), *Language and thought: Interdisciplinary themes*, pp. 162–183. Cambridge: Cambridge University Press.

Clark, A. (2000). *A theory of sentience*. Oxford: Oxford University Press.

Clark, A. (2001). *Unsupervised Language Acquisition: Theory and Practice*. Ph. D. thesis, School of Cognitive and Computing Sciences, University of Sussex.

Clayton, N. S., T. J. Bussey, and A. Dickinson (2003). Can animals recall the past and plan for the future? *Nature Reviews Neuroscience 4*, 685–691.

Cleary, T. (1994). *Zen antics: 100 stories of enlightenment*. Boston, MA: Shambhala.

Cohen, F. (1987). A cryptographic checksum for integrity protection. *Computers and Security 6*, 505–510.

Cohen, J. (1964). Dependency of the spectral reflectance curves of the Munsell color chips. *Psychonomic Sciences 1*, 369–370.

Cohen, M. R. and W. T. Newsome (2004). What electrical microstimulation has revealed about the neural basis of cognition. *Current Opinion in Neurobiology 14*, 169–177.

Colby, C. L. (1998). Action-oriented spatial reference frames in cortex. *Neuron 20*, 15–24.

Conant, R. C. and W. R. Ashby (1970). Every good regulator of a system must be a model of that system. *Intl. J. Systems Science 1*, 89–97.

Connor, C. E., D. C. Preddie, J. L. Gallant, and D. C. Van Essen (1997). Spatial attention effects in macaque area V4. *J. of Neuroscience 17*, 3201–3214.

Conradt, L. and T. J. Roper (2003). Group decision-making in animals. *Nature 421*, 155–158.

Conway, A. R., M. J. Kane, and R. W. Engle (2003). Working memory capacity and its relation to general intelligence. *Trends in Cognitive Sciences 7*, 547–552.

Cooper, L. N., N. Intrator, B. S. Blais, and H. Z. Shouval (2004). *Theory of Cortical Plasticity*. Singapore: World Scientific.

Coricelli, G., H. D. Critchley, M. Joffily, J. P. O'Doherty, A. Sirigu, and R. J. Dolan (2005). Regret and its avoidance: a neuroimaging study of choice behavior. *Nature Neuroscience 8*, 1255–1262.

Cosmides, L. and J. Tooby (1996). Are humans good intuitive statisticians after all? Rethinking some conclusions of the literature on judgment under uncertainty. *Cognition 58*, 1–73.

Cosmides, L. and J. Tooby (1997). Evolutionary psychology: A primer. Available online at http://www.psych.ucsb.edu/research/cep/primer.html.

Craig, A. D. (2005). A new view of pain as a homeostatic emotion. *Trends in Neurosciences 26*, 303–307.

Craik, K. J. W. (1952). *The nature of explanation*. Cambridge, England: Cambridge University Press.

Crick, F. (1994). *The Astonishing Hypothesis: The Scientific Search for the Soul*. New York: Charles Scribner's Sons.

Crick, F. and C. Koch (1990). Towards a neurobiological theory of consciousness. *Seminars in the Neurosciences 2*, 263–275.

Crick, F. and C. Koch (1998). Consciousness and neuroscience. *Cerebral Cortex 8*, 97–107.

Croft, W. (2001). *Radical Construction Grammar: syntactic theory in typological perspective*. Oxford: Oxford University Press.

Croft, W. and D. A. Cruse (2004). *Cognitive Linguistics*. Cambridge: Cambridge University Press.

Culicover, P. W. (1999). *Syntactic nuts: hard cases, syntactic theory, and language acquisition*. Oxford: Oxford University Press.

Culicover, P. W. and R. Jackendoff (2005). *Simpler Syntax*. Oxford: Oxford University Press.

Cummins, R. (1989). *Meaning and mental representation*. Cambridge, MA: MIT Press.

Cutzu, F. and S. Edelman (1996). Faithful representation of similarities among three-dimensional shapes in human vision. *Proceedings of the National Academy of Science 93*, 12046–12050.

Cutzu, F. and S. Edelman (1998). Representation of object similarity in human vision: psychophysics and a computational model. *Vision Research 38*, 2227–2257.

da F. Costa, L. and O. Sporns (2006). Hierarchical features of large-scale cortical connectivity. *Eur. Phys. J. B 48*, 567–573.

Dabrowska, E. (2004). *Language, mind, and brain: some psychological and neurological constraints on theories of grammar*. Georgetown University Press.

Dabrowska, E. and J. Street (2006). Individual differences in language attainment: Comprehension of passive sentences by native and non-native English speakers. *Language Sciences 28*, 604–615.

Dahl, Ö. (2004). *The Growth and Maintenance of Linguistic Complexity*. Amsterdam: John Benjamins.

Dale, R. A. and M. J. Spivey (2006). Unraveling the dyad: Using recurrence analysis to explore patterns of syntactic coordination between children and caregivers in conversation. *Language Learning -, –*. In press.

Daneman, M. and P. A. Carpenter (1980). Individual differences in working memory and reading. *Journal of Verbal Learning and Verbal Behavior 19*, 450–466.

Dawkins, R. (1976). *The Selfish Gene*. Oxford: Oxford University Press.

Dawkins, R. (1998). Postmodernism disrobed. *Nature 394*, 141–143. Available online at http://www.physics.nyu.edu/faculty/sokal/dawkins.html.

Dawkins, R. (2006). *The God delusion*. Boston, MA: Houghton Mifflin.

Dawson, E., T. Gilovich, and D. T. Regan (2002). Motivated reasoning and performance on the Wason selection task. *Personality and Social Psychology Bulletin 28*, 1379–1387.

De Brabanter, P. (2001). Zellig Harris's theory of syntax and linguistic reflexivity. In *Belgian Essays on Language and Literature*, pp. 53–66.

de Unamuno, M. (1972). *The tragic sense of life in men and nations*. Princeton, NJ: Princeton University Press.

Deary, I. J. (2001a). Human intelligence differences: a recent history. *Trends in Cognitive Sciences 5*, 127–130.

Deary, I. J. (2001b). Human intelligence differences: towards a combined experimental-differential approach. *Trends in Cognitive Sciences 5*, 164–170.

Deary, I. J. and G. Der (2005). Reaction time explains IQ's association with death. *Psychological Science 16*, 64–69.

Decety, J. and P. L. Jackson (2004). The functional architecture of human empathy. *Behavioral and Cognitive Neuroscience Reviews 3*, 71–100.

Decety, J. and J. A. Sommerville (2003). Shared representations between self and other: a social cognitive neuroscience view. *Trends in Cognitive Sciences 7*, 527–533.

Dennett, D. C. (1984). *Elbow room: the varieties of free will worth wanting*. Cambridge, MA: MIT Press.

Dennett, D. C. (1987). *The intentional stance*. Cambridge, MA: MIT Press.

Dennett, D. C. (1991). *Consciousness explained*. Boston, MA: Little, Brown & Company.

Dennett, D. C. (1993). Learning and labeling. *Mind and Language 8*, 540–547.

Dennett, D. C. (1995). *Darwin's Dangerous Idea: Evolution and the Meanings of Life*. New York: Simon & Schuster.

Dennett, D. C. (2003). *Freedom evolves*. New York: Viking.

Dennett, D. C. (2006). *Breaking the Spell: Religion as a Natural Phenomenon*. New York: Viking.

Descartes, R. (1641). *Meditations on first philosophy*. New York: The Liberal Arts Press. This edition published in 1960.

DeSchepper, B. and A. Treisman (1996). Visual memory for novel shapes: Implicit coding without attention. *Journal of Experimental Psychology: Learning, Memory and Cognition 22*, 27–47.

Deutsch, D. (1997). *The fabric of reality*. Allen Lane.

Dewey, J. (1903). Logical conditions of a scientific treatment of morality. *Decennial Publications of the University of Chicago, First Series 3*, 115–139.

Dewey, J. (1916). *Democracy and education*. New York: Macmillan.

Dick, P. K. (1968). *Do Androids Dream of Electric Sheep?* San Francisco: Del Rey Books.

Diessel, H. (2004). *The Acquisition of Complex Sentences*, Volume 105 of *Cambridge Studies in Linguistics*. Cambridge: Cambridge University Press.

Dijksterhuis, A. and J. A. Bargh (2001). The perception-behavior expressway: automatic effects of social perception on social behavior. In M. P. Zanna (Ed.), *Advances in Experimental Social Psychology*, Volume 33, pp. 1–40. New York: Academic Press.

Dobzhansky, T. (1973). Nothing in biology makes sense except in the light of evolution. *The American Biology Teacher 35*, 125–129.

Dolezal, H. (1982). *Living in a world transformed: perceptual and performatory adaptation to visual distortion*. New York: Academic Press.

Dominey, P. F. (2005). From sensorimotor sequence to grammatical construction: Evidence from simulation and neurophysiology. *Adaptive Behavior 13*, 347–361.

Doubell, T. P., T. Skaliora, J. Baron, and A. J. King (2003). Functional connectivity between the superficial and deeper layers of the superior colliculus: an anatomical substrate for sensorimotor integration. *Journal of Neuroscience 23*, 6596–6607.

Draaisma, D. (2000). *Metaphors of memory*. Cambridge: Cambridge University Press.

Du Bois, J. W. (2001). Towards a dialogic syntax. Unpublished manuscript.

Duncan, J., R. J. Seitz, J. Kolodny, D. Bor, H. Herzog, A. Ahmed, F. N. Newell, and H. Emslie (2000). A neural basis for general intelligence. *Science 287*, 457–460.

Dunning, D. and G. L. Cohen (1992). Egocentric definitions of traits and abilities in social judgment. *Journal of Personality and Social Psychology 63*, 341–355.

Duvdevani-Bar, S. and S. Edelman (1999). Visual recognition and categorization on the basis of similarities to multiple class prototypes. *Intl. J. Computer Vision 33*, 201–228.

Eco, U. (1979). *The role of the reader: Explorations in the semiotics of texts*. Bloomington, IN: University of Indiana Press.

Eco, U. (1986). Casablanca: cult movies and intertextual collage. In *Travels in hyperreality*, pp. 197–211. New York: Harcourt Brace Jovanovich.

Eco, U. and T. A. Sebeok (1988). *The Sign of Three: Dupin, Holmes, Peirce*. Indiana University Press.

Edelman, S. (1987). Line connectivity algorithms for an asynchronous pyramid computer. *Computer Vision, Graphics, and Image Processing 40*, 169–187.

Edelman, S. (1995). Receptive fields for vision: from hyperacuity to object recognition. Unpublished manuscript, available online at http://kybele.psych.cornell.edu/~edelman/Watt/watt-rfs/watt-rfs.html.

Edelman, S. (1998a). Representation is representation of similarity. *Behavioral and Brain Sciences 21*, 449–498.

Edelman, S. (1998b). Spanning the face space. *Journal of Biological Systems 6*, 265–280.

Edelman, S. (1999). *Representation and recognition in vision*. Cambridge, MA: MIT Press.

Edelman, S. (2000). Brahe, looking for Kepler: review of *Neural Organization* (M. A. Arbib, P. Érdi and J. Szentágothai, MIT Press, 1998). *Behavioral and Brain Sciences 23*, 538–540.

Edelman, S. (2002). Constraining the neural representation of the visual world. *Trends in Cognitive Sciences 6*, 125–131.

Edelman, S. (2003). But will it scale up? Not without representations. *Adaptive Behavior 11*, 273–275. A commentary on *The dynamics of active categorical perception in an evolved model agent* by R. Beer.

Edelman, S. (2006). Mostly harmless: review of *Action in Perception* by Alva Noë. *Artificial Life 12*, 183–186.

Edelman, S. (2007). Bridging language with the rest of cognition: computational, algorithmic and neurobiological issues and methods. In M. Gonzalez-Marquez, I. Mittelberg, S. Coulson, and M. J. Spivey (Eds.), *Proc. of the Ithaca workshop on Empirical Methods in Cognitive Linguistics*, pp. 424–445. John Benjamins.

Edelman, S. (2008). *Computing the mind: how the mind really works*. New York: Oxford University Press.

Edelman, S. and T. Flash (1987). A model of handwriting. *Biological Cybernetics 57*, 25–36.

Edelman, S., K. Grill-Spector, T. Kushnir, and R. Malach (1998). Towards direct visualization of the internal shape representation space by fMRI. *Psychobiology 26*, 309–321.

Edelman, S. and N. Intrator (2000). (Coarse Coding of Shape Fragments) + (Retinotopy) ≈ Representation of Structure. *Spatial Vision 13*, 255–264.

Edelman, S. and N. Intrator (2002). Models of perceptual learning. In M. Fahle and T. Poggio (Eds.), *Perceptual learning*. MIT Press.

Edelman, S. and N. Intrator (2003). Towards structural systematicity in distributed, statically bound visual representations. *Cognitive Science 27*, 73–109.

Edelman, S., N. Intrator, and J. S. Jacobson (2002). Unsupervised learning of visual structure. In H. H. Bülthoff, C. Wallraven, S.-W. Lee, and T. Poggio (Eds.), *Proc. 2nd Intl. Workshop on Biologically Motivated Computer Vision*, Volume 2525 of *Lecture Notes in Computer Science*, pp. 629–643. Springer.

Edelman, S., S. Ullman, and T. Flash (1990). Reading cursive handwriting by alignment of letter prototypes. *Intl. J. Computer Vision 5*, 303–331.

Edelman, S. and H. R. Waterfall (2007). Behavioral and computational aspects of language and its acquisition. *Physics of Life Reviews 4*, 253–277.

Edelman, S. and D. Weinshall (1998). Computational approaches to shape constancy. In V. Walsh and J. Kulikowski (Eds.), *Perceptual constancy: why things look as they do*, Chapter 4, pp. 124–143. Cambridge, UK: Cambridge University Press.

Egan, G. (1994). *Permutation City*. London: Orion.

Egan, G. (1997). *Orphanogenesis*. New York: HarperCollins. Excerpt from *Diaspora*. Available online at the author's website.

Egan, G. (1998). *Distress*. New York: HarperPrism.

Egan, G. (1999). Transition dreams. In *Luminous*. London: Orion/Millennium.

Ehrsson, H. H. (2007). The experimental induction of out-of-body experiences. *Science 317*, 1048.

Ehrsson, H. H., C. Spence, and R. E. Passingham (2004). That's my hand! Activity in premotor cortex reflects feeling of ownership of a limb. *Science 305*, 875–877.

Eichenbaum, H. (2000). Hippocampus: Mapping or memory? *Current Biology 10*, 785–787.

Eichenbaum, H., P. Dudchenko, E. Wood, M. Shapiro, and H. Tanila (1999). The hippocampus, memory and place cells: is it spatial memory or memory space? *Neuron 23*, 209–226.

Elio, R. (2002). Issues in common sense reasoning and rationality. In R. Elio (Ed.), *Common sense, reasoning and rationality*, pp. 3–36. New York: Oxford University Press.

Epley, N. and T. Gilovich (2005a). The anchoring-and-adjustment heuristic. *Psychological Science 17*, 311–319.

Epley, N. and T. Gilovich (2005b). When effortful thinking influences judgmental anchoring: differential effects of forewarning and incentives on self-generated and externally provided anchors. *Journal of Behavioral Decision Making 18*, 199–212.

Erman, B. and B. Warren (2000). The idiom principle and the open-choice principle. *Text 20*, 29–62.

Estes, W. K. (1957). Of models and men. *American Psychologist 12*, 609–617.

Evans, J. S. B. T. (2005). Deductive reasoning. In K. J. Holyoak and R. G. Morrison (Eds.), *The Cambridge handbook of thinking and reasoning*, pp. 169–184. New York: Cambridge University Press.

Evans, V. (2006). The evolution of semantics. In *Encyclopaedia of Language and Linguistics*. Elsevier. 2nd edition.

Evans, V. and A. Tyler (2004). Spatial experience, lexical structure and motivation: The case of *In*. In G. Radden and K. Panther (Eds.), *Studies in Linguistic Motivation*, pp. 157–192. Berlin: Mouton de Gruyter.

Ferreira, F. and K. G. D. Bailey (2004). Disfluencies and human language comprehension. *Trends in Cognitive Sciences 8*, 231–237.

Ferreira, F., K. G. D. Bailey, and V. Ferraro (2002). Good-enough representations in language comprehension. *Current Directions in Psychological Science 11*, 11–15.

Fillmore, C. J. (1985). Syntactic intrusion and the notion of grammatical construction. *Berkeley Linguistic Society 11*, 73–86.

Finch, S. and N. Chater (1991). A hybrid approach to the automatic learning of linguistic categories. *Artif. Intell. and Simul. Behav. Qtrly. 78*, 16–24.

Fitch, W. T., M. D. Hauser, and N. Chomsky (2005). The evolution of the language faculty: Clarifications and implications. *Cognition 97*, 211–225.

Fitzgerald, E. (1983). *Rubaiyat of Omar Khayyam*. London: St. Martin's Press.

Fivush, R. and C. A. Haden (2003). *Autobiographical Memory and the Construction of a Narrative Self: Developmental and Cultural Perspectives*. Mahwah, NJ: Erlbaum.

Flash, T. (1987). The control of hand equilibrium trajectories in multi-joint arm movements. *Biological Cybernetics 57*, 257–274.

Floridi, L. and J. Sanders (2004). On the morality of artificial agents. *Minds and Machines 14*, 349–379.

Fodor, J. A. (1998). *Concepts: where cognitive science went wrong*. Oxford: Clarendon Press.

Fogassi, L., P. F. Ferrari, B. Gesierich, S. Rozzi, F. Chersi, and G. Rizzolatti (2005). Parietal lobe: from action organization to intention understanding. *Science 308*, 662–667.

Fogelin, R. (2003). *Walking the Tightrope of Reason: The Precarious Life of a Rational Animal*. Oxford: Oxford University Press.

Fortin, N. J., K. L. Agster, and H. B. Eichenbaum (2002). Critical role of the hippocampus in memory for sequences of events. *Nature Neuroscience 5*, 458–462.

Foster, D. H. (2003). Does colour constancy exist? *Trends in Cognitive Sciences 7*, 439–443.

French, R. M. (1999). Catastrophic forgetting in connectionist networks. *Trends in Cognitive Sciences 3*, 128–135.

French, R. M. (2000). The Turing Test: the first fifty years. *Trends in Cognitive Sciences 4*, 115–121.

French, R. M. (2002). The computational modeling of analogy-making. *Trends in Cognitive Sciences 6*, 200–205.

Frith, C., R. Perry, and E. Lumer (1999). The neural correlates of conscious experience: an experimental framework. *Trends in Cognitive Sciences 3*, 105–114.

Gallagher, S. (2000). Philosophical conceptions of the self: implications for cognitive science. *Trends in Cognitive Sciences 4*, 14–21.

Gallant, J. L., R. E. Shoup, and J. A. Mazer (2000). A human extrastriate area functionally homologous to Macaque V4. *Neuron 27*, 227–235.

Gallese, V. (2005). Embodied simulation: from neurons to phenomenal experience. *Phenomenology and the Cognitive Sciences 4*, 23–48.

Gallese, V. and A. Goldman (1998). Mirror neurons and the simulation theory of mind-reading. *Trends in Cognitive Sciences 12*, 493–501.

Gallese, V., C. Keysers, and G. Rizzolatti (2004). A unifying view of the basis of social cognition. *Trends in Cognitive Sciences 8*, 396–403.

Gallian, J. A. (2004). The first sixty-eight years of the Putnam Competition. *American Mathematical Monthly 111*, 691–699.

Gandolfo, F., F. A. Mussa-Ivaldi, and E. Bizzi (1996). Motor learning by field approximation. *Proceedings of the National Academy of Science 93*, 3843–3846.

Garey, M. R. and D. S. Johnson (1979). *Computers and intractability: a guide to the theory of NP-completeness*. San Francisco, CA: W. H. Freeman.

Garrod, S. and M. J. Pickering (2004). Why is conversation so easy? *Trends in Cognitive Sciences 8*, 8–11.

Gell-Mann, M. and S. Lloyd (1996). Information measures, effective complexity and total information. *Complexity 2*, 44–52.

Gelman, R. and C. R. Gallistel (2004). Language and the origin of numerical concepts. *Science 306*, 441–443.

Geman, S., E. Bienenstock, and R. Doursat (1992). Neural networks and the bias/variance dilemma. *Neural Computation 4*, 1–58.

Gerken, L. (2006). Decisions, decisions: infant language learning when multiple generalizations are possible. *Cognition 98*, B67–B74.

Gerstner, W. and W. M. Kistler (2002). Mathematical formulations of hebbian learning. *Biological Cybernetics 87*, 404–415.

Gibbs, R. W. (1994). *The Poetics of mind: Figurative thought, language, and understanding*. Cambridge: Cambridge University Press.

Gibson, J. J. (1933). Adaptation, after-effect, and contrast in the perception of curved lines. *J. Exp. Psychol. 16*, 1–31.

Gibson, J. J. (1979). *The ecological approach to visual perception*. Boston, MA: Houghton Mifflin.

Gier, N. (2002). The virtues of Asian humanism. *Journal of Oriental Studies 12*, 14–28.

Gier, N. (2007). Hebrew and Buddhist selves: a constructive postmodern proposal. *Asian Philosophy 17*, 47–64.

Gier, N. and P. K. Kjellberg (2004). Buddhism and the freedom of the will. In J. K. Campbell, D. Shier, and M. O'Rourke (Eds.), *Freedom and Determinism: Topics in Contemporary Philosophy*, pp. 277–304. Cambridge, MA: MIT Press.

Giese, M. A., I. A. Thornton, and S. Edelman (2003). Metric category spaces of biological motion. *Journal of Vision 3*(9), 83.

Gigerenzer, G. and D. G. Goldstein (1996). Reasoning the fast and frugal way: models of bounded rationality. *Psychological Review 103*, 650–669.

Gil-White, F. J. (2005). Common misunderstandings of memes (and genes): The promise and the limits of the genetic analogy to cultural transmission processes. In S. Hurley and N. Chater (Eds.), *Perspectives on Imitation: From Mirror Neurons to Memes*. Cambridge, MA: MIT Press.

Gilbert, A. L., T. Regier, P. Kay, and R. B. Ivry (2006). Whorf hypothesis is supported in the right visual field but not the left. *Proceedings of the National Academy of Science 103*, 489–494.

Gilbert, D. T. and R. Buckner (Friday, January 19, 2007). Time travel in the brain. The Time Magazine.

Gilbert, D. T., M. D. Lieberman, C. K. Morewedge, and T. D. Wilson (2004). The peculiar longevity of things not so bad. *Psychological Science 15*, 14–19.

Gintis, H. (2003). The hitchhiker's guide to altruism: Gene-culture coevolution, and the internalization of norms. *Journal of Theoretical Biology 220*, 407–418.

Girkin, C. A. and N. R. Miller (2001). Central disorders of vision in humans. *Survey of ophthalmology 45*, 379–405.

Girosi, F., M. Jones, and T. Poggio (1995). Regularization theory and neural networks architectures. *Neural Computation 7*, 219–269.

Gleitman, L. and A. Papafragou (2005). Language and thought. In K. J. Holyoak and R. G. Morrison (Eds.), *The Cambridge handbook of thinking and reasoning*, pp. 633–661. New York: Cambridge University Press.

Gleitman, L. R., K. Cassidy, R. Nappa, A. Papafragou, and J. C. Trueswell (2005). Hard words. *Language learning and development 1*, 23–64.

Glenberg, A. M. (1997). What memory is for. *Behavioral and Brain Sciences 20*, 1–55.

Glimcher, P. W., M. C. Dorris, and H. M. Bayer (2005). Physiological utility theory and the neuroeconomics of choice. *Games and Economic Behavior 52*, 213–256.

Glimcher, P. W. and A. Rustichini (2004). Neuroeconomics: The consilience of brain and decision. *Science 306*, 447–452.

Glymour, C. (2001). Another way for nerds to make babies: the Frame Problem and causal inference in developmental psychology. In *The Mind's Arrows*, Chapter 3, pp. 19–46. MIT Press.

Glymour, C. (2004). We believe in freedom of the will so that we can learn. *Behavioral and Brain Sciences 27*, 661–662.

Gobet, F., P. C. R. Lane, S. Croker, P. C.-H. Cheng, G. Jones, I. Oliver, and J. M. Pine (2001). Chunking mechanisms in human learning. *Trends in Cognitive Sciences 5*, 236–243.

Gobet, F. and H. A. Simon (1998). Pattern recognition makes search possible: Comments on Holding (1992). *Psychological Research 61*, 204–208.

Gold, J. I. and M. N. Shadlen (2002). Banburismus and the brain: decoding the relationship between sensory stimuli, decisions, and reward. *Neuron 36*, 299–308.

Goldberg, A. E. (2003). Constructions: a new theoretical approach to language. *Trends in Cognitive Sciences 7*, 219–224.

Goldberg, A. E. (2005). *Constructions at work: the nature of generalization in language*. Oxford: Oxford University Press.

Goldsmith, J. (2001). Unsupervised learning of the morphology of a natural language. *Computational Linguistics 27*, 153–198.

Goldsmith, J. A. (2005). The legacy of Zellig Harris: Language and information into the 21st century. vol. 1: Philosophy of science, syntax and semantics, Bruce Nevin, ed. (review). *Language 81*, 719–736.

Goldstein, M. H., A. P. King, and M. J. West (2003). Social interaction shapes babbling: Testing parallels between birdsong and speech. *Proceedings of the National Academy of Science 100*, 8030–8035.

Goldstone, R. L. (1994). The role of similarity in categorization: providing a groundwork. *Cognition 52*, 125–157.

Goldstone, R. L. (2000). Unitization during category learning. *Journal of Experimental Psychology: Human Perception and Performance 26*, 86–112.

Goldstone, R. L. and L. W. Barsalou (1998). Reuniting perception and cognition: the perceptual bases of similarity and rules. *Cognition 65*, 231–262.

Golledge, R. G. (Ed.) (1999). *Wayfinding Behavior: Cognitive Mapping and Other Spatial Processes*. Baltimore MD: The Johns Hopkins University Press.

Good, I. J. (1965). Speculations concerning the first ultraintelligent machine. In F. L. Alt and M. Rubinoff (Eds.), *Advances in Computers*, Volume 6, pp. 31–88. Academic Press.

Goodman, J. T. (2001). A bit of progress in language modeling: Extended version. Technical Report MSR-TR-2001-72, Microsoft Research.

Gopnik, A., C. Glymour, D. M. Sobel, L. E. Schulz, T. Kushnir, and D. Danks (2004). A theory of causal learning in children: causal maps and Bayes nets. *Psychological Review 111*, 3–32.

Gopnik, A. and L. Schulz (2004). Mechanisms of theory formation in young children. *Trends in Cognitive Sciences 8*, 371–377.

Gordon, R. M. (2004). Folk psychology as mental simulation. In E. N. Zalta (Ed.), *The Stanford Encyclopedia of Philosophy*. Avaliable online at http://plato.stanford.edu/archives/fall2004/entries/folkpsych-simulation/.

Gottfredson, L. S. (2003). Practical intelligence. In R. Fernandez-Ballesteros (Ed.), *Encyclopedia of psychological assessment*, pp. 740–745. London: Sage.

Gottfredson, L. S. (2004). Life, death, and intelligence. *Journal of Cognitive Education and Psychology 1*, 23–46.

Gottfredson, L. S. (Winter 1998). The general intelligence factor. *Scientific American Presents 9*(4), 24–29, 51.

Gottfredson, L. S. and I. J. Deary (2004). Intelligence predicts health and longevity, but why? *Current Directions in Psychological Science 13*, 1–4.

Gottlieb, G. L., D. M. Corcos, S. Jaric, and G. C. Agarwal (1988). Practice improves even the simplest movements. *Exp. Brain. Research 73*, 436–440.

Gray, J. R., C. F. Chabris, and T. S. Braver (2003). Neural mechanisms of general fluid intelligence. *Nature Neuroscience 6*, 316–322.

Graziano, M. S. A., C. S. R. Taylor, T. Moore, and D. F. Cooke (2002). The cortical control of movement revisited. *Neuron 36*, 1–20.

Greene, J. and J. Haidt (2002). How (and where) does moral judgment work? *Trends in Cognitive Sciences 6*, 517–523.

Greene, J. D. (2003). From neural 'is' to moral 'ought': what are the moral implications of neuroscientific moral psychology? *Nature Reviews Neuroscience 4*, 847–850.

Greene, J. D. and J. D. Cohen (2004). For the law, neuroscience changes nothing and everything. *Philosophical Transactions of the Royal Society of London B 359*, 1775–1785.

Griffiths, T. L. and A. Yuille (2006). Technical introduction: A primer on probabilistic inference. *Trends in Cognitive*

Sciences 10, supplementary material. Available online at http://dx.doi.org/doi:10.1016/j.tics.2006.05.007.

Grill-Spector, K., R. Sayres, and D. Ress (2006). High-resolution imaging reveals highly selective nonface clusters in the fusiform face area. *Nature Neuroscience 9*, 1177–1185.

Grodner, D., E. Gibson, and D. Watson (2005). The influence of contextual contrast on syntactic processing: evidence for strong-interaction in sentence comprehension. *Cognition 95*, 275–296.

Groh, J. M. and U. Werner-Reiss (2002). Visual and auditory integration. In V. S. Ramachandran (Ed.), *Encyclopedia of the Human Brain*, pp. 739–752. San Diego, CA: Academic Press.

Grosbras, M.-H. and T. Paus (2003). Transcranial magnetic stimulation of the human frontal eye field facilitates visual awareness. *European Journal of Neuroscience 18*, 3121–3126.

Grosenick, L., T. S. Clement, and R. D. Fernald (2007). Fish can infer social rank by observation alone. *Nature 445*, 429–432.

Grünwald, P., I. J. Myung, and M. Pitt (Eds.) (2005). *Advances in Minimum Description Length: Theory and Applications*. MIT Press.

Gutfreund, Y., W. Zheng, and E. I. Knudsen (2002). Gated visual input to the central auditory system. *Science 207*, 1556–1559.

Guttman, N. (1963). Laws of behavior and facts of perception. In S. Koch (Ed.), *Psychology: a study of a science*, Volume 5, pp. 114–178. New York: McGraw-Hill.

Hafting, T., M. Fyhn, S. Molden, M.-B. Moser, and E. I. Moser (2005). Microstructure of a spatial map in the entorhinal cortex. *Nature 436*, 801–806.

Hale, J. (2004). The information-processing difficulty of incremental parsing. In F. Keller, S. Clark, M. Crocker, and M. Steedman (Eds.), *Proceedings of the ACL Workshop on Incremental Parsing: Bringing Engineering and Cognition Together*, pp. 58–65.

Hamilton, W. D. (1964). The genetical evolution of social behaviour I and II. *Journal of Theoretical Biology 7*, 1–16 and 17–52.

Hammitt, W. E. (1982). Cognitive dimensions of wilderness solitude. *Environment and Behavior 14*, 478–493.

Hammitt, W. E., K. F. Backman, and T. J. Davis (2001). Cognitive dimensions of wilderness privacy: an 18-year trend comparison. *Leisure Sciences 23*, 285–292.

Harnad, S. (Ed.) (1987). *Categorical Perception: The Groundwork of Cognition*. New York: Cambridge University Press.

Harnad, S. (1990). The symbol grounding problem. *Physica D 42*, 335–346.

Harris, C. L. (1998). Psycholinguistic studies of entrenchment. In J. Koenig (Ed.), *Conceptual Structures, Language and Discourse*, Volume 2. Berkeley, CA: CSLI.

Harris, C. L. and E. A. Bates (2002). Clausal backgrounding and pronominal reference: A functionalist approach to c-command. *Language and Cognitive Processes 17*, 237–270.

Harris, C. L., J. B. Gleason, and A. Aycicegi (2006). When is a first language more emotional? psychophysiological evidence from bilingual speakers. In A. Pavlenko (Ed.), *Bilingual minds: Emotional experience, expression, and representation*. United Kingdom: Clevedon.

Harris, Z. S. (1951). *Methods in structural linguistics*. Chicago, IL: University of Chicago Press.

Harris, Z. S. (1954). Distributional structure. *Word 10*, 140–162.

Harris, Z. S. (1968). *Mathematical Structures of Language*. New York: Wiley Interscience.

Harris, Z. S. (1991). *A theory of language and information*. Oxford: Clarendon Press.

Hartman, E. J., J. D. Keeler, and J. M. Kowalski (1990). Layered neural networks with Gaussian hidden units as universal approximations. *Neural Computation 2*, 210–215.

Hastie, T. (1984). Principal curves and surfaces. Technical Report 276, SLAC (Stanford Linear Accelerator Center). Available online at http://www.slac.stanford.edu/pubs/slacreports/slac-r-276.html.

Hauser, M., N. Chomsky, and T. Fitch (2002). The faculty of language: What is it, who has it, and how did it evolve? *Science 298*, 1569–1579.

Hay, J. B. and R. H. Baayen (2005). Shifting paradigms: gradient structure in morphology. *Trends in Cognitive Sciences 7*, 342–348.

Hayden, M. H. (2004). Yoko Ono: Remember Love. Galleri 5, Kulturhuset, Stockholm, 29 may – 8 august 2004. *Konsthistorisk Tidskrift 73*, 248–252.

Hebb, D. O. (1949). *The organization of behavior*. Wiley.

Heider, F. and M. Simmel (1944). An experimental study of apparent behavior. *American Journal of Psychology 57*, 243–249.

Heit, E. (2000). Properties of inductive reasoning. *Psychonomic Bulletin & Review 7*, 569–592.

Hemmi, J. M. and J. Zeil (2003). Robust judgment of inter-object distance by an arthropod. *Nature 421*, 160–163.

Hemphill, C. T., J. J. Godfrey, and G. R. Doddington (1990). The ATIS spoken language systems pilot corpus. In *Proceedings of a workshop on speech and natural language*, pp. 96–101. San Francisco, CA: Morgan Kaufmann.

Henrich, J. and F. J. Gil-White (2001). The evolution of prestige: Freely conferred status as a mechanism for enhancing the benefits of cultural transmission. *Evolution and Human Behavior 22*, 165–196.

Hertwig, R. and G. Gigerenzer (1999). The 'conjunction fallacy' revisited: how intelligent inferences look like reasoning errors. *Journal of Behavioral Decision Making 12*, 275–305.

Hesslow, G. (2002). Conscious thought as simulation of behaviour and perception. *Trends in Cognitive Sciences 6*, 242–247.

Heyes, C. M. (1998). Theory of mind in nonhuman primates. *Behavioral and Brain Sciences 21*, 101–134.

Heyes, C. M. (2005). Imitation by association. In S. Hurley and N. Chater (Eds.), *Perspectives on Imitation: From Mirror Neurons to Memes*. Cambridge, MA: MIT Press.

Hobson, J. A., E. Pace-Schott, and R. Stickgold (2000). Dreaming and the brain: toward a cognitive neuroscience of conscious states. *Behavioral and Brain Sciences 23*, 793–842.

Hoey, M. (2005). *Lexical priming: a new theory of words and language*. Abingdon, UK: Routledge.

Hofstadter, D. R. (1979). *Gödel, Escher, Bach: an Eternal Golden Braid*. New York: Basic Books.

Hofstadter, D. R. (1985a). Variations on a theme as the crux of creativity. In *Metamagical Themas*, Chapter 12, pp. 232–259. Harmondsworth, England: Viking.

Hofstadter, D. R. (1985b). Who shoves whom around in the careenium? In *Metamagical Themas*, pp. 604–630. Harmondsworth, England: Viking.

Hofstadter, D. R. (2001). Analogy as the core of cognition. In D. Gentner, K. J. Holyoak, and B. N. Kokinov (Eds.), *The Analogical Mind: Perspectives from Cognitive Science*, pp. 499–538. Cambridge MA: MIT Press.

Hofstadter, D. R. and M. Mitchell (1995). The Copycat project: a model of mental fluidity and analogy-making. Chapter 5, pp. 205–265. NY: Basic Books. in Fluid Concepts and Creative Analogies.

Holyoak, K. J. and R. G. Morrison (Eds.) (2005). *The Cambridge handbook of thinking and reasoning*. New York: Cambridge University Press.

Honey, C., R. Kötter, M. Breakspear, and O. Sporns (2007). Network structure of cerebral cortex shapes functional connectivity on multiple time scales. submitted.

Hong, L. and S. E. Page (2004). Groups of diverse problem solvers can outperform groups of high-ability problem solvers. *Proceedings of the National Academy of Science 101*, 16385–16389.

Hopcroft, J. E. and J. D. Ullman (1979). *Introduction to Automata Theory, Languages, and Computation*. Reading, MA: Addison-Wesley.

Hopfield, J. J. (1982). Neural networks and physical systems with emergent collective computational abilities. *Proceedings of the National Academy of Science 79*, 2554–2558.

Horn, B. K. P. (1974). Determining lightness from an image. *Computer Vision, Graphics, and Image Processing 3*, 277–299.

Horner, V., A. Whiten, E. Flynn, and F. B. M. de Waal (2006). Faithful replication of foraging techniques along cultural transmission chains by chimpanzees and children. *Proceedings of the National Academy of Science 103*, 13878–13883.

Hubel, D. H. and T. N. Wiesel (1959). Receptive fields of single neurons in the cat's striate cortex. *J. Physiol. 148*, 574–591.

Hume, D. (1740). *A Treatise of Human Nature*. Available online at http://www.gutenberg.org/etext/4705.

Hume, D. (1748). *An Enquiry Concerning Human Understanding*. Available online at http://eserver.org/18th/hume-enquiry.html.

Hume, D. (1779). *Dialogues Concerning Natural Religion*. Published posthumously. Available online at http://www.anselm.edu/homepage/dbanach/dnr.htm.

Hurford, J. R. (2003). The neural basis of predicate-argument structure. *Behavioral and Brain Sciences 26*, 261–316. Available online at http://www.isrl.uiuc.edu/~amag/langev/paper/hurford01theNeural.html.

Hutchins, E. (1995). *Cognition in the Wild*. Cambridge, MA: MIT Press.

Hutchins, E. (2000). Distributed cognition. In W. Kintsch (Ed.), *International Encyclopedia of the Social & Behavioral Sciences*, pp. 2068–2072. Elsevier.

Hyde, P. S. and E. I. Knudsen (2002). The optic tectum controls visually guided adaptive plasticity in the owl's auditory space map. *Nature 415*, 73–76.

Ikegaya, Y., G. Aaron, R. Cossart, D. Aronov, I. Lampl, D. Ferster, and R. Yuste (2004). Synfire chains and cortical songs: Temporal modules of cortical activity. *Science 304*, 559–564.

Imamizu, H., T. Kuroda, T. Yoshioka, and M. Kawato (2004). Functional magnetic resonance imaging examination of two modular architectures for switching multiple internal models. *Journal of Neuroscience 24*, 1173–1181.

Itti, L. and P. Baldi (2006). Bayesian surprise attracts human attention. In *Advances in Neural Information Processing Systems, Vol. 19 (NIPS*2005)*, Cambridge, MA, pp. 1–8. MIT Press.

Itti, L. and C. Koch (2001). Computational modeling of visual attention. *Nature Reviews Neuroscience 2*, 194–203.

Itti, L., C. Koch, and E. Niebur (1998). A model of saliency-based visual attention for rapid scene analysis. *IEEE Transactions on Pattern Analysis and Machine Intelligence 20*, 1254–1259.

Jackendoff, R. (1995). The boundaries of the lexicon. In M. Everaert, E.-J. v. Linden, A. Schenk, and R. Schreuder (Eds.), *Idioms: structural and psychological perspectives*, pp. 133–165. Hillsdale, NJ: Erlbaum.

Jackendoff, R. and S. Pinker (2005). The nature of the language faculty and its implications for evolution of language (reply to Fitch, Hauser, and Chomsky). *Cognition 97*, 211–225.

Jaffe, D. B. (2005). Action potential initiation in hippocampal neurons: computations, clocking, and cognitive function. *Cellscience Reviews 1*(3).

James, W. (1890). *The Principles of Psychology*. Available online at http://psychclassics.yorku.ca/James/Principles/.

Jaynes, J. (1976). *The origin of consciousness in the breakdown of the bicameral mind*. Boston, MA: Houghton Mifflin.

Ji, D. and M. A. Wilson (2007). Coordinated memory replay in the visual cortex and hippocampus during sleep. *Nature Neuroscience 10*, 100–107.

Jing, J. and K. R. Weiss (2005). Generation of variants of a motor act in a modular and hierarchical motor network. *Current Biology 15*, 1712–1721.

Joerges, J., A. Küttner, C. G. Galizia, and R. Menzel (1997). Representations of odors and odor mixtures visualized in the honeybee brain. *Nature 387*, 285–288.

Johnson, K. E. (2004). On the systematicity of language and thought. *Journal of Philosophy CI*, 111–139.

Johnson, N. F. (1965). The psychological reality of phrase-structure rules. *J. of Verbal Learning and Verbal Behavior 4*, 469–475.

Jones, B. C., A. C. Little, I. S. Penton-Voak, B. P. Tiddeman, D. M. Burt, and D. I. Perrett (2001). Facial symmetry and judgements of apparent health — support for a 'good genes' explanation of the attractiveness-symmetry relationship. *Evolution and Human Behaviour 22*, 417–429.

Jones, J. L. and A. M. Flynn (1993). *Mobile robots: inspiration to implementation*. Natick, MA: A. K. Peters.

Joris, P. X., P. H. Smith, and T. C. T. Yin (1998). Coincidence detection in the auditory system: 50 years after Jeffress. *Neuron 21*, 1235–1238.

Judd, D. B., D. L. MacAdam, and G. Wyszecki (1964). Spectral distribution of typical daylight as a function of correlated color temperature. *Journal of the Optical Society of America 54*, 1031–1040.

Jungman, N., A. Levi, A. Aperman, and S. Edelman (1994). Automatic classification of police mugshot album using principal component analysis. In S. K. Rogers and D. W. Ruck (Eds.), *Proc. SPIE-2243 Conference on Applications of Artificial Neural Networks*, Orlando, FL, pp. 591–594.

Juniper, A. (2003). *Wabi sabi: the Japanese Art of Impermanence*. Boston: Tuttle.

Kaan, E. and T. Y. Swaab (2002). The brain circuitry of syntactic comprehension. *Trends in Cognitive Sciences 6*, 350–356.

Kahneman, D. and S. Frederick (2005). A model of heuristic judgment. In K. J. Holyoak and R. G. Morrison (Eds.), *The Cambridge handbook of thinking and reasoning*, pp. 167–293. New York: Cambridge University Press.

Kahneman, D. and A. Tversky (1982). The simulation heuristic. In D. Kahneman (Ed.), *Judgment Under Uncertainty: Heuristics and Biases*, pp. 201–208. Cambridge: Cambridge University Press.

Kalansuriya, A. D. P. (1993). The Buddha and Wittgenstein: a brief philosophical exegesis. *Asian Philosophy 3*, 103–112.

Kaminski, J., J. Call, and J. Fischer (2004). Word learning in a domestic dog: Evidence for "fast mapping". *Science 304*, 1682–1683.

Kanazawa, S. and J. L. Kovar (2004). Why beautiful people are more intelligent. *Intelligence 32*, 227–243.

Kandel, E. R. (2003). The molecular biology of memory storage: A dialog between genes and synapses. In H. Jörnvall (Ed.), *Nobel Lectures, Physiology or Medicine, 1996-2000*. Singapore: World Scientific.

Kane, M. J. (2003). The intelligent brain in conflict. *Trends in Cognitive Sciences 7*, 375–377.

Karov, Y. and S. Edelman (1998). Similarity-based word sense disambiguation. *Computational Linguistics 24*, 41–59.

Kawato, M. (1999). Internal models for motor control and trajectory planning. *Current Opinion in Neurobiology 9*, 718–727.

Keenan, J. P., M. A. Wheeler, J. G. G. Gallup, and A. Pascual-Leone (2000). Self-recognition and the right prefrontal cortex. *Trends in Cognitive Sciences 4*, 338–344.

Keil, F. C. (1989). *Concepts, kinds and cognitive development*. Cambridge, MA: MIT Press.

Keil, F. C. (2003). Folkscience: coarse interpretations of a complex reality. *Trends in Cognitive Sciences 7*, 368–373.

Kemp, C., A. Bernstein, and J. B. Tenenbaum (2005). A generative theory of similarity. In *Proceedings of the Twenty-Seventh Annual Conference of the Cognitive Science Society*.

Kersten, D., P. Mamassian, and A. Yuille (2004). Object perception as Bayesian inference. *Annual Review of Psychology 55*, 271–304.

Keysers, C. and D. I. Perrett (2004). Demystifying social cognition: a Hebbian perspective. *Trends in Cognitive Sciences 8*, 501–507.

King, A. J. (2004). The superior colliculus. *Current Biology 14*, R335–R338. A primer.

Kirby, S. (2000). Syntax without natural selection: how compositionality emerges from vocabulary in a population of learners. In C. Knight, M. Studdert-Kennedy, and J. R. Hurford (Eds.), *The evolutionary emergence of language*, pp. 303–323. Cambridge: Cambridge University Press.

Knill, D. and W. Richards (Eds.) (1996). *Perception as Bayesian Inference*. Cambridge: Cambridge University Press.

Knudsen, E. I. and M. Brainard (1991). Visual instruction of the neural map of auditory space in the developing optic tectum. *Science 253*, 85–87.

Knuth, D. E. (1982). The concept of a meta-font. *Visible Language 16*, 3–27.

Knuth, D. E. (1986). *The METAFONTbook*, Volume C of *Computers and Typesetting*. Reading, MA: Addison-Wesley.

Kobatake, E. and K. Tanaka (1994). Neuronal selectivities to complex object features in the ventral visual pathway of the macaque cerebral cortex. *J. Neurophysiol. 71*, 856–867.

Kobatake, E., G. Wang, and K. Tanaka (1998). Effects of shape-discrimination training on the selectivity of inferotemporal cells in adult monkeys. *J. Neurophysiol. 80*, 324–330.

Koch, C. and K. Hepp (2006). Quantum mechanics in the brain. *Nature 440*, 611–612.

Koch, C. and N. Tsuchiya (2007). Attention and consciousness: two distinct brain processes. *Trends in Cognitive Sciences 11*, 16–22.

Köhler, W. (1947). *Gestalt psychology*. New York: Liveright.

Körding, K. P. and D. M. Wolpert (2006). Bayesian decision theory in sensorimotor control. *Trends in Cognitive Sciences 10*, 319–326.

Koriat, A. (1995). Dissociating knowing and the feeling of knowing: Further evidence for the accessibility model. *Journal of Experimental Psychology: General 124*, 311–333.

Koriat, A. and M. Goldsmith (1996a). Memory metaphors and the laboratory/real-life controversy: correspondence versus storehouse views of memory. *Behavior and Brain Sciences 19*, 167–188.

Koriat, A. and M. Goldsmith (1996b). Monitoring and control processes in the strategic regulation of memory accuracy. *Psychological Review 103*, 490–517.

Koriat, A., M. Goldsmith, and A. Pansky (2000). Toward a psychology of memory accuracy. *Annual Review of Psychology 51*, 483–539.

Kövecses, Z. (2000). The concept of anger: Universal or culture specific? *Psychopathology 33*, 159–170.

Krakauer, J. W. and R. Shadmehr (2006). Consolidation of motor memory. *Trends in Neurosciences 29*, 58–64.

Kreiman, G., I. Fried, and C. Koch (2002). Single-neuron correlates of subjective vision in the human medial temporal lobe. *Proc. Nat. Acad. Sci. 99*, 8378–8383.

Krueger, J. and R. W. Clement (1994). The truly false consensus effect: An ineradicable and egocentric bias in social perception. *Journal of Personality and Social Psychology 67*, 596–610.

Kuhl, P. K. (2000). A new view of language acquisition. *Proceedings of the National Academy of Science 97*, 11850–11857.

Kuhl, P. K. (2004). Early language acquisition: Cracking the speech code. *Nature Reviews Neuroscience 5*, 831–843.

Kuncel, N. R., S. A. Hezlett, and D. S. Ones (2004). Academic performance, career potential, creativity, and job performance: can one construct predict them all? *Journal of Personality and Social Psychology 86*, 148–161.

Kupers, R., A. Fumal, A. Maertens de Noordhout, A. Gjedde, J. Schoenen, and M. Ptito (2006). Transcranial magnetic stimulation of the visual cortex induces somatotopically organized qualia in blind subjects. *Proceedings of the National Academy of Science 103*, 13256–13260.

LaBerge, S. (1990). Lucid dreaming: psychophysiological studies of consciousness during REM sleep. In R. R. Bootzen, J. F. Kihlstrom, and D. L. Schacter (Eds.), *Sleep and Cognition*, pp. 109–126. Washington, DC: American Psychological Association.

Laforte, G., P. Hayes, and K. Ford (1998). Why Gödel's theorem cannot refute computationalism. *Artificial Intelligence 104*, 265–286.

Lakoff, G. (1970). *Irregularity in Syntax.* New York: Holt, Rinehart and Winston.

Lakoff, G. (1987). *Women, Fire and Dangerous Things: What Categories Reveal about the Mind.* Chicago, IL: University of Chicago Press.

Lakoff, G. and M. Johnson (1980). *Metaphors we live by.* Chicago, IL: University of Chicago Press.

Lamb, S. M. (2004). *Language and reality.* London: Continuum.

Lamme, V. A. F. (2003). Why visual attention and awareness are different. *Trends in Cognitive Sciences 7,* 12–18.

Lamme, V. A. F. (2006). Towards a true neural stance on consciousness. *Trends in Cognitive Sciences 10,* 494–501.

Lamme, V. A. F., K. Zipser, and H. Spekreijse (1998). Figure-ground activity in primary visual cortex is suppressed by anesthesia. *Proceedings of the National Academy of Science 95,* 3263–3268.

Lamotte, É. (1973). Trois sūtra du *saṃyukta* sur la vacuité. *Bulletin of the School of Oriental and African Studies 36,* 313–323.

Land, E. H. and J. J. McCann (1971). Lightness and retinex theory. *Journal of the Optical Society of America 61,* 1–11.

Landauer, T. K. and S. T. Dumais (1997). A solution to Plato's problem: the latent semantic analysis theory of acquisition, induction, and representation of knowledge. *Psychological Review 104,* 211–240.

Langacker, R. W. (1987). *Foundations of cognitive grammar,* Volume I: theoretical prerequisites. Stanford, CA: Stanford University Press.

Langacker, R. W. (1998). Conceptualization, symbolization, and grammar. In M. Tomasello (Ed.), *The new psychology of language,* pp. 1–39. Mahwah, NJ: Erlbaum.

Larson, R. W. (1997). The emergence of solitude as a constructive domain of experience in early adolescence. *Child Development 68,* 80–93.

Lashley, K. S. (1923). The behavioristic interpretation of consciousness. *Psychological Bulletin 30,* Part I, 237–272; Part II, 329–353.

Lashley, K. S. (1951). The problem of serial order in behavior. In L. A. Jeffress (Ed.), *Cerebral Mechanisms in Behavior,* pp. 112–146. New York: Wiley.

Lau, C. H. and R. E. Passingham (2006). Relative blindsight in normal observers and the neural correlate of visual consciousness. *Proceedings of the National Academy of Science 103,* 18763–18768.

Laureys, S. (2005). The neural correlate of (un)awareness: lessons from the vegetative state. *Trends in Cognitive Sciences 9,* 556–559.

Lavie, R. J. (2003). *The analogical speaker or grammar put in its place*. Ph. D. thesis, University of Paris 10.

Le Guin, U. K. (1985). *Always Coming Home*. New York: Harper and Row.

Lebedev, M. A. and M. A. Nicolelis (2006). Brain-machine interfaces: past, present and future. *Trends in Neurosciences 29*, 536–546.

Lee, D. (2006). Neural basis of quasi-rational decision making. *Current Opinion in Neurobiology 16*, 191–198.

Lehky, S. and T. Sejnowski (1999). Seeing white: qualia in the context of decoding population codes. *Neural Computation 11*, 1261–1280.

Lenggenhager, B., T. Tadi, T. Metzinger, and O. Blanke (2007). Video ergo sum: manipulating bodily self-consciousness. *Science 317*, 1096–1099.

Leopold, D. A. and N. K. Logothetis (1999). Multistable phenomena: changing views in perception. *Trends in Cognitive Sciences 3*, 254–264.

Lewis, M. D. (2005). Bridging emotion theory and neurobiology through dynamic systems modeling. *Behavioral and Brain Sciences 28*, 169–245.

Lieberman, P. (2005). The pied piper of Cambridge. *The Linguistic Review 22*, 289–301.

Lieven, E., M. Tomasello, H. Behrens, and J. Speares (2003). Early syntactic creativity: a usage-based approach. *Journal of Child Language 30*, 333–370.

Lin, D. (1998). An information-theoretic definition of similarity. In *Proc. 15th International Conf. on Machine Learning*, pp. 296–304. Morgan Kaufmann, San Francisco, CA.

Lin, L., R. Osan, S. Shoham, W. Jin, W. Zuo, and J. Z. Tsien (2005). Identification of network-level coding units for real-time representation of episodic experiences in the hippocampus. *Proceedings of the National Academy of Science 102*, 6125–6130.

Lin, L., R. Osan, and J. Z. Tsien (2006). Organizing principles of real-time memory encoding: neural clique assemblies and universal neural codes. *Trends in Neurosciences 29*, 48–57.

Linden, E. (2002). *The Octopus and the Orangutan*. New York: Dutton.

Lindsay, P. H. and D. A. Norman (1972). *Human information processing: an introduction to psychology*. New York: Academic Press.

Linsker, R. (1990). Perceptual neural organization: some approaches based on network models and information theory. *Ann. Rev. Neurosci. 13*, 257–281.

Llinás, R. R. (2001). *I of the Vortex*. Cambridge, MA: MIT Press.

Lloyd, D. (2002). Functional MRI and the study of human consciousness. *Journal of Cognitive Neuroscience 14*, 818–831.

Locke, J. (1690). *An essay concerning human understanding*. Available online at http://www.ilt.columbia.edu/publications/locke_understanding.html.

Loftus, E. F. (2003). Our changeable memories: legal and practical implications. *Nature Reviews: Neuroscience 4*, 231–234.

Long, C. R. and J. R. Averill (2003). Solitude: an exploration of benefits of being alone. *Journal for the Theory of Social Behaviour 33*, 21–44.

Loomis, J. M., R. L. Klatzky, R. G. Golledge, J. G. Cicinelli, J. W. Pellegrino, and P. A. Fry (1993). Nonvisual navigation by blind and sighted: Assessment of path integration ability. *Journal of Experimental Psychology: General 122*, 73–91.

Lormand, E. (1990). Framing the Frame Problem. *Synthése 82*, 353–374. Available online at http://www-personal.umich.edu/~lormand/phil/cogsci/holorobophobe.htm.

Lubinski, D. (2004). Introduction to the special section on cognitive abilities: 100 years after Spearman's (1904) "'General intelligence,' objectively determined and measured". *Journal of Personality and Social Psychology 86*, 96–111.

Lubinski, D., C. P. Benbow, R. M. Webb, and A. Bleske-Rechek (2006). Tracking exceptional human capital over two decades. *Psychological Science 17*, 194–199.

Lyubomirsky, S. (2001). Why are some people happier than others?: The role of cognitive and motivational processes in well-being. *American Psychologist 56*, 239–249.

Lyubomirsky, S., K. M. Sheldon, and D. Schkade (2005). Pursuing happiness: The architecture of sustainable change. *Review of General Psychology 9*, 111–131.

Mach, E. (1886). *Contributions to the analysis of the sensations*. New York: Open Court.

Mack, A. (2003). Inattentional blindness: looking without seeing. *Current Directions in Psychological Science 12*, 180–184.

MacWhinney, B. (2000). *The CHILDES Project: Tools for Analyzing Talk*. Mahwah, NJ: Erlbaum. Volume 1: Transcription format and programs. Volume 2: The Database.

Macy, M. W. and R. Willer (2002). From factors to actors: computational sociology and agent-based modeling. *Annual Review of Sociology 28*, 143–166.

Maguire, E. A., D. G. Gadian, I. S. Johnsrude, C. D. Good, J. Ashburner, R. S. J. Frackowiak, and C. D. Frith (2000). Navigation-related structural change in the hippocampi of taxi drivers. *Proceedings of the National Academy of Science 97*, 4398–4403.

Makkai, A. (1995). *Homo Loquens* as 'sender-receiver' (i.e., *tranceiver*) and the *raison d'être* of sememic, lexemic and morphemic prefabs in natural language structures and language use. In M. E. Landsberg (Ed.), *Syntactic iconicity and linguistic freezes*, pp. 91–116. Berlin: Mouton de Gruyter.

Maoz, I., A. Ward, M. Katz, and L. Ross (2002). Reactive devaluation of an "Israeli" vs. "Palestinian" peace proposal. *Journal of Conflict Resolution 46*, 515–546.

Marchand, H. (2003). An overview of the psychology of wisdom. Available online at http://www.prometheus.org.uk/Files/MarchandOnWisdom.PDF.

Marian, V. and M. Kaushanskaya (2005). Autobiographical memories and the self in bicultural bilinguals. In *Proceedings of the International Symposium on Bilingualism*, Somerville, MA, pp. 1478–1486. Cascadilla.

Markman, A. and D. Gentner (1993). Structural alignment during similarity comparisons. *Cognitive Psychology 25*, 431–467.

Markman, E. (1989). *Categorization and naming in children*. Cambridge, MA: MIT Press.

Marr, D. (1970). A theory for cerebral neocortex. *Proceedings of the Royal Society of London B 176*, 161–234.

Marr, D. (1971). Simple memory: a theory for archicortex. *Phil. Trans. Royal Soc. London 262*, 23–81.

Marr, D. (1982). *Vision*. San Francisco, CA: W. H. Freeman.

Marr, D. and T. Poggio (1977). From understanding computation to understanding neural circuitry. *Neurosciences Res. Prog. Bull. 15*, 470–488.

Marr, D. and T. Poggio (1979). A computational theory of human stereo vision. *Proceedings of the Royal Society of London B 204*, 301–328.

Marshall, J. B. (2002). Metacat: a self-watching cognitive architecture for analogy-making. In *Proceedings of the 24th Annual Conference of the Cognitive Science Society*, pp. 631–636.

Martin, A. and J. Weisberg (2003). Neural foundations for understanding social and mechanical concepts. *Cognitive Neuropsychology 20*, 575–587.

Mason, M. F., M. I. Norton, J. D. Van Horn, D. M. Wegner, S. T. Grafton, and C. N. Macrae (2007). Wandering minds: the default network and stimulus-independent thought. *Science 315*, 393–395.

Massimini, M., F. Ferrarelli, R. Huber, S. K. Esser, H. Singh, and G. Tononi (2005). Breakdown of cortical effective connectivity during sleep. *Science 309*, 2228–2232.

McCarthy, J. (1990). Some expert systems need common sense. In V. Lifschitz (Ed.), *Formalizing Common Sense: Papers by John McCarthy*, pp. 189–197. Norwood, NJ: Ablex. Originally published in 1984.

McCarthy, J. and P. J. Hayes (1969). Some philosophical problems from the standpoint of Artificial Intelligence. In D. Michie and B. Meltzer (Eds.), *Machine Intelligence*, Volume 4, pp. 463–502. Edinburgh: Edinburgh University Press.

McCulloch, W. (1956). Toward some circuitry of ethical robots or an observational science of the genesis of social evolution in the mind-like behavior of artifacts. *Acta Biotheoretica 11*, 147–156. Reprinted in *The Embodiments of Mind* (1965).

McCulloch, W. S. (1947). Machines that think and want. Lecture to American Psychological Association. Reprinted in Embodiments of Mind, pp.307-318, MIT Press, 1965.

McCulloch, W. S. (1951). Why the mind is in the head. In L. Jeffress (Ed.), *Cerebral mechanisms in behavior*, pp. 42–111. New York: Wiley.

McCulloch, W. S. (1952). Finality and form. Publication No.11 in the American Lecture Series (Springfield, IL; Charles C. Thomas). Reprinted in Embodiments of Mind, pp.256-275, MIT Press, 1965.

McCulloch, W. S. (1965). *Embodiments of mind*. Cambridge, MA: MIT Press.

McCulloch, W. S. and W. Pitts (1943). A logical calculus of ideas immanent in nervous activity. *Bulletin of Mathematical Biophysics 5*, 115–133. Reprinted in Embodiments of Mind, pp.46-66, MIT Press, 1965.

McKenzie, C. R. M. (2003). Rational models as theories – not standards – of behavior. *Trends in Cognitive Sciences 7*, 403–406.

McKinnon, D. W. (1962). The nature and nurture of creative talent. *American Psychologist 17*, 484–495.

Medin, D. L., R. L. Goldstone, and D. Gentner (1993). Respects for similarity. *Psychological Review 100*, 254–278.

Medin, D. L. and E. E. Smith (1984). Concepts and concept formation. *Annual Review of Psychology 35*, 113–138.

Melinger, A. and C. Dobel (2005). Lexically-driven syntactic priming. *Cognition 98*, B11–B20.

Melis, A. P., B. Hare, and M. Tomasello (2006). Chimpanzees recruit the best collaborators. *Science 311*, 1297–1300.

Mellers, B. A., A. Schwartz, and A. D. J. Cooke (1998). Judgment and decision making. *Annual Review of Psychology 49*, 447–477.

Meltzoff, A. and M. Moore (1977). Imitation of facial and manual gestures by human neonates. *Science 198*, 74–78.

Merker, B. (2004). Cortex, countercurrent context, and dimensional integration of lifetime memory. *Cortex 40*, 559–576.

Merker, B. (2007). Consciousness without a cerebral cortex: a challenge for neuroscience and medicine. *Behavioral and Brain Sciences 30*, 63–81.

Mesoudi, A. and A. Whiten (2004). The hierarchical transformation of event knowledge in human cultural transmission. *Journal of Cognition and Culture 4*, 1–24.

Mesoudi, A., A. Whiten, and K. N. Laland (2006). Towards a unified science of cultural evolution. *Behavioral and Brain Sciences -, -.* In press.

Metzinger, T. (2003). *Being No One: The Self-Model Theory of Subjectivity.* Cambridge, MA: MIT Press.

Metzinger, T. (2004). The subjectivity of subjective experience: A representationalist analysis of the first-person perspective. *Networks 3-4*, 33–64.

Metzinger, T. (2005). Précis: Being No One. *Psyche 11*(5). Available online at http://psyche.cs.monash.edu.au/symposia/metzinger/precis.pdf.

Meyer, J.-A., A. Guillot, B. Girard, M. Khamassi, P. Pirim, and A. Berthoz (2005). The Psikharpax project: towards building an artificial rat. *Robotics and Autonomous Systems 50*, 211–223.

Miller, E. K. and J. D. Cohen (2001). An integrative theory of prefrontal cortex function. *Annual Review of Neuroscience 24*, 167–202.

Miller, G. A. and J. A. Selfridge (1961). Verbal context and the recall of meaningful material. In S. Saporta (Ed.), *Psycholinguistics: a book of readings*, pp. 198–206. New York: Holt, Rinehart and Winston.

Millikan, R. (1995). *White Queen Psychology and other essays for Alice.* Cambridge, MA: MIT Press.

Minsky, M. (1961). Steps toward artificial intelligence. *Proceedings of the Institute of Radio Engineers 49*, 8–30.

Minsky, M. (1985). *The Society of Mind.* New York: Simon and Schuster.

Minsky, M. (2000). Commonsense-based interfaces. *Communications of the Association for Computing Machinery 43*, 66–73.

Minsky, M. (2006). *The Emotion Machine: Commonsense Thinking, Artificial Intelligence, and the Future of the Human Mind.* New York: Simon & Schuster.

Mitchell, M. (1993). *Analogy-making as perception: a computer model.* Cambridge, MA: MIT Press.

Mitchell, M. (2001). Analogy-making as a complex adaptive system. In L. Segal and A. Cohen (Eds.), *Design Principles for the Immune System and Other Distributed Autonomous Systems.* New York: Oxford University Press.

Miyashita, Y. (2004). Cognitive memory: cellular and network machineries and their top-down control. *Science 306*, 435–440.

Moore, T. and K. M. Armstrong (2003). Selective gating of visual signals by microstimulation of frontal cortex. *Nature 421*, 370–373.

Moore, T. and M. Fallah (2001). Control of eye movements and spatial attention. *Proceedings of the National Academy of Science 98*, 1273–1276.

Moran, J. and R. Desimone (1985). Selective attention gates visual processing in the extrastriate cortex. *Science 229*, 782–784.

Moser, E. I. and M.-B. Moser (2003). One-shot memory in hippocampal CA3 networks. *Neuron 38*, 147–148.

Mueller, E. T. (2001). Common sense in humans. Available online at http://www.signiform.com/erik/pubs/cshumans.htm.

Müller, R.-A. and S. Basho (2004). Are nonlinguistic functions in 'Broca's area' prerequisites for language acquisition? FMRI findings from an ontogenetic viewpoint. *Brain and Language 89*, 329–336.

Muller, R. U. and J. L. Kubie (1989). The firing of hippocampal place cells predicts the future position of freely moving rats. *Journal of Neuroscience 9*, 4101–4110.

Mumford, D. (1994). Neuronal architectures for pattern-theoretic problems. In C. Koch and J. L. Davis (Eds.), *Large-scale neuronal theories of the brain*, Chapter 7, pp. 125–152. Cambridge, MA: MIT Press.

Murphy, G. L. (2002). *The big book of concepts.* Cambridge, MA: MIT Press.

Murray, S. O., D. Kersten, B. A. Olshausen, P. Schrater, and D. L. Woods (2002). Shape perception reduces activity in human primary visual cortex. *Proceedings of the National Academy of Science 99*, 15164–15169.

Muzur, A., E. F. Pace-Schott, and J. A. Hobson (2002). The prefrontal cortex in sleep. *Trends in Cognitive Sciences 6*, 475–481.

Nagel, T. (1974). What is it like to be a bat? *Philosophical Review LXXXIII*, 435–450. Available online at http://members.aol.com/NeoNoetics/Nagel_Bat.html.

Naigles, L. G. (1990). Children use syntax to learn verb meanings. *Journal of Child Language 17*, 357–374.

Nakayama, K., Z. J. He, and S. Shimojo (1995). Visual surface representation: a critical link between lower-level and higher-level vision. In S. M. Kosslyn and D. N. Osherson (Eds.), *Visual Cognition*, pp. 1–70. Cambridge, MA: MIT Press.

Nation, P. and R. Waring (1997). Vocabulary size, text coverage and word lists. In N. Schmitt and M. McCarthy (Eds.), *Vocabulary: Description, Acquisition and Pedagogy*, pp. 6–19. Cambridge: Cambridge University Press.

Navon, D. (1977). Forest before trees: The precedence of global features in visual perception. *Cognitive Psychology 9*, 353–383.

Needham, C. J., P. E. Santos, D. R. Magee, V. Devin, D. C. Hogg, and A. G. Cohn (2005). Protocols from perceptual observations. *Artificial Intelligence 167*, 103–136.

Neisser, U. (1967). *Cognitive Psychology*. New York, NY: Appleton-Century-Crofts.

Neisser, U. (Ed.) (1982). *Memory Observed: Remembering in Natural Contexts*. San Francisco: Freeman.

Neisser, U. (1997). Rising scores on intelligence tests. *American Scientist 85*, 440–447.

Neisser, U. and R. Fivush (Eds.) (1994). *The Remembering Self: Construction and Accuracy in the Self Narrative*. Cambridge: Cambridge University Press.

Nelson, K. and R. Fivush (2004). The emergence of autobiographical memory: A social cultural developmental model. *Psychological Review 111*, 486–511.

Newell, A., J. C. Shaw, and H. A. Simon (1959). Report on a general problem-solving program.

Newell, A. and H. Simon (1972). *Human Problem Solving*. Englewood Cliffs, NJ: Prentice-Hall.

Newell, K. M., Y.-T. Liu, and G. Mayer-Kress (2001). Time scales in motor learning and development. *Psychological Review 108*, 57–82.

Newmeyer, F. J. (1996). *Generative linguistics: a historical perspective*. London: Routledge.

Newport, E. L. and R. N. Aslin (2004). Learning at a distance: I. statistical learning of non-adjacent dependencies. *Cognitive Psychology 48*, 127–162.

Newsome, W. T. and J. A. Stein-Aviles (1999). Nonhuman primate models of visually based cognition. *ILAR Journal V40(2)*.

Nichols, S. and R. Mallon (2006). Moral dilemmas and moral rules. *Cognition 100*, 530–542.

Nilsson, D.-E., L. Gislén, M. M. Coates, C. Skogh, and A. Garm (2005). Advanced optics in a jellyfish eye. *Nature 435*, 201–205.

Nilsson, N. J. (2006). How are we to know?

Noelle, D. C. (2001). Exorcising the homunculus: there's no one behind the curtain. *Free Inquiry 21*(2). Available online at http://www.secularhumanism.org/fi/.

Nolfi, S. and D. Floreano (2000). *Evolutionary Robotics: The Biology, Intelligence, and Technology of Self-Organizing Machines*. Cambridge, MA: MIT Press.

Ochsner, K. N., C.-Y. P. Chiu, and D. L. Schacter (1994). Varieties of priming. *Current Opinion in Neurobiology 4*, 189–194.

O'Connor, T. (2006). Free will. In E. N. Zalta (Ed.), *The Stanford Encyclopedia of Philosophy*. Available online at http://plato.stanford.edu/archives/spr2006/entries/freewill/.

Ohbayashi, M., K. Ohki, and Y. Miyashita (2003). Conversion of working memory to motor sequence in the monkey premotor cortex. *Science 301*, 233–237.

Oja, E. (1989). Neural networks, principal components, and subspaces. *International Journal of Neural Systems 1*, 61–68.

O'Keefe, J. and J. Dostrovsky (1971). The hippocampus as a spatial map: Preliminary evidence from unit activity in the freely moving rat. *Brain Research 34*, 171–175.

Op de Beeck, H. and R. Vogels (2000). Spatial sensitivity of Macaque inferior temporal neurons. *J. Comparative Neurology 426*, 505–518.

Op de Beeck, H., J. Wagemans, and R. Vogels (2001). Inferotemporal neurons represent low-dimensional configurations of parameterized shapes. *Nature Neuroscience 4*, 1244–1252.

Opris, I. and C. J. Bruce (2005). Neural circuitry of judgment and decision making. *Brain Research Reviews 48*, 509–526.

O'Regan, J. K. (1992). Solving the real mysteries of visual perception: The world as an outside memory. *Canadian J. of Psychology 46*, 461–488.

O'Regan, J. K. and A. Noë (2001). A sensorimotor account of vision and visual consciousness. *Behavioral and Brain Sciences 24*, 883–917.

O'Reilly, R. C. (2006a). Biologically based computational models of high-level cognition. *Science 314*, 91–94.

O'Reilly, R. C. (2006b). The division of labor between the neocortex and hippocampus. In G. Houghton (Ed.), *Connectionist Modeling in Cognitive Psychology*. Psychology Press. in press.

O'Reilly, R. C. and M. J. Frank (2006). Making working memory work: a computational model of learning in the frontal cortex and basal ganglia. *Neural Computation 18*, 283–328.

O'Reilly, R. C., D. Noelle, T. S. Braver, and J. D. Cohen (2002). Prefrontal cortex and dynamic categorization tasks: Representational organization and neuromodulatory control. *Cerebral Cortex 12*, 246–257.

O'Reilly, R. C. and K. A. Norman (2002). Hippocampal and neocortical contributions to memory: Advances in the complementary learning systems framework. *Trends in Cognitive Sciences 6*, 505–510.

Österbauer, R. A., P. M. Matthews, M. Jenkinson, C. F. Beckmann, P. C. Hansen, and G. A. Calvert (2005). Color of scents: Chromatic stimuli modulate odor responses in the human brain. *J. Neurophysiol. 93*, 3434–3441.

Oudeyer, P.-Y. (2005). How phonological structures can be culturally selected for learnability. *Adaptive Behavior 13*, 269–280.

Paine, R. W. and J. Tani (2005). How hierarchical control self-organizes in artificial adaptive systems. *Adaptive Behavior 13*, 211–225.

Paton, J. J., M. A. Belova, S. E. Morrison, and C. D. Salzman (2006). The primate amygdala represents the positive and negative value of visual stimuli during learning. *Nature 439*, 865–870.

Patten, S. B. and J. Arboleda-Flórez (2004). Epidemic theory and group violence. *Journal of Social Psychiatry and Psychiatric Epidemiology 39*, 853–856.

Paul, G. S. (2005). Cross-national correlations of quantifiable societal health with popular religiosity and secularism in the prosperous democracies: A first look. *J. of Religion and Society 7*(11).

Paz-y-Miño, G., A. B. Bond, A. C. Kamil, and R. P. Balda (2004). Pinyon jays use transitive inference to predict social dominance. *Nature 430*, 778–781.

Pearl, J. (2001). Causal inference in statistics: A gentle introduction. In *Computing Science and Statistics: Proceedings of Interface '01*, Volume 33. Avaliable online at http://ftp.cs.ucla.edu/pub/stat_ser/R289.pdf.

Pearl, J. and S. Russel (2003). Bayesian networks. In M. A. Arbib (Ed.), *Handbook of Brain Theory and Neural Networks*, pp. 157–160. Cambridge, MA: MIT Press. Available online at http://ftp.cs.ucla.edu/pub/stat_ser/R277.pdf.

Peirce, C. S. (1960). *Collected Papers of Charles Sanders Peirce 1931-1958*. Cambridge, MA: Harvard University Press. Edited by C. Hartshorne and P. Weiss.

Pelgrims, B., M. Andres, and E. Olivier (2005). Motor imagery while judging object-hand interactions. *Neuroreport 16*, 1193–1196.

Pereira, F. (2000). Formal grammar and information theory: Together again? *Philosophical Transactions of the Royal Society 358*(1769), 1239–1253.

Perrett, D. I., D. M. Burt, I. S. Penton-Voak, K. J. Lee, D. A. Rowland, and R. Edwards (1999). Symmetry and human facial attractiveness. *Evolution and Human Behavior 20*, 295–307.

Perrett, D. I., A. J. Mistlin, and A. J. Chitty (1987). Visual neurones responsive to faces. *Trends in Neurosciences 10*, 358–364.

Phillips, C. (2003). Syntax. In L. Nadel (Ed.), *Encyclopedia of Cognitive Science*, Volume 4, pp. 319–329. London: Macmillan.

Pickering, M. J. and H. P. Branigan (1999). Syntactic priming in language production. *Trends in Cognitive Sciences 3*, 136–141.

Pickering, M. J. and S. Garrod (2004). Toward a mechanistic psychology of dialogue. *Behavioral and Brain Sciences 27*, 169–225.

Pietroski, P. M. (2003). The character of natural language semantics. In A. Barber (Ed.), *Epistemology of Language*, pp. 217–256. Oxford, UK: Oxford University Press.

Pinker, S. (1997). *How the mind works*. New York: Norton.

Pinker, S. (2002). *The Blank Slate: the modern denial of human nature*. Harmondsworth, Middlesex, England: Viking.

Pinker, S. and R. Jackendoff (2005). The faculty of language: What's special about it? *Cognition 95*, 201–236.

Plato (360BCE). *Theaetetus*. Translated by B. Jowett. Available online at http://www.gutenberg.org/etext/1726.

Plomin, R. and F. M. Spinath (2002). Genetics and general cognitive ability (g). *Trends in Cognitive Sciences 6*, 169–176.

Poggio, T. (1990). A theory of how the brain might work. *Cold Spring Harbor Symposia on Quantitative Biology LV*, 899–910.

Poggio, T., M. Fahle, and S. Edelman (1992). Fast perceptual learning in visual hyperacuity. *Science 256*, 1018–1021.

Poggio, T., R. Rifkin, S. Mukherjee, and P. Niyogi (2004). General conditions for predictivity in learning theory. *Nature 428*, 419–422.

Popper, K. R. (1950). Indeterminism in quantum physics and in classical physics. Part i. *The British Journal for the Philosophy of Science 1*, 117–133.

Popper, K. R. (1992). *Conjectures and refutations: the growth of scientific knowledge*. London: Routledge. 5th ed.

Port, R. F. and A. P. Leary (2005). Against formal phonology. *Language 81*, 927–964.

Posner, M. I. and A. Pavese (1998). Anatomy of word and sentence meaning. *Proceedings of the National Academy of Science 95*, 899–905.

Postal, P. M. (2004). Junk linguistics. In *Skeptical linguistic essays*. New York: Oxford University Press. Part II.

Povinelli, D. J., J. M. Bering, and S. Giambrone (2000). Toward a science of other minds: escaping the argument by analogy. *Cognitive Science 24*, 509–541.

Prokosch, M. D., R. A. Yeo, and G. F. Miller (2005). Intelligence tests with higher g-loadings show higher correlations with body symmetry: evidence for a general fitness factor mediated by developmental stability. *Intelligence 33*, 203–213.

Pullum, G. K. and B. Scholz (2002). Empirical assessment of poverty of the stimulus arguments. *The Linguistic Review 19*, 9–50.

Pulvermüller, F. (2002). A brain perspective on language mechanisms: from discrete neuronal ensembles to serial order. *Progress in Neurobiology 67*, 85–111.

Putnam, H. (1975). The meaning of 'meaning'. In K. Gunderson (Ed.), *Language, Mind, and Knowledge*, pp. 131–193. Minneapolis, MN: University of Minnesota Press.

Putnam, H. (1988). *Representation and reality*. Cambridge, MA: MIT Press.

Putnam, H. (2004). *Ethics without ontology*. Cambridge, MA: Harvard University Press.

Quine, W. V. (1961). The problem of meaning in linguistics. In S. Saporta (Ed.), *Psycholinguistics: a book of readings*, pp. 251–261. New York: Holt, Rinehart and Winston.

Quine, W. V. (1972). Methodological reflections on current linguistic theory. In D. Davidson and G. Harman (Eds.), *Semantics of Natural Language*, pp. 442–454. Dordrecht: Reidel.

Quine, W. V. O. (1953). Two dogmas of Empiricism. In *From a Logical Point of View*, pp. 20–46. Cambridge: Harvard University Press.

Quine, W. V. O. (1960). *Word and object*. Cambridge, MA: MIT Press.

Quiroga, R. Q., L. Reddy, G. Kreiman, C. Koch, and I. Fried (2005). Invariant visual representation by single neurons in the human brain. *Nature 435*, 1102–1107.

Raby, C. R., D. M. Alexis, A. Dickinson, and N. S. Clayton (2007). Planning for the future by western scrub-jays. *Nature 445*, 919–921.

Radford, G. P. (2002). Beware of the Fallout: Umberto Eco and the making of the model reader. In *Proc. of the 93rd Annual Conference of the Eastern Communication Association*, New York. Available online at http://www.themodernword.com/eco/eco_papers_radford.html.

Raichle, M. E. (2006). The brain's dark energy. *Science 314*, 1249–1250.

Ramachandran, V. S. and W. Hirstein (1997). Three laws of qualia. *Journal of Consciousness Studies 4*, 429–458.

Ramachandran, V. S. and W. Hirstein (1999). The science of art: A neurological theory of aesthetic experience. *Journal of Consciousness Studies 6*, 15–51.

Rapoport, A. and J. N. Bearden (2005). Strategic behavior in monkeys. *Trends in Cognitive Sciences 9*, 213–215.

Raz, A. and J. Buhle (2006). Typologies of attentional networks. *Nature Reviews Neuroscience 7*, 367–379.

Reali, F. and M. H. Christiansen (2005). Uncovering the richness of the stimulus: Structural dependence and indirect statistical evidence. *Cognitive Science 29*, 1007–1028.

Recanzone, G. H., M. M. Merzenich, W. M. Jenkins, A. G. Kamil, and H. R. Dinse (1992). Topographic reorganization of the hand representation in cortical area 3b of owl monkeys trained in a frequency discrimination task. *Journal of Neurophysiology 67*, 1031–1056.

Reitman, W., R. Nado, and B. Wilcox (1978). Machine perception: what makes it so hard for computers to see? In C. W. Savage (Ed.), *Perception and cognition: issues in the foundations of psychology*, Volume IX of *Minnesota studies in the philosophy of science*, pp. 65–87. Minneapolis, MN: University of Minnesota Press.

Rensink, R., J. K. O'Regan, and J. J. Clark (1997). To see or not to see: the need for attention to perceive changes in scenes. *Psychological Science 6*, 368–373.

Rensink, R., K. O'Regan, and J. J. Clark (1995). Image flicker is as good as saccades in making large scene changes invisible. *Perception 24 (suppl.)*, 26–27.

Reps, P. (1989). *Zen Flesh, Zen Bones*. New York: Anchor Books.

Reynolds, J. R. and R. Desimone (1999). The role of neural mechanisms of attention in solving the binding problem. *Neuron 24*, 19–29.

Richards, W. (1982, December). How to play twenty questions with nature and win. A.I. Memo No. 660, Artificial Intelligence Laboratory, Massachusetts Institute of Technology. Available online at ftp://publications.ai.mit.edu/ai-publications/pdf/AIM-660.pdf.

Richardson, D. C. and R. A. Dale (2005). Looking to understand: The coupling between speakers' and listeners' eye movements and its relationship to discourse comprehension. *Cognitive Science 29*, 39–54.

Rilling, J. K., S. K. Barks, L. A. Parr, T. M. Preuss, T. L. Faber, G. Pagnoni, J. D. Bremner, and J. R. Votaw (2007). A comparison of resting-state brain activity in humans and chimpanzees. *Proceedings of the National Academy of Sciences 104*, 17146–17151.

Rissanen, J. (1987). Minimum description length principle. In S. Kotz and N. L. Johnson (Eds.), *Encyclopedia of Statistic Sciences*, Volume 5, pp. 523–527. J. Wiley and Sons.

Rizzolatti, G. and M. A. Arbib (1998). Language within our grasp. *Trends in Neuroscience 21*, 188–194.

Rizzolatti, G. and L. Craighero (2004). The mirror-neuron system. *Annual Review of Neuroscience 27*, 169–192.

Roediger III, H. L. and K. McDermott (1995). Creating false memories: Remembering words not presented in lists. *Journal of Experimental Psychology: Learning, Memory, & Cognition 21*, 803–814.

Roelfsema, P. R. (2005). Elemental operations in vision. *Trends in Cognitive Sciences 9*, 226–233.

Roelfsema, P. R., V. A. F. Lamme, and H. Spekreijse (1998). Object-based attention in the primary visual cortex of the macaque monkey. *Nature 395*, 376–381.

Roelfsema, P. R., V. A. F. Lamme, and H. Spekreijse (2004). Synchrony and covariation of firing rates in the primary visual cortex during contour grouping. *Nature Neuroscience 7*, 982–991.

Roland, D., J. L. Elman, and V. S. Ferreira (2005). Why is *that*? Structural prediction and ambiguity resolution in a very large corpus of English sentences. *Cognition 98*, 245–272.

Rolls, E. T. (2000). *The Brain and Emotion*. Oxford: Oxford University Press.

Rorie, A. E. and W. T. Newsome (2005). A general mechanism for decision-making in the human brain? *Trends in Cognitive Sciences 9*, 41–43.

Rosch, E. (1978). Principles of categorization. In E. Rosch and B. Lloyd (Eds.), *Cognition and Categorization*, pp. 27–48. Hillsdale, NJ: Erlbaum.

Rosch, E., C. B. Mervis, W. D. Gray, D. M. Johnson, and P. Boyes-Braem (1976). Basic objects in natural categories. *Cognitive Psychology 8*, 382–439.

Ross, K. L. (1999). Zen and the Art of Divebombing, *or* The Dark Side of the Tao. Available online at http://www.friesian.com/divebomb.htm.

Rudolph, U. and B. Antkowiak (2004). Molecular and neuronal substrates for general anaesthetics. *Nature Reviews Neuroscience 5*, 709–720.

Rudrauf, D., A. Lutz, D. Cosmelli, J.-F. Lachaux, and M. le van Quyen (2003). From autopoiesis to neurophenomenology: Francisco Varela's exploration of the biophysics of being. *Biological Research 36*, 27–65.

Rumelhart, D. E. (1980). Schemata: The building blocks of cognition. In R. J. Spiro, B. Bruce, and W. F. Brewer (Eds.), *Theoretical Issues in Reading and Comprehension*. Hillsdale, NJ: Erlbaum.

Saffran, J. R. (2001). Words in a sea of sounds: the output of infant statistical learning. *Cognition 81*, 149–169.

Saffran, J. R., R. N. Aslin, and E. L. Newport (1996). Statistical learning by 8-month-old infants. *Science 274*, 1926–1928.

Sag, I. A., T. Baldwin, F. Bond, A. Copestake, and D. Flickinger (2002). Multiword expressions: A pain in the neck for NLP. In *Proceedings of the Third International Conference on Intelligent Text Processing and Computational Linguistics (CICLING 2002)*, pp. 1–15. Mexico City, Mexico.

Sagan, C. (1973). *Cosmic connection: an extraterrestrial perspective*. Cambridge, UK: Cambridge University Press.

Sakai, K. and Y. Miyashita (1991). Neural organization for the long-term memory of paired associates. *Nature 354*, 152–155.

Salzman, C. D., K. H. Britten, and W. T. Newsome (1990). Cortical microstimulation influences perceptual judgements of motion direction. *Nature 346*, 174–177.

Sandbank, B., S. Edelman, and E. Ruppin (2007). From ConText to grammar: a step towards practical probabilistic context free grammar inference. In *Proceedings of the 6th Israeli Symposium on Computational Linguistics*.

Sanfey, A. G., G. Loewenstein, S. M. McClure, and J. D. Cohen (2006). Neuroeconomics: cross-currents in research on decision-making. *Trends in Cognitive Sciences 10*, 108–116.

Sanjana, N. and J. B. Tenenbaum (2002). Bayesian models of inductive generalization. In S. Becker, S. Thrun, and K. Obermayer (Eds.), *Advances in*

Neural Information Processing Systems, Volume 15, Cambridge, MA, pp. 51–58. MIT Press.

Sapir, E. (1921). *Language: An Introduction to the Study of Speech.* New York: Harcourt, Brace. Available online at http://www.bartleby.com/186/.

Saxe, R. (2006). Uniquely human social cognition. *Current Opinion in Neurobiology 16*, 235–239.

Saxton, M., C. Houston-Price, and N. Dawson (2005). The prompt hypothesis: Clarification requests as corrective input for grammatical errors. *Applied Psycholinguistics 26*, 393–414.

Schaal, S. (1999). Is imitation learning the route to humanoid robots? *Trends in Cognitive Sciences 3*, 233–242.

Schaal, S., A. Ijspeert, and A. Billard (2003). Computational approaches to motor learning by imitation. *Philosophical Transactions of the Royal Society of London: Series B 358*, 537–547.

Schacter, D. L. and D. R. Addis (2007). The cognitive neuroscience of constructive memory: remembering the past and imagining the future. *Philosophical Transactions of the Royal Society of London B 362*, 773–786.

Schaeffer, J., N. Burch, Y. Björnsson, A. Kishimoto, M. Müller, R. Lake, P. Lu, and S. Sutphen (2007). Checkers is solved. *Science 317*, 1518–1522.

Schall, J. D. (2001). Neural basis of deciding, choosing and acting. *Nature Reviews Neuroscience 2*, 33–42.

Schank, R. C. and R. P. Abelson (1977). *Scripts, Plans, Goals and Understanding: an Inquiry into Human Knowledge Structures.* Hillsdale, NJ: L. Erlbaum.

Scharfstein, B. (1998). *A Comparative History of World Philosophy: From the Upanishads to Kant.* Albany, NY: SUNY Press.

Schooler, J. W., D. Ariely, and G. Loewenstein (2003). The pursuit and monitoring of happiness can be self-defeating. In J. Carrillo and I. Brocas (Eds.), *Psychology and Economics*, pp. 41–70. Oxford: Oxford University Press.

Schrauf, R. and D. Rubin (2003). On the bilingual's two sets of memories. In R. Fivush and C. Haden (Eds.), *Autobiographical memory and the construction of a narrative self*, pp. 121–145. Mahwah, NJ: Erlbaum.

Schütze, C. T. (1996). *The empirical base of linguistics: grammaticality judgments and linguistic methodology.* Chicago, IL: University of Chicago Press.

Schwartz, B., A. Ward, J. Monterosso, S. Lyubomirsky, K. White, and D. Lehman (2002). Maximizing versus satisficing: Happiness is a matter of choice. *Journal of Personality and Social Psychology 83*, 1178–1197.

Searle, J. (1980). Minds, brains, and programs. *Behavioral and Brain Sciences 3*, 417–424.

Seebach, B. S., N. Intrator, P. Lieberman, and L. N. Cooper (1994). A model of prenatal acquisition of speech parameters. *Proceedings of the National Academy of Science 91*, 7473–7476.

Selfridge, O. G. (1959). Pandemonium: a paradigm for learning. In *The mechanisation of thought processes*. London: H.M.S.O.

Shadmehr, R. (1995). The equilibrium point hypothesis for control of posture, movement, and manipulation. In M. A. Arbib (Ed.), *Handbook of Brain Theory and Neural Networks*, pp. 370–372. Cambridge, MA: MIT Press.

Shadmehr, R. and S. P. Wise (2005). *Computational Neurobiology of Reaching and Pointing: A Foundation for Motor Learning*. Cambridge, MA: MIT Press.

Shaw, P., D. Greenstein, J. Lerch, L. Clasen, R. Lenroot, N. Gogtay, A. Evans, J. Rapoport, and J. Giedd (2006). Intellectual ability and cortical development in children and adolescents. *Nature 440*, 676–680.

Sheldon, K. M., T. Kasser, K. Smith, and T. Share (2002). Personal goals and psychological growth: Testing an intervention to enhance goal-attainment and personality integration. *Journal of Personality 70*, 5–31.

Shepard, R. N. (1962a). The analysis of proximities: Multidimensional scaling with unknown distance function. Part I. *Psychometrika 27*(2), 125–140.

Shepard, R. N. (1962b). The analysis of proximities: Multidimensional scaling with unknown distance function. Part II. *Psychometrika 27*(2), 219–246.

Shepard, R. N. (1968). Cognitive psychology: A review of the book by U. Neisser. *Amer. J. Psychol. 81*, 285–289.

Shepard, R. N. (1980). Multidimensional scaling, tree-fitting, and clustering. *Science 210*, 390–397.

Shepard, R. N. (1987). Toward a universal law of generalization for psychological science. *Science 237*, 1317–1323.

Shepard, R. N. (2001). Perceptual-cognitive universals as reflections of the world. *Behavioral and Brain Sciences 24*, 581–601.

Shepard, R. N. and S. Chipman (1970). Second-order isomorphism of internal representations: Shapes of states. *Cognitive Psychology 1*, 1–17.

Shipp, S. (2004). The brain circuitry of attention. *Trends in Cognitive Sciences 8*, 223–230.

Shomstein, S. and M. Behrmann (2006). Cortical systems mediating visual attention to both objects and spatial locations. *Proceedings of the National Academy of Science 103*, 11387–11392.

Siegal, M. and R. Varley (2002). Neural systems involved in 'theory of mind'. *Nature Reviews Neuroscience 3*, 411–486.

Simon, H. A. (1957). *Models of man — social and rational.* New York: Wiley.

Simon, H. A. (1973). The organization of complex systems. In H. H. Pattee (Ed.), *Hierarchy theory: the challenge of complex systems*, Chapter 1, pp. 1–28. New York: George Braziller.

Simon, H. A. (1996). *The Sciences of the Artificial* (third ed.). Cambridge, MA: MIT Press.

Simons, D. J. and C. F. Chabris (1999). Gorillas in our midst: sustained inattentional blindness for dynamic events. *Perception 28*, 1059–1074.

Simons, D. J. and D. T. Levin (1997). Change blindness. *Trends in Cognitive Sciences 1*, 261–267.

Simons, D. J. and D. T. Levin (1998). Failure to detect changes to people during a real-world interaction. *Psychonomic Bulletin & Review 5*, 644–649.

Simons, D. J. and R. A. Rensink (2005). Change blindness: past, present, and future. *Trends in Cognitive Sciences 9*, 16–20.

Sloman, A. and R. Chrisley (2003). Virtual machines and consciousness. *Journal of Consciousness Studies 10*, 113–172.

Smart, J. J. C. (2004). The identity theory of mind. In E. N. Zalta (Ed.), *Stanford Encyclopedia of Philosophy*. Stanford University. Available online at http://plato.stanford.edu/archives/fall2004/entries/mind-identity/.

Smith, B. (1995). The structures of the common-sense world. *Acta Philosophica Fennica 58*, 290–317.

Smith, B. (2003). Ontology. In L. Floridi (Ed.), *Blackwell Guide to the Philosophy of Computing and Information*, pp. 155–166. Oxford: Blackwell.

Smith, B. and R. Casati (1994). Naive physics: An essay in ontology. *Philosophical Psychology 7*, 225–244.

Smith, E. E. (1990). Categorization. In D. N. Osherson and E. E. Smith (Eds.), *An invitation to cognitive science: Thinking*, Volume 2, pp. 33–53. Cambridge, MA: MIT Press.

Smith, J. D., W. E. Shields, and D. A. Washburn (2003). The comparative psychology of uncertainty monitoring and metacognition. *Behavioral and Brain Sciences 26*, 317–373.

Smith, L. B. and M. Gasser (2005). The development of embodied cognition: Six lessons from babies. *Artificial Life*, 1113–1130.

Smith, P. L. and R. Ratcliff (2004). The psychology and neurobiology of simple decisions. *Trends in Neuroscience 27*, 161–168.

Smulders, T. V., A. D. Sasson, and T. J. DeVoogd (1995). Seasonal variation in hippocampal volume in a food-storing bird, the black-capped chickadee. *Journal of Neurobiology 27*, 15–25.

Smullyan, R. (1983). *5000 B.C. and other philosophical fantasies*. New York: St. Martin's Press.

Snippe, H. P. and J. J. Koenderink (1992). Discrimination thresholds for channel-coded systems. *Biological Cybernetics 66*, 543–551.

Snow, R. E., P. C. Kyllonen, and B. Marshalek (1984). The topography of ability and learning correlates. In R. J. Sternberg (Ed.), *Advances in the psychology of human intelligence*, Volume 2, pp. 47–104. Hillsdale, NJ: Erlbaum.

Snyder, A., J. Mitchell, T. Bossomaier, and G. Pallier (2004). The creativity quotient: an objective scoring of ideational fluency. *Creativity Research Journal 16*, 415–420.

Sokal, A. and J. Bricmont (1998). *Fashionable Nonsense*. Picador.

Solan, Z., D. Horn, E. Ruppin, and S. Edelman (2005). Unsupervised learning of natural languages. *Proceedings of the National Academy of Science 102*, 11629–11634.

Solomonoff, R. J. (1964). A formal theory of inductive inference, parts A and B. *Information and Control 7*, 1–22, 224–254.

Sommer, M. A. and R. H. Wurtz (2006). Influence of the thalamus on spatial visual processing in frontal cortex. *Nature 444*, 374–377.

Sperber, D. (1990). The epidemiology of beliefs. In C. Fraser and G. Gaskell (Eds.), *The social psychology of widespread beliefs*, pp. 25–43. Oxford: Clarendon Press.

Spivey, M. J. (2006). *The continuity of mind*. New York: Oxford University Press.

Spivey, M. J. and R. Dale (2006). Continuous dynamics in real-time cognition. *Current Directions in Psychological Science 15*, 207–211.

Squire, L. R. (2004). Memory systems of the brain: A brief history and current perspective. *Neurobiology of Learning and Memory 82*, 171–177.

Stanfill, C. and D. Waltz (1986). Toward memory-based reasoning. *Communications of the ACM 29*, 1213–1228.

Stanovich, K. E. and R. F. West (1998). Cognitive ability and variation in selection task performance. *Thinking and Reasoning 4*, 193–230.

Steedman, M. (2001). Information structure and the syntax-phonology interface. *Linguistic Inquiry 31*, 649–689.

Sternberg, R. J. (1999). Successful intelligence: finding a balance. *Trends in Cognitive Sciences 3*, 436–442.

Sternberg, R. J. (2003). *Cognitive Psychology*. Belmont, CA: Thompson Wadsworth.

Steyvers, M., J. B. Tenenbaum, E. J. Wagenmakers, and B. Blum (2003). Inferring causal networks from observations and interventions. *Cognitive Science 27*, 453–489.

Stickgold, R. (2005). Sleep-dependent memory consolidation. *Nature 437*, 1272–1278.

Stickgold, R. and M. Walker (2004). To sleep, perchance to gain creative insight? *Trends in Cognitive Sciences 8*, 191–192.

Stork, D. G. (Ed.) (1997). *HAL's Legacy: 2001's Computer as Dream and Reality*. Cambridge, MA: MIT Press. Available online at http://mitpress.mit.edu/e-books/Hal/.

Stringer, S. M., E. T. Rolls, and T. P. Trappenberg (2005). Self-organizing continuous attractor network models of hippocampal spatial view cells. *Neurobiology of Learning and Memory 83*, 79–92.

Stuphorn, V., E. Bauswein, and K. P. Hoffmann (2000). Neurons in the primate superior colliculus coding for arm movements in gaze-related coordinates. *Journal of Neurophysiology 83*, 1283–1299.

Sugihara, T., S. Edelman, and K. Tanaka (1998). Representation of objective similarity among three-dimensional shapes in the monkey. *Biological Cybernetics 78*, 1–7.

Sugrue, L. P., G. S. Corrado, and W. T. Newsome (2005). Choosing the greater of two goods: neural currencies for valuation and decision making. *Nature Reviews Neuroscience 6*, 1–13.

Sumner, P., P.-C. Tsai, K. Yu, and P. Nachev (2006). Attentional modulation of sensorimotor processes in the absence of perceptual awareness. *Proceedings of the National Academy of Science 103*, 10520–10525.

Suppes, P., B. Han, and Z.-L. Lu (1998). Brain-wave recognition of sentences. *Proceedings of the National Academy of Science 95*, 15861–15866.

Sutton, J. (2002). Cognitive conceptions of language and the development of autobiographical memory. *Language & Communication 22*, 375–390.

Sutton, J. (2006). Distributed cognition: Domains and dimensions. *Pragmatics & Cognition 14*, 235–247.

Szathmáry, E. and J. M. Smith (1995). The major evolutionary transitions. *Nature 374*, 227–232.

Tanaka, J. and I. Gauthier (1997). Expertise in object and face recognition. In D. Medin, R. Goldstone, and P. Schyns (Eds.), *Mechanisms of Perceptual Learning*, pp. 85–125. Academic Press.

Taylor, J. G. (2002). Paying attention to consciousness. *Trends in Cognitive Sciences 6*, 206–210.

Tegmark, M. (2000). Importance of quantum decoherence in brain processes. *Physical Review E 61*, 4194–4206.

Tenenbaum, J. B. (1999). Bayesian modeling of human concept learning. In S. A. Solla, T. K. Leen, and K.-R. Müller (Eds.), *NIPS (Advances in Neural Information Processing Systems)*, Volume 12, Cambridge, MA. MIT Press.

Tenenbaum, J. B. (2000). Rules and similarity in concept learning. In S. Solla, T. Leen, and K. Muller (Eds.), *Advances in Neural Information Processing Systems*, Volume 12, Cambridge, MA, pp. 59–65. MIT Press.

Tenenbaum, J. B. and W. T. Freeman (2000). Separating style and content with bilinear models. *Neural Computation 12*, 1247–1283.

Tenenbaum, J. B. and T. L. Griffiths (2001). Generalization, similarity, and Bayesian inference. *Behavioral and Brain Sciences 24*, 629–641.

Tenenbaum, J. B., T. L. Griffiths, and S. Niyogi (2006). Intuitive theories as grammars for causal inference. In A. Gopnik and L. Schulz (Eds.), *Causal learning: Psychology, philosophy, and computation*. Oxford University Press.

Theakston, A. L. (2004). The role of entrenchment in children's and adults' performance on grammaticality judgment tasks. *Cognitive Development 19*, 15–34.

Thomas, E., M. M. Van Hulle, and R. Vogels (2001). Encoding of categories by noncategory-specific neurons in the inferior temporal cortex. *J. Cognitive Neuroscience 13*, 190–200.

Thompson, R. K. R. and D. L. Oden (2000). Categorical perception and conceptual judgments by nonhuman primates: the paleological monkey and the analogical ape. *Cognitive Science 24*, 363–396.

Toga, A. W. and P. M. Thompson (2005). Genetics of brain structure and intelligence. *Annual Review of Neuroscience 28*, 1–23.

Tolkien, J. J. R. (1954). *The Lord of the Rings*. London: George Allen & Unwin.

Tolman, E. C., B. F. Ritchie, and D. Kalish (1946). Studies in spatial learning: II. Place learning versus response learning. *Journal of Experimental Psychology 37*, 385–392.

Tomasello, M. (Ed.) (1998). *The new psychology of language*. Mahwah, NJ: Erlbaum.

Tomasello, M. (2000a). The item-based nature of children's early syntactic development. *Trends in Cognitive Sciences 4*, 156–163.

Tomasello, M. (2000b). Primate cognition: introduction to the issue. *Cognitive Science 24*, 351–361.

Tomasello, M. (2003). *Constructing a language: a usage-based theory of language acquisition*. Cambridge, MA: Harvard University Press.

Tomasello, M. (2006). Acquiring linguistic constructions. In R. Siegler and D. Kuhn (Eds.), *Handbook of Child Psychology*, pp. 1–48. Oxford.

Tong, F. (2003). Primary visual cortex and visual awareness. *Nature Reviews Neuroscience 4*, 219–229.

Tootell, R. B. H., E. Switkes, M. S. Silverman, and S. L. Hamilton (1988). Functional anatomy of macaque striate cortex. II. Retinotopic organization. *Journal of Neuroscience 8*, 1531–1568.

Torralba, A., K. P. Murphy, W. T. Freeman, and M. A. Rubin (2003). Context-based vision system for place and object recognition. In *Proc. IEEE Intl. Conference on Computer Vision (ICCV)*, Nice, France, pp. 273–281.

Treisman, A. (1986). Properties, parts, and objects. In K. R. Boff, L. Kaufman, and J. P. Thomas (Eds.), *Handbook of Perception and Human Performance*, Volume 2, Chapter 35, pp. 1–70. New York: Wiley.

Treisman, A. and G. Gelade (1980). A feature integration theory of attention. *Cognitive Psychology 12*, 97–136.

Trivers, R. L. (1971). The evolution of reciprocal altruism. *The Quarterly Review of Biology 46*, 35–57.

Tsao, F.-M., H.-M. Liu, and P. K. Kuhl (2004). Speech perception in infancy predicts language development in the second year of life: A longitudinal study. *Child Development 75*, 1067–1084.

Tsotsos, J. K. (1990). Analyzing vision at the complexity level. *Behavioral and Brain Sciences 13*, 423–445.

Tsunoda, K., Y. Yamane, M. Nishizaki, and M. Tanifuji (2001). Complex objects are represented in macaque inferotemporal cortex by the combination of feature columns. *Nature Neuroscience 4*, 832–838.

Turing, A. M. (1936). On computable numbers, with an application to the Entscheidungsproblem. *Proceedings of the London Mathematical Society, Series 2 42*, 230–265.

Turing, A. M. (1950). Computing machinery and intelligence. *Mind 59*, 433–460.

Tversky, A. and D. Kahneman (1983). Extension versus intuititve reasoning: The conjunction fallacy in probability judgment. *Psychological Review 90*, 293–315.

Tye, M. (2003). Qualia. In E. N. Zalta (Ed.), *Stanford Encyclopedia of Philosophy*. Stanford University. Available online at http://plato.stanford.edu/archives/sum2003/entries/qualia/.

Ullman, S. (1984). Visual routines. *Cognition 18*, 97–159.

Urry, H. L., J. B. Nitschke, I. Dolski, D. C. Jackson, K. M. Dalton, C. J. Mueller, M. A. Rosenkranz, C. D. Ryff, B. H. Singer, and R. J. Davidson (2004). Making a life worth living: Neural correlates of well-being. *Psychological Science 15*, 367–372.

Valentine, D. E., S. R. Sinha, and C. F. Moss (2002). Orienting responses and vocalizations produced by microstimulation in the superior colliculus of the echolocating bat, *Eptesicus fuscus*. *Journal of Comparative Physiology A 188*, 89–108.

Valentine, T. (1991). Representation and process in face recognition. In R. Watt (Ed.), *Vision and visual dysfunction*, Volume 14, Chapter 9, pp. 107–124. London: Macmillan.

Van Boven, L. and T. Gilovich (2003). To do or to have: That is the question. *Journal of Personality and Social Psychology 85*, 1193–1202.

Varzi, A. C. (2001). The best question. *Journal of Philosophical Logic 30*, 251–258.

Vidyasagar, T. R. (1998). Gating of neuronal responses in macaque primary visual cortex by an attentional spotlight. *Neuroreport 9*, 1947–1952.

Vinge, V. (1993). The coming technological singularity: how to survive in the post-human era. *Whole Earth Review Winter*. Available online at http://www-rohan.sdsu.edu/faculty/vinge/misc/singularity.html.

Vogeley, K. and G. R. Fink (2003). Neural correlates of the first-person perspective. *Trends in Cognitive Sciences 7*, 38–42.

Voltaire (1752). *Voltaire's philosophical dictionary*. New York: Knopf. Translated by H. I. Woolf (1924). Available online at http://history.hanover.edu/texts/voltaire/volindex.html.

Vrij, A., R. Fisher, S. Mann, and S. Leal (2006). Detecting deception by manipulating cognitive load. *Trends in Cognitive Sciences 10*, 141–142.

Wagner, U., S. Gais, H. Haider, R. Verleger, and J. Born (2004). Sleep inspires insight. *Nature 427*, 352–355.

Wang, R. F. and E. S. Spelke (2002). Human spatial representation: Insights from animals. *Trends in Cognitive Sciences 6*, 376–382.

Warneken, F. and M. Tomasello (2006). Altruistic helping in human infants and young chimpanzees. *Science 311*, 1301–1303.

Waterfall, H. R. (2006). *A little change is a good thing: Feature theory, language acquisition and variation sets*. Ph. D. thesis, University of Chicago.

Watt, W. C., H. Sakano, Z. Y. Lee, J. E. Reusch, K. Trinh, and D. R. Storm (2004). Odorant stimulation enhances survival of olfactory sensory neurons via MAPK and CREB. *Neuron 41*, 955–967.

Watts, A. (1994). Biting an iron bull. In M. Watts (Ed.), *Talking Zen*, pp. 124–137. New York: Weatherhill.

Wegner, D. M. (2003). The mind's best trick: how we experience conscious will. *Trends in Cognitive Sciences 7*, 65–69.

Wegner, D. M. (2004). Precis of *The Illusion of Conscious Will*. *Behavioral and Brain Sciences 27*, 649–692.

Weisberg, R. W. (1986). *Creativity: genius and other myths*. New York: W. H. Freeman.

Weisberg, R. W. (1993). *Creativity: beyond the myth of genius*. New York: W. H. Freeman.

Welchman, A. E., A. Deubelius, V. Conrad, H. H. Bülthoff, and Z. Kourtzi (2005). 3D shape perception from combined depth cues in human visual cortex. *Nature Neuroscience 8*, 820–827.

Wertenbaker, C. and I. Gutman (1985). Unusual visual symptoms. *Survey of Ophthalmology 29*, 297–299.

Whiten, A. (2000). Primate culture and social learning. *Cognitive Science 24*, 477–508.

Wickelgren, I. (1997). Working memory linked to intelligence. *Science 275*, 1581.

Wierzbicka, A. (1996). *Semantics: primes and universals*. Oxford: Oxford University Press.

Wiggs, C. L. and A. Martin (1998). Properties and mechanisms of perceptual priming. *Curr. Opin. Neurobiol. 8*, 227–233.

Wigner, E. P. (1960). The unreasonable effectiveness of mathematics in the natural sciences. *Comm. Pure Appl. Math. XIII*, 1–14.

Willshaw, D. J., O. P. Buneman, and H. C. Longuet-Higgins (1969). Non-holographic associative memory. *Nature 222*, 960–962.

Wilson, M. A. and B. L. McNaughton (1993). Dynamics of the hippocampal ensemble code for space. *Science 261*, 1055–1058.

Wilson, M. A. and B. L. McNaughton (1994). Reactivation of hippocampal ensemble memories during sleep. *Science 265*, 676–679.

Wilson, R. A. and F. C. Keil (Eds.) (2001). *The MIT Encyclopedia of the Cognitive Sciences (MITECS)*. Cambridge, MA: MIT Press.

Wilson, T. D. and D. T. Gilbert (2005). Affective forecasting: Knowing what to want. *Current Directions in Psychological Science 14*, 131–134.

Wise, S. P. and R. Shadmehr (2002). Motor control. In V. S. Ramachandran (Ed.), *Encyclopedia of the Human Brain*, Volume 3, pp. 137–157. San Diego, CA: Academic Press.

Wittgenstein, L. (1958). *Philosophical Investigations* (3rd ed.). Englewood Cliffs, NJ: Prentice Hall. Translated by G. E. M. Anscombe.

Wittgenstein, L. (1972). *On certainty*. New York: Harper Torchbooks.

Wolfe, J. M. and S. C. Bennett (1997). Preattentive object files: Shapeless bundles of basic features. *Vision Research 37*, 25–43.

Wolff, H. W. (1974). *Anthropology of the Old Testament*. Philadelphia: Fortress Press. Translated by Margaret Kohl.

Wood, E., P. A. Dudchenko, R. J. Robitsek, and H. Eichenbaum (2000). Hippocampal neurons encode information about different types of memory episodes occurring in the same location. *Neuron 27*, 623–633.

Wray, A. (2000). Holistic utterances in protolanguage: the link from primates to humans. In C. Knight, M. Studdert-Kennedy, and J. R. Hurford (Eds.), *The evolutionary emergence of language*, pp. 285–302. Cambridge: Cambridge University Press.

Xiao, Z. and N. Suga (2002). Modulation of cochlear hair cells by the auditory cortex in the mustached bat. *Nature Neuroscience 5*, 57–63.

Yates, F. A. (1966). *The Art of Memory*. Chicago: University of Chicago Press.

Yu, B. and M. P. Singh (2003). Detecting deception in reputation management. In *AAMAS'03: Proceedings of the Second International Conference on Autonomous Agents and Multiagent Systems*, New York, NY, pp. 73–80. ACM Press.

Yuille, A. and D. Kersten (2006). Vision as Bayesian inference: analysis by synthesis? *Trends in Cognitive Sciences 10*, 301–308.

Zaslaw, N. (January 27, 1997). Der neue Köchel. *Mozart Society of America Newsletter 1*(1).

Zwaan, R. A. (2001). Language comprehension as guided experience. In L. Degand, Y. Bestgen, W. Spooren, and L. van Waes (Eds.), *Multidisciplinary Approaches to Discourse*, pp. 1–9. Amsterdam: Uitgaven Stichting Neerlandistiek VU.

Credits

THE ORACLE: Michelangelo Buonarroti (1475-1564). The Delphic Sibyl (1510). Fresco, Cappella Sistina, Vatican. Wikimedia Commons image – *3* ᶒ BRAIN AND MIND RIDDLE: Man and woman: van Meckenem, Israhel (1445-1503), *Self-portrait* and *Wife*, engravings (ca. 1490). Wikimedia Commons image, public domain. Chartreuse cat: Wikimedia Commons photograph, released into public domain by user Evil woolf78 (2007). Siamese cat: Wikimedia Commons photograph, released into public domain by user Gramoleros (2005). Marmot: *Marmota olympus*, National Park Service photograph via Wikimedia Commons, public domain. Drk8080 robot photograph ⓘ Michael Kuroda, licensed under Creative Commons Attribution 2.0 License – *4* ᶒ PSIKHARPAX AND A FRIEND: Animat image © courtesy Benoît Girard, AnimatLab, France – *6* ᶒ NINE FRUIT, THREE WAYS: Photograph courtesy of Angie's Groves, www.angiesgroves.com – *7* ᶒ LIGHTNESS: A setup for studying lightness of surfaces, from Katz, D., 1935. *The World of Colour* (London: Kegan Paul, Trench, Trubner & Co) – *7* ᶒ PROMETHEUS: Füger, Heinrich Friedrich (1751-1818). *Prometheus Brings Fire to Mankind* (c. 1817). Oil on canvas. Liechtenstein Museum. Public domain – *13* ᶒ DANCE AND (MIS)COMMUNICATION: © Cartoonbank.com, a division of The New Yorker Magazine – *14* ᶒ A SIGN: Illustration courtesy of Alexei Sharov – *15* ᶒ ABACUS: Wikimedia Commons image. Public domain – *17* ᶒ REFLEX ARC: Drawing by René Descartes (1596-1650). Public domain – *18* ᶒ PINYON JAY: *Gymnorhinus cyanocephalus*. Photograph by Dave Menke, US Fish and Wildlife Service, via Wikimedia Commons – *19* ᶒ ARMILLARY: Wikimedia Commons image. Public domain – *20* ᶒ TIME AND SPACE: Dalí, Salvador (1904-1989). *Soft Watch at the Moment of First Explosion*. 1954. Oil on canvas. © 2007 Salvador Dali, Gala-Salvador Dali Foundation / Artists Rights Society (ARS), New York – *21* ᶒ APLYSIA: The sea slug *Aplysia californica*. Photograph courtesy of Columbia University, placed in the public domain by the National Human Genome Research Institute (NIH) – *22* ᶒ PROUST'S MANUSCRIPT: The last page of the manuscript of *À la recherche du temps perdu* by Marcel Proust. Wikimedia Commons image – *22* ᶒ LASCAUX: A sketch by A. Glory of a paleolithic painting from the Lascaux cave in Dordogne, France. Wikimedia Commons image. Public domain – *23* ❧ ONE IF BY LAND: Paul Revere's ride. Wikimedia Commons image. Public domain – *23* ❧ TREACHERY OF IMAGES: Magritte, René (1898-1967). *Treachery of Images*. 1928-1929. Oil on canvas. © 2007 C. Herscovici, Brussels / Artists Rights Society (ARS), New York – *24* ❧ CLAIRVOYANCE: Magritte, René (1898-1967). *Clairvoyance*. 1936. Oil on canvas. © 2007 C. Herscovici, Brussels / Artists Rights Society (ARS), New York – *24* ❧ CAT BOUNCING OFF A WALL: Photograph ⓘ (2006) Flickr user tetraconz, made public under Creative Commons Attribution licence 2.5 – *25* ❧ INFINITE REGRESS: *A Recursive Homunculus*, computer drawing ⓘ Shimon Edelman (1987), made public under the Creative Commons Attribution license 2.5 – *25* ❧ TURING MACHINE: Redrawn after Petrov, P., *Church-Turing Thesis as an Immature Form of Zuse-Fredkin Thesis (More Arguments in Favour of the 'Universe as a Cellular Automaton' Idea)* (2003) – *27* ❧ PRIME MOVER: Raphael (Raffaello Sanzio) (1483-1520). *Astronomy*, from the ceiling of the Stanza della Segnatura. Stanze di Raffaello, Vatican Palace, Vatican State. Photo credit: Scala / Art Resource, NY – *28* ❧ DYNAMICAL SYSTEM: Image courtesy of O. Knill, http://dynamical-systems.org – *29* ❧ DRAGONFLY: Photograph ⓘ Shimon Edelman (2007), made public under the Creative Commons Attribution license 2.5 – *30* ❧ HIERARCHICAL ABSTRACTION: Redrawn after Rudrauf et al. (2003, fig.3) – *30* ❧ CASSINI SPACECRAFT: Image courtesy NASA/JPL-Caltech – *32* ❧ PROMETHEUS: Moreau, Gustave (1826-1898). *Prometheus*. Oil on canvas. 1868. Photograph placed in public domain by the Yorck Project: 10.000 Meisterwerke der Malerei. Courtesy of DIRECTMEDIA Publishing GmbH – *32* ❧ DIAGRAM OF THE BRAIN: Miniaturist, English (active c. 1300). Diagram of the brain, after Avicenna. Illumination on parchment. University Library, Cambridge – *37* ❧ PYRAMIDAL NEURON: Image courtesy of R. Hevner – *38* ❧ ACTION POTENTIALS: Redrawn after Jaffe (2005) – *39* ❧ SYNAPSE: Electron microphotograph courtesy of Pati S. Irish, University of Washington – *40* ❧ RETINA: A drawing by Santiago Ramon y Cajal (1901) – *40* ❧ HYRAX: Cape hyrax, *Procavia capensis*. Photograph released into the public domain by Wikimedia Commons user Anthony Steele (2005) – *41* ❧ MICROELECTRODES: Microphotograph of in vitro recording from NG108-15 neuroblastoma cells courtesy of Dr. Peter Molnar, NanoScience Technology Center, University of Central Florida – *42* ❧ FACE TUNING: Monkey photograph ⓘ Wikimedia Commons user Rob, released under Creative Commons Attribution 2.0 License. Karl Marx photograph: public domain – *44* ❧ MRI SCANNER: Varian 4T MRI scanner, at the Brain Imaging Center, Helen Wills Neuroscience Institute, University of California, Berkeley. Photograph released into the public domain by Wikimedia Commons user Semiconscious – *45* ❧

RETINOTOPY: Redrawn after Tootell et al. (1988, figs.1,2) – *45* ❧ TONOTOPY: Redrawn after Xiao and Suga (2002, fig.1) – *45* ❧ OPTIC CHIASM: Drawing 722 from Gray's *Anatomy*. Wikimedia Commons image. Public domain – *47* ❧ VARIABLE-RESOLUTION EYE CHART: Redrawn after Anstis (1974, fig.3) – *48* ❧ SOMATOSENSORY HOMUNCULUS: Illustration courtesy of C. D. Smith, MD, via Wikimedia Commons – *48* ❧ SOMATOSENSORY PLASTICITY: Redrawn after Recanzone, Merzenich, Jenkins, Kamil, and Dinse (1992) – *49* ❧ STAIRWAY TO HEAVEN: Lyrics excerpt © Led Zeppelin – *50* ❧ THE ZIGGURAT OF UR: Wikimedia Commons image, released into the public domain by Tla2006 – *50* ❧ COMPLEX RECEPTIVE FIELD: Redrawn after Hubel and Wiesel (1959) – *52* ❧ FIDDLER CRAB: *Uca longisignalis*, NOAA image. Public domain – *53* ❧ VISUAL-MOTOR COORDINATION: Churchland (1986, fig.2). Reproduced by permission of Oxford University Press – *53* ❧ CROSSBAR NETWORK: Churchland (1986, fig.9,10). Reproduced by permission of Oxford University Press – *54* ❧ COMPOUND EYE MAN: Figure 7c from *The resolution of lens and compound eyes*, in *Neural principles in vision*, K. Kirschfeld, Springer Verlag, Berlin Heidelberg 1976. Image courtesy of K. Kirschfeld – *57* ❧ VISUAL-MOTOR COORDINATION: Drawing by René Descartes (1596-1650). Public domain – *58* ❧ MULTIDIMENSIONAL CUBES: Images courtesy Miqel.com – *62* ❧ FRONTISPIECE OF *Novum Organum*: Bacon, Francis. *Instauratio Magna*, 1620. Photo credit: Image Select / Art Resource, NY – *65* ❧ COLUMNAR STRUCTURE OF MT CORTEX: Redrawn after Newsome and Stein-Aviles (1999, fig.4) – *66* ❧ THE MOTION COHERENCE TASK: Redrawn after Newsome and Stein-Aviles (1999, fig.5) – *67* ❧ THE RECEPTIVE FIELD OF AN MT NEURON: Redrawn after Newsome and Stein-Aviles (1999, fig.3) – *67* ❧ MICROSTIMULATION IN AREA MT: Redrawn after Newsome and Stein-Aviles (1999, fig.6) – *68* ❧ CHICKEN CROSSING: Image courtesy of Jackie Damrau and STC Lone Star Community – *69* ❧ BARN OWL: A drawing of a barn owl, *Tyto alba*, from Thomas Bewick's *History of British Birds* (1847) – *71* ❧ BINAURAL HEARING: Owl photograph: ⓘWikimedia Commons user Stevie B, licensed under Creative Commons Attribution 2.0 License. Mouse photograph: Wikimedia Commons, courtesy NIH, public domain – *72* ❧ BARN OWL: Redrawn after Carew (2001, ch.3) – *73* ❧ BARN OWL: Redrawn after Carew (2001, ch.3) – *74* ❧ BARN OWL, NUCLEUS LAMINARIS: Redrawn after Carew (2001, ch.3) – *75* ❧ NEURON ON A CHIP: Scanning electron micrograph © (1987) courtesy Judy Trogadis – *78* ❧ LEOPARD: Photograph ⓘ Patrick Giraud (2006), made public under the Creative Commons Attribution license 2.5 – *85* ❧ WORDS AND IMAGES: A composition patterned after a fragment (3rd column, 4th row from the top) from René Magritte's

Gallery, London / Art Resource, NY – *114* ⋙ A SILLY WALK: Image of John Cleese from *Monty Python's Flying Circus*, © courtesy of Python (Monty) Pictures, Ltd – *115* ⋙ COLOR SPACE: Image from Isaac Newton's *Optics* (1660). Public domain – *116* ⋙ SHEPARD'S COLOR SPACE: Shepard (1962b, p.236). © 1962 by the Psychometric Society – *116* ⋙ GENERALIZATION GRADIENTS: Shepard (1987). Reprinted with permission from AAAS – *116* ⋙ KAKURU: Illustration by Carl Buell – *119* ⋙ BAYESIAN VISION: Kersten et al. (2004, p.274). Reprinted, with permission, from the Annual Review of Psychology, Volume 55 © 2004 by Annual Reviews www.annualreviews.org – *120* ⋙ NEURON-LEVEL VERIDICALITY: Redrawn after Op de Beeck et al. (2001) – *128* ⋙ RAPHAEL: Raphael (Raffaello Sanzio) (1483-1520). Self-portrait. 1506. Uffizi, Florence, Italy. Photo credit: Scala / Art Resource, NY – *130* ⋙ REMBRANDT: Rembrandt Harmensz van Rijn (1606-1669). Self-portrait, 1629. Oil on wood. Alte Pinakothek, Munich, Germany. Photo credit: Scala / Art Resource, NY – *130* ⋙ ATHENA: Phidias (c. 480 BC - c. 430 BC), *Athena Lemnia*. Photograph © The Art Archive / Dagli Orti – *131* ⋙ ZEUS: Phidias (c. 480 BC - c. 430 BC), *Zeus* – *131* ⋙ PARTHENON: The temple of Pallas Athena on the Acropolis, in Athens, Greece. Photograph released into the public domain by Wikimedia Commons user Mountain (2006) – *132* ⋙ RYOAN-JI: The Ryoan temple in Kyoto, Japan. Photograph released into the public domain by Wikimedia Commons user Fg2 (2005) – *132* ⋙ DUBYA TO DICK: Cartoon by Bill Day © Commercial Appeal, distributed by United Feature Syndicate, Inc – *133* ⋙ MR. SPOCK: Leonard Nimoy as Mr. Spock, in Robert Wise's film *Star Trek, The Motion Picture* (1979). Photograph © Paramount / The Kobal Collection – *133* ⋙ *Almond blossom*: Photograph ⋒ Shimon Edelman (2004), made public under the Creative Commons Attribution license 2.5 – *135* ⋙ *Wabi-sabi*: Photographs ⋒ Shimon Edelman (2003-2005), made public under the Creative Commons Attribution license 2.5 – *135* ⋙ FROM ONE DAY TO ANOTHER: Magritte, René (1898-1967). *D'un jour a l'autre*. © ARS, NY. Photo credit Herscovici / Art Resource, NY – *138* ⋙ TOMATOES: Photograph released into the public domain by Wikimedia Commons user Stegano (2006) – *138* ⋙ THE BIRTH OF ATHENA: Athena issuing from the head of Zeus. Attic black-figured amphora, 5th BCE. Louvre, Paris, France. Photo Credit: Erich Lessing / Art Resource, NY – *139* ⋙ VISUAL RECEPTIVE FIELDS IN AREAS V4, IT: Kobatake and Tanaka (1994) – *144* ⋙ VISUAL RECEPTIVE FIELDS IN AREA IT: Op de Beeck and Vogels (2000). Reprinted with Permission of Wiley-Liss, Inc., a subsidiary of John Wiley and Sons, Inc – *144* ⋙ *Iron horse*: Photograph ⋒ Shimon Edelman (2004), made public under the Creative Commons Attribution license 2.5 – *146* ⋙ SCENE AND OBJECT VISION BY

175 ❧ RAT PATHS RECONSTRUCTED FROM NEURAL ACTIVITY: Wilson and McNaughton (1993). Reprinted with permission from AAAS – *176* ❧ COGNITIVE MAPS: Eichenbaum et al. (1999, fig.5,6), © Elsevier – *176* ❧ USING PLACE CELLS: Burgess (2002). Reproduced by permission of Taylor & Francis Ltd., http://www.informaworld.com – *177* ❧ BLACK-CAPPED CHICKADEES: *Poecile atricapillus*. Acrylic painting (1974), Bob Hines, United States Fish and Wildlife Service. Wikimedia Commons – *178* ❧ A LONDON CAB: Photograph courtesy of Ed Sanders (2003), via Wikimedia Commons – *178* ❧ WHAT DOES EVERYONE KNOW?: Quote from Elio (2002, pp.3-36), reproduced by permission of Oxford University Press, Inc – *179* ❧ CARTOON GRAVITY: Top panel of *Cartoon Physics* (⚖) (2007) courtesy of Greg Williams and the Wikimedia Commons – *179* ❧ *A Day in the Life*: Excerpt © Apple Corp. (The Beatles) – *181* ❧ COWS (MEDIEVAL): © 1996 Dover Books – *183* ❧ A TREBUCHET: © 1996 Dover Books – *183* ❧ COW (AN OUTLINE): Image public domain – *183* ❧ *View of the World from 9th Avenue* (S. STEINBERG): Cover of *The New Yorker*, March 29, 1976. Copyright © 1976 The Saul Steinberg Foundation / Artists Rights Society (ARS), New York. Cover reprinted with permission of *The New Yorker* magazine. All rights reserved – *184* ❧ VITRUVIAN MAN: Da Vinci, Leonardo(1452-1519). *Vitruvian Man* (1492). Pen and ink on paper. Photograph courtesy Luc Viatour via Wikimedia Commons – *187* ❧ WOTAN: Fritz Feinhals (1869-1940) singing Wotan in Wagner's *Der Ring das Nibelungen* (1903) – *188* ❧ A RUBE GOLDBERG CONTRAPTION: *How to keep your boss from knowing when you are late* by Rube Goldberg ® and © of Rube Goldberg, Inc – *191* ❧ REMEMBER LOVE: The façade of the Kulturhuset Museum, Stockholm, which in the summer of 2004 hosted an exhibition of Yoko Ono's works, titled *Remember Love* (Hayden, 2004). Photograph (⚖) Shimon Edelman (2004), made public under the Creative Commons Attribution license 2.5 – *195* ❧ ORANGUTAN WITH A *Neesia* FRUIT: Illustration © (2007) Perry van Duijnhoven – *196* ❧ LEARNING TO PLAY TENNIS BY IMITATION: Billard et al. (2004) © Royal Society of London – *197* ❧ IMITATION FLOW CHART: Schaal (1999, fig.3), © Elsevier – *197* ❧ WHAT WOULD JESUS DRIVE?: Cartoon by Bill Schorr © United Feature Syndicate – *201* ❧ CHIMPANZEES JUDGING GAZE DIRECTION: Povinelli et al. (2000, fig.10), © Cognitive Science Society – *202* ❧ THE VALUE OF SIMULATION: Off the mark 1/13/1998 Atlantic Feature © 1998 Mark Parisi – *204* ❧ DIMENSIONS OF HIPPOCAMPAL ACTIVATION: Lin et al. (2006), © Elsevier (2006) – *208* ❧ HIERARCHICAL REPRESENTATIONS IN THE HIPPOCAMPUS: Lin et al. (2005, fig.4) © 2005 National Academy of Sciences, USA – *210* ❧ MIRROR NEURONS: Gallese and Goldman (1998, fig.1), © Elsevier – *211* ❧ RASHOMON:

A scene from Akira Kurosawa's film *Rashomon* (1951). Image public domain – *214* ❧ OVERCONFIDENCE IN RECOGNITION MEMORY: Redrawn after Koriat (1995) – *215* ❧ MEMORY ACCESS: Redrawn after Koriat and Goldsmith (1996b) – *216* ❧ *The Memory of a Journey III* (R. MAGRITTE): Copyright © 2007 C. Herscovici, Brussels / Artists Rights Society (ARS), New York – *217* ❧ FALSE MEMORY: Loftus (2003, fig.1) – *218* ❧ MNEMONICS: Excerpt from *Memory Course*, © courtesy of Python (Monty) Pictures, Ltd – *219* ❧ GIULIO CAMILLO'S MEMORY THEATER: A reconstruction by Yates (1966), courtesy of the University of Chicago Press – *220* ❧ THE MAN OF THE SEA: Magritte, René (1898-1967). *The Man of the Sea*. Oil on canvas. 1927. © 2007 C. Herscovici, Brussels / Artists Rights Society (ARS), New York – *222* ❧ THE FUNNIEST JOKE: Excerpt from *Monty Python's Flying Circus*, © courtesy of Python (Monty) Pictures, Ltd – *225* ❧ THE MEANING OF LIFE: Photograph (ⓘ) Shimon Edelman (2007), made public under the Creative Commons Attribution license 2.5 – *227* ❧ LETHE: Spencer Stanhope, John Roddam (1829-1908). *The Waters of Lethe by the Plains of Elysium* (1880, detail). Oil on canvas. Manchester Art Gallery, UK / The Bridgeman Art Library – *228* ❧ *Once in a Lifetime*: Lyrics excerpt © Talking Heads – *233* ❧ ARS MAGNA: Kircher, Athanasius (1602-1680). A woodcut from *Ars Magna Sciendi* (1669), courtesy Department of Special Collections, Stanford University Libraries – *235* ❧ MALKOVICH-MALKOVICH: John Malkovich as himself in *Being John Malkovich*, a film by Spike Jonze (1999). Photograph © Universal / The Kobal Collection – *236* ❧ WORD PERMUTATIONS: Lull, Raymond (1235-1315). A woodcut from *Ars Magna* (1305). Wikimedia Commons image, public domain – *237* ❧ TWO CAMOUFLAGED PTARMIGAN: Photograph © (2007) courtesy of Andrew Leenheer – *238* ❧ LEON TROTSKY: Wikimedia Commons image. Public domain – *239* ❧ THE PHILOSOPHICAL LANGUAGE OF JOHN WILKINS: Image public domain – *242* ❧ SURPRISED INFANT: Photograph © (1987) by Shimon Edelman – *247* ❧ TWITTERING MACHINE: Klee, Paul (1879-1940) © 2007 Artists Rights Society (ARS), New York / VG Bild-Kunst, Bonn. *Twittering Machine*. 1922. Watercolor and pen and ink on oil transfer drawing on paper, mounted on cardboard. The Museum of Modern Art, New York, USA. Digital image © The Museum of Modern Art / Licensed by SCALA / Art Resource, NY – *248* ❧ A SPECTROGRAM OF SPEECH: A spectrogram of a Japanese woman from Shinagawa, Tokyo, saying minato. Image (ⓘ) ishwar (2005), made public under the Creative Commons Attribution license 2.0 – *249* ❧ BRIAN MEETS PILATE: Excerpt from *Monty Python's Life of Brian*, © courtesy Python (Monty) Pictures, Ltd – *250* ❧ CAVALRY OF CORTÉS: Sixteenth century depiction of the battle for Tenochtitlan between the Aztecs and the

army of Hernán Cortés. Wikimedia Commons image, public domain – *251* ❧
LEARNING LANGUAGE: THE FIRST YEAR: Redrawn after Kuhl (2004, fig.1) –
251 ❧ THE VEGETABLE GARDENER: Arcimboldo, Giuseppe (1530-1593).
The Vegetable Gardener (c. 1590). © The Art Archive / Museo Civico Cremona /
Dagli Orti – *254* ❧ NOW THEN!: Excerpts from *Monty Python's Flying Circus*,
© courtesy of Python (Monty) Pictures, Ltd – *256* ❧ HUNGARIAN PHRASE-
BOOK: Excerpt from *Monty Python's Flying Circus*, © courtesy of Python (Monty)
Pictures, Ltd – *258* ❧ THE VIRTUES OF TELECONFERENCING: © Cartoon-
bank.com, a division of The New Yorker Magazine – *258* ❧ GRAMMAR AND
LEXICON: Redrawn after Bates and Goodman (1999) – *262* ❧ THE MAN-
DARIN VERB-NOT-VERB CONSTRUCTION: Image courtesy of Mark A. Baker,
www.chinese-outpost.com – *263* ❧ ROMANES EUNT DOMUS: Excerpt from
Monty Python's Life of Brian, © courtesy of Python (Monty) Pictures, Ltd – *272* ❧
THE LONDON TUBE MAP: © London Transport – *274* ❧ GRAMMAR: De la
Hyre, Laurent (1606-1656), *Allegorical Figure of Grammar* (1650). Oil on canvas.
© National Gallery, London. Reproduced by permission – *276* ❧ RICO, THE
BORDER COLLIE: Photo by Manuela Hartling, © (2004) Reuters. Reproduced by
permission – *278* ❧ THE JABBERWOCKY: Tenniel, John (1820-1914). *Jabber-*
wocky. An illustration to Lewis Carroll's *Through the Looking-Glass* (1872). Public
domain – *279* ❧ NO CLASS WARFARE: © Cartoonbank.com, a division of
The New Yorker Magazine – *280* ❧ GIVE PEACE A CHANCE: Recording of
Give Peace a Chance at the 1969 bed-in, showing John Lennon and Yoko Ono, with
Timothy Leary in front. Photograph ⓹ Roy Kerwood, made public under Creative
Commons Attribution 2.5 license – *281* ❧ TROUBLE AT THE MILL: Excerpt
from *Monty Python's Flying Circus*, © courtesy of Python (Monty) Pictures, Ltd –
283 ❧ MOTOR HOMUNCULUS: Fig. 22, p.57 of *The Cerebral Cortex of Man* by
Penfield/Rasmussen (1950). Reprinted with permission of Gale, a division of Thom-
son Learning: www.thomsonrights.com. Fax 800 730-2215 – *289* ❧ GREEK
TRIREME: Wikimedia Commons image (U.S. Air Force Air War College). Pub-
lic domain – *296* ❧ FIGS: *Ficus carica*, leaves and fruit. G. Eric and Edith
Matson Photograph Collection, Library of Congress. Public domain – *296* ❧
WADING GODWITS: Marbled godwits (*Limosa fedoa*) near Malibu, California.
Photograph ⓹ Shimon Edelman (2004), made public under the Creative Commons
Attribution license 2.5 – *296* ❧ SENTENCE SPACE: Modified from a map of
the Bear seamount, Stocks, K. 2005. *SeamountsOnline: an online information sys-*
tem for seamount biology. Version 2005-1. http://seamounts.sdsc.edu – *298* ❧
BASHŌ'S HAIKU: Translation © Alan Watts – *299* ❧ A 3D SWITCHYARD:
Image courtesy Phil Saunders © www.saunderscreative.com – *301* ❧ LINGUIS-

TIC INCOMPETENCE: Excerpt from *Monty Python's Flying Circus*, © courtesy of Python (Monty) Pictures, Ltd – *302* ❧ ENJOYING WINE: Heracles visiting the centaur Pholus. Offering wine to his guest Pholus carries game hanging from a tree over his shoulder. Black figure hydria (calpis), ca. 520-510 BCE. Photo: Hervé Lewandowski. Louvre, Paris, France. Photo Credit: Réunion des Musées Nationaux / Art Resource, NY – *304* ❧ THE WASTE LAND: Excerpt from *The Waste Land* © 1922 T. S. Eliot. Reprinted by permission of Harcourt, Inc – *305* ❧ A CAT IN MEDITATION: Burroughs gazing at a wall. Photograph courtesy Jennifer Cramlet (2007). A drawing of a similarly predisposed cat appears on p.60 of *Old Possum's Book of Practical Cats*, T. S. Eliot, Faber & Faber, London (1962) – *306* ❧ THE NAMING OF CATS: Excerpt from *The Naming of Cats* in *Old Possum's Book of Practical Cats*, © 1939 by T. S. Eliot and renewed 1967 by Esme Valerie Eliot, reprinted by permission of Harcourt, Inc – *306* ❧ BODHIDHARMA (DARUMA) IN MEDITATION: Sesshū Tōyō (1420-1506). Ink on paper (detail) – *306* ❧ THE THOUGHT WHICH SEES: Magritte, René (1898-1967). Copyright © 2007 C. Herscovici, Brussels / Artists Rights Society (ARS), New York. *The Thought Which Sees*, 1965. Graphite on paper. Gift of Mr. and Mrs. Charles B. Benenson. The Museum of Modern Art, New York, NY, USA. Digital image © The Museum of Modern Art / Licensed by SCALA / Art Resource, NY – *315* ❧ A CLAY DISH FROM BAMIYAN: Kabul Museum, Afghanistan – *316* ❧ A VEHICLE BRAIN: Adapted from Jones and Flynn (1993) – *317* ❧ APOLLO 13, DAMAGED SERVICE MODULE: Photograph courtesy NASA/JPL-Caltech – *318* ❧ THE TOWER OF HANOI STATE SPACE GRAPH: Diagram courtesy of Salvador Gutierrez – *319* ❧ STATE SPACE SEARCH IN CHESS: Campitelli and Gobet (2004) – *322* ❧ CHUNKING IN CHESS: Gobet et al. (2001) – *323* ❧ LIMPETS: Excerpt from *Monty Python's Flying Circus*, © courtesy of Python (Monty) Pictures, Ltd – *324* ❧ LIMPETS: Image courtesy of Alasdair Hamilton and the Scottish Natural Heritage Image Library – *324* ❧ GO: A Go game board. Wikimedia Commons photograph ⓕ Dmitri Lechtchinski, made available under Creative Commons Attribution 2.5 license – *324* ❧ THE APOLLO SPACECRAFT IN THE LUNAR TRANSIT CONFIGURATION: Illustration courtesy of NASA/JPL-Caltech – *327* ❧ APOLLO 13 CO_2 SCRUBBER ADAPTOR: Photograph courtesy of NASA/JPL-Caltech – *328* ❧ BETTER OR WORSE: Calvin and Hobbes, © Universal Press Syndicate. Reprinted by permission – *331* ❧ SPANISH INQUISITION: Excerpts from *Monty Python's Flying Circus*, © courtesy of Python (Monty) Pictures, Ltd – *332* ❧ LOGIC: Bierce, Ambrose. *The Unabridged Devil's Dictionary*. © (2002) The University of Georgia Press – *335* ❧ ARGUMENT CLINIC: Excerpt from *Monty Python's Flying Circus*, © courtesy of Python (Monty) Pictures, Ltd – *336*

(1881-1973) © 2007 Estate of Pablo Picasso / Artists Rights Society (ARS), New York. *Bull's Head (seat and handles of a bicycle)*, 1942. Photo: Beatrice Hatala. Musee Picasso, Paris, France. Photo credit: Réunion des Musées Nationaux / Art Resource, NY – *380* ❧ THE DUNCKER CANDLE PROBLEM: Wikimedia Commons image. Public domain – *380* ❧ VARIATIONS ON A THEME: Redrawn after Hofstadter (1985a, ch.12) – *381* ❧ ELEPHANT: Calder, Alexander (1898-1976) © 2007 Calder Foundation, New York / Artists Rights Society (ARS), New York. *Elephant*, c. 1928. Wire. Private collection. Photo credit: Art Resource, NY – *383* ❧ GOLDFISH BOWL: Calder, Alexander (1898-1976) © 2007 Calder Foundation, New York / Artists Rights Society (ARS), New York. *Goldfish Bowl*, 1929. Wire. Private collection. Photo credit: Art Resource, NY – *383* ❧ BLUE FEATHER: Calder, Alexander (1898-1976) © 2007 Calder Foundation, New York / Artists Rights Society (ARS), New York. *Blue Feather*, c. 1929. Wire. Private collection. Photo credit: Art Resource, NY – *383* ❧ THE WRIGHTS' FLYER: The first successful flight at Kitty Hawk on Dec. 17, 1903. Photograph by John T. Daniels. Public domain – *385* ❧ REPRODUCTION PROHIBITED: Magritte, René (1898-1967) © 2007 C. Herscovici, Brussels / Artists Rights Society (ARS), New York. *La Reproduction Interdite* (Portrait d'Edward James). 1937. Oil on canvas. Museum Boymans van Beuningen, Rotterdam, The Netherlands. Photo credit: Banque d'Images, ADAGP / Art Resource, NY – *387* ❧ THE SON OF MAN: Magritte, René (1898-1967) © 2007 C. Herscovici, Brussels / Artists Rights Society (ARS), New York. *The Son of Man*. 1964. Oil on canvas. Private collection. Photo credit: Banque d'Images, ADAGP / Art Resource, NY – *395* ❧ *Upper Tse'elim Canyon, the Judean Desert*: Photograph ⓘ S. Edelman (2005), made public under the Creative Commons Attribution license 2.5 – *396* ❧ *Schrödinger's Cat*: photograph ⓘ S. Edelman (2005), made public under the Creative Commons Attribution license 2.5 – *399* ❧ VOLTAIRE: Dalí, Salvador. (1904-1989). *Slave Market with a Disappearing Bust of Voltaire*. 1940. Oil on canvas. Copyright © 2007 Salvador Dali, Gala-Salvador Dali Foundation / Artists Rights Society (ARS), NY – *402* ❧ ATTENTION IN AREA V4: Redrawn from Moran and Desimone (1985) – *405* ❧ MICROSTIMULATION OF FRONTAL EYE FIELDS: Moore and Fallah (2001, fig.3) – *406* ❧ THE FUNCTIONAL ARCHITECTURE OF ATTENTION: Redrawn from Shipp (2004, fig.2g) – *407* ❧ THERE IS NO SPOON: Photograph by Shimon Edelman, inspired by a scene from *The Matrix*, a film by Andy and Larry Wachowski (1999) – *410* ❧ GAVAGAI!: Photograph © (2006) Shimon Edelman – *411* ❧ EYE: Escher, Maurits Cornelius (1898-1972). *Eye*. 1946. Lithograph. © The M. C. Escher Company. Photo Credit: Art Resource, NY – *412* ❧ AGENCY AND OWNERSHIP: Redrawn from Gallagher (2000, fig.1) – *413* ❧ A

PIERSON'S PUPPETEER: Illustration © courtesy Carl Buell – *416* ❧ TELEP-
RESENCE: Photograph courtesy NASA – *416* ❧ GOTTLIEB ON DESCARTES:
Excerpt from *Think Again: What did Descartes really know?*, Anthony Gottlieb,
The New Yorker, Nov. 20, 2006, pp.86-92, © (2006) The New Yorker – *418* ❧
A RECEPTIVE FIELD FROM THE CAT'S SUPERIOR COLLICULUS: Groh and
Werner-Reiss (2002, fig.1), © Elsevier – *422* ❧ VISUAL-MOTOR CONTROL
AS A NEURAL MAPPING: Churchland (1986, fig.6). Reproduced by permission
of Oxford University Press – *422* ❧ THE LOCATION OF THE SUPERIOR
COLLICULUS: Human Brain, sagittal section: Wikimedia Commons illustration ⊛
Patrick J. Lynch, medical illustrator and C. Carl Jaffe, MD, cardiologist, released un-
der Creative Commons Attribution 2.5 license – *423* ❧ MULTIMODAL TUNING
OF RECEPTIVE FIELDS IN THE SC: Gutfreund et al. (2002, fig.3). Reprinted
with permission from AAAS – *423* ❧ A SUPERIOR COLLICULUS CELL
RESPONDING TO VISUAL AND AUDITORY STIMULI: Groh and Werner-Reiss
(2002, fig.3,6), © Elsevier – *424* ❧ A VIEW THROUGH MY LEFT EYE: Figure 1 from Ernst Mach's *Analysis of the Sensations* (1886). Image public domain –
426 ❧ SCALLOP EYES: Wikimedia Commons image. Public domain – *427*
❧ "SEEING AS": A garter snake in the Robert Treman State Park, Ithaca, NY.
Photograph ⊛ (2007) Shimon Edelman, made public under the Creative Commons
Attribution license 2.5 – *427* ❧ CAT CONTEMPLATING A JUMP: © Cartoon-
bank.com, a division of The New Yorker magazine – *428* ❧ LOBSTER: Image
courtesy of US Department of Interior, Fish and Wildlife Service – *430* ❧ AC-
CESS CONSCIOUSNESS: Redrawn after Lamme (2003, fig.4) – *430* ❧ WE THE
PEOPLE: A key to *Signers of the Constitution* (1940) by Howard Chandler Christy.
US Capitol, Washington, DC. Courtesy of the Architect of the Capitol – *432* ❧
RIVALROUS GRATINGS: Redrawn after Leopold and Logothetis (1999) – *433* ❧
AN AMBIGUOUS IMAGE: Photograph and image processing by Shimon Edelman
(2007) – *434* ❧ TRANSCRANIAL MAGNETIC STIMULATION: Brain scan
photograph used in this illustration placed in public domain by Wikimedia Com-
mons user Cajolingwilhelm – *435* ❧ CHE GUEVARA: Image released into the
public domain by Wikimedia Commons user Arrenlex (2006) – *436* ❧ A BAT:
Brown big-eared bat, *Plecotus auritus*. E. O. Schmidt. Woodcut (1927). Wikimedia
Commons image. Public domain – *437* ❧ A CHARIOT: Assyrian war chariot
of the later period. Plate XCII, No.II, *The Seven Great Monarchies Of The Ancient
Eastern World*, Volume 2 (of 7): Assyria. The History, Geography, And Antiqui-
ties Of Chaldaea, Assyria, Babylon, Media, Persia, Parthia, and Sassanian or New
Persian Empire; With Maps and Illustrations by George Rawlinson (1812-1902).
Public domain – *438* ❧ COGITO: Bierce, Ambrose. *The Unabridged Devil's*

media Commons – *497* ❧ A GALAXY: Photograph courtesy NASA, ESA, and the Hubble Heritage Team (STScl/AUSA) - ESA/Hubble Collaboration – *498* ❧ AFTER THE SINGULARITY: Ho, David. *World Order*. Reprinted by permission of the artist – *505* ❧ OLDUVAI GORGE, SEEN FROM SPACE: Photograph courtesy NASA/JPL-Caltech – *506* ❧ Note: all lyrics and poetry are property and copyright of their respective owners and are quoted in this book strictly for educational purposes. For the sources of illustrations and quotes from scholarly publications, see the corresponding entries in the general reference list.

Index

Colophon

This book was designed and typeset by the author, using free open-source software: the Free Software Foundation GNU Emacs text editor, the Unix `TeXLive-2007` distribution of Leslie Lamport's LaTeX system (based on Donald Knuth's TeX), and the memoir class written by Peter Wilson.